The Missing Myth

A New Vision of Same-Sex Love

~

Gilles Herrada

SelectBooks, Inc.
New York

This edition published by SelectBooks, Inc.
For information address SelectBooks, Inc., New York, New York.

First Edition

ISBN 978-1-59079-242-1

Cataloging-in-Publication Data

Herrada, Gilles.
  The missing myth : a new vision of same-sex love / Gilles Herrada. -- 1st ed.
     p. cm.
  Includes bibliographical references and index.
  Summary: "Using a transdisciplinary and developmental approach, the author presents his vision of the role of homosexuality in human evolution by reconciling biological, sociocultural, historical, ethical, psychological, ontological, and spiritual dimensions. Stressing connections between the mythic representation and social status of homosexuality, he advocates creation of a modern mythos of same-sex love largely inspired from the scientific narrative"--Provided by publisher.
  ISBN 978-1-59079-242-1 (pbk. : alk. paper)
  1. Homosexuality. 2. Homosexuality--Genetic aspects. I. Title.
HQ76.25.H464 2012
306.76'6--dc23
                    2012013781

Manufactured in the United States of America

10 9 8 7 6 5 4 3 2 1

To my father

To Marguerite Yourcenar

CONTENTS

P A R T III The Beautiful

Acknowledgments

First I want to express my immense gratitude to my friends Dean Papademetriou, Tanya Henderson, and Jay Kauffman, who spent countless hours correcting the earliest versions of this manuscript. I doubt that this book would have ever taken form without their selfless support. I would like to extend my deep appreciation to my earliest readers, Jaime Arango, Judson Morrow, and Daniel Piateck, for their time, advice, and precious encouragement. I am also profoundly thankful to those who have contributed in one way or another to this endeavor: Goran Tkalec, Barbara Larish, Fiona Doetsch, Grace Hochheiser, Cameron Pollard, James Jayo, Malaga Baldi, Claudia Vergara, Kazem Abdullah, Marcy Auerbach, Erik von Hahn, Owen Coffey, Elizabeth Debold, and Rebecca Kline.

Among those who have played a part in the emergence of this book, two have a special place in my heart. The first one is Olivier Grenier, who suggested the title. The second encompasses the nearly three hundred participants of the Partnership Course led by Angela Amado in Los Angeles in 2004. Their incredible spirit, monumental appreciation, and unconditional listening gave birth to the man who would eventually become the author of this book. I also wish to thank the team at SelectBooks, Nancy Sugihara, and particularly Kenzi Sugihara for his refreshing curiosity and for trusting the value of my work.

However, I cannot end those acknowledgments without mentioning the names of the few scholars and writers who have profoundly influenced my thought and consequently the substance of this book: Ken Wilber, who provided the philosophical foundation of this work; Michel Foucault, whose contribution to the fields of gay, gender, and cultural studies still remains an unmatched source of inspiration; Mircea Eliade and Joseph Campbell, who revealed to me the paramount importance of symbolic realities in human existence; David F. Greenberg, author of the pivotal *The Construction of Homosexuality*, which first exposed me to the idea that homosexuality was not a biological problem only; Kathy Gaca (and her remarkable *The Making of Fornication*), R.C. Kirkpatrick, Vivienne Cass, Richard Wrangham, Frans de Waal, Edward O. Wilson, Stephen Murray, Gilbert Herdt, and Bernadette Brooten, who also played a decisive role in the maturation of the many of the claims that I make in *The Missing Myth*.

PREFACE

Why is homosexuality an issue? Has anyone yet found the answer to that question? In fact, one must admit that at the dawn of the twenty-first century homosexuality remains surprisingly enigmatic, if not obscure. By that I mean that homosexuality makes no sense, either to those who refuse to accept its existence or to those who have to defend their right to love. And this has been a reality for so long that we forget that millions of individuals across the world live with an identity that does not make sense. This book is an attempt to make sense of homosexuality—a quest for that which is most important for human beings and what homosexuality has been missing the most: meaning.

Investigating the homosexual phenomenon today feels like opening Russian dolls, leaving nearly all questions unanswered. Why was homosexuality accepted in some cultures but not in others, and why did Christian culture in partic-ular censure this type of sexuality so brutally? The Bible—Leviticus 20:13 in particular—has been widely held responsible for this.[1] However, the Scriptures of the Judeo-Christian tradition contain a significant number of prohibitions and other abominations that are also punishable by death: blasphemy,[2] curs-ing one's parents,[3] being a medium,[4] and Sabbath breaking,[5] to name only a few. Even rape did not invoke the same level of severity in the Judeo-Christian world.[6] Until recently, it was essentially considered a crime against the property of a father or a husband, when it was not simply seen as the rightful reward of victorious warriors. Why such a hysteria about homosexuality and so much flex-ibility regarding other biblical prohibitions?

One could truly wonder why the condemnation of homosexuality as a capital sin—a sin against God calling for nothing less than the death of the sinner—eventually enjoyed such an immense consensus in the Christian world. Blaming the Bible becomes increasingly questionable as one continues to sift through history. The laic, anti-religious, and atheist doctrines that progressively emerged after the Age of Enlightenment and the rise of modernity rejected the authority of the Bible. Nonetheless they quickly adopted this apparently fundamentally Christian prejudice. How can one use the Bible to explain why Nazi Germany sent thousands of homosexuals to the death camps? Commu-nist regimes in the Soviet Union, China or Cuba were and still are notoriously atheist. Yet, they too have brutally repressed homosexuality at some point.

The repression of homosexuals persisted and sometimes even intensified in non-Christian cultures well after their decolonization by Western countries. Indian and Muslim societies, for instance, traditionally relatively tolerant toward homosexuality, became highly homophobic in the twentieth century, and this regrettable evolution did not involve any conversion to the Christian faith. If the Bible can no longer serve as a common denominator for the anti-homosexual stances of Paul the Apostle, Saint Augustine, Hitler, Stalin, and Ayatollah Khomeini, then what can?

If you think that we can make better sense of homosexuality's more recent history, you might be disappointed. The explosion of freedom that marked the historical recognition of gay rights during the second half of the twentieth century is hardly explainable. As recently as the 1950s, homosexuals were still the object of hateful discrimination that was very effectively relayed by the police force, the psycho-medical body, and the media. In those years, the disclosure of one's homosexuality, voluntarily or not, constituted social suicide, and commonly resulted in losing a job, abandonment by friends and family, or worse repercussions. Only thirty years later, however, things had changed considerably. During the 1970s and '80s, gay activism became surprisingly tolerated by a majority of governments all across Western Europe and North America at a time when their respective police forces were best equipped to repress it. Why did they refrain? A major change happened in the twentieth century that not only affected gay rights, but also our entire cultural perception of personal freedom, and we do not really know what caused it.

Thus, the difficulty is rarely about finding out the possible origin of an idea, such as the interdiction of homosexual acts. Rather, the difficulty is in knowing the mechanisms by which entire civilizations end up embracing or rejecting that very idea. This is the real thorny question that we should try to address with regard to homosexual history and the cultural success of homophobia. The fact is that attempts to determine the subtle mechanisms that have influenced homosexuality's fate have been scarce. According to the general scholarly consensus, homosexual history appears to be the consequence of the persuasive influence of historical figures, such as the writers of Leviticus, Saint Paul, Harvey Milk, or Act-Up leaders. But were the moral views on homosexuality over centuries and among millions of individuals the mere product of collective manipulations? Experts in psychocultural development have recently argued that, contrary to general belief, the history of cultures is not determined by the views of their leaders. Instead, these leaders appear to be the direct expression of hidden undercurrents that relentlessly transform human cultures.

We must therefore humbly acknowledge that we do not understand very well the cultural dynamics that are implicated in the acceptance of homosexuality in human societies. We still have very little idea about why homosexuality turned out to have such a tragic fate. Even today, addressing those questions feels daunting.

Homosexual history unfolds like a saga of epic dimensions that we comment on profusely, but seldom comprehend.

This is nonetheless only one of many peculiarities that homosexuality seems to exhibit. Not only is the problem of its approval and integration in human society still an unresolved mystery thus far, but its cultural substance also appears—oddly—to lack the scope of all other foremost cultural identities. If I were to ask a question as basic as "What does being homosexual mean?" most people, including an overwhelming majority of homosexuals like me, will undoubtedly answer that it means "to be sexually attracted to people of the same sex," or a close version of that. And the fact is that this answer is absolutely accurate. But if you were to tell a woman that being a woman means simply "to be sexually attracted to men and produce babies," most women might legitimately feel disconcerted. Not that the statement itself would be incorrect, but mainly it would sound horrifyingly reductive and impoverishing—in other words, so incomplete that it simply becomes risible.

What about the female body, its world of specificities, its pleasures, its cycles, its fragility, and its strength; what about the female social and economic presence, women's historical role, and its meaning in the future of our civilization; what about the female mind, the power of its sensitivity, inclusiveness, and intuitiveness; what about female love, motherhood, or non-motherhood; what about the eternal feminine, the Goddesses, Gaia, Eve, the Virgin Mary, and so forth. And I am just skimming through some of the most obvious aspects of womanhood that any woman can choose to identify with or not. Womanhood is a massive topic that necessitates encyclopedic knowledge to be seriously covered.

This difference between the way people describe what it means to be homosexual and what it means to be a woman is something noticeably peculiar. Both womanhood and homosexuality are psychocultural identities that are essential in Western society today. Yet womanhood appears to have a level of complexity—a depth—that the concept of homosexuality, in spite of the profusion of stereotypes about it, fails to convey. In one, we see an identity that holds a vast world of meanings and multiple connections to all sorts of aspects of our humanity: womanhood. In the other, we see an identity that is reduced to a particular type of behavior: homosexuality.

When looking more carefully, this drastic reductionism also applies to the concept of heterosexuality, which quickly brings us to an interesting conclusion. The reason heterosexuals of both sexes do not think of themselves as much in terms of their heterosexuality (besides the fact that they represent a large majority of the population) is that although heterosexual life entails to pair sexually and emotionally with people of the opposite sex, heterosexuals are never reduced to defining themselves only by this fact. That is why the concept of heterosexuality, a term which appeared along with that of homosexuality only toward the end of the nineteenth century, had never been much of a cultural reality before then and is still not really one today. The idea of heterosexuality, which is a by-product of the concept of homosexuality, had until then remained undistinguished from an entire collection of realities representing the whole of life, much the same way we view womanhood. While the concept of heterosexuality, which feels so artificial, has never really achieved the status of a psychocultural identity in our culture, homosexuals have been doomed to endure the disconnection of their homosexual identity from the rest of human existence. Whether this is the result of our mere ignorance or the fact that homosexual identity is narrow by nature, we are still left with an unsettling question: how can one be comfortable living with this?

Leaving the questions concerning the nature of homosexuality and the reasons of its troubled history unanswered, other questions can be asked: Where does homosexuality originate? What can explain its presence in all human populations throughout history? What makes a minority and, intriguingly, only a minority of people homosexual? Suddenly, the conceptual vacuum metamorphoses into a swirl of discordant theories. Psychologists, sociologists, and biologists have been actively involved in bitter academic battles over the primordial cause of homosexuality. Unresolved Oedipus complex, queer theory, or the gay gene: make your choice! In fact, after decades of heated discussion, the most recent reviews on the topic often opt for a more pacifying approach by giving each protagonist a piece of the pie: nature and nurture would both contribute to the onset of homosexuality. A truce has been signed—a truce instead of the truth. This consensus emerged regardless of the fact that psychologists have no explanation to offer about the causes of homosexuality that might qualify as scientifically serious. It also avoids acknowledging the disastrous impact of nearly one century of dogmatic and plainly erroneous psychoanalytic theory of homosexuality. Wisely, no one has ever attempted to articulate genetic and environmental causes of homosexuality together. For instance, how does the gay gene actually induce the identification of a future gay boy with his mother in order to get the father's attention? The answer seems so out of reach that nobody dares to even mention it. Clever is the scholar who will adopt a prudent silence on those issues today.

We have to confront the fact that our current culture and even gay culture have been unable to offer a coherent understanding of homosexuality, of its "what," "why," and "how," and that we have left unanswered crucial questions concerning its complex historical journey.

In the end, I fear that the vast majority of homosexuals across the world still think of themselves as a mistake rather than as a mystery of nature. After having realized and accepted their difference, after having come out and finally healed, one last question keeps resonating in the heart of many homosexuals on this planet: "Why me?" Even if with age and the practice of life we have become numb to the persistent and uncomfortable self-doubt, this subliminal message is always there, hidden in the shadow. Homosexuality is seen by most homosexuals as well as the great majority of the people around them as . . . bad luck.

I had to address that issue for myself. I discovered that the gay world provided neither relief nor solution. Instead, it kept returning the same echo to my ears. Many others just like me were wrestling with a lingering malaise, a subtle and nonetheless persistent sorrow about being homosexual, and ultimately the feeling that fate had made a cruel choice for us. I realized then that most if not all the writings about homosexuality had a particular tone to them, or more exactly, a peculiar aftertaste. Skimming through the abundant scholarly literature about homosexuality, I was struck by the pervasive sadness and insidious resignation that is present all over the so-called "homosexual discourse," which the "supportive" or "gay-friendly" sticker could not really mask.

For instance, this is how Richard A. Isay, who remains after his death an undisputed authority on the subject and practice of psychotherapy for gay people (and whom I otherwise truly respect for his sincere humanism) concludes his book *Being Homosexual* published in 1989: "[. . .] it takes enormous effort for gay men to maintain their sense of dignity and self-worth in a society that remains inimical to them and their sexuality. It will take an even greater effort and conviction for our society to encourage the self-worth and emotional health and well being of gay men by sanctioning loving relations of all kinds."[7] Seventeen years later, as if nothing had changed, Isay reiterates: "Even when the time does come when society is less ambivalent, it will take several generations for parental attitudes to change so that the unique feelings and needs of gay children are valued and not denied [. . .] For the foreseeable future, many if not most gay men will have a hard time believing that they are worth the effort it takes to find a partner or seeing the benefits of loving and being loved by one other person over a long period of time."[8] Now, take a deep breath.

Despite the compassion and the hope that they intend to convey, these lines sound a lot like a life sentence. In fact, the affliction expressed in these excerpts is very representative of the gloomy atmosphere found in today's scholarly writings about homosexuality. By and large, the tone is either melancholic, angry, or emotionally anesthetized. Not only is our vision of homosexuality reductive and barely intelligible, but we cannot even manage to find any beauty in it. Behind the flamboyant "proud to be gay" mantra, homosexuals are, in their great majority, disconnected from their roots, from their heart, and from their soul. No one can then blame them for feeling the way they feel.

I read in a 2007 issue of the French gay magazine *Têtu* that "[. . .] more and more gays and lesbians complain about the state of their culture. For various reasons, doubt persists. Is our community still the leader in innovating? Our closest friends start to make definitive statements such as 'it's not how it used to be' or 'gay culture gets on my nerves.'"[9] Then followed an impressive addendum of "1001 secrets" intended to reawaken the interest of gays in their culture.

There might very well be a "homosexual malaise," that is to say, a growing dissatisfaction of homosexuals with the culture that bears their name. Accumulating evidence seems to signal that the homosexual community and its culture are heading toward a crisis. In fact, gay culture may have already reached a point of no return. And if this phenomenon is mostly visible in urban centers of Westernized countries, it is however present everywhere homosexuals have had enough time to enjoy the relative freedom of being open about their sexuality. Only half a century since the onset of gay liberation, it looks as if today the gay community might be losing its soul before finding one. Since such a strong statement calls for more compelling evidence, I would like to present a succinct inventory of some of the most obvious and troubling manifestations of today's homosexual malaise.

According to an article published by *Time* magazine in October 2005, gay youth appears less and less attracted by the gay label, and this despite the fact that gayness is incomparably easier for them to embrace than it was for previous generations.[10] In 2007 one could read again in *Têtu*: "LGBT seniors talk about the old good times. People in their 40s are wary of what is new. Those in their 30s feel torn between memories of an uneasy youth and the present, so obvious and natural. And young people tend to reject all that gay and lesbian stuff [. . .]."[11] Echoing this, Ritch C. Savin-Williams relayed in *The New Gay Teenager* the edifying reactions of the numerous young people he has interviewed, which range from a mere indifference to a total aversion for the gay label and gay culture.[12] Apparently many gays in their teens and early twenties are having increasing difficulties relating to the gay manifesto of their elders and gay identity in general.[13]

I will certainly refrain from using these observations to generalize about an entire generation.[14] Yet, when others report that "[. . .] the gay movement [does not] understand the extent to which the next generation just wants to be normal kids,"[15] it seems reasonable to believe their thirst for belonging is simply eclipsing their need to assert themselves as gay, which had been so vital for the generations before them. What is it about "normality" that pushes so many of these supposedly "post-gay" teens to give up on a sociocultural victory that their elders made so easy for them? And what does it mean for them to be "normal" and at the same time faithful to their own psychosexual integrity? Unlike Savin-Williams, I am far from validating too quickly their denial of gay identity. Their cautiousness toward the gay label is a response to a simple arithmetic: for many, it feels more comfortable to rest in the entitlement resulting from years of gay activism and ensure their integration into normality than to keep the fighting spirit alive to defend and promote an identity that does not attract them that much.

But if for gay youth the appearance of normality appears more attractive than gay identity, I hear an urgent invitation to reexamine the culture that we have collectively created. We must fundamentally question why gay identity does not feel like home to many homosexual and bisexual kids. Even if this issue is difficult to pin down, one can already acknowledge that for many young homosexuals and bisexuals, "gay" is neither an appealing label nor a future so worth battling for. If it is true that gay youth's craving for normality is a reflection of their legitimate need for belongingness, this might simply remind us how much previous generations have been blindly resigned to being eternal outlaws.

One also notices that a growing majority of adult homosexuals are losing interest in their homosexual "specificity." Instead, they eagerly opt for a life style that is a carbon copy of centuries-old heterosexual models, which have definitely proved their value in terms of providing a comfortable, healthy, and fulfilling existence. Stable and loving relationships, faithfulness between partners, long-term material and emotional support, marriage, and eventually adoption and surrogacy . . . nothing of that has been invented under the cover of homosexuality. Today, in one of the most touching reversals of history, the institution of marriage that had been dynamited and left in flame by the feminist movement, is in the process of being rescued by homosexuals.

At the same time, many homosexuals experience a sense of loss and sorrow (once again) from abandoning a piece of hard-won identity after so many years of struggle.[16] Gay identity, unlike others, seems doomed to either survive in adversity or dissolve into an integration process.[17] But is the path to happiness so narrow that it can explain a cultural exodus from subversiveness into plain normality? At this point, one can only observe the failure of modern gay culture to include the full range of human relationships without fading into the cultural norm that has been denying its mere existence for the longest time—in other words, without losing itself.

Another sign that times are changing: urban homosexual life seems to be undergoing a surprisingly early decline today. In cities that have been historical gay havens like New York[18] and Paris,[19] and also in Boston,[20] Atlanta,[21] Provincetown,[22] and Cape Town,[23] gay neighborhoods are slowly and ineluctably fragmenting. Even the well-established Castro neighborhood in San Francisco appears to be exposed to the same centrifugal forces.[24] Gay neighborhoods are becoming gentrified and gay businesses are scattering. The trend is more obvious in places where gay culture has had enough time to experience and enjoy the fruit of its recent emancipation (a "luxury" that does not yet apply to cities like Istanbul, Beijing, or Kansas City). In New York, where I live now, the stretch of Eighth Avenue, which used to host the heart of gay Chelsea, is turning into a succession of fashion chain-stores and fancy restaurants. The last "officially" gay coffee shop has closed. Candles have replaced most books on the shelves of the last gay gift store. Gay Chelsea is slowly but surely disappearing from the map.[25]

The gentrification process is substituting the original gay neighborhoods, with their funky blend of bookstores, sex shops, bars of all sorts, clubs, cafés, and restaurants, with a constellation of trendy gay bars in scattered areas of the city. And the disappearance of gay neighborhoods is only reflecting the fact that gay communities themselves, which once embodied the front-line of social, intellectual and artistic creativity movements, are blending in. Are we witnessing the end of an era? Some, like Andrew Sullivan, have wondered whether we were already heading toward a post-gay world.[26] Yet, is this again no other than the familiar resignation infused throughout the gay discourse which I was talking about earlier? And are we not simply reenacting our morbid fascination for the cursed fate of homosexuality?

Despite the converging evidence of a crisis, no one can deny the remarkable transformation that occurred in the last forty years. Gay liberation was nothing less than a miracle with regard to Western history. The sexual revolution changed the cultural landscape of the West in depth. For many women and men, straights, gays, and bisexuals, the 1970s provided a breath of liberty of unprecedented intensity. Boundaries were broken. Many social taboos could suddenly be challenged. All those extraordinary changes happened also at a time of unmatched progress for women's, civil, and social rights. With a wind of freedom blowing under their wings, homosexual communities incarnated, more fully than any others, a revolution that promised to reinvent human relationships. "This was the era of the post-Stonewall new left, of the Castro and the West Village, an era where sexuality forged a new meaning for gayness: of sexual adventure, political radicalism, and cultural revolution," recalls Andrew Sullivan.[27]

Then the pendulum swung back. The wave of neoconservatism that followed aimed to end an era of moral subversion. The parallel rise of the AIDS epidemic certainly made this moment even more difficult and painful for gays. The AIDS crisis arrived as a terrible reminder of the implacable vulnerability of human beings when they are cut off from a solid social and cultural network. Andrew Sullivan summarized nicely the dilemma that homosexual communities across the world had to face: "A ghetto was no longer an option."[28] Reinventing the world was no longer an actuality. Instead, surviving was. The AIDS carnage imposed a dramatically different rhetoric on homosexual activism that we all must admit, produced unparalleled results. In just three decades, homosexuality was decriminalized and gay unions legalized in many countries. The transformation of the social and moral environment of gays in countries like England, Belgium, Spain, and South Africa was simply unimaginable only thirty years ago. Even in China, attitudes toward homosexuality are evolving quickly.[29] And if countries like Russia and many areas of the United States are still lagging behind, it all seems just a matter of time before criminalizing homosexuality becomes marginalized.

The objective of gay revolution seems within reach. One country, one state, and one city at a time, gays are securing their right to love, desire, meet, and unite. This represents an amazing accomplishment. And yet, is that all what gay liberation was, is, or should be about? Is the only raison d'être of the gay movement to defeat homophobia? Can gay revolution be complete without also exploring what homosexuals want to embody in today's world? If that is the case (and I believe it is), we might have stopped short of delivering the full potential of our revolution. Have we simply given up? I believe we know very well that, to a large extent, we have. Today a majority of homosexuals, self-doubting, skeptical, or sometimes even blasé, cannot overcome a feeling of helplessness.

Andrew Sullivan's remarkably insightful article in *The New Republic* in 2005, "The End of Gay Culture and the Future of Gay Life," landed like a bombshell in the gay world. But instead of acting as a salutary electroshock, its subtle and painless pessimism has remained largely unchallenged, let alone addressed. In fact, many sighed from relief in recognizing a familiar fate: a return to nothingness.[30] The AIDS crisis alone cannot explain the phenomenon that we are currently observing. Gay teenagers may just be rebelling against gayness insofar as gayness has become the new norm that is imposed on them; it may be legitimate for the gay couples who desire children to leave behind them a culture that has failed to integrate family values; and the forces at work in real estate economics may make gay businesses more difficult to develop today than twenty years ago; nonetheless, it is time that we recognize the converging signs of a crisis. And could this crisis, which I indeed consider to be an identity crisis, be a historical opportunity rather than a predicted death?

Now that we are aware of the symptoms, we need a diagnosis, and, if possible, a solution or at least the beginning of one, starting by answering this question: Where and why did homosexuality lose its soul? I believe that the homosexual discourse and as a consequence, gay culture, which homosexuals have collectively generated since the emergence of modern homosexuality since World War II, have failed on two major counts.

The first one is that gay culture, stretched precariously among abstract academic discourse, hard-core political activism, and the sparkles of urban gay life, is still incapable of offering an image of homosexuality that would be not only diverse but also whole, complete, at peace with itself, and connected to all the various facets that constitute a true human being—in body, mind, and soul. As a result, gay identity as current gay culture conveys it, is still not a match for the deep aspiration of a growing majority of homosexual individuals. Homosexuals, young and old, increasingly aware of and free to be themselves, can less and less recognize themselves inside a gay identity that fails to embrace all of life.

What is the promise of gay life today? At best, living homosexuality is translated into a successful healing process. At best, homosexuals can legitimately hope for a healthy life style . . . once they have managed sorting it all out. Is there anything in the so-called gay culture that can reflect a deep sense of happiness about being gay? Is there anything in it that is helping us find our true essence as homosexual beings, some inner peace, or some sense of purpose? For an increasing number of homosexuals of all generations, personal fulfillment means leaving the gay specificity behind. Homosexuals do not know who they are as homosexuals, and modern gay culture offers few clues about the deep nature of homosexuality.

After having been stigmatized as a sin or a perversion by two millenniums of homophobic culture, a mere half-century of well-intentioned pro-homosexual discourse has left homosexuality impoverished, truncated, disjointed, and ripped apart. Why is this? Modern homosexual identity only started to emerge in the nineteenth century and really grounded itself no earlier than the second half of the twentieth century. In this respect, this identity is extremely young, and because of the historical cultural context in which it was born, modern homosexuality has essentially been conceived and theorized within a biological, psychoanalytic, and sociological, and hence profoundly materialist context.

As a result, modern homosexuality exists in body and mind but has no soul. Modern homosexuality has been analyzed and rationalized by modernists, contextualized and even deconstructed by postmodernists, but not many have dared trying to give meaning to it. Twentieth century and twenty-first century academia would never dare to venture far into the domain of symbolism, let alone spirituality. As a consequence, the sacred dimension of modern homosexuality—symbolic and spiritual, inevitably—has remained largely ignored by the homosexual discourse, leaving its brutal rejection by traditional religions still unanswered.

By submitting to endless quarrels inside the humanities and sciences, homosexual identity has fragmented into multiple theories—all opposed to each other, all profoundly limiting and highly politicized, and all with depressing consequences. "Homosexual by choice" versus "homosexual nature," "biologically determined" versus "culturally constructed," "same-sex marriage" versus "invented life styles," "polymorphous perversity" versus "normality," . . . same-sex love was turned into a battlefield and gay identity into a laboratory animal by the very people who intended to protect it. Decades later, after Boswell, Foucault, the gay gene, queer theory and so on, do we know what it means to be homosexual? We have no idea. We do not know what it is, and even less why it is. Homosexuality has been reduced to a set of sexual behaviors, a therapeutic process, or, for better or worse, gender transgression. Most regrettably, homosexuals are always presented as victims—whether victims of their parents, society, history, or the "gay gene"— they are always viewed as victims.

My conclusion is that the vision of homosexuality that today's culture conveys is desperately shallow. But by shallow, I do not mean simplistic or frivolous. Historians, psychologists, scientists, social scientists, and writers have been fairly prolific and some remarkably insightful regarding this topic. Instead I mean that modern homosexuality lacks wholeness, and that in its inability to cover the full spectrum of body, mind and soul, it also dramatically lacks depth. Deprived of depth, modern homosexual identity is simply insubstantial, in other words, flat, just like the thousands of pages of theories written about it. Many homosexuals can no longer fit into such a cramped space. We see the impact of this disastrous limitation on the gay community: Unattractive for the youngest gay generations, scanty for many gay adults, and even debilitating for many individuals for whom hyper-sexuality and substance abuse have become the only possible response to spiritual deprivation, gay culture seems deserted by a growing number of gays. Something is really going sour between homosexuals and homosexual identity, and for a good reason. Not surprisingly, the survival of gay culture seems to be at stake from the mere perspective of the homosexuals' assimilation into "normality." Today, gay identity is close to schizophrenia, and nothing a mentally-sane human being would strive for. Hiding in the shadow of gay pride is a feeling of resignation that a few undeniably are starting to notice.

The second count is that the pro-homosexual discourse has failed at understanding the spectrum of anti-homosexual reactions that we commonly label "homophobia." The homosexual discourse (defensive, probably from fear of being perceived as being weak) has refused to explore the world of homophobia from the perspective of the homophobic person and has discounted any perspectives on homosexuality that it deemed homophobic. As a result we have no understanding of the dynamics of acceptance and rejection of homosexuality. Nobody, let alone homosexuals, has any idea about the forces that have decided the fate of homosexuality in humanity's history.

Homophobia, from a pro-homosexual perspective, exists as an untamed monster. And the growing tolerance toward homosexuality in Western countries should not hide from view the desperation of the large majority of homosexuals around the world. Homophobia is still a major problem today, from the revolting hanging of homosexuals in a country like Iran to the mere fact that many gays in developed countries undergo psychotherapy in order to come to terms with their homosexual essence.[31] Still today, homosexuals are vulnerable targets, and we can neither understand why this is nor can we explain the mechanism behind such hatred. Without a rigorous and honest deconstruction of the rationale behind homophobia, unbiased by our own moral views, it will be impossible to understand the dynamics of acceptance and rejection of homosexuality in the past, today, and in the future. We will keep fighting symptoms but not the cause. In fact, we will be able to address the problem of homophobia only when it becomes intelligible to us.

Let me be absolutely clear about my present argument. By no means is "understanding" homophobia the same as "accepting" or "tolerating" it. Understanding homophobia requires probing anti-homosexual reactions from the inside and not just from the outside. It is about deconstructing homophobia from its own inner perspective and its own worldview rather than our own. The current pro-homosexual discourse is nowhere near that.

Homosexuality is now at a crossroads, having to choose between dissolving into normality and inventing a future that honors its true essence. For the majority of homosexuals today, one's pride and self-esteem, which should emerge naturally from our collective vision of same-sex love, instead end up being grafted onto one's gay identity after years of self-reflection (and more often than not, years of committed therapeutic work). I find it urgent that we generate a cultural landscape that celebrates homosexuality. In that sense, the original and somewhat humble premise of *The Missing Myth* is that homosexuality has yet to discover itself.

My intention here is not merely to overcome the current identity crisis of homosexuality. It is to create the foundation of a renovated homosexual discourse from which homosexuality can start to expand in all the domains of human experience, an all-encompassing, truly human vision of itself, from its biological foundations to its numerous psychological, cultural, and spiritual ramifications—in body, mind, and soul. How can one then accomplish such an ambitious goal? We are going to embark on an uncommon journey by revisiting the many aspects of homosexuality, but with a novel intention: to find out how it all fits together and begin to create a richer picture of same-sex love supported by an open-minded, pluralistic, and positive discourse.

In recent decades, advances in neuroscience, psychology, anthropology, and primatology have revolutionized the notion of human nature. These discoveries have profound implications particularly with respect to the way we interpret sexual behavior. Not only does the role of sex largely exceed the strict domain of reproductive needs, but this evolution occurred way before the apparition of humankind. Among many primates and most great apes (i.e., chimpanzees, bonobos, gorillas, and humans), sex facilitates bonding and conflict resolution, thereby ensuring the social coherence of the group. In fact, in both humans and bonobos, sex makes social interactions extremely rewarding by making them greatly pleasurable. Homosexual behavior, which is widely distributed in the animal kingdom, is highly organized among chimpanzees, bonobos, gorillas, and humans. We will see that, far from being the expression of some randomness of wildlife, let alone an anomaly of nature, homosexual behavior in apes is crucial to their social development. We will explore the brain and behavior, in both apes and humans, and distill from this all the information we need so that homosexuality stops being the conundrum that it never was.

Identifying the subtle evolutionary dynamics that connect the biological and the psychocultural domains will be crucial to understanding homosexuality, homosexual behavior, and the complex reactions that they have elicited throughout history. Since our prehistory, human behavior has been shaped by the same basic need for security, and the same constant fear of the unknown. Exploring the drastic effects of these needs and fears on the mind will help us unravel why human beings and human societies act and react the way they do.

Since the emergence of the first human cultures, our inability to objectively grasp all the dangers and mysteries of life and the world has been soothed by the existence of myths. Myths have played an essential role in providing all civilizations a familiar representation of all that was unknown: the shape of the universe, the cycle of seasons, the inevitability of time, the enigma of our origins, the mystery of our fate, birth and death, diseases, power, setbacks, and, of course the cause of all our passions and desires. Myths have described the creation of the world, the life of the gods, and the origin of humanity. They have given a sacred, universal, and timeless representation of everything human beings knew about the world, and, more importantly, about themselves.

We will see that the fate of homosexuality has been tied to its mythic representation. Whenever homosexual behavior is positively depicted in the mythic narrative, homosexual relationships were socially accepted. In other words, this has constituted the *sine qua non* condition of their sociocultural viability. Diverging from nearly all other religious traditions, the Judeo-Christian lineage stands out for its complete absence of positive representation of same-sex love and desire in its mythology.

Eventually, we will explore the reemergence of homosexuality inside the current mythic space, a curious and convoluted blend of religious myths, historical narratives, global media culture, art, and, increasingly, of scientific concepts. The role of science in our modern and postmodern culture will be examined carefully. Science is far more than a technological revolution. Science is the womb inside of which human knowledge about the universe and ourselves is transforming. And for an increasingly significant part of the world population—particularly in postindustrial societies—science is now the new great storyteller. Scientific theories are progressively replacing the old religious myths in their fundamental function of providing explanation for all the mysteries human beings are confronted with—where we come from, where we are heading to, and . . . who we are.

It will then be just the right time to reframe the scientific research on homosexuality and its historical importance. Science, like any other human activity, is susceptible to failure, and, like any other aspect of human culture, susceptible to moral biases. Yet by looking at the biological roots of homosexuality, science is accomplishing a seminal act as revolutionary as those of Galileo and Copernicus when they uncovered the rotation of planet Earth around itself and around the sun. The rest of human reality had to reorganize around these discoveries and not the other way around. By exploring the origin of homosexuality, science offers a unique historical opportunity to expand our knowledge of same-sex love, and give it a depth that it is still terribly lacking today. At the same time, science works in the long term. To elucidate the causes and origins of homosexuality will take science some time. Therefore, "sit back, relax, and enjoy the show."

I intend in this book to create a totally new epistemological context from which one can view homosexuality. This requires becoming a truly pluralistic thinker. The homosexual discourse must escape the monologue in which it is trapped today and move forward. Concretely, that means that we ought to envision homosexuality in body, mind, and soul, not out of a kind of political negotiation (the "truce instead of the truth" that I was regretting earlier) but instead out of a process that seeks to integrate all the knowledge coming from totally different fields—a meta-analysis, in short.

Finally, we ought to integrate the dimension of time inside the homosexual discourse. Biological evolution, cultural and psychological development, moral progress . . . everything unfolds in a timely fashion. It is impossible to ignore this important aspect of human reality anymore. In fact, looking at everything about homosexuality in terms of development, which is to say, throughout all the dimensions of time, will be essential for the success of this endeavor. Our knowledge of homosexuality must be rearranged at all levels using a totally different context to start with. We must give the homosexual discourse a new architecture that is all-encompassing, transdisciplinary, and evolutionary. To achieve this, I will essentially perform the work of a mason attempting to renovate an old and uncomfortable mansion: patiently, systematically, and with passion.

Inspired from the profoundly innovative work of the philosopher Ken Wilber and what he terms the Integral Approach, I will contemplate homosexuality through the three Platonic domains of human existence—the True, the Good, and the Beautiful—three basic and irreducible perspectives that give their title to the three parts of *The Missing Myth*. After having explored the objective aspects of homosexuality in the True, and the question of its moral recognition in human cultures in the Good, same-sex love ultimately reveals itself as being an infinite space of inner exploration and creation—the Beautiful, so dear to Plato. Homosexuality is incarnated and spiritual, personal and cultural, and it has a past, a present, and a future. Homosexual identity ought to recapitulate all the domains of human existence. Only then can our pride, instead of a rebelling statement, emerge from the profound sense that homosexuality is an honor and a gift, that it is sacred.

I have one daring ambition, or it could be said that I want to take on an uncommon challenge: to bring homosexuals—individually and as a community—to a real and deep sense of closure with regard to their personal history as well as the grand history of homosexuality, and by doing so, help them metamorphose into authentic and responsible actors in history. With all humility, this is the work that I intend to begin in this book.

Notes to the Reader

In order to avoid predictable doubts and misinterpretations regarding my original intention, I want to specify a few important points.

First, I often refer to "homosexuality" or "homosexuals," yet I never intend to exclude bisexuals. A repetition of "homosexuals and bisexuals" would be soon tiresome to the reader. Bisexuality is fully acknowledged and honored in this book, albeit silently. I define—and this will become hopefully obvious as the book unfolds—two fundamental principles that are heterosexuality and homosexuality, and bisexuality partakes from both principles. Bisexual readers will have to sort it out for themselves, individually. If eventually this simplification proves to constitute a mistake, I will certainly apologize for it. But, to the best of my knowledge, considering bisexuality as the vehicle of the two fundamental principles that homo- and heterosexuality define seems to me to be an appropriate and judicious choice. As I will demonstrate, homosexual desire is widely present (yet not omnipresent) in human populations, beyond the minority—homosexuals and bisexuals—that embody same-sex love in their flesh. Ultimately homosexuality goes far beyond homosexuals, bisexuals, and homosexual desire. That is also what this book is about.

Second, I chose to use the words "homosexuality" and "homosexual" to define the transcultural and transhistorical reality of same-sex desire. I have used the word "gay" in the strictly limited context of modern homosexuality, which will be clearly defined in the section that will address the evolution of homosexual culture. It might be risky to set a precise time-period, but essentially homosexual culture following World War II can be referred to as gay. Importantly, and unless specified, my use of words "gay" and "homosexual" encompass gay/homosexual men and lesbians. I seldom use the word "queer," a term which I personally poorly relate to for multiple reasons, to qualify individuals. Queer theory specifically shifts the focus from the reality of distinct sexual identities to the equally valid one of a constellation of sexualities outside of the heterosexual norm. The intention behind queer theory was to pull gays out of the stereotypical views and pre-cast sexual identities that were defined by and from a normative discourse, and reclaim a freedom that seemed lost. But, as we will see, queer liberation was a reaction against the dominant order, but by no means an authentic inner deliverance. In addition, while I certainly do not deny the important insights provided by this approach, queer theory avoids inquiring into the essence of homosexuality, as if trying to escape another form of determinism and control.[32] *The Missing Myth* conversely does not oppose the concept of freedom with the one of determinism, but instead sees them as running parallel in two different realms.

Third, I would like to warn my reader that I have barely delved into what the psychoanalytic field has to say about homosexuality. To the best of my knowledge, all psychoanalytic theories on homosexuality presented thus far are, without exception, dogmatic, self-justified, and non-experimental. In other words, I find them quasi-irrelevant. A critical approach of their content has a place in a study of psychoanalytic theory but is unsuited for an essay on same-sex love. I instead focus on the abundant and compelling material originating from rigorous and experimental approaches to homosexuality. This should naturally reveal the lack of substance in the various psychoanalytic conceptualizations of homosexual desire which I came across. However, it would be absurd to minimize the profound impact of psychoanalytic theory and Sigmund Freud on homosexuality in Western culture and their pivotal role in homosexual history during the twentieth century. This will be explored.

Finally, I truly regret that *The Missing Myth* suffers from the implacable limitation of its author—that is, from having been written by a man. Nature made the choice for me, and I must admit at this point that this book is clearly less knowledgeable about female homosexuality than it is about male homosexuality. Part of this bias clearly stems from the fact that my perspective on the world is colored by both my gender and my sexuality. Another reason for this is that male homosexuality is far better documented than female homosexuality. The disparity will be most noticeable when exploring homosexual history. Many have deplored this situation. It is, however, how things are. Nevertheless, I believe from deep in my heart that, overall, the vision that I present in *The Missing*

Myth applies to both male and female homosexuality. As often as I could, I tried to include female concerns and specificities in my work. Never, however, did I intend to impose my views on a world that I cannot access interiorly. I therefore invite female readers, homosexual or not, to approach *The Missing Myth* while bearing in mind my humble apology for not providing a fair and equal treatment to their experience.

Gilles Herrada
New York, December 20, 2012

～

A Renovated Homosexual Discourse

You never change things by fighting the existing reality. To change something, build a new model that makes the existing model obsolete.

Attributed to Richard Buckminster Fuller

Perhaps the new age will focus not just on the buildup of more knowledge but also on the fashioning of new relationships to the knowledge we already have.[33]

Robert Kegan and Lisa Lahey

A good gardener gives as much attention to the soil in his field as to what grows on it. The creation of a great wine begins with choosing the right land, soil chemistry, and light exposure. Only then can you obtain a result that will not only exceed your greatest expectations but also one that will get better over the years. Therefore, I will proceed as good gardeners do.

If the intention is to expand the homosexual universe so that it encompasses the body, the mind, and also the soul, we ought to ask ourselves how we are going to do that. The space in which this conversation will take place needs to be prepared. And very specifically, if the goal is to generate a vision of homosexuality that includes meaning, there must first be created a form of discourse that can welcome meaning. We are condemned either to come up with a new methodology or merely regurgitate a version of what has already been said and written before. It must therefore be defined as to how this vast topic can be talked about—and specifically, how differently in comparison with past discussions. Defining my methodology (which will eventually be recognized as an integral approach), is not a mere prerequisite to this inquiry. It constitutes the foundation of an authentically new vision of same-sex love. And we need to become solidly grounded in this foundation so that the rest of this investigation can flow flawlessly.

We must however remain vigilant. If we are talking about meaning, soul, and spiritual depth, two major pitfalls need to be avoided. Failing to distinguish them would seriously jeopardize the chances to build a rigorous and authentically renovated homosexual discourse. The first one of these pitfalls is to be content with recycling ancient religious beliefs that either incorporate same-sex desire and/or gender transgressions in their mythologies or at least offer teachings that are more positive toward sex than those of the Judeo-Christian tradition. In that situation, one finds a constellation of minor movements that are generally affiliated with the New Age culture (e.g., male tribes, gay Wicca, or Tantra for gay men), and whose spiritual roots range from paganism to oriental philosophies.[34]

The second pitfall involves a "forced" reinterpretation of the sacred texts (essentially the Judeo-Christian ones) in order to reveal attitudes more favorable to homosexuals. Some scholars took advantage of the fact that it is indeed difficult, if not impossible, to know for certain what the authors of Leviticus 20:13, for instance, meant exactly. Even the writings of Paul the Apostle on homosexuality are in many ways subject to multiple interpretations, as we will see in later chapters. Some have even argued about possible romantic relationships between Jesus and other men, John the Apostle or Lazarus. I respect their work and contribution; yet I believe that none of that will help us build a convincing case for homosexuality, let alone understand the history of homosexuality.

On the one hand, homosexual spiritualities (if there is such a thing yet) that involve a return to ancient rituals and beliefs neglect the fact that more than two thousands years of monotheism, three centuries of modernity, and half a century of postmodernity have gone by. We cannot offer a convincing future for homosexuality by simply worshiping ancient gods and goddesses or by performing sacred dances in the woods. On the other hand, those who try to explain the clash between same-sex love and Judeo-Christianity as resulting from a mere misinterpretation of religious texts are simply in denial, even if their claims appear backed up with a solid expertise in linguistics. No one can ignore the overall homophobic character of Judeo-Christian culture.

Our quest for meaning cannot indulge in attempts to revive or deny the past. Discovering homosexuality's depth should represent a move forward, not backward. In other words, depth needs to be created, not reprocessed. It ought to emerge from a synthesis of all the various parts that compose the homosexual reality in the present, including, not in spite of, history. Having clarified this point, let me dive into the heart of the matter.

PERSPECTIVE AND CONTEXT

How can one reconcile the fact that the pro and con homosexual discourses always see themselves as being equally grounded, equally justified, and equally right? Usually, and this is particularly true of the pro-homosexual discourse, we dismiss the issue by simply assuming that the other side is either ill-intentioned, ignorant, or mentally limited. In all cases, we disregard their opinions and feel perfectly justified to do so.

But very quickly, the crystalline simplicity of this way of thinking forces us to confront a shocking reality: Your homophobic neighbor might indeed be intellectually limited; however, Saint Augustine was not. He nonetheless condemned homosexual behavior unreservedly. So did Saint Thomas Aquinas, who theorized on the crime of sodomy in the twelfth century, thereby laying down the moral standard of the Church for the centuries to come. The philosophers of modernity, despite a flicker of hesitation at the time of the Enlightenment, quickly endorsed the anti-homosexual views of Christianity. Their rhetoric changed, yet their incomprehension of same-sex love remained surprisingly the same. And throughout the nineteenth and twentieth centuries the medical institution and, later, psychoanalysts, reinforced the prejudice even more. (Remember that it was not until 1973 that the American Psychiatric Association removed homosexuality from its list of mental disorders.) The interminable list of theologians, philosophers, scientists, and other thinkers who have chastised homosexual behavior for centuries demonstrates how much the line that separates the acceptance of same-sex love from its rejection has little to do with their level of education or intelligence. One must be blind to believe that, generation after generation, homophobes were merely uncultured and barbarous. They were for the most part as balanced, intelligent, and educated as you and I, and sometimes among the most visionary individuals of their time.

How can human intelligence produce such different results as having one person vilify an "abominable" act and another fight for his or her right to love? This astonishing and yet so familiar reality reveals the extent of our current ignorance. Here lies the key to understanding homosexuals' personal and collective fate, and yet we have been unable to resolve this paradox. This failure encapsulates the limitations that have traditionally plagued the current homosexual discourse, as much as the limitations that a renovated homosexual discourse ought to transcend.

Overall, the debate around homosexuality (homophobia included) has been very consistent on one point: one's analysis of the issue is always consistent with one's moral views on the topic. Simply said, pro-homosexuals have been very busy trying to defend and justify their own views on homosexuality while anti-homosexuals were doing the exact opposite. Not surprisingly, each side has made no effort to understand the rationale of the adversary, as one would expect from adversaries, after all. Rare are those who tried to break this pattern. Each camp is trapped in a monologue, and the rule of the game is to listen (really listen) only to those who agree with you. One may call this way of thinking "monological" insofar as it only considers one logic or perspective, which is that of the one expressing it. Accordingly, the discourse thereby generated is informed unilaterally by only one context: the one of the person expressing it. I would like to examine that mechanism more closely. It is our reluctance to think beyond monological views that is at the root of our dichotomized vision of the world (between right and wrong, we and them, whatever side one takes) and has led us to the current impasse. Monological thinking has impaired the pro-homosexual discourse since its creation and, therefore, constitutes the first limitation that we must overcome.

There are two concepts with which we must now become deeply acquainted: perspective and context. They represent the angle and space, respectively, from which one thinks, feels, and, logically, acts. When one grows curious about the context and the perspective from which a given person speaks, one starts quickly to see how much both dramatically affect the way we understand things. Any conversation, any opinion, but truly anything, should always be considered along with the context and the perspective from which it emerges. Such a statement might sound obscure to some of you or obvious to others; it is however the most difficult thing for human beings to do, and let me illustrate what I mean with a simple example.

Let us pick a hypothetical situation, one that will trigger, without doubt, emotional reactions and moral judgments: Peter grabs his gun and shoots a man before him. Those are mere facts. Nevertheless, the action took place within a certain context or setup. In Peter's case, how is that context going to affect our view on what happened? If Peter was sitting at the counter of a neighborhood bar and the unlucky fellow who was shot to death had just made a deplorable joke at the expense of Peter, our most likely interpretation would be that Peter committed plain bloody murder. In contrast, if Peter and the other man were enemies on the battlefield, our most probable interpretation would be that Peter responded like one would expect from a soldier. The action of killing someone, within two different contexts, gives rise to at least two alternative interpretations, two moral judgments, and consequently two very different stories. One is about a criminal, the other about a hero. Yet things are not always that simple. Imagine that Peter was walking on the street when a stranger stole his wallet. Peter shot the man in order to retrieve his wallet. You and I might not agree any longer on what to think of it. In this context, the shooting is likely to evoke a range of different interpretations and opinions, insofar as no large cultural consensus exists regarding the right to kill in order to protect one's property.

There are several lessons that one can learn from this simple case study. First of all, notice how our interpretation of the facts is a function of the context that surrounds the action as much as the action itself. Second, we always face multiple perspectives, or levels of reality, at once. A first level describes objective facts and only objective facts (e.g., Peter shoots a guy on a battlefield) that can be measured and/or recorded. This perspective, exterior, so to speak, reflects a concrete and neutral reality observed from the outside. Nevertheless, we become quickly aware of another level of reality: you and I are going to interpret and judge the facts immediately: "Peter killed someone"; "Peter protected himself"; "this is bad"; "what Peter did is brave, I would have run away"; or "Peter has no heart." We are going to have an opinion about it, whether we want it or not, because this is what the human mind does, automatically. Even if that opinion is neutral or undetermined at this point, it is still an opinion, which implies a moral judgment based on emotional reactions and a certain understanding of the fact. Hence in addition to the exterior perspective given by objective facts, a new perspective emerges simultaneously, or will emerge as soon as we become aware of the facts, which consists of our perception and interpretation of the facts. This constitutes a second perspective, this time interior or subjective, because it depends on the existence of a "subject" to perceive this reality.

So, on the one hand, we have an objective reality: exterior, factual, and measurable, and on the other hand, a subjective reality: interior and hosted by the mind. Subjective reality includes not only personal interpretations, but also moral (good or bad) and aesthetic (beautiful or ugly) judgments—what one feels, thinks, or intends in response to, for instance, Peter's situation, the Mona Lisa, Osama Bin Laden, or gay sex. Those judgments are altered and informed by the exterior context in which the facts occur (the bar, the war, or the wallet in Peter's example), but they are also informed by the interior context of the individual. If your own son is in the army, you may manifest a special compassion for soldiers, regardless of the details of what might have really happened. On the contrary, if your father was in the military and left you negative memories, your judgment might end up being harsher, colored with personal resentment. If one of your loved ones committed a murder, you may show more mercy. Overall, objective facts will be perceived very differently as a function of one's personal experiences, culture, age, mood, education, spiritual beliefs, moral development, and so on. Even for perfectly valid reasons, our views are always biased.

We still need to distinguish one last basic perspective. Subjective perspectives come in infinite numbers: my perspective, yours, plus the perspective of everyone who is neither you nor me. That said, your subjective perspective is only another version of mine and vice versa, in that they both are individual subjective perspectives, each composed of beliefs, opinions, moral judgments, aesthetic tastes, and so forth, and each contingent upon its own inner context. The third basic perspective derives directly from individual perspectives, yours, mine, or theirs, in fact from all of them put together. This new perspective has different names, all very familiar to you: agreement, consensus, collective opinion, collective consciousness, etc. It sums up all that a group of people agrees upon, thinks, feels, understands, believes, and so forth—one vast collective interior perspective based upon shared views and shared values.

Anything can be contemplated through three fundamental perspectives, three different prisms, each of them with its own context: (1) the facts—objective reality—and their factual context; (2) one's perception of the facts—individual subjective perspective—and its own interior context; and (3) the collective perception of the facts—collective subjective perspective—and its own subjective interior context. But now that we have distinguished those three perspectives, it is equally crucial to understand how they relate to each other, and let me illustrate this with another example.

"Thou shalt not kill" is typically the expression of an agreement among a group of people, hence a collective subjective view. None of us invented "Thou shalt not kill," yet it deeply influences us. For many of us it is part of the context that determines our moral individual judgment. This shows us that the collective subjective context affects one's individual subjectivity (interpretations, moral judgments, tastes, and so forth) in a very significant manner. So, individual and collective subjective perspectives are intimately connected.

The following example illustrates the interdependence between individual and collective perspective: A plantation owner in the seventeenth century American South possesses African slaves. Because the cultural consensus in that part of the world and at that time of history approved slavery, hardly anyone in the same historical and geographical context condemns that man. Let us now assume that he treats his slaves humanely, in comparison with other local slave owners. How do you in retrospect assess the moral value of this particular situation? Is that man another slave master that has participated in the atrocity of slavery or a man of exception, knowing that, in the seventeenth century American South, slaves were barely considered human beings? This will certainly depend on the collective subjective context that you are coming from. From the vantage point of the twenty-first century, one is most likely to feel appalled by anything involving slavery. In contrast, we can safely assume that a contemporary of these facts, even with an abolitionist sensitivity, would have come from a totally different moral context and, as a result, expressed a more positive outlook. Notice however that even if you live in the twenty-first century, nothing stops you from transposing yourself (virtually speaking of course) to the context of that place and time and understanding that from a seventeenth century American South viewpoint, this was a rather good man. The point of this conversation is not to debate moral views on slavery, but only to emphasize how interdependent individual and collective subjective domains are. We will explore those mechanisms in great detail later, but for now, we have enough material to move along.

As soon as human beings become aware of something, a spectrum of interpretation, feelings, and opinions about this something invades their minds. But the fact is that in the end what we usually call "reality" is not so much composed of objective facts, but rather of facts deeply and irreversibly embedded in our interpretation of the facts. Our world is systematically colored by a multitude of interpretative processes, one layer over the other. We can also reasonably assume that two different persons evolving in two different cultural contexts are likely to process information differently, reach dissimilar conclusions, and ultimately build very distinctive views of the world that surrounds them, which in turn will alter how the next information will be perceived. The system "feeds itself." The more our individual opinions are backed up by a strong cultural consensus, the more we feel validated in our illusion that what we think and feel is simply reality.

One fact, and already there are three different perspectives and contexts from which to see it: three dramatically different agendas that are going to have a tremendous impact on the way we are going to perceive things. For those of you who enjoy semantics, these three fundamental and irreducible perspectives correspond to the three pronouns: third person singular, IT (which includes he and she), first person singular, I, and first person plural, WE. Any occurrence can be viewed objectively as mere facts and things, which corresponds to the third person IT perspective of a neutral observer. The same occurrence is grasped subjectively through the individual perspective of the first person singular I, opening the gate of interpretation, thoughts, and feelings. And from the sum of all those I perspectives arises a collective subjective perspective, WE. We will soon see how useful these three perspectives—IT, I, and WE—will be in our exploration of the homosexual phenomenon. Yet we still have one last distinction to outline in order to complete this part.

Let us come back to Peter's action for a moment. So far, the source of the subjective perspective was always somehow similar: you or me. You and I, albeit different, have in common that we are outside the action. We are both external observers capable—presumably—of articulating an IT, I, or WE perspective on the facts. Now if we leave the perspective of the observer and try instead to put ourselves in Peter's shoes, the actor's position, let us see what happens. When Peter faced an enemy soldier on the battlefield, he might have felt authentically life-threatened. Using his gun was an appropriate response in order to protect his life. But without changing anything about the facts but only what happened in his head, what if Peter acted out of cold blood? Similarly, in the case of robbery, we would look at Peter's action very differently depending on whether his wallet contained the money to pay for his daughter's vital surgery or only a few bucks. Why? Because in the first case we may assume that Peter felt deeply desperate, but not in the second one. Perhaps the stranger had a particular racial type, which could constitute crucial information on a battlefield or the rationale for a racist murder in a western city. Hence, our views and moral judgment are likely to be profoundly altered depending on whether Peter acted out of an irrepressible fear or in cold blood, or whether he was prejudiced or not. The same action will sound either justified, questionable, or clearly reprehensible. Eventually, it will determine whether you are going to feel compassion for this man, or not. What was Peter's true intention? What did he think and feel? This piece of information—the "why" of the issue—is critical. It holds the key to our puzzle.

By attempting to see the event through Peter's eyes, we may very well reach a conclusion that is very different from the one we would have otherwise chosen. Yet, the interior reality of Peter is held within a context that is totally different from ours, as exterior observers. To access Peter's subjective world requires experiencing "being" Peter, at least for a moment. And in general, since brains, unlike computers, cannot synchronize their respective contents, entering someone's inner reality is a rather complicated task for human beings. Peter himself would have to sort out layers of lies, denials, self-protection, and self-justification in order to unearth his true intentions.[35]

The most common way to achieve this is to enter in a dialog with the other and listen carefully to what the person says. You genuinely let yourself intuit, embrace, and eventually experience the inner world or first person perspective of another individual (or group of individuals). You put yourselves in someone else's shoes, and by doing so, you get a vivid picture of his or her world, thoughts, intentions and feelings, without the interferences resulting from personal judgments.

Entering the interior space of another necessitates a lot of sensitivity, trust, fair judgment, and an authentic curiosity. It requires above all an acute awareness of our own context, the one that constrains and drives us, your or my "I," which unfailingly gets dragged into the picture. This unique way to relate to another is called empathy.[36] Empathy is relating with nothing else in the way. Empathy implies a non-judgmental listening to another, and this is probably one of the most difficult things for human beings. And the more one integrates the subjective reality of an "other," the more one is able to deconstruct the rationale behind the actions, thoughts, and emotions of that "other." But when that other is someone with whom we can barely emotionally, psychologically, or culturally identify with, or someone who denies your right to love or even your right to live, developing empathic feelings for that other constitutes an authentic tour de force. Being a pluralistic thinker requires the willingness to slide into the first person perspective of someone, regardless of our point of view. This is neither voodoo nor sainthood. This is only intellectual rigor.

Now, what if the occurrence in question is no longer Peter or slavery but a law criminalizing homosexuality, a ban against same-sex marriage, a hostile speech delivered by a religious leader, or a fatwa against homosexuals? What if it is opening civil partnership to same sex-couples or allowing gay bishops in the Anglican Church? And what if it is about closing gay sex clubs or distributing condoms in high school in order to prevent the spread of HIV? The same exact mechanisms apply to the world of gay politics and homosexual history in general. Oversimplifying very little, one observes that from a pro-homosexual perspective homophobia is the problem, and that, not surprisingly, from an anti-homosexual perspective, homosexuality is the problem—two different contexts, two different conclusions, and two statements grounded in a monological thinking. Moreover, each standpoint, being validated by a strong consensus within its own group and its own culture, ends up looking so much like "reality" that nobody ever questions it. But if instead one begins to assume that these two statements are equally valid when considered inside their own contexts, one can then start to ask the first really interesting question: What about context(s) can make same-sex love appear so different depending on what side of the fence one stands? And if, while coming from a pro-homosexual moral standpoint, one suddenly stops denying the context-dependent validity of homophobic claims, one is revolutionizing the homosexual discourse.

Throughout this inquiry into the homosexual phenomenon, you and I will have to stay acutely aware of the fact that IT, I, and WE perspectives always come in two distinct "flavors," a pro-homosexual one and an anti-homosexual or homophobic one. From an integral perspective, we must offer a comprehensive rationale to both and not just to one or the other. Let me give you a sense of what these six minimal perspectives may look like with a very simple example.

Imagine that the occurrence in question is two men having sex, and let us consider it first from the standpoint of one of the men involved in the act. From an IT perspective, sex evokes a world of body reactions and physical sensations which all occur into a particular physical context—two bodies that appear designed to enjoy this sort of experience. From an "I" perspective, one desires, love, but one also makes sense of this moment through emotions, feelings, and thoughts, all connected with a vast inner world (his inner context) of memories, knowledge, beliefs, preferences, and so on. From a WE perspective, one contemplates how sex between two men is perceived by homosexuals, starting with the two involved in the act, along with the network of beliefs and moral views that surrounds them, which also have their own cultural and historical context. So, in a nutshell, a man sleeps with a man (IT perspective), hopefully, he enjoys it (I perspective) and feels good or bad about it as a function of the beliefs and morals that he shares with his partner and the culture he lives in (WE perspective).

Now, from the viewpoint of a homophobic observer (most presumably), those three perspectives are diametrically different, yet just as real and just as important. It may involve reactions of repulsion, the activation of some brain areas that will elicit aggressive behavior, and/or a sudden surge of adrenaline in the bloodstream (IT perspective). One may experience all sorts of negative emotions—fear, anger, disgust, and so forth—resulting in hostile thoughts and feelings (I perspective). And the unpleasant experience is automatically framed into the particular type of homophobic discourse that is available through the culture in which that individual grows (WE perspective). To recapitulate, one witnesses homosexual behaviors (IT), is grossed out by it and perhaps also angry (I), and immediately understands why, thanks to his inherited homophobic beliefs (WE).

Having to cover each one of those six perspectives in a rigid manner for each and every conversation about homosexuality would be excruciating. Moreover, such clear-cut dichotomy between pro- and anti-homosexual perspectives is not representative of the complexity of the real world. Rather, our entire discourse needs to become aware that what we call reality is usually nothing else but our clever interpretation of the facts, which itself is largely under the influence of greater dynamics that will be explored in depth in the following chapters, and that human deeds, opinions, and emotions remain incomprehensible as long as one takes them out of the objective and subjective context from which they arose.

Ultimately, homosexuality and homophobia, just like any kind of human experience, can be accessed from two very different I perspectives: that of an insider or that of an outsider. From the I perspective of an insider, one feels; from the I perspective of an outsider, a YOU perspective, one judges. And there is nothing morally wrong about that, other than, when one is limited to judging, one is not only excluded from another's inner reality but also doomed to remain at the effect of a dynamic that one cannot comprehend. This is exactly why homosexuals and homophobes still cannot understand each other and keep seeing themselves as each other's victims. We need to transcend the binary choice of I versus YOU,

I versus "other," and develop an ability to get profoundly related with the inner experience of another, as different as a homophobe may be from a homosexual. It may still look abstract at this point, but there lies our only chance to understand where the blindness, the fear, and the violence come from, and deconstruct the elements of a tragedy that has been going on for centuries now. And in opening ourselves to a multi-perspective view of reality, we are taking a first step toward creating the foundation of a truly pluralistic homosexual discourse.

CULTURAL PARADIGM

We have now become accustomed to the idea that people's views and actions are, first, consistent with their own personal subjectivities and not necessarily someone else's, and second, that far from being free-moving entities, they are extensively constrained by the context in which they emerge. What exactly influences one's subjectivity? And what do we know about its environment? Postmodern thinkers, Michel Foucault in particular, have abundantly debated those questions. I would like now to revisit their brilliant insight, which today is perhaps the central tenet of postmodern thought.

Our subjective world, our psyche, is filled with an unmeasurable mass of preexisting information. This mass of preexisting information, whose existence precedes anything that comes out of our mind, has a singularly familiar name: the culture. According to postmodern thinkers, cultures are the inevitable filters through which one sees the world and oneself—through which one thinks, feels, judges, and operates his or her entire life. For instance, we can easily see how two civilizations as introverted and extroverted as Japan and Brazil, respectively, can give rise to two distinct flavors of human beings. Growing up Japanese or Brazilian will have a decisive influence on the way one understands things such as honor, love, and individual freedom. Similarly, any culture and subculture, whether based on class, race, socio-economics, age, religious beliefs, sexuality, or life style, will unavoidably play a determinant role in shaping individuals. We tend to be more or less aware of how much the sum of all those layers—cultures and subcultures—alters the way that we experience life and understand the world and ourselves. Usually travelers and those living abroad become extremely conscious of their cultural specificities. Crossing social class boundaries, or simply paying a visit to a different age group, will quickly shed light on the striking influence of subcultural contexts also. Often one feels like he/she is on a different planet.

Now, what postmodern thinkers tell us is that all this is actually only the tip of the iceberg. It is only what ordinary mortals like you and I can see of the cultural yoke that girdles their mind. We are deeply unaware of the full extent in which who we are, what we think, feel, and even create is controlled by the cultural context in which we grow. For the most part, this process is totally invisible to us. The very foundation of our access to knowledge resides in this blind area, deeply buried inside our collective psyche. In *The Order of Things*, Michel Foucault defined what he called an episteme (from "knowledge" in Greek). Each episteme delimits an epistemological unit, or more exactly, the epistemological unity—the particular capacity of knowing—of a certain culture at a given time of history, which Foucault describes as follows: "This *a priori* is what, in a given period, delimits in the totality of experience a field of knowledge, defines the mode of being of the objects that appear in that field, provides man's everyday perception with theoretical powers, and defines the conditions in which he can sustain a discourse about things that is recognized to be true."[37]

A set of a priori assumptions that fixes the conditions of knowledge and of the discourse about this knowledge, in other words, that determines what people spontaneously see as true and how they are going to grasp that truth . . . that is quite a concept. The dictionary tells us more simply that an episteme corresponds to "the body of ideas that determine the knowledge that is intellectually certain at any particular time." Eventually, Michel Foucault himself, certainly out of compassion for his readers, condensed his thought into the idea of "cultural subconscious" (not to be confused with Carl Jung's notion of collective unconscious). An episteme represents the few hidden basic principles that govern any given cultural paradigm, a little like the underwater part of an iceberg.

Without becoming religiously attached to the concepts of episteme and cultural paradigm themselves, we absolutely need to realize what they imply: In order to be able to know something, human beings must first see it and, second, accept that it is real and true. Knowing does not occur in a blank space, but instead relies on the existence of a body of predetermined rules that allow and shape the process of knowing. All mental processes arise and evolve within a cultural field, itself organized according to a set of invisible assumptions, which are going to constrain the quality of our thoughts, feeling, moral views, and aesthetic judgments, at the most primordial level. At the end, the cultural context—episteme, cultural paradigm, and so on—operates very much like the operating system of a computer. Its main task is to provide the basic framework in which all software functions. It both defines and limits the performance of the computer by fixing the perimeter of what can be done with it.

Just as we were starting to get used to the idea that everything that we think, feel, or intend, emerges from a vast pool of collective elements, most of them below consciousness level, we have yet to realize that the epistemological context of a given (sub)culture, far from being a fixed entity, evolves. And this process occurs in a very particular fashion. First the cultural context does not merely change but actually expands through history. At each pivotal time in history, such as the Axial Age, the Enlightenment, the rise of modernity, postmodernity, or globalization, to name only a few, the paradigm/episteme shift manifests itself in the form of a significant expansion of the space of awareness. Almost suddenly, more things can be recognized and understood, that is, seen and accepted as true. As a consequence of that, an entire field of knowledge, beyond the one that was previously available, becomes accessible. And this implies that each new paradigm/episteme includes the one that precedes it. Let me illustrate that with a concrete example.

The concept of universal gravitation, as Isaac Newton conceptualized it in the seventeenth century, was consistent with a vision of a universe governed by the law of cause and effect, which structured the scientific paradigm of the time. Although it constituted an amazing breakthrough, Newton's theory of universal gravitation is no match—complexity-wise—for the mind-boggling subtleties of quantum theory, born three centuries later, which sees elementary particles in terms of probability events and proclaims the virtual impossibility of absolute measurement. Scientists in the seventeenth century were grounded in a world of assumptions—an epistemological context—that was incompatible with the kind of ideas associated with quantum theory. Those ideas could not possibly fit in a mind of the seventeenth century scientist, and most likely it would have occurred as pure fantasy. On the other hand, a twentieth century scientist can easily comprehend a seventeenth century scientific theory, such as the law of universal gravitation, simply because his epistemological context surpasses and includes the one that fostered the scientific revolution in the seventeenth century. Twentieth century scientists can adopt the epistemological context of seventeenth century scientists, but the reverse is not possible. By no means was this an issue of intellectual limitation on the part of seventeenth century scientists, especially when that scientist is named Isaac Newton.

Even the brightest minds in human history have been trapped into the particular cultural context of their time. There is and will be no exception to this. And this applies to Isaac Newton as much as Augustine, Thomas Aquinas, and the many thinkers that have expressed anti-homosexual opinions. Open mindedness, just like knowledge, is not a mere matter of intelligence or selflessness. In fact, those qualities are, by and large, secondary. No matter what, the set of basic assumptions that define the prevalent cultural paradigm/episteme of a given time remains unquestioned by those who are lost in it: for them, it is reality. Like water for fish (and air for us), people are never aware of the "cultural subconscious" that undergird the act of knowing. Yet, taken out of the water, a fish might quickly notice that something is missing. Likewise, the epistemological roots of a particular cultural context can only be seen when you step out of it. Hence, cultural historians can only identify and analyze a given paradigm/episteme in a retrospective manner. They remain blind to the one to which they belong. Not only can we not recognize our "cultural subconscious," but it is impossible to distance ourselves from it, and therefore to grasp how much it colors our views of the world.

Contrary to what they believe, human beings cannot experience the world directly. Rather, they are like a fish in an aquarium, observing the outside through the deforming thickness of multiple translucent layers, completely oblivious to the presence of the water and the glass wall, and convinced that things out there really are like what they see. We see and speak of the world through multiple interpretive lenses. And the fact is that we not only borrow most of those lenses from our culture, but, for a large part, this process is beyond our understanding. These invisible cultural boundaries define our space of awareness. Whether we want it or not, they constrain the scope of what we can grasp and what we can create.

Any endeavor to explain the rise or decline of particular moral views must take this essential insight of postmodernity into account, and this is especially true for those who attempt to decode the logic of homosexuality's history. We must then shift our focus from the moral views themselves to the contexts from which those moral views emerged. It is inside those contexts that they will make sense, and inside those contexts that we will be able to articulate them together within a larger framework. Many have told the story of those moral views. This book is about the story of the contexts in which those moral views unfolded.

THE TIME DIMENSION, FROM INDIVIDUAL DEVELOPMENT TO SPECIES EVOLUTION

Nothing is fixed. Everything is in movement. And so is our so-called reality—human awareness, oblivious traveler, surreptitiously drifting on an invisible raft. By unveiling the inescapable pull of cultures over individual psyches and how the epistemological context of any culture evolves throughout history, postmodern thinkers pointed to one essential variable: time. Time is the ultimate context for everything, particularly when it involves human beings. Every aspect of human reality unfolds in a timely fashion. Not only do we rarely see time as being an active dimension of human life, but we may also start to view time as being flexible, complex, often distorted, and occasionally discontinued ("Einsteinian" as opposed to "Newtonian" time) and still, an omnipresent force, constantly transforming every aspect of human existence. And this applies to the three major timescales in which human life unfolds: individual life, the span of a culture, and the evolution of the human species.

Time is inherently going to affect who we are, how we see ourselves, and what we are aware of; hence it will deeply alter what we think, believe, say, and what we can create. When one chooses time as the basic context to describe everything, everything becomes a developmental process. What I call "developmental process" is significantly more complex than the simple alternation of birth, maturation, aging, and eventually death. Most, if not all, aspects of what Pierre Teilhard de Chardin called the "phenomenon of man" seem to unfurl over time according to some master plan. My declared goal here is to reframe the entire homosexual phenomenon so as to reveal the various developmental dynamics that animate it. Chapter by chapter, I intend to demonstrate that homosexuality contains the blueprints of its unfolding with time, and on multiple planes, each one corresponding to a different timescale.

First, consider the shortest timescale: the duration of one's lifetime. Developmental psychologists have extensively studied how sexual desire, sexual behavior, and sexual identity (heterosexual or homosexual) progressively emerge from childhood to adulthood. They all concur that homosexual identity—one's self-awareness of being homosexual—does not work like an "off-on" switch as often imagined. To embrace a homosexual identity entails more than simply finding out one day that you are gay. Rather, it grows via a complex process of expansion of one's awareness about oneself and the cultural environment. Homosexual identity crystallizes sequentially, through discrete steps recapitulated through six emblematic stages of development, which I will present in chapter 15.

Let us next take a larger temporal framework, now counting in centuries: cultural history. What we call homosexuality today is in fact a recent concept. Until approximately the mid-twentieth century, the idea of two men or two women involved in a loving, monogamous, long term, and equal-in-status relationship, which epitomizes the current homosexual ideal in the West, was largely foreign. In all other cultures across the world and throughout history, homosexual relationships obeyed very different moral and aesthetic rules. Just to give you an idea, "Greek love" was rigidly codified as the love of a mature man for an adolescent boy and strictly restricted to that type of relationship. Homosexual love, as we know it today, was invented anew. It was the result of a centuries-long historical process, that is, a cultural developmental process.

One can zoom out even more and contemplate the homosexual phenomenon at an even wider timescale, over hundreds of thousands, if not millions, of years throughout the evolution of the human species. In recent decades the contribution of zoologists, neuroscientists, and geneticists to this topic has been nothing short of astounding. But if homosexual behavior was shown to be extremely common in the animal kingdom, far more compelling is the fact that the social organization of homosexual behavior in apes presents striking parallels with what anthropologists and historians have reported regarding early human societies. Little by little, the meticulous study of sexual life of apes allows us to reconstruct nearly twenty-five million years of sociobiological evolution of homosexual behavior. Keep in mind however that because of its unprecedented development in the cultural sphere, the human species has brought the homosexual sociocultural repertoire to an entirely new level of refinement.

The story of homosexuality is not one, but several. Each one of those stories gives us a different piece of the puzzle. All together, they tell us the grand story of the unraveling of the homosexual phenomenon through time. Homosexuality is not so much a state of fact, but rather a dynamic reality—an evolutionary impetus.

Now, homosexuality is not the only phenomenon that I intend to observe through the lens of time. Homophobia, from an integral perspective, ought to receive an equal treatment, which means that it must be investigated by following the same guidelines. Putting aside whether we like it or not, homophobia must also be understood in developmental terms (biological, psychological, and cultural) rather than as an expression of man's evil. At the same time, an essential difference distinguishes the development of homosexuality and the one of homophobia. Homosexuality is a mode of being, which includes multiple dimensions of what a human being can embody or embrace. But, most importantly, homosexuality exists for its own sake. Homophobia, in contrast, is no more than a reaction against homosexuality, a particular form of hostility. As such, it is part of a much larger dynamic, to which I dedicate an entire chapter: the acceptance or rejection of the "other."

CONTEXT-DETERMINED VERSUS CONTEXT-AWARE

The Integral Approach proves particularly powerful, for it allows people to tackle any problem at a depth and with a breadth that is seldom reached when using more restrictive approaches. Yet any new, improved, or more effective methodology, while able to solve old problems, inevitably creates new ones. Notice what happened when modernity took over in seventeenth and eighteenth centuries Europe. Under the impulse of geniuses such as Nicholas Copernicus, René Descartes, and Isaac Newton, critical thinking progressively imposed itself as the prevalent mode of thinking, aiming to replace an old medieval paradigm, in which truth was principally determined on the basis of collective agreements and build through rhetoric. Until that point, for instance, the stories of the Scriptures were true by virtue of the cultural consensus that held them as true. Any scientific and philosophical claims had to be consistent with the words of the Bible in order to be accepted (a mode of thinking that still prevails in traditionalist and fundamentalist religious cultures today). But by challenging the oppressing and omnipresent authority of belief systems, critical thinking liberated the discovery process from the cultural dogma. Objective knowledge was set apart from the world of beliefs and, from that point on, beliefs would no longer determine "truth" (at least theoretically). This major shift in European culture paved the way for the emergence of the modern paradigm. The birth of modern science and technology, the rise of democratic regimes, the end of slavery, the establishment of market economies, to name only a few, are direct consequences of this epistemological revolution.

However, moderns faced a new and daunting challenge. Their empirical and objective approach to the world inherently depended on the quality of their assessment of the reality that they were trying to grasp. Logically, the precision of the measurement became the new obsession of the modern world. Sciences such as physics and natural history, and also economics, history, education, and political science, all grew hungry for increasingly powerful methods that would help them gauge as precisely as possible the validity of their hypotheses (and we will see later how that process has been instrumental in the evolution of cultural views concerning homosexuality).

If we mean to develop an "integral approach" to human affairs and, in our particular case, of homosexuality, what new excruciating problem must "integral" thinkers therefore confront? The central difficulty in any integral approach revolves around one's awareness of the many possible perspectives and contexts.

This is where the quality of integral thinking lies. Integral thinkers ought to wrestle with the depth generated by the multiplicity of perspectives, each one coming with its own epistemological context, just like the moderns did with the precision of their experimental measurements.

But my argument raises another question: how are integral thinkers supposed to accomplish such a feat? You remember that everything we know, we know within, and thanks to a web of preexisting information—the epistemological context. What we already know (or believe we know) dramatically affects how we learn new information. Depending upon whether the latter is congruent or not with one's epistemological context, one either adopts, rejects, disregards, or fails to notice it. In point of fact, for most of their lives human beings are totally unaware of or uninterested in the context from which they discover the world. They have no control over it. By and large, human beings are context-determined, "determined" as in the result of a determinism.

Take the landing of the first human being on the moon, for instance. Depending on one's context, one might view this historical feat very differently: an extraordinary accomplishment from the viewpoint of the advance of science, a heroic exploit as seen through the eyes of a child or a tribe member, a terrible waste of money according to a humanitarian activist, a proof of men's arrogance from the viewpoint of a religious ultra-conservative, or as uninteresting information for one undergoing an existential crisis. Now, one can see that all those perspectives are valid—seen from their own contexts. Sending a man to the moon was a remarkable scientific and human achievement, but was horrifyingly costly, barely improving the quality of life for human beings on the planet, particularly for those living in miserable conditions, and was, all things considered, rather insignificant in the scale of the cosmos. Everybody is "right" from his/her own perspective.

To turn this insight (the importance of context) into an epistemological context is no small feat. Integral thinkers, if conscientious, must learn to work with a kaleidoscope of perspectives/contexts and stop limiting themselves to their personal opinions about everything. This implies to transition from being context-determined to being context-aware. To be context-aware demands intellectual discipline, a long-term and rigorous effort to unearth the perspectival depth of anything, just like modernity strived for always more refined assessments of objective reality.

Applying this principle to the study of homosexuality, as I will do, will enable us to solve many mysteries and unlock some of the core issues of the homosexual debate. That, however, entails examining the moral views of the current pope from his particular context, the organization of same-sex relationships in different cultures from their particular contexts, homosexual desire from its many different contexts, and "gay pride" from the many possible contexts from which it can emerge. As can be imagined, we are due for a serious update.

Since I am contemplating the omnipresence and quasi omnipotence of contexts, I should say something about the context of my arguments. I will often sound critical of both a certain kind of gay activism and the homosexual discourse more or less up to and including the advent of queer theory, which I deem as being both dangerously fragmented and manipulative and fundamentally Manichaean. I nonetheless deeply acknowledge the astonishing courage of gay activism without which I would not be able to tell my own story today. If gay marriage is now possible in several countries, and tomorrow in many others, nobody can deny the preeminent role of gay activism. My gratitude for all those men and women who gave me the freedom to live how I live today is immense. I similarly salute the remarkable insights of the many outstanding intellectuals who have contributed to the emergence of a pro-homosexual discourse. My work is built on theirs. And yet, I am challenging the context which they all come from.

But my challenge does not come from the conviction that those before me did wrong or that they should have proceeded differently. As a matter of fact, I do not believe that things should have been different. The homosexual discourse is also an evolutionary phenomenon, that is, a story that unfolds through time. The questions that arise and the solutions that are offered are always a function of the sociocultural context of the time. Many of the questions and solutions that I present here would have been irrelevant, even inappropriate, at times when the church sentenced sodomites to burn at the stake, when governments sent homosexuals to concentration camps or psychiatric hospitals, or when staying in the closet was the only way that one could keep a job, a family, and friends. But we are now, collectively, in a very different place. Hence my challenge is a call for more growth. Not only because we can afford it now, having harvested the results of several decades of gay activism, but mostly because it is today the vital step forward that we need to make.

The True, the Good, and the Beautiful

We are now equipped with an integral—pluralistic, context-aware, and evolutionary—worldview. This means that we can tackle a problem such as the acceptance of homosexuality in human societies knowing that our personal opinions and those of others are unavoidably trapped into the cultural web from which they are born. We then know that this cultural web is not fixed, but overall expands along with the culture itself in the historical process that we call cultural development. Now, I would like to pin down more precisely where and why gay culture and the homosexual discourse got stuck.

As I have stated, something about homosexuality today does not quite work. Accepted or even integrated, there is still something unsettling about it. Coming out is a mere relief, "gay pride" no more than a survival trick. What is this nagging discomfort that homosexuals keep feeling? And if this unpleasant feeling no longer results from their oppression, what causes it? The intuition that the adventure initiated in the 1970s with gay liberation was still incomplete kept lingering in the back of my head—a taste of wanting more, without being able to tell what it was. After searching so hard and so well, I still did not really know how to cope with, address, or let alone comprehend the disappointment of my people. And this feeling secretly tormented me.

In the meantime, gay culture was clouded by the fumes of a fratricidal war between the various clans of gay activism. Gay liberation had engendered an ideological kaleidoscope worthy of a council of the early church—no debate about the sex of angels or the divine nature of Jesus, but instead the relentless confrontation between the proponents of gay identity versus queer identity, social integration versus cultural rebellion, nature versus nurture, essentialists against constructivists, and so on. The result on the homosexual community was toxic. I eventually became seriously frustrated about the issue. Let me share with you the four insights that I had over the years, in the order in which I became aware of them.

First, the young research scientist that I was back then came to realize to what extent the scientific research on homosexuality (which included the data from neuroscience, genetics, and zoology) was seriously misunderstood and how the fundamental role played by science in the homosexual debate was totally missed. During the 1990s, scientists accumulated compelling evidence that demonstrated (1) the widespread distribution of homosexual behavior among the animal kingdom; (2) the genetic inheritance of homosexuality, at least to some degree; and (3) the probable involvement of discrete areas in the limbic system in sexual orientation. Still, the debate was fierce, particularly regarding the genetic and neurobiological aspects of homosexuality. Some gay activists did not hesitate to accuse scientists of playing into the hands of oppressive homophobic institutions, when they were not suspecting them of setting the ground for future eugenic politics. Some scholars in the humanities dismissed the very validity of their research. Others saw in the scientific inquiry into homosexuality's biology a betrayal or some sort of profanation. For them the scientific approach was at best reductive, at its worse, dangerous. Their discourse, which undoubtedly aimed at defending the political integrity of the homosexual minority, was too often reminiscent of the dark ages. Curiously, while an entire section of gay activism went ballistic, most of my gay friends and other "LGBT" acquaintances appeared to welcome scientific news without any particular concern, if not enthusiastically. For them, being homosexual was as natural as having two hands or one nose.

As years went by, it became clear to me that the humanities' mistrust of biological sciences was dictated by fear more than reason. An integral discourse on homosexuality cannot disregard that fear. It must address it. So, it is about time that we offered a serious answer to these questions: Why should science look into the world of homosexuality? Why are we fascinated but also sometimes threatened by the explanations that science gives us? Not only was the whole impact of the scientific culture on the collective psyche being ignored (which we will explore in time), but the homosexual discourse lacked the solid epistemological context that it needed to assimilate a scientific demystification of same-sex desire. Up to this point, the homosexual discourse has tried its best to "cope" with scientific information. It is time for the homosexual discourse to instead become hungry for what science has to say.

The second problem was that gay activism did not hesitate to conflate scientific information with moral issues in order to promote its own agenda. To take a concrete example, searching for the "gay gene" became morally and politically charged, which quickly generated unsolvable contradictions in the gay agenda. In one sense, the gay gene was a "good thing," insofar as people appeared generally less hostile to homosexuals if it was demonstrated the homosexuality was some sort of "birth defect" rather than the voluntary adoption of a depraved life style. On the other hand, the gay gene was a "bad thing" that would soon allow discrimination against homosexuals in utero. For some, the existence of a gay gene denied homosexuals the authorship of their lifestyle. Homosexuals were stripped of their free will. Homosexuality was being turned into another form of determinism, and the genome was becoming the ultimate "oppressor."

How incongruous would it be to argue that slavery should be abolished on the basis that African American people have no say in the color of their skin! Why should homosexuals tolerate a gay political agenda built upon the belief that they are genetically "doomed"? The connection is absurd. In fact, history shows that the belief that same-sex desire results from one's innate disposition, which was widespread from antiquity to the nineteenth century, never fostered any tolerance for those who acted upon this desire. Conflating science and morality was a short-sighted strategy. It estranged homosexuals from the concept of homosexuality even more, and turned the fragile quest for a homosexual consciousness into a lobbying campaign.

Third, the homosexual discourse has, by and large, failed to present homosexuals other than as the victims of the heterosexual order. After nearly one hundred years of pro-homosexual discourse, which started with the work of remarkable pioneers such as Karl Heinrich Ulrichs (1825–1895) and John Addington Symonds (1840–1893), the overly dominating tone has desperately been the one of victimization. Guy Hocquenghem, in his groundbreaking manifesto *Homosexual Desire*, published in 1972, wrote that "the establishment of homosexuality as a separate category goes hand in hand with its repression."[38] In 2002, thirty years later, queer theorist David M. Halperin added his own personal touch to the problem by confessing that "[his] purpose in historicizing homosexuality was to denaturalize heterosexuality, to deprive it of its claims to be considered as a 'traditional value' and ultimately to destroy the self-evidence of the entire system on which the homophobic opposition between homosexuality and heterosexuality depends."[39] Even Michel Foucault could not imagine homosexuality other than in terms of dominance and repression (the "ruse of power" as

Halperin puts it).[40] According to their claim, homosexual rebels around the world had one common enemy: the heterosexual authority.

In the end, homosexual culture was of no help when it came to giving me a real sense of who I am, deep inside. Why should I be proud to be gay? Essentially, there was no valid reason to feel ashamed of it, but that was about it. Something was missing. Homosexual identity felt incomplete, truncated. It did not convey a sense of wholeness and depth, let alone beauty. Next to this, heterosexual life was showing me a world that had no equivalent in mine: dating, marriage, children, family . . . Heterosexuality embodied the miracle of life, homosexuality did not. Not only did heterosexuality dominate all sociocultural structures, but it was also omnipresent in all traditional representations of love from Adam and Eve to Sleeping Beauty and her Prince Charming. Even the laws of physics convinced me that, in nature, only opposites attract each other. An electric plug, a magnet . . . everything expressed some symbolic version of heterosexuality. The universe was not telling me anything about homosexuality, about who I am, and how I love. Instead, it constantly reminded me of heterosexuality's universality. In that universe I was a guest but not a participant, some sort of mutant unlikely to procreate (a separate "species," as Michel Foucault puts it). In other words, I did not belong.

Despite a multitude of definitions, homosexual identity is meaningless. Imprisoned in a schizophrenic and victimized vision of itself, it has failed to provide a solid ground for what homosexuals, like any other human beings, strive for: happiness. I then began to wonder whether anybody had tried to make sense of homosexuality. The truth is, many people had, but the picture was too fragmented to be recognizable. The pieces of the puzzle had to be reorganized. Yet this had to be done in a way that would not repeat the failure of the past. We must therefore complete the foundations of our renovated homosexual discourse and pick up the conversation where we left it.

First, I propose that a transformed homosexual discourse—pluralistic, context-aware, and evolutionary—also fulfills the three following conditions: (1) it ought to integrate all fields of knowledge—that is, to be transdisciplinary; (2) it should keep distinct, yet mutually informed scientific knowledge, moral considerations, and political agenda; and (3) it must absolutely confront the problem of homosexuality's lack of meaning. At which point, I assert that such a discourse needs to address the three fundamental questions that follow:

- What is homosexuality?

- How is it collectively perceived?

- What constitutes one's personal inner experience of homosexuality?

Differently put, I suggest that the whole homosexual reality can be divided into three non-reducible separate perspectives. Collapsing those three questions into one indiscernible blob will only perpetuate the shortcomings that I have described earlier. And you may also recognize in those three themes the three primordial perspectives—IT, WE, and I, respectively—that we have defined earlier.

The first question—"what is homosexuality?"—represents all the objective aspects of homosexuality—homosexuality as object. Hence it corresponds to the IT perspective of a detached observer (even though you and I know now that an observer, always trapped into a particular cultural context, can never be neutral). It encompasses homosexuality's factual reality in today's world and throughout history, its sociocultural organization, as well as its biological and behavioral aspects. I like to call that section "facts and numbers," which is to say what one can count and measure, the best one can.

The second question—"how is homosexuality collectively perceived?"—summarizes the WE perspective, that is, the cultural reality of homosexuality. Homosexuality has a geography and a history. This is the part where one should address all the moral questions related to same-sex love and desire and, in particular, make sense of homosexuality's chaotic history.

The third and last question is by far the more complex and until recently the least explored of the three: the perspective of the "I," someone's personal experience. What is it like for me, the "I" who is talking? What does it mean that "I" am homosexual? And what does one do with that? Every homosexual must at some point face the daunting, solitary, and yet heroic task of building an authentic and coherent self-identity in order to feel whole again. Every homosexual must at some point give meaning to his or her own existence.

Every aspect of homosexuality falls inevitably into at least one of those three distinct perspectives, three distinct domains, and three distinct conversations. By keeping those three distinct conversations rigorously separated, we will avoid the political ruses and overall confusion that have plagued the homosexual discourse up to this time. But even more importantly, by reinstating personal subjectivity as a major concern and giving it back its just place in a renovated homosexual discourse, we will be forced to confront the vast space that today's homosexual culture has left astonishingly empty: the realm of meaning.

As suggested by Ken Wilber, founder of the Integral Approach and to whom I feel immensely indebted, we can trace those three conversations throughout the history of philosophy. They are what Wilber calls the "Big Three":

> Likewise, Habermas's three validity claims, for truth (objects), truthfulness or sincerity (subjects), and rightness or justice (intersubjectivity) . . . And in the broadest sense this is Plato's the True (or propositional truth referring to an objective state of affairs, it), the Good (or cultural justice and appropriateness, we), and the Beautiful (or the individual-aesthetic dimension, I). The Big Three are likewise Kant's three critiques: the Critique of Pure Reason (theoretical it-reason), of Practical Reason or intersubjectivity (we), and of personal Aesthetic Judgment (I). Thus, although other items are included as well, these three great domains—the Big Three—are especially the domains of empirical science, morality, and art.[41]

The True, the Good, and the Beautiful symbolize three distinct and fundamental domains or perspectives through which homosexuality, can be looked at. They give their names to the three parts of this book. We are now to embark on a very singular quest: to gather the scattered fragments of the homosexual reality and integrate them into one grand integral vision of same-sex love. And let us start with objective reality, or, according to Plato, the True.

PART I

The True

The Homosexual Presence

As promised, facts and numbers:

According to the 2005 nationwide survey ordered by the British government, which intended to gauge the economic impact of its new national gay Civil Partnership, nearly 6% of the British population self-identified as homosexual.[42] Yet another survey by the Office for National Statistics in 2010 determined that only 1% of the U.K. population identified as gay or lesbian and 0.5% as bisexual.[43] Other surveys realized in the United States in recent decades offers numbers that oscillate those two extremes.[44] Most recent studies, still in the United States, estimate to ~1.7% the ratio of self-identified gay and lesbian adults (similar counts were found in Canada: 1.9%, Australia: 2.1%, and Norway: 1.2%).[45] The same studies acknowledge that those numbers are most probably undervalued, and homosexuals are more likely to represent 2 to 3% of the adult population.[46]

DEMOGRAPHICS

Evaluating the real incidence of homosexuality among a given population has constituted a serious challenge. The major reason for this is rather obvious. Homosexuals have tended to hide their sexual identity for fear of social alienation. Not a single culture has ever stood out for its total absence of homophobic prejudice (I will substantiate this unusual claim later on). Hence researchers never had at their disposal a truly reliable, unbiased, population sample to perform their studies. Social scientists, acutely aware of the issue, have devised strategies in order to bypass this obstacle.

Rather than directly questioning people about their sexual identity—which people experienced as being both threatening and insensitive given the strongly homophobic context encountered in Europe and North America back then—previous studies focused on the sex of past and current sexual partners.

Indeed, it appears easier to disclose having same-sex experiences rather than admitting to being homosexual, just as it often feels easier to confess having stolen something rather than being a thief. And, as we will soon see in detail, while the two phenomena—self-identification as homosexual, on the one hand, and homosexual behavior, on the other—are tightly linked, they are nevertheless fundamentally distinct. To assume that homosexual behavior equals homosexual identity or that it offers an accurate measure of one's degree of self-identification as homosexual is tempting; it is nonetheless inaccurate. Combining these two elements into one unique and blurry "homosexual reality" has engendered a tremendous confusion and caused numerous headaches among those who have candidly strived to delineate the sociocultural presence of homosexuality.

This was however how Kinsey chose to proceed in his revolutionary survey of sexual practices among American people (*Sexual Behavior in the Human Male* published in 1948 and *Sexual Behavior in the Human Female* in 1953). This was a spectacular start on two accounts. First, the absence of homophobic prejudice in Kinsey's questionnaires and his vigilance regarding the moral neutrality of his team members during the interviews had almost certainly no precedent in the history of social science. Second, the study revealed that 37% and 13% of the male and female population respectively have had at least one same-sex experience.[47]

In 1948 America, the news was hard to swallow. But it also soon generated even more confusion. It quickly became obvious that Kinsey's methodology had significant flaws, particularly regarding the composition of his sample, which was far from being representative of the general population. In addition, Kinsey's results reflected the sexual history rather than the inner (subjective) experience of the people that they had interviewed. Methodological limitations and reductionism aside, the Kinsey Report had opened an irreversible breach in America's moral foundation.

The years that followed saw the research on the demographics of homosexuality, which was complicated and always produced debatable results, turn into a battle of statistics. Governments and other conservative organizations would usually end up with numbers around 1% if not below, while estimates from pro-gay associations often sky-rocketed to 15%. Between the 1% and 15%, one could vaguely discern the nebulous presence of a sexually hard-to-define group of people—individuals who occasionally indulged in "anomalous" practices according to some, or were closeted homosexuals according to others, depending on which side of the fence one stood. Yet, "waverers" constituted one sixth to one fifth of the population, which was definitely more than any conservative could bear.

How can one make sense of such disparity? One simply needed to remember what question pollers asked: "what do you do?" or "what are you?" For many people these two questions have very different answers. What one "does" does not tell about what one "is" until you have a solid experimental ground to assume so. After all, perhaps people did not lie as much as one originally thought.

Already, the history of homosexuality should have raised a red flag. Throughout centuries of homophobic Western culture, the sexual life of homosexuals has never been a trustworthy indicator of their deep desires. Homosexuals have commonly married and lived "honest" heterosexual lives, repressing anything that could not fit inside the sociocultural frame in which they lived. Homosexuals have lied by necessity in order to survive. And that was only one side of the problem. Homosexual behavior is much more fluid than we generally think. It is more frequent among teenagers and in mono-sexual environments, such as boarding schools, prisons, or monasteries. Equally mysterious is the fact that the prevalence of homosexual behavior varied dramatically throughout history. It was routinely practiced in highly developed civilizations—ancient Greece, imperial Rome, pre-Muslim India, imperial China, and pre-Meiji Japan—and was present in most tribal cultures across North America, Asia, Oceania, and Africa. Then, in the space of only a few centuries (a short time on a historical scale), the frequency of homosexual behavior that the Christian West deemed shameful suddenly plummeted, a pattern that European colonization would eventually spread across the world. And yet, unexpectedly, homosexual behavior reappeared during the twentieth century in Europe and North America, and exploded (comparatively speaking) in the last decades.

The assumption that same-sex experience could somehow "measure" one's homosexual identity is a risky one. (Having personally been in a sexually enjoyable relationship with a woman for a period of three years never made me feel other than what I always felt—that is, homosexual.) Why should same or opposite-sex experiences automatically define or alter one's sexual identity? Why presume that one either lies or made a mistake? When they find themselves unable to solve a paradox, human beings often prefer to deny its existence.

I regard as particularly useful, if not necessary and urgent, that homosexual behavior be once and for all distinguished from homosexual identity. It is impossible to reconcile the psychological, sociocultural, and historical reality of homosexuality otherwise. "What do you do" and "what are you" are two very different phenomena that arise in two different realms. The first one—homosexual behavior—represents an objective reality that can be broken down into observable measurable events: an erection, a touch, a penetration, a secretion, or an orgasm. On the other hand, "what you are" is a subjective reality that can only be accessed from the inside. Only through a conversation can one find out whether someone feels gay, lesbian, straight, bisexual, or something else. No machine can determine that yet, which is why scientists are so prone to ignore the subjective side of homosexuality and reduce homosexuality to its behavioral, and hence observable aspects; it was not that they denied the existence of a homosexual subjectivity, but did so rather for the good and valid reason that subjective realities still lie for a great part beyond the reach of the current scientific technology.

The difference between 1% and 15% is not so difficult to interpret in the end. It largely depends on the category in which you put the people that have had both same and opposite-sex sexual experiences. If the term homosexual is restricted to those who never touched anyone from the opposite sex (i.e., exclusively homosexual behavior), then one obtains something close to 1%. Opponents of homosexual rights, eager to deny the reality of homosexuality, feel much happier with that sort of arrangement (and I would not even qualify as homosexual myself). Next to the ~1% of individuals with a pristine homosexual pedigree, one encounters a broader range of individuals who have experienced sex with both genders, regardless of their sexual identity, emotional involvement or their overall satisfaction with the experience. Self-identified gays and lesbians who have sex with opposite-sex partners at some point of their lives (as I did) are not rare, just as many straight-identified people have sex with same-sex partners at some point of their lives, not to mention bisexuals. According to recent surveys, between 10 to 15% of adults report having engaged in same-sex sexual behavior, even though half of them self-identify as heterosexual.[48] Interestingly, these numbers have increased in recent years, proof that people feel more inclined to acknowledge homosexual experiences now than they did twenty or fifty years ago. They may very well keep climbing up in the future if the homophobic prejudice keeps losing its strength. In the end, by announcing that ~25% of adults have experienced at least one same-sex relationship or more, Alfred Kinsey, who was so severely criticized for choosing volunteers instead of a representative population sample for his research, might have been unknowingly prophetic.

To renounce any monolithic conception of the homosexual reality obliges us to specify first which "homosexuality" is being talked about, starting with myself. Unless specified otherwise, homosexuality, as I define it, partakes of both homosexual identity and homosexual behavior, even when homosexual identity remains concealed and/or homosexual behavior suppressed. So, I consider homosexual anybody for whom same-sex desire is an essential part of one's self-identification, (1) regardless of the fact that such self-knowledge is culturally relevant or not, and (2) regardless of the fact that mate choice is limited to a specific subcategory of same-sex partners. Others might offer other definitions, but I find this one most comprehensive and relevant for this discussion. And I hope that the following chapters will make the reasons and implications of my choice clear.

Accordingly, I call homosexual those who consider that creating sexual and emotional bonds with people of their own sex is a true expression of their sexual nature, and only those. Just bear in mind that this by no means precludes the possibility of other enjoyable or exploratory sexual experiences beyond those virtual boundaries, nor does it guarantee that same-sex experience will actually occur.

The next question that naturally comes to mind is: if today homosexuals constitute about 2–3% of the population in the United Kingdom and the United States, what about the rest of the world and, most importantly, was it also the case in the past? From an absolute standpoint, we do not know and probably never will. Notwithstanding this inescapable limitation, one may cautiously attempt to trace the contours, even if blurry, of homosexuality's transcultural and transhistorical reality by extrapolating from the many discoveries that historians and anthropologists have accumulated in the last decades. Today, the presence of homosexuality throughout human history is richly documented. It appears fairly certain at this point that, as R.C. Kirkpatrick wrote, "homosexual behavior has existed throughout human history and in most, perhaps all, human cultures."[49] If you still need to convince yourself of this, I invite you to read remarkable and undisputed scholarly works such as David Greenberg's *Construction of Homosexuality*, Louis Crompton's *Homosexuality and Civilization*, and Stephen O. Murray's *Homosexualities*. The evidence is too compelling today for anybody to argue otherwise in a serious manner.

Homosexual behavior, whose presence has been abundantly documented among numerous animal species,[50] is common among apes (bonobos, chimpanzees, and gorillas) including humans. In fact, it appears deeply ingrained in human sexual nature, and has most probably been so since prehistory.[51] Yet not all human beings show interest in same-sex partners, even when the cultural taboo placed on this behavior remains minimal. In that respect, humans are surprisingly different from all other apes. Among non-human apes and numerous species of monkey, while the frequency of homosexual behavior can vary as a function of the species and circumstances, they never are the attribute of a subset of the population only. Instead, they are more or less homogeneously displayed by the entire group. Among all primates, only the human species possesses a subgroup of individuals that show predominant interest for same-sex partners. Thus, if bisexuality turns out to be the common trait among primates, homosexuality appears to be a characteristic of the human species.

Scientific studies, from the Kinsey report in 1948 to Dean Hammer's publication in 1993, are very consistent regarding this fact: Human sexuality manifests itself through a spectrum of preferential sexual "habits." A majority of individuals are only interested in opposite-sex partners, a variable minority shows attraction to partners of both sexes in various degrees, and a smaller minority is preferentially drawn to same-sex partners.[52] Today we have many good reasons to believe that since its differentiation as a separate species, human populations have—always and everywhere—included individuals more inclined to homosexual behavior. What we unfortunately cannot trace at this point is the moment when, in the course of its evolution, our species switched from generalized homosexual behavior to some sort of homosexual "specialization." We may only assume that this shift had occurred very early in the evolution of modern humans.

Yet homosexual behavior is only half of the equation. What about the distribution of homosexual identity in space and time? That issue must be handled carefully. Knowing how problematic determining the percentage of homosexual population still is today, trying to trace this parameter back in other cultures in history, let alone prehistory, is in most cases beyond daunting. I honestly believe that, unless a significant methodological breakthrough occurs, this goal might very well be unachievable.[53]

Explicit forms of homosexual identity have been found in many cultures other than ours. Radically different from what we understand as homosexual or gay identity today, those homosexual identities entailed some degree of self-identification that was intimately associated with same-sex desire and/or love. They can be traced back as far as tribal-shamanic levels of cultural development, which included various groups in pre-Colombian North America and Siberia.[54] Tribal-shamanic cultures are believed to date back to the Upper Paleolithic period, more prosaically called the late Stone Age (40,000–10,000 BCE).[55] Today researchers are prone to believe that psychoculturally defined homosexual identities have been part of human cultures as early as 12,000 BCE, and possibly earlier.[56] At this point, we can reasonably assume that explicit forms of homosexuality antedate the apparition of agriculture (~ 9,000 BCE) and the birth of the first cities (~ 7 to 5,000 BCE). Homosexuality seems to have been part of human history before the latter even began.

AN ELUSIVE VARIABLE: HOMOSEXUAL IDENTITY

As mentioned earlier, to talk about homosexual identity is to step into muddy waters and it will take several chapters to untangle this multifaceted reality (and you will probably understand why so many scientists have been reluctant to include this slippery variable in their studies, to the point of eventually dodging the entire issue of homosexuality's subjectivity). But let us start here.

To state that homosexuality existed since the Stone Age (as I just did) is a bit of a short cut, which fails to take into account the infinite complexity of subjective realities. "Feeling homosexual" necessitates that an individual acquires some concept of what being homosexual means first. Without it, one might simply feel different, "special," without being able to put words to it. Or one might never become aware of it. As long as the surrounding culture does not provide the conceptual blueprint for a particular subjective reality, isolated individuals cannot build the necessary mental structure that will help them grasp that interior reality (this insight was the great contribution of postmodern thinkers). Cultures provide the necessary templates from which people are able to see and understand themselves. (Chapter 15 shows how the development of one's homosexual identity follows the same trajectory.) I can understand myself as being gay only because I learned this concept from my culture. In fact, homosexuality remains formless until the culture allows it to take a particular shape, whether gay, lesbian, queer, and homosexual in recent times; sodomite and tribade in the Middle Ages; two-spirit among Native North American tribes; *erastes*, *eromenos*, and *kinaidos* in ancient Greece; *catamitus* and *cinaedi* in imperial Rome; *aikāne*, *māhū* and *fa'afafine* in Polynesian cultures and so forth.[57] Hence, if on the one hand homosexuality appears to be a transhistorical and transcultural constant, each particular form of homosexuality constitutes a distinct cultural construct.

At this point, I would like to question the persistent belief among postmodern academia that homosexuality was invented only in the nineteenth century when the word homosexuality itself was introduced; before that time, it is claimed, there were only homosexual acts.[58] I instead strongly agree with authors like Stephen O. Murray, Gilbert Herdt, Louis Crompton, and (to a lesser extent) Randolph Trumbach who have seriously challenged that opinion. As far as we can tell, the sodomite of the Middle Age, the queen of eighteenth century England, and the two-spirit of North America, to name only a few, were types of individuals, not mere bundles of homosexual behaviors.[59] What was born during the nineteenth century is not homosexuality itself, but instead the scientific conception of same-sex desire with which we still live today, and I will discuss this extensively later in the section on The Good. There were many premodern homosexual identities before the nineteenth century, such as those listed in the previous paragraph.

One's self-identification as homosexual is inseparable from the cultural context in which it arises; it is, however, not reducible to a cultural artifact. Homosexual identity, as demonstrated by psychological studies (discussed in chapter 15), preexists within one's subjectivity as a formless potential—a proto-homosexual identity, if you will—well before the moment when the culture provides a form and a language to represent and manifest it. I adhere to the idea that sexual (homo or hetero) identity is primarily rooted in our biological makeup, and we will soon see why and how that is possible. Sexual identity is originally formless and language-less and requires cultural models to take shape. And in that, homosexual identity is not very different from male and female gender identities.

Homosexualities

Throughout history, homosexuality has taken many forms significantly different from what we call homosexuality today. And in all the cultures where homosexuality was an integrant part of the sociocultural landscape, same-sex relationships were highly codified. Complex social conventions stipulated same-sex relationships very precisely as far as who was with whom, and why, when, and how long. Extremely little was left to individual creativity and even less to randomness.

The existence of these diverse forms of homosexuality pushed forward the notion of "homosexualities," whose conceptualization by the structuralist movement during the second half of the twentieth century represented a major development of our understanding of same-sex love. Today, a large consensus among historians, anthropologists, and social scientists informs us that homosexuality had overall taken three major forms: transgenerational, transgender, and egalitarian/modern.[60] (Notice that heterosexuality has also its own sociocultural variants—monogamy, polygamy, patriarchy, matriarchy, gender co-dominance, and so forth—and homosexuality is by no means special in this respect.) This minimal typology faithfully recapitulates the sociocultural reality of homosexuality in all past and present cultures.[61]

Before we explore these three sociocultural variants of homosexual relationships in more detail, one must first discern through these what is, I believe, one of the basic principles of homosexuality's geohistorical reality. In any given culture, homosexual relationships were always given a particular form, maintained by a set of rules, customs, social norms, aesthetics, rituals, belief system, and/or institutions. Those psychocultural models have shaped homosexual identities and channeled homosexual behavior. Hence, beyond the existence of various forms of same-sex relationships, it is crucial to understand that cultures always felt the compelling need to shape homosexual behavior. Even in the least coercive cultural environment, one always observes some degree of social pressure on the nature of homosexual relationships.[62] Homosexual behavior among teenagers represents a major exception to this rule in that most cultures regarded them as being essentially playful, benign, and (justly!) non-indicative of the future adult's sexuality. But this was almost never the case for adults of mating age. In most instances, those constraints were uncompromising, and sometimes suffocating.

Moreover, the sociocultural form, as important as it appears, is not a perfect indicator of the reality of homosexual behavior inside a given culture. "Thou shalt not kill" has never and nowhere been a reliable clue regarding the occurrence of murder. A given sociocultural form of homosexuality is therefore only the collective representation of what homosexual behavior ought to be, not of what homosexuals truly do and feel. Nor does it tell us what same-sex lovers really desire.[63] This said, human beings are profoundly influenced and limited by their cultural milieu, as we have seen. I can hardly imagine reasons why people in other times and other places would have been more capable than we are of distancing themselves from their own inherited cultural models. Hence, if the cultural norm does not directly reflect individual behavior, it is still representative of the behavioral "center of gravity" of a population; it remains a valid indicator of the behavior of the majority. It does not say much about what same-sex lovers really did in their bed, but it tells a lot about what people were willing to see and know about their neighbors, their children, and even themselves, and overall, what people were more prone to enjoy. And with this solid context as a backdrop, we are now ready to explore homosexualities.

Transgenerational homosexuality was well known in the Greek and Roman worlds, probably in the whole Indo-European lineage, as well as in ancient China and Japan.[64] In the twentieth century, it was still reported among populations of northern and central Africa, the Amazon basin, and in Australian and Melanesian cultures.[65] This form of homosexuality, which is typically represented by Greek pederasty and by the ritualized homosexuality among Melanesians cultures, is centered around the temporary sexual relationship between a sexually mature man and a youth. The age difference, or more precisely the sexual immaturity of the youngest partner, is crucial for the social acceptance of the relationship.

In Classical Greece, every male citizen—the *erastes*, according to the Athenian terminology—was encouraged to pursue and establish a stable relationship with a young man—the *eromenos*—between the age of fourteen and twenty. The presence of a beard was typically a sign that the *eromenos* had reached the age limit. Beyond that point, any sexual interaction became inappropriate. The relationship was supposed to transform into friendship and lose its sexual character. It was imperative that the youth be the receptive partner and the adult the insertive one.[66] Reversing this polarity was seriously frowned upon, insofar as it would jeopardize the social status of the adult. Past the age limit, the passive role became a source of humiliation for a youth, having reached maturity. The sexual relationship was condemned to end, the *eromenos* expected to convert into an *erastes*, and the *erastes* invited to seek another *eromenos*.

In Melanesia, the Sambia people displayed another archetypical variant of transgenerational homosexuality.[67] Homosexual acts were integrated into coming-of-age rituals in which boys were abducted by older bachelor males, taken into the forest and totally isolated from their families, particularly from their mothers. "Female traces are removed through painful rites . . . they are inseminated through oral intercourse so they can grow, become strong, and reproduce. All younger males between the ages of seven and fourteen are inseminated by older bachelors, who were once themselves semen recipients."[68] Unlike Greek or Roman homosexuality, Sambia homosexual relationships were confined to rituals and usually short-lived.[69] Members of the tribe describe them as a "playful duty" (at least on the sperm-donor side) rather than opportunities for strong emotional bonding. Ritualistic homosexual relationships in Melanesia are ideologically concerned with making boys into men, not with love, sharply contrasting with pre-Christian Europe in that regard.[70]

In transgender homosexuality, one of the individuals involved in the relationship has switched gender, usually at a very young age. Transgender individuals belong to their new reassigned gender, female or male, or more often to a particular category—a third sex. People with a reassigned gender commonly see themselves as souls trapped in the wrong body and, in many cases the gender reassignment aims to restore the integrity of the individual. Transgender homosexuality involves cross-dressing, various cross-gender behaviors, and, in some instances, castration. Needless to say, but this is crucial, transgender males ought to assume the sexually receptive role in their relationships with other males. Accordingly the sexual and gender identity of their partner stays absolutely intact. One man can enjoy anal intercourse with his transgender male lover, and in some cultures even marry him; he is still fully a man, as much as any other man. But of course, everybody assumes that he is the insertive partner.

Transgender homosexuality was found in Europe, Asia, Africa, the Americas, and the Pacific region. Two-spirits (also known as berdaches) were encountered among many North-American Native Indian tribes.[71] Not surprisingly, the tradition progressively disappeared in the aftermath of European colonizations.

In India, *hijras* have existed as a third sex for ages. Becoming a *hijra* originally required one to undergo a castration procedure, but today an increasing number opt to conserve their genitalia. In Polynesia, Samoan *fa'afafines* and Hawaiian *māhūs* still constitute defined social groups and separate sexual identities. Two-spirits, *hijras*, *fa'afafines*, and *māhūs* have in common to be socially included (which by no means implies to be socially valued). To some extent eunuchs, whose fates extraordinarily ranged from slave to statesman, also formed a group of individuals well integrated within the social fabric.[72] However, this was not always the case: the Greek *kinaidos*, the Roman *cinaedi*, as well as the transvestites and transsexuals of Western culture can hardly be viewed as socially integrated. At best, they were tolerated. Notice also that most transgender homosexual traditions involved males. The two-spirit tradition, which offers many examples of female-to-male transgender individuals, represents a rare exception.

In many cultures, transgender homosexuality was also associated with magic or religious functions (the term "role-specific homosexuality" is often used to describe this particular subclass of transgender homosexuality), which was typically the case in the shamanic tradition of the Asia-Pacific zone and the alleged sacred prostitution around the Mediterranean basin during antiquity. Among many Native Indian tribes (e.g., Navajos and Zunis), two-spirits were granted a spiritual significance, which entailed foretelling the future, healing skills, and/or performing religious rituals.[73] To lesser degree, Indian *hijras* also performed religious ceremonies on some particular occasions (for the most part however, *hijras* were prostitutes).

Egalitarian/modern homosexuality represents the last and most recent form of homosexuality.[74] Modern homosexuality, which became the prevalent model in homosexual (gay) culture sometime around the second half of the twentieth century, implies "equal social status between partners, particularly, similarity in age, prestige, gender representation, and access to resources" and is, unlike the two previous categories, never determined by a rigid sexual polarity between partners.[75] Importantly, according to modern standards, both the active-insertive "top" and the passive-receptive "bottom" are homosexual. If sexual versatility is not a requirement in modern homosexuality, it is nonetheless a possibility. Not that sexually symmetrical homosexual relationships never existed in the past. Seneca the Elder already commented on those youths "assaulting one another's chastity while neglecting to defend their own."[76] Such a thing was known not only in Rome, but also in Greece, Muslim countries, and China.[77] But by no means were those relationships a sociocultural norm before the twentieth century. As stated previously, one would be wise to hold modern homosexuality as a still-emerging psychocultural model. Modern homosexuality in 1970 and modern homosexuality in 2010 are two very distinct animals. The emergence of gay rights, AIDS, marriage and civil unions, and the right to adopt have already altered homosexuality's expression in our culture and will continue to do so.

LESBIAN LOVE

Some of you might have noticed my relative silence regarding lesbianism. Scholars have desperately tried to match female homosexual relationships with the transgenerational and transgender models.[78] Yet the result is by and large unconvincing. The "mummy-baby" relationship, a standard case of so-called transgenerational socially structured female homosexuality that started in Lesotho during the nineteen fifties, essentially involves adolescent girls and can hardly be compared to male transgenerational relationships, which unmistakably imply a drastic difference in term of sexual maturity between the two partners.[79] The "marriage resistance movement" represents a second case of alleged structured lesbian relationships (which, for reasons that still escape me, was labeled as transgender elsewhere).[80]

During the nineteenth and first half of the twentieth century in China, near the Pearl River delta region, female silk workers succeed in avoiding marriage and achieving economical independency by forming sisterhoods.[81] In some cases (but how representative are they?), sworn sisters engaged in sexual relationships. Still, the fact that these women were unmarried, earned cash, and combed their hair in the fashion of married women is a little slim to label them as "transgender." They were still bona fide females. Besides, in these two cases, female relationships developed largely away from men's eyes. Albeit socially structured, they barely qualify as socially recognized, let alone integrated forms of lesbianism. On the other hand, the Roman tribades and the modern North American butch lesbian, two significantly more convincing instances of transgender lesbianism, have without fail elicited hostility and contempt among their contemporaries. As far as we can tell, only female two-spirits and female transgender shamans who took a wife constitute convincing forms of socially integrated transgender lesbianism.[82] But those cases were extremely uncommon, let alone historically representative of lesbianism.

In conclusion, not only were integrated forms of female homosexuality very rare, but overall, the social organization of female homosexuality is dramatically different from that of males. Evelyn Blackwood perfectly encapsulated the historical specificity of lesbian relationships: "[Anthropological studies] suggest that female homosexuality is less institutionalized, less well-developed, less important or less visible than male homosexuality."[83] Not only do we have good reasons to believe that the incidence of female homosexuality is lower than that of males, but because human societies in their great majority have been male-dominated, female relationships had to stay hidden from public eye.[84]

Female relationships had to coexist with marriage and the essential duty of reproduction. Hence, lesbian love flourished secretly in the harems of the Middle-East, among concubines in polygamist cultures like China, and probably in most societies structured around a strict segregation between sexes. Elsewhere sisterhoods, whether in monasteries, béguinage (lay Roman Catholic sisterhoods that appeared in the late Middle-Age Northern Europe), all-female factories, wash-houses, brothels, or even widowhood offered other favorable contexts for secret loving relationships between women.

The transgenerational and transgender models, so relevant to the world of male homosexuality, cannot help us decrypt the sociocultural logic of female homosexuality, a startling difference that will be explored in subsequent chapters.[85] I concur with Blackwood when she claimed that, instead, the "range of lesbian behavior that appears cross-culturally varies from formal to informal relations."[86] Informal relations are socially hidden (sex among unmarried young women, harems, and polygynous households). Formal relations are more socially integrated (bond friendships, sisterhoods, schools, woman-marriage, and cross-gender females), yet always extremely discreet regarding sexual intimacy. "Where women have control over their productive activities and status, both formal and informal relations may occur. Where women lack power, particularly in class societies, they maintain only informal lesbian ties or build institutions outside the dominant culture."[87] Throughout history, overwhelmingly the existence of female homosexual relationships depended on the way females were able to negotiate their sexual freedom with the male establishment by gaining some level of socio-economical independence.[88]

Ironically, men were seldom fooled. In most cases, anthropological data about female love were obtained from men through the literature, gossip, or interviews conducted by researchers. More often than not they chose to close their eyes. More often than one may expect, men in premodern cultures ignored sexual affairs between women as long as they remained sufficiently discreet. They were too busy keeping up with what has constituted their main preoccupation since prehistory: making sure of the paternity of their children.

DEBUNKING THE HOMOSEXUAL "CONUNDRUM"

What is the most nonsensical belief about homosexuality? This one: that homosexuality is a biological paradox. Some book titles could not be more explicit: *Conundrum: The Evolution of Homosexuality*[89] and *The Puzzle: Exploring the Evolutionary Puzzle of Male Homosexuality*.[90] Let me recapture for you the sheer logic of the homosexual "conundrum." A fundamental tenet of species evolution is that genetic traits carried exclusively by individuals that do not mate actively are doomed to disappear from the surface of the planet. Homosexual sex does not lead to reproduction; hence, homosexuality should have vanished long ago. But insofar as homosexuals keep being born here and there, that is, everywhere, homosexuality has quickly turned into an unsolvable evolutionary paradox. And this idea is so entrenched in our culture that even a publication as prestigious as the scientific journal *Nature* mentions it as if it were an uncontested truth.[91]

So, what is that mystery about? The truth is that putting aside the most recent evolution of homosexual relationships in the last fifty years or so (which represents two to three generations at the most), homosexuals have always actively reproduced. First of all, the strongly homophobic culture that has dominated the West and eventually the entire world since the rise of Christianity has forced the great majority of homosexuals to conceal, at least to a certain degree, their true sexual desires. In Europe and North America, most homosexual men married and fathered children. Nor could lesbian love resist the omnipresent control over female reproductive power by males. In a general manner, homosexual behavior was often repressed and homosexual extramarital relationships prudently hidden.

Second, from a larger historical standpoint, exclusive homosexuality has almost never been the rule. Rather, bisexuality was. Sexual freedom—which in antiquity, as in the rest of the world, implied almost exclusively the legitimate sexual self-gratification of males—was always second to the duty of reproduction. Greek philosophers had, along with their young male lovers, a wife and children. Marrying was a vital duty for Greek citizens at large, both in Athens or Sparta, and Greek culture never compromised on this. The same was true in Rome, China, India, and Japan. That homosexual relationships among Japanese Buddhist monks did not coexist with heterosexual reproduction was due to the vow of celibacy, not to homosexuality.[92] In many Native American cultures, marrying a two-spirit/berdache was, in most cases, only possible for men who already had fathered children. Moreover, those unions were notably unstable. Men often abandoned their male two-spirit partners for "real" women who could give them children.[93] In Sambia culture, men cannot attain full personhood unless they marry.[94] Arabic culture in the classical age was known to close its eyes to the man enjoying the favor of a male youth as long as he fulfilled the active role and married, and this mentality is still deeply ingrained in Middle Eastern countries today.

Across the board, men and women who have or might have felt drawn toward same-sex partners have most of the time married and produced offspring, willingly or not. In contrast with what we see today, homosexual relationships in the past have never excluded parallel unions with opposite-sex partners. Most of time, the duty of procreation was mandatory (gender-transformed males and the rare instances of gender-transformed females constitute the only true exception to this rule; their case will be discussed later).

So, if that covered homosexuality from the dawn of humanity to, say, the mid-twentieth century, what has happened since? Is homosexuality as we know it today, which presuppose desires for same-sex partners exclusively, a true exception to what we have just seen? At first glance, modern homosexuality does look like a reproductive dilemma. Now, one needs to acknowledge two important points.

The first one is that today the non-procreative character of homosexuality is largely amplified by the extraordinary rigidity that characterizes the status of the wife and the parental ideal in contemporary society. Roman culture,

Christianity, and later modernity have always emphasized the responsibility of husbands toward their wives and strongly encouraged the creation of exclusive and lasting bonds between spouses. Marital responsibility as we know it today in the West has almost no equivalent in the ancient world. Not only were male Greek citizens free to enjoy the company of boys, but this never jeopardized their authority as males, husbands, and fathers. Modern homosexuals, on the other hand, must consider engaging in heterosexual relationships very carefully. For a man to impregnate a woman involves a drastically different level of commitment today. Even for lesbian couples, the social pressure to maintain the father figure in the equation remains overwhelming. In all cases, homosexuals today are still strongly discouraged to venture outside the classic model—"natural" and "perfect"—of the heterosexual family, that is, the father, the mother, and their kids all living happily together. Yet, provided that exclusive homosexual behavior for an entire lifetime is fairly rare (probably fewer than 1% of the population), I suspect that in a cultural setup not as rigid as ours regarding parental norm, many homosexuals of both sexes would have happily procreated outside of and in addition to their homosexual relationships. And there is no reason to believe that they would have not been good and responsible parents.

Second, homosexuality today is still a work in progress and we ought to be very prudent in our sociocultural assessment of what constitutes modern homosexuality. The progressive legalization of gay marriage and the increasing occurrence of stable relationships within the homosexual community are already reshaping the concepts of gay love. For instance, the number of same-sex couples in the United States grew by more than 30% between 2000 and 2005 (from 600,000 couples to 777,000).[95] Moreover, the number of homosexual couples that seek to have children is clearly on the rise, despite the long struggle that it almost always entails. It often takes male couples years before being able to adopt or find a surrogate mother. Likewise, the procedure of artificial insemination is rarely an easy one for lesbian couples. Because reproduction is still such an arduous process for homosexual couples, it is quasi-impossible to gauge the real incidence of "homosexual reproduction." Certainly, not all homosexuals, male and female, are interested in raising their own families, just like they are not all interested in monogamous or exclusively homosexual relationships. But that is also true of heterosexuals.

Ultimately, I regard it as absurd to consider exclusive same-sex behavior as part of modern homosexuality's definition, and likewise to exclude from it the many and tenacious strategies developed by homosexual couples in order to achieve procreation. It did not take long for homosexuals with "exclusive same-sex behavior" to reclaim their right to parenthood. The future might not even remember that homosexuality and parenthood were at one point viewed as being disconnected. What is certain, however, is that, unless morals and laws discourage homosexuals to reproduce by outlawing their own strategies and their own version of parental responsibility, homosexuality is hardly an evolutionary paradox. In fact, it is hardly a paradox at all.

HOMOSEXUALITY TODAY

Transgender homosexuality (including sacred prostitution) was methodically wiped out by Christianity and later Islam. Modernity brought it to near extinction all over the world. *Hijras*, whose religious status is far from being central in modern Indian culture and who are far from being immune to the strong homophobic prejudice of the rest of the population, have nevertheless managed to survive. The same is true of Pacific transgender traditions, *fa'afafines* and *māhūs*. The trend is however indisputable. Transgender homosexuality is increasingly marginalized in our world. And as a culturally imposed form of homosexuality, it has become obsolete.

Transgenerational homosexuality also has largely disappeared today, at least as a socially integrated form of homosexuality. The emergence of the moral status of the youth, which so strongly distinguished the Romans from the Greeks, progressively brought the sexual use of teenage males beyond the limits of morality. Not that the sexual desire for the youth has vanished. It has progressively become socially and morally unacceptable (remember, cultural standards tell little about the actual spectrum of desires among people). Today, pederasty (the love of youth), often confused with pedophilia (the sexual use of children), carries a powerful moral stigma. And in only two decades transgenerational homosexual rites, once common among Melanesian cultures, have become things of the past.[96]

Today gay culture is slowly but surely diffusing beyond the North-American and European continents, and everywhere the introduction of modern-gay identity is slowly displacing local-traditional homosexual identities.[97] Gay culture, which quickly came to embody the dazzling success of modern homosexual identity in the West, has since the 1970s fostered an unprecedented revival of same-sex love. Gays and lesbians are now found in positions of leadership. Paris and Berlin have gay mayors. The Anglican Church has gay bishops and Judaism gay and lesbian rabbis. Today, the visibility of homosexuals in arts, literature, cinema, and media is nothing less than astonishing. And civil unions, registered partnerships, and marriage of gays and lesbians are celebrated in many countries (e.g., Denmark, England, Spain, South Africa, the Netherlands, Canada, New Zealand, Uruguay, and France) and few American states (e.g., Massachusetts, Vermont, Iowa, Connecticut and New York). Fortunately this list keeps growing over the years.

In the meantime, many countries still enforce brutal anti-homosexual legislations. Saudi Arabia, Iran, Mauritania, Sudan, Somalia, Nigeria, and Yemen still apply the death penalty against male homosexuals in 2011.[98] The living conditions of homosexuals in Africa, the Middle East (with the notable exception of Israel), and the south-west quadrant of Asia are more than alarming. In countries like Poland and Russia, homophobia remains incredibly virulent. In 2011 homosexuals were still sentenced to imprisonment, corporal punishment, or death penalty in seventy-six countries and five territories; in comparison, and only thirty-two countries and thirty territories recognize same-sex relationships, at least at some level.[99] The difference is shocking. Yet the trend is slowly moving in the right direction.

Today however, the economic impact of the homosexual community is undeniable. As a matter of fact, the gay and lesbian community has recently emerged as a highly tangible world-size target market. U.K. companies are now "chasing the pink pound," the cumulated income within the gay community, a nearly £60 billion estimate in 2005.[100] And according to the 6th edition of *The U.S. Gay and Lesbian Market*, the total buying power of the U.S. lesbian, gay, bisexual, and transgender adult population reached 743 billion "pink" dollars in 2010.[101] With marketing, advertisements, and original products developed in order to meet the specific needs of gays and lesbians (whatever those needs might be) and enhance their lifestyle (whatever that means), the pragmatic qualities of the free-market economy have made a surprising contribution to the diffusion of gay culture and the development of gay rights.

Some recent trends in the gay world are increasingly evident. In order to escape the unbearable loneliness and the secrecy inherent in their condition, homosexuals often migrated to larger cities. As early as the nineteenth century, emerging metropolises such as New York, Paris, and London were the host of distinct and vibrant homosexual communities, which all developed their own subculture and social network—the seeds of the gay culture. In the decades following World War II, that movement took off. San Francisco and New York turned into gay meccas. Gay "ghettos" mutated into gay neighborhoods, and gay neighborhoods—against all odds—became fashionable.

Today however, the forces of gravity seem to operate differently. The disappearance of well-established gay neighborhoods such as Greenwich Village, and the increasingly apparent gentrification of many others, reminds us how much of what we have been calling gay culture since the 1970s is an elusive target. I moved to New York, the gay metropolis *par excellence* in 1994, the year of the twenty-fifth anniversary celebration of the Stonewall riots. That same year New York City was also hosting the fourth Gay Games. The power and liveliness of these events were simply astonishing. Fifteen years later however, the flame is seemingly dying. The incredible spirit of my first gay parades appears increasingly diluted amid marketing concerns, perhaps the unexpected cost of social integration. And if the gay community overall remains prosperous, the "community" itself seems to be less and less the preferred channel for the expression of homosexuals and less and less an important part of their social identity. In "The End of Gay Culture," the October 2005 cover story in *The New Republic*, Andrew Sullivan commented: "It is indeed hard not to feel some sadness at the end of a rich, distinct culture built by pioneers who braved greater ostracism than today's generation will ever fully understand. But, if there is a real choice between a culture built on oppression and a culture built on freedom, the decision is an easy one."[102] I can only agree. Today homosexuals enjoy a freedom, at least in the West, that has not been experienced for centuries. Homosexuals are winning the battle for their integration and acceptance in human society. And this is an extraordinary achievement and the hard-won result of our elders and those who keep fighting today.

Another striking characteristic of gay culture is its global character. Born from the postmodern revolution of the nineteen seventies, gay culture has quickly embodied the planetary consciousness that has lately become increasingly noticeable through other global issues as diverse as the inter-dependence among national economies, the fight against climate change, terrorism and global security, and humanitarian intervention. Gay villages, no longer isolated islands, have given birth to a global culture—gay culture—for better or worse. Gay pride parade replicates have popped up all around the world, and not just in Sydney and Rome, but also in Moscow, Jerusalem, and Mumbai. The creation of the Gay Games (originally named Gay Olympics) in 1982 made the transnational character of gay culture even more patent. The AIDS tragedy has also helped to develop a global consciousness among homosexual communities across the globe. The rapid spread of HIV made the common fate of homosexuals in all continents almost palpable. They shared the same desires, the same risks, and the same social isolation. And if a solution was to be found, it had to be global as well. And now, the Internet, undoubtedly the most spectacular manifestation of the new global culture, is giving an unprecedented impetus to the universalization, or homogenization, perhaps, of gay culture. Planet-wise, gays and lesbians are far from being as alone and isolated as they were conditioned to believe. For the first time in history, homosexuals have become aware of their presence in the world. And for the first time also, so has everybody else.

C H A P T E R   T W O

~

The Homosexual Phenomenon

Now that we have skimmed through facts and figures about homosexuality's presence in the world and introduced some basic elements of homosexual reality, we can progress one step further. I would like to untangle two key aspects of homosexuality—homosexual behavior and homosexual identity—that are too often confused, conflated, or misused. That distinction will be central to our model.

A Two-Component System

Homosexuality has been frequently reduced to homosexual behavior, and for several good reasons. The first is that, given the strong homophobic tone of Western culture until today, many people were unable or unwilling to disclose their homosexual identity. Surveys would dangerously fluctuate as a function of people's self-awareness, honesty, and courage. This alone was already unworkable. Second, the very nature of "feeling" homosexual appeared highly contingent upon cultural variables. That was too much to handle for researchers, even with the best intentions. Science always tries to reduce things to their measurable tangible components. Starting with Kinsey, the overall consensus in sociobiology became that the sex of one's partners (whom one had sex with) was the only data that could reliably estimate one's sexual tendencies. Sexuality turned into grades, from 0 to 6 (that is, from exclusively heterosexual to exclusively homosexual).

Despite the powerful cathartic effect of Kinsey's studies (and those that followed) at the time of their publication and their profound impact on the course of homosexual history, the scope of this methodology proved to be limited. They left totally unexplained the many atypical variations in the occurrence of homosexual behavior during (1) one's individual sexual development, (2) in relation to the social environment, and (3) throughout history. If numbers could measure homosexual behavior, they still could not make sense of homosexuality.

Rather than trying to reduce homosexual reality in order to fit it into a comprehensible questionnaire, which is to say, in order to avoid methodological difficulties, let us posit here that homosexuality among humans is a dual reality comprised of two distinct and interdependent parts: one that is primarily objective, homosexual behavior; and another that is primarily subjective, homosexual identity. And I would like to show you that splitting homosexual reality into these two distinct basic components can bring some clarity to an otherwise tremendously complex phenomenon. In fact, I consider the distinction between homosexual behavior and homosexual identity necessary and sufficient to account for the full complexity of homosexual reality.

Homosexual behavior refers to the observable display of sexual interaction with individuals of the same sex. However, in the particular context of an exploration of homosexuality, only sexually motivated homosexual behavior is instructive about someone's homosexual experience.[103] Homosexual behavior must be generated from desire and, potentially, elicit pleasure (desire-less same-sex behavior automatically involves other sorts of motivations that I do not find relevant to our inquiry). Homosexual behavior that results either from force or necessity, such as rape and prostitution, or from a chemically induced state of confusion, should be either dismissed as being non-informative, or at least be considered very cautiously.

I thus put subjective conditions on the meaningfulness of homosexual behavior, well aware that those conditions are extremely difficult to evaluate. Defining and evaluating one's desire or one's motivation constitute a serious challenge. Furthermore, these concepts are also subject to cultural variability. For instance, wanting to kiss someone on the lips might be interpreted very differently in the United States from the way it is in Russia. Intention, desire, and pleasure may occasionally contradict each other when individual experience becomes too complex or troubled. Yet the difficulty of defining experimental modalities cannot constitute a valid excuse to ignore what is beyond their limits. It is more important at this point to delineate as specifically as possible what is truly relevant about the homosexual reality, even if the contours remain fuzzy.

Homosexual identity refers to the immutable and compelling evidence of knowing oneself as such.[104] Just like any other identity, it is primarily subjective, hence not directly measurable. One must engage in a conversation with someone to know how that person sees him or herself. One might be able to guess sometimes, but no more than guess. Homosexual identity is a defining aspect of one's self, emerging within a spectrum of sexual identities whose complexity can exceed or differ from the current choice between being heterosexual, bisexual, or homosexual. Homosexual identity can be expressed through homosexual behavior, but not necessarily. One can engage from the beginning in a strictly celibate or a purely heterosexual lifestyle and still experience the compelling evidence of feeling homosexual inside his or her soul. Yet, provided that no extraordinary psychological or cultural factor comes to interfere, a healthy homosexual identity is naturally expressed through a pleasurable homosexual sexuality (even if not exclusively).

Homosexual identity and homosexual behavior have nonetheless an important feature in common: they are both culturally constrained. This point deserves a particular attention. Homosexual identity is culturally constructed, and modern homosexual identity (gay identity, as I defined it here) is only one particular cultural variant of homosexual identity. Historians and anthropologists have traced those identities back to the earliest types of sociocultural organizations: transgender shaman, *erastes-eromenos*, sodomite, two-spirit, and so forth. The great majority of traditional cultures included one or more psychocultural identities associated with same-sex desire and pleasure, just not exclusively. In the Melanesian tribes that practiced boy-inseminating rituals and sexual relationships between boys and young adults, the homosexual acts were limited to the duration of ceremonies. All the adult men at the age to participate in these rites engaged in homosexual behavior with boys. And they did so willingly. Hence, in Melanesian culture, homosexual desire was embedded within male identity itself, without defining a particular subgroup. "A" homosexual identity was somehow integrated—undistinguished though not erased—within a larger identity, such as manhood in this case. The males of the Sambia tribe did not know themselves as homosexuals, yet they knew themselves as males who eventually would enjoy being fellated by boys amid coming-of-age rites. As a matter of fact, in most cultures that practiced transgenerational homosexuality, male identity constituted the wider carrier for homosexual desire and, sometimes, love.

Sambia people have another important point to teach us. Indeed, Gilbert Herdt reports that "a few males do not or cannot make the transition from same-sex to opposite-sex erotic relations" and "more than one of them continue to prefer boys."[105] Although Sambia had no particular role or label associated with this particular taste, these men knew themselves as men who preferred boys over females. Herdt's finding illustrates how a formless (potential) homosexual identity can exist in the absence of any elaborate cultural construct. Individuals might become aware of their atypical desires or not, and the rest of the group might notice it as a specific category or not. Homosexual identity, in its simplest form, manifests itself as an irrepressible desire for same-sex partners.

Homosexual behavior in humans is not without constraint either. If nature gives us plenty of evidence that among animals homosexual behavior, as any sexual behavior, is essentially biologically driven, the situation is dramatically different in our species. In fact the expression of homosexual behavior among humans varies tremendously according to the sociocultural environment. It also fluctuates significantly throughout one's psychosexual development. I see at least three major instances where homosexual behavior appears "regulated":

First, the biological clock that initiates puberty appears also to elicit the typical surge of homosexual behavior observed during adolescence. The fact that many teenagers in most and possibly all cultures tend to engage in playful homosexual activities among themselves, and that despite a long century of intense angst regarding this issue, such behavior has no consequence on their adult sexual identity, is largely accepted.[106] When behavior and identity are viewed as two separate modules that are interconnected, yet with each one having its own developmental dynamic, the adolescent "homosexual phase" may simply be interpreted as a transient step in human sexual development during which homosexual behavior is temporarily switched on or, more likely, when sexual desire is still little restricted and often opportunistic. At any rate, the phenomenon seems tightly associated with the hormonal changes that trigger the onset of sexuality. Homosexual behavior is therefore likely to be biologically modulated so as to facilitate the psychosexual maturation of the future adult. In that sense, adolescent homosexual behavior is relatively peripheral to the development of adult homosexuality.

Second, the cultural variability of homosexual behavior is patent and has baffled many. As far as we can tell, the Athenian citizen from the third century BCE and the Englishman from the Victorian Era belong to the same species. Still, the respective frequencies of homosexual behavior in those two male populations contrast strikingly. In Classical Greece, homosexual behavior was common, culturally integrated, and the sign of an educated mind. In Victorian England, it was associated with sin and perversity and the shame of a tiny minority. Those who, like Oscar Wilde, found the courage to brave the taboo against same-sex behavior were the exceptions. They often paid a high price for their audacity. Numerous others revealed their desire only under the seal of secrecy. Still, unlike ancient Greeks, the great majority of Queen Victoria's subjects could live without engaging in same-sex behavior comfortably.

One must then admit that the cultural setup has the power either to favor or inhibit the expression of homosexual behavior in adults. The historical prevalence of homosexual behavior fluctuates between a minimum point—reduced to the people who like Wilde are ready to infringe the norm—and a maximum point—resisted only by those who are totally refractory to same-sex pleasures. We must then infer the existence of a significant portion of the population (at least among males) whose interest for same-sex partners is strongly influenced by the sexual mores of their time. For those people, homosexual behavior is optional and not necessary to their emotional well-being. Later in life, cultural imprinting, life experiences, and personal inclination will determine to what degree those individuals find homosexual interactions appealing or not. As introduced in the previous chapter, from a homosexual standpoint the spectrum of sexualities among humans can be roughly divided into three subgroups: (1) individuals who feel ineluctably attracted to same-sex partners; (2) those who are only optionally interested in same-sex partners; and (3) those who manifest no interest in homoerotic contacts. Cultures appear essentially to modulate the frequency of homosexual (and heterosexual) behavior in the middle group, a little like the custom of not eating pork meat in Judaism and Islam.

Third, some environments appear to bring on homosexual behavior among certain individuals, independently from one's age and cultural background. In particular, all-male environments are known to favor homosexual behavior: military service increases the likelihood of same-sex behavior by 50% and attending public school in England by 100%[107]; the all-male miner communities found in South Africa constitutes another striking example of so-called "situational homosexuality."[108] I would like to focus on two exemplary cases: prisons and wars.

Recent studies and the rising number of victims' confessions disclosed in the media have outed the reality of homosexual abuse in many jailhouses in the United States, Venezuela, Brazil, England, and Uganda.[109] Reports from Human Right Watch have showed that nearly one in five male American inmates has been subject to sexual abuse. Perpetrators typically target younger, smaller, weaker, less masculine, or less aggressive individuals. The rapist "alpha male" asserts his dominance and at the same time ensures sexual gratification in an environment that in most cases offers none. Within the scope of our inquiry, only the homosexual behavior of the rapist is informative to us, provided that he is the only one who intends and enjoys the interaction. Reminiscent of premodern forms of homosexuality, the dominant inmate never perceives himself as homosexual or gay. His status as insertive partner leaves his masculinity intact. In nearly all cases those men are exclusively heterosexual outside the prison. Thus, the confinement within a brutal all-male environment prompts homosexual behavior in men that do not seem to be particularly disposed to it otherwise.

War is another example of a ruthless male environment. Unlike female rape, which is well-documented today, male rape remains incredibly taboo. It has however been present since ancient times: "The rape of a defeated male enemy was considered the prerogative of the victor in battle and served to indicate the totality of the former's defeat. Even in ancient times we find the widespread belief that an adult male who is sexually penetrated, even by force, thereby 'loses his manhood, and hence can no longer be a warrior or ruler [. . .] Gang-rape of a male was also considered an ultimate form of punishment, and as such was known to the Romans (for adultery) and Iranians (for violation of the sanctity of the harem)."[110] While rarely brought to public attention and often avoided in the statistics, male rape seems to be a normal casualty of war, even today.[111] The sexual abuse of black male slaves has also been documented during slavery time in America (and its true occurrence probably underestimated).[112] In addition to reminding us of the enduring symbolic power of one's anal penetration by another's penis, the specificities of male rapes in war and prison settings prove once more how much homosexual behavior follows its own dynamic and obeys its own set of triggers, whether from a testosterone burst, culture, education, inter-male competition, or simple opportunity.

When homosexuality is seen as a monolithic reality, I defy anyone to reconcile its various peculiarities in a model that truly makes sense. I suggest that homosexuality is best understood as a two-component system including homosexual identity and homosexual behavior, one being primarily subjective and the second primarily objective with each one having its own individual and sociocultural dynamics and, I presume, its own neuronal structure to support its existence. Instantly homosexuality becomes logical from prehistory to now.

A two-component model can accommodate the existence of the so-called "homosexual phase" of adolescence and the fact that the form and frequency of homosexual behavior vary dramatically with cultures and the level of stress (e.g., war and prison). It can explain why some individuals, male and female, can enjoy same-sex interactions without feeling homosexual, for the simple reason that homoerotic desire does not automatically define who one is. Many are the women who have experienced meaningful homoerotic relationships with other women in their life, and yet have argued their non-identification with lesbian, gay, or homosexual identity.[113] The fluidity of love between women, that is, the protean connection between women's sexual desire and their sexual identity, has rarely been included in the "homosexual equation." Too often, their experience was invalidated by hard-core activists who needed a clear-cut pledge to the homosexual cause and scholars who could not cope with any fragmentation of homosexual experience.

HOMOSEXUAL ORIENTATION AND HOMOSEXUAL PREFERENCE

Having the preceding information as a background, I would like to define and redefine a few concepts that I believe will prove valuable for future research. First of all, we have seen that sexually motivated homosexual behavior comes in two flavors. For some people it is an essential condition to their well-being and happiness. It is deeply connected to their sexual identity, either homosexual or bisexual, and their overall sense of self. I call this type of homosexual behavior "essential." For others, homosexual behavior appears more recreational or exploratory in nature. Whatever their frequency might be, one can live perfectly well without it, and rarely does it end up becoming part of one's sexual identity. I call this second type of homosexual behavior "optional."[114]

However, such a clear-cut dichotomy between essential and optional homosexual behavior is unlikely to reflect the reality of human life perfectly. First, a gross division of homosexual behavior between essential and optional types does not preclude the existence of a spectrum of sexual motivations between those two extremes. Nor should anyone feel obliged to validate his or her homosexual desire as belonging to one or the other category. However, by acknowledging the existence of two distinct psychological variables and two distinct evolutionary dynamics, this division allows us to account for the extraordinary variability of homosexual behavior during one's psychosexual development as a result of one's sociocultural environment, and throughout history.

Next I would like to redefine two poorly agreed-upon concepts: homosexual orientation and homosexual preference. The first term has mostly been employed by scientists to describe tangible factors associated to one's homosexuality, while the second was preferred by those who emphasized the primordial role of subjectivity in one's homosexuality. Since my model considers behavior and subjectivity as being two concomitant and irreducible aspects of one's (homo) sexual experience, I cannot help refining the definition of (homo)sexual orientation and (homo)sexual preference.

Let me reframe the concept of sexual orientation in order to describe specifically the pattern of arousal and sexual behavior that directly correlates with sexual identity. Naturally, homosexual orientation correlates with homosexual identity. This implies that, by definition, the homosexual behavior of homosexually-oriented people is essential in nature (in contrast, homosexual behavior without homosexual or bisexual identity is optional). People with a homosexual identity and orientation need same-sex interactions to feel sexually and emotionally fulfilled. However, by no means does homosexual orientation presuppose that one's sexual behavior is exclusively or even predominantly homosexual. Nor should one mistake predominantly or even exclusively homoerotic sexual habits for a homosexual orientation, at the risk of having to come up with another theory to explain what happens during puberty and other cases of situational homosexuality.

The concept of homosexual orientation becomes particularly useful when no obvious equivalent to homosexual identity can be found in a given culture (e.g., Sambia people in Melanesia).[115] This gives me the opportunity to clarify my position. Converging historical and anthropological evidence, from classical Greece to the Pacific cultures and from the Native Indians of North American plains to African tribes, leads us to believe that individuals for whom homosexual behavior was essential have probably existed in all human cultures. It is on the universal presence of essential homosexual behavior that I base the claim that homosexuality is a transcultural and transhistorical phenomenon. And it is by tracing essential homosexual behavior, that is, homosexual orientation (as I define it here), throughout history, and by noticing the various sociocultural identities and practices to which it was associated (even if not exclusively) that one can lay out a history of homosexuality.

Symmetrically, sexual preference, as I wish to define it here, encompasses the particular domain of subjectivity—distinct from sexual identity—that correlates sexual behavior: sexual fantasies, desires, curiosities, and anticipated pleasures. Unlike sexual identity and orientation, which tend to fall into discreet categories (hetero-, bi-, and homosexual), sexual preference is as fluid and convoluted as sexual desire can be. In that sense, sexual preference is the subjective counterpart of all "sexually motivated" sexual behaviors. Consequently, to speak of homosexual preference suggests a psyche where same-sex desire dominates at a particular moment of one's life, regardless of one's overall sexual identity. The notion of homosexual preference is well suited to describe previously hard-to-define situations—a woman involved in a same-sex relationship but who does not however identify as lesbian, and the homosexual phase of adolescence—where the concepts of sexual identity and orientation are not easily applicable. What is more, evaluating one's sexual preference is more relevant than reviewing one's overall sexual behavior insofar as not all sexual acts are sexually motivated. For some people, none are. Hence, evaluating one's homosexual preference aims to bypass the many constrains and biases that result from peer pressure, social conventions, fear, and limited life opportunities.

Ultimately, it all depends on what you are interested in: what one does (sexual behavior), what one would like to do (sexual preference), how one sees oneself in sexual terms (sexual identity), or what type of sexuality is indispensable to one's long term psychological fulfillment (sexual orientation). This said, "The map is not the territory." This model is only a symbolic representation of homosexual reality, not reality itself. We should still hold this model fluidly. Life offers enough examples of individuals who, at one point in their life, enjoyed an intense but completely atypical passion for a person of their own sex. Their desire might indeed feel totally essential at the time; I would not necessarily doubt their heterosexual identity. In the end, accessing authentically our deepest feelings and desires is only an impossible dream. At best, it is a work in progress. The complexity of human sexual life will never fit neatly into four categories. Still, to the best of my knowledge, this organic model of homosexuality accounts for all the basic aspects of homosexual reality that have been described in the literature on homosexuality, as well as the complex evolutionary, biological, psychological, and sociocultural dynamics at work through it.

CHAPTER THREE

The Homosexual Body

Much ink has been spilled over the issue of the biological origins of homosexuality. Science in general exerts an irresistible fascination upon modern culture and we cannot help but be all ears at each one of its discoveries. No matter what we say, we are under its spell. And this is particularly true of "gay science"—the science that inquires into the biology of homosexuality—so magnetic on the one hand and so frustrating on the other. Many in the pro-homosexual camp, scholars and gay activists, have had tremendous difficulties accepting, trusting, or even simply understanding what gay science was doing and what it was saying. For that reason, the first thing we need is a context to help us make sense of this conversation. Before wondering about the gay brain or the gay gene, one should ask first: Why should we be interested in the biological mechanisms of homosexuality in the first place? In other words, why bother?

EPISTEMOLOGICAL DEPTH

Since classical antiquity, and even more so since the Renaissance, science has excelled at opening our eyes to the wonders of the physical world. In the last century especially, the mass of scientific information available to us has expanded phenomenally. What could previously fit in one book now necessitates a multi-volume encyclopedia. Look through a telescope: what was a small bright little dot is now a cluster of galaxies, each one composed of billions of stars in all different colors and magnitudes. Look through a microscope: what used to be a mere smear is now an intricate network of microscopic organisms, each one composed of countless sub-elements—a nucleus, mitochondria, cilia, chromosomes, and other minute details. The deeper one looks through the Hubble telescope or an electron microscope or the large Hadron collider, the more one finds. The more the world becomes complex, diverse, and multiple.

Science expands our vision of the universe not only by spotting new galaxies, discovering new sources of energy, or alerting us about global climate change; it does it also by probing into our own physical nature. For nearly five centuries (if we start counting from the time of Leonardo da Vinci's dissection drawing), science has been obsessed with describing and understanding the mechanisms of the human body. By doing so, the "scientific eye" has given an epistemological depth to the body that was unthinkable earlier. Today many men and women have a sense of their own biology that is deeper and richer than that of geniuses like Aristotle and Newton.

Science plays a pivotal role in modern culture first and foremost because it has forever transformed our perception of the physical world and how we relate to it. Scientific depth is all around us. We know what a galaxy and the surface of the planet Mars looks like. Dinosaurs are so familiar to us today that we almost forgot that they disappeared millions of years ago. We can visualize strands of DNA delivering their vital information within each cell of our body. The fetus in the mother's womb is no longer a stranger. It has a body, a face, and a life of its own. So much of what we see today is inaccessible to the naked eye. We forget how much this was not the case for the generations that preceded us. But today the scientific eye does more than simply perceive things beyond the limits of the biological eye, revealing the microscopic, the infinite, the hidden, and the distant past. Progressively, science is penetrating the mystery of our origins. Many scientific theories—the big bang theory, the birth of life, the evolution of species, or human prehistory—are central today to the way we understand ourselves and the universe that surrounds us.

Science has been very curious about homosexuality and the homosexual community would be poorly advised to ignore its contribution. Why? Because the scientific exploration of the biological reality of homosexuality is slowly deciphering the mystery of homosexuality's distant origins. Just like the big bang tells us the story of our cosmic roots, the stories you are about to read here will eventually reveal where homosexuality comes from, evolutionarily speaking. They may appear to be about the brain, genes, and apes, but in fact these stories begin to tell a greater story: the origins of homosexuality since the dawn of humanity.

Predict and Control

Gay science is like a time-bomb, always ready to explode. The entire field is mined, charged with fear and anger. For the few scientists brave enough to step into this type of research, publishing the results of their work has often meant facing attacks from gay activists. The criticisms were by no means consistent. The "gay gene" of Dean Hammer was all at once a proof of homosexuality's inevitability, and the gateway to eugenic politics aiming to eliminate homosexuals by means of genetic screening. And when Simon LeVay described how the sexual orientation of his particular population sample correlated to the size of some nuclei located in the hypothalamus, which also happened to vary between sexes, he was immediately accused of perpetuating old normative stereotypes that regard homosexuals as feminized males and masculinized females.[116]

Too often the tone of the debate evoked the dark times of the Holy Inquisition when, Copernicus, like many others, hesitated to share his revolutionary theory beyond a small circle of trusted friends, and Galileo was almost burned at the stake. Four hundred years later, the homosexual discourse and gay political activism are plagued with the same disease (although not the same political power as the Church in medieval times). Just consider the conclusion of the entry titled "Scientific approaches to homosexuality" in *Gay Histories and Cultures: An Encyclopedia* published in 2000: "There is no persuasive evidence that sexual orientation is biological. Historically, much of the research that has been undertaken served primarily the political agendas of those conducting it. This holds true even for ongoing research. The ethical and political question is whether etiologic sexual orientation research should be undertaken in homophobic societies."[117] Accusations are all over the place, and the incomprehension is total.

The truth is, every new discovery comes with its share of hopes and fears. And every new understanding comes with new moral choices. Anything in the human world always emerges simultaneously in the realms of the True (the discovery), the Beautiful (hopes and fears), and the Good (moral choices). Yet the True, the Beautiful and the Good constitute three distinct conversations, not one. To conflate them into one single un-sortable moralistic hodgepodge is to force the homosexual discourse into a dead end. The truth is the truth, even if relative, regardless of the fact that it does not feel good or beautiful in the moment. This said, an integral approach of gay science cannot ignore that while for centuries the scientific institution represented the only shield against the abuse of religious power, today it elicits real concerns and outright fear among a significant number of scholars, activists, and lay people. But what do people fear exactly in science?

Since prehistory, the top issue on human beings' agenda has been to ensure their own safety. In order to maintain this safety, human beings are compelled to predict and control everything around them. Better than any other animal species before them, they have been able to foresee potential perils by quickly recognizing patterns and piecing huge amounts of information together. Even among themselves, human beings know how to detect the faintest signs in the body language of other people that can help guess their next move. As it happens, human societies have shown exactly the same predisposition. Most, if not all, authority figures, be they governments or Churches, have automatically manifested the same tendency to predict and control the behaviors of whoever lies within the limits of their jurisdiction. Naturally, sexual outlaws—sodomites, lesbians, homosexuals, and other "deviants"—have constituted usual targets of their invasive scrutiny. As early as late antiquity and throughout the Middle Ages, far before the rise of modern science, physiognomists, chiromancers, and astrologers had already devised sophisticated ways of discerning the signs of a sexually deviant soul through the analysis of facial features, lines on the palm of the hands, and the geometry of planetary positions.[118]

Modern empirical science strives to predict too, but its rationale is very different. In fact, predicting is at the heart of the scientific method. The analytical power of science resides in its ability to imagine a model or theoretical framework that could explain a given phenomenon and then test this model by designing experiments that can confirm or contradict the various predictions drawn from it. A model is experimentally validated when it allows scientists to predict the behavior of the system in question better than any other model. Inevitably the political, judiciary, medical, and psychiatric institutions found in science an unexpected ally. By devising means to predict or at least surmise one's homosexuality, scientists offered legal authorities an undreamed-of leverage in their incessant effort to prevent, punish, or marginalize suspicious individuals. And indeed many scientists have been happy to help.

Despite their apparent similarity and occasional convergence of interest, one must absolutely avoid confusing science's thirst for knowledge with society's inherent need to control individuals. In other words, one should refrain from mixing up scientific curiosity and political moralism—the True and the Good. Conflating them results in a gross reductionism. My argument specifically challenges Michel Foucault's canon (largely endorsed by queer theorists): Science in the nineteenth and twentieth centuries cannot be understood solely in terms of a tool of oppression, even if it occasionally was a tool of oppression. As Simon LeVay reminds us, "untold thousands of gay men have been subjected to psychoanalysis, castration, testicle grafts, hormone treatments, electric shock therapy, and brain surgery in attempts to 'cure' them of their unfortunate condition."[119] Therefore, it is not that scientists themselves had no historical responsibility. Nor is it that the scientific methodologies should not be subject to moral scrutiny. It simply is that accusing science of being an instrument of political control is to mistake the illness for its symptoms. It is aiming at the wrong target. What needs to be readjusted is not science but a cultural context that deems homosexual behavior abnormal, regardless.

What is more, scientific research involves numerous trial and error steps . . . and missteps. The mass of scientific data published each year is astonishing. High-quality data represents only a minor fraction. In that sense, science is not different from art and philosophy. Some publications are better than others. Many do not deserve to be read at all, or at least not with the same level of trust. Media tend to generate even more confusion: They rarely discriminate between high- and low-quality scientific information provided that journalists seldom have the necessary expertise to evaluate it appropriately, and more importantly, because the focus is often on hunting for the sensational rather than on critical analysis of the data's claim and value.

Scientific discovery is a historical process. As knowledge expands, older knowledge often becomes obsolete. At the same time, knowledge does not appear *ex nihilo*. New knowledge emerges from the misconceptions of the past, just like future knowledge will emerge thanks to our current misconceptions. When Copernicus discovered that the earth rotates around the sun and not the other way around, he could do so because Ptolemy's geocentric model was unable to predict subtle irregularities in planetary movements. Although the model of Ptolemy was inaccurate, its existence was a prerequisite for Copernicus' insight. By failing to address Copernicus' more sophisticated measurements, it offered our revolutionary astronomer a unique chance to challenge and eventually surpass Ptolemy's theory. In short, the genius of Copernicus relied on that of Ptolemy.

A lot was written about homosexuality in previous centuries that went as far as people could understand the issue back then. Although we may see their views as naive, if not sometimes devious, they still were the prerequisite for what is possible to know now. There is no question that overall our age can produce better quality data than past centuries. More powerful technologies allow science to be more insightful. This hierarchy results from science's natural growth, that is, from an evolutionary process. We would be wise to refrain from ridiculing or vilifying too rapidly what people in the past thought was true. We would be even wiser to remain modest about what we hold as true today. Sooner or later, our "truth" too will become obsolete. In the end, the only thing that an exploration of the True must absolutely stand for is truth. The Good and the Beautiful will adjust automatically and naturally.

The primary focus in exploring the scientific research on homosexuality should be the exactness of the theories. I will comment very little on hypotheses that have proven to be erroneous. It would be inappropriate to discuss here the archaic physiognomic and anthropometric studies from the nineteenth century, which identified quite a few interesting typical facial and body features among homosexuals (e.g., dilated anal sphincter and bizarre penis shape). Similarly, scientists concur today that homosexuality does not result from hormonal imbalance during puberty or in the mother during gestation. The rationale of these experiments was simplistic and their design lacked the necessary rigor.[120] Subsequent studies have ruled out their claims. One cannot present obsolete hormonal theories on an equal footing with the others. Yet obsolete theories should not be ruled out because they sound offensive, but because they belong to the history of science and no longer to the field of scientific knowledge. Rather than sifting through a long catalog of unsorted theories, I intend to integrate the current data regarding homosexuality's biology into one possible model and—cautiously—to speculate on what the mechanism underlying homosexuality might be.

Scientific research has investigated the depth of the homosexual phenomenon by asking three basic questions, each one defining a particular modality of approach of reality: (1) what is homosexuality; (2) how does it appear; and (3) why does it exist. The first two questions—what and how—originally the domain of medicine and psychiatry, are currently the field of exploration of neuroscience and genetics. The third question—the why of homosexuality—has been the department of sociobiology and anthropology and will be treated subsequently in the last two chapters of the first part of the book, "The True." This last question will offer a seamless transition to the discussion in the second part of this book, "The Good."

Analyzing what homosexuality is and how it appears in some individuals involves two distinct and complementary branches of science: the one that describes and the one that explains. Descriptive science aims to characterize, identify, recognize, correlate, group, sort, and hierarchize. It observes, draws limits, offers definitions, recognizes structures and patterns. Hence, it is a purely outside view, a quintessentially third person/exterior/IT perspective on homosexuality. In contrast, when one asks how homosexuality arises, one shifts perspective. One must stop looking at how homosexuality manifests physically to focus instead on the biological structures that give birth to it. How homosexuality emerges from our biological nature represents a more "interior," so to speak, assessment of homosexuality's objective reality. One then tries to explain mechanisms and identify particular chains of events and their unfolding during the life of an individual. One deals with genetic program, developmental pattern, and adaptive behavior. This is the world of mechanistic sciences—developmental genetics and developmental molecular biology. Let us begin by exploring the material reality of homosexuality from the outside.

HOMOSEXUALITY, VIEWED FROM THE OUTSIDE

Descriptive sciences—zoology, botany, astronomy, and so forth—have been and still are the pioneers. They have cleared the way long before mechanistic sciences got into the picture. We must remember for instance that Charles Darwin was a naturalist, and that his discovery of the principle of the evolution of species through natural selection stemmed from years of patient and laborious observations of animal species in the wild. It took more than a century for molecular genetics to start grasping the inner reality of Darwin's theory.

But when science turned its eyes to the issue of homosexuality, it had first to redefine in objective terms what had mainly been described in moral and aesthetic terms as an abject and ugly sin. Science had to decide first what to look at and that, as you may already guess, still is a matter of debate and a source of confusion today. We have seen that since Kinsey's work, scientists have often reduced homosexuality to homosexual behavior, primarily because subjective realities are often viewed as being unworkable from a scientific standpoint. Science treated homosexuals no differently than any other subjects of interest—orchids, butterflies, savages, women, or even men. Everything had to be ordered into species and sub-species, categories and subcategories. Homosexuals were no exception. Nineteenth and early twentieth century "gay science," the science of Karl Heinrich Ulrichs, Richard von Krafft-Ebing, Magnus Hirschfeld, and Sigmund Freud, although caught in the dominant paradigm and totally tangled up in the anti-homosexual prejudice of their time, achieved a great deal of work by observing homosexuals, sorting them into categories, and attempting to find ways to describe people's sexual taste rationally. (That particular segment of history of "gay science" will be explored in more details in chapter 9).

Even if their visions of homosexuality were all biased, morally charged, and proved to be inaccurate later on, nineteen century scientists transformed the discourse on homosexuality. Homosexual acts became a subject of debate and competing theories. Most importantly, because science aims to describe, measure, and classify, homosexual behavior entered the regular pipeline of scientific affairs. For decades scientists surveyed homosexual behavior and published their observations, making them available to the public. Both homosexuals and their behaviors became part of the population data. Regardless of the moral tone of these reports, anyone could read about this topic. Even if by and large the early scientific discourse on homosexuality did not sound more positive than the religious discourse of its time, the unspeakable sin could now be talked about, studied, counted, measured, and possibly predicted. This shift was crucial. It progressively broke apart the wall that had surrounded same-sex desire since the fall from grace of homosexuality in the early time of Christianity (see chapter 8). One step at a time, science stripped homosexuality of the clandestine and impenetrable aura in which it had been trapped for centuries. For the first time, same-sex acts left the heavy silence of the confessional. The discourse about homosexuals stopped being the exclusivity of moralists, religious or not. The "sin of Sodom"—now perversion, gender inversion, or mental pathology—could experience the natural fate as any other element of conscious discourse: to evolve. And science, even the most prejudiced, has always succeeded at challenging and constantly remodeling its own dogma, its own assumptions and most certain beliefs.

Today, descriptive gay science is alive and well and keeps struggling with the issue of homosexuality's "physicality." It still battles to transform an inconvenient subjective truth into something tangible, observable, measurable, and predictable. Anthropometric measurements are not the prerogative of old-fashion medicine and pre-molecular biology. Each year, the various parts of the homosexual body are measured, and the corresponding results compiled and shared with the rest of the scientific community—a mere routine.[121]

Several recent studies associated homosexuality with subtle changes in the ratio between the lengths of the second and fourth fingers, the so-called 2D:4D ratio.[122] The 2D:4D ratio is sexually dimorphic, which means that it is statistically different between the sexes, men having a lower ratio than women. The sexual variation of the 2D:4D ratio has been linked to a difference in prenatal exposure to androgens, the masculinizing hormones, which can either be due to higher levels of androgens or to a variation in the sensitivity of their target receptor, the androgen receptor.[123]

The results are both intriguing and incredibly confusing. Studies show that homosexual women exhibit lower (so-called "masculinized") ratios than heterosexual women, though this alteration seems hand specific. It gets more complicated when looking at homosexual men. Studies conflict with each other, some showing a higher (so-called "feminized") 2D:4D ratio, others a lower ("hyper-masculinized") ratio. Some show a hyper-masculinized ratio but only in the case where those men have two or more elder brothers.[124] A more recent publication reports that the 2D:4D ratio is not only sexually dimorphic but also ethnicity dependent.[125] A feminized 2D:4D ratio was present in the white gay population of their samples but not among Asian and Black participants. Even within the white population, research teams report a higher ratio among homosexuals and bisexuals in the United States and the United Kingdom, but a lower one in continental Europe.[126] Taken all together, the logic of those results remains inscrutable, to say the least, and I would rather stop there.

What can we learn from the 2D:4D ratio studies nonetheless? First of all, those articles published between 2000 and 2008 illustrate how much science has by no means abandoned its old ambition to "measure" homosexuality. Second, very clearly one cannot directly correlate sexual orientation with prenatal exposure to androgen. Results vary too much from group to group and according to the origin of the population. It would however be too easy simply to dismiss these results altogether. If sexual orientation is unlikely to be determined by or associated with a sex-atypical exposure or sensitivity to androgens in utero, it is however reasonable to believe that homosexual orientation can still be affected by a change in this key signaling pathway, but only indirectly.[127] Different alterations in the androgen signaling pathway could produce different results, if any, in skeletal growth (the 2D:4D ratio) and sexual orientation, depending on the overall biological background (sex, ethnicity, population subgroup, etc.). Scientists are probably looking at peripheral (i.e., remotely associated) and opportunistic (i.e., only occasionally associated) correlative factors of sexual orientation, but not at direct causes. This could easily explain the discordance between the different studies and the variation among various ethnic groups. In the end, the case of women suffering from congenital adrenal hyperplasia supports such a conclusion. Exposed to higher levels of prenatal androgen, those women exhibit slightly to significantly masculinized genitalia. Still, despite a higher frequency of homosexual orientation,[128] the majority ends up identifying themselves as heterosexual.[129] This further demonstrates the unlikeliness of a direct correlation and the likeliness of an indirect one.

The consistency issue is by no means limited to 2D:4D ratio studies. I share, for instance, the same reservations regarding similar works that have looked at other subtle sexual dimorphic features, such as fingerprint patterns (beautifully named dermatoglyphics), the frequency of oto-acoustic emissions (which are tiny sounds emitted by the cochlea, a structure located within the inner ear), or particular aspects of skeletal growth.[130] In fact, we will see that scientists have often misinterpreted their own data. And we will eventually understand why.

Other attempts to reveal homosexuality's physical reality have been more straightforward and, in my opinion, more relevant and promising than those above. The rationale was simple. However you turn it—behavior, identity, orientation, or preference—one is most likely to find the source of one's homosexuality in the organ that "hosts" the human soul: the brain. The work of Simon LeVay in 1991, which succeeded brilliantly at catching the media's attention at the time, represents a major breakthrough in the field. Despite its flaws, no one can possibly ignore it today.

Previous studies in rodents had paved the way to LeVay's discovery. They had observed subtle size differences between males and females in a particular subregion of the limbic system (a set of brain structures that have been demonstrated to be involved in the formation of innate behavior) called the hypothalamus. The hypothalamus is subdivided into various nuclei. One of them, known as the preoptic area, is five times larger in males than in females.[131] Other groups confirmed the existence of sexually dimorphic structures in the human hypothalamus.[132] But when LeVay's collaborators surveyed the size of a particular nucleus named INAH3, they found, in addition to the somehow expected male-female dimorphism, a significant difference between homosexual and heterosexual men. INAH3 was on the average two to three fold bigger in heterosexual men than in women and homosexual men.[133]

Nonetheless, this study was challenged by a second one which claimed that if the volume occupied by INAH3 in homosexual men is indeed smaller than in heterosexual men, the number of cells did not significantly vary with sexual orientation (the difference between males and females was, however, confirmed).[134] Furthermore, LeVay's methodology faced much criticism insofar as the brains that his team used came from corpses of HIV positive men, which might have affected the results for one reason or another. Methodological differences can account for the discrepancies among the various results, not to mention the unreliability resulting from having to process biological samples originating from dead people. But in spite of all this, recent studies confirm that LeVay had stuck his scalpel in the right spot.

Spectacular technological breakthroughs have recently given scientists a new chance to explore the human brain, but this time without having to slice cadavers. Functional magnetic resonance imaging (FMRI) confirmed that the hypothalamus lights up when individuals are sexually aroused by means of erotic images, especially in men.[135] This activation of the hypothalamic zone upon visual activation is consistent with the self-declared sexual orientation of those individuals: the hypothalamus of hetero and homosexual men appears to respond to straight-oriented and gay-oriented erotic stimuli respectively, but not the other way around.[136] So, the hypothalamus has indeed a lot to do with sexual arousal in humans.

Recently, Ivanka Savic and Per Lindström published two consecutive studies that I find particularly convincing.[137] Using positron emission tomography (PET) to monitor the activation of specific areas in the brain, they exposed heterosexual men, heterosexual women, and homosexual men to two very special chemicals—a testosterone derivative (4,16-androstadien-3-one) and an estrogen-like steroid (estra-1,3,5(10),16-tetraen-3-ol)—which are believed to act as pheromones. We will have a more specific conversation about pheromones in the following chapters, but here is what you need to know for now: pheromones are odors, usually not recognized in a conscious manner, that are secreted by the body (e.g., in sweat and urine) and that trigger sexual arousal in other individuals who happen to be sensitive to them. Basically, when two animals sniff their respective behinds, they instinctively seek pheromonal cues. If the pheromone cocktail matches their liking, which to say if one animal's pheromones stimulate the other's hypothalamus, it triggers sexual arousal. Savic and Lindström have then exposed individuals to the two presumptive human pheromones, either the male one (testosterone-derived) or the female one (estrogen-derived), while monitoring the activity of various areas of their brains using PET. They found that the hypothalamus of both heterosexual women and homosexual men lights up when exposed to the male pheromone but not the female one. They observed the opposite pattern with heterosexual men and lesbian women who, as expected, responded to the female attractant chemical but not the male one.

Unfortunately, what those studies cannot tell is whether the differences that we observe are the cause or the result of a homosexual lifestyle, that is, whether they are innate or acquired. Psychocultural conditioning added to obvious moral restrictions upon experimental design render studies with human subjects difficult to interpret. It happens however that another animal model, the sheep, may help us sort this out. Sheep present a nearly identical sexually dimorphic difference in the preoptic/anterior hypothalamic area.[138] Rams too exhibit sexual diversity, and about 6% to 8% prefer other males and can be considered as being exclusively homosexual.[139] In those homosexual rams, the average size of the sexually dimorphic hypothalamic nucleus is similar to that of females and twice smaller than that of heterosexual rams. Therefore the similarity with humans is striking. Very importantly, while the equivalent experiment would be technically impossible to perform with humans for moral reasons, the same team was able to demonstrate that the hypothalamic sexual dimorphism occurs during the last month of gestation.[140] That means that this sexual dimorphism, at least in rams, is not the result of experience but instead of a genetic program, whose unfolding appears to be sensitive to testosterone level.[141] Hence, if all the dots are far from being connected, they already align pretty convincingly.

Before we conclude this section, I must mention that differences among homosexual men and women have been found in other areas of the brain: the size of the anterior commissure[142] (the structure that connects the right and left hemispheres of the brain), asymmetry between the left and right cerebral hemispheres, and connection of the amygdala with other areas of the brain.[143] And often indeed homosexual patterns resemble that of the opposite sex. Those studies corroborate other studies that highlighted the difference in neurocognitive abilities between homosexual and heterosexual men and women: for skills like basic spatial perception, location memory and verbal capabilities, gay men tend to perform—on the average—like women.[144] Yet those results have been difficult to reproduce and should be considered prudently.

It appears that the brain is able to modulate its own sexual differentiation in a manner that is not strictly tied to the so-called "genital sex." Using mechanisms that are still unknown, the brain is able to adopt a conformation that biologists often describe as being "sex atypical." This means that, anatomically speaking, male homosexual orientation/preference might rely, to a degree that remains to be determined, on the same neural organization that ensure female heterosexual orientation/preference. The same applies to female homosexual and male heterosexual orientation/preference.

However, when dealing with anatomical data such as those presented here, one must remain particularly vigilant. First, those anatomical differences reflect average difference between the homosexual and heterosexual populations, but not systematic individual difference. In other words, those anatomical differences are only statistically significant, and cannot alone predict the sexuality of a given individual, whether in a human being, a ram, or a mouse. One must always keep that important fact in mind.

Second, whatever anatomical differences are observed on the basis of sexual orientation/preference, we must remember that those differences do not match gender identity. As far as we can tell, the majority of homosexual individuals used in those studies still identify closely with their "genital gender." Hence those anatomical differences would be better defined as determining attraction to males or females, independently from genital sex and gender identity. The scientific discourse might be well inspired to use a language that states its conclusions in a more conservative fashion, particularly when it comes to qualifiers such as "sex atypical," "masculinized," and "feminized." Not that one should feel offended by the concept of gender inversion. I am simply advocating for more clarity. Rigorously speaking, if homosexual-specific motifs in the brain emerge independently from gender identity, the latter, which I anticipate to have a neural basis as well, must rely on distinct sexually dimorphic features. Logically, the concepts of masculinization and feminization should be reserved to qualify anatomical differences that match gender rather than sexual orientation/preference. Other qualifiers sound more pertinent to describe these patterns: male/female-inclined or -orientated (as used in ram studies), andro/gyno-philic, or andro/gyno-tropic (which literally translate into "turned towards male or female," and would definitely be my term of choice).[145]

More must come. Viewed from the outside, homosexuality still reveals a vague and uncertain visage at this point. The data on homosexuality's anatomy are convincing but too imprecise. Brain imaging needs to reach far better definition levels in order to break through into the mystery of human sexuality. Yet, as time goes on, scientists are drawing an increasingly detailed map of homosexuality's anatomy. Key elements of this map are likely to lie within the hypothalamus, this small subunit of our limbic system that appears to preside over our deepest instinctive needs and desires: hunger, thirst, and sex. And converging evidence points to this almond-size structure as being the likely host of human sexual orientation/preference. Although a work in process, this map is an essential piece of our integral map. Yet it has another side to it, an insider view, so to speak: a temporal map of how the homosexual brain emerges, which is what we are going to explore next.

HOMOSEXUALITY, VIEWED FROM THE INSIDE

By what process is a homosexual being generated? To grasp homosexuality's physical reality viewed from the inside is the domain of sciences that study mechanisms and seek causes. And while the "outside" map of homosexuality talks about hypothalamus and differences in the brain, the "inside" map tells us stories of twins and genes.

Attempts to understand the physiological origins of homosexuality are ancient. Apparently Aristotle believed that a man's desire to be anally penetrated originate from a diversion of semen to the anal region, "causing congestion that seeks relief."[146] Centuries later, in the logic of his revolutionary theory of individual psychosexual development, Freud imagined the primordial cause of homosexuality as being primarily subjective and the result of a developmental arrest. He understood homosexual desire fixation in adults as a failure to overcome the bisexual phase characteristic of adolescence, that is, as an unresolved Oedipal dilemma.[147] Hence, for Freud, homosexuality was a perversion. And if today many of Freud's conclusions, particularly with respect to homosexuality, have lost all relevance, his developmental logic was visionary.

In 1986 Bailey and Pillard published the first reliable study of genetic inheritance of homosexuality.[148] Others followed and, as usual, it quickly degenerated into a battle of numbers.[149] The rationale of these studies is simple, perhaps as we will discover later, a little too simple. In theory identical twins share the same genome, in other words, exactly the same genetic information. They are natural "clones." If homosexuality is genetically transmitted, identical twins should exhibit the same pedigree, either homosexual or heterosexual, in 100% of the cases. Sexual orientation among non-twin brothers (which includes fraternal twins) who have only 50% of their genome in common should coincide in 50% of cases on the average. And the less related two individuals are, the less their genetic backgrounds overlap and the less their sexual orientation should match, until you reach the average incidence in the whole population, which is probably around 2–3%. (One important caveat to this is that familial influence might vary exactly the same way: twins tend to be raised more uniformly than regular siblings. Because twin studies cannot discriminate very well between these two possibilities, they have been overtly criticized by psychologists, even though as far as we can tell, no one knows of any family-related psychological cause to homosexuality. The fact that there is no statistical difference in the sexual orientation of children raised by homosexual and heterosexual families should urge social scientists to reconsider their most basic assumptions regarding homosexuality's etiology. We will soon see that, unlike social sciences, biologists have accumulated much evidence in their own favor.)

In their great majority, genetic studies consistently reveal higher levels of co-inheritance among siblings compared to non-siblings, with the highest rates among identical twins, which is clearly indicative of "some" degree

Selected Data on the Co-Inheritance of Homosexual Orientation among Twins and Non-Twin Siblings

Study (year)	A (1986)	B (1993)	C (1999)	D (1991)	E (1993)	F (2000)	G (2000)	H (1992)	C (1999)	E (1993)	F (2000)
Sex of the sample	Male only						Male + Female		Female only		
Identical twins				52%	64%	20%	31%	25%		48%	24%
Fraternal twins				22%	28%		8%	12%		16%	
Siblings	22%	13.5%	7–10%						3–4%		
Adoptive siblings				11%						6%	

Results are expressed in % of sibling pairs in which homosexuality (or bisexuality) is shared by both siblings.[150]

of genetic causality. However, as you can see in the following table, the data accumulated thus far have failed to show the clear-cut correlation that geneticists had hoped for.

Surveys with the highest convergence rates generally recruited twin pairs through advertising. They were therefore accused of over-selecting individuals "drawn" to discuss their homosexuality and that of their siblings. On the other end of the spectrum, one finds a recent survey conducted in Australia indicating only 20% convergence among twins. Rather than using advertising, researchers opted to contact twin pairs whose information was compiled in a pre-existing national registry that contained no indication about their sexual orientation.[151] Despite the claim of the authors, I am tempted to believe that cultural prejudice against homosexuals that is allegedly virulent in Australia may have biased the results even more than in other studies, negatively this time. But, insofar as psychocultural biases appear inevitable in this sort of study, one should simply acknowledge the existence of a mosaic of data. Overall, numbers oscillate somewhere in the middle, around 50% genetic heritability.[152] The final and logical conclusion to these studies was that homosexuality is a "moderately inherited" genetic trait, the other unaccounted-for 50% being arbitrarily attributed to the sociocultural environment and psychological predispositions.

The story does not stop there. Geneticists went a step further in their quest for the biological origin of homosexuality. In their 1993 publication, the group of Dean Hammer and Angela Pattatucci pointed to the fact that homosexuality often appeared co-inherited from the maternal lineage: that is, from the mother's branch of the family. Maternal cousins and uncles of homosexuals are more likely to be homosexual, compared to those from the paternal side. Using molecular genetic analysis, they discovered a particular segment of the X chromosome, which appeared to be highly correlated with the transmission of homosexuality: the Xq28 marker—the famous "gay gene."[153]

It did not take long however for this to become more complicated, as usual. First, Hammer's team found no linkage between Xq28 and female homosexuality.[154] Second, a similar project, led by another group using a male Canadian population sample, failed to confirm the role of the Xq28 marker.[155] Eventually, Hammer's team published a new genetic investigation, focusing on the transmission of male homosexuality only, that revealed the possible implication of multiple chromosomal locations (7q36, 8p12, and 10q26, on chromosome 7, 8, and 10 respectively).[156] Their original candidate, Xq28, appeared to play an ambiguous and unequal role depending on the choice of population samples.[157] A new research project with the full support of the National Institute of Health and coordinated by Alan Sanders at the Evanston Northwestern Healthcare Research Institute is currently underway.[158] Thus, the saga is not yet over.

But before one can try to make sense of those confusing results, I'll mention two recent developments that also seem to imply a maternal regulation of male homosexuality, at least to some degree. The first one holds the barbaric name of "extreme skewing of X chromosome inactivation." Unlike men, who have an X and a Y chromosome, women have two X chromosomes. But having two X chromosomes creates a dangerous imbalance: having two copies of all the genes carried by the X chromosome while men have only one means women would end up producing twice the necessary amount of the corresponding products. To compensate for this potentially toxic situation, one of the X chromosomes is automatically chemically modified so as to lose all activity. Therefore, all the cells in a female body contain only one active X chromosome, randomly picked. As it happens, in the mothers of gay men, this process appears—on the average—to favor one X over the other. And in the mothers of two or more gay sons, this phenomenon is even more accentuated.[159] Mothers of gay sons display another curious peculiarity. They exhibit higher fecundity levels.[160] Beyond Freud's wildest dreams, mothers appear once again "complicit" in their sons' sexual tendencies.

Variation in the frequency of male homosexuality has been also linked to another mysterious process, the "fraternal birth order effect." Put simply, the more elder brothers a man has, the higher his odds of being homosexual are (the rate increasing by ~33% with each older brother).[161] Authors have imagined some sort of slow immunization mechanism taking place in the mother's womb which counter-selects heterosexual male embryos or affects the development of their brain in utero,[162] a theory which I find not only "exotic," but also theoretically unsupported and, taken globally, extremely weak.[163] The fraternal birth order effect will be discussed again later.

If none of those mechanisms is likely to explain the global occurrence of homosexuality, they nonetheless add to what we have reviewed earlier, at least in the case of male homosexuality. In the end, beyond a wise "wait and see" attitude, what can one possibly conclude from all these complex, partial, and often contradictory results? Mostly because of the semi-conclusive character of studies of twins, people, including biologists, have quickly settled for the equally shared influence of biological information and environmental factors.[164] Today this "50/50" theory is widely accepted, even though no study has ever shown any convincing causal link between one's homosexuality and environmental factors.[165] The battle between biological and social sciences was over without a victor. For nearly a century now, social sciences have been able to spread their views on the cause of homosexuality without any experimental support.[166] And if the legend of "the possessive mother and the distant father" might be finally losing ground, one may wonder what the other plausible suspects are today. Now, do the twin studies really argue in favor of a mixed influence between the biological and the psychological? Let me tell you why I believe they do not.

First of all, identical twins are not as identical as we previously thought. The genome is not the static database scientists believed it was. It is, on the contrary, a surprisingly dynamic structure. The expression of numerous genes gets modified and sometimes even impaired through a mechanism that is called "imprinting." It has been recently shown that the imprinting process modifies the genome of each twin in an unequal fashion. While identical twins start with perfectly identical genetic information, differences in gene imprinting will accumulate throughout their lifetime.[167] This means that identical twins no longer constitute the perfect genetic duplicates we thought they were and we should no longer expect a 100% match between them. This new fact only already forces us to reconsider the current consensus. Yet I wish to clarify some other important points by refreshing our memory regarding some of the basic tenets of genetics.

Classically, in order to find genes involved in a particular trait, geneticists attempt to obtain mutants defective for this trait. If the trait is hair, for instance, they look for either hairless or over-hairy mutants. The genetic comparison between mutant and normal ("wild-type") animals enables researchers to locate the defective gene, or at least the particular chromosomal segment carrying that gene. Almost certainly, this gene plays a role in the establishment of this trait. In most cases, mutant animals (mice, flies, and fish) are produced artificially in the laboratory. For obvious ethical reasons, geneticists working on humans have been limited to the rare mutations nature provides them with: albinos, color-blinds, hemophiliacs, diabetics, those having a sixth finger, and other precious rarities. This is the scientific logic behind the twin-studies, Dean Hammer's research, and in general the hunt for the "gay gene." Observe that as far as I can tell, geneticists have all based their research on the same fundamental assumption: Homosexuality results from an impairment of the prevalent—"normal"—trait, heterosexuality. Geneticists knew that what the media had been calling the "gay gene" was in fact the "gay-mutated" version of still-to-be-discovered gene (whose normal function was likely to promote "normal" heterosexual pairings). Whether it is the "gay gene" or the "gay-variant" of that gene, the unquestioned belief was always that homosexuality itself was a mutation, in one form or another—a defect in the reproductive instinct.

Scientists are right about one point: There must be a biological mechanism to ensure the proper reproduction of the human species, which is to say, that makes sure that males and females get together and mate efficiently. Such a mechanism exists everywhere in the animal kingdom, and there is no good reason to believe that our species constitutes an exception to that rule (we will investigate those mechanisms in the next chapter). Scientists were therefore right to assume that homosexuality implied a modification of the "heterosexual instinct." But that is about it.

In the meantime, geneticists failed to take into account a key piece of information: according to all anthropological records accumulated thus far, homosexual behavior has been present in all human populations, everywhere on the planet and almost certainly since prehistory. We do not know of any group where homosexual behavior was indubitably absent. Despite the great variability of body features and cultural habits displayed by human beings across the globe, "homosexual-less" populations have never been observed convincingly. Moreover, not only is homosexuality ubiquitously distributed among human populations, but it is also always limited to a minority. We do not know of any culture where everybody happened to be interested in same-sex partners, even though, as we know, this would by no means hinder the reproductive process that requires very limited amounts of heterosexual pairing to work perfectly.

All this is an extremely odd pattern for a mutation. Either a mutation is detrimental and progressively selected out by the mating process, or it provides a reproductive advantage (even if indirect or cryptic) and tends to spread throughout the population. Given enough generations, it should either disappear or disseminate. Even if the mutation or trait in question is neutral, that is, neither really detrimental nor really advantageous, it still tends to "cluster," which is to say, to spread among some group and vanish from others (e.g., skin or hair color, height, etc.). If homosexuality were an inherited trait/mutation, one would expect to see significant differences among populations that history has kept segregated for a long-enough time. Centuries of either pro or anti-homosexual cultural selection should have generated visible disparities. But this is not what we see. Exposed to similar cultural backgrounds, human populations across the planet exhibit the same distribution of sexual behaviors: (1) a small minority of "recalcitrant" homosexuals, irrespective of the level of social acceptance, (2) a larger group of individuals whose sexual preferences are flexibly altered by psychocultural conditions, and (3) an essentially heterosexual majority.

This can mean only one thing: that the prevailing theoretical model that sees homosexuality as being a mutation, a so-called Darwinian trait, is inaccurate. It is incompatible with anthropological data and leaves too many gray areas with respect to twins and genetic linkage studies. As previously stated when considering the 2D:4D ratio, I contend that the genetic factors shared by identical twins, carried by the markers Xq28, 7q36, 8p12, and 10q26, or those behind the "fraternal birth order" and "extreme skewing of X chromosome inactivation" effects, are peripheral rather than central to the establishment of one's sexual orientation/preference. They involve mechanisms capable of positively influencing the occurrence of homosexuality but not those directly implicated in it. And insofar as peripheral genetics tend to be population specific, we can now explain why those results were often inconsistent with each other. They might apply to a North American genetic background, but not to an Australian or European one.

The trait that geneticists should have considered from the beginning is not homosexuality but the spectrum of sexualities defined by the sexual orientation/preference (hardly differentiable in the data accumulated this far). In that respect, nature has already done the experiment for us: this spectrum of sexualities has been maintained in virtually all known human populations, which is absolutely remarkable considering how much humans can differ with respect to other traits. In the meantime, we still have no clue about the genes that are decisive for the organization of sexual orientation/preference in the brain and its peculiar distribution. We might reasonably suspect that it involves multiple genes and complex mechanisms. One may instead imagine sexual orientation/preference as a "loose switch," geared preferably toward opposite-sex, either sex, or same-sex partners, provided that opposite-sex attraction seems always to prevail. The mechanism would be stochastic in nature, that is, its variations randomly determined and hardly predictable on an individual basis, and yet, statistically speaking, relatively stable among human populations. Such a model can accommodate homosexuality's biological reality.

And even if we have no good genetic model to explain this phenomenon, we do have a famous precedent: left-handedness. Just like homosexuality, left-handedness is present among other primates, yet is particularly frequent in humans.[168] And beyond this, the similarities between homosexuality and left-handedness are absolutely striking:

> Left-handedness has a frequency of around 10% in the general population with a slightly higher frequency in the male population compared to the female population. [. . .] Left-handedness is highly correlated with cerebral asymmetry. [. . .] The genetics of left-handedness is a highly debated issue and both environmental and genetic models have been proposed. However, twin, family and adoption studies support a genetic background to human handedness. Several proposed genetic models [suggest] that handedness is determined by chance due to the accumulation of stochastic events during embryonic development. [. . .] the exact genetic model of human handedness remains to be elucidated.[169]

Only recently have molecular geneticists identified a first gene, LLRTM1, which appears to influence left-handedness in some populations depending on their geographic origin. Therefore LLRTM1, which is suspected to influence neural development, constitutes a "susceptibility" gene rather than a causal one. I intuit that the case of left-handedness and LLRTM1 illustrates perfectly the difficulty and pitfalls of behavioral genetics. Homosexuality and left-handedness appear among a minority in human populations. Neither can be traced down to a single gene responsible for the expression of that specific trait (likewise, we are still unable to grasp the mechanisms which generate the unique pattern of our fingerprints and the color of our irises).

For those interested in speculating a little further, the size variation of the INAH3 hypothalamic nucleus may represent a good starting point. However, a closer look at the original data reveals that if the average volume appears to be larger in heterosexual males compared to women and homosexual men, some heterosexual men have a smaller INAH3, while some heterosexual women and gay men have a larger one. Therefore, the size of INAH3 alone cannot predict sexual preference/orientation other than statistically. The variability of INAH3 may very well participate in the overall process and promote the stochastic distribution of sexual orientation/preference, but it cannot explain the entire phenomenon.[170] Most likely, size difference reveals (but does not always) more subtle functional differences at the cellular and/or molecular level. Still, try to imagine for a moment: what if . . .

. . . the INAH3 nucleus was the source of a still-to-be-discovered "X" molecular signal, whose strength would vary among individuals. A strong X signal would prime areas of the brain involved in mating behavior to respond preferably to female stimuli, that is, the presence of a female. Alternatively, a weak X signal would reinforce one's interest in male partners. The strength of this X signal could fluctuate as a function of the size of the INAH3 nucleus as well as other factors (the number of synapses and the levels of neurotransmitters could also play a critical role in the process).[171] Yet the final intensity of the X signal in adults would be set once and for all during gestation, whether produced or not (a little like the amount of light that an electric bulb generates when it is turned on depends on how it was originally manufactured, even if it remains off for a while). This in utero setting could be influenced by multiple factors, such as:

- sexual hormones produced by the gonads (e.g., testosterone), which would explain why the majority of a given sex are primarily or only attracted to the opposite sex.

- hormonal signals in the brain itself, including (1) hormones (e.g., estradiol, testosterone, and dihydrotestosterone), (2) enzymes involved in the production of those hormones (e.g., the aromatase, the enzyme that transforms testosterone into estradiol in the brain), or (3) their receptors (variations in the 2D:4D ratio suggest that the androgen receptor is a likely candidate)

- and probably many other yet-to-identify factors. In mice for instance, a recent study demonstrated that key sex-specific behaviors such as aggression and maternal care remain strongly influenced by unknown elements located on the sex chromosomes, completely independent from the presence of testes or ovaries, and testosterone levels.[172]

Through a series of subtle variations, some males would increasingly "deviate" from the prevailing heterosexual pattern, showing a less and less interest in females to the point of becoming exclusively interested in other males. And the reciprocal would be true for some females. This would explain the existence of a spectrum of mate preference among each sexes instead of a strict mate choice dictated by gonadal sex—a "loose switch" instead of a "clear-cut switch."

According to my theory, genetics studies did not uncover the (probably many) genes directly involved in the formation of the loose switch but only mutations capable of displacing the standard distribution of sexual preference/orientation among particular groups that results from the existence of a loose switch. This would explain why different genetics studies pointed at different positions in the genome, depending on the population sample. On the other hand, twin studies show that, all things being more or less equal at the genetic level (given the differences due to gene imprinting), the loose switch can still fluctuate within a 50% range. Genetic influences cannot impose more than ~50% convergence, the rest being left to meticulously orchestrated molecular randomness.

Speculations are endless. Still I hope this discussion gives you a sense of what an etiological biological theory of sexual attraction that does not see homosexual desire as an unexplainable "oddity" might look like. Goodbye then to "*the gay gene*," which was merely a reductionist illusion fostered by a culture that equates homosexuality with reproductive malfunction and evolutionary paradox.

~

The Biology of Desire

. . . hope and pride and not despair are the ultimate legacy of genetic diversity. . .

Edward O. Wilson, *On Human Nature*

As Dick F. Swaab observed, "Neurobiological research related to sexual orientation in humans is only just gathering momentum."[173] Molecular geneticists, neuroscientists, and behavioral neuroscientists are still investigating the homosexual phenomenon today. More data will come and more controversies will arise. But when one, no longer fearful or defensive, chooses to come to terms with the insatiable curiosity of the scientific community, one will still have to develop critical awareness with regard to the scientific discovery process. Put in more simple terms, it would be wise to prepare ourselves for the harvest of future scientific data. Gay or not, science is and will be speaking more and more about how the "homosexual brain" and the "homosexual mind" function. The homosexual world can neither remain passive nor defiant. Nor can it rely on tabloid journalism to integrate scientific knowledge. An integral homosexual discourse is poised to take on such a challenge. We must, therefore, endow ourselves with a context that can measure up to the task by creating a solid foundation of knowledge from which future knowledge can branch. Therefore, I would like to continue our exploration of the fascinating world of biological science a little longer.

A Post-"Nature versus Nurture" Homosexual Discourse

The strict distinction between nature and nurture, a modern avatar of the ancient body vs. soul dichotomy, is conceptually obsolete. In other words, it is simply not how things work. Nature and nurture exist as a continuum. They interact constantly and in a circular fashion. The concept of neuroplasticity epitomizes more than any other the reality of this nature-nurture continuum. Neuroplasticity manifests itself in two different manners.

First, genomic information, albeit essential, not only uses but also needs the physical environment to complete its own unfolding. This is particularly so in the case of brain development during infancy. The example of the visual system in that regard is most compelling. If one covers an eye of newborn monkeys for the first six months of their life by suturing one eyelid, their visual system will be forever impaired.[174] While the sutured eye appeared to be perfectly functional once reopened, the neural connections between the retina and the brain as well as the areas involved in processing visual information have failed to develop properly. Past a certain age (which appears to be species-specific), the visual system can no longer, or only poorly, recover from stimulus deprivation.

Even more interestingly, if you raise a kitten for five months after birth in an environment that only includes either horizontal or vertical lines, they eventually displayed major defects in their visual system: "Their head movements were jerky when following moving objects; they tried to touch distant objects and often bumped into things. Most important of all, they seemed to be blind to stripes orthogonal to the orientation of the environment in which they were reared. [. . .] In each case, the majority of cortical cells responded to the stimuli that were present in their environment and responded very weakly to anything else."[175] Without the environment, genetic information alone is not sufficient to establish a fully functional visual system. And past a certain age, the defects become irreversible.

These experiments teach us an important lesson. Environmental cues are sometimes indispensable for the full maturation of the brain, and without external stimulation, some neuronal networks degenerate completely. Biological systems have the capacity to utilize the environment. Genes provide the master plan, but the final result is only obtained in conjunction with the environment, within a relatively short period of time after birth. However, the degree of variability observed during the period of neuroplasticity is limited to and by the biological template. The environment cannot introduce information that the biological template is not programmed to recognize in the first place. Essentially, the environment only awakens a biologically determined potential.

Second, some neural structures are designed to host a wide range of information. This extraordinary property of the brain accounts for the vast psychological and cultural heterogeneity that we witness in the world. Notwithstanding, this diversity, as extraordinary as it looks, hides subtle yet very real limits directly imposed by the neural structures that host the mental process. So, if in many ways the psyche looks like a blank slate, we are nevertheless clearly limited in our choice of chalks. And this second aspect of neuroplasticity is perfectly illustrated by the organization of human languages.

Language is fascinating in that it might represent the most remarkable achievement of our species. It expresses our humanness and constitutes the basis of our self-identity and consciousness. With about 4,000 to 6,000 identified variants, the diversity of human languages is exceptional. Yet, despite their astonishing creativity, all human languages contain a quasi-invisible template—"a universal grammar, not reducible to history or cognition, [which] underlies the human language instinct."[176]

The exact nature of this universal grammar is highly debated among linguists. In spite of this, I would like to give you a sense of what the concept means. For instance, sentences are typically constructed around the relation between participants and events, and that is reflected through the symbolic relation between the arguments of the sentence (subject, direct object, and indirect object) and the verb.[177] The same way, in all human languages, sentences can be expanded indefinitely through what linguists call "recursion." Basic sentence-unit can be embedded within a larger sentence, hierarchically and with no other limitation than people's memory (e.g., [1] I noticed that [2] Brian wrote on his notebook that [3] Judith was traveling to New York City in July). These simple rules appear to constitute a universal paradigm governing all human languages. The incredible speed at which children are able to acquire language strongly argues in favor of the existence of a pre-existing grammatical "groove" in the brain's language center also. The linguistic creativity of human beings has structural requirements that are biologically defined, hence genetically determined.

And yet, nowhere more than through language have human beings experienced the dichotomy between nature and nurture. Nowhere more than through language have they tasted the absolute freedom to invent. What human beings have viewed as being the most exquisite evidence of their separateness from nature is none other than a subtle continuum. The environment is used to awaken an already programmed information and create a perfectly controlled diversity. One can thus define neuroplasticity as the use of variable yet predictable factors of the environment so as to (1) complete the development of the nervous system and (2) generate controlled levels of psychocultural diversity. Ultimately, this concept radically contradicts the concept of a human mind as a *tabula rasa*.

With respect to homosexuality, what do we learn from the concept of neuroplasticity? I suspect that, for a good part, the dogma of psychological science presents the dynamic of psychosexual development backward. Despite indisputable exceptions (e.g., psychological traumas), the causal effect of the environment upon individual psychosexual development, which psychology and social science have championed yet never experimentally substantiated, is being seriously challenged. The same way kittens pick up vertical and horizontal visual cues to ensure the full maturation of their visual system, human beings are likely to select cues in their psychocultural environment that match—resonate with—their "inner template." Over the years, successive iterations would progressively allow individuals to build an adult mind.

A lot is still to be learned and I believe that psychologists will increase their chances to decipher the connections between psychosexual development and childhood environment by embracing rather than denying the fact that the mind at birth is not a blank slate (rare are those who, like Isay, acknowledge that homosexuality is most likely innate).[178] And by no means should one understand from this that the psychocultural environment does not play an important role. But, as far as we are concerned, the nature vs. nurture debate is over.

GENETIC? BIOLOGICAL? . . . WHAT?

Insofar as everything about human beings relies, in one way or another, on biological structures and consequently on their genetic makeup, what do the terms "genetic" and "biological" exactly mean when specifically applied to homosexuality? Both terms have been so misused and misinterpreted in the media that it seems necessary at this point to clarify, not so much what they mean for scientists, but rather, what the real concepts behind their use in the homosexual discourse are.

In journalistic language, "biological" is a shorthand for "biologically determined." Indeed, the big question in the homosexual discourse, which has tortured generations of gay activists, is whether homosexuality is determined (i.e., primarily caused) by the biological structures generated by the natural unfolding of our genetic information. However, the question "is homosexuality biological?" hides another one, a preliminary question, that we have to address first: Is homosexuality in adults immutable or can it be changed at will? Because, indeed, being biologically determined and being immutable are not necessarily tied to one another. To begin with, as William Byne wrote, "it is clear that learned behavior can nonetheless be immutable."[179] But the opposite is also true: biologically determined behavior can be modified to some degree and even sometimes suppressed. For instance, infants, like so many animals, are biologically programmed to enjoy sweetness and dislike bitterness and sourness in food.[180] As it happens, natural products that are either bitter or sour tend to be toxic, that is, rotten or poisonous, while sweet ones are usually loaded with sugar, a highly beneficial nutrient. Yet most adults manage to educate themselves so as to appreciate flavors that they are "biologically determined" to avoid (like vinegar and French cheese), a phenomenon that is highly guided by cultures. And they do so very happily.

So, is homosexuality immutable? Well, it all depends on which homosexuality is being talked about, which is why people kept disagreeing on this issue. As seen in chapter 2, homosexual behavior is either essential or optional. One's homosexual desire is likely to feel immutable in the first case but not (or much less) in the second one. For the same reason, this sense of immutability differentiates homosexual orientation from homosexual preference (as previously defined). Similarly, homosexual identity tends to be more accentuated and more permanent in men and more subtle and fluid in women (see chapter 15). It is undeniable that for many homosexuals the longing for same-sex partners, and the fact that this longing constitutes a core element of their sense of self, does feel immutable and true. And the many heartbreaking accounts of "ex-gays" only remind us of this blatant fact.

Now, is the source of this immutability—(homo)sexual orientation—biological, and is one's sexual repertoire—(homo)sexual preference—biologically restricted (provided that those two aspects of homosexual reality are culturally shaped as well)? I have addressed that question in the previous chapter, as well as I could at that point. That (homo)sexual orientation or preference, and most likely both of them, are primarily dictated by the particular conformation of defined structures in the brain can hardly be dismissed today. Hence, if the psychocultural environment "makes" someone homosexual, that is, gives one's homosexuality a defined shape and substance, one's sexual orientation/preference is essentially biologically determined. In other words, human (homo)sexuality is biologically primed and culturally shaped. And in that, sexuality might not be so different from gender. Remember that, despite the vast psychocultural diversity that the concepts of maleness and femaleness entail, sex determination, which matches gender in nearly all individuals, result from the presence or absence of one single gene carried by the Y chromosome, *sry*.[181]

This point clarified, what does the claim that "homosexuality is genetic" mean? "Genetic" stands for "genetically inheritable," which more or less comes down to say that homosexuality is inherited from the parents. We have ruled out that possibility in the previous chapter. Homosexual orientation/preference is not a "mutation" that would be genetically inherited like the color of the eyes, diabetes, or hemophilia. What scientists have found are yet-to-be-defined genetic factors that appears to increase homosexuality's frequency, but that is all. What is inherited is the mechanism(s) by which the unique and relatively stable spectrum of sexual orientation/preference is established, which I have called a sexual orientation/preference switch or "loose switch," as previously discussed. That "loose switch" mechanism is inherited at 100%. Take any two 100% heterosexual human beings on the planet, one male and one female, and allow them to breed long enough so as to generate a large group of people. You will find that, regardless of the cultural environment, the great majority of the adult population thereby generated will only be interested in opposite-sex partners; a small minority will be mostly or exclusively drawn to same-sex partners, and in between the two, will be a group of people potentially interested in both sexes. (Again, this is based only on sound assumptions, not data, and nature might prove me wrong.)

THE SMELL OF DESIRE

Inasmuch as the hypothalamus plays a key role in orchestrating sexual behavior, and if we agree that, as we might reasonably expect, it is also the area in the brain where the sexual orientation/preference switch is maintained, let me then ask a question: How does the hypothalamus know what sex it prefers? We tend to forget that behind the whole issue of homosexuality lies a very simple question: Whom do you desire and whom are you ready to love? Thus one cannot close this chapter without devoting a few pages to the biology of desire. More specifically, I would like to explore a particular branch of neuroscience that I consider particularly promising if we want to elucidate the etiology of homosexuality: the science of smell. The works of Savic and Lindström using brain imaging already pointed in that direction. As it happens, numerous research studies suggest an involvement of smell in the regulation of human sexuality. In a nutshell, it appears that we tend to desire the most those whose odor we like.

Of all our senses, the sense of smell is the most connected to emotions. It awakens memories (Proust's madeleine, which, unlike what most people think, involved primarily the sense of smell and very little of the taste buds). It is the most instinctual sense and the most difficult to tame. We like an odor or we do not, often without concession. Odors elicit highly impulsive responses that are often beyond our control. This said, compared to other animals, the sense of smell is quite reduced in humans.[182] While most animals depend on the nose to locate food, detect predators, and choose a mate, adult humans clearly rely mostly on vision to sample their environment.

As a matter of fact, human beings survive very well without a functional sense of smell. But let us not jump too quickly to a conclusion here. Indeed, while anosmia (the loss of the sense of smell) affects ~1% of the human population (~5% of individuals above 45 year old), very curiously, congenital anosmia, a genetically caused inability to detect odors from birth, is an extremely rare condition, with no more than 1 in 10,000 individuals. Moreover, in most of those cases, congenital anosmia is associated with Kallmann syndrome, a severe condition resulting from a failure of the development of olfactory-related hypothalamic structures.

Hence, contrasting remarkably with deafness and blindness, people suffering from true congenital anosmia as a result of an impaired olfactory system (the system in charge of detecting odors) are astonishingly scarce: so far, only a few families have been identified in the entire world.[183] And in those families, none of the few genes known to be critical for a functional sense of smell was found to be defective.[184] All this is to say that if human beings appear not to be the greatest noses in the animal kingdom, and if the sense of smell is certainly dispensable in adults, still, enormous pressure is placed upon maintaining a functional olfactory sensitivity. Somehow, the sense of smell must still play a critical function in humans.

How does the olfactory system affect sexual behavior in animals? It happens that in most of the animal kingdom the sense of smell is in fact twofold. Smells come in two very different sorts. The first class of chemicals encompasses everything we commonly call odors—the smell of rose, vanilla, wet dog, garbage, gas leak, sweaty armpits, and so forth. Odorant cues are directly transmitted to and processed by the brain's cognitive centers, which analyze them, match them with preexisting information stored in memory centers, associate them with past personal experiences, and (in humans) put them in language.[185] This occurs within a fraction of a second, every time one sniffs. Try to smell the odor emanating from a pot of freshly brewed coffee right now, and you will know perfectly what I am talking about.

Pheromones accounts for the second class of chemical that animals can detect. Pheromones are little known molecules found in bodily secretions such as sweat, urine, saliva, tears, and anogenital emissions,[186] whose primary function is to inform individuals about the sex, fertility status (i.e., in heat or not), and social rank (essentially among males) of other individuals in the same species.[187] But while the signal resulting from the detection of common odors is transmitted to the brain's cognitive centers, pheromones activate discrete areas in the limbic system instead, primarily in the hypothalamus. The hypothalamus is not only essential in the formation of innate behaviors, such as hunger, thirst, sex, and maternal behavior, but it also orchestrates key neuroendocrine responses associated with emotions and reproduction. Therefore pheromones can potentially activate the various nuclei of the hypothalamus that I have previously mentioned, and that scientists suspect to be involved in mate choice (e.g., INAH3).

It was known that eliminating pheromone sensitivity by means of surgery completely abolishes sex drive in virgin animals (these experiments being typically done in rodents).[188] But genetically engineered impairment of the pheromone recognition pathway in mice produced even more striking results: Male mutants no longer showed any particular sexual preference.[189] They attempted to mate with any cage mates, regardless of their sex, and no longer displayed aggressive behavior toward strange males introduced in the cage by the experimenter (regular males would commonly attack). Impairing the pheromone sensory system in mice led to a loss of sexual discrimination.

As one may expect, numerous studies have tried to uncover the role of pheromones in our species.[190] And among the flurry of behavioral analyses on the potential role of pheromones in humans, one study stands out, which presented the first believable evidence of people's ability to recognize pheromones. In 1998 the team of Martha McClintock started to monitor hormonal responses rather than behavior in order to determine the possibility of pheromonal communication among people.[191] It was already known that women living in communities, such as convents and college dormitories, develop synchronized menstrual cycles.[192] McClintock's research demonstrated that the synchronization of women's menstrual cycles could also be achieved by simply placing underneath the noses of female volunteers a little pad containing undetectable amounts of sweat collected from the armpit of another woman. The frequent exposure to another women's bodily secretion slowly but surely shifted the timing of their periods so that they eventually synchronized. And this constituted the first convincing proof of human pheromonal communication.

Still, evidence of a connection between bodily secretion and sexual preference remains meager, let alone compelling.[193] However, as seen in the preceding chapter, the spectacular development of brain imaging techniques have recently allowed the team of Ivanka Savic to show that the hypothalamus of female volunteers lit up in a PET readout when the volunteers sniffed androgen-like compounds, male pheromone candidates. Symmetrically, men's hypothalamus responded to estrogen-like substances.[194] Ivanka Savic and Per Lindström later demonstrated that these activation patterns depended upon sexual orientation. Pheromonal hypothalamic responses presented a similar pedigree in male-attracted individuals (heterosexual women and homosexual men) and in female-attracted individuals (heterosexual men and homosexual women). Yet, which one comes first—sexual orientation or hypothalamic activation patterns—still constitutes a mystery, a limitation that we have already discussed in the previous chapter. And this is where the scientific research in sexual orientation/preference stands at the moment I am writing these lines.

However, I now have a chance to refine my theory of the "loose switch": A sexual orientation/preference switch could be generated by altering the neural connections that link pheromonal signals to areas in the brain involved in sexual arousal. As explained in the previous chapter, this would happen during embryonic life, well before sexual desire actually emerges. Genetic information would ensure that, in the majority of cases, regions in the hypothalamus responsible for the adult sexual drive get wired so as to predominantly respond to pheromonal cues from the opposite sex. The same genetic information would also allow that in, a significant number of individuals, sexual orientation/preference is not exclusive but instead broader or malleable, that is, potentially sensitive to both male and female pheromones; and in a reduced number (around 2–3%?) the polarity would be reverse with individuals responding more strongly, if not exclusively, to pheromonal cues from partners of their own sex. Remember that this switch is not merely random, in which case one would expect a symmetry between the demographics of heterosexuals and homosexuals. The switch is clearly biased toward heterosexual pairing.

After birth, pheromones would help the brain associate someone's sex with a myriad of other sensory cues: body odors, the pitch of a voice, the shape of the body, the texture of the skin, the body hair, and so on, and later, with sex-specific behaviors and increasingly complex cultural norms, this would progressively turn the originally simple information into an elaborate assessment of one's human social environment. I expect those steps take place during infancy. We know, for instance, that newborns rely massively on smell to recognize their mothers and that odors are essential to the infant-mother interaction. Once the brain is fully imprinted, pheromones, while perhaps still pleasurable, would nonetheless become dispensable. From that point on, the brain is primed to respond to a specific range of stimuli and not to others, even if it does not know it yet.

When, at the onset of puberty, sexual hormones elicit a sudden burst of sexual desires, the particular conformation of the hypothalamic switch that resulted from early imprinting would be progressively awaken and reinforced with experience. The notorious "pan-sexuality" of adolescent, which is to say, their ability to enjoy sex without much consideration for their partner's sex would result from a delayed or slow activation of the sexual orientation/preference switch compared to sexual desire, inducing a phase when sexual behavior remains little constrained. Eventually, a more defined sexuality crystallizes. A sexually adult individual is born.

A pheromone-based etiological theory of sexual preference could also account for the fraternal birth order effect. It is by no means unreasonable to conceive that mothers could alter the sexual orientation of their sons, not through some hypothetic antibodies as suggested elsewhere, but instead by sending particular pheromonal cues in utero.[195] The fetus drinks four hundred milliliters of amniotic fluid a day, and olfactory neurons in the nasal cavity are constantly exposed to the mother's womb's chemicals. Recent studies have demonstrated that children's preference for certain flavors (e.g., carrot, garlic, or fruits) is strongly affected by the type of food that their mothers absorbed during pregnancy and breast feeding.[196] Children clearly favor substances to which they have been exposed during uterine life and shortly after birth. That the mother's alimentation changes the taste of her milk has been known since ancient times. However, that mothers' feeding behavior could alter the chemical environment of the fetus in the womb is new. Even more importantly, those studies show that not only chemical communication between the mother and the fetus occurs through the amniotic fluid, but also that it has a lasting effect on the child, most likely by reinforcing particular neuronal circuits in the fetus's brain.

Similarly, prenatal activation of the pheromonal olfactory pathway by maternal pheromones released in the amniotic fluid could influence the patterning of the hypothalamus of the fetus by gently favoring neural connections consistent with a homosexual orientation/preference. By activating a particular set of sensory neurons and not others, the mother's pheromones released in the amniotic fluid would enhance (or alternatively inhibit) some neural pathway versus others. Using pheromonal cues, the mother's reproductive history could remotely affect the neuroplasticity of the hypothalamic (loose) switch and therefore, increase the odds of their sons being homosexual.

This model, if proven true, could provide a solid and basic rationale to explain the "core reality" of human sexual diversity. Yet homosexuality and, more generally, sexual diversity must involve more than just a "loose switch." We have yet to understand why some sexual impulses are essential while others are optional. Sexual preference itself is an intricate mosaic made of many desires, pleasures, fantasies, and fears. We are also still far from addressing differences between women's and men's sexuality. As for sexual identity, scientists have yet to give us a first hint about where in the brain that might take place.

Yet more data will come. Scientific knowledge is a building process. Yesterday's science, despite all its mistakes and imperfections, was the foundation without which today's science could not have emerged. Today's science, in spite of its errors and limitations, will be the foundation of tomorrow's science. Neuroscience is dramatically changing the way we understand the human brain. It will undoubtedly transform how we conceive human nature, just like astrophysics and quantum physics have already revolutionized our knowledge of the cosmos. It is however essential to understand that biological determinism does not make us less human . . . or less divine.

Regardless of the validity of my hypothesis, I hope to have shown you that a biological theory of homosexuality, when appropriately informed by all fields of natural and social sciences, can convey not only depth but also beauty. Each cell in our body contains a story. One just needs to listen to what the story tells us. This is, however, only the beginning. We have only explored "how" homosexuality emerges. We have still to ask the most important question: why did homosexuality emerge? And to answer this, we must now turn our attention to our distant cousins, the great apes. They hold the key to the evolutionary logic of human homosexual behavior.

CHAPTER FIVE

Up from the Jungle

Comment s'est-il pu faire qu'un vice destructeur du genre humain s'il était général, qu'un attentat infâme contre la nature, soit pourtant si naturel? Il paraît être le dernier degré de la corruption réfléchie; et cependant il est le partage ordinaire de ceux qui n'ont pas encore eu le temps d'être corrompus. Il est entré dans des coeurs tout neufs, qui n'ont connu encore ni l'ambition, ni la fraude, ni la soif des richesses. C'est la jeunesse aveugle qui, par un instinct démêlé, se précipite dans ce désordre au sortir de l'enfance, ainsi que dans l'onanisme.*

Dictionnaire Philosophique, Voltaire, 1764

Primates teach us a great deal about the evolutionary logic of homosexual behavior. The world of primates is roughly divided among—in evolutionary order—lemurs (the best known of a larger family, the prosimians), monkeys, and apes.[197] Lemurs, with their pretty fur and their large expressive eyes, are unmistakable; monkeys are widely spread across Central and South America, Africa, South Asia and Japan, and count among them a few celebrities such as the baboon and the macaque; and great apes—which are going to constitute our main object of attention in this chapter—encompass chimpanzees, bonobos, gorillas, orangutans, and . . . humans.[198] Interestingly, homosexual behavior is far from being equally distributed in the primate family.[199] It is absent in lemurs and all prosimians in general, yet widespread among monkeys and apes. Split early on between the Old and New Worlds, monkeys themselves have evolved into two geographically and evolutionarily distinct groups. Among New World monkeys, homosexual behavior is rare. In contrast, it flourishes among many (but not all) species of Old World monkeys and even more so among apes. Not only does the repertoire of homosexual interactions in both sexes become much more diversified, but this explosion of creativity comes also with a cohort of new features: a preference for particular partners, stable relationships, and . . . sexual pleasure. In short, one sees

---

* "How did it come about that a vice destructive of mankind if it were general, an infamous outrage against nature, is yet so natural? It appears to be the highest degree of deliberate corruption, and is nevertheless the ordinary lot of those who have not yet had time to be corrupted. It has penetrated unspoilt hearts that have not yet known ambition nor fraud nor the thirst of wealth; it is blind youth that flings itself into this disorder [as well as in onanism] upon leaving childhood, by an instinct still little understood."[200]

in primates the emergence of increasingly complex homosexual behavior. And, in order to understand their evolutionary logic in humans specifically, I will focus here on the remarkable research that has been performed on our immediate genetic family, the great apes.

Apes are, genetically speaking, highly related to each other and evolutionarily separated by some twenty-five million years from all other monkeys. The orangutan was the first species to branch off the ape family tree about fifteen million years ago, followed by the gorilla, around ten million years ago. Humans and chimpanzees started to diverge around five million years ago, and the latest species that separated from the chimpanzee was the bonobo, about two or three million years ago. And to scientists' great surprise, chimpanzees and bonobos proved to be genetically closer to us than they are to gorillas. Thus, if the great apes are our cousins, chimps and bonobos happen to be our "first" cousins.

Provided our evolutionary proximity with bonobos and chimpanzees, humanity might start thinking of itself as being located right in the middle of the ape family tree, which does not mean that human beings have not drastically changed since they have left the African savanna. Most recent calculations have estimated to around 94% the genomic similarities between the human and chimpanzee genomes. Out of ~ 22,000 genes total, 1418 human genes do not seem to have an equivalent in chimpanzees.[201] At the same time, most recent data obtained from the differential analysis of the human and chimpanzee genomes have failed to show very clear signs of the uniqueness of the human brain (ironically, the maximum divergence between the two species is observed among the genes expressed in testes!).[202] Ultimately, if the dissimilarities between humans and apes are striking, they should not overshadow the similarities and vice versa.

In recent decades the study of great apes has cast new light on human nature. Of all apes, the humanness of chimpanzees and bonobos especially is all at once disturbing, disconcerting, and deeply moving. In the wild as in captivity, they fascinate us, acting like mirrors of our own behavior. If their communication skills appear to be quite basic in the wild, their ability to learn fairly sophisticated languages in a human environment is astonishing. Moreover, after over nearly one and a half centuries of patient observation of chimpanzee groups in Africa, primatologists (the zoologists specialized in the study of primates) have identified thirty-nine endogenous chimpanzee cultures in the wild.[203] Chimps can use tools. They can break nuts with a stone and use stems to fish ants out of their nest and quickly slurp them. But this technical knowledge is not innate but group specific. As youngsters learn from older group members, the information is passed from one generation to the next.

Certainly, one contemplates cultural emergence at its most primordial level. What we see with chimpanzees can hardly compare with highly sophisticated human cultures. Yet it is undeniable that the basic principle that ensures the birth of a culture, which is to say a reliable learning process allowing the safeguarding of knowledge through generations, is already in place in chimpanzees. Our relatedness with the great apes and even more so with bonobos and chimpanzees largely exceeds the genetic plan, and in the last decades human beings have been forced to reconsider their uniqueness. Humanity can no longer be defined by the use of language or the manufacture of tools. The line that separates humanity from all other great apes has become blurry to a point of invisibility. For instance, researchers have recently reported an unusual habit unique to male chimpanzees in the Uganda forest that I find simply astonishing: they clean their penises after sex by using either a leaf or their fingers.[204] The human soul did not appear with our split from the bonobos-chimpanzee line, but rather, it has slowly emerged over the fifteen million years or so of ape evolution.

In the earlier days of primate research, zoologists observed gorillas, chimpanzees, baboons and other primates always through a particular lens. They kept recognizing in our cousins what they could not tolerate to see in humans. In accordance with Darwin's theory of the evolution of species, monkeys and apes symbolized the savage and brutal nature that human beings had escaped from. Angry gorillas pounding their chest epitomized the horror of an untamed violence and reminded us of the patent superiority of our intellect. In the aftermath of World War II and its unsurpassed atrocities, the distance that separated us from the rest of the animal kingdom took a different meaning. Human beings became the "killer ape," the only animal in creation that indulges in wars, murders, rapes, and other monstrous brutality.[205] People started to see in monkeys and apes an incarnation of the "good savage," the image of a paradise lost. Peacefully living in harmony with nature and untouched by men's bloody madness, they had preserved the primordial innocence and good nature that we had long forgotten. And of course, both pictures turned out to be deceptive and it took the literary success and remarkable speaking skills of contemporary primatologists, such as Frans de Waal and the world famous Jane Goodall, to shake the old black-and-white paradigm.

The filiation between apes and humans is biological, behavioral, and ultimately sociobiological. Scientists have traced the origins of many features previously thought to be exclusively human in apes back to our former home, the African savanna. Thousands of years of human cultural evolution have by no means erased the primate in us. It is still present, deeply embedded through the multiple layers of our psyche and hidden behind millenniums of cultural diversification. But human natural history, to which the evolution of homosexuality is tied, is hardly a peaceful story. Human beings, just like the universe, our planet, and life itself, are the fruits of incessant cataclysms. Violence is omnipresent and cannot be ignored when speaking of sex and love.

ON SEX AND VIOLENCE

Let us start with our most distant cousin in the ape family, the orangutan.[206] Orangutans live exclusively in the wild of South East Asia, mostly in the deep forest of the islands of Borneo and Sumatra, far from their African relatives—chimpanzees, bonobos, gorillas, and humans. Many of us remember images of massive and slow-moving male Orangutans, either encountered in a zoo or through the pages of a book. In the wild, these overweight males represent a particular type of males, the so-called "big males." And by big, you should understand that they are about twice the size of females. Big males are not merely solitary; they are overtly antisocial. Encounters between two big males always result in confrontations. They either fight or chase one another.

Yet there exists a second type of males, the small ones. About the size of females, they were for a long time simply mistaken for young males. However, many of them are adults. Their development appears somehow blocked. Small males do not behave like big males. They do not give the typical long calls so characteristic of big males. They are not as loud and aggressive, and thanks to their light weight, they can move swiftly. Occasionally, small males start growing and turn into the big type, thanks to a mechanism that still puzzles scientists today.

Solitary by nature, orangutans exhibit rare, nonetheless consistent, same-sex behavior in comparison to their more social African cousins (predictably, the frequency of same-sex interactions increases dramatically in captivity). Same-sex behavior is part of the normal repertoire of young (sexually immature) and small (sexually mature) males and all females. In the wild, traveling individuals pair up in temporary consort that may last up to a few days. Young adult and teenage males, penis erect, were seen enjoying "ventro-ventral contact of the anogenital region."[207] They wrestle playfully, hug for long minutes, kiss, insert their fingers into their partner's anus, closely examine each other's "private parts," have oral and sometimes anal sex.[208] Females are no slouches themselves at this game. They insert their fingers into their partner's vagina, while sometimes masturbating themselves with the foot (a sexual prowess that is of course only possible when one has been gifted four hands). Those interactions can carry on for ten to twelve minutes, which in the animal world is pretty remarkable.

Yet, by only considering homosexual behavior, our enterprise would miss the point. Never isolated, same-sex behavior is always part of a network of social behaviors that also includes reproductive and non-reproductive heterosexual sexual behaviors. If our goal is to unearth the dynamics that have shaped homosexual behavior in human societies, we therefore need to explore how those various behaviors have coexisted inside the global sexual strategy of a given species. And thanks to the orangutans, we can start solving a fifteen-million-year-long puzzle.

What about the orangutan heterosexual world then? Between big and small orangutan males, size does matter, but not only for aesthetic reasons. Females love the big males, but they profoundly despise the small ones. When females copulate with big males, they "look relaxed, engaged, and willing," in other words, totally happy.[209] Systematically ignored by the females, small orangutan males have developed a drastic tactic to satisfy their needs: they routinely rape the females. "The females showed fear and tried to escape from the males, but they were pursued, caught and sometimes struck and bitten [. . .] The male usually grasped the female by her thighs or round the waist with his prehensile feet, but by pulling herself about by her arms a female can keep moving and the male is forced to follow. One mating started at the top of a tree and ended on the ground. Such rape sessions lasted about ten minutes."[210] Depending on the study, between 50 to 88% of the matings observed within a specific orangutan population were identified as rapes.

The violence of the mating behavior of orangutan males is shocking, but also strangely familiar. Compared to other species with potential male rapists, such as elephant seals, the highest concentration of rapists is observed in the ape family. Rapes are observed among chimpanzees with frequencies similar to those encountered in humans. In contrast, rape seldom occurs among gorillas and bonobos. The reason for this difference resides in the fact that, unlike orangutan, chimpanzee, and human females, gorilla and bonobo females live in troops with strong inter-individual bonds that allow them to resist attacks by males. We are going to see how much male innate aggressiveness is effectively counterbalanced in species that have evolved strong social cohesion and sophisticated relational skills. This is only the beginning of a long history of sex and violence among the ape family, our family. And if in the world of brutality humans have proved to be quite skilled, they have not invented anything.

Second on our genetically-ordered list is the gorilla. Gorilla groups are of two kinds. Most typically, they live in small polygynous communities comprised of one alpha-male—the so-called silverbacks—and a harem of females with their youth. At some point, young adult males abandon their group of origin to form long-lasting all-male parties. Homosexual behavior is frequent among females of the same harem.[211] They typically embrace each other and rub their genitals against each other, all that being accompanied with a great deal of joyful screaming. Contrary to heterosexual copulations, lesbian sex seems essentially concerned with achieving mutual pleasure. Moreover, females show clear preferences for some particular females. In the meantime, the dominant male can enjoy his heterosexual monopoly and, occasionally, the few male youths available in the group.

What happens in all-male parties is, however, a different story. Same-sex is not only the rule, but it is also plentiful, diverse, and often loud. Like females, males often show preferences for another male, which they court, fight, and ardently compete for. But while teenagers and young males mount each other indiscriminately, silverbacks never allow anyone to mount them (a point which is crucial to notice, as we will soon understand).[212] In fact, "the dominant silverback males of this band [treat] the younger males as a harem, competing over ownership in the same way known of bisexual units."[213] So, one can recapitulate the above by stating that gorilla females are largely bisexual while gorilla males appear more to be sequentially bisexual, which is to say homosexual in all-male parties but mostly heterosexual when females are present.[214]

Compared to orangutans and chimpanzees, gorillas are of a very peaceful nature. They are the most quiet and affectionate of all apes. But this apparent gentleness should, nonetheless, not fool us. Infanticide is widespread in gorilla communities, and the strategy works in the following way.[215] A young adult male, ready and very willing to mate and create his own group, locates a group and starts to spy on the females. Taking advantage of a moment of distraction from the alpha-male (or the latter might have died), the stranger male attacks an isolated female and kills her youth. Invariably, the female gorilla ends up following the murderous male. This might sound incomprehensible to us, but the reason seems to be that she recognizes in the killer a male more powerful than her previous mate, the father of her deceased baby, which proved to be incapable of defending her progeny. The killer constitutes a stronger, hence safer, potential father. Instinctively, she will abandon the harem and partner with the murderous male. The reproductive logic of the female gorilla is, to say the least, uncompromising: she cannot afford to put up with a weak father. Yet the crescendo of male brutality does not stop with gorilla infanticide.

In chimpanzees, male violence targeted against individuals of their own species becomes part of a larger scheme: warfare.

> It began with a border patrol. At one point they sat still on a ridge, staring down into Kahama valley for more than three-quarters of an hour until they spotted Goliath, apparently hiding only twenty-five meters away. The raiders rushed madly down the slope to their target. While Goliath screamed and the patrol hooted and displayed, he was held and beaten and kicked and lifted and dropped and bitten and jumped on. At first he tried to protect his head, but soon he gave up and lay stretched out and still. His aggressors showed their excitement in a continuous barrage of hooting and drumming and charging and branch-waving and screaming. They kept up the attack for eighteen minutes, then turned for home, still energized, running and screaming and banging on the tree-root buttresses. Bleeding freely from his head, gashed on his back, Goliath tried to sit up but fell back shivering. He too was never seen again. So it went. One by one the six adult males of the Kahama community disappeared [. . .].[216]

This scene occurred during the 1970s and startled the scientists who witnessed it. Yet the story does not end there. The Kasekela chimpanzees started a relentless and merciless war against the Kahama group (to which Goliath belonged) until all the males of the Kahama group were killed, one after the other. Eventually the Kahama group was only composed of females. The three adult females were either killed under the researchers' eyes or were never seen again, almost certainly killed or mortally wounded as a result of brutal attacks by their neighbors. Young females experienced a different fate. They were integrated into the Kasekela group. By extending their territory, the winners increased their resources of food. But they also earned fertile females as war trophies. And in that process, they significantly boosted their reproductive potential.

Since the "Kahama war," raids have been observed in chimpanzee populations across the entire African continent. From Senegal to Tanzania, researchers monitored chimpanzees practicing the art of war in ways strangely reminiscent of our own horror. A team working in Kibale national park in Uganda reported three cases of male killing. There the palette of brutality comprised, among other things, the ripping of the testicles.[217] The script is invariably the same: several male chimpanzees, mostly adults but also sometimes teenagers, rarely females, gather together. At some point the party begins to move resolutely toward the territorial border of a neighboring group. They patiently patrol the area until isolated individuals are spotted. From that moment on, and in a very systematic manner, they assault individuals in vulnerable situations until all males are decimated. The killing is always done by males and the brutality is limitless. Ultimately, males murder all infants, finish off undesirable older females, and take the young females back with them. The progeny of the vanquished males is wiped out, and with it, their genes. War is genetic competition made conscious. And in this game, there can only be one victorious genome.

This discovery took conservationists by surprise. In Niokolo-Koba National Park in Senegal, they had to stop the reintroduction into the wild of chimpanzees raised in captivity due to violent raiding by native chimpanzees. It is essential, however, to understand that this phenomenon is tightly associated with the reproductive strategy of the chimpanzees. "The social world of chimpanzees is a set of individuals who share a communal range; males live forever in the groups where they are born, while females move to neighboring groups at adolescence."[218] In effect, females do not like to mate with their brothers. The latter may attempt to copulate with her and even rape her, but she will resist.[219] By instinct, females avoid sexual interaction with their siblings and migrate to a neighboring group upon reaching sexual maturity. As a consequence "the range is defended, and sometimes extended with the aggressive and potentially lethal violence, by groups of males related in a genetically patrilineal kin group; [and] out of four thousand mammals and ten million or more other animal species, this suite of behaviors is known only among chimpanzees and humans."[220]

In both chimpanzee and human societies, male bonds are dramatically favored. In any given chimp group or human tribe, males are related to each other while females are not. And this appears to be the rule for most if not all early human cultures across the globe, including for the few known matrilineal societies (whose number seems almost anecdotal compared to the overwhelming majority of patrilineal societies reported on all continents and throughout history).[221] In addition to being all blood-related, male chimpanzees are political animals. Through mutual grooming and food sharing, they build alliances with other males that will ensure reciprocal support in case of conflict with other members of the group.[222] This results in the formation of male coalitions, which will not only affect the status of each male in the group, but also decide eventually which one will occupy the position of alpha-male.

Therefore, what we see emerging in chimpanzees is a reproductive strategy based on male dominance and inter-community competition, often merciless. In humans, just like in chimpanzees, the primeval link between warfare and reproduction is undeniable. When one looks at human societies, wars have historically been waged by men. And on the rare occasions where women are involved in combat (e.g., the former Soviet Union, Israel, and many modern armies), female soldiers are unfailingly directed by male officers. The methodic rape of women has always been part of the horrific routine of war, even today, when war is waged by the armies of highly developed countries and officers are trained in military academies. The spiral of violence that war generates has the potential to awaken a five-million-year-old instinct in the brain of men. The taste for fighting, killing, raping, and raiding has been carried over from one generation to the next. Humans, chimpanzees, and to a lesser extent gorillas and orangutans, have been selected over millions of years to excel at this game. Male violence, deeply imbedded in men's brain and channeled through thousands of years of cultural evolution, resurfaces through wars, gang fights, and the competition for sex, money, and power.

History demonstrates how much men are capable of regressing and reconnecting with their most primal instincts. A study of the genetic diversity of populations across Latin America has recently given us a real-life measure of the impact of this dynamic on our species. The data attests that Central and South American populations are predominantly descended from immigrant European men and Native and African women.[223] What this means is that from the moment they took possession of the Americas, the Spanish and other European conquerors successfully hindered the access of both native males and "imported" African males to all females, whom they kept for their own use. And naturally, this operation was achieved mainly through killing and enslavement. Male violence is a fundamental element of the male biological setup. In other words, in each man lays dormant a Paleolithic brute.

I would like to refine my point. First, bear in mind that male aggressiveness has allowed the human species to survive in a particularly hostile environment. Despite their big brains, human beings are not especially well endowed to hunt big prey and defend themselves from predators. Without this extraordinary capacity for coordinated violence, our species would have probably never made it to this day. It appears that throughout evolution men have been assigned the dirty tasks—hunting and raiding—thereby minimizing females' exposure to violent acts. Any injury that increased the risk of miscarriage would be extremely costly for females and would affect the entire group. The investment of human females in their offspring is almost without equivalent among primates.

Second, the price paid by males for engaging in inter-group violence is astonishing, yet often ignored. Most of the killing for which males are responsible is perpetrated on males. From an exclusively male perspective, this was clearly not a comfortable deal at all. Third, females are not total strangers to violence.

Fatal attacks involving females have been described in several species of monkeys, such as white-faced capuchins, red colobus, and Diana monkeys.[224] In fact, female chimpanzees themselves occasionally participate in the raiding of neighboring groups. Physically weaker than males, they wait for the victim to be visibly weakened to take part in the violence.[225]

Our goal here is not to accumulate evidence against the male sex but only to uncover the biological logic of a reproductive strategy that males and females have co-developed throughout evolution.[226] Besides, male violence is by no means inevitable. By denying it or, at the other end of the spectrum, by reducing maleness to violence, one only misses the point. First, human's mental development has allowed much more than a mere translation of our primordial instincts into cultural customs. Second, you and I have yet to explore the life of the bonobos in order to make up our mind regarding what the full range of our biological heritage might be. Male violence is only one part in the complex kaleidoscope of innate behaviors that constitutes the underlying prehistoric shadow of our species. What is more, we have not yet addressed the most important question: How can male chimpanzees manifest such a high level of aggressiveness toward strangers, particularly males, to the point of exterminating them, and at the same time develop such a remarkable degree of cooperation and social cohesion with the males of their own group?

Like any well-constituted ape, female and male chimpanzees engage in same-sex play. The palette of sexual behavior, which includes mutual masturbation, mounting, fellatio, cunnilingus, and kissing, is not dramatically different from what we have already seen among other apes.[227] Yet homosexual interactions in chimpanzees are far from exuding the playfulness of gorillas or the refreshing innocence of bonobos. And the reason for this is that, far from merely being a leisure activity, sex in chimpanzees is often a bargaining chip. Sexual favors are regularly traded for food.[228] Because dominant males and their allies tend to monopolize the food, particularly the meat brought back from hunting, all the females, other males, and youths are constrained to beg, having very little to offer other than grooming time or sex.[229]

Moreover, in chimpanzees, non-reproductive sex—particularly between males— is crucial to what scientists have called "post-conflict resolution."[230] Chimpanzees make out in order to make up. Reconciliatory sex is not rare among primates in general. Bonobos for instance have mastered this practice.[231] In chimpanzees, albeit less frequent as a mode of reconciliation (compared to mutual grooming for example), make-up sex constitutes the bulk part of non-reproductive sexual contacts. In the minutes following a clash, one male presents his behind to appease the other male, they mouth kiss and, possibly, one mounts the other.[232] And if chimpanzees do not display the sensuality and the level of arousal showed by their two cousins, bonobos and humans, it does look like a promising beginning.

Reconciliation mechanisms are absolutely essential to ensure the continuation of cooperation among individuals that share the same collective interest.[233]

Accordingly, reconciliatory behaviors—including homosexual behavior—are key to the survival of male alliances. Without them, the spiral of male violence would simply be kept unchecked. It is this balance between aggression and reconciliation that makes possible the coexistence between the social cohesion of the group and the dynamic of competition. And sex, heterosexual and homosexual, plays a decisive role in keeping this precarious equilibrium intact. This said, what appears to be an interesting start in chimpanzees—make-up sex—becomes an art in bonobos, our last ape relatives on the list.

THE INVENTION OF SEX

Bonobos were mistaken for dwarf chimpanzees for a long time. Only at the beginning of the twentieth century were they defined as a new species of ape. Their habitat in current Congo extends on the south bank of the Zaire River, which separates them physically from chimpanzees that live on the north bank. They suddenly became popular in the mid-1990s, thanks to the books of primatologists like Frans de Wall and Richard Wrangham. Nicknamed the "ape from Venus," the "gentle ape," and the "sexy ape," bonobos fascinate us.

Altogether, comparing bonobos and chimpanzees informs us a great deal about what may be the complex rationale of homosexual behavior and homosexuality in human beings. First, bonobos' sexual behavior and social organization, strikingly different from that of chimpanzees in many ways, shows us how quickly evolution works, which is to say, how minute changes at the genomic level can engender significant behavioral differences. Second, when put together, behaviors in chimpanzees and bonobos recapitulate a large chunk of the human behavioral repertoire. And as it happens, we sometimes look more like chimpanzees and at other times more like bonobos.

Everything about bonobos sounds different from chimpanzees. Even their typical call does not have the throaty depth of chimpanzees' call. Rather, they sound like birds. They exude gentleness. What characterizes bonobos at first glance is their insatiable sexuality. They all participate enthusiastically, regardless of age and sex. In addition, bonobos are incredibly creative in terms of sexual act and position. I still have vivid memories from attending Richard Wrangham's class on primate behavior at Harvard University. I remember blushing during a video projection on bonobo sexual behavior, which definitely qualified for the most severe movie rating.

In bonobos, sex not only feels good but, as in chimpanzees, it also helps release tensions, especially when a new source of food is discovered. The rush toward food supplies generates both overexcitement and nervousness among the members of the group. One can quickly observe a flurry of sexual activities all over the place. A few minutes later everybody is eating quietly. But behind this living representation of the Kama Sutra, bonobo society hides a sociological jewel: "Among bonobos there are no reports of males forcing copulations, battering adult females, or killing infants [. . .] the sexes are co-dominant."[234] If a male dares to harass or attack a female, other females quickly join in to defend her and drive the aggressive male away. This indeed constitutes a major improvement regarding female rights. On the other end, male bonobos do not exhibit the same bonding quality that females have. When a male, even the alpha-male, is being chased off by a gang of angry females, other males do not try to rescue him. As a matter of fact, no male can resist a group of females determined to get rid of him.

The male dominance observed in chimpanzees springs from their patrilineal organization. Males are blood-related while females migrate to neighboring groups of their free will, or sometimes as a war trophy. But female bonobos also migrate at puberty just like their chimpanzee sisters. What can therefore explain the emergence of diametrically different social models? There too, sex constitutes the linchpin of this social revolution. In bonobos, intense sexual interactions catalyze the formation of powerful and lasting bonds between females, allowing a unique cohesion of the female group. By nearly reversing the balance between sexes, lesbian sex may have caused nothing less than a little evolutionary revolution.

A very popular practice between females is G-G rubbing (G-G stands for genitalia-genitalia), which bears the exotic name of *hoka-hoka* locally. In *Demonic Males*, Wrangham and Peterson report a typical scene, which occurred after a young female migrated from her group of origin and arrived in a new one:

> The adolescent female sits watching the older one. When the older female wants *hoka-hoka* and has seen that the adolescent is waiting, she lies on her back and spreads open her thighs. The adolescent quickly approaches and they embrace. Lying face to face, like humans in the missionary position, the two females have quick, excited sex. Their hip movement are fast and side to side, and they bring their most sensitive sexual organs—their clitorises—together. Bonobo clitorises appear large (compared to those of humans or any other apes) and shifted ventrally compared to chimpanzees. [. . .] their location and shape have evolved to allow pleasurable *hoka-hoka*—which typically end with mutual screams, clutching limbs, muscular contractions, and a tense, still moment. It looks like orgasm.[235]

This is how female bonobos develop a network of friendships that will protect them and their babies very efficiently. Aggressiveness between females is low and usually sex takes care of it. Sex clears out tensions and stress, and restores the harmony in the female party. What about the males? In general male bonobos are much less aggressive than their chimpanzee brothers, albeit they do fight and compete for status. Fight intensity and the drive for dominance are simply not as high as in chimpanzees. As we have already mentioned, male bonobos, although blood-related, do not form the type of alliances that encourage intergroup hostilities in chimpanzee males. They can access females more easily with little concern regarding rank competition. Everybody gets his share of fun. This is quite different from chimpanzees, yet not quite like humans either.

Another very interesting reason that explains bonobos' ease around mating resides in the unusual reproductive physiology of female bonobos. Fertile female chimpanzees undergo very visible physical changes. Their genitalia become tumescent, exuding a very typical smell—a cocktail of pheromones—which drives males totally crazy. On the other hand, female bonobos exhibit swollen genitalia for extended periods of time and lack the typical "love smell" that signals the time of ovulation. In point of fact, male bonobos cannot tell whether a female is fertile or not. To counter this problem, bonobos simply mate all the time. Human males face exactly the same problem as their bonobo cousins. They cannot tell when a human female is fertile. And just like bonobos, human sexual activity does not significantly fluctuate with the female fertility cycle, to say the least.

What about sex among male bonobos? They too have fun together, performing sex in every position and variation imaginable. Mirroring female *hoka-hoka*, males mutually rub their genitalia in what has been coined as "penis fencing." As you may remember, male bonobos do not form alliances like females and they do not self-organize into hawkish all-male parties like male chimpanzees. Nobody has observed male bonobos going beyond mild combats, even though bloody wounds do sometimes happen. Nothing remotely resembling killer gangs has ever been reported. Impossible in chimpanzees, the meeting of two bonobo groups generally result in friendly interactions, food sharing, mutual grooming, and of course . . . sex. Although much more gentle than their chimpanzee and human cousins, male bonobos do however compete for status, food, and sometimes females, but the tension that results from this competition dissipates through mutual sexual gratification. Unlike females, males do not create long term networks of friendship through sex. For male bonobos, homosexual sex is merely a pleasurable social activity and a means for conflict resolution. They indeed make love, not war. So, now, what do orangutans, gorillas, chimpanzees, and Bonobos teach us about human homosexuality?

THE EVOLUTIONARY LOGIC OF HOMOSEXUAL BEHAVIOR

As Mary McDonald Pavelka wrote very justly, "our pre-cultural evolutionary history is not so remote as to render us unique in all respects and isolated in the world of living things. Human sexuality is primate sexuality, and an understanding of human sexuality requires that we know something about our basic primate sexuality."[236] All behavioral studies recently conducted on apes (and other primates) corroborate the fact that homosexual behavior was positively selected throughout evolution in all ape species—humans included. They also confirm very clearly that homosexual behavior, even as omnipresent as in bonobos, is absolutely compatible with an effective reproduction of the species.[237] Claims that systematically posit the contrary are arbitrary and have no scientific basis.[238]

Yet the evolutionary logic of homosexual behavior, like that of many social and altruistic behaviors, such as mutual grooming, reassurance behavior, assistance to allies, and non-reproductive sexual behavior in general, cannot be elucidated only in terms of providing a reproductive advantage directly to the individual enacting those behaviors. Evolution is a complex dynamic that occurs in parallel through competition between individuals but also through competition between groups.[239] Without group selection, it is not just homosexual behavior that becomes problematic; all altruistic behaviors and the entire cultural development that we see starting in chimpanzees and triumphing in humans are turned into evolutionary non-sense. If individual competition was the only driving force of evolution, altruism would never have resisted the competition with selfish behavior inside a given group.[240] Logically, why would one teach another how to use a tool to obtain food (a rock to crack nuts, a stick to fish ants, or a spear to kill deer) instead of keeping this food for oneself if that were the case? Yet this is not what we observe. Instead, we see the emergence of more and more cooperative species like the great apes, and ultimately the planetary triumph of one of the most cooperative and yet most competitive species of all time, humans. Homosexual behavior must then be understood as providing an evolutionary advantage to the entire group against other groups, and not necessarily to the individual. It benefits the reproductive success of the group as a whole. However, if homosexual behavior provides an evolutionary advantage in the framework of altruistic behavior and group selection, one should not interpret altruism as being nice or even generous with another.[241] Altruism, evolutionarily speaking, is the propensity (largely unconscious) of any given individual to invest in relationships and/or the well-being of the group at large in order to achieve more complex and long term goals.

If we want to use cross-species comparison to decipher the evolutionary logic of human homosexuality behavior, prudence is recommended. Human behavior is sometimes reminiscent of that of chimpanzees and at other times that of bonobos. Humans share with chimpanzees a high level of male violence, a widely spread domination of males over females, the quasi-universal practice of wars and gang violence by males, a strong taste for hunting and meat, and, occasionally, cannibalism. On the other hand, both human and bonobo females conceal their fertility status, a particularity that seems to correlate with an abundant and largely deregulated sex life. Ultimately, humans, chimpanzees, bonobos, and gorillas all enjoy frequent and pleasurable sexual activities which include a large repertoire of sexual practices unrelated to reproduction such as masturbation, oral sex, and, of course, homosexual sex.

Now that we have established the ground rules of this conversation, let us explore the specifics of homosexual evolution. What could be the reproductive advantage of human homosexual behavior? As always, the answer to that crucial question is multiple.

As advocated by leading primatologists such as Frans de Wall and Richard Wrangham, sexual behavior has evolved in order to mitigate aggressiveness, particularly from males. Unchecked, male violence becomes rapidly devastating. In only a few years, entire groups of chimpanzees were exterminated under the eyes of human observers as the result of the premeditated and relentless elimination of individuals in vulnerable situations. In humans the development of higher intelligence, quite unique in the animal kingdom, must have dramatically changed the scale and reach of male violence. Unmatched skills in the manufacture of tools as well as analytical faculties capable of conceiving increasingly effective strategies multiplied the forms this violence could take exponentially. For our distant ancestors, addressing this challenge must have been of vital importance. Not surprisingly, sex as an efficient means to dissolve tensions within the group was preserved in humans. Insofar as human evolution combined both an extraordinary intelligence and high levels of aggressiveness, "social" sex—little concerned with reproduction—may have acted as a safety valve. One could even speculate that by protecting the community from the destructive effects of intra-group violence, "social" sex provided a favorable ground for the extraordinary development of humans' intelligence.

Efficiently balanced with reconciliation mechanisms (kissing, hugging, and sex), aggressiveness, rather than an antisocial instinct, allows individuals to compete within an overall cooperative social environment. Social life among chimps, bonobos, and humans entails a succession of fights and reconciliation and, as a matter of fact, relies heavily on the equilibrium between the two.[242] Sexual behavior in general and homosexual behavior in particular form the bulk of the social glue that makes life in society possible. And it is widely accepted that an intense social life was the *sine qua non* condition for the extraordinary development of human intelligence and culture.[243]

So, the first answer to our question is that homosexual sex, like the majority of sexual interactions in apes, obeys the logic of social cohesion. If that were true, one would expect sex frequency to reflect the size of the group: sex should be more frequent in larger groups. And while chimpanzee parties rarely include more than nine individuals,[244] bonobo parties average seventeen members.[245] This correlates with the fact that, unlike chimps, bonobos' prolific sexuality is essentially driven by pleasure and largely disconnected from the temporal constraints of the female reproductive cycle. And in that respect, we have seen that humans are like bonobos. Considering the impressive size of human communities, nonconceptive sex seems to have fulfilled its soothing role to perfection in our species.

More specifically, complex homosexual relationships have emerged in the periphery of their heterosexual counterparts so as to fulfill three specific goals: (1) sex in general constitutes a low-cost token easily redeemable for valuable goods and services, such as political alliance and material security; (2) homosexual behavior specifically reinforces ranking and promote cohesion between males; and (3) it allows bonding and mutual support between females. Let me now develop each point in the same order as above.

(1) We have seen that in chimpanzees sex is often a leverage to bargain for food with dominant males. And the reason this phenomenon is especially

true for chimpanzees is largely explained by the fact that, unlike gorillas and bonobos, which are both vegetarian species, chimps love meat. Male chimpanzees are formidable hunters. Incidentally, hunting skills give chimpanzee males a decisive edge over all other members of the group. Males end up owning the most coveted good: meat.[246] That places them in a unique position of dominance towards other all females, youths, and any male too young or inexperienced to catch prey. Such a dependence seems less likely in groups relying mostly on gathering leaves and fruits to feed themselves. And to that extent, human males are just like their chimpanzee cousins: they have a high control over material goods.

Prehistoric records demonstrate that humans have appreciated animal flesh. Men are remarkable hunters, far better than chimps. They would not have been able to impose their supremacy over the entire planet otherwise. This implies that, since prehistory, the dominance of the human male has not only been physical and political, but also economic. Obviously, for most human beings, meat no longer constitutes the most coveted good. Culture and technology have diversified the nature of what human being craves into the vast range that we know today: material property, land, gold, money, honorific title, political connection, knowledge, and so forth. Yet, from the very beginning, adult males had an edge that they never lost.

In humans, just like in chimps, sex has been a bargaining chip for political and economic support,[247] which sociobiologists refer to as "reciprocal altruism," that is, an exchange of services from which both parties benefit. Historical records show that same-sex relationships have often been highly instrumental in the formation of such alliances, in which material and political support was exchanged for sexual favors and prestige.[248] In ancient Greece homosexual relationships guaranteed material support, education, and access to a social network to the youth. It was the duty of the *erastes* to provide guidance to his *eromenos* and to help him become a model citizen. In return, the beauty of the latter was a source of pleasure and endless pride for the former. In Sparta warriors taught their young lovers how to surpass themselves on the battlefield. Male pairs were renowned for their bravery in combat and their selflessness in protecting each other. In Crete, men without same-sex partners were reputedly at a social disadvantage.[249]

Transgenerational homoerotic pairing between an experienced warrior and his novice was the basis of the Mamluk institution in the Ottoman Empire and Egypt, the powerful Azande army in Congo, as well as the samurai tradition in pre-Meiji Japan. Also in Japan, the essential part of the religious education of young Zen apprentices was fostered amid a sexual friendship with an older monk. In Melanesia and pre-Columbian Americas, male homosexual pairs supported each other in the field, in hunting, and in battle in exchange for food and education. Homosexual relationships in tribal societies were often embedded within complex marital traditions, such as the practice of sister exchange, which gave men the right to use the younger brother of their future bride as a sexual outlet.[250] Among the Sambia people of New Guinea, the ritualistic insemination of adolescents must imperatively lead to the youths' maturation into men. Pleasure is traded for the masculinizing virtue of semen. Albeit magic in essence, Sambia rituals represent a fine example of men giving away their most precious possession: their status as males. All other cases, including the short-lived resurgence of homosexual cultures in Florence and Venice in the fifteenth century and the pirate tradition during the seventeenth century, obey to the same logic.[251]

The overwhelming majority of transgenerational male relationships—by and large the predominant form of male homosexuality in human cultures[252]—were centered around economic and political alliances. Homosexual relationships have channeled adult male altruistic behavior in the direction of the younger generation, and this, beyond the strict limit of kin.[253] From this, one may easily infer that they have helped foster social cohesion in groups composed of multiple kin. And insofar as homosexual desire has facilitated, if not forced, male altruism toward male youths, same-sex relationships may have greatly eased the transfer of knowledge—technological, economic, or related to the art of warfare—from one generation to the next. And in that respect, homosexual behavior has certainly provided human groups a critical advantage against competitors.

(2) We have now understood that in humans as in apes, sex plays a pivotal role in the network of relationships that secure the cohesion of the group. Sex offers a solution to conflicts, it can be exchanged for favors like food and political alliances, and it allows bonding. Yet, it also happens that homosexual relationships have specifically evolved to play a distinct function in each sex.

Let us take a closer look at the flurry of male-male mounting among our cousins in the African and Asian jungles. From an anthropologist's viewpoint, the organization of male homosexual behavior differs dramatically between chimpanzees, gorillas, and orangutans on the one hand, and bonobos on the other. For instance, "the contest for dominance is more elaborate among chimpanzees. Chimpanzees have ritualized signals of status recognition; bonobos don't. [. . .] In chimpanzees, signals of reassurance or reconciliation exaggerate the hierarchy—such as when a subordinate crouches and approaches a dominant while panting softly, and the dominant reaches out and pats the outstretched hand of the subordinate."[254]

Sexual interactions tend to reenact the ranking difference.[255] In other words, the polarity of the sexual interaction often (but not always) reminds which one is the dominant male. More often than not, the dominant male is the one that mounts the other: "[Chimpanzees] present their anogenital region in a gesture of submission or appeasement, often followed by a genital inspection by the recipient."[256] Even when mounting does not occur, "grooming and appeasement frequently involve the fondling of the dominant male's scrotum by the subordinate male."[257]

However, remember that homosexual interaction among male chimpanzees is scarce and, as far as we can tell, pleasureless. The impact of the dominance status on the mounting polarity is most obvious among gorillas. Here, the correlation is clear: Silverbacks [mature gorillas] mount the younger individuals; however, they are never mounted themselves.[258] Even in orangutans, in a rare case of male same-sex relationship observed in the wild, scientists noticed that "the larger and presumably dominant male mounted the smaller male in a ventro-ventral [aka missionary] position."[259]

On the opposite side of the spectrum, homosexual behavior among bonobos is symmetrical, two males mounting each other in turn with excitement.[260] While a strong male dominance sets the tone of homosexual relationships in chimpanzees, gorillas, and orangutans, the male bonobos, considerably softened by the social dominance of females, enjoy each other sexually in a relaxed and unconcerned fashion that seems to be unique in the ape world. Undoubtedly, apart from modern homosexuality (for reasons that I will make clear later), humans have behaved more like gorillas and chimpanzees than like bonobos. As a matter of fact, the obsession of the human male with ranking is undeniable in nearly all cultures and throughout history.[261]

In all cases of transgenerational male homosexuality (the most prevalent form), there is a very clear affirmation of the ranking/social status: the adult male always dominates the younger one sexually. To be more specific, the adult male is the insertive partner, and not the other way around. In Greece and in the Roman Empire, for an adult male to be penetrated by a younger male or a slave prostitute, who were both totally acceptable sex partners otherwise, was a cause of humiliation and profound dishonor. Likewise, the Shudo tradition—"the Way of the Young"—was central to the highly misogynistic Samurai culture that prevailed in feudal Japan from medieval time to the nineteenth century. Not surprisingly, the young novice, the *wakashu*, endorsed the receptive part with his tutor, the *nenja*.[262] The erotic relationships between Buddhist bonzes and their acolytes, also known as *chigo*, were structured in the exact same fashion. The same rigid sexual hierarchy prevailed during the short revival of homosexual cultures in Florence and Venice in the early Renaissance and in the Islamic world in the classical age. Needless to say, during the coming-of-age rituals widespread among Melanesian tribes, the initiated youth was the receptacle of the semen ejaculated by his older partner, never the other way around. I have come across only one exception where younger partners allegedly penetrated older ones: the Nkundó people, in what was then Belgian Congo. Yet that interesting oddity has only been reported by one person, a conservative Belgian missionary named Gustave Hulstaert, in 1938.[263]

In transgender forms of homosexuality one of the partners becomes female or female-like, hence, by definition, sexually receptive. Two-spirits, *hijras*, and *faàfafines* are culturally defined as quasi-females (or at least no longer bona fide males), exempt from reproductive duty. Yet, the counterpart of all this is equally important: a "stud" male can be sexually involved with a transgender male, as long as he fulfills the insertive role that is expected of him, his (dominant) male status remains unchallenged. This is also true in contemporary Latino culture: a macho who fornicates with a *maricon* is still a man. And from a Western perspective, the implacable logic of gender transformation observed all over Latin America can sometimes proves quite disconcerting: in Brazil, for instance, sexual encounters between *bichas* (the Brazilian equivalent of *maricones*) is regarded as a form of lesbianism; and, while sex between a *bicha* and a ("real") male is acceptable, sex between *bichas* is not (similar views were reported among Nigerian Hausa people).[264]

He who penetrates asserts his higher rank over the other. Males maintained their dominant status by sleeping with youths, prostitutes, slaves, eunuchs, socially inferior individuals, or war prisoners—always assigned the receptive role—or with feminized males.[265] Across the globe, transgressions to that basic tenet were considered despicable. Sex between two sexually mature men of similar status would necessitate that at least one of them takes on the submissive role, and that was universally unacceptable.

In fact, it is possible to imagine retroactively how the various sociocultural forms of homosexuality may have emerged historically. As long as human groups were organized around the relatively absolute power of an alpha-male and his cohort of political allies, male homosexual relationships probably had a lot in common with what we have seen in chimpanzees and gorillas. Muscular strength and political skills determined the relative dominance of each male in the group, as well as how homosexual interactions went. But very early on, human cultures acquired rigid class systems. Members were sorted out according to a social status: leaders, members of the elite, warriors, women, elders, and youths. Eventually, larger groups were divided into a more complex mix of upper and lower classes: priests, healers and physicians, farmers, military, nobles and aristocrats, slaves, and so forth.

This transition generated an unexpected problem. Ranking polarities, which were originally fluid and easy to sort out with a good fight, became fixed, inborn, and eventually hereditary. Equal-in-status males could no longer simply use sex to evacuate tensions, insofar as no sensible male would risk letting himself be penetrated by another male of his own class for fear of being automatically socially demoted. Consequently, who lies with whom, and how, became a very big deal in human cultures. Male homosexual desire had to be carefully organized, that is, ritualized and culturally embedded so as to soothe the prehistoric anxiety of males regarding their status and ensure that same-sex interactions would continue to play their unique role in preserving the social cohesion of the group. And at that moment, homosexuality entered history.

The rigid ranking pattern in which the homosexual behavior of the human male has been trapped evolutionarily is further evidenced in situational homosexuality. You remember that the term "situational homosexuality" delineates homosexual relations involving men who display sexual interest for other men only when confined in all-male environments—prisons, boarding schools, monasteries, and the military. Often secret, situational homosexuality is poorly documented. Yet, as discussed in a previous chapter, a few recent scandals involving rape cases have shed light on the hidden world of jails in America, Brazil, and Venezuela.[266] And the way situational homosexual relationships are consistently organized sounds startlingly familiar.

Dominant males, the most aggressive ones, get to pick other males for their sexual needs. All accounts corroborate the fact that the polarity of the sexual act matches the ape dominance code. The penetration of one's body, orally and even more so anally, reaffirms the superior status of the one who performs it. Symmetrically, the one whose physical integrity has been invaded ends up defeated, demeaned, and subdued. And other males do not need any manual to perceive the significance of the act. They interpret it from instinct. Sexual hierarchy includes rapes, forced prostitution, sex slavery, and gang rape. One statistic on U.S. penitentiaries claims that nearly 7% of male inmates have been subjected to sexual assault during their detention. As one would predict, the insertive aggressor does not perceive himself as homosexual. Nor is he some sort of closeted homosexual. Most of these men would show no interest for males outside this particular setup. The hierarchical organization of situational homosexualities demonstrates only one thing: how quickly the human male can awaken, from some mysterious place deep inside his brain, a prehistoric dormant instinct that uses sexual performance to manifest dominance.[267]

(3) The comparison between the sexual habits of bonobos and chimpanzees offers a unique opportunity to understand the distinct evolutionary logic of female homosexuality. Females are less aggressive and less preoccupied with their social status than males. Instead, human females had to tackle more pressing problems such as increased infant dependence, increasing but still unreliable assistance from the biological fathers, and the coexistence with a number of other unrelated females in the same territory.[268]

One must remember that bonobo and chimpanzee females migrate at puberty, leaving behind all the females they were related to. This phenomenon, called female exogamy, is similarly observed in a majority of human societies. Upon their arrival in their new group, young females are particularly vulnerable to male aggressions. At this point, females bonobos, unlike their chimpanzee sisters, work on obtaining support from older females by initiating sex (remember *hoka-hoka*).[269] Same-sex behavior creates powerful bonds between females, which prove to be particularly efficient to shield them and their progeny from aggression attempts. Hence, while sex between males seems commonly tainted with tension and status affirmation, lesbian sex is essentially bonding in nature. Between females, sex appears to promote the emergence of egalitarian sororities, which have no real equivalent among males. This seems particularly true among bonobos, gorillas, and, to a much lesser extent, chimpanzees (the central role of female same-sex relationships is also abundantly documented in two species of monkey, the rhesus monkeys and the Japanese macaque).[270] The egalitarian quality of female homosexual interactions is seldom encountered in the frame of male homosexual behavior. Male apes—with the relative yet notable exception of male bonobos—are always obsessed with ranking (by no means does this imply that female homosexuality is systematically egalitarian and male homosexuality rank-based, as we shall see).

This difference provides a compelling starting point to help us understand the unequal natures of male and female homosexualities. If both ensure bonding and cohesion among each sex, they appear to manifest two distinct evolutionary logics—ranking in males and security in females. Therefore, male and female homosexualities, while symmetrical at first glance, have quite different sociobiological rationales.

This explains why, as we have seen in previous chapters, cultural anthropologists had all the difficulties in the world trying to fit female homosexuality in the transgenerational and transgender categories, which both had primarily been defined in order to accommodate variations among male homosexual relationships. Female homosexuality is fundamentally untouched with the problem of ranking that has shaped all premodern forms of male homosexuality. Male-dominated cultures have been much more concerned about female adultery with other males than female's encounters with other females. Lesbianism did not directly threaten the male urge to "spread their genes." Females had to conceal their desire by reason of their vulnerability to males' physical, political, and economic power. Then, rather than ranking, female homosexuality has been constrained by the omnipresent dominance of males, the coercion exerted over the crucial issue of reproduction, and the all-important male obsession regarding the paternity of the children they bore. Anthropological studies on primates and human cultures are remarkably congruent in the matter. Therefore, in total agreement with Blackwood, female homoerotic relationships appear better defined as either informal or formal (see chapter 1).[271]

If women have traditionally been dominated by men in most cultures, same-sex relationships have consistently played a central part in the rare historic instances that saw the development of female emancipation movements. Homoerotic relationships played a critical part in the marriage resistance movement in China[272] (which took place in the Pearl River Delta surrounding Canton from approximately 1865 through 1935, and included up to one hundred thousand women), among Moslem Mombasa women of Kenya, and Lesotho "mummy-baby" pairs for instance, who all were able to create small sustainable communities, independently from men (see chapter 1).[273]

It is also clear that female homosexuality is more fluid than male homosexuality. Male sexual orientation tends to be more clear-cut than women's, which is to say, males tend to identify with and stick to the same sexual orientation for their entire lives. Women are more likely than men to go back and forth between heterosexual and homosexual relationships. Homosexuality in the human female may have evolved in a way to be more opportunistic than deterministic, reflecting the prehistoric necessity to address their physical vulnerability, their dependence on males, and the need to cope with the intensive care that their babies require.[274] Yet more research is necessary to uncover all the details of female homosexuality's unique evolutionary meaning.

PRETTY BOYS

The particular organization of male homosexual behavior and its subtle translation into cultural norms may have offered another unexpected evolutionary advantage in humans. In numerous species, but this is especially true for great apes, evolutionary pressure stems essentially from two parallel dynamics: (1) the female's preference for particular mates and (2) the competition among males to attract the favor of the females. The fittest males of the group secure their access to the females by excluding other males from the reproductive process, *ipso facto* guaranteeing the expansion of their genetic lineage. Weak males, unable to compete efficiently, see their genes slowly eliminated from the gene pool of the group and eventually, from the species.

In the meantime, females appear to play the same evolutionary game, but in their own ways. Although often the subject of males' forceful advances, females nonetheless show a consistent interest in high-ranking males, especially alpha-males. And despite their aesthetic preferences, females wisely remember that high-ranking males also bring more food and are more efficient at protecting their young. Yet we must take a closer look at what "fittest" means among apes. Among chimpanzees, humans, and bonobos, fittest does not always equal strongest. In other words, muscles aren't everything. Male chimpanzees, for instance, have developed an interesting feature to help them win the reproductive race—the sperm war. It happens that female chimpanzees are quite promiscuous during the period of estrus, mating successively with different partners. In response, chimpanzee's testicles are absolutely enormous with respect to their body size and produce impressive amounts of sperm. So, by overflowing the female genitalia with their sperm, males maximize their odds to win the sperm-race to the egg. Moreover, chimp sperm tends to solidify into a quasi-hermetic plug, making the work of subsequent competitors even more difficult. Thus, size truly matters, but not only that of muscles.

We have seen earlier that sexual interactions were also highly instrumental in the formation of alliances among males. Those alliances, in many ways, function like friendships. They provide assistance in case of danger and facilitate the sharing of food. In the competition game with other males, the ability of a given individual to generate a network of powerful alliances is as essential as body strength. Therefore, high-ranking individuals are not necessarily the strongest, but also those that can mobilize the most support.[275] Among chimpanzees, as among humans, brutal shifts in male alliances can have dramatic effects on male hierarchy and, in turn, the sex life of the individuals implicated in the "coup." So size still matters, but not only that of body parts.

To recap, mating opportunities in chimps and humans appear to be a function of social rank, which itself combines physical and political strength. This said, recent observations have demonstrated that political alliances among male chimpanzees have another payoff beside the usual mutual grooming, food sharing, and assistance in conflict.[276] While the alpha-male monopolizes access to fertile females by brutally interrupting matings involving other males, he nonetheless rewards his allies with preferential access to females.[277] Therefore, mating opportunities also reflect one's ability to win the favors of a high-ranking male.[278]

Scientists have observed a similar correlation between rank and mating opportunities in humans. Genetic studies have demonstrated very precisely that early human populations—across the world—were primarily polygamist.[279] This means that before the relatively recent implementation of monogamy in human cultures, a minority of males has monopolized the access to females and excluded all other males from the mating game. And if in humans as in chimpanzees, a restricted number of high-ranking males have kept control over the females, one can also reasonably assume that political and sexual alliances with these powerful individuals have probably helped young males overcome the limitations inherent to their lower social position.

Therefore, one can conceive the following scenario: Let us imagine a population where dominant males develop a consistent sexual interest for young males that is not random but rather is a function of their attractiveness, whether this is based on (depending on the culture) fitness, physical beauty, skillfulness, good temper, or character strength. Those homosexual relationships associated with a rewarding mechanism in which a dominant male assists his young male lover in his quest for a female mate offer a clear evolutionary advantage.[280] The fittest males would increase their chances to procreate by being preferred not only by the females (for whom they have to compete fiercely with other males), but also by older males in position of power. In that case, the evolutionary pressure would result from the convergence of three dynamics: (1) heterosexual selection by females, (2) homosexual selection by males, and (3) inter-male competitions in games (1) and (2). One would then anticipate this triple level of selection to widen the pool of competing genes passed from one generation to the next, insofar as the number and diversity of young males "selected" to breed increase significantly. The selective pressure from males on males boosted the evolutionary dynamic in the population.

Homosexual alliances may also help extend the selection process by helping males reproduce on the basis of individual qualities, such as strength and attractiveness, and not just on the basis of political alliances (i.e., helping your political friend to find a mate) or kinship (i.e., helping your own children to find a mate).[281] And history shows that overall males have carefully picked their male partners.[282] We know that the *eromenos-erastes* relationship largely benefited the youth at both social and material levels. "Lovers" were held responsible for turning their young "beloveds" into accomplished citizens, that is, meant to marry and father the future citizens of the polis. It is hardly disputable that transgenerational homosexual cultures overall fostered strong alliances among males that greatly facilitated the social and reproductive success of the younger partner. And while my hypothesis requires further validation, I am arguing that humans might have become the most successful apes also by having reinforced and refined the mechanisms of selection thanks to homosexual relationships between dominant males and their protégés.

WHEN LESS IS MORE

I believe that we have now in our hands a solid rationale to help us understand the evolution of homosexual behavior in humans. Balancing male aggressiveness, community building in females, ranking and political alliances in males, and ultimately a brilliant refinement of the selection mechanism all constitute a compelling string of "Darwinian advantages," viewed from a sociological context that values the importance of altruistic behavior and group selection. Echoing others, I have also argued on numerous occasions that, when considering one's sexual behavior independently from one's sexual identity, a great majority of homosexuals are in fact behaviorally bisexual. For this reason, homosexuality hardly qualifies as an evolutionary paradox in the first place. Yet I have commented little on the existence of the tiny minority of individuals (most likely below 1%) who show zero interest for the opposite sex.

One can detect the presence of "exclusive behavioral homosexuals" across history, often associated (or confused) with gender inversion. The *kinaidos* and *malakos* in Greece and the *cinaedus* and *pathicus* in Rome, customarily defined as effeminate and sexually passive men, faced public dishonor rather than submitting to the reproductive norms of their time. More generally though, transgender males and rare females, in societies where those identities were integrant part of the psychocultural landscape, were simply excused from reproductive duty without further ado. Asian literature also often reports stories of uncompromising same-sex lovers.[283] Although still difficult to define precisely at this point, it seems that very real, dyed-in-the-wool exclusive homosexuals have existed since the beginning of recorded history, and possibly since prehistory.[284] Nevertheless, exclusive behavioral homosexuality is unheard of among other apes. Clearly, it is a human particularity.

It seems that in humans, homosexual behavior is distributed differently than in other apes. If great apes are fundamentally all bisexual, humans display a discrete spectrum of sexualities from strictly heterosexual to strictly homosexual. Why is the human evolutionary strategy different from that of other apes? I doubt whether anyone can answer that question for certain at this point. One can only acknowledge that human beings have propagated better than all other primates. So, whatever the reason was, nature certainly did not make such a bad choice for us. This said, exclusive behavioral homosexuality would constitute an evolutionary paradox if it were not totally overshadowed by the only very real Darwinian conundrum of the human species: menopause.

Simplistic Darwinian reasoning would require the reproductive cycle to match longevity, insofar as animals normally have no reason to survive if they cannot reproduce. Nevertheless, and regardless of the big fuss about the non-reproductive aspect of homosexuality, it appears that human evolution resulted in a significant limitation of the reproductive pool that is almost unique among mammals: Virtually all middle-age women undergo menopause because of a depletion of their reserves of eggs that makes them totally unable to reproduce. A state similar to menopause is observed in just a few mammal species, such as whales. It occurs briefly before death in chimpanzees[285] and gorillas[286] in the wild, and it is unseen in orangutans.[287] Longer menopausal states were reported among a few aging gorilla[288] and chimpanzee[289] females, but only in captivity, where many other factors are likely to disturb the reproductive cycle. The true occurrence of menopause in apes other than humans remains arguable and is still seriously challenged by leading primatologists like Richard Wrangham and Jane Goodall.[290] If individual reproductive power were the ultimate goal of evolution, menopause would constitute the worst aberration displayed by the human species, not homosexuality: 20 to 40% of human females cannot reproduce at all. This is astounding!

One may wonder how removing middle-age females from the fertile pool helps increase the reproduction rate. The most accepted theory for the existence of menopause contends that forcing older females out of motherhood and turning them into grandmothers enhances the care and protection given to infants and youths. Motherhood associated with grand-motherhood would be more effective than motherhood alone. Once again, the logic of human evolution comes to light when including both individual and group selection, instead of flattening the whole phenomenon to the individual level. When Richard Dawkins offered his vision of the "selfish-gene," he unfortunately reduced the dynamic of species evolution to a competition between genes. Non-reproductive sexualities and menopause therefore constitute two strong empirical evidences in favor of the importance of group selection. Genes are able to expand themselves through wider dynamics, which involve gene, whole organism, and/or group competition. Evolution does not hesitate to sacrifice the reproductive faculties of some individuals to the benefit of the entire group. The other words, the gene's "selfishness" proves to be more complex and more efficient than the mere instant-gratification provided by immediate inter-individual competition.

No matter what you and I believe, despite homosexual behavior and menopause, we cannot but agree on the fact that the reproductive success of the human species has been phenomenal, to a point where it has actually become a major problem today.

THE ROOTS OF HOMOPHOBIA

Homosexual behavior has played a major role in the emergence of humans as sociocultural beings. They have ensured the cohesion of the first human groups that left the African savanna to conquer the world. Increasingly complex and diversified homosexual cultures have propelled humans on an evolutionary trajectory that has been nothing but astonishing. Naturally, I do not intend to singularize homosexual behavior, or ignore other essential human virtues that have also played an essential role in our evolution: selflessness, sense of honor, sense of sacrifice, and, of course, love . . . Yet, I dare argue here that deciphering the evolutionary function of homosexual behavior is key to understanding how human beings, at one point in their history, stopped being mere reproductive machines.

Evolutionarily speaking, homosexual behavior liberated men and women from the crushing logic of procreation.

This said, biology does not justify anything. The fact that homosexuality is the result of evolution makes it neither acceptable nor unacceptable. It only makes it the result of an evolutionary process. Both male violence and homosexuality are the result of evolution. Both are "natural" (as in "products of nature"). Nature does not make homosexuality good or bad, beautiful or ugly. It only makes it true. It will take more than one chapter to explore the moral substance of homosexuality. In the meantime, I cannot but concur with Walter Williams: "What is even more important for anthropologists to understand is why a minority of cultures stigmatize this pleasurable genital stimulation between persons of the same sex. Thus [. . .] it is not homosexual behavior which most needs to be analyzed by anthropologists but homophobia."[291] Well put. Rarely however does one see the idea of the biological origin of homophobia reach the headlines. From a homophobic perspective, by far the most common, homophobia is either divine inspiration or common sense. It is seldom viewed as an expression of prehistoric instincts, even by the pro-homosexual camp, terrified at the idea of finding any biological justification to its worst nightmare.

Now, before we start exploring the prehistoric roots of homophobia in the general framework of targeted social violence, observe also that, historically speaking, female homosexuality has seldom been the target of homophobic violence.[292] Ensuring the paternity of their progeny constituted the major problem of males. In almost all cultures, the sexual freedom of all females was severely restricted. Until the European Renaissance and the rise of modernity, love between women was generally kept secret, if not ignored, and simply of little interest to male storytellers. Yet we know through the mythologies that female love was far from being unknown. But unlike male love, female love is symmetrical. It involves neither penetration nor ranking. In contrast, inasmuch as male homosexual behavior has very early on stirred up high anxiety levels among males, males have also been the primary focus of homophobic attacks.

Can the great apes give us a hint as to the biological origins of homophobia? I believe they can not only give us a hint, but they actually can help us understand a fundamental aspect of homophobia. But to get a glimpse of homophobia's obscure biological origins, one must first remember an invariant property of homosexual behavior among humans, chimpanzees, gorillas, and orangutans: the polarity of male homosexual behavior scrupulously reflects ranking; in the sexual act, the insertive male dominates; his receptive partner is dominated. Immediately after a conflict, a lower ranking male will present its bottom to appease the other. Inspection of the anogenital region, penetration, and occasionally ejaculation usually follows, like an imprinted ritual.[293] Gorilla silverbacks and adult orangutans never let anyone mount them, let alone penetrate them. And for adult chimpanzees, it often depends on the balance of power at the moment.

How cultures have structured male homosexual relationships demonstrates unequivocally that human males ubiquitously tend to associate sexual penetration with domination and sexual receptiveness with submission. In most if not all cases of premodern homosexuality, the dominant male could not be penetrated without jeopardizing his status of male. Males should only penetrate other males who are inferior in status: youths, slaves, eunuchs, transgender males, and so forth. As I have suggested earlier, human societies had to solve a problem that no other ape species had to face.

Humans very early on organized themselves into relatively egalitarian societies:[294] all males within the same social group, class, or caste are by definition equal in status. This radically new social arrangement rapidly sent out an urgent warning: equal-in-status adult males could not sleep together without taking the risk of being accused of sexual passiveness. For this reason, the so-called cultural forms of homosexuality, which all aimed to fix homosexual behavior by determining who could do what to whom, when, and often even where, became an absolute necessity. By electing youths, slaves, eunuchs, prostitute, enemies, and/or feminized males as acceptable partners, all homosexual cultures of the past have guaranteed a scrupulous respect to ranking and the status of the male. Thus, thanks to precise rituals and immutable customs, all traditional cultures—from ancient Greece to Melanesia, and from pre-Meiji Japan to pre-colonial Africa—managed to reconcile the irreconcilables: ranking order and intraclass egalitarianism.

However, we should not lose sight of the fact that those who did not submit to the uncompromising rule of male ranking—the effeminate, soft and passive adult males—were ostracized across the board. Submitting one's body to sexual penetration—without a solid symbolic context to justify it (as in the case of transgender homosexuality for instance)—has been a cause of angst, contempt, or even rage, on the part of males in probably all human cultures. Everywhere, for a mature male to be penetrated was a source of humiliation. Assyrians and Egyptians wrote about it some 4,000–3,000 year ago.[295] In ancient Greece, at the height of the pederastic tradition, *malakoi* (soft men) and the *kinaidoi* (effeminate men) were banished from the two most primordial male institutions, the popular assembly and the gymnasium.[296] The *galli*, effeminate priests of the goddess Cybele, were barely tolerated.[297] *Depilati* (men who shaved their body hair), *effeminati*, and *cinaedi* were subject to constant criticisms by their Roman contemporaries. And soft males were systematically ridiculed in Greco-Roman literature.[298]

From Rome to Japan, men's insertive role in the sexual act was as much a prerogative as it was a mandatory symbolic manifestation of their status as males. Almost without exception, those who did not abide by this law were despised by their peers, deemed weak and untrustworthy, and often socially demoted. Males who voluntary relinquish their rank, hence their status and honor as males, by seeking to be sexually penetrated, constituted "natural" targets of hatred for the other males. I infer from this that the primeval source of homophobia is that males are, by instinct, primed to interpret the act of being penetrated as a loss of status, and consequently, to perceive sexually passive adult males as males of inferior rank. Transgender males, boys, novices, and other young acolytes escaped that fate only insofar as the culture did not symbolically identify them as bona fide males. And, as we will see in subsequent chapters, this immunity was sometimes subject to change.

As you may certainly already suspect, homophobia is a sociobiological phenomenon embedded into a cultural dynamic, which we will continue to explore in the second part of this book in detail. The transgression of the rules of male ranking is not the whole story. Alone, it cannot explain the size and scope of the homophobic wave that engulfed Europe and eventually the entire world. It can only help us spot a specific sociocultural tension, which is to say, understand why this type of individual could potentially become the target of collective hatred. The historical triumph of homophobia was fueled by another primordial aspect of our animal nature: the fear of the unknown. It is indeed human beings' visceral dread of what is beyond their comprehension and control that turned homophobia into organized violence. Naturally, the fear of the unknown will constitute the next and last item in our inventory of the True.

The Fear of the Unknown

We have seen that the evolutionary advantage of homosexual relationships resides specifically in the use of sex as a medium of social cohesion and, potentially, in refining the selection process of males. We were also able to make an important prediction. Congruent with the fact that male homosexual relationships in the premodern world were systematically fashioned according to the rule of male ranking, the idea that the polarity of the penetrative act is instinctively interpreted in terms of dominance by all the males in the group does not appear so far-fetched. Sexual receptiveness—"built-in" for females but only optional, if not voluntary, for males—is the sign of one's inferior status. The rule of male ranking can perfectly explain the antipathy for sexually passive males that was observed across the world, thereby providing a cogent starting point to begin to decode the complex phenomenon that we call homophobia today.

Yet, as hinted earlier, male ranking cannot account for the violence and nor the ostracism that came to be imposed indiscriminately on the perpetrators of both passive and active homosexual acts, as well as on lesbians. Nor can it explain the rise, spread, and persistence of exceptionally virulent homophobic attitudes, first throughout Western culture, and eventually across the entire world. To elucidate how homophobia as we know it today emerged will require two steps. In the second part of this book, the Good, we will investigate how Christianity gave birth to a distinctive homophobic culture, more fanatical than any other culture before it and, most importantly, extended to all homosexual acts. But before that, we need to explore what is perhaps the most fundamental feature of human cultures, more ubiquitous than religion and more ancient than patriarchy. Human beings everywhere have divided the world in which they lived along the same line: on one side, what and whom they liked, accepted, supported, and shared with; and on the other side, everything else—what and whom they feared, fought, and avoided at all cost. And it is where this fundamental division of the world, so deeply entrenched in our animal nature, comes from, and how it has altered human cultures that I wish to explore now.

The Unknown

All animals strive naturally to live in an environment that is as safe as possible. Their ears and eyes wide open, animals detect anything that might sound or look suspect. If this were not enough, their exquisite olfactory system, capable of sampling the environment over great distances, can sense the invisible approach of even more remote predators. And human beings have also inherited the primal need to recognize and protect themselves from danger.

The brain utilizes enormous resources to detect potential menaces from the environment, constantly collecting and analyzing a phenomenal amount of sensory information at each second. When facing danger, no animal can afford to take the time to think the matter through, or rely exclusively on past experience. Danger—the roaring of a wild beast, a brutal shock, or the smell of fire—must be addressed immediately. The response is instinctive, emotional, and it has a very familiar name: fear. The structure responsible for the fear response is located in one of the most primitive parts of the brain, and you also know its name: the amygdala. In response to a threat, this tiny organ hosts a dichotomous choice that will prove particularly decisive: we either fight or flee.

However, fear in human beings, unlike in other animals, is not only caused by danger as it arises in the present moment, but also by perils that they are able to foresee. Because of the extraordinary development of the human mind, fear is also triggered by the mere anticipation of danger. And in human beings, this mechanism has become particularly intense. At every instant, the mind calculates all foreseeable scenarios. Every second, millions of synapses are firing in our brain so as to quench our subliminal obsession with anticipating potential dangers. In point of fact, the human mind is a formidable predicting machine.

The evolution of ape behavior has already pointed to that direction. Chimpanzees go to war against neighboring groups so as to secure their control over larger supplies of food and acquire extra females. Their anticipation of a threat (a potential lack of food) arises from a sophisticated genetic programming of their brain, not from mental deduction. In that, humans seem to be the only primates capable of holding a conceptual vision of their future in their mind. But insofar as the mental representation of future dangers has no other limits than those of human imagination, the predictive process can quickly get out of hand: the harvest looks abundant on the other side of the hill where a neighboring tribe dwells but desperately meager on yours; they may then grow too strong and become a threat; a stranger installs his new workshop in the village and could jeopardize your own business; a gang of unidentified men is spotted walking through your land; a handsome man shows up at a party drawing the attention of all the women. In the world of eventualities, threats come in infinite forms.

As a result, human beings live in a world of phobias, more often than not completely absurd. Those phobias (understood here as non-pathological intense and irrational fears/aversions for a specific object) are a response to what humans neither see nor understand, and which they can neither predict nor control. At the most fundamental level, human beings loathe the unknown.[299] As much as possible, they will avoid it. And if they cannot, they will attack. Flee or fight, the amygdala offers its verdict. "Human beings are strongly predisposed to respond with unreasoning hatred to external threats and to escalate their hostility sufficiently to overwhelm the source of the threat by a respectably wide margin of safety,"[300] wrote the sociobiologist E.O. Wilson. Yet, if fear generates either avoidance or aggressiveness, what determines the choice between the two? What makes someone prefer fighting over fleeing, and vice versa?

THE TESTOSTERONE DILEMMA

[. . .] during the nineteen-fifties, twenty-two middle class, white, protestant, well-adjusted, eleven-year-old boys were invited to camp. The psychologists working with the camp then split the boys into two groups that were kept apart. Friends were separated as much as possible. The experimenters' aim: to find how easily group hostility would emerge. It took a week for each group to give themselves an identity, a leader and a culture. One group called themselves the Rattlers, and they prided themselves on being tough, refusing for instance to complain about injuries. The other group, the Eagles, concentrated on vilifying homesickness. Finally, a grand tournament was announced. For five days the Rattlers and the Eagles would compete for trophies. It started well enough, with a baseball game played fairly. The Eagles lost. But that night, in a sneak raid, the Eagles burnt the Rattlers' flag. Next day, the Rattlers' leader started a fight by challenging the Eagles' leader to admit the burning of the flag. When other kids joined in, experimenters felt they had to intervene. The intervention stopped the fight for the time being, but then, hours later, it escalated. That night the Rattlers raided the Eagles; the Eagles retaliated with a raid on their own. This time the boys were fighting with sticks and bats, and they were prepared to arm themselves with stones. But then the Rattlers stole the Eagles trophies, and when the Eagles negotiated to get them back, the Rattlers insisted on humiliating the Eagles by making them crawl on their bellies. Finally, the experimenters, seeing that things were getting out of hand, restored a degree of friendly relation among the boys by setting goals that could be accomplished only by the two groups working together.[301]

There is a great lesson to learn from this experiment. We already know about one thing. It is highly unlikely that the same protocol applied to two groups of girls would have produced the same result. Physical violence, in humans as in other apes, is primarily a male problem. Across the world and throughout history, men have overwhelmingly been the perpetrators of violent acts—hunting, wars, genocides, murders, torture, you name it. And behind all these sociocultural manifestations of male brutality lay the influence of the most powerful molecule on our planet: testosterone.

During fetal development and again at the time of puberty, the male hormone tends to freeze the fight-or-flight switch into the fight position, priming males to attack and if necessary kill, rather than run away. Obviously all men are not equally testosterone-driven. Many succeed in finding healthy substitutes, expressing their taste for competition through sport, money making, power, sex, or rhetoric. Even so, violence is still highly rewarded in many cultures or subcultures. And recent history demonstrates that when fate places men into stressful situations such as prison, war, fighting, or in extremely competitive environments, even the most educated ones can turn into a prehistoric beast.

In the end, seen from a distant planet, human history might very well be summarized into one key issue: managing testosterone. This said, if women rarely participate in violence, they consistently reward it, starting with sexual favors. The victorious soldier is welcomed back home and into the bed of his female admirer(s). After slaughtering some villains, the fearless knight wins the heart of his beloved. Those examples may be clichés, yet they illustrate perfectly well how much women have played their part in collective violence by providing an irresistible incentive.

The experiment with the Rattlers and the Eagles gives us another crucial piece of information. It demonstrates how the boys, artificially split into two teams, rapidly generated two distinct antagonistic sub-cultures, and how they meticulously hunted for signs of "differentness" in order to set themselves apart from the "others." And it is the process of creating "otherness" that we now need to investigate very carefully.

THE MAKING OF OTHERNESS

When it comes to individuals, what distinguishes known from unknown? Which is to say, how and why is someone going to be viewed as either same or other, either belonging or not belonging, either kin or not-kin, either in or out, and so forth? For chimpanzees this choice never gets much more complex than recognizing members of their own group. But we know that, for human beings, this game has become much more complex. For our inquiry, this is a key issue. Homophobia stems from the fact that, from a homophobic standpoint, homosexuality is recognized as a sign of otherness and, therefore, tends to elicit aggressiveness. We learned from chimpanzees that in the "in" scenario, aggressive behavior finds itself effectively balanced by rituals of reconciliation, but also that in the "out" scenario, male violence is potentially unleashed. And humans, it appears, behave the same way.[302]

However, we also know that homophobia as we define it today is neither a biological nor a cultural given. In pre-Christian traditional cultures, homophobia never had the scope and strength that it eventually found during the Christian and modern eras. The strong homophobic current that appeared around the turn of the first millennium gained an enormous momentum, globally shifting the sexual mores in what used to be the Roman Empire and beyond (i.e., all of Europe, the Middle East, and North Africa). Eventually, homophobic hate diffused across all continents, taking roots everywhere it stepped. This teaches us two very important points. First, homophobia is neither inherent to human beings nor human cultures. Second, the spread of homophobia was far too efficient not to be supported by some deeper mechanism. Homophobia's history strongly suggests that the making of otherness is a dual phenomenon, part cultural and part innate.

Cultures do not expand in all possible directions, restricted only by mankind's capacity to create. Rather, their diversity appears curiously limited. For instance, the overwhelming majority of human societies are patriarchal, structured around the basic social unit represented by the nuclear family, engage in wars with their neighbors, entail some form of cooking, endorse specific religious beliefs, and practice some form of divination.[303] And, more often than not, the origin of the mechanisms that influence human cultures lies within our biological nature.[304] Likewise, not all biological imperatives are reflected through human cultures, and when they are, they do not manifest with the same intensity everywhere. Cultures did not all develop the same angst, fear, and/or need to control in connection with such and such aspects of our biology (e.g., male dominance over females, male ranking, social hierarchy, gender differences, and so forth). In fact, cultures can sometimes overturn some of our most powerful instincts: the incest taboo, already present in chimpanzees, was overridden by one of the greatest civilization in antiquity, the Egyptians. Human cultures are incredibly elastic.

Therefore, different (sub)cultures can channel violence toward different categories of victims. The culturally defined target of hatred can be women (misogynistic culture), foreigners (xenophobia), people of different ethnic origins (racism and anti-Semitism), and so on. In other words, cultures create stigmas. Those stigmas are neither permanent nor inherent to all human cultures. Throughout history, we see them surface, disseminate, and then often disappear. Similarly, the "homosexual," defined as a target of collective hatred, is a cultural invention. Yet, this can only be the visible tip of the iceberg. Beyond the obvious cultural heterogeneity of collective hates, why is the process of creating an unknown "other"—one who does not belong—always so easy? Fire can only thrive upon a flammable terrain.

To explain homophobia's rapid diffusion, one may reasonably hypothesize the existence of a neural template (as in the case of language). Anthropologists, sociobiologists, and psychologists concur that the human mind is inherently prone to dichotomize the world that surrounds them between same and other, friend and foe, familiar and unknown, safe and unsafe, and so forth.[305] Thanks to this neural "groove," the violence so easily triggered by the presence of the unknown and boosted by a surge of testosterone at puberty in males can quickly disseminate into the cultural sphere. Just like a virus requires a specific docking site to invade an organism and spread throughout an entire population efficiently, a given stigma needs to be recognized in the brain as a bona fide criterion of otherness in order to invade the collective psyche of a whole community.

We are then due to explore the origins of the mechanisms of inclusion and rejection, and how these have expanded from the individual to the collective levels, that is, from the biological to the cultural levels. And we are about to find out that, in the animal world as well as in humans, you are suspect . . . until you prove not to be so.

BELONGING

Humans do not live in constant fear. Why? Because, like any other animals, human have effective ways to identify very quickly the intrusion of danger, either real or potential, within their security space. Besides, when it comes to individuals of our own species, we are, from the moment we are born, drawn to differentiate the members of our group from all others. It all naturally starts with the distinction between the mother and what is not the mother. Quickly, the world splits between kin and non-kin. And as they slowly reach adult age, human beings keep differentiating between safe and unsafe by extending the same dichotomous rule to everything. Throughout individual psychosocial development as well as species evolution, one can see the mechanisms of kin recognition increase in complexity. Yet, despite its elaborate cultural refinements, kin recognition remains a constant need in humans. But how does kin recognition work exactly?

In mammals kin recognition is mainly ensured by the sense of smell. All the way up to apes, animals rely essentially on odors and pheromones to identify their kin. Even if the olfactory system is significantly reduced in humans, we know however that infants, who are nearly blind during the first months of their lives, depend heavily on smell to recognize their mother and her breast, and familiarize themselves with the presence of other members of the family, such as the father and siblings.[306] Only later will vision take over that important role, and in adults, kin recognition will for the most part depend on visual memory. Yet, at this point, kinship is essentially defined by blood-relatedness and instinctively recognized through our senses.

As the field of social interactions expands to distant family members, neighbors, other clans, other countries, and so on, kinship recognition, which was originally essentially instinctive, becomes first and foremost a cognitive process involving learning and memory. Now, why can you so easily relate to a distant maternal aunt, a member of your soccer team, or a fellow citizen as members of your kin? The answer to this is simple. You have something special in common: your mother, a passion of a particular sport/team, a country. This means that, at one point of human development, kinship does not only result from having genes or odors in common but also from having something meaningful in common. Sameness turns into commonality, yet the logic remains unchanged. The following example illustrates my point: I am in the New York City subway waiting for my train to show up. From a distance, I observe a couple of people desperately trying to find their location on the subway map. I suddenly notice that they speak French. From that moment, I feel driven to approach them and offer my help.

Why? Because the couple and I are native French speakers, and only because of that. The common cultural element alone justifies my trust and motivates my intention. We share a fragment of culture, which somehow works as a substitute for blood kinship, even if the bond only lasts the time of a subway ride.

Overflowing from the objective into the intersubjective domain, commonality, which originally was exclusively biological, becomes primarily cultural. Cultural commonality allows kinship to transcend the narrow bond of genetic relatedness, while still including it. It acts as social glue (just like sex). But cultural kinship allows for the development of stable communities at a totally different level. As the sense of commonality keeps expanding, human societies have been able to grow from clan to tribe to nation-state to multinational organization, and more recently to a global level. Accordingly, people originally only relate to their own clan, then to their own ethnicity, their own nationality, and ultimately all people. And even if not all people go through all these stages of expansion of kinship, history nevertheless shows us very clearly that, overall, it is the direction in which human communities grow: by granting the bond of cultural commonality to an increasingly larger circle.

How will this help us decipher the dynamics of homophobia and the fate of homosexuality? If I summarize what we have covered so far in this chapter, we have seen that human beings fear the unknown above all things. Like any other animals, they distinguish kin from non-kin, their own group versus "the others." Yet humans are by and large cultural beings. Culture composes the bulk part of the social cement that has enabled humans to cohabit and coalesce into increasingly larger communities. But sometimes the cement can crumble. The bond of cultural kinship becomes reversible. If, in the midst of a cultural upheaval, the sudden emergence of cultural differences succeed in overriding the cultural commonality, some people find themselves expelled from the space of cultural kinship. They do not "fit in" anymore with the rest of society. Going down the spiral that we had previously climbed, they become "others," by definition unknown, unpredictable, hence potentially dangerous. We commonly call this scapegoating. As the scapegoating process gains impetus, violence, particularly that of males, is no longer tethered. "We are strongly predisposed to slide into the deep, irrational hostility under definable conditions," E.O. Wilson warned us, which is exactly what happened between the Rattlers and the Eagles.[307] Adults artificially fostered the emergence of a sense of otherness by creating two different teams with distinct basic identities, and this mini-cultural shift was enough to turn the boys into savage brutes.

Now, what more can we learn about those enigmatic "elementary particles" of human cultures that have the power to grant or deny commonality and decide the fate of people?

KNOWING

Humankind has reached a level of awareness that is probably unique in the animal kingdom. But excellence has come at a price. The first *Homo sapiens*, intelligent but also highly vulnerable to predators, opened their eyes on a world that must have been terrifying. And for them, the unknown took a very particular face—death. Never before has a species had such an acute sense of its own destiny; and never before has a species had a knowledge of its own mortality. Humans might not have invented language, tools, strategies, and even culture, but they might have been the first and only species to become aware of the intolerable reality of their ultimate fate.

The fear of death, and its denial—the quest for immortality—propelled the human race out of the African savanna across the entire world. It has shaped the individual minds as well as the collective psyche of humanity. It also inoculated humans with the urge to create. It enjoined people to build temples, pyramids, and cathedrals, and to send ships across oceans and space. But even more importantly, the fear of death transformed our relationship to time and forever altered our relationship to the universe.[308]

Aware of their collective history, human beings were doomed to dread dangers even before experiencing them: cold, drought, famine, war, murder, rape, dishonor, isolation . . . Moreover, with the expansion of kinship, they feared not only for themselves but also for their own kin and loved ones. Keeping the children safe, protecting the girls and the women from being raped, worrying about the men on a hunting trip or engaged in a battle . . . became inescapable aspects of human life. Awareness does indeed come at a price. The extraordinary development of human consciousness and the ability to conceptualize danger multiplied the number and diversity of possible threats exponentially, and with it may have brought humankind's existential anxiety to unbearable levels. But of course, human cultures have addressed the fear of the unknown brilliantly.

From instinct, a male chimpanzee knows how to shake the branches of a tree to convey his anger and readiness to attack. The meaning of his behavior is clear to all the parties involved. Meaningful behaviors, whether warning signs of imminent aggression or courtship, constitute an essential mode of communication between individuals of the same species. Although common in the animal kingdom, they appear to acquire an unusual depth as you go up the evolution tree. Already in monkeys, social communications based on behavior (e.g., grooming, kissing, and hugging) are not merely innate. Studies have demonstrated that to a certain extent, individuals can learn from the rest of the group, which is to say that these behaviors are partly culturally acquired.[309] And when humans grew into cultural beings, the association of particular behaviors with specific meanings became a highly elaborate creative act.

The presence of a group of unknown men walking in my direction might worry me. But if one of them comes forward and offers to shake hands, I will assume that their intentions are friendly. Hence "shaking hands," very much like "shaking a branch," communicates a precise and fixed information that is understood the exact same way on both sides. Nonetheless, hand shaking did not merely emerge from the brain's genetic programming. The gesture is not innate; it is acquired and culture-specific. Shaking hands is one among myriad behaviors that have the power to convey meaning. In areas as basic as greeting, food sharing, courting, and hunting, human beings have used culturally defined behaviors to communicate their intentions, and this, despite or in addition to spoken language. Altogether these acquired, meaningful behaviors represent an essential pillar of human cultures, and, as we will see, their extraordinary diversity reflects precisely that of cultures.

To do justice to such a complex and fascinating topic requires more extensive exploration. All we need to understand here is that in all human cultures certain behaviors acquired a particular symbolic meaning that was collectively accepted, culturally determined, and ultimately culturally maintained. The form and meaning of these behaviors have been faithfully transmitted from one generation to the next, learned by example. Human behavior has then the power to embody symbolic subjective realities. They inform others of one's intention, desire, goal, duty, or rank. Those symbolic associations are shared by all the individuals of the group over time. They are often regarded as eternal and universal truths.[310] And just as in language, human beings are biologically equipped to create, use, and learn symbolic behaviors. In fact, they are driven to do so. Human beings are, by nature, meaning-driven creatures.

For our distant ancestors, trying to decode the chaotic and impenetrable logic of life, and perhaps have some control over it, became a vital necessity.[311] Will the sun rise again tomorrow? Will the harvest be abundant this year and the hunt successful? Will the children grow strong and healthy? Will the new wife prove fertile and give sons? How do we make sure that the soul of the deceased reaches the afterworld? What should we do to appease the gods? All human societies had to collectively deal with the unbearable unpredictability of life, the ultimate unknown.

Insofar as humans since the Paleolithic Age have had a tendency to imagine the outer world in their own image, they naturally started to converse with the world and the hidden forces that operated through it using the same symbolic language that they had been using among themselves since as far as they could remember.[312] (Would you not similarly approach aliens from a distant planet by communicating in your own language?) And as cultures kept growing in complexity, symbolic behaviors progressively coalesced into sophisticated rituals.[313]

Rituals are meaningful collective behaviors with a repetitive and fixed structure. Just like the symbolic fragments that composed them, the form and meaning of rituals are shared by the whole group and remain largely unaltered though the generations. Rituals have provided two complementary functions. First, since prehistory, they have constituted the primordial mode of communication of humanity with the rest of the universe and the unknown—gods, spirits, dead ancestors, and other life forces. Second, rituals have crystallized all the most important aspects of human life into a predictable form: marriage, pregnancy, birth, inaugurations, death, mourning, reconciliation, sleeping, greeting, feeding, meeting, hunting, battling, and of course, cohabiting with the invisible world. All these areas of human life are meticulously ritualized. Cultures have resolved once and for all how, when, and why those things should happen.[314] Because they have provided templates for every particular moment of the life of human beings, rituals have succeeded in controlling the uncontrollable. In all cultures, rituals are connected to the knowledge of a time of perfection—a golden age—before the split between humanity and the gods, when the unknown did not yet exist. So, by reenacting ancient deeds perpetrated by a god or a hero at the beginning of time, they also ensure the perfect unfolding of human life in harmony with the cosmos and the divine sphere.[315]

Notice that even today, our institutions, governments, justice system, and, of course, religions are built upon hundreds of rituals entangled together so that human affairs can unfold in a perfectly orderly and predictable fashion. Generation after generation, rituals recreate a collective "truth" that people do not need to question anew every day of their lives. They make the uncertainty of the world and human life tolerable. And as Malinowski wrote, "by sacralizing and thus standardizing the other set of impulses, [they bestow] on man the gift of mental integrity."[316]

Yet rituals are much more than mere symbolic behaviors. Rituals have the power to channel the deepest layers of the collective psyche, where their immaterial "alter egos"—the myths—reside.[317] Often inseparable from rituals, myths replace the unknown with stories that can magically explain all the mysteries—life, birth and death, health and illness, defeat and victory, love and hate, fear, inspiration, anger, hunger, and so forth. They turn the unknown into something comprehensible. They give the unknown a known substance—a concrete representation of what is and why it is that way. (Carl Jung asserted that "myths of a religious nature can be interpreted as a sort of therapy for the sufferings and anxieties of humankind in general."[318])

By connecting concrete reality to symbolic meanings, myths and rituals embody humankind's dialogue with the unknown. And by doing so, they generate and reinforce the sense of kinship among the people that share them. Myths and rituals are those elementary particles of human cultures that determine belongingness. They are the foundation of sociocultural kinship that we have been seeking. They are the "keys to the kingdom": when shared, they include; when betrayed, they divide. They pull the string of people's social destiny.

But we are getting ahead of ourselves. Myths, immaterial inhabitants of our collective soul, do not live in the True, which is the domain of objective things and facts, but in the Good. To this point, we still have not reviewed some fundamental differences between the objective and the subjective realms. We must wait a little more, bearing in mind that myths and rituals emerge from the fear of the unknown. It is on them that we will later focus most of our attention. Understanding the dynamics of the acceptance of homosexuality will depend on it.

SEX AND THE MIRACLE OF LIFE

Humanity's fascination for the miracle of birth has never faded. The act of giving life connects human beings to all origins: their own, that of the world, that of time, and that of all living creatures. Birth not only keeps the community growing, but it also repeats the primordial event from which stems everything human beings know: the sun also is born every morning, so is the moon every month, and spring every year. Without this cyclically and orderly reiteration of this miracle (a perfect ritual indeed!), the world would fall apart. Then, more than in anything else, human beings have seen in the power of giving birth a reflection of the reassuring regularity of the universe they live in and, at the same time, the embodiment of the unknown in their own flesh. Upon giving birth, all hopes and all fears converge.

Procreation promotes the survival of the group and throughout most of human history, having the largest population possible generally offered the best chance to outcompete other groups. For all traditional cultures, it was an imperative necessity, and it was viewed as such. As much as with death, people's concerns about procreation have been overwhelming. They have haunted human cultures since prehistory.[319] They have kept shamans busy for thousands of years, tormented religions, obsessed states, and fascinated science. As it happens, not many other areas of life have been more constrained by rituals than the procreative act. For the primitive as well as for the modern, the scrupulous respect of birth rites has been the best means to confer procreation some degree of predictability.

Our ancestors seem to have understood the connection between the sexual act and birth very early on. Most prehistoric religious representations unearthed by archeologists depict erect penises, voluptuous Venuses with dangerously swollen bellies and gigantic breasts, and other well-endowed figurines carved in stone. Here too, the fear of the unknown turned sexual life into a myriad of rituals, which, beyond their cultural diversity, invariably intended to maximize the reproductive success of the group. Rites of passage, circumcision, sexual initiations, betrothal, marriage, anniversaries, and even Valentine's Day betray our compulsive need of control and predictability. And in today's ultra-modern maternity hospitals, those rites are called "medical protocols." In vitro fertilization may have been substituted for the sperm wars that rage among male chimps, yet the logic is exactly the same: humans will do anything to ensure their reproductive success. And if each one of these rituals has its own symbolism, rationale, and history, they all aim to alleviate our prehistoric anxiety regarding procreation by promising a favorable outcome.

It is crucial to understand to what degree reproductive sexuality has always been ritualized. Throughout history, societal views on reproductive sex have been highly dogmatic and the pressure placed upon individuals relentless. In other words, heterosexuality—by essence "conceptive," according to its historic definition—has been culturally shaped in its finest details. The omnipresence of the institution of marriage—the "supernaturally sanctioned bond, superadded to the primarily biological fact: the union of man and woman for lifelong partnership in affection, economic community, the procreation and rearing of children"[320]—illuminates the historical and global significance of the issue for human beings. So, the constraints historically placed on homosexual behavior should not be viewed as an independent issue but rather as just another consequence of people's incessant apprehension regarding procreation and sex in general.

If indeed the ancient world seldom divided sexuality between homosexual and heterosexual behaviors, it clearly discerned between appropriate and deviant sexual acts. Stepping outside the boundaries defined by local customs was often costly, if not fatal: the single mother hidden away from public eyes by her family; the individuals whose sterility constituted the only valid excuse to break the most sacred commitment of all, marriage; the unfaithful wife stoned by the angry crowd; and the effeminate man exiled from the city. In heterosexual as much as in homosexual matters, cultures have seldom tolerated randomness.

All homosexual relational forms that I have described in earlier chapters ensued from a ritualization process. Actually, any cultural "form" is, in itself, ritualistic. The so-called ritualized homosexuality observed among Melanesian tribes is a developmentally ancient ritualistic form of homosexuality, but by no means the only ritualized one. Rituals designate fixed and repetitive collective behaviors that convey powerful symbolic meanings. Today's institutions may be more complex forms of rituals than primitive rites, yet the rationale remains fundamentally the same.

Furthermore, it would be largely inaccurate to believe that homosexual behavior was viewed as unrelated to reproduction. On the contrary, homosexual behavior was traditionally organized around the same concerns as reproductive sex. The ancients knew perfectly that homosexual behavior could not lead to reproduction, of course, but they seldom opposed homosexual and reproductive behaviors. By and large, they simply found it natural that both desires cohabited in the same individuals, a rule that suffered only rare exceptions. Homosexual behavior did not define alternative cultures or identities. They were an integral part of the sexual norms of the times, as long as they were integrated into the ritualistic space, and as long as they did not hinder the reproductive success of the group.

Transgenerational homosexual cultures, which represented the great majority of the traditional forms of same-sex relationships, always made sure that receptive young males turned into breeding males in due time. In fact, the particular ritualistic organization of each transgenerational homosexual culture defined precisely when the transition from receptive to insertive male should occur and how. The case of transgender homosexuality appears more intricate. In most cases, "stud" males seldom engaged in long-term or exclusive relationships with transgender males. In antiquity, transgender people were, in most instances, prostitutes or courtesans. This was generally the case of eunuchs in Persia and India,[321] and this is still the case of *hijras* in India. In those cultures, gender reversal, castration, and prostitution were often compatible with religious functions (e.g., the Roman *galli*, priests of Cybele, and other male sacred prostitutes who might have existed in the cultures of the Mediterranean basin and the Middle East), but almost never with marriage.[322] In Pacific cultures, the *Māhū* and *fa'afafine* generally officiate as servants or sometimes even concubines, yet not as head wives.[323]

American Indian two-spirits and transgender shamans have constituted a relative exception in that they did marry other men.[324] But there were often drastic prerequisites to relationships with two-spirits, which appear particularly worth noticing here: Among Lakota and Zapotec people, men were only allowed to marry two-spirits as secondary spouses after having started their own family. Among the Hidatsas, relationships with two-spirits were only acceptable for old men past their childbearing years. Among Crow and Mohave peoples, two-spirits' partners were the object of constant sarcasms; relationships with two-spirits were notoriously unstable; sooner or later, men would commonly leave, marry a woman, and have children. In *The Spirit and the Flesh*, Walter Williams concluded unambiguously on that issue: "[. . .] by keeping the majority of male marriages short-term, the joking ensures that most men mate with women at some point and have children. Other cultures accomplished the same goal by restricting male marriages to those men who have already had children. Thus it is only acceptable for the berdache to become a second or third wife in a polygynous family where the female wife has already reproduced. [. . .] None of these patterns of marriage threatens the reproduction of the population."[325] Therefore, while usually socially well accepted, most transgender relationships occurred on the side of a heterosexual institution. The symbolic integration of sexually-receptive transgender individuals as adequate partners in bed, but not in life, prohibited insertive males from engaging in long term relationships with receptive males. Despite rare exceptions, sex with a transgender was fine as long as it did not involve any socioeconomic bond.

In the end, this leads to the following conclusions. First, the great majority of traditional cultures included a ritualistic form of homosexual behavior, which I have previously discussed under the label of "cultural forms of homosexuality" and "homosexualities." (Notice that I have intentionally ignored modern homosexuality in this conversation. Modern homosexuality operates very distinctly. Its rationale can only be fathomed from a totally different context that will only be explored later.) Second, human cultures have structured homosexual relationships so as to take into account a dual concern: male ranking and the overall reproductive success of the group. And third, in their vast majority, transgenerational and transgender-ritualized homosexualities, which is to say, pretty much all premodern forms of homosexuality can be viewed as an endeavor to shield reproduction from the excesses of same-sex desire. Ultimately, the social acceptance of homosexual behavior always correlates with the existence of a homosexual ritualistic space. Without it, the ritualistic fellowship is broken, and the fear of the unknown unleashed. And the consequences, as we will soon see, are dreadful, to say the least.

We have reached the end of the True. In the process, we have explored what homosexuality is, how it emerges, and why it has represented a competitive advantage for our species. But we have not yet made sense of homosexuality's fate. This constitutes our next task. To accomplish this we shall leave the realm of objective certainties and enter the immaterial world of shared values, morals, and beliefs. And together, we are now crossing the Rubicon that separates the True from the Good.

PART II

The Good

Immaterial Realities

In the previous part, the True, we have explored homosexuality as a fact, as an object, an "IT." We have discovered that homosexuality is better understood as a dual phenomenon with homosexual behavior on one side and homosexual identity on the other, which although tightly linked, have distinct dynamics, distinct histories, and distinct evolutionary paths. We now know that among males, homosexual relationships have taken different forms in different cultures, and that with the remarkable exception of modern homosexuality, traditional models (transgenerational and transgender) have all scrupulously abided by the rule of male ranking while ensuring the reproductive success of males. Along the way, we have clarified a few important questions. First, homosexuality is neither a disorder, nor a mutated trait, nor an evolutionary paradox. On the contrary, homosexual behavior has increased the reproductive success of the group by promoting social harmony and bonding among its members. Second, homosexual behavior and, most likely, homosexual identity, are the products of a genetically generated sexual diversity in the human population. Scientific evidence seems to suggest that the asymmetrical distribution of homosexual and heterosexual desires might result from stochastic variations in the organization of the brain (the "loose switch"). Finally, although biologically determined, how sexual orientation and sexual preference manifests in one's life remains largely under the influence of the cultural environment.

Homosexual behavior is a key element of our evolutionary heritage, as much as language, technology, culture, and spirituality. But the same thing can also be said about warfare and rape. So, we are now facing a serious dilemma: at this point of our inquiry, we still cannot tell the good from the bad. Why? Because, intrinsically, the things and facts that compose the realm of True, are neither good nor bad nor beautiful nor ugly. They just are what they are. A purely objective approach of reality, such as the one chosen by science, is not designed to convey a sense of goodness or beauty (nor their opposite, badness and ugliness).

Goodness and beauty are perspectives, not immanent attributes. They totally depend on one's subjectivity.

Freeing ourselves from the constraint of morality while exploring the True was crucial in our endeavor thus far but it cannot be the entire story. The True, the Good, and the Beautiful are three distinct conversations that one should absolutely refrain from conflating, yet none can be ignored. So we now have a colossal problem ahead of us, that is, to answer the second key question of this book: "how is homosexuality collectively perceived?" In other words, how does homosexuality fit into the cultural views of its time and what mechanisms determine its integration into the sociocultural fabric? To address those questions, one must now enter the realm of the intersubjective realities—shared values, culture, morals, beliefs and so forth. But inasmuch as the intersubjective domain involves feelings, ideas, and intentions that people have in common, it inevitably requires some kind of communication, sensitivity, or understanding (language being one possible modality) to allow feelings, thoughts, and intentions to flow between individuals. It follows that the intersubjective space is not merely a collection of individual subjective spaces. It is the network of communication that emerges between individuals.

Unveiling the intersubjective dynamics that have decided on the fate of homosexuality in human cultures will be determinant for the success of our enterprise. And if, as I have claimed earlier, we first have to make sense of homophobia if we are to get rid of it, let us see what it is going to take.

THE DYNAMICS OF THE INVISIBLE

Remember when in the section about the True we investigated, for instance, homosexual behavior among chimpanzees. I relied on published peer-reviewed data, which altogether allowed me to discern particular patterns, a "big picture," with respect to the role of homosexual behavior during human evolution. Those data consisted of various reports, which in turn originated from real life observations, video recordings, genetic studies, and so forth, in other words, from objective facts.

Whether considering a behavior, a gene, a morphology, or a neural network, that is, any tangible thing or event occurring in the physical universe, the paradigm is fundamentally the same as if you consider a stone. There is only one "truth" about this stone. It has only one color, one hardness, one molecular composition, one origin, and so forth. Moreover, the stone exists independently of the one who observes it. We can all disappear; the stone will still be there. The stone is an object—an IT. That is what the True (as we defined it here) is made of, things like stones, and science has become a master at deciphering its mysteries. Now, it might sound like I am stating the obvious but we are going to see how much human beings tend to lose sight of basic realities as simple as this.

Consider shared values and morals. How does one "measure" those things? Cultures, morals, and beliefs are very real, yet they are immaterial in essence. They inhabit a world of intersubjective communications, but not of things and facts. Despite the claims of scientific materialism, their immaterial character does not make them less real. By the same token, we should be very careful not to confuse subjective and intersubjective realities with their material correlates. For instance, sexual desire co-emerges with all sort of neuronal activities and behaviors. Yet the experience of desire itself is fundamentally immaterial and absolutely distinct from the physical events that accompany it. By living it, one brings it into existence. The respect of the national flag is not a tangible thing either. Even the most accurate neural recording will fail to capture the thoughts, feelings, and intentions of the people who experience it. And the same applies to everything people think and feel, whether it is about death penalty, global warming, the presidential election, Marilyn Monroe, or . . . homosexuality. The intersubjective world is fundamentally immaterial, and—unlike stones—morals, cultures, and beliefs are not palpable and measurable realities. Notwithstanding, it appears that most people believe that morals and beliefs are just like stones. And clarifying this issue will help us explain a great deal about why humanity has gone mad for the last fifty thousand years or so.

If you and I disagree about the color of a stone, we can together define colors in terms of wavelengths of visible light and measure that. Measurement can reveal only one truth and only one of us can be accurate (or the most accurate). Our disagreement has been settled. So now, take a subjective reality such as freedom. Freedom manifests itself in the world in many different ways—abolition of slavery and other castes systems, democratic values, civil rights, education, equality of chances, free trade, egalitarian society, etc.—yet these manifestations are nothing but objective correlates of freedom. Those are only things and facts that we associate with the concept of freedom. They relate to freedom because some people say they do, even if we do not all agree on those various meanings of freedom. Freedom itself is not a tangible reality but an immaterial one, made of thoughts, feelings, and intentions. Unlike stones, freedom cannot live without human beings to conceive it. (Inter)subjective realities need consciousness to arise, and consciousness needs brains to exist (as far as I can tell). And if humankind were to disappear, freedom would disappear with it, automatically.

This has a major consequence. If the concept of freedom is the "object" you are trying to grasp, there are in fact as many conceptions of freedom as there are conscious minds in the universe. What is more, freedom exists also as a vast collection of cultural agreements in the intersubjective space. So, try to imagine that you do not have one stone—an object called "freedom"—but, instead, an astronomical number of stones (individual concepts) organized in separate heaps (cultural agreements) and all different from each other. Each concept and each cultural agreement is as real as another. Just come up with a new one; as long as you can hold it in your consciousness, it is real, as a subjective reality. Subjective realities exist only by virtue of people experiencing them, and intersubjective realities only by virtue of people agreeing about them.

While we could argue about the properties of a stone, we are now facing a very novel situation: in the (inter)subjective universe, all the different concepts of freedom are all equally real. One is not more accurate or closer to the truth than another; they are just different concepts. But how often do we remember that? In the (inter)subjective world, one can no longer use the true-false dichotomy. Immaterial things—ideas, feelings, and points of view—obey fundamentally different laws and dynamics. Notice, a stone will fall according to the laws of gravity. The concept of freedom will not. But if one annihilates all consciousness in the universe, stones will be just fine. Yet freedom will be gone forever.

Rigorously speaking, you cannot measure the good and the bad. You cannot prove the goodness or badness of something, you can only claim it. Pretending that you can prove it is a fallacy, that is, to confuse moral values with stones. Morals rely on consciousness and agreement and nothing else. We agree or disagree, and that is all. When freedom, killing, war, stealing, taxes, government, institutions, marriage, hygiene, clothing, or anything else is understood in terms of goodness, your opinion is as valid as mine. And that is also true if you consider different opinion groups, political parties, religious faiths, and cultures. One cannot prove the other wrong because different opinions are equally valid in the intersubjective space.

Morals regarding the acceptance of homosexuality abide by the same rules. One camp believes that it is an abomination and another that it is a totally appropriate way of being. Who is wrong and who is right? The answer is: neither or both. It is like being a vegetarian. Some people believe that eating meat is a bad thing. I personally think it is fine. But you cannot, on a moral ground, tell that one diet is good and the other bad, or less good. They are two different moral views on the same objective reality. Any moralistic approach based on the principle that good and bad are as self-evident as true and false is inevitably pointless. There is no possible resolution in such a context. And that is why the interminable debate about who is right and who is wrong has been going on for thousands of years.

But if nobody is either right or wrong, if people can only agree or disagree about their moral views and if all opinions are equally valid, the world becomes a quite sinister place to live in. How do you then distinguish between Gandhi and Hitler, democracy and dictatorship, peace and war, happiness and pain, or love and hate? If you keep trying to sort (inter)subjective realities as if they were stones, which is to say, in terms of right/true and wrong/false, you actually cannot demonstrate the moral difference that you intuitively discern between the various aspects of human life. You can only scream louder than your opponent. And if this sounds really awful, it is the absurd situation in which monological views have led the world.

Now, we all possess a deep and compelling sense of good and bad. Moral values are absolutely central to human consciousness. Without them, our understanding of the world would feel terribly incomplete. But we have to deconstruct the old paradigm in order to build a new one. There is more to say about moral views and subjective realities in general. Because, indeed, "equally valid" does not mean "equal in value."

You remember that people's views are inescapably trapped in the context from which they emerge and that it is that context that determines the moral value of everything that occurs in their world. Let me illustrate my point by comparing food diets from a moral standpoint. As I said, I am not a vegetarian. In my views, chickens and cows are part of the food chain. Animals deserve fair treatment when they are alive, but my eating meat is consistent with the way the ecosystem has been organized for millions of years. So for me, given my context, eating meat is "good." Let us now consider a vegetarian standpoint. For many vegetarians, eating meat implies the suffering of animals. Provided that proteins can easily be obtained from other sources, meat is thus dispensable and animal suffering is unnecessary and cruel. That too makes sense. Seen from one's own context, each moral view is perfectly consistent.

By the same token, seeing homosexuality as good or bad is essentially a matter of context. For example, opponents of homosexual rights often argue that same-sex relationships offend the sacrosanct complementarity between male and female principles and/or that homosexual acts are disgusting and unaesthetic. That is obviously not my context for looking at homosexuality, as this book demonstrates. But viewed from their referential frame, the disapproval of same-sex relationships is nothing but a logical continuity. I cannot oppose any valid evidence to prove them wrong, because there is none (nor can they prove me wrong). And more often than we would like to admit, many homophobic people are otherwise intelligent and well-educated, which makes it so puzzling.

However, we have now moved the conversation one level deeper. Rather than wrestling with nebulous moral opinions, we are now contemplating the contexts from which they arise, that is, people's worldview. Very much like epistemes and cultural paradigms (see introduction), worldviews constitute the global context from which one person or one group operates. Worldviews encompass all the fundamental assumptions from which one sees all things. They offer all at once an epistemological frame, a belief system, basic moral directives, and a meaning of life. Worldviews co-arise automatically with complex consciousness. Since the moment human beings tried to make sense of the world they lived in, they have constituted the invisible foundation of the very act of knowing.

Human cultures have generated many different worldviews since the Stone Age, each new worldview yielding new ideals and new mores perfectly consistent with it. Now, all these worldviews may be equally valid; they are not, however, equal in value. They fall into a hierarchy. And it is on this hierarchy that I would like to focus now. This is where we find again a directionality that we had lost.

The Evolution of Morals

I will be neither the first nor the last one to notice the disconcerting silence of the Bible—the book that has constituted the moral foundation of Western culture—regarding the horror of slavery. And this absence is beyond mere ambiguity. Nowhere in the Bible is slavery condemned (either in the Hebrew or the Christian version). In order to overcome this embarrassing detail, many today point to the biblical message of universal love. Since, by definition, "universal" encompasses "all" people, it has to include slaves. However, considering the great deal of detail that both the Torah/Pentateuch and the New Testament go into specifying the moral value of all sort of acts and things, slavery represents an astonishing omission. Keep in mind that, in Biblical times, slave masters had total power over their slaves. They could treat them in ways that we would definitely view as criminal these days, even with animals. Torture, harsh physical punishment, sexual abuse, and killing were commonplace. Slaves had no moral status, only an economical value. They were often nothing more than a piece of property of which one could dispose at will. Nevertheless, even though the Bible is mute regarding slaves' suffering, it offers precise directions to both slave owners and slaves:

> If a man beats his male or female slave with a rod and the slave dies as a direct result, he must be punished, but he is not to be punished if the slave gets up after a day or two, since the slave is his property. (Exodus 21:20–21)

> If you buy a Hebrew servant, he is to serve you for six years. But in the seventh year, he shall go free, without paying anything. If he comes alone, he is to go free alone; but if he has a wife when he comes, she is to go with him. If his master gives him a wife and she bears him sons or daughters, the woman and her children shall belong to her master, and only the man shall go free. But if the servant declares, 'I love my master and my wife and children and do not want to go free,' then his master must take him before the judges. He shall take him to the door or the doorpost and pierce his ear with an awl. Then he will be his servant for life. (Exodus 21:2–6)

The New Testament does not prove more sensitive to slaves' horrible life conditions than the Old Testament. In fact, it demonstrates a clear commitment to preserving the social status quo:

> Slaves, obey your earthly masters with respect and fear, and with sincerity of heart, just as you would obey Christ. (Ephesians 6:5)

> That servant who knows his master's will and does not get ready or does not do what his master wants will be beaten with many blows. But the one who does not know and does things deserving punishment will be beaten with few blows. From everyone who has been given much, much will be demanded; and from the one who has been entrusted with much, much more will be asked. (Luke 12:47–48)

And when Paul deliberated on the fate of ancient Jewish customs as elemental as circumcision and the customary diet restrictions inside the Christian faith, most were simply abolished. He, however, neglected the case of slavery.

By no means do I intend to denigrate the moral value of ancient sacred texts such as the Bible. That would be as absurd as to turn a blind eye on their limitations. On the one hand, the Bible professes a message of universal love, sublime and eternal, but on the other, it fails to discern slavery (among other things) as a major moral issue of its time. The paradox is only an apparent one. Neither morally conflicted nor totally convinced, the integral explorer knows that, once again, these contradictions cannot be resolved monologically. The inconsistency between universal love and the practice of slavery is blatant for whoever judges them from today's worldview, hence, today's moral context. Instead, one should try to understand empathically (as discussed in the introduction) the issue of slavery from the perspective of the people who lived some twenty to twenty-seven centuries ago. The Bible overlooked the issue of slavery because its authors, even if "divinely" inspired, had absolutely no concept of a world without it. They simply could not conceive of such a thing, just like they would have been unable to grasp concepts such as general relativity or man-caused climate change. In other words, the Bible was written neither by angels nor by insensitive monsters but only by the people of the time.

The worldview that spawned the biblical texts was blind to the horror of slavery. The same was true for all the great thinkers of antiquity who universally endorsed the institution of slavery, including Plato and Aristotle, whom one might consider as the founders of Western civilization.[326] Augustine and Thomas Aquinas thought slavery was part of a natural universal order. Buddhism was as circumspect as Christianity about this issue even though slavery was common all across Asia. This paradox is a direct consequence of what we have seen in the introduction. Individual and collective minds are invariably trapped into a particular worldview, which defines the boundaries inside of which things can be known; what lies beyond its limits is simply invisible.

Therefore, while the Bible and the various teachings of the world's major spiritual traditions contain numerous invaluable insights that remain relevant to modern life, we ought to remain aware of the historical contexts from which they emerged. The *Declaration of Human Rights* of the French Revolution from 1789 and the *Universal Declaration of Human Rights* of the United Nations from 1948 (which addressed issues such as slavery and the rights of minorities, women, and children) were overall more inclusive and more in tune with the moral landscape of their time than those centuries old traditions. Over time, humanity has moved along. Its field of awareness has undeniably expanded, even if this process has proved chaotic and heterogeneous, to say the least. We are nonetheless starting to get a sense of the dynamics that have constantly reshaped moral standards of human cultures.

Developmental psychologists, such as Abraham Maslow, Jean Piaget, Erik Erikson, Jean Gebser, Robert Kegan, Jane Loevinger, Susanne Cook-Greuter, Lawrence Kohlberg (this list is by no means exhaustive), and before them the spiritual leader Sri Aurobindo, have all emphasized the fact that the human mind matures through an orderly succession of discrete stages of increasing complexity. And their models, albeit focusing on different facets of psychosocial development, proved to be remarkably congruous with each other. The works of those pioneers culminated with a model of psychocultural development named Spiral Dynamics, originally theorized by Clare W. Graves and later popularized by Don Beck, Christopher Cowan, and Ken Wilber.[327] Their model represented a decisive breakthrough in the way that we understand cultural evolution and here is what we all need to retain from it: "Different times give different minds."[328]

Throughout history, human societies have exhibited an irresistible tendency towards increasing levels of integration, which involved groups of increasing size and populations of increasing diversity. Most primitive societies were centered around clans, in which only a few families stuck together to ensure a better survival of their kin. Later in (pre)history people started to aggregate into larger communities, clans into tribes, and tribes into nation-states. More recently, nation-states have begun to merge into multi-state organizations, and in the last century we have witnessed the emergence of global structures on the scale of the whole planet.

Each stage automatically relies on a different conception of what constitutes a sane and safe environment, which directly derives from the particular worldview that people at this stage hold as true. Clan organization confers superior levels of protection against predators and attacks from neighboring groups as well as a more systematic gathering and sharing of food. It facilitates the practice of highly cooperative tasks such as hunting and raiding. Congruent with that, a clan's worldview tends to focus on the harmony with nature, the honoring of elders, and the cult of the ancestors. At the tribal stage, the larger population size enables greater specialization among the many members of the group in cooperative farming, and also the raising of powerful armies capable of conquering large territories. Reflecting those changes, tribal worldviews gave birth to sophisticated polytheistic mythologies in which each god would represent and protect a given social function—farmer, warrior, merchant, leader, priest, and so on.

Nation-states strengthen the authority of a central government. For that purpose they elect kings, emperors, consuls, and sultans. They enforce the respect of written laws and rely on a complex social hierarchy. And at a multi-national level, people tend to value communication, diplomacy, international cooperation, and problem resolution at a global level as the best guarantee for stability. We typically see this happen today with the issue of global warming. Each time, the new worldview embraces larger and more heterogeneous populations, more specialized sociocultural roles, and increasingly diverse sub-cultures, in other words, an increasingly intricate space of kinship. Each time, it confronts and tries to solve new issues. And each time, it generates more complex sociocultural architecture to hold that new level of complexity together. The next chapters will illustrate how key that dynamic is.

Each worldview is transmitted from one generation to the next, just like genetic information. Notice also that each new worldview includes the knowledge and concerns of all prior worldviews. As we have seen in the introduction, the fact that cultural evolution proceeds through an expansion process automatically generates an asymmetry. People at a later stage of cultural development have the enough knowledge to make sense of previous stages; yet the same is not true the other way around. We can study the way clans, tribes, and nation-states function. We can decrypt their psychology, cultures, and worldviews. However, early stages do not have the means to apprehend more complex worldviews. For clan members, clan life is not only the norm, but also the only lifestyle available in their worldview. Accordingly, they perceive their own social organization, ethics, and belief system as wisdom and common sense. Damaging nature is bad in a clan worldview not because of global warming but because you might offend the spirits. We moderns may think that respecting spirits is archaic and global warming common sense, but for tribal consciousness, respecting spirits is common sense and global warming nonsense. By the same token, for the authors of the Bible a world without slavery would not have been the promise of a brighter future but an absurdity, because they could not conceive of any social and economical alternative to the use of slaves.

Individuals and civilization at an earlier psychocultural stage of development cannot mentally grasp more complex worldviews and what later stages are about. They do not see the following stages as a "promising future" at all. They see them as foolish. In the path of cultural development, all previous steps of development occur as passé, too simple, obsolete, or archaic; still, they are comprehensible because any worldview includes all the ones that came before. On the other hand, all the steps ahead represent a leap into the unknown. And, as you certainly remember, human beings are not very keen on the unknown. In human psychocultural evolution, the next step forward seldom resembles progress; generally, it is just chaos.

The evolution of moral views proceeds from the exact same dynamic. But first, it would be useful to redefine the concept of morals in a way more relevant to our inquiry and, in doing so, remind you of some of our earlier insights. We have seen in chapter 5 that social cohesion among primates hinges on altruistic behavior. Altruistic behavior is central to conflict resolution, bonding, alliance formation, food sharing, and so forth, and without it, human communities would have been unable to grow beyond the size of clans. Evolutionarily speaking, altruism and morals are directly connected. By and large, morals are none other than culturally codified altruism. "You shall not murder," "steal," or "covet your neighbor's house" (Exodus 20) are perfect illustration of codified altruism.

Remember also that altruistic behavior operates only inside of the space of kinship. As a result, the reality of human beings ends up split in two parts.

The first one—the safe part—is delineated by the space of kinship. In this part of the world, people can relate empathically; altruistic behavior flourishes; and morals apply. Any transgression of the rules must be severely punished. The other part—the unsafe one—lies beyond the limits of kinship. There lies the world of the "others," those from whom problems may come, those from whom one should keep away, and those that might soon have to be eliminated. Many primitive cultures did not even conceive the people outside their own tribe as human beings.[329] And in this part of the reality, empathy is absent; altruistic behavior is suppressed and morals do not apply.[330]

Since ancient times, the Golden Rule has enjoined people to "in everything, do to others what you would have them do to you"[331] (which represents a fair definition of reciprocal altruism) or, according to a relatively close version, "love your neighbor as yourself"[332] (which is somehow almost what empathy is about). However, the real and only problem has always been defining who your neighbor is. Another individual? Another tribe? Another race? Another social caste, religious community, gender, sexual identity group, or even species? As E.O. Wilson sagaciously observed: "Human beings are consistent with their code of honor but endlessly fickle with reference to whom the codes apply."[333]

Now, we have seen in chapter 6 that kinship that originally was only blood-related has extended to the symbolic realm very early in history of humanity. In most human societies, it is not blood but cultural commonality—myths and rituals—that have held communities together. In other words, kinship is primarily defined by the worldview. Thanks to this extraordinary transition, unique to the human species as far as we can tell, the space of kinship could expand, with people's worldview being the only limit. Moral evolution directly results from this widening of the boundaries of the space of kinship, which I also like to call the space of empathy (or "empathic space"; the philosopher Peter Singer speaks of an expanding "circle of care" to describe the same thing).[334] People are suddenly able to include individuals whom they previously viewed as unknown, alien, and hence, potentially dangerous. They can relate to them from a first person perspective, that is, as themselves. And human history is relatively consistent in that respect: the limits of the space of empathy of the dominant group have expanded by integrating individuals and communities which previously were viewed as outsiders or inferiors, bestowing on them the privilege of sharing equal rights and equal status.

Look at the outlawing of slavery, for instance. The process was initiated in Portugal, England, and France in 1761, 1772, and 1794 respectively. The United States abolished slavery in 1865 and Brazil, as nearly the last country to do so, waited until 1888. But despite the persistence of slavery in a few countries around the Indian Ocean and the Middle East, most nations had banned slavery, which had been an essential aspect of most if not all civilizations since antiquity, in a remarkably short time-period. In the past, all the rebellions of slaves had sooner or later been repressed by bloodshed. But this time, history operated differently. Over the course of a century, a new moral standard spread across the world. Slaves, who by then were mostly of African origin, were invited to join the institutional kinship because enough people could relate to them empathically.

The same is true regarding the legalization of women's right to vote during the twentieth century. The bravery of women activists certainly had a part in that change; yet in most cases the laws implementing women's political rights were passed by men only. One cannot downplay the impact of men's new state of mind in this institutional revolution. For a majority of men, the space of empathy had expanded to include women. And the same thing can be said about laws of religious freedom, civil rights, women's and gay rights, or even children's rights (adopted by the United Nations only recently in 1989). And this list is by no means exhaustive. But always, what was viewed earlier as the privilege of a few is later seen as the norm for all.

However, until a population is ripe for an expansion of the space of kinship (which often but not always correlates with a shift in worldview, as we will see in detail later), what you get is a fierce resistance against the very idea of accepting these new "others." People feel threatened. Obviously humanity has not progressed linearly toward a generalized state of empathy for others. What I am presenting here is a broad evolutionary trend that involved many pauses, temporary regressions, fragmentations (e.g., a century separates the abolitionist and civil right movements), and complex oscillations (we will see that the history of homosexuality exemplifies this perfectly). The world's global moral evolution did not hinder the horror of two world wars, the concentration camps, and the many genocides across Europe, Asia, and Africa. What is more, moral development is inevitably heterogenous among large populations. All people in a given culture are not at the moral front line of their time. As I wrote earlier, "you shall not commit murder" will never give you an estimate of the murder rate, yet it will still give you an accurate idea of the level of moral development of a given culture. Today's global level of moral development is significantly different from what it was in the past. It would be hypocritical to deny that taken globally, modern mores show that people feel far more empathy for their neighbors than they did in the past.[335]

The Logic of Homosexual Rights

Advocates and opponents of gay rights and same-sex marriage cannot hear each other for the simple reason that each camp fails to relate empathically with the other camp. From a homophobic viewpoint, a world that includes same-sex love is not a world with "more love," it is a world doomed to fall into chaos. Homosexual relationships are outside of their space of empathy because homosexual love is outside of their worldview. And as long as people are not ready for the shift, what lies ahead on the path of moral development is sensed as a loss of their value system. Even if they can see one on television and sometimes even around them, the "homosexual" remains an "unknown," just like ghosts, sea monsters, aliens, and other demons. As a consequence, they cannot easily relate to the pain and frustration of same-sex partners.

My point is that the various claims of the homophobic discourse are nothing but intellectual elaborations and justifications. Whether in a discussion about God, nature, aesthetics, or psycho-medical theories of all sorts, it does not matter; the arguments that homophobes use to demonstrate the immorality and wrongness of homosexual behavior are just all that is available in the prevalent worldview that can support their urgent need to keep the danger at bay. They simply build a shield against a reality that they cannot grasp. What counts is to avoid the threat. By continually arguing with the specifics of homophobic discourses instead of addressing the threat that homosexual acts and same-sex love represent in homophobic consciousness, the pro-homosexual discourse keeps talking to a wall. All attempts by homosexual activists to challenge and mute the homophobic hatred have fallen flat. A renovated—integral—discourse on homosexuality ought to avoid sterile confrontations with homophobic cultures and focus more on the reasons homosexuality remains fundamentally incompatible with a homophobic worldview.

Although anti- and pro-homosexual camps are both equally deaf to the position of the other side, there is a difference between the lack of empathy of the homophobes' camp and ours. I infer that the pro-homosexual camp, in its great majority, is perfectly equipped to decipher the logic of homophobic dynamics. On the other hand, the homophobes' camp is seldom able to comprehend the homosexual world and connect it to its moral values. This asymmetry—which is none other than the one we have discussed earlier regarding moral evolution—gives the pro-homosexual camp a very special responsibility. Simply said, because we are more "adult" than they are, we should behave more like "adults" than they do.

At the same time, the pro-homosexual camp would be well inspired to remain extremely humble. By no means does its agenda constitute the ultimate point of humankind's moral evolution. Homophobia is not the "last acceptable prejudice," as suggested by some.[336] It is only the last prejudice we can see at the horizon of our own worldview. How could we possibly recognize all the things that we are now willing to tolerate for the sake of our own comfort—animal mistreatment, ecological irresponsibility, third-world poverty, no universal access to knowledge, prison violence, and, even more so, all that we cannot even conceive yet—which will be considered as cruel, inhuman, or absurd for generations to come? We all are conservative in the face of what we do not know. And we all have our own version of what chaos could look like.

Sexual identity is the latest moral frontier, but not the last one. It is one that many countries in the world are crossing today. Nevertheless, at a global level, the fight for gay rights must remain a top priority. Homosexual people cannot be denied the right to meet, love, live, marry, have or adopt children, the right to be socially recognized as well as institutionally and economically treated like any couple, the right to public dignity, respect, and happiness, and as children and teens, the right to grow up in a safe and nurturing environment. Those rights must become inalienable and sacred, and capitulating has never been an option. Yet we also need to understand as we go forward that some people are terrified by the future we are offering them because they cannot understand it. What we need to address is not how they justify their aversion and their violence but rather what causes the terror behind it. But now that we have accepted the fact that homophobic views have their own logic and that, no matter what, they cannot hear what we tell them, how on earth are we supposed to promote gay rights? My answer to this question is threefold.

First, let us remind everybody that we all benefited from that same evolutionary process at one point of our collective history. African people are no longer slaves, women are no longer men's servants, and Jews are no longer confined to ghettos, thanks to an empathic process. Take Japan and the United States, or European nations: these countries are no longer engaging in warfare today, also thanks to an empathic process. For the same reason, our justice system no longer uses torture (at least routinely). Democracy, which is a form of government more empathic than despotism, is more widespread today than it ever was. Social justice, which is more empathic than reckless socioeconomic competition, is also more common now. While this list is not exhaustive, and despite numerous ups and downs, today's world displays globally far more empathy than it did in the past. It is therefore undeniable that bestowing empathic feelings upon an always greater circle has fueled humanity's moral evolution.

Thus any moral framework that we see today, even the most conservative one, is the product of a historical process, that is, of an expansion of the space of empathy. Said very simply, today's conservatives, despite claims to the contrary, are the liberals of the past. They too have evolved. They still stand for maintaining the status quo; yet their status quo has changed. (As the American philosopher Susan Neinam responded in a recent interview, "To imply that the way things *are* is the way they *have to be* is to be blind to philosophical developments, to be blind to historical developments"[337]). They are no longer those who fought against civil rights and women's rights in the 1960s. Now they oppose gay rights because this is where the moral frontier lies. This implies also that the dignity that all of us enjoy today is only possible thanks to an empathic transformation of past mores. How paradoxical then to see that the great majority of the people hostile to gay rights can express their views today thanks to the empathic process that they now refuse to grant gays. None of these people—women, racial minorities, workers, descendants of immigrants and so forth—would have been allowed to speak up in the past, but they have forgotten this. It might be time to remind them.

Second, some homophobic activists have reasoned that accepting homosexuality would eventually lead to legalizing other "alternative" sexualities such as polygamy, incest, pedophilia, or bestiality.[338] Since we now understand that from a homophobic standpoint, homosexuality is not different from any other illicit sexual acts since they are perceived as equally unknown and dangerous, we can now challenge their point of view very specifically.

In order to evaluate the moral values of "non-conventional" sexualities, the mental and physical integrity and the free will of all parties involved in the act ought to honored, which implies to take into account the first-person perspectives of all the parties participating in the sexual act (a selective empathy would be the opposite of empathy). All forced sexual acts, whatever their nature or context, obviously failed the test. But what about other sexual acts?

To the best of my knowledge, pedophilia presupposes the free expression of the sexual desires of an adult at the expense of a child's integrity. Children are psychologically and emotionally too vulnerable to resist the advances and psychological manipulations of a grown-up. Their free will is still developing; hence the prudence principle must apply. So, pedophilia fails the test. Regarding incest, a parent has a unique power over his or her own child, even when the child becomes an adult. Nothing should jeopardize the protective role that is demanded from a father or a mother. In all cases, incest betrays the sacred bond between the parent and the child. Incest between adult siblings should be looked at differently. When taking into account all possible perspectives, one must still consider the perspective of potential offspring who might suffer from genetic defects as a result of inbreeding. Sibling incest appears moral only when it is between two responsible adults who consent not to conceive. And unless someone convinces me not only that an animal consented freely to copulate with a human being (provided that it did not involve the rape of an animal), but also that the animal's consent emerged from a similar level of consciousness as that of the human partner, the case of bestiality can also be easily ruled out.

What about polygamy then? The traditional practice of polygamy essentially bestows on men the right to have many wives. Traditional polygamy undervalues women's dignity and cannot, therefore, constitute a moral improvement in a modern context. In the case of multiple romantic relationships among consenting and responsible adults, provided that there is no gender, socioeconomic, or cultural bias (which appears to be the case in "polyamory") one cannot deny their right to love or refuse their social acceptance.

On the other hand, modern homosexuality involves consenting individuals, fully aware of who they are and fully responsible for their lives. Homosexuals have proved that, when given a chance, and often despite being given none, they were able to create relationships based on love, self and mutual respect, and reciprocal care. And with all our respect and empathic feelings for those who cannot understand or accept that, the repression of homosexuals must stop and homosexual love must start being honored in all parts of the world.

Third and very importantly, we need to find efficient ways to alter homophobic worldviews in order to foster the complete assimilation of gays (including couples) within the empathic space. This will be investigated in several of the chapters that follow.

THE PROBLEM OF HOMOSEXUALITY

Before we begin exploring the history of homosexuality, you may have noticed that, in the previous paragraph, I did not mention homosexuality in vague terms but specifically referred to it as "modern homosexuality." Modern homosexuality is perfectly compatible with modern moral standards. No rational argument can today justify the arbitrary prohibition of sexual and romantic relationships between two consenting adults of the same sex. However, the homosexual discourse has overall been remarkably oblivious, often ambiguous, and unfortunately sometimes, plainly hypocritical, about the moral status of traditional forms of homosexuality.

While premodern homosexual cultures were congruent with the prevailing morals of their time, they clash across the board with contemporary moral views. Typically, transgenerational homosexuality implied a sexual relation between a mature and often married man and a youth, which these days would qualify as both pedophilia and adultery. During the Classical Age, the sexual eligibility of a youth was determined by beardlessness and near adult height, which mostly comprised youths from the age of twelve to nineteen. On top of that, the youth ought to be the sexually receptive partner (either anally or intercrurally, depending on the city they came from), no matter what their preference (if any) was. Remember that in ancient times, sexual versatility, so central to modern homosexual culture, was total nonsense.

Ritualistic homosexual practices would encounter some serious opposition, were they to be translocated outside their Melanesian cultural microcosm. Young adolescents were literally kidnapped by their male elders, brutally carried away from their mother and family to the forest, and either anally penetrated or forced to fellate older males until ejaculation. According to the local symbolic narrative, sperm possessed the magical power to transmit the maleness of the adult into the immature body of the juvenile; spitting never was an option. Cases of boys having anal intercourse with more than seven men during the same night were reported.[339] Melanesian homosexual rituals had absolutely no concern for things like consent or mutual pleasure, to say the least (even if they sometimes occurred). Today, everybody would denounce those rites as sexual abuse of minors.

Transgender homosexual relationships did not bestow more freedom on same-sex lovers either. Social norms demanded that the stud male penetrate the feminized male. Often, feminization presupposed the ablation of the genitals, at least partially. If transgender homosexual relationships exist today in the midst of gay culture, they result from an authentic choice but no longer from a social convention. And so does genital ablation.

What is more, traditional homosexualities had no tolerance for same-sex relationships as we understand them today: a loving bond between two individuals of equal status regarding age, gender, sexual role, and social rank. This type of relationship was unimaginable in ancient Greece, Islamic culture, Asia, pre-Meiji Japan, and

New Guinea. Never would you have encountered symmetry and balance between same-sex partners. Instead, traditional homosexual cultures were obsessed with the symbolic complementarity between maleness and femaleness, insertive and receptive, in other words, with ranking. Premodern homosexualities were less preoccupied with the mental well-being and sexual fulfillment of both partners than they were with making sure that homosexual desires would not disrupt the reproductive process. This did not happen out of mere indifference or even rigidity, but only because those concepts were absent from their worldview. Believe it or not, when it comes to sex and sexual identity, happiness and inner integrity are remarkably recent ideas.

Yet, that premodern homosexualities are inconsistent with modern moral views would not be so important if it were not for the following consequence. Grounded in our current worldview, we—defenders of same-sex love—would disown most and possibly all traditional forms of homosexuality if they were to be transposed into our own sociocultural setup, among our own people, or into our own lives. We could not honestly tolerate them. Hence, it may be legitimate for a more evolutionary advanced moral framework grounded in a more inclusive worldview and a wider empathic space to challenge and possibly reject archaic forms of homosexuality. Keep that in mind. This will be the new context through which we will be looking at homosexual history.

Let us face it, our recurrent nostalgia for other times and other places where homosexuality was celebrated or at least practiced, stems largely from an illusion. The hard-won freedom that gay men and lesbians enjoy today has never existed before. Modern homosexuality demonstrates not only the remarkable resilience of homosexual desire and homosexual love, but even more so its extraordinary capacity to reinvent itself. Note that the phenomenon is not unique to homosexual relationships. Premodern heterosexual cultures ("heterosexualities"), which had been for the longest time centered around polygamy, male dominance, bridal virginity, and so on, have also become largely obsolete today.

The emergence of modern homosexuality in the Judeo-Christian West is nothing short of revolutionary, not only regarding the history of the Western world, but also regarding the entire evolutionary journey of homosexuality. Yet the long transition between premodern and modern homosexual culture was also a time of great sorrow. For nearly fifteen centuries, sodomites lived in fear and in shame, and their desires were often silenced in bloodshed. But now, homosexual history can reveal its logic. We have a solid context to understand what happened and we are now ready to read the story again, with new eyes.

The Fall from Grace

How and why did Western civilization develop a brutal aversion to all forms of same-sex behavior? As you know, the prohibition against same-sex activities was only one among many others in the Torah. In that regard, historians David Greenberg and Marcia Bystryn asked particularly pertinent questions:

> If the early Christian church abandoned some Jewish practices (such as dietary restrictions, circumcision, and observance of Saturday as the Sabbath), why did it preserve others? If, in the course of centuries, Christians modified or abandoned some early doctrines, such as the prohibition of usury and, for Protestants, priestly celibacy, why not all? If the condemnation of homosexuality in other religions had little if any impact on popular attitudes, why did it have such a powerful impact on Jews and Christians?[340]

The Jews themselves had managed to restore the practice of usury by the end of the third century CE, even though the latter appears to violate no less than six times the laws of the Torah.[341] Equally unexplained is the fact that female homosexuality, a relatively minor concern in the civilizations of antiquity, was first prohibited and second, systematically associated with male homosexuality, starting from the first centuries of our era. Lesbian love, which is nowhere mentioned in the Torah, appears suddenly and concomitantly in both the Christian and Rabbinic discourses. Why? The historical singularity of same-sex love is all at once baffling and captivating.

It is justly held that the history of homosexuality can only be understood inside the larger context of the history of sexual mores and morals. This said, few scholars have offered solutions to our problem. John Boswell linked the acceptance of homosexuality to the variation in the level of urbanization. While his thesis appears weakly supported by historical data, it retrospectively had the merit to try cracking an enigma that most historians had simply neglected to mention. Greenberg and Bystryn remind us that "early Christian views of sexuality were formed in the context of a broad trend toward asceticism in the Hellenistic and late Roman Empires and of the competition between what was eventually recognized as the Orthodox Christian Church and other religious cults, including the Gnostics,"[342] which became the prevalent view after the groundbreaking publication by Michel Foucault of his *History of Sexuality*. It is true that in the centuries around the beginning of the Common Era, we progressively see develop a profound shift in the sexual mores of the cultures located around the Mediterranean. This "sexual revolution," which would irremediably alter the fate of homosexuality, was initiated independently—geographically and conceptually—by the two peoples that have most influenced Western culture: the Jews and the Greeks.

Still, the rise of ascetic morals may explain the timing but hardly the astonishing intensity of this phenomenon. It would also be of very little help when considering modernity's enthusiastic rallying to the Christian homophobic discourse, the planetary triumph of homophobia in the nineteenth and twentieth centuries, and its remarkable resilience in many African and Muslim countries today. We are still missing many pieces of our puzzle. It might then be the right time to try to interpret homosexuality's sociocultural past against the backdrop of the sociobiological and evolutionary constraints placed upon human culture, which were patiently laid out in the earlier chapters. But before delving further into this new chapter, I wish to draw your attention to two important points.

First, we will have to come to terms with the fact that, any way you view it, homosexual history is mostly a history of male homosexuality. Until the twentieth century, female homosexuality is overall far less documented than its male counterpart.[343] In a species where almost universally males strove to curb the sexual temptations of their females, lesbian loves remained concealed from the public eye most of the time. Denouncing this as an injustice, resenting it, or blaming it on men or on me, is unlikely to change the facts. Yet the patent asymmetry between the respective visibilities of male and female homosexualities has had another major consequence: males engaging in homosexual acts were by far the main targets of homophobic hatred and violence.[344]

Second, at no point does this chapter pretend to be historically exhaustive. It concentrates on Mediterranean cultures and covers a period that we commonly call classical antiquity, overall ignoring all other cultures where traditionally homosexual behavior was not a major issue (provided that it was congruent with the prevailing sociocultural model). The paragraphs that follow do not even intend to offer a complete account of historical events, nor even a short history of homosexuality. Excellent works have been published elsewhere.

However, I intend to show here why the paradigm change that led to the general prohibition of all types of homosexual acts in the West became increasingly attractive for the populations located inside the limits of the Roman Empire at the beginning of the Christian Era. Rather than trying to be exhaustive, my analysis aims at grasping, through selected examples, where, when, and, most importantly, why homosexual love ended up having the destiny that we know. I want to illustrate how an integral analysis of homosexual history—and by integral I mean pluralistic, evolutionary, and informed by all fields of knowledge, as defined earlier in this book—can help us untangle this issue. In other words, I would like to demonstrate that we do now have a necessary and sufficient epistemological framework to accomplish a mini-miracle: to make sense of homosexual history.

THE JEWS: DIFFERENCE AND PURITY

Starting around the twelfth century BCE, nomadic tribes from the Canaan central highlands began slowly to coalesce into what eventually became the kingdom of Israel. Jews were racially indistinct from their Semitic neighbors. Very early on in Jewish history, defining their difference became a matter of survival, and building a Jewish identity imposed itself as a political priority. Archeologists have noticed, for instance, that pork bones vanish from Jewish settlements specifically as early as the ninth century BCE, proof of very ancient drive to set cultural boundaries. The exile to Babylon, and the quasi-continuous occupation of their land by Persians, Greeks, and Romans only exacerbated this vital necessity. Thus, for the Jews, religion represented a powerful tool geared to consolidate a fragile national identity, so often on the verge of collapsing.

Jewish religious culture combined an unprecedented theological creativity with a relentless emphasis on their ethnic difference. Admittedly, Jews appear to have been the first people to introduce a clear prohibition of homosexual acts in their book of laws. (That Jews were influenced and possibly preceded by Zoroastrianism, which developed in Persia around the same time, regarding this issue remains an open question; similarities are striking.) The outlawing of male same-sex behavior is indisputable and appears in the Torah twice: "Thou shalt not lie with mankind, as with womankind: it is abomination." Leviticus 18:22 and "If a man also lie with mankind, as he lieth with a woman, both of them have committed an abomination: they shall surely be put to death; their blood shall be upon them." Leviticus 20:13.[345] And I now would like to revisit with you the complex rationale behind this prohibition.

First, it is crucial to notice the Torah's barring of male but not female homosexual behavior. This contrast, quite stunning at first glance, reminds us how much we need to free ourselves from modern cultural norms and, instead, endeavor to grasp the logic of ancient morals within their own historical background. The differential treatment between male and female homosexual behavior emphasizes a point already raised that should no longer surprise us: sexual activities of males and females have elicited very distinct responses in premodern cultures. Men often closed their eyes to women's affairs with other women as long as they jeopardize neither the paternity of their children nor their reputation. In addition, in Jewish culture (and many other cultures of antiquity), women's activities came under their father or husband's authority, and, for the most part, the Torah addresses women through men.

Scholars, such as Daniel Boyarin, have argued that the biblical prohibition concerns only male anal intercourse.[346] Sexual enjoyment between males other than anal penetration, he contends, qualified as masturbation, which is not forbidden in the Torah. But regardless of how stringent the two prohibitions of Leviticus might have been for their authors, male Jews were certainly not immune to the implacable rule of male ranking. Jews—so often under the domination of their neighbors and constantly struggling to maintain the integrity of their state and culture—must have feared the degradation of status and the feminization associated with the passive part. Leviticus 18:22 and 20:13 can be viewed as a legitimate attempt to culturally structure their terror of being dominated by foreign males. (According to recent historical analyses, the Holy Code of Leviticus, which contains both prohibitions, appears to have been written during the exile to Babylon, which would justify even more the stress put on preventing the sexual penetration of Jewish males.)

In that regard, Jews exhibited the same anxiety concerning male sexual receptiveness as any other culture of their time.[347] If early Mesopotamian[348] law codes were silent about homosexuality, spreading false rumors on someone's passive homosexuality was fined, and the homosexual rape of a neighbor condemned by law during the Middle Assyrian period (fifteenth to tenth century BCE). In Hittite culture (which flourished in what is now Turkey from the eighteenth to twelfth centuries BCE), law codes prohibited father-son incest only. In Egypt, one can still discern the negative moral charge placed upon the anal receptiveness of males through their mythology, and in particular, in the complex relationship between the gods Seth and Horus.[349] Egyptian mythology recounts how Horus and Seth competed for Osiris's succession in front of the other gods. During the night, Seth covertly inseminated Horus anally. This fact horrified Horus's mother, Isis. On the other hand, it authorized Seth to proclaim his maleness before the other gods: "Let me be awarded the office of Ruler [. . .] for as to Horus, the one who is standing [. . .], I have performed the labor of a male against him." Immediately, "The Ennead [the nine gods involved in the trial] let out a load cry. They spewed and spat at Horus's face."[350]

Thus, while Seth could afford to brag publicly about having inserted Horus anally, Horus only receives contempt for having played the receptive part, even against his will. And of course, we have seen that Greeks and Romans, who became the successive masters of Palestine in the footsteps of Alexander the Great (fourth century BCE), and who profoundly influenced Jewish culture, were highly preoccupied by maintaining the integrity of the status of the adult male—one that shall not let anyone penetrate his body.

In sharp contrast, the Zoroastrian canon proves to be strangely similar to that of the Torah: "The man that lies with mankind as man lies with womankind, or as woman lies with mankind, is the man that is a *Daeva* [demon]; this one is the man that is a worshipper of the *Daevas*." "The guilty may be killed by anyone, without an order from the *Dastur* [high priest]."[351] Because indeed, similar to

Zoroastrianism, Leviticus 20:13 contends that both partners shall be put to death, as "both" committed an abomination. Hence, it does appear the Jews innovated in that they opted for a brutal outlawing of anal sex regardless of the receptive or active role. And we now need to explain this.

Jewish monotheism crystallized a radically new vision of the spiritual universe. Which ones, among the many innovations operated by Judaism, have been the most significant with regard to Western history is, obviously, a debatable matter. Yet, as far as we are concerned here, the most novel property of Yahveh, the unique God of the Jews, is to be sexless and still, of a predominantly male gender.[352] Yahveh's invention by Jewish monotheism bares an unprecedented sexual revolution in its design. In all polytheist religions, sexual energy, procreative or not, was an omnipresent element of the divine.[353] Sexual desire, sexual acts, and sexual creation were represented in all ancient polytheist mythologies (this connection between sex and the sacred is still strongly engrained in Hinduism and Shinto, for instance). As scholar Richard Hoffman justly points in his remarkably insightful article, *Vices, Gods, and Virtues*, Yahweh creates by his word, not through sexual intercourse.[354] With the advent of Jewish monotheism, sex is simply deleted from the domain of the sacred.

Parallel to this, the paradoxically sexless maleness of Yahveh introduced a sharp gender polarization, which, as we are going to see, constitutes a cornerstone of Judaism as much as monotheism itself. The relationship of Yahveh with his people is also that of an active masculine principle—God—with a receptive feminine element—the people of Israel. This sacred connection defines a "divine axis," God and the chosen people. At the same time, it institutes a gendered and sacred hierarchy, in which, needless to say, the masculine principle reigns. It does so also because the masculine principle is associated with the power to create. Yahveh is not only the totality of the divine, but he is also the creator of the universe and mankind (and I intentionally use mankind here only to remind you how much the concept of "universal" has traditionally been viewed as masculine, for the exact same reason). This attribute is unusual in the ancient world. In most, if not all, other mythologies, creator gods—"sky gods"—are often obscure, abstract rather than anthropomorphic, remote from people, and rarely worshipped.[355] In contrast, male-gendered Yahveh combines both aspects of creator and omnipresent master.

His superiority over the world is unchallenged, and so is that of males over females. The social supremacy of males, patriarchy, in short, has existed since prehistory (the alleged existence of prehistoric matriarchies is not supported by anthropological data). So Jews were not particularly innovative in that domain. What Judaism invented is an exclusively male symbolic representation of the divine. Probably for the first time in human history, the feminine principle becomes archetypically subordinate to the masculine principle. Notice for instance how mankind's creation reiterates and reinforces this primordial hierarchy. Eve does not directly emanate from God but is created from a fragment of

Adam's body only to put an end to his solitude. "Adam said, this is now bone of my bones, and flesh of my flesh: she shall be called woman, because she was taken out of man." (Genesis 2:23)[356]

It is impossible to understand the logic of Abrahamic monotheism without realizing the utmost importance of this hierarchical polarity. Why? Because this polarity—primordial and sacred, since it is connected to the divine; hierarchical, since the masculine prevails over the feminine; and unique, insofar as monotheism unlike polytheism offers no other spiritual alternative—reflected the perfection of the origins. It mirrored the fundamental complementarity at the source of all life. It was the one ultimate truth. This new spiritual polarity of Jewish monotheism gave birth to a symbolic ideal—an eternal and universal template—after which everything in Jewish life ought to be modeled. And of course the practice of sexual intercourse ought to be in the image of God's relationship to Israel.

The impact of Jewish monotheism was paramount. In fact, an entirely new cultural paradigm emerges from it: (1) there is only one God; therefore there is only one truth, one moral, and one law; (2) the primal archetype of human relationships is contained in the special alliance between God and Israel; and (3) God—almighty masculine power and life giver—protects and, when necessary, punishes his obedient beloved—Israel, the chosen people, God's feminine counterpart. Congruent with those views, ancient Jewish laws enforced a rigorous discipline regarding sexual relationships:

> If a man commits adultery with another man's wife—with the wife of his neighbor—both the adulterer and the adulteress must be put to death. If a man sleeps with his father's wife, he has dishonored his father. Both the man and the woman must be put to death; their blood will be on their own heads. If a man sleeps with his daughter-in-law, both of them must be put to death. What they have done is a perversion; their blood will be on their own heads. If a man lies with a man as one lies with a woman, both of them have done what is detestable ["an abomination" in King James version]. They must be put to death; their blood will be on their own heads. If a man marries both a woman and her mother, it is wicked. Both he and they must be burned in the fire, so that no wickedness will be among you. If a man has sexual relations with an animal, he must be put to death, and you must kill the animal. If a woman approaches an animal to have sexual relations with it, kill both the woman and the animal. They must be put to death; their blood will be on their own heads. (Leviticus 20:10–16)

Now the prohibition of all (male) homosexual acts, regardless of the role, suddenly makes a lot of sense. Everything that threatens the monotheist ideal is outlawed, and in most cases, the issue is quickly settled by killing the transgressor. In that regard, we must resist the temptation to introduce a modern sensitivity when reading Leviticus 20 and, in general, the entire Torah. For instance, adultery—whose banning constitutes nothing less than the tenth commandment (Exodus 20:14), which is prohibited again in Leviticus 18:20, and sentenced to death according to Leviticus 20:10—is not a crime because it shows disrespect for the spouse, which would constitute a contemporary reinterpretation of the scriptures, but only because it challenges God's primordial order. Men should not cheat on their wives because God would never cheat on Israel. We then ought to understand the prohibition of male homosexual behavior (confined to anal sex or not) in that context. A disciplined sexuality was to mirror the exclusive and sacred relationship of Yahveh with his people. While polytheism was able to accommodate as many modes of existence as there were gods, monotheism established a unique standard, in the image of God's love.[357]

Yet, once again, we ought to avoid judging the monotheist paradigm shift with modern eyes. Despite its authoritarian and obsessive ethos, the monotheist "simplification" constituted a major sociocultural evolution because truth and morals became a sacred collective good—God's law—which was fixed in time and identical for all (at least in principle). The monotheist worldview offered people a way out from ego-driven societies in which the mood of the ruler, the will of the victor, or the oracle of the priests determined the collective truth and the fate of entire societies. It represented not only a reassuring stabilization of moral values, but also a relative and yet real emancipation for human beings, regardless of their sex, and, equally ironically, regardless of their sexual tastes.

Insofar as Jews hindered by all means possible a dilution of their culture ("I am the Lord your God, who has set you apart from the nations" Leviticus 20:24), the reinforcement of strict sexual restrictions became as instrumental in the definition of Jewish identity as their diet was. The sin of idolatry, as defined in the Torah, shielded Jewish people from practices that were socially integrated in foreign cultures and very often embodied the worship of sexualized gods. Yahveh was never to be worshipped sexually, but, on the contrary, through a disciplined sexuality. All sexual activities outside or in addition to the worshiping of Yahveh constituted direct rebellion against Yahveh.[358] Anti-idolatry laws reinforced the limitation of sexual acts within the kinship delineated by the Jewish faith, ensuring the Jews would not be tempted to enjoy sex in forms that were severely forbidden by the Torah. Provided that cultic homoerotic practices were not uncommon among their polytheistic neighbors, the prohibition of male homosexuality may have helped prevent idolatry, but by no means was this limited to homosexual acts: Inter-religious marriages were strictly banned.[359] And this rule, which scholars define as "religious endogamy," is a pillar of Judaic culture even now.

Now, let us try to decipher the spiritual logic hidden behind the Torah's apparent obsession with controlling sexual behavior. In those times, people believed that the gods, or God, were at the origin of the incomprehensible and unpredictable jolts of their souls.[360] People had no concept of individuality as we understand it today. That concept would emerge much later in humanity's history. What animated people's thoughts, emotions, and, of course, desires was simply invisible to them. Psychological reality, so omnipresent in our culture today, resided far beyond the space of awareness of people in early antiquity. The direct consequence of this was that concepts, such as self-discipline and self-control, were also largely foreign in early antiquity. Unlike most of their contemporaries (with the notable exception of the Greeks, as we will soon find out), it seems that the writers of the Torah understood perfectly the dangerous power of unrestrained erotic impulses over the mind. Jewish leaders, very early on, intuited the necessity of channeling sexual instincts so as to serve Israel and its God. If not, chaotic sexual desire could only weaken the will of people and their faith, and undermine the purity of their soul.

By the same token, Jews found any kind of gender transgression distasteful. Cross-dressing was also deemed an "abomination": "The woman shall not wear that which pertaineth unto a man, neither shall a man put on a woman's garment: for all that do so are abomination unto the Lord thy God " (Deuteronomy 22:5).[361] Remember that the very straightforward monotheistic cosmology, based upon one unique ideal model and one unique truth, was ill-equipped to accommodate both sexual and gender ambiguities, which pervaded polytheistic cosmologies.[362] As suggested by some historians, Leviticus 18:22 and 20:13 may have also helped eradicate sacred male prostitution, feminized male priesthood, and ritual orgies, which were commonplace among their neighbors. It might have specifically targeted the *kadeshim*, Canaanite priests whose exact identity is still poorly documented. Most likely, they were cross-dressing and/or transgender males, which was rather common in the Middle East in those times. As it happens, in the seventh century BCE, King Josiah ordered their extermination across the land of Israel.[363]

This said, something important must be stressed regarding the sexual mores of the Jews. In early Judaism, sexual desire, albeit unpredictable and potentially dangerous, is by itself pure. Their special covenant with Yahveh lived through the strict respect of the Torah's sexual laws. Hence, in Jewish philosophy the emphasis is on the obedience to Yahveh's orders, not on the repression of one's sexual drive. Enjoying sexual intimacy with a mate is legitimate. Sex and pleasure—although no longer divine—remain integrant parts of the relation to God. In other words, the Yahveh of the Torah is a jealous god, not a puritanical one.

There is one last circumstance that could also explain why Jewish culture fostered a unique aversion to males' promiscuity. Early Jewish culture developed very strict purity laws. What would enter their mouths and what would touch their penises was not a simple matter of pleasure. Impurity/uncleanness was an unforgivable leap away from God's perfect order, that is to say, from God himself. It erased the difference that allowed Yahveh to discern his people. Notice, for instance, how intercourse with menstruating women was strongly prohibited.[364] In many cultures, including Hebraic culture, menstrual blood and excrement are symbolically evocative of death. In the logic of a world divided between pure and impure, clean and unclean, those two matters should not mix with semen—a substance that brings life—which was seen transculturally as sacred. This said, anal sex between a man and a woman is ignored in the Torah, indicating that purity is unlikely to have constituted the chief justification for the outlawing of male anal sex, or that, alternatively, more demand was put on males when it came down to sexual purity. We may safely conclude that the prohibition of homosexual acts epitomized, as much as the pork-free diet, the central role of bodily purity in structuring and reinforcing Jewish identity.

In the next section, we are going to see that the same fundamental concerns—order, control, and purity—although also extremely present, took a significantly different turn in Greek thought.

GREEK LOVE

Despite appearances to the contrary, Leviticus 18:22 and 20:13 would have never achieved world fame without the radical changes that operated at about the same time by the Greek thinkers, changes that will change the face of Western civilization forever. Now, to speak of the role that Greek culture played in the discredit of homosexual love may seem odd. Has the term "Greek love" not often been used as a tactful substitute for the word "homosexuality"? Nevertheless, it is through the evolution of Greek thought and its follow-up in the Greco-Roman world that one can find the roots of the West's attitudes toward sexuality. It is impossible to decode Christian sexual morals without recognizing the fundamental role of their double—Jewish and Greek—heritage. By the same token, it is only through the synergy between the philosophies of these two cultures in the first centuries of our era that one can understand why Christianity came to orchestrate a "dehomo-sexualization" of Western civilization. But even before exploring the progressive shift that started around the sixth century BCE, let us review the state of the sexual mores in ancient Greece at the apogee of "boy love."

At that time it was common and socially rewarding for Greek men to engage in romantic and sexual liaisons with attractive young men. As we know, the age difference was an essential element of its acceptance in Greek society. The age gap was sometimes minimal in terms of number of years, it was however crucial that it reflected a difference in the male status of the two partners. There could be only one "man," the *erastes*, and one "boy," the *eromenos* (both terms according to the Athenian terminology) and these roles were not interchangeable.[365] This ritualistic form might have tolerated borderline cases and possibly rare transgressions, it was nonetheless the only socially accepted form in ancient Greece. According to Classical Greek literature on the topic, beardlessness and nearly adult height characterized the *eromenos*, and, generally, age twenty represented the informal limit after which the *eromenos* was invited to switch gear and become an *erastes* himself.[366] Moreover, so as to not jeopardize the integrity of his future status as male, the *eromenos* ought to be indifferent to the sexual performance and unconcerned with his own pleasure. Arousal would only constitute a suspicious sign of a passive or effeminate nature, which, as we will see below, Greeks despised mightily. The Greek pederastic model—boy love—institutionalized complex rules that were designed to protect the honor of the males while asserting their inalienable right to sexual self-gratification. In addition to relationships with young men, Greek males were allowed to have concubines, visit prostitutes, and abuse slaves, a freedom that they of course never granted to their wives.

Yet one should not reduce the pederastic institution to a mere one-way process. It also entailed an efficient system of patronage, in which young men would offer their company and sexual favors in exchange for social connections and an education that aimed to prepare them for their future role as citizens and warriors. More explicitly, the *erastes*'s duty was to protect but also teach wisdom to his lover. The *erastes* represented a role model. In exchange, the *eromenos* offered his beauty—physical, intellectual, and moral—to his benefactor.[367] Often the *eromenos* was regarded as a kind of "trophy boy," an infinite source of pride for his *erastes*.[368] As Michel Foucault concluded, "in Greece, [. . .] sex served as a medium for initiations into learning."[369]

In many respects, the Greek pederastic model constitutes a typical example of reciprocal altruism. The *erastes-eromenos* relationship was the foundation of ritualized mentorship in which the masculine virtues were transmitted from adult to youth, according to a complex set of rules, customs, and morals, which have been extensively described in the specialized literature.[370] However, according to what we have seen in earlier chapters, it would seem quite surprising if all Greek males, in Athens, Sparta, or Thebes, three cities famous for valuing male relationships very highly, engaged in sexually active relationships with young men. The exact prevalence of homosexual relationships in Greek society is impossible to determine. As discussed in chapter 1, historical data tell us about how people ought to behave rather than what they actually enjoyed and often concealed behind doors. In that sense, I tend to concur with historian Robert Allen in that "many young men and older men who had little or no real interest in same-sex unions actively sought each other out so that they might pretend publicly to be lovers, constituting what we may call a heterosexual underground."[371] Ironically, the nonsexual character of many same-sex relationships was probably kept "in the closet."

Lesbian love, despite Sappho's indisputable notoriety, was largely underrepresented in a Greek culture where women were essentially seen as breeding material. It seems that Spartan women engaged in transgenerational homosexual relationships, just like their husbands, yet that is as much as we can learn from Greek authors, who, as always, paid little attention to women.[372] Only through the virulent writings of the early Fathers of the Christian Church, such as Clement of Alexandria and John Chrysostom for instance, do we find out that lesbian eroticism was far from unknown among the people that surrounded the Mediterranean Sea, which I will explore with you in due course.

Now, the existence of boy love should not hide from view that Greeks, like numerous cultures of antiquity, felt a profound contempt for feminized and sexually receptive adult males. Although the *malakos* (literally "soft man") and the *kinaidos* (effeminate) escaped public punishment and were somehow relatively well-tolerated, they were forbidden to hold public office, participate in public assembly, and have access to the gymnasium.[373] Greeks did not give a warm welcome to the *galli*, castrated and cross-dressing priests of the goddess Cybele, whose cult was imported to Greece around the eighth century BCE (a few centuries later, Romans also frowned upon their indecent parading in the cities of the Empire).[374] Non-masculine males were widely mocked in Greek literature.[375] And classically, their behavior and sexual tastes were viewed by Greek thinkers such as Aristotle as reflecting an intrinsic feminine nature, as opposed to being seen as mere acts or temporary phases.

Softness and sexual passivity were perceived as a sign of moral weakness incompatible with the responsibility and strength of character required of a citizen. For the Greeks, and probably for any other cultures lacking a defined symbolic function for transgender males, feminized males were deemed untrustworthy. In perfect agreement with the fundamental law of male ranking, they constituted a class of sub-males, a position of inferiority that was incompatible with bonding with "real" males.

It is actually worth noticing that this suspicion regarding the civic loyalty of feminized and sexually receptive males has endured in the Western collective psyche to this day. During the years of World War I, England, still fevered by the revelations of the Oscar Wilde trial, went on a crusade against homosexuals accused of representing ideal targets of blackmail for the German secret services.[376] In the 1950s, United States Senator Joseph McCarthy accused all homosexual perverts of disloyalty toward the community and the state and sought to have them banned from the military and other public functions.[377] The "don't ask, don't tell" policy that was reluctantly implemented by the Clinton administration and only repelled in 2011 during the Barack Obama presidency demonstrates the spectacular longevity of this prejudice.

In order to understand the changes that later undermined the sociocultural basis of the pederastic institution, let me remind you about a fundamental difference about the peoples that lived during early antiquity. Ordinary people viewed their gods as the ultimate origin of the energies that affected their souls, thoughts, emotions, and desires.[378] Regarding sexual impulses in particular, Greeks held the strong belief that "eros [was] a divine force emanating from the gods Aphrodite and Eros that stimulate[d] people to yearn to make love. Aphrodite had 'tamed' human beings, gods and animals."[379] Therefore, human beings were compelled to act upon Aphrodite and Eros's injunctions. Eros and Aphrodite clouded people's minds by instilling love and sexual desire in their souls, and disobeying the gods constituted a serious peril.

Ordinary people in antiquity saw themselves as powerless, totally at the mercy of the gods' whims. They did not have the same sense of individuality as we understand it today, two or three thousand years later. We already touched upon some aspects of that critical point as we were trying to understand the evolutionary logic of Judaic laws. Self-centered concepts, such as self-discipline and self-control, were foreign to people during early antiquity who did not see themselves as intellectually or emotionally independent minds. They did not have a fully differentiated ego, so to speak. Thus, their existences channeled forces that were much larger than themselves, unfathomable for ordinary mortals. What was at the source of their thoughts, emotions, and desires was so totally unknown that they only could grasp it through their mythologies. For lack of anything better, the ancients equated the incessant impulses that they experienced with the various attributes of their gods. Given the prevalent worldview of the time, this was the only natural explanation that they could find to help them make sense of who they were.

However, around the sixth and fifth century BCE, a radically new paradigm emerged in various parts of the Old World. This cultural revolution is called the Axial Age. Extraordinary thinkers— Siddhartha Guatama (aka the Buddha) in India, Lao-Tzu and Confucius in China, Zoroaster (the founder of Zoroastrianism) in Persia, and the Hebrew Prophets Isaiah, Jeremiah, and Ezekiel, in the Middle East—altered the very foundation of civilization. In the West, the Axial revolution was set in motion just a century before Socrates and Plato by another eminent figure of ancient Greece, more famous however for his geometry than for his cosmology: Pythagoras.

A DISCRETE CULTURAL REVOLUTION

Pythagorean communities started to develop in the sixth century BCE under the leadership of Pythagoras of Samos in Croton, south of Italy. And if Pythagoras is essentially remembered for the famous theorem that bears his name, he may also be considered as one of the most influential thinkers of the Western world. Not only did his spiritual views influence Plato's directly, but, thanks to the diffusion of Platonism throughout Western philosophy, the Pythagorean conception of the divine and Pythagorean ethics would, six centuries later, shape entire segments of Christian thought.

Pythagorean spiritual views of the universe were highly innovative in that they were radically dualistic. Pythagoreans saw the world as split between good and evil and read everything in terms of geometric dualities: limited vs. infinite, odd vs. even, oneness vs. plurality, right vs. left, male vs. female, fixed vs. moving, straight vs. crooked, good vs. bad, square vs. oblong, and so forth. Logically, Pythagoreans understood human nature itself as dual, torn between its material aspect—the body—which was bad in essence, and its immaterial aspect—the soul—which was good, perfect, and, in essence, divine.[380] And the urgent needs and brutal impulses of the body constituted a constant threat for the soul. In other words, the soul was imprisoned in the body. From a Pythagorean perspective, dual literally meant "duel."

The human soul belonged to the realm of geometric perfection, not to the unbearable chaos of earthly existence. Pythagoreans desperately sought to liberate the soul from the hold of the body. Scholar Kathy Gaca intuited perfectly the logical implication of such a worldview. For Pythagoreans, she writes, "human beings should lead their lives like a symphony, not like the dissonant squeaks and squawks in the warm-up before the performance. The attainment of harmony, further, requires intense constraints on human behavior, not liberties to do as one pleases."[381] Pythagoreans grew particularly worried about people's three instinctual drives—drink, food, and . . . sex. They deduced that only a strict control over people's sexuality and diet could alleviate the suffering of their soul, ease their temper, but also strengthen their progeny.

For that purpose, Pythagoreans authored the first procreative and eugenic sexual mores. Sexual relations should be performed infrequently, solely with the goal of reproduction, within marriage, and unconcerned with physical pleasure.[382] Following that same logic, procreationism forbids all other sexual activity as morally irresponsible, whether homoerotic, autoerotic, or heterosexual other than strictly dedicated to reproduction within marriage.[383] Charondas, one of Pythagoras' pupils, could not have made it clearer: "Each man must love his legitimate wife and procreate from her. Into nothing else should he ejaculate [. . .] the seed of his children [. . .]. He must not waste or abuse that which is honorable in nature and custom. Nature made seed [. . .] for the sake of producing children [. . .], not licentiousness."[384] Note that we are in fifth century BCE.

Just emerging from a Hellenic culture in which prevalent moral views were highly sympathetic of non-reproductive pleasures, Pythagorean rules did not in fact convey the strong prejudice that one might assume at first glance after reading the lines above. Pythagoreans were primarily worried about the conditions of conception and protecting the soul from the brutal violence of our bodily instincts. They valued temperance and self-control with sex, food, or alcohol. Their compulsive need to control all aspects of human life to perfection is exquisitely symbolized by the so-called "nuptial number." According to Plato's *Republic* (fourth century BCE), Pythagoreans had devised a way, notoriously complex, to determine the most auspicious timing to conceive their progeny.[385] This system aimed at producing children with strong minds, healthy bodies, and favorable destinies. However, do not let yourself be fooled again. More than expressing a genuine concern for their youths, Pythagoreans understood that the fate of the communities depended upon the quality of the future generations.

Pythagorean procreationism seldom affected Hellenistic sexual mores. Limited for centuries to relatively isolated communities, the Pythagorean sexual revolution proved nonetheless to be astonishingly prophetic. Little by little, it gained the favors of prominent thinkers. Plato and Aristotle quickly joined in. Later, the Roman Musonius, Epictetus, Seneca, and the Jewish Philo introduced a distinct homophobic tone to their own interpretations of Pythagorean asceticism. However, it was the Christian Church and its Fathers who not only devised the most radical version of Pythagorean dualism by far, but also ensured its planetary triumph.

Plato (429–347 BCE), more than any other, symbolizes the transition that would alter the fate of same-sex love in the West. When it comes down to the "love of boys," one can hardly believe that the *Symposium* and the *Laws* were written by the same man. In the first, Plato celebrated same-sex love through the voice of Phaedrus: "For I know not any greater blessing to a young man who is beginning life than a virtuous lover [*erastes*], or to the lover than a beloved youth [*eromenos*]."[386] But in his last book, Plato offered the first homophobic statement in Western culture: "I think that the pleasure is to be deemed natural which arises out of the intercourse between men and women; but that the intercourse of men with men, or of women with women, is contrary to nature, and that the bold attempt was originally due to unbridled lust."[387]

The shift is often attributed to the frequent contacts between Plato and Pythagorean communities. Most certainly inspired by Pythagorean views, nonetheless distinct from them, Plato saw sexual desire, hunger, and thirst as three primal needs and three legitimate sources of pleasure. Sexual drive, like any other, is inherent to the human body as originally and intentionally designed by the gods.[388] Yet Plato's major concern is that, albeit natural, instinctive drives are irrational. Unless tightly bridled, sexual passions can tyrannize and dominate the most precious gift of the human mind, reason, that is, *logos*.[389]

For Plato, sexual desire, toward either boys or women, must set itself free from lower instincts so as to reach the higher realms of pure beauty and goodness— Platonic love. (Later, Aristotle will also believe that pederastic relationships ought to remain chaste.)[390] In that regard, Plato's concept of eros is radically different from that of a mere appetite begotten by the gods, which was the prevalent idea in fourth century BCE Greece, as we have seen. While severing eros from sexual drive, Plato elevates the concept of Platonic love-eros to a spiritual dimension.

At the end of his life, Plato embraced procreative morals highly reminiscent of Pythagorean sexual ethics. According to Plato's utopian vision of the ideal city, "guardians and citizens also must reproduce only during their prime of life so as to give birth to the healthiest possible offspring."[391] During this time, young men are discouraged to masturbate. Their bodies and their souls should be geared toward producing strong and healthy young citizens, and the most accomplished individuals are selected to mate more frequently, just like stallions. Only when that essential duty was accomplished could they indulge in sterile sexual pleasures, such as the company of boys. In Plato's later ideal, carnal desire is to be channeled through reproduction and eugenic goals, for the good of the entire community.

Other Greek philosophers, while voicing a similar worry about people's untamed instincts, offered strikingly different solutions to the issue. Early Stoics, like Zeno (335–263 BCE) and Chrysippus (280–207 BC), untouched by Pythagorean angst, opted for more nuanced views, which are interesting to compare to Plato's. Early Stoics held a more holistic and inclusive view of the universe, devoid of any polarization between the body and the soul. Zeno, for instance, held a resolutely pantheist conception of the universe—the divine and nature are one.

The soul is an integral part of nature. Accordingly, eros does not hinder the mind's highest function—logos—as long as one keeps away from irrational passions and immoderate impulses.

So, if early Stoics indeed expressed a similar concern about the excesses of human nature, they refused to partition their spiritual universe. Rather, eros constitutes the primordial energy that moves the soul and allows it to grow, and sexuality, the very essence of the creative power of the gods.[392] Early Stoics held a midway position in that their eros, distinct from senseless erotic passion (thereby opposing the popular beliefs of the time, as seen earlier), composes the very substance of friendship, including sexual friendship (thereby contradicting Plato and Pythagoreans). Thanks to eros, a youth learns the art of reasoning, he acquires wisdom and moral rigor. The pederastic model, which involves not only sexual pleasure but more importantly the nurturing bond between an older male and a young one, was still highly valued by early Stoics.[393] Masculine friendships transcend naturally the physical interaction without having to suppress it, once again, in great contrast to Plato's views. For the early Stoics, sexuality is meaningful; it deserves its just place among other essential functions of the mind, like seeing, speaking, and thinking.

Stoics condemned all forced sexual acts against women or youths (female or male). Sexual acts were not to be performed before age fourteen. Insofar as popular Greek morals granted dominant males full power over whoever they sexually coveted, early Stoic views regarding the moral status of women and youth and the stress that they laid on mutual consent were quite revolutionary, to say the least. It is even more fascinating to learn that Zeno and Chrysippus encouraged female homoerotic activities, also for didactic purposes.[394] They encouraged symmetry between sexes. Wise adult women should, just like men, seek to establish sexual relationships with adolescent males or females. And homoerotic relationships should prevail over male-female ones.[395] In that regard, early Stoic ethics may sound absolutely remarkable; yet notice how they deeply embodied the spirit of the Axial Age, which from Greece to China, saw everything in geometric terms, symmetries and hierarchies. Inasmuch as Stoic eros remained divine and homosexual pederastic relationships were morally valued, their reasoning applied to males and females equally. Likewise Plato in his *Laws*, antithetically, condemns both male and female homosexual acts. The architecture of the early Stoic universe may differ from that of Pythagoreans and Plato but their spiritual ideals shared the same basic epistemological framework.

Even Epicurus of Samos (341–270 BCE), despite his legendary philosophical emphasis on pleasure, was in tune with the ascetic revolution of the Axial Age:

> When we say that pleasure is the goal, we do not mean the pleasure of debauchery or sensuality. Despite whatever may be said by those who misunderstand, disagree with, or deliberately slander our teachings, the goal we do seek is this: freedom from pain in the body and freedom from turmoil in the soul. For it

is not continuous drinking and revelry, the sexual enjoyment of women and boys, or feasting upon fish and fancy cuisine which result in a happy life. Sober reasoning is what is needed, which decides every choice and avoidance and liberates us from the false beliefs which are the greatest source of anxiety.[396]

THE DESACRALIZATION OF SEX

Thus, while their solutions differed significantly, Greek philosophers altogether encouraged their contemporaries to abandon a vision of themselves that reduced them to being the mere puppets of the gods. In that regard, they totally reinvented the concept of individual freedom, which until this time had meant instant gratification and essentially entailed two things: pleasure and power. From then on, a free man is a "reasonable" man, that is, a man driven by his ability to think rationally and curb his animal instincts. People are no longer conceptualized as hostages of the gods' dictates, an image that for us could be translated into people's inability consciously to control unconscious impulses. Human beings became thought of as creatures distinct from all other animals, aware of their soul, accountable for their thoughts, emotions, and desires, morally answerable for their actions, responsible for their destiny and that of the entire community. And this radical shift, which starts in Greece with the Pythagoreans, imposed *logos*, the principle of supreme reason, as the new master of the Western mind.

The rise of logos led to a serious readjustment of the sexual morals. With more self-awareness came more responsibilities. Sex became humankind's business and no longer god's. Put differently, sexuality reflected directly the quality of the individual—body, mind, and soul. To a large extent, Greek thought, just like Judaism, desacralized sex. However Greek and Jewish thinkers operated differently. In the Jewish tradition, sexual discipline represents a tangible reality by which God measures people's ability to free themselves from their psychobiological randomness. Individual liberation is contingent on Yahveh's universal and omnipotent order. Greeks did not care whether their sexuality demonstrates their obedience to a possessive god. Instead, the morality of the Greeks was of an aesthetic nature. As Michel Foucault puts it, the Greeks developed "an aesthetics of existence, the purposeful art of a freedom perceived as a power game."[397] Individual beauty, whether it was the outer beauty of the body or the inner beauty of the soul, was the foremost value of Greek philosophy. Love and (depending on who was talking) sex became an aesthetic act, which is to say, a creative act. Aesthetic rules were present all over the highly ritualized courtship of the eromenos by the erastes. "Among the Greeks there was a whole moral aesthetics of the boy's body; it told of his personal merit and of that of the love one felt for him. Virility as a physical mark should be absent from it; but it should be present as a precocious form and as a promise of future behavior: already to conduct oneself as the man one has not yet become."[398] And yet, this paradigm shift had a terrible cost. The link between sex and the sacred was severed. Sexuality left the spiritual world to become an object, an "IT," a topic of study.

Before we move on, allow me to review again the differences between the early Stoics and the Platonic-Pythagoreans camp. Doing this will tremendously help us follow how and why the concept of boy love and the moral views associated with it evolved so dramatically in the centuries that followed. In the early Stoic cosmology, the divine includes sex. The sexual acts of the gods channel their creative impulses, and the same is true of human beings. Sex and logos are not enemies, and conscious self-control suffices to harmonize their transformative power. Furthermore, early Stoics valued reproduction without reducing sexuality to strict reproductive needs. As a consequence, same-sex love preserves its spiritual essence and, logically, remains morally unproblematic.

On the other hand, Plato and Pythagoreans concurred about sex being a mere instinct that defies the logic of temperance and constitutes a threat to logos. In various degrees, they emphasized the social responsibility of the reproductive act, its importance in strengthening the community, and the primacy of collective necessities over selfish desires. Sterile homosexual love represented a disturbance of that perfect order. Reduced to an instinctual behavior, it lost its spiritual and symbolic essence, hence its moral value. Homosexual love was negated as a virtue. Instead, it became a lust one must refrain from. According to Plato's more moderate views, the love of boys ought to transmute itself from the desire of the flesh into the pure love of beauty.

Observe that the connection of sexuality to the sacred comes forth as the critical factor to explain the divergence between a worldview that praises same-sex love and one that disapproves of it, even moderately. Keep that in mind. I will have much more to say about how the relation between sexuality and the sacred plays a key role in the acceptance of same-sex love. For now, we are only starting to trace the historical origins of their divorce. In the centuries to come, the spread of Neoplatonic philosophies slowly but surely gained momentum among the populations that the Roman Empire had absorbed within its borders. The early Stoic non-dualistic vision of the universe, which kept flourishing in the East, quickly faded in the West. For better or for worse, logos gradually imposed itself as the sole master of Western thought. Extraordinary things came from it. And yet, from that time on, Greek love—the love of the youth—was doomed.

THE BROTHELS OF ROME

The contrast between two great Roman emperors who both reigned during the second century CE—Hadrian, whose lasting passion for the young Antinous represents one of the most eloquent accounts of male love to this day, and Marcus Aurelius, the Stoic philosopher who discouraged the love of boys—captures perfectly the hesitant yet irreversible transition that was occurring.[399] First, the desacralization of same-sex pleasure, and sex in general, only amplified under Roman rule. Second, we see the homosexual social space shrink step-by-step and eventually collapse. In many ways, by gradually sanctioning the departure of homosexuality from the public sphere, the Roman Empire paved the way to Christianity. And if in the Greek world the origin of this paradigm shift was primarily of a theological nature, in the Roman Empire, this evolution operated more visibly at the social level, and resulted in a spectacular improvement of the moral status of the wife and the freeborn youth. In point of fact, the so-called Christian family as we conceive it today is a Roman and purely pagan invention.

The marital institution became pivotal in the sexual morals of Roman thinkers. Unlike their Greek predecessors, late Stoic Gaius Musonius Rufus (first century CE) argued that only male-female pairs that are united in marriage as husband and wife and working on producing offspring are deemed appropriate. Seneca and Epictetus (two other Stoics of the first and second century CE) shared the position that human nature was essentially heterosexual, and childbearing was the ultimate goal of sexual relationships. They both concurred in conceiving eros as a negative energy that overwhelmed reason, logos, and were in agreement with Pythagorean thinking rather than that of early Stoics.

In the Empire, the nuclear family was increasingly seen as the fundamental unit of Roman society and marriage as the cornerstone of sexual morals. Mutual faithfulness among spouses was suddenly valued as a manifestation of virtue, inner strength, and self-mastery.[400] Marriage stabilized men by channeling their dangerous appetites and untamable temper into socially beneficial behaviors. Unlike their married counterparts, male bachelors were now viewed as potential predators. Marriage was the only proper institution for sexual relationships. Other relationships, such as homosexual bonds, were considered mere substitutes, if not socially undesirable.[401] Marriage—preferably procreative—became a patriotic act.[402]

Marital life was very different in ancient Greece. Husbands and wives evolved in socially and culturally separate worlds. The life of Greek wives was limited to running households and the reproductive duty. Greek men reserved their true passions for young males. Regarding marriage, they were essentially concerned with the legitimacy of their offspring. John Boswell explains that "At Athens and in the Roman Republic, legal heterosexual matrimony was essentially the transfer of power over a woman, who had been under the control of her father (or brother, or uncle, or some adult male), to that of her new husband (or his father, if the husband was not head of his own household), who then stood in this role as her controller/protector."[403]

In comparison, Roman wives in the Empire enjoyed a far superior level of recognition and respect from their husbands.

> [. . .] a different form of marriage became common under the Empire. Technically, the new form was *sine manu* 'without authority': the wife did not become the property of her husband, or even legally a part of his *familia*, but was conceptualized as an adult person in her own right or as an extension of her former family, now joined to the husband's (i.e., as opposed to her becoming a member

of his *familia*). Within the household (though certainly not outside it) there was a semblance of equality.[404]

In Rome, the morality of marriage proceeded from a sense of reciprocity. Marriage underwent a rapid evolution from a private into a public institution.[405] And the concept of the master and mistress of the house began to impose itself.[406]

Notice also that if the change mostly benefited women, it essentially occurred in the minds of men. It was the men who stopped seeing women as personal goods. Instead, they began to acknowledge their humanity and dignity. Women deserved to be the recipient of men's love. Their feelings were seen as being as valid as men's. Their sadness in having to share their husband with other sexual partners, which included other women, prostitutes, slaves, and boys, was perceived as being unacceptable. In the space of a few generations, Roman culture offered a new image of the husband-wife relationship, as demonstrated by the unambiguous disapproval of adultery in the Empire.[407] Extra-marital relationships, no longer the legitimate expression of male privilege, became infidelities. Increasingly, popular novels praised the notion of passionate and romantic love between the spouses. Women became objects of romantic passion and, at the same time, objects of respect.

Plutarch's dialogues in his *Eroticus* exemplify the new male-female relationship that emerged in the first centuries: "It is ridiculous to maintain that women have no participation in virtue. What need is there to discuss their prudence and intelligence, or their loyalty and justice, when many women have exhibited a daring and a great-hearted courage which is truly masculine? [. . .] They are, in fact, fond of their children and their husbands; their affections are like a rich soil ready to receive the germ of friendship; and beneath it all is a layer of seductive grace."[408] The premise of the marital revolution could be foreseen nearly three centuries earlier in the revolutionary gender-egalitarian ethics of early Greek Stoics.

Roman homosexual mores differed sharply from that of their Greek neighbors. The sexual use of male youths, which had characterized Greek culture at its apogee, and to some extent, the Roman Republic, fell into complete disgrace in the Roman Empire. Already Plutarch (circa 46–120 CE) noticed with curiosity that Roman men "absolutely refrained from free boys."[409] Remember that the Mediterranean-type of pederastic relationship was founded on a principle of inequality not only in terms of status but also in terms of pleasure. The *eromenos* was expected to accommodate his *erastes'* desires, not to enjoy his caresses. Beauty and valor as much as self-restraint and a reserved demeanor characterized the virtuous *eromenos*, and was by no means sensuality. Hence, the evolution of moral status of freeborn youths throughout the first centuries inevitably bumped into an unsolvable dilemma: When consenting, the *eromenos* shows a feminine nature that only deserves contempt; when coerced or forced, he is humiliated and legitimately vengeful.

The pederastic tradition centered around the gymnasium institution, which had distinguished Hellenic aesthetics, continued to lose its spiritual, moral, and, more importantly, its educational values. Instead, the citizens of the empire sent their children to school. Roman mothers, far more present socially and more educated than their Greek sisters, played an increasingly large role in the lives of their children. More importantly, fathers, not some older male lover, were now regarded as solely responsible for their son's instruction.[410]

Logically, Roman moralists became increasing critical of what they liked to call the "Greek custom."[411] The Skeptic philosopher and physician Sextus Empiricus (circa 160–210 CE) agreed that "homosexual sex is shameful—or rather has actually been deemed illegal."[412] Ammianus Marcellinus, the great Roman historian who lived in the fourth century CE, reported on the barbarian peoples living in Scythia that "among them the young men are coupled with adult males in unmentionable sexual unions, and spend the flower of their youth in these unseemly relationships."[413] And by the third century CE, seducing young free male citizens was severely punished by the still pagan Roman Empire.[414]

The reason freeborn Roman boys were no longer acceptable as sexual outlets for adult males is twofold: first, Roman youths were viewed as bona fide citizens of the Empire, and second, any attempt on their sexual integrity constituted a violation of the honor of the *paterfamilias*.[415] The fundamental tenet of Roman sexual mores was that no Roman male citizen was to be penetrated, regardless of his age. This said, although the evolution of collective morals is our primary focus, let us keep in mind that there have always been people to transgress these social taboos. The scandalous lives of the Roman emperors Galba, Nero, and Elagabalus remind us that some men enjoyed or even preferred the hard body of masculine adult males. But Romans disapproved greatly of this behavior, and their contempt for penetrated and/or effeminate males was limitless.

The evolution of freeborn youth's social status had a consequence that is rarely fully grasped in the specialized literature. Indeed, as a result of all that I have described, the homosexual social space shrank dramatically. Roman men enjoyed homosexual intercourse mostly with slaves (occasionally favorites) and prostitutes. While Greek love essentially revolved around the gymnasium, Roman homosexual culture flourished in brothels and slave markets. The contrast is striking. The alleged wide acceptance of homosexual behavior in the Roman Empire reported by many historians and scholars should be taken with a grain of salt; this acceptance was in fact seriously restricted. The significant shift that Roman homosexual culture represented, and how much that evolution in values opened the way to the Christian attitudes toward homosexuality, has rarely been acknowledged (or realized).[416] Christianity merely completed a process that had been largely initiated amid a polytheistic society. What early Christianity deplored was not the love between two adult homosexual men or women as we conceive it today, a kind of relationship that was disapproved in Roman society and in any other culture before the twentieth century. What was deplored was the sexual use—and abuse—of slaves, prostitutes, and, when available, boys.

LOVE YOUR NEIGHBOR AS YOURSELF

In recent years, a few scholars, all outstanding linguists, have offered bold reinterpretations of biblical texts in order to soften their homophobic tone. On that matter, I intend to be both prudent and conservative. When aware of an ambiguity in the translation of the Scriptures, I will mention the issue and, when possible, include specific references in footnotes so that readers can make up their own mind. I will discuss directly in the body of the text cases in which Paul's language concerning homosexual acts is subject to interpretation, insofar as I believe these ambiguities to be incredibly revealing. This said, insofar as nearly all Christian theologians shared the same disgust for homosexual behavior, my focus will be on trying to make sense of the Church's general fury against same-sex love and same-sex lovers rather than discussing whether the early Church was not as homophobic as we thought on the basis of arguable linguistic details. Not that those are uninteresting. They have simply diverted scholars from what, I believe, is really the heart of the problem: the profound incompatibilities between the Christian dogma and same-sex love.

Homosexuality is mentioned in none of the four gospels.[417] The sermons of Jesus, as they appear in the gospels, express little concern regarding the sin of "fornication"—the classical term for non-reproductive sex. In sharp contrast, Paul and later Augustine, Jerome, and Chrysostom, to name only a few, were clearly tormented by the issue. The source of the Church's implacable hostility must then be found not in the gospels' narrative but in the very foundation of the Christian doctrine, which are two different things. For that matter, by combining Jewish monotheism and Neoplatonism, Christianity constitutes one of the most brilliant philosophical and religious syntheses ever achieved. And as predicted, same-sex love found itself quickly trapped right at the intersection of two philosophical traditions that had both independently developed a fierce antipathy to homosexual behavior. We are now going to see how the merging of those two doctrines gave birth to the sociocultural tsunami that would eradicate homosexual behavior from the social sphere (or at least its visible part) of Western culture.

It is neither oversimplifying nor meaningless to acknowledge the central role of the Apostle Paul in that process. However, it would be difficult or even impossible to understand Paul's ideas and the evolution of the sexual morals of Christianity without mentioning first the pivotal influence of a contemporary of both Jesus and Paul: that of Philo of Alexandria. A Jewish philosopher well versed in Greek philosophy, who lived from 20 BCE to 50 CE, Philo of Alexandria produced a breakthrough synthesis of Judaism and Neoplatonism, which impacted early Christian thinkers immensely. Not only can we consider Philo as an influential figure in the history of Christian thought, but we can also recognize him as a key character in homosexual history. We will encounter his name more than once.

Philo combined the Jewish concern about the propensity to disobey God's laws with the (neo)Platonic problem of excessive physical appetites for the pleasures of food, drink, and sexual activity.[418] According to Philo's Neoplatonism, the deliberate path to the liberation of reason (logos) from the tyranny of eros becomes the *sine qua non* condition to one's relationship to God. Through this, Philo doubly justifies God's hostility against sexual desire. Sexual desire and pleasure, which in Jewish history had essentially been treated as an element of cultural differentiation from their polytheistic neighbors, is transmuted into the worst of evil—the original sin of Adam and Eve: "And this desire caused likewise pleasure to their bodies, which is the beginning of iniquities and transgressions, and it is owing to this that men have exchanged their previously immortal and happy existence for one which is mortal and full of misfortune."[419] And in this context, inevitably, the worshiping of all foreign gods amounted to the adoration of Satan.

In the same period the early leaders of the Christian Church, Paul and Peter on the front line, found themselves confronted with exactly the same issue as the Jews ten centuries earlier: how to differentiate Christians from their non-Christian neighbors. Paul took on the challenge passionately. One of his most urgent concerns was to reconcile imperatively the universal scope of Christ's message, embracing all people as God's people and, at the same time, clearly draw the limits of Christendom. To set Christians apart from non-Christians, Paul discarded all the old dietary restrictions of the Torah, the respect of Sabbath and other holy days, and even the utmost sacred ritual of circumcision of all males. In fact, for Paul the old Jewish laws stipulated in the Torah had no authority over Christians. Not only was the old Jewish covenant with Yahveh obsolete, but the mere observance of the law was no longer enough. Christians had to earn their salvation by deliberately transforming their soul. The liberation of the mind through rigorous self-discipline and the strong emphasis on individual responsibility championed by Greek thinkers constituted the perfect basis for a new alliance between Christians and God. And in that, there is little doubt that Paul imitated Philo. Yet, unlike the now Christian Paul, Philo the Jew did not discard the ancient laws of the Torah. Philo's procreationism sees as "against nature" (*para physin*) a series of sexual acts that cannot lead to producing an offspring, such as male homosexuality and bestiality, but also included sexual relations with menstruating females and even remaining married to an infertile wife.[420] Where Philo saw similarity and continuity, Paul saw a rupture. Paul recognized in logos—the *sine qua non* condition of free will and clear conscience—the very foundation of the Christian mind and its new faith. Logos became the cornerstone of the new covenant between Christians and God-Christ. It is the purifying power of logos that Paul held in mind when he taught the basis of the Christian way of life.

The control of sexuality was as central to the new paradigm that Paul preached as it was to Philo. Paul summoned Christians and non-Christians alike to renounce the sin of idolatry, which represented in Paul's mind the sensual worship of sexualized gods. Christian life, as Paul defined it, required a strict discipline that

The Fall from Grace • 141

included the renunciation of all sexual pleasures and a sublimation of all sexual desires. It demanded of Christians that they examine their inner world ceaselessly, to foresee, control, and repress any manifestation of bodily evils absolutely. And repeating a logic that we have already seen in Pythagorean thought, sexual acts among Christians must be limited to procreative purposes.

Yet Paul also had in mind to secure the survival of Christianity and its Church. He appropriated the old Jewish laws that favored religious endogamy and applied them to Christians. Consequently, sex should occur only within the indissoluble sanctified marriage and only between two Christians.[421] Outside the limits of the strict observance of sexual rules—procreationism and religious endogamy—lay the horrendous sin of fornication. Fornication constituted surrender to the force of evil, that is to say, to the influence of Satan.[422] And, not too surprisingly, homosexuality fell into that category.

Christianity inherited the meticulous desacralization, objectification, and disrepute of sexuality pronounced by Greek thinkers. In fact, it embraced the concept avidly. That said, Greek and Christian attitudes toward sexual matters were far from identical. Foucault expressed perfectly the subtle, yet critical, paradigm shift: "[. . .] while [for the Greeks] it was all right to 'use' pleasures, one had to be careful not to be carried away by them—the reason was not that sexual activity was a vice, nor that it might deviate from a canonical model; it was because sexual activity was associated with a force, an *energeia*, that was itself liable to be excessive [. . .] this force was potentially excessive by nature, and the moral question was how to confront this force, how to control it and regulate its economy in a suitable way." That is very different from Christian morals: "In the Christian doctrine of the flesh, the excessive force of pleasure had its principle in the Fall and in the weakness that had marked human nature ever since."[423] The Church reserved some of its most visceral and bitter criticisms to sexual pleasure and non-reproductive sex. Greeks' foremost concern was to help people grow wiser; Christianity's urgent mission was to ensure the salvation of their souls.

From this, a new question arises: Why did the Christian doctrine become so polarized? While the Christian universe represented a significant departure from the Jewish one, its many similarities with the Pythagorean cosmology are striking. Christianity believed in a profoundly dualistic spiritual vision of the world. The material world, which seemed to offer only chaos, pain, and tears, was a foreshadowing of hell (a feeling that must have considerably amplified as the Roman Empire kept collapsing). On the other hand, God, unique and immaterial, represented the essence of perfection (truth), goodness, and beauty. This duality between good and evil became an obsession. It structured the entire Christian universe. And more than Judaism and later Islam, Christianity put the material world at the spiritual antipode of God.[424] Christianity's only path to salvation was through a distant divinity, a God alien to his own creation. For the Church, flesh anchored humankind to a fallen world away from God's divine light. Flesh was the source of constant suffering and constant temptation. Sexual impulses hampered human access to the divine. And with Augustine (as with Philo earlier), sex turned into the original sin itself.

As astonishing as it may sound for us, Paul and Philo offered quite moderated views on sexuality. As a matter of fact, Christian theologians in the first centuries argued bitterly about whether Christians should have sex at all. Tatian the Assyrian (second century CE), whose major contribution to the Christian dogma was a harmonized version of the four gospels, professed a total renouncement to sexual activities in order to save the soul.[425] Extreme versions of Christian asceticism like Tatian's gained a significant momentum during the second century CE, particularly in the early Syrian church and various Gnostic sects across the Middle East.[426] But for many other theologians, a Christianity without reproduction would have condemned itself to an absurd death. Clement of Alexandria (second century CE), another very important protagonist in the definitions of Christian sexual morals, urged that sex within marriage was acceptable, and in that regard was more in tune with Paul's positions. Reproduction was an honorable Christian duty as long as it was kept untainted by lust and pleasure.

Ultimately Paul's and Clement's positions prevailed in the early Church, sealing the ultimate triumph of a nearly eight-century-old Pythagorean sexual revolution. Theological teachings that involved a rejection of the reproductive duty were soon dismissed as heretic. By tolerating the production of heirs for the sake of its own survival on earth, Christianity pushed the logic of duality between God and flesh to its near-end logic but not further. (God would have to wait a little longer to gather all his children in heaven!) Christianity confirmed its limitless antipathy to sexual pleasures, even within marriage and even with strictly pro-creationist goals. Above all, the Church valued life-long virginity.[427] Do not forget that for Paul, marriage was the second best choice after chastity, and that the leaders of the Church imposed on themselves the strictest rule of all: an uninterrupted sexual abstinence (even if it took centuries to be fully enforced).

Greek asceticism aimed to free human beings from their primeval nature as well as from selfish gods. The Christian Church brought them back to God thanks to the limpid authority of its dogma. The sophisticated philosophy of the intellectual elite became a universal religion that was accessible and open to all. It would indeed be inaccurate to believe that the doctrine was imposed on a reluctant population. As Gaca wrote, "the stimulus was not one of merely irrational frenzy due to some undetectable potion that early Christians drank."[428] Before Christianity became the official religion of the Empire, its devotees suffered terrible persecutions from Roman power, and yet Christianity kept rising. As far as one can tell, the citizens of the Roman Empire embraced its views eagerly and so did the barbarian tribes that invaded Europe after them. Ascetic practices were embraced by Christians in high numbers with monks voluntarily choosing celibacy as women chose chastity and married couples limited their sex lives to the strict necessity of childbearing. Christianity, whatever one may think about it, made the revolution of the Axial Age available to the community at large, regardless of their ethnic group and social class.

INVENTING THE SODOMITE

Even before the Church found itself in a position to influence the head of the Roman state, the homosexual social space had already diminished tremendously and homosexual love had already lost its moral foundation. In imperial Rome same-sex love meant primarily sleeping with prostitutes and slaves, and less and less openly with youth. True, not everybody abided by the new moral code, and the sexual extravagances of many Roman emperors remind us of that fact. Yet the virulent critics that these transgressions elicited underline the increasing success of the ascetic ideal among Romans. Even the sexual use of slaves was harshly criticized ("What need is there to say that it is an act of licentiousness and nothing less for a master to have relations with a slave?" says Musonius).[429] Despite all this, the Empire remained extremely tolerant of such practices. This ambiguity is clearly illustrated by the fact that by the fourth century CE, male prostitution was forbidden, but that in practice the law against prostitution was never enforced and taxes were still collected from male prostitutes. In the Roman Empire as in Greece, it took more than the indignation of philosophers to change people's sexual mores (and the reasons for this will be uncovered in subsequent chapters).

Roman moralists and Christian leaders shared the same abhorrence for the lack of self-discipline, gross satisfactions, and vulgar pleasures. Equally unanimous was the contempt of Romans for soft, effeminate, sexual passive men, and lesbians (the so-called tribades), which reminds us that homophobia existed well before and far beyond Judeo-Christianity, although the targets were not rigorously identical.[430] In addition, homosexual pleasures could no longer coexist with the new and improved moral status of the wife and that of the youth that characterized Roman society (which entailed an expansion of the "empathic space" or "circle of care," as discussed in the earlier chapter). The men who refused or were unable to fit the role of faithful husband and responsible father that the new moral code demanded from them inevitably became increasingly visible to their peers. Their social integration grew increasingly difficult and their legality increasingly volatile. Christianity only gave the final blow to a practice that was already being pushed out of history.

Just like Yahveh, the God of Christianity—God the Father—was also of a male gender despite his sexlessness. He was incarnated into a male, Jesus. The divine pair that God and the Church constituted manifested the ultimate perfection, the hierarchized union between the male and female principles. Thus Christianity inherited the same gender polarity as Judaism, with the same implications as those we have seen. But the incompatibility between same-sex love and the nascent Christian doctrine was even more profound. For Christians, God had surrendered material reality to Satan since the Fall of Adam. Christianity—dualistic and discarnate—disowned the manifest world. It repudiated the body as the intrinsic source of vulnerability of humankind. At the antipode of the Christian ideal, homosexual desire, already demoted to the status of lustful behavior, expressed the voice of the flesh. The Christian ascetic dogma had absolutely no space for non-procreative love, even within heterosexual marriage. It refused homosexuality as it rejected any form of fruitless pleasure or anything that would validate humankind's materiality. To its eyes, homosexual desire could only be evil.

And yet Christianity did not simply prohibit homosexual acts. It unconsciously performed a seminal act of phenomenal importance in homosexual history. And once again, we owe Philo of Alexandria—brilliant intellectual, fervent Jew, and virulent homophobe—the original "stroke of genius." Plato's final stance against homoerotic relationships, which essentially concerned males of reproductive age, was transformed by Philo's logic into an absolute outlawing of any sort of same-sex interactions, regardless of age and gender differences:

> Much graver than [sex with a menstruating woman] is another evil, which has rammed its way into the cities, namely pederasty. In former days the very mention of it was a great disgrace, but now it is a matter of boasting not only to the active but to the passive who habituate themselves to endure the disease of effemination [. . .]. These persons are rightly judged worthy of death by those who obey the law [. . .] And the lover of such [the active partner] may be assured that he is subject to the same penalty. He pursues an unnatural pleasure [. . .] and does his best to render cities desolate and uninhabited by destroying the means of procreation.[431]

Notice how in a single diatribe Philo piles up active and passive partners, pederasty, and effeminacy, as one evil.[432] We ought to grasp the extent of Philo's reinvention of the prohibition of Leviticus. A man who lies with another man is no longer a mere abomination that deserves death. It defines those who indulge in it, passively as well as actively. Philo identified those sinners as a "particular species" (to plagiarize Foucault). Moreover, for Philo, the partner of the boy lover—the pederast—is the effeminate man, which is in total disagreement with the sexual standards of his time. You certainly remember that people in antiquity were essentially preoccupied by the issue of dominance. They cared only about who was the one who penetrated versus who was being penetrated. With Philo, the receptive-effeminate and insertive-pederast partners are united together under the same label, the same injunction and the same penalty, probably for the first time in history. Individuals who until then had been archetypically totally unrelated were now regrouped under one unique concept. If there is one moment in Western culture when one can situate the emergence of a homosexual character as we understand it today, blurring the fundamental distinction that the act of penetrating had constituted since the dawn of civilizations, I recognize it here, in Philo's discourse. It is Philo who first invents the "proto-modern" homosexual (regardless of the fact that the word "homosexual" was coined only centuries later; the psycho-medical discourse in the nineteenth century only recycled a concept that was already centuries-old; that will be explored in great detail in the next chapter).

Paul incorporated the condemnation of homosexual acts in the Christian doctrine from its inception:

> Because of this, God gave them over to shameful lusts. Even their women exchanged natural relations for unnatural ones. In the same way the men also abandoned natural relations with women and were inflamed with lust for one another. Men committed indecent acts with other men, and received in themselves the due penalty for their perversion. (Roman 1:26–27)

> Do you not know that the wicked will not inherit the kingdom of God? Do not be deceived: Neither the sexually immoral nor idolaters nor adulterers nor male prostitutes [*malakoi*] nor homosexual offenders [*arsenokoitai*] nor thieves nor the greedy nor drunkards nor slanderers nor swindlers will inherit the kingdom of God. (1 Corinthians 6:9–10)

Paul's silence regarding the sexual roles played by homosexual partners according to their differences in age or status, which were so important in Greco-Roman culture, is without precedent in the ancient world. Paul's use of the term *arsenokoitai* is actually particularly revealing. Paul is apparently the first to coin this word.[433] Derived from *arseno* (men) and *koitai* (*koiten*, to lie in bed or, by extension, to have sex with), scholars have largely debated on its meaning in Paul's discourse. The church's consensus was that the *arsenokoitai* represented the active insertive partners of *malakos* (meaning literally "soft"), who are the effeminate, passive men.[434] Today however, the meaning of *arsenokoitai* is again open to multiple interpretations and the focal point of a heated debate between pro- and anti-homosexual linguists.[435] But perhaps Paul did not intend to convey anything more specific than the vague image of two men sleeping together. Scholars have desperately tried to deconstruct the genealogy of the word *arsenokoitai*, disregarding the possibility that Paul may have constructed a new word deliberately, for the very good reason that he meant to describe something that was convincingly novel, a new concept of the all-encompassing sin of same-sex fornication. In the footsteps of Philo, Paul's discourse catalyzed the emergence of a new sin—the unnatural vice—and therefore a new species of sinner, still vaguely defined: the future homosexual.

Paul made no clear reference to Leviticus 18:22 and 20:13.[436] More importantly, he uses the Platonic concept of "unnatural" (*para physin*) not the Jewish one of "abomination." Remember that the law of the Torah no longer applied to Christians. Paul inherited the Neoplatonic abhorrence of anything that represented a threat to logos, so central to the Christian faith. For him, *malakoi* and *arsenokoitai* cannot inherit the kingdom of God because they refuse to embrace the knowledge—logos—of God.

Yet Paul operated another paradigm shift in Roman 1:26–27 that proved to be decisive for the way the West theorized homosexual desire in the centuries to come and foundational for our modern concept of same-sex love. Along with male homosexuality, Paul also condemned sexual acts between women, the first and only time lesbian sex is mentioned in the Scriptures. This change is critical. Never before had lesbian love been subject to anything more than contempt, disgust, or social disapproval, and never before had it been amalgamated with male homosexual relationships, with only one remarkable exception, Plato in his *Laws*: "[. . .] the intercourse of men with men, or of women with women, is contrary to nature [. . .]."

By forbidding women to have sex with women, Paul first acknowledged the new moral status of women in Roman and Christian society. Homosexual lust became a moral choice that women had to confront directly and individually. Paul's injunction contrasted sharply with the general attitude toward women during early antiquity. As mentioned earlier, female conduct was usually under the authority of a man, either the woman's father or her husband. That is still the case, for instance, in the Neoplatonic version of Judaism envisioned by Philo. Remaining faithful to Leviticus, Philo ignored the "lust" among women.[437] Later however, rabbinic Judaism begun to discuss sexual contacts between women as well. We find them mentioned in both the Jerusalem Talmud and the Babylonian Talmud, demonstrating that this change was by no means limited to Christianity.[438]

However, Paul's logic only reveals its ironical beauty if one puts it back in the context of Axial thought. Remember that Axial thinkers conceived of the cosmos and human nature in geometric terms. They saw polarities, symmetries, and symbolic complementarities everywhere—good and evil, male and female, heat and cold, yin and yang, and so on. The Axial philosophies, such as Pythagoreanism, Platonism, Christianity, Buddhism, and Taoism, all sought to reveal the hidden order of the cosmos. Their concepts of good and bad derived directly from the cosmic order. What did not conform to this universal order was deemed "against nature" or "unnatural" (*para physin*). This concept is fundamentally different from the pre-Axial one of "*toevah*"—taboo or impurity, poorly translated into "abomination" in the King James version of the Bible. As long as lesbian relationships remained quasi-invisible in pre-Axial cultures, meaning all cultures in antiquity, they did not constitute "*toevah*." Only male homosexuality could be taboo-*toevah*. But both male and female homosexuality challenged the typically Axial cosmic order of Christianity, in which, needless to remind you, sexual pleasure was on the side of evil. Hence, Paul chastised the love between women for symmetry's sake. Thus his logical reasoning reiterated that of previous Axial thinkers, Plato and, only the other way around, the early Stoics, who some three centuries earlier strongly encouraged sexual affairs between mature and younger women also for the sake of symmetry.

Everything else that follows could be viewed as mere footnotes of Philo's and Paul's writing. Clement of Alexandria condemned the love of boys and the effeminate man (*kinaidos*) also for being unnatural in his *Paidagogos*, echoing the same homophobic anxiety as Philo and Paul.[439] Very interestingly, Clement pushed Paul's "homosexual synthesis" a step further, as Bernadette Brooten demonstrated very precisely in her remarkably documented work, *Love Between*

Women.[440] Clement employed constructs such as *arrenomixia* ("male-mixing") highly reminiscent of *arsenokoitai* from 1 Corinthians 6.[441] Even more notable, he put together a unique term—*allelobasiai*—to designate sexual contacts between men or between women indifferently, which was unheard of in the ancient world. Literally, *allelobasiai* means "going into one another sexually" and nothing more.

Another Father of the Church who played a central role in defining the sexual morals of Christianity was the Greek John Chrysostom (circa 347–407), archbishop of Constantinople, who preached against the "heinous sin" with a particular vehemence: "[The Greeks] were addicted to the love of boys, and one of their wise men made a law that *pædrasty*, as well as anointing for wrestling, should not be allowed to slaves, as if it was an honorable thing; and they had houses for this purpose, in which it was openly practiced. And if all that was done among them was related, it would be seen that they openly outraged nature, and there was none to restrain them [. . .] For as to their passion for boys, whom they called their '*Pædica*,' it is not fit to be named."[442] Elsewhere, Chrysostom recommended that they be "driven out and stoned."[443] And, commenting directly on Paul's Romans 1:26–27, he reiterated the parallel between male and lesbian loves. "All these affections then were vile, but chiefly the mad lust after males; for the soul is more the sufferer in sins, and more dishonored, than the body in diseases [. . .] And a yet more disgraceful thing than these is it, when even the women seek after these intercourses, who ought to have more sense of shame than men [. . .] For even women again abused women, and not men only."[444]

In his *Confessions*, Augustine of Hippo (354–430 CE) also embraced the Platonic idea of crime against nature: "Therefore are those foul offences which be against nature, to be every where and at all times detested and punished; such as were those of the men of Sodom: which should all nations commit, they should all stand guilty of the same crime, by the law of God, which hath not so made men that they should so abuse one another."[445] And many centuries later Thomas Aquinas (1225–1274), the other central figure of Christianity, directly quoting Augustine, sealed the anti-homosexual dogma of the Roman Catholic Church:

[. . .] it is contrary to the natural order of the venereal act as becoming to the human race: and this is called 'the unnatural vice.' This may happen in several ways. First, by procuring pollution, without any copulation, for the sake of venereal pleasure: this pertains to the sin of 'uncleanness' which some call 'effeminacy.' Secondly, by copulation with a thing of undue species, and this is called 'bestiality.' Thirdly, by copulation with an undue sex, male with male, or female with female [. . .]: and this is called the 'vice of sodomy.' Fourthly, by not observing the natural manner of copulation, either as to undue means, or as to other monstrous and bestial manners of copulation.

Therefore, since by the unnatural vices man transgresses that which has been determined by nature with regard to the use of venereal actions, it follows that in this matter this sin is gravest of all. After it comes incest [. . .][446]

Christianity thus guaranteed the disgrace of same-sex love. In 309 the Council of Elvira adopted the first anti-homosexual canon of the Church by condemning sexual acts with boys. Four years later, under the ruling of the first Christian Roman emperor Constantine the Great, the Edict of Milan marked the beginning of a new era for Christianity. It not only ended persecutions against Christians (and started those against Jews), but it eventually bestowed on the Church its immense political power. From this point on, the Church's hostility against same-sex lovers amplified rapidly. In 533 the Byzantine emperor Justinian enacted the first laws that sentenced the men who indulge in same-sex acts to death. Around the same time, the Visigoth rulers of Iberia (today's Spain) proscribed homosexual behavior by punishing both partners, passive and active, by excommunication, banishment, and castration.

In spite of this, medieval Christianity did not immediately succumb to the most extreme forms of homophobia; nor was this evolution homogeneous in all that was left of the Roman Empire. Anti-homosexual laws were not equally harsh and were variably applied among Christian nations. For centuries the Church was essentially trying to curb same-sex relationships among the clergy and in monasteries. (In fact, the Church struggled to impose celibacy and chastity on its members, but opposite-sex much more than same-sex acts among priests remained the dominant issue during the Middle Ages). It is only with the rise of the powerful inquisition in the twelfth century and throughout the Renaissance that the fear of the sodomite turned into a collective hysteria. This tragic period of homosexual history has been extensively described elsewhere.

Altogether, the discourse of the early Fathers of the Church and other moralists of the time, such as Philo, confirms the progressive emergence of a new sexual category that included all homoerotic pleasures. By coalescing the effeminate male, the lover of boys, the receptive and the insertive partners, as well as male and female same-sex lovers into a unique category, they helped crystallize a new identity of sinners. A few centuries later, this new category would define the infamous "sodomite" archetype of the Middle Ages and the Renaissance (under the label of sodomy one finds a mixed bag of various sexual activities including sex between males, regardless of the type of sexual act, any kind of anal penetration, either homosexual or heterosexual, and occasionally lesbian sex) and eventually the "homosexual." The coinage of novel terms, such as *arsenokoitai, arrenomixia,* and *allelobasiai* greatly supports this thesis.[447]

Second, it is important to understand that for Christianity at large, from Paul to Aquinas, same-sex acts were first and foremost unnatural (*para physin*), which is a typically Axial concept, and not "*toevah*" (abomination). Christian thinkers no longer felt bound to the old Jewish law. They mostly inherited their views on same-sex erotic practices from Greek and other Neoplatonic thinkers. That the unnatural vice is also presented as *toevah*-abomination in the Torah is almost a coincidence.

This epistemological shift also helps us understand the prohibition of lesbian sex, which is very difficult to justify otherwise. Unlike male relationships, female relationships seldom constituted a threat in male-dominated societies and they were rarely ritualized. But with the advent of the Axial Christian worldview added to the improved social status of women in the Roman Empire, lesbian relationships became, just like their male counterparts, "unnatural," for they were incompatible with the new cosmic order. It might not be so far-fetched to suggest that as it was falling from grace, male homosexual love dragged lesbian love down with it. What is certain, however, is that from that point on, male and female homosexual love shared the same destiny.

In the meantime, all other cultures preserved some sort of connection between sex and the sacred. They did not develop the same antipathy for the flesh and earthly pleasures as Christianity. Sex remained spiritually meaningful.[448] Asia did acknowledge the cost of uncontrolled desires on the body's vital energies, but its answers were very different. Buddhism, for instance, which is to a large extent also a very dualistic doctrine, advocated a conscious detachment from all desires, but not their eradication. Buddhists hoped to reach nirvana in their lifetime. Christians saw death as the only path to liberation. Eastern cultures—from India to Japan—invented erotic arts. Rather than trying to kill the evil, the East made it dance.

HOMOSEXUALITY'S DESTINY

Progressively, the two classical forms of same-sex relationships—pederasty (transgenerational) and the sexual use of effeminate males (transgender), who were commonly prostitutes—became increasingly marginalized and eventually outlawed across the Roman Empire. Ultimately, slaves constituted the only available sexual outlet for same-sex desire. But despite its gradual rejection, it is striking to observe the remarkable inertia of Greco-Roman homosexual culture in the same period. Roman and Greek letters of the first centuries confirm the absence of any attempt to redefine homosexual love according to the new ethic, such as the respect for the sexual integrity of youth, the dignity of the wife, and mutual faithfulness within marriage. Instead, we read lengthy debates about the love of women versus that of boys, ignoring any other alternative. Latin homoerotic novels kept celebrating the love of boys. Petronius's famous *Satyricon*, for instance, which depicts the homoerotically charged adventures of Encolpius and Ascyltos, and their mutual passion for the sixteen-year-old slave Giton, failed to break from the homosexual standard of its time. And apparently, the idea of granting effeminate men some dignity did not cross anybody's mind either.

The incapacity of Greco-Roman homosexual culture to adapt is particularly revealing of the root of the problem. What we observe in the first centuries is the inability of homosexual culture to disengage from its prehistoric structure. All traditional homosexual relations vigilantly maintained the male hierarchical order. Most ancient cultures bestowed on men a limitless and guiltless access to all sorts of sexual gratifications. At the antithesis of that, the new sense of individuality that emerged in classical philosophy and Jewish religion emphasized the necessity to reach higher levels of self-awareness, self-control, and self-responsibility. This new paradigm promoted a social reorganization (i.e., an expansion of the empathic space) that simultaneously aimed at stabilizing men. To achieve this goal, the new social order elevated the family to the status of cornerstone of society and encouraged loyalty within marriage. By doing so, it flanked men with two newcomers: the wife, as a moral anchor; and his children, whose honor ought now to be defended as his own in order to secure the moral integrity of the next generation.

I suggest therefore that it is the clash between the rise of logos and a shift to a more collective value system, on the one hand, and a homosexual culture unable to disengage itself from the prehistoric rule of male ranking, on the other hand, that led to the fall from grace of homosexuality at the turn of the Common Era in Western culture. While the moral and spiritual emphasis put on logos promoted an unprecedented social and spiritual evolution, male Mediterranean homosexual culture kept holding on to a social model inherited from the jungle. This is—I believe—the grand lesson of the homosexual history in the first centuries.

We ought to grasp fully what such a finding implies. Homosexual victimization originates, among other things, from a "withdrawal" from history. Somehow homosexuals have collectively convinced themselves that they had absolutely no involvement in the historical process that resulted in a generalized backlash against them. But homosexuals have been part of history, not simply spectators. When one gives a closer look at the moral shift that coincided with the rise of Christianity and resulted in the bloody oppression of homosexuality for nearly fifteen centuries, no one can reasonably doubt the fact that homosexuals also participated in this historical evolution. Not only did the homosexual culture of the time fail to evolve but I find hard to believe that same-sex lovers in late antiquity, unlike the rest of the population, refused to embrace a new value system that emphasized reason, discernment, personal responsibility, self-awareness, and commitment to the well-being of the community over their own individual needs and impulses. They did, of course embrace this. But by doing so, they unknowingly espoused a cultural revolution that also fostered the rise of homophobia.

In the centuries to come, the sodomite—fallen hero of love in antiquity, stripped of all dignity, socially isolated, emotionally alienated, and culturally labeled with an identity designed to unleash the collective wrath—was to carry the weight of the moral failure of ancient homosexual culture on his shoulders. However, the sodomite archetype contained the seeds of another transformation to come. By collapsing the entire spectrum of same-sex acts—active, passive, pederastic, transgender, male, and female—under a unique concept, the Christian discourse unknowingly created the conditions of a new alchemical transformation. Out of this emerged a new form of homosexuality, totally unimaginable before: modern homosexuality.

CHAPTER NINE

The Great Transformation

Perpetuating a long tradition of Greek, Roman, and Jewish thinkers, the Church made the battle against human animal instincts its own. Since Christianity saw in the weaknesses of the flesh the origin of the Fall of the race of Adam, repressing sex for pleasure (both heterosexual and homosexual) quickly became a priority. Eventually the rift between same-sex love and the collective morals that had inexorably deepened over the centuries reached a point of no return. The love between men and between women, which were deemed sterile physically as well as spiritually, lost public approval. Homophobia, which since prehistory had essentially targeted effeminate, soft, weak, and hence passive males, suddenly took an entirely new dimension. No longer restricted to the antediluvian logic of male ranking, homophobic hatred at the turn of the Common Era broadened its scope significantly. By conflating the passive and the active partners of homosexual acts into one unique "animal"—the sodomite archetype—the West invented a new concept and new target all at once. Being indiscriminately insertive and receptive, the sodomite dishonored—by definition and by default—the rule of male ranking. In the meantime, lesbians had to confront the anti-sodomite prejudice along with another prehistoric prejudice: misogyny.

The new cultural homophobia that emerges in the first centuries succeeded remarkably well in rerouting an animosity originally aimed at sexually passive males and sexually insubordinate females. To survive, homosexual love took refuge in secrecy. It concealed itself, often under the priestly vow of celibacy, protected behind the walls of convents and monasteries.[449] Sometimes it dared exhibit itself at the court of the kings of England or France, but those were exceptions to the rule. Overall, despite its remarkable resilience, same-sex love vanished from the social/ritualistic space. Christendom banished the sodomite from the collective space of empathy. Sodomites were subjected to ostracism, threats, and, for the most unfortunate ones, tortures, horrendous mutilations, and sometimes atrocious deaths. Ironically, sodomites ended up being degraded to the same sub-human status as that of the last acceptable objects of their desire in Roman times: slaves.

While disconcerting at first glance, the emergence of cultural homophobia is remarkably congruent with the emerging epistemological context of the time. In the first centuries CE both pagan philosophers and the early Fathers of the Church enjoined crowds to adopt a lifestyle that would help free their reasonable mind—logos—from blind greed and the brutal urges of the body. It is primarily an obsessive and unyielding defense of logos that pushed Western cultures toward ascetic mores. The repression of sexuality and the condemnation of homosexual acts were a means to specific goals, but were not the point of the new Christian faith. The Church never advocated the suppression of all non-procreative sexual acts for its own sake. On the contrary, it was the price that Christians had to pay to liberate their soul. Remember that for the Church love between men and between women was unproblematic, as long as it was not expressed sexually.

In point of fact, same-sex lovers were not the sole victims of the Christian moral upheaval. Men, while preserving their superior status, suffered a major drawback in their traditional privileges. The new morals of marriage demanded faithfulness on the part of the husband too. The reform of the marital institution aimed at enhancing the wives' dignity. Moreover, women encountered in the Christian praise of female virginity and chastity the only good excuse to avoid marriage.[450] On the other hand, these virtues also constituted a virtual prison for many generations of women. Notwithstanding this, men and women in large numbers converted to the new faith, often risking persecutions at the price of their lives. Many same-sex lovers must have made a similar choice. Early Christians, regardless of their sex and sexual tastes, did not merely behave like a flock of brainless sheep.

Equally important was to acknowledge the fact that for the great majority, ancient forms of homosexual relationships are inconsistent with our current morals, whether a person is straight or gay. One can sift through thousands of pages of homosexual history and cultural anthropology and not find a single mention of this issue. How can one dissect Paul's discourses without conceding first that Paul essentially witnessed men visiting bordellos or buying handsome youths on the slave market for their personal use? Even the intense passion between the emperor Hadrian and the handsome Antinous, which strongly impressed my adolescent soul, would today qualify as sexual harassment by a fifty-year-old man of his nineteen-year-old subordinate.

The homosexual discourse can no longer ignore that in nearly all cases homosexual relationships in the ancient world were just another expression of male privilege. In 1871 when John Addington Symonds recognized that "The peculiar status of Greek women is a subject surrounded with difficulty; yet no one can help feeling that the idealization of masculine love, which formed so prominent a feature of Greek life in the historic period, was intimately connected with the failure of the race to give their proper sphere in society to women. The Greeks themselves were not directly conscious of this fact . . ."[451] he actually demonstrated a double and rare courage: defending same-sex love and, at the same time, acknowledging the patent conflict of interest between male love in classical Greek culture and an improvement of the living conditions of other members of society. The inability of Greco-Roman homosexual culture to reconsider its moral basis and explore new social models is, retrospectively, completely mesmerizing. Incidentally, it reveals how difficult it must have been to imagine a world outside the prehistoric logic of male ranking.

Now I would like to dissipate the halo of mystery that surrounds a second pivotal moment in the history of homosexuality: its resurrection nearly two millenniums after its fall into disgrace. These two moments are key issues in the homosexual collective psyche. The integrity of today's homosexual identity depends on our ability to make sense of both.

THE CONTEXT OF A NEW REVOLUTION

Fast-forwarding shamelessly through history, I will summarize a millennium and a half of homosexual history in a nutshell: the "unspeakable sin" of the Middle Ages became the "abominable vice" during the Renaissance, and later became "pederasty" and "effeminacy" and then "sexual inversion" in the scientific literature in the nineteenth century, and eventually "sexual perversion" in the psychoanalytic discourse that dominated in the twentieth century. Still, the invert, the pederast, the queen, and the sexual pervert were largely based on the same central character—the sodomite—simply translated into different worldviews. Knowing this, if we are to tackle the issue of the miraculous reemergence of homosexuality after World War II, we now need to provide an answer to two questions.

The first one is the following: What are the conditions of the resurgence of homosexuality in the second half of the twentieth century? Just as in the previous chapter, we need to unearth the multilayered context—biological, social, and psychocultural—in which the readmission of homosexuals within the social space occurred. In their introduction to *Historical Perspectives on Homosexuality*, Salvatore Licata and Robert Petersen asked very pertinent questions that perfectly illustrate my point: "Why did the homosexual rights movements appear when they did? Why did the first known protests against sodomy laws occur in Germany in the latter half of the nineteenth century? Why did the movement in the United States first take hold in the 1950s after Henry Gerber's attempt had failed in the 1920s?"[452] The question is really: Why then, and not before or later? And as in the previous chapter, we will have to lay bare the various evolutionary trends that have decided recent history, and see whether they converge on this incredible moment that we call "gay liberation."

The second question is: What is the nature and place of modern homosexuality within the grand scheme of homosexual evolution? In other words, is there an evolutionary logic to the emergence of this entirely novel form of homosexual relationship that we call modern homosexuality? However, to address this question, we will have to get around an issue that we have already faced many times. Until the end of twentieth century, homosexual desire was typically studied and portrayed by individuals whose sole goal was to eradicate this sort of behavior. Historians have been forced to observe homosexuals and their desires through deforming mirrors. The birth date of modern homosexuality in Western history is difficult to trace for that reason. And yet, even the most biased accounts of homosexual reality have helped researchers discern the progressive genesis of new identities and new ways of relating among same-sex lovers.

I will address these two questions in that order. The following discussion aims to offer some answers, not a definitive explanation. More details will need to be fleshed out, later and elsewhere. Rather, this inquiry intends to lay out what an evolutionary approach of homosexual history may look like. In an integral context, the direction of history is determined by the evolutionary dynamics that animate it more than the particular charisma of a certain leader. If people in the first centuries had not been craving a discourse consistent with how they felt about themselves, Paul would have ended being the leader of yet another failed Jewish sect. Visionaries are individuals capable of revealing what in the collective psyche is ready to emerge. All the names that you have heard and will hear—Plato, Augustine, Voltaire, Freud, Kinsey, and so forth—are individuals who intuited the concerns and hopes of their generation before people even became conscious of the changes to come. They only represent the visible waves of complex evolutionary undercurrents. I will show here that the fall of homosexuality and its resurgence obey the same basic rules.

We are going to see how the very context that had fostered the disgrace of homosexuality ended up being challenged, undermined, and eventually broken into pieces by the rise of two radically new paradigms, modernity and postmodernity.

Modernity and the Art of Measuring

In the sixteenth century the era of the great explorations began. Thanks to Christopher Columbus (1451–1506) and Vasco di Gama (1460 or 69–1524), and (for better or worse) the conquest of the Americas, the size of the world virtually doubled. Yet the transformation that started in the Renaissance went far beyond the discovery of new lands. Altogether, Renaissance luminaries in all domains of knowledge opened new eyes to the world that surrounded them. Leonardo da Vinci (1452–1519), multidisciplinary thinker, artist, scientist, and prolific inventor, epitomizes the new spirit that was slowly materializing. Just a generation prior to da Vinci, a Florentine architect, Filippo Brunelleschi (1377–1446), had introduced his peers to a revolutionary technique: linear perspective. From that time on, proportions in drawings and paintings would represent the relative position of each object in space accurately. They would no longer reflect the subjective hierarchy, spiritual or thematic, which had been so central to the medieval worldview. Renaissance art strived to portray the world objectively and free itself from the weight of the collective subjectivity that medieval art had embodied magnificently. And as often in history (I personally believe that it is always the case), artists led the way.

The need to represent and, more generally, comprehend the world in an objective fashion opened a new era: modernity. No other domain of knowledge has embodied the values of modernity more thoroughly than modern science. Rational thinking, which is at the very core of modern science, was nothing new. It can be traced back to primitive cultures as distinct from magical or mythical thinking.[453] Since ancient times human beings were able to differentiate two sorts of realities, those that involved the intervention of spirits or gods and those that resulted from a simple chain of events. Medieval architects knew perfectly that the arches of their cathedrals stood up thanks to a precise balance between the different physical forces involved, and not thanks to the angels. However, before modernity, truth (i.e., the ultimate knowledge) was primarily demonstrated by the power of rhetoric. Truth, in the medieval paradigm, was generated through language and on the basis of the collective agreement that was delineated in the prevalent belief system.

For instance, in order to support his brilliant reasoning, Thomas Aquinas referred to Aristotle and Augustine, in other words, the cultural consensus, but he did not validate or even challenge the truthfulness of his theology by means of objective observation. Insofar as the Scriptures constituted the foundation of the Christian worldview and the primordial source of truth of Western medieval culture, everything that was not consistent with their content was denied. But by electing rational thinking, no longer restricted to solving technical issues, as the supreme and only valid way to reveal truth and by putting it at the center of its new worldview, modernity altered Western culture irreversibly. With the modern worldview came a new methodology to approach the world and determine truth: scientific empiricism. In this new paradigm, observation supplanted belief. And modern science would soon become the main instrument of this revolution.

While a lot can be said about this fascinating topic, I would like to focus here on two highly symbolic figures of the scientific revolution: Copernicus (1473–1543) and Galileo (1564–1642). The consequence of their discoveries is of utmost importance in the Western collective psyche. By placing the sun at the center of the universe and rejecting the earth at the periphery, Copernicus and Galileo accomplished much more than a simple scientific readjustment. They expelled humankind from the center of the Universe. One could not possibly embrace Copernicus's heliocentric model without, at the same time, having to reevaluate the spiritual position of human beings in the universe entirely. The resistance of the Church was therefore not only coherent, but also in many ways justified (even if its methods were by no means excusable). The Church understood immediately the threat that this new knowledge represented, and not merely against its own dogma. Christianity's sacred cosmology was being dismantled, and with it, the representation of the divine perfection through the geometry of the cosmos. If the gracious and audacious architecture of the Copernican universe still celebrated the majesty of God, the unique status of humankind in relation to God was erased. Copernicus and Galileo broke into pieces the tangible manifestation of the exclusive covenant between God and humanity. We have seen earlier how much the God-God's people dyad had a double meaning in the Judeo-Christian cosmology. It first symbolized the fundamental and absolute complementarity between the masculine (God) and the feminine (Christendom), thereby revealing the inherent order of the cosmos. Second, in claiming the existence of a cosmic perfection, the Christian worldview posited the existence of one, and only one, truth: its own.

Suddenly Westerners had to fill an immense void, which is to say, to re-imagine their place in God's creation. When three centuries later, Darwin published his theory of the evolution of the species, he involuntarily brought to completion the cosmological enterprise that Copernicus and Galileo had initiated. After Darwin, all the material evidence of God's unique alliance with humankind was demolished. Science, on the other hand, leaving behind the shadowy workshops of alchemists, began to monopolize the cultural sphere. Scientific thinking—rational and empirical—infiltrated all the disciplines of knowledge and all human activities. Politics, economics, populations, communication, and even warfare became scientific. And the economic and geopolitical triumph of the West in the nineteenth and twentieth centuries would eventually confirm the spectacular success of the modern paradigm.

The modern universe, according to Isaac Newton (1643–1727), perhaps the greatest and most representative genius of modernity, was ruled by the laws of cause and effect. Deciphering its whole mechanism was simply a matter of time. To reach that goal, the methodology was fundamentally always the same: to turn everything into object, an "IT." And, as we already know from our exploration of the True, scientists started to observe and measure everything—plant, river, fossil, trade, agricultural and industrial production, idea, behavior, language, people, body parts, and so on. They collected all sorts of information on everything that came under their scrutiny. They searched for unique features, repetitive patterns, similarities, symmetries, and hierarchies. Each object was to be classified, labeled, and attributed its just place in a perfectly organized universe. In doing so, scientists hoped to bring to light the hidden mechanisms that had brought all those objects into existence. Science would finally fulfill on the grand dream of the Axial Age: to unveil the glorious architecture of the universe. But one of the ironies in history is that thanks to this revolutionary methodology, the laws of science also ended up pulling apart the Axial ideal of a universal order, which the West seemed to have forever triumphed with the advent of Christianity. In the same breath, it would disintegrate the centuries-old consensus about homosexuality and homosexuals. But we are getting ahead of ourselves.

Note also that if scientists undertook to monitor everything they saw, it was not always with optimal accuracy or irreproachable honesty. Scientists are and will always be like any other human beings, trapped into layers of cultural conditioning, limited by their ignorance, and manipulated by their most secret fears. Yet science is first and foremost a collective and historical endeavor. With the scientific method, even though biased and flawed, knowledge is constantly reevaluated. New observations complement or replace the previous ones. New ideas challenge the old ones. Science always strives for more accuracy and more resolution. How far we are now from premodern worldviews founded on the certainty of already possessing the ultimate truth.

Modern science operated with human beings as with any other object. But when they confronted the mystery of our sexual behavior, scientists did not begin their quest on a neutral ground. Western science emerged from a culture that had abhorred sex and despised flesh for centuries. On top of its discomfort regarding sexual matters, Western culture had forged an enduring consensus (to say the least) around its conception of normality: the goal of sex is to reproduce. In consequence, all "natural" sexual acts ought to involve a man and a woman. Anything outside of this perimeter constituted an aberration from the logic of nature. Until the nineteenth century, morality remained by and large the domain of predilection of religions and philosophy. Modern science in comparison had still very little weight. In the meantime, scientists did what they knew best: to measure and classify. In that respect the second half of the nineteen century witnessed an unprecedented flurry of novel theories about homosexuality. Let me give you a sense of what they sounded like.

Dr. Paul Moreau, a French psychiatrist, convinced that same-sex desire resulted from a degenerescence of the "genital sense," explained in his *Des Aberrations du Sens Génésique* published in 1887 that "among the most frequent causes of aberrations in the genital sense, heredity comes first," and that "a pathological aberration in reproductive feelings [*"sentiments génésiques"*] must be assimilated to a neurosis completely, and, as such, its existence is compatible with the highest intelligence." This said, for Moreau, non-hereditary causes could also favor the development of this condition in predisposed individuals, for instance extreme poverty, age, constitution, temperament, seasons of the year, climate, and food.[454] In the same period, the renowned Italian criminologist and forensic expert, Cesare Lombroso, explained among many other things that the "unnatural vice" was frequent among horses, donkeys, cattle, insects, fowls, dogs, and (believe it or not!) ants, and usually associated with cases where the male animal has been excluded from intercourse with females.[455]

Dr. Ambroise Tardieu, a very influential medico-legal expert in Paris, bragged about having personally examined over three hundred pederasts and other sodomites. According to him, those individuals were widely distributed among all ages, professions, and social classes, contradicting the prevalent stereotype of the degenerate aristocrat, which was by far the most common throughout the eighteenth and nineteenth centuries. He also offered infallible ways to identify sodomites that are worth detailing (and not to mention, hilarious). Our French expert claimed with authority that passive pederasts could be recognized by their flaccid buttocks, a deformed anus, and a loose anal sphincter; and active pederasts could be recognized by their penises, either thin and pointy or long and tapered, and their large muzzle-like glans.[456]

You certainly noticed that most of those people pontificated about homosexuals as if they were grasshoppers. And they did so very seriously. A century later, many still take offense at the way nineteenth century science talked about homosexuals. One must however read their discourse in its historical context; in other words, compare it to what was there before rather than to what came after. First, while the theories often proved awfully biased and obviously inaccurate, the mode of thinking was nonetheless radically novel. All those theories may have been trapped in a cultural consensus openly hostile to homosexuals; still, nineteen century scientists were not concerned about abiding with the collective consensus. They did not hesitate to contradict, argue, and compete with one another. We may laugh at their ideas retrospectively, but their intellectual creativity was nonetheless very real. We often forget how much this was not the case before modernity. Second, we need to keep in mind that people had very limited access to the homosexual population back then. The few that they had the opportunity to meet had often been arrested, put either in jail or a psychiatric institution. Or they were desperate individuals seeking medical or psychological help.

Finally, we should not forget that nineteenth century intellectuals could not possibly understand the modern homosexual. Modern homosexual identity did not even exist then, and homosexuals themselves had few clues about what their desires and feelings were all about. All that emerged progressively later. Rather, what physicians and psychiatrists endeavored to decipher was the same old mystery—the sodomite. But in doing so, they succeeded in taking the lead in the public discourse on homosexuality, even overwhelming the Church itself. They initiated the debate that still goes on today and gave a new impetus to a discourse that had not evolved for centuries.

Along the way, a few of them, who were often homosexual themselves, undertook the courageous mission to try to comprehend a world under seal. In complete opposition to the consensus of their time, they often urged for the decriminalization of homosexuality. Those men operated within the exact same epistemological framework as their contemporaries, which demanded to provide both a taxonomy and an etiology of the object of study. That was the time of the invention of the world *homosexualität* by the Austro-Hungarian activist Karl Maria Kertbeny (1824–1882), of Havelock Ellis's "sexual inversion," and Freud's concept of "perverse polymorphism." Dr. Gustav Jäger, who adopted some of Kertbeny's theory and was instrumental in the diffusion of the word *homosexualität*, sorted homosexuals between *mutuelle*, those who practice mutual masturbation, and *pygisten*, those who engage in anal sex.[457]

Others divided lesbians between sapphists who perform oral sex with other women and tribades who mutually rub their genitals.[458]

The epistemological foundation of modern thought is most brilliantly illustrated by the complex classification system of Karl Heinrich Ulrichs (1825–1895), one of the first modern homosexual activists. Like most of his contemporaries, Ulrichs found it natural and useful to sort same-sex lovers into categories and subcategories, and this, despite his acquaintance with the word *homosexualität* (the word was coined for the very first time in 1868 by Kertbeny in a letter to Ulrichs).[459] He divided sexual orientation between *dioning* (heterosexual masculine man) and *urning*[460] (homosexual man, which Ulrichs defined as a man with a female psyche who is attracted to other men) from which the English "uranian" originated. Then, *urnings* come in different flavors: *Mannlinge* are masculine and drawn to effeminate men, *weiblinge* are feminine, and *zwischen-urnings* prefer adolescent males. *Uranodionings* represent the category of bisexual males. Ulrichs' classification gets even more refined: *Virilisierte Mannlinge* are *urnings* who pass as heterosexual men, which is to say as *dionings* (somehow equivalent to closeted homosexuals). *Uraniasters* are heterosexual men who can occasionally engage in same-sex activities. Women were similarly divided among *dioningins* (heterosexual), *urningins* (homosexual, that is, a female body with a male psyche), and *uranodioningins* (bisexual). Ultimately, *zwitters*, the hermaphrodites, stand right in the middle of this kaleidoscope of gender and sexual orientation combinations.

In order to counteract the negative impact of the many epithets used to describe homosexuals—sodomite, pederast, sexual pervert, degenerate, and so on—early advocates of the homosexual cause had to be clever. And they indeed proved to be quite imaginative in this matter, as demonstrated by the abundant terminology that they came up with. Unfortunately, this contrasts sharply with their relative lack of originality with respect to the etiology of same-sex desire, which can only remind us how difficult their task must have been in such an inhospitable cultural context. Most of them viewed homosexual desire through the lens of gender deviance, an old idea that dates back to antiquity. English writer John Addington Symonds (1840–1893), German Karl Heinrich Ulrichs, Austro-German sexologist, psychiatrist, and author of *Psychopathia Sexualis*, Richard von Krafft-Ebing (1840–1902), British sexologist Havelock Ellis (1859–1939), author of *Sexual Inversion*, and later Magnus Hirschfeld (1868–1935), founder of the Institute for Sexual Research in Berlin, all conceptualized homosexuality as "a female soul in a male body" and vice versa (more rarely as "psychic hermaphrodites").

In that respect, Freud (1856–1939) and Karl Maria Kertbeny constitute interesting exceptions. In *Three Contributions to the Sexual Theory*, Freud was very explicit on that issue:

> The Sexual Object of Inverts: The theory of psychic hermaphroditism presupposed that the sexual object of the inverted is the reverse of the normal. The inverted man, like the woman, succumbs to the charms emanating from manly

qualities of body and mind; he feels himself like a woman and seeks a man. But however true this may be for a great number of inverts it by no means indicates the general character of inversion. There is no doubt that a great part of the male inverted have retained the psychic character of virility, that proportionately they show but little the secondary characters of the other sex, and that they really look for real feminine psychic features in their sexual object.[461]

Freud was among the first intellectuals to differentiate clearly between homosexual attraction and gender inversion, thereby marking a major step forward in the evolution of our Western conception of homosexual desire.

Kertbeny never came close to Freud's notoriety. Nor did he have a real influence in the early pro-homosexual movement, if not for his coining of the word "homosexuality." Yet, just as Freud emphasized the distinction between same-sex desire and gender inversion, Kertbeny insisted on the need to differentiate homosexuality from pederasty: "The great majority of northerners in whom this inclination is innate have a great horror of the boyish, the effeminate in their own sex and all the more passion, not for the youth, but for the guy (to which category soldiers usually belong), indeed for the man, even in the mature man who had already passed forty."[462]

The case of Marc-André Raffalovich (1864–1934), an unknown to most non-specialists, illustrates further the discreet emergence of a new vision of the homosexual (mostly male at this point), distinct from the effeminate man and the pederast. Raffalovich, a French poet expatriated in London, was himself very conflicted about his homosexuality. He despised effeminate men whom he considered perverts. Without any particular degree, he nonetheless published several studies on the topic. Raffalovich dismissed the link between same-sex desire and degeneracy, as well as the division between active and passive individuals. For him, homosexual desire was fundamentally normal. Yet he may be most remembered for his unapologetic defense of virile homosexuality, a concept that he also applied by symmetry to women and that he called "unisexuality," hence challenging the quasi omnipresent dogma of sexual inversion frontally.[463]

Modern intellectuals, from Tardieu to Raffalovich, reexamined the cryptic character that the sodomite symbolized up until then. They dissected and laid flat the different parts of a convoluted stereotype. Methodically, they challenged the accuracy of any unverified assumptions. Even if many were highly prejudiced, they succeeded in demonstrating that few of those assumptions were inconsistent with what they observed. Eventually, the consensus about what constitutes a homosexual would shatter irreversibly and they all played a role in this process, even if inadvertently. Because they were no longer expected to be reliably effeminate, criminal, mental degenerate, or carriers of particular bodily stigma (at least not systematically), homosexuals became "normal" in appearance—that is, invisible. To detect those elusive menaces, the twentieth century had to rely on more complex procedures: denunciation, interrogation, and eventually it would find a powerful weapon: psychoanalysis.

Yet modernity had one last stunning contribution to make in the person of Alfred Kinsey. Alfred Kinsey (1894–1956), in my opinion probably the most important figure of modern homosexual history, truly deserves a special mention. His work marked the apotheosis of more than a century of modern exploration of homosexuality, but also paradoxically the end of the modern era. The impact of *Sexual Behavior in the Human Male* (published in 1948) and *Sexual Behavior in the Human Female* (in 1953) on Western culture was, to say the least, transformative. Kinsey's revelations undercut the very foundation of Judeo-Christian sexual morals. Regarding homosexual behavior specifically, the verdict was earth-shattering. First, Kinsey demonstrated the existence of a spectrum of sexual behavior and desire ranging from exclusively heterosexual to exclusively homosexual, replacing the strict dichotomy between normal and deviant. Second, the occurrence of homosexual behavior within the population was much higher than previously thought, which came as a total surprise. Third, Kinsey's publications anchored once and for all the fact that homosexual desire was only marginally associated with effeminacy and pederasty. Last, sexual desires for same and opposite-sex persons were not mutually exclusive. Altogether, the Kinsey report busted the very idea that a homosexual stereotype existed.

We have already inquired into the specifics of Kinsey's data, their originality as well as their flaws. Notice that Kinsey's methodology is quintessentially modern, that is, to measure and classify. Kinsey's epistemological frame is the same as that of Ulrichs, Hirschfeld, and others. Nonetheless, and I will keep stressing this crucial fact: science is a historical process that unfolds with time. Kinsey benefited from the long struggle and the many mistakes of his predecessors. He had access to a large population of volunteers that included students, prisoners, and prostitutes. Despite its obvious imperfection, Kinsey's sample contrasted sharply with the homosexual microcosm routinely studied until that point, which was composed of individuals who had either been arrested for public offenses or were actively seeking relief for their emotional suffering by consulting a therapist.

Another difference of importance, Kinsey was an accomplished biologist, a botanist by training and a staunch entomologist. Prior to his famous reports, he had already published several studies ranging from the study of wild plants to the classification of gall wasps. On the other side of the spectrum, Ulrichs was a legal adviser; Symonds and Raffalovich, poets; Karl Maria Kertbeny, a political activist; Hirschfeld and Krafft-Ebing, physicians; and Ellis, almost one. Yet not a single one was a biologist. And as for Freud and his successors, there is no need for me to comment on their poor understanding of the scientific process, let alone biology.

Did the modern discourse on homosexuality really make a difference? After all, the voices of early proponents of homosexual emancipation were but a discreet minority among the scientific discourse, that overall remained homophobic until more or less the nineteen eighties. Modern science may not have attempted to challenge the morals of its time directly, but it did however slowly erode the old moral consensus around same-sex desire. By turning the "abject" into an "object," science extricated homosexual behavior from the netherworld in which it had been trapped thus far. Homosexuality entered the regular pipeline of scientific affairs, just like flu epidemics, oil extraction, or the laws of gravity. Books and articles were published about pederasts, inverts, and occasionally lesbians. Homosexuals were studied by physicians, experts in forensic medicine, and psychiatrists. They were described and occasionally exhibited in medical schools.

As degrading as those occurrences might feel today, we owe them a great deal. Because it turned out to be so prolific, the scientific and pseudo-scientific discourse on homosexuality had a significant impact on the general public. Albeit feared, hated, and despised, homosexuals started to become familiar. If neither modernity nor the nineteenth century invented the concept of homosexuality, modern or not (despite claims to the contrary by postmodern thinkers), they succeeded remarkably in making their new theories known by all. Homosexuals started to hear about homosexuals as well. They could begin thinking of themselves as something more complex than mere sinners. Their disease had a biological cause, their perversion a developmental logic, and their lifestyle some rare champions. Same-sex love was still devoid of any goodness or beauty; yet it started to have some objective depth to it. That was not great, but it was certainly better. No matter what, times were changing. And in less than a century, homosexuality's fate would be turned upside down.

The twentieth century was the scientific century *par excellence*. Health, education, creation, and warfare—nothing escaped the modern paradigm. From the moment of their birth to their death, people in increasingly high numbers saw their lives unfold within a scientific framework. But because of its insatiable appetite for more precision, science ended up bumping into the very limits of the paradigm that had nurtured its own birth. From this paradox emerged a new era—postmodernity—that started to question the very possibility of knowing the universe in which we live or ourselves. And the postmodern paradigm, which discreetly began to infuse Western popular culture from the 1960s on, succeeded where modernity had fallen short. By surfing the wave of sociocultural revolutions that shook America and Europe in the 1970s, gay liberation movements would achieve the unthinkable: the rehabilitation of same-sex love.

POSTMODERNITY AND THE FACE OF THE UNKNOWN

Art always seems to be first to embody the changes to come. While science in the nineteenth century—hyper-confident—already celebrated its undoubted triumph against all the mysteries that had baffled humanity since the dawn of history, Romantic painting began to betray the artist's increasingly problematic relation with objective reality. The unavoidable and overwhelming presence of the painter's emotions made fictitious, perhaps even treacherous, any attempt to represent objective reality scrupulously. The meticulousness of the Classical period, which had championed visual accuracy and negated the artist's subjectivity, disappeared progressively. Outlines became increasingly blurry; shapes uncertain. Impressionists kept deconstructing reality, increasingly merging their objective and subjective perceptions of things. In the musical world, composers such as Brahms and Malher operated a similar transformation of musical forms. Each successive artistic movement that the twentieth century witnessed helped free art from the tyranny of form even more, until nothing was left other than a pure concept. To regain possession of our inner world, art killed the "object."

Nevertheless science, now a powerful driving force in Western culture, was to make the postmodern paradigm palpable to all. The daughter of modernity, science ended up dissolving the very foundation of our relationship to reality. And this rupture is best embodied by the works of two of the most emblematic intellectual figures of the twentieth century, Albert Einstein (1879–1955) and Sigmund Freud.

After Albert Einstein's publication in 1917 of his "Cosmological Considerations on the General Theory of Relativity," the universe would never to be the same again. The cultural shift that his theory generated was at least of the magnitude of the Copernican revolution, if not beyond. Mass and energy, the two fundamental essences of the Newtonian universe were now equivalent and transmutable: $E = mc^2$. Matter can melt into energy and energy can condense into matter. Bill Bryson captured quite well the emotionally disturbing nature of Einstein's revolutionary theory: "The most challenging and nonintuitive of all the concepts in the general theory of relativity is the idea that time is part of space. Our instinct is to regard time as eternal, absolute, immutable—nothing can disturb its steady tick. In fact, according to Einstein, time is variable and ever changing. It even has shape. It is bound up [. . .] with the three dimensions of space in a curious dimension known as spacetime."[464] In Einstein's universe, an object with a mass deforms the fabric of spacetime; gravitational fields cause light to bend; objects traveling at a near-light speed experience time passing more slowly than immobile ones (according to that theory, astronauts on a spaceship moving through the cosmos at the speed of light and coming back to earth after a year or so, would find out that everybody they knew had died of old age in the meantime). And if that was not enough already, Einstein's general theory of relativity predicted that the universe was either expanding or contracting; it made plausible the existence of black holes, objects so dense that even light can no longer escape from their gravitational fields. Einstein's general relativity blew apart the old Newtonian paradigm—the soul of modernity. But, like everything in science, it was doomed to become obsolete one day.

Today physicists have produced theories that are even more extraordinary and even less intelligible. Quantum mechanics exploded reality into probabilistic dust, a world where particles behave like waves and waves like particles. More recently, superstring and M theory uncovered the possible existence of multiple dimensions, far beyond the four (tridimensional space plus time) that we already know. By the end of the twentieth century, the mechanics of the universe had become rather counterintuitive, to put it mildly.

Quantum mechanics teaches us a tough lesson: the impossibility to know an object in minute detail. For instance, it is impossible to confirm the position of an electron by observation. You can either calculate its positions or observe it, but not both at the same time, because the very act of observing or measuring disturbs the object, and hence alters the reality you are trying to grasp. The validation of knowledge through measuring—mantra of modernity and pillar of modern science—was now demoted to the status of an impossible dream. The modern paradigm was simply neutered. But before recapitulating the dramatic consequence that this new vision of the universe had on Western culture, let us first explore the other epistemological revolution that was occurring in parallel in the salons of Vienna.

While physicists were orchestrating the death of the Newtonian paradigm, another kind of explorer was focusing not on the secrets of matter and the cosmos, but on the uncharted territory also known as the human mind. Freud's discovery of the unconscious brought to life an obscure and fascinating world, full of mysteries and paradoxes as manifold, deep, and exuberant as those generated from the theory of general relativity and quantum mechanics. Yet I would like to let Freud explain his discovery in his own words:

> A conception—or any other mental element—which is now present to my consciousness may become absent the next moment, and may become present again, after an interval, unchanged, and, as we say, from memory, not as a result of a fresh perception by our senses [. . .] We were accustomed to think that every latent idea was so because it was weak and that it grew conscious as soon as it became strong. We have now gained the conviction that there are some latent ideas which do not penetrate into consciousness, however strong they may have become. Therefore we may call the latent ideas of the first type *preconscious*, while we reserve the term *unconscious* (proper) for the latter type [. . .] It designates not only latent ideas in general, but especially ideas with a certain dynamic character, ideas keeping apart from consciousness in spite of their intensity and activity [. . .] Certain deficiencies of function of most frequent occurrence among healthy people, e.g. *lapsus linguae*, errors in memory and speech, forgetting of names, etc., may easily be shown to depend on the action of strong unconscious ideas in the same way as neurotic symptoms [. . .] The unconscious idea is excluded from consciousness by living forces which oppose themselves to its reception, while they do not object to other ideas, the preconscious ones. Psychoanalysis leaves no room for doubt that the repulsion from unconscious ideas is only provoked by the tendencies embodied in their contents.[465]

The parallels between Freud's theory and quantum mechanics are striking. Just like electrons, our thoughts become nearly impossible to locate in the psyche;

they are selected out of consciousness by an unpredictable operation, buried in the mysterious depth of the unconscious, and yet manifest themselves through the cryptic encoding of our involuntary slips. Undetectable thoughts and emotions can alter other thoughts and emotions from a distance, just like light bends because of the invisible presence of a gravitational field. Secret dimensions open at every corner. According to Freud, the human soul is, by definition, unknowable, just like the universe of quantum physics. Human beings are left with only one solution—to devote themselves to the endless routine of examining their mind and decrypting the coded signals from their unconscious, in hope of establishing some harmony in an irreversibly flawed mechanism.

And it is not so much the detail of Freud's psychoanalytic theory, Einstein's general relativity, or quantum mechanics that is of interest for us here. Those theories are valuable to us first and foremost because they were the precursory signs of a paradigm shift: the advent of postmodernity. Notice first that these three theories quickly encountered an immense success within the general public. The notion of the unconscious spread through Western culture like wildfire. So did general relativity. Black holes, the big bang, and the idea of an expanding universe, three predictions based on Einstein's equations, are deeply engrained in today's popular culture. On the other hand, the synchronicity between the rise of conceptual art, post-Newtonian physics (i.e., starting from Einstein's theories of general relativity), and the discovery of the unconscious, is nothing short of astonishing.[466] These three concomitant revolutions all conveyed the same subliminal message: to know the universe or oneself with certainty is an illusion. If there is such a thing as truth, it is inaccessible. Instead, truth is always subjective. It all depends on the observer and everybody is entitled to his or her own perspective, his or her own subjective opinion of what is true, good, and beautiful, and what is not. Hence one can no longer tell who is right. The era of certainty gave way to the era of relativism.

One century later, we are so accustomed to these concepts that we have forgotten how earth-shattering they must have been. "To know"—the goal of modernity, the divine mission of Christianity, and the grand dream of classical philosophy— was declared structurally impossible. Reality was now a moving target—a world of statistical possibilities. No longer God's present to the sons of Adam, nor the perfect mechanic of an invisible watchmaker, the universe became the ultimate unknown—human beings' worst nightmare. Human beings had worked really hard to conceal the unknown behind their mythologies and in the dark recesses of their unconscious so as never to deal with it. And if for postmodern thinkers the idea that the only thing one can know for certain is the fact that one cannot know anything for certain constituted an existential predicament, altogether inevitable and delightful, it was torture for normally constituted human beings.

In the meantime, two world wars and the dreadful threat of nuclear annihilation ended up throwing the illusions of modernity on the trash heap of history. Technical progress alone failed to provide freedom and happiness. Not only had reason not protected people against their worst instincts, but in fact, it had amplified their destructive power exponentially. Modernity, despite its undeniable success—the end of slavery, the rise of democracies, and the invention of modern science—could not bring humanity beyond a certain point. Logos had reached its limits. By the 1960s the divorce between modernity and Western culture was fully consummated. And Western society was ready to explode.

Now, postmodernity was by no means the first time in human history that some people chose to confront the unknown. Facing the impenetrable mystery of the universe, that is, allowing the unfathomable presence of the Divine, had been part of a long tradition known as mysticism. Since the beginning of the Axial Age, in the East as in the West, in the mysteries of ancient Greece and Egypt, in Buddhist and Christian monasteries, and among the Sufis, men and women across the world had withdrawn from mundane existence and dedicated their lives to contemplating the unknown. Yet this "culture of the mystery" had always been confined to monasteries. The outside world, "the" world, had remained totally unprepared, to say the least. It would then be inaccurate to pretend that postmodern science, whether it was quantum physics or psychology, has reconciled the Western world with spirituality. Let us nonetheless remember that in the backdrop of the sociocultural turmoil that started in the 1960s and '70s, there unfolded another revolution—this one spiritual. Betrayed by modernity and surrounded by the unknown on all sides, including within themselves, millions of Westerners welcomed with open arms the religious leaders of the East, who unlike their Western colleagues were more than willing to share their "pathway to bliss." Gay liberation also happened at a time when dozens of Indian gurus and Buddhist teachers rushed to enlighten crowds in America and Europe. And today, we are so used to the smiling presence of the Dalai Lama that we tend to forget the time when spiritual diversity in the West consisted in having a few Jews in the neighborhood and nothing more.

In order to complete this vivid picture of the epistemological context that fosters gay liberation, there remains one last element of the puzzle to uncover that we owe largely to Freud's creative genius. Despite the numerous patent misconceptions of his psychoanalytic theory, Freud shall still be regarded as one of the most, if not the most seminal thinker of the twentieth century. Already, the discovery of the unconscious had been a first stab in the back of modernity. But to make things even worse, Freud's revolutionary vision of the human nature gave sex—Christianity's old foe—a central place. Sexual impulse was now at the heart of human psychological development. Not only did sexuality channel the fundamental energy that animates all human beings, but in fact sex was the life force itself. Everything, from personality traits to relationships to social life, resulted from complex iterations between one's sexual impetus and the external world. Human activities, whether social, work-related, or creative, were sublimated forms of sexual energy. With Freud, sex—or Satan, according to the Christian mythos—is not merely rehabilitated. It outranks God.

It is not so much whether Freud was right or not with respect to the primordial role of sex that is important here; once again, it is the fact that Western culture massively adopted those views. People believed the claims of psychoanalytic theory, eagerly. Needless to say, the West was in for trouble. The enforcement of puritanical morals had necessitated centuries of coordinated effort from all Christian Churches. It took just a few decades after Freud's seminal ideas started to diffuse to see the old repressive culture collapse. From a historical point of view, the scale and speed of this cultural reversal is mind-blowing. As the old Christian morals went crumbling down, generations of Westerners rediscovered the pleasures of sex, and the West underwent its second sexual revolution.

All things considered, Freud never really understood homosexuality. While being one of the rare intellectuals to recognize that homosexual desire does not automatically entail gender deviance, Freud was still unable to grasp the fundamental normality of homosexual desire, let alone its evolutionary purpose. For him, homosexuality was a benign form of immaturity—a developmental arrest—an idea very much with in agreement with the spirit of his time, even among homosexual intellectuals. And if Freud shared a genuine empathy for homosexuals, which strongly contrasted with the overall homophobic tone of the rest of psychoanalytic movement, he was not unique. Carl Jung, another great master, shared the same moderate open-mindedness toward homosexuals. Other intellectuals, as preeminent as Leo Tolstoy, Hermann Hesse, Thomas Mann, Emile Zola, Stefan Zweig, and Albert Einstein, made public statements in favor of repelling German anti-homosexual laws. Nevertheless, Freud's contribution to homosexual liberation is nothing short of astonishing.

Freud's unique role stems from his notion of the primordial bisexuality of all human beings. Dwelling on completely erroneous theories of embryonic hermaphroditism, Freud introduced in *Three Contributions to the Sexual Theory* in 1910 the idea that the undifferentiated soul of a human newborn carries a bisexual disposition within itself.[467] Later, as the individual develops throughout childhood into a "normal" adult, only the sexual impulses congruent with reproduction prevail. Accordingly, homosexuality corresponds to a failure in the psychosexual maturation process, resulting in the persistence of inadequate desires. In that sense, Freud's concept of bisexuality appears better defined as a "bisexual potentiality," distinct from the mere "sexual ambidexterity" that one might get at first. Freud's idea is fundamentally developmental, and very different from what we call bisexuality today.

This concept is at the heart of Freud's psychoanalytic theory and, according to Freud, at the heart of human nature.[468] It is our original bisexual state that allows Freud to explain phenomena such as infantile sexuality, autoeroticism, the Oedipus complex, and, of course, homosexuality. (To some degree, Jung's notion of animus and anima is analogous to the Freudian concept of primordial bisexuality. Similarly, Jung utilized the animus/anima to theorize homosexual desire.) But, as always, it is the impact on people that is most meaningful. At first, the news about people's primordial bisexuality landed as an omnipresent threat. Parents' urgent mission was now to ensure the masculinization of their sons. Overbearing and overprotective mothers constituted a risk that ought to be watched carefully. Eventually, the concept of bisexuality turned into insurmountable evidence. And during the 1970s bisexuality nearly became synonymous with sexual liberation.

What Freud did was to re-actualize de facto the ancient concept of a bisexual divine, but this time, expressed within a (post)modern framework. He rediscovered the fundamental ambiguity of human nature, so familiar to polytheist cultures, and which had been concealed in the West since the monotheist revolution. After Freud (and Jung, to a lesser extent), it became increasingly difficult, if not impossible, to define people's sexual essence. To make things worse, Kinsey transformed the concept of masculinity and femininity into moving targets. Just like the electrons of quantum mechanics, their "relative positions" turned into probabilistic realities, into waves. They were literally changing too fast to be observable. Uprooted, sexual identities were set loose. Suddenly, men turned into sexual objects (e.g., Elvis Presley, James Dean, Marlon Brando, and my favorite, Paul Newman), and women into celebrated intellectuals (e.g., Simone de Beauvoir and Susan Sontag). But this is only the tip of the iceberg. The development of effective and affordable contraceptive methods, which had a staggering impact on the collective psyche, is beyond the scope of this book. We will limit ourselves to noticing the odd synchronicity between all of this and the unprecedented change in the reproductive strategy of the human species. We are now getting a sense of the kind of world that witnessed the emergence of gay rights. At this point, the postmodern cultural revolution was ready to turn into riots.

GAY LIBERATION

It is only with the age of Enlightenment, in the eighteenth century, that modernity really started to reassess the moral consensus. The great majority of philosophers of the Enlightenment—Charles de Montesquieu (1689–1755), Denis Diderot (1713–1784), and Voltaire (1694–1778) in particular—recommended more tolerance for a vice that appeared to them so distasteful and yet, also, a private matter. Voltaire was a regular guest and friend of Frederick the Great, King of Prussia, who loved men, at least during his young age.[469] In his *Confessions*, Jean Jacques Rousseau shared a story about his involuntary involvement with a Moorish man who tried to molest him during his youth.[470] Overall, if the philosophers of the Enlightenment had a difficult time understanding both homosexual behavior and the need to punish those who practiced them by death, they also expressed that paradox very prudently in their writings.

The shift was subtle, nonetheless real. In 1791 the French Revolutionary Assembly decriminalized sodomy, along with heresy and blasphemy.[471] Through this formidable progress, one may discern the influence of the philosophy of Enlightenment as much as a desire to challenge and weaken the moral authority of the Church, which had always faithfully supported the absolute monarchy. The Napoleonic Code maintained the decriminalization of same-sex acts between consenting adults (a surprising fact, given that the Napoleonic law repealed the abolition of slavery). More importantly, the Napoleonic Code provided an ideal template to the many countries eager to reform outdated law codes. In the footsteps of Napoleon's armies, the Netherlands, Bavaria, Spain, and Portugal also decriminalized homosexual acts, and, thanks to the highly symbolic character of the French Revolution, so did the young republics of South America.[472] Elsewhere however, particularly in Anglo-Saxon countries such as England and the United States, sodomites had yet to see the light of the Enlightenment. Sometimes, the repression worsened. In England the death penalty against the crime of sodomy survived until 1861, when the crime of sodomy was finally commuted into a life sentence.[473] Bear in mind also that even in supposedly liberal countries, decriminalization never meant freedom, let alone dignity. Sodomites remained regularly harassed and under tight police surveillance, not to mention being subject to blackmail.

In the late-nineteenth century, especially in Germany and England, a wind of change started to blow. In 1836, at the heart of the Romantic period, which in many aspects marked the dawn of the postmodern era, the Swiss German Heinrich Hössli published a seven hundred-page treaty—*Eros, On the Love of Men*—which constituted the first defense of male love in modern times.[474] Later, a few other intellectuals whose names I mentioned earlier—John Addington Symonds, Karl Maria Kertbeny, Karl Heinrich Ulrichs, Richard von Krafft-Ebing, Havelock Ellis, Magnus Hirschfeld, and Freud—strived to redefine and explain a phenomenon that they were the first to approach positively or, at least, more positively. All endeavored to clear homosexual desire of its aura of evil and fought courageously to instill new ideas in a culture that frowned upon their mere interest in the matter.

Pro-homosexual political activism began in Germany in the figure of Magnus Hirschfeld. In 1897 Hirschfeld founded the Scientific Humanitarian Committee in an attempt to create the first pro-homosexual lobby. He successfully convinced prominent intellectuals of his time—among them, Richard von Krafft-Ebing, Leo Tolstoy, Rainer Maria Rilke, Hermann Hesse, Thomas Mann, Emile Zola, Gerhart Hauptmann, Stefan Zweig, and Albert Einstein—to sign a petition that demanded the repeal of the German anti-homosexual law, the infamous Paragraph 175.[475] Hirshfeld would, however, fail. Nazism soon put an end to the whole adventure. With World War II, the communist purges in the Soviet Union, and China's Cultural Revolution, the fury that the human race had carried in its collective psyche since prehistory seemed to reach its peak. Against a backdrop of general horror, the brutal repression of homosexuals was no exception. Their elimination in concentration camps, gulags, and other reeducation camps, was just more of the same, but now, at an industrial level.

And yet, miracles always remain possible and times of crisis often contain the seed of the next sociocultural transformation. World War II created the ferment of a new cultural shift, not in Europe this time, exhausted after years of warfare, but in the United States. Why did gay liberation reemerge there, in perhaps the most puritan of all Western countries? If it appears difficult to tell for certain, one can still identify a series of favorable conditions.

First of all, the United States had a long tradition of cohabitation, often precarious, among distinct cultural minorities. Gays and lesbians in America found in the ethnic communities that surrounded them a providential role model that their European counterparts seldom had. I maintain that it's impossible to understand the emergence of the gay liberation movement without taking into account community dynamics. The preliminary genesis of a self-identified gay community was an indispensable step toward the inception of an effective gay political movement. At the same time, the extraordinary political dynamism of the black community helped propel an unprecedented wave of protests that sent shock waves throughout all layers of society. Surely one cannot ignore the catalyzing effect of the civil rights movement on all other post-World War II liberation movements to serve both feminists and gays.

Second, World War II had very different consequences on American homosexuals, away from the horror of the Nazi camps. The massive mobilization of millions of American males and thousands of females, combined with the fierce homophobia present in the military and civil administrations, promoted an unprecedented geographical redistribution of the homosexual population.[476] The American army, sticking to its regular drafting procedure, systematically excluded thousands of gay men and lesbians after they mistakenly confessed to having had homosexual experiences or attractions. With a dishonorable discharge from the United States army in their pocket and forever labeled as gay, many young men and women preferred not to go back to their hometowns and families. Instead many migrated to big cities where, on the one hand, it was easier to achieve larger anonymity and where on the other hand, hospitable gay subcultures existed already. New York, San Francisco, Chicago, and Washington D.C. saw their homosexual populations swell, bringing together gays and lesbians in large numbers as never before in world history.

Third, in the wake of World War II and the onset of the Cold War, homosexual communities in the United States found themselves caught in an absurd contradiction. Homosexuals had never been geographically so grouped. Yet amid the anticommunist and anti-homosexual tide of McCarthyism, they found themselves extremely vulnerable to political persecutions. During the 1950s thousands of homosexuals lost their jobs thanks to the diligence of the Federal Bureau of Investigation set up by Senator McCarthy.[477] However, the greatest harm was inflicted more discretely. For decades psychoanalysts and other psychologists continued to treat homosexuals for a sickness they did not have and taught them with total impunity to deny who they were.

The fourth favorable condition for the emergence of a viable gay movement in the United States ensued from the fact that the American government system is unparalleled in its reliance on the influence of political lobbies to promote specific agendas. Since, for the first time in history, gays and lesbians had gathered into sizable and highly visible communities in major cities across the country, it became manifest that the homosexual community had an opportunity to exercise political influence at the local and national level.

Last but not least, Alfred Kinsey published his two reports: *Sexual Behavior in the Human Male* (in 1948) and *Sexual Behavior in the Human Female* (in 1953)—modernity's greatest gifts to the homosexual community—using data collected within the United States. If Kinsey's work had a transformative effect worldwide, in the United States it was experienced like an earthquake.

Altogether, America had a perfect mix: an authoritarian Puritanism, a political system that gave a voice to well-organized minorities, and a homosexual population concentrated in major urban areas at an unprecedented level. But that cannot explain everything. It is equally important to acknowledge and understand why society somehow let it happen. So, always keep in mind that those victories became achievable goals only as the postmodern paradigm and its correlate, relativism, pervaded Western culture during the 1950s and continued forward. Then the evolution appears logical, almost predictable. To put all the historical responsibility of gay liberation on gay activism would be missing half of the story, even though I by no means intend to minimize the role of political activism. Without the extraordinary courage of those men and women, nothing would have been possible. But a new consciousness had emerged: there is not one single truth; there might even be no truth at all. The old moral order—the time of certainties—had become increasingly "porous" since the Copernican revolution. By the late 1960s, it had irreversibly decayed and doubt was spreading all over Western culture.

In retrospect, it all went very fast. The Mattachine Society, which was to become the first efficient and lasting homosexual organization in the United States, was founded in 1950 by a small group of gay men in Los Angeles. Two years later, Mattachine launched *One*, the first homosexual publication of any significance in America. In 1955 a group of women split and created a separate lesbian group, the Daughters of Bilitis. By the late 1950s, San Francisco had some thirty gay bars, more than New York City.[478] By the 1960s legendary artists and thinkers like Alan Ginsberg, Jack Kerouac, William Burroughs, Paul Goodman, Tennessee Williams, and Truman Capote were no longer afraid to speak about men's feelings for each other, setting a very new tone in American literature. In the meantime, the black community won its first battle under the transformational leadership of Martin Luther King, Jr. and the relentless support of President Lyndon B. Johnson. The Civil Right Act was signed on July 2, 1964. And on the night of June 27, 1969, a disparate group of gay men, lesbians, and drag queens quietly hanging out at the Stonewall bar in Greenwich Village would make history. Instead of tolerating— once more—a humiliating raid by the New York City police, those unlikely heroes decided to rebel.

The so-called Stonewall riots marked a turning point. From then on, the history of achievement of homosexual rights accelerated. Unlike the Mattachine Society and the Daughters of Bilitis which had primarily focused on public education and community support, new organizations emerged that would turn the gay political cause into a radical fight. The Gay Liberation Front was created, then the Gay Activist Alliance, and in 1973 the National Gay Task Force. Those organizations challenged politicians and lobbied for gay rights openly. In 1973 the American Psychiatric Association removed homosexuality from its list of mental illness, another victory for individual rights and also one of symbolic importance. In 1974 an openly gay woman, Elaine Noble, was elected for the first time to the Massachusetts House of Representatives, and in 1977 Harvey Milk was elected to the board of supervisors of the city of San Francisco.[479] That same year the people of the state of California rejected "Proposition 6," which sought to ban homosexuals from teaching in public schools. And I will stop here.

In twenty years homosexuals went from being fired from their jobs to being elected. I know very well how much that progress was far from being homogeneous in the world. Even in the United States today, many homosexuals do not benefit from the same level of freedom as their peers in San Francisco or New York. Nevertheless, historically speaking, the success of the gay liberation movement is dazzling. It cannot be explained only by the courage and the intelligence of its leaders. Why were the Stonewall riots not repressed by bloodshed? The story turned out the way that it did not only because of the unique fighting skills of a group of heroic drag queens, but mostly because the New York City police did not risk responding with the same level of brutality as it had in the past. In the same way, Proposition 6 was defeated in 1977 and not only because of Harvey Milk's formidable charisma. People had changed, too, and so had many of their leaders.

Everything occurs within a context, and everything is the result of an evolutionary process that unfolds with time. This has been our working hypothesis since the beginning. The rapid reintegration process of homosexuals within the empathic space that had its origin in the United States in the second half of the twentieth century did not happen in a contextual vacuum. Instead, I argue that it may be viewed as the product of the convergence of four interrelated evolutionary dynamics:

First, four centuries of modernity and half a century of postmodernity had reduced the foundation of the Christian cosmology to dust. Humankind had lost its centrality in a universe that it would never comprehend anyway. The Freudian concepts of original bisexuality and sex as life's primordial force had blurred the limpid division of the world between the male and female principles, men and women, God and his creation, soul and body, good and bad, and so forth, which had been a cornerstone of the Western worldview since the Axial Age.

Second, one century of objective scientific discourse, in spite of all its flaws and limitations, had revealed homosexuality's existence to the world and, even more importantly, to homosexuals. Kinsey's splendid contribution disclosed to the entire planet that homosexual behavior was common and that the homosexual and heterosexual worlds did not constitute two separate realms, but in fact, a continuum.

Third, the postmodern paradigm had occasioned a cultural shift that has no known precedent in human history: relativism. Postmodern relativism holds that because human beings are trapped inside their own subjectivity, truth is an unreachable target. From relativism emerged a series of eclectic movements—the civil rights campaign, the hippy wave, feminism, pacifism, gay liberation, queer theory, and so forth—that all aimed to liberate people from unquestioned "cultural truth" and rejected any cultural norm as a form of oppression.

The fourth dynamic, which we are going to explore next, helped homosexuals break free from an evolutionary logic that had constricted male homosexual relationships since prehistory. It would create a novel relational form, so obvious today that we tend to forget its revolutionary character: modern homosexuality.

FOR THE LOVE OF COMRADES: THE EMERGENCE OF MODERN HOMOSEXUALITY

Before proceeding further, let me warn you once again that, even today, modern homosexuality is still evolving, disparate, and difficult to grasp with certainty. Any description, including the one that follows, ought to be revisited sooner or later, refined, and perhaps readjusted. Notice also that what I call modern homosexuality (in agreement with the current terminology) is not, rigorously speaking, modern, in that it is not a product of modernity. Modern homosexuality was constructed step by step starting from the first centuries of our era, and took its current form around the 1950s and '60s. Hence, it would be more accurate to speak of contemporary or postmodern homosexuality. Yet, in order to maintain some consistency with the prevalent homosexual discourse (and doubtful the term "postmodern homosexuality" could ever take hold), I will continue to use the term "modern homosexuality," hoping that it will not create too much confusion in the readers' minds.

Throughout this book, I have often united transgenerational and transgender homosexualities under one larger category, traditional/premodern homosexualities, whose hallmark is (1) the status of the "stud" male is always guaranteed by his active role in the penetrative act and (2) female homosexuality, unconcerned with ranking polarities and rarely culturally defined, developed little in the public arena.

Modern homosexuality is drastically different from traditional homosexualities and by no means represents a revival of traditional/premodern homosexualities. Contrary to the two forms of homosexual relationships of the past (transgenerational and transgender), equal status between the two partners constitutes the signature of modern homosexuality. Transgender homosexuality still exists, in various forms and degrees: transgendered/transsexual women and men, transvestites, drag queens, and butch lesbians. And so does transgenerational homosexuality, in the attraction of older men exclusively to young males. Yet those relationships are no longer the prevalent model—the archetypical "center of gravity"—among homosexual communities in North America, Europe, and parts of Asia today. What is more, modern homosexuality emerged from a cultural paradigm—postmodern relativism—that challenges society's divine right to normalize people's sexuality and professes the right of each individual to be different, two notions that are diametrically opposed to the spirit of traditional homosexualities.

Can we, retrospectively, discern the discrete presence of "modern-like" homosexual relationships in the distant past? It is hard to tell. Remember that what we know about sexuality in the past is mostly what people were comfortable sharing, bragging about, and occasionally exposing to the public eye. We do not know for sure what Greek males really did in their bedrooms. It is nonetheless irresistibly tempting to scrutinize history and try to recognize same-sex relationships that were certainly not "modern" as I define it, yet more equal or more free from the tyranny of male ranking.

The passionate friendships of Achilles for Patrocles and of King David for Jonathan, showed a quasi-negligible age gap, no sign of feminization on either side, but nonetheless, a significant status difference. Nor do we know whether those friendships had a sexual component to them. It's true that aside from the presence of a beard, one can hardly recognize in the famous statue that represents Harmodius or Aristogeiton—the pair of lovers and fierce warriors who helped free Athens from its tyrants in 514 BCE, losing their lives in the process,—which one was the *erastes* and which one was the *eromenos*.[480] Aristotle also mentioned the case of Philolaus, a great law giver at Thebes, and his lover Dioclese, an Olympic athlete, who lived together and were buried beside each other.[481] The martyrdom of Saints Serge and Bacchus in the third century also inspired many commentaries. John Boswell in particular held their fervent companionship as a prototype of accepted masculine unions during the early time of Christianity. But ultimately, examples of quasi-equal status lovers in antiquity are so rare, and overall, too dubious to have any significance for us.

Throughout the Middle Ages, the Renaissance, and the onset of modernity, official records of trials for sodomy show no clear sign of emergence of a new kind of homosexual relationships. Even Oscar Wilde, during his trial in 1895, defined "the love that dare not speak its name" as the spiritual affection of an elder for a younger man. However, things seem to change in the eighteenth and nineteenth century. People became increasingly aware of the existence of a minority of adult males who enjoyed playing the passive role while having sex with other men.[482] "Queens" and "mollies" were essentially women-like creatures, effeminate men, weak and untrustworthy, at least from the public perspective. They thought, spoke, and dressed like women; it was therefore inevitable that they would also express the same desire as women. Noticeably, we begin to find instances (mainly from police reports) where the sexually passive and actives roles were reversible between partners. In post-revolutionary France, the decriminalization of sodomy other than those involving children or rape provided an unexpected freedom to homosexual lovers. At the same time, as private and consensual same-sex relationships tend to vanish from criminal records, their sudden lack of visibility becomes problematic for historians. And yet in 1804, for instance, we do hear of the case of a relationship between two domestic servants at the respective age of twenty eight and thirty five.[483] Later, Karl Maria Kertbeny (the one who first coined the word homosexuality), carefully avoiding to acknowledge that he was probably speaking for himself, described the "passion [. . .] for the man, even in the mature man who had already passed forty."[484] And around the same period, homoeroticism began to reemerge in the arts and literature with the works of Oscar Wilde and Edward Carpenter in England, and, in France, Rimbaud, Verlaine, and Baudelaire. Times were changing.

The American poet Walt Whitman may very well be considered the herald of modern homosexual love. His 1860 version of *Leaves of Grass*, which included the *Calamus* poems, revealed the "manly love of comrades" and the "athletic love" to a large audience. His lyrical and nonetheless subtle celebration of male love, incredibly bold for the times, enchanted homosexual writers on the other side of the Atlantic—Wilde, Carpenter, and Symonds.[485] Thanks to Whitman, who was and still is the most celebrated poet in America, people discovered that the ardent and lasting friendships between men could also be erotic.

A century separates the *Leaves of Grass* from the Mattachine Society, just the time it took for the new spirit of the time to coalesce into a new form of same-sex relationship—modern homosexuality, the love between same-sex equals—and eventually into a new identity. This equality between partners is twofold. It first manifests in the form of a striking symmetry between partners—almost twin-like—with respect to age, education level, social class, and cultural experience. Obviously, perfect symmetry in the relationship is not a requirement. Differences and diversity are often (but not always) welcomed. Yet adequate symmetry regarding psychological maturity, life goals, and/or physical attractiveness, for instance, does correspond to a prevailing ideal in modern gay culture.

The second aspect—the symmetry in the sexual roles—is, I believe, even more crucial. I have emphasized how premodern homosexual cultures were obsessed by the status of the dominant male. All ancient cultures spent a tremendous amount of energy defining and maintaining the sociocultural identity of sub-male categories—youth, transgender, slave, and so forth. All that disappears in modern homosexuality. All conventions rooted in male ranking are abrogated. In its place, modern homosexuality values the versatility between partners for the sake of mutual sexual fulfillment. The insertive and receptive roles ("tops" and "bottoms") have not disappeared; however, any "specialization" in one role or the other tends to be perceived as a limitation and usually characterized as missing out on the full spectrum of the homosexual experience. And by no means does it constitute an affirmation of status. We clearly are a world away from ancient models.

At this point, notice that paradoxically, while the modern homosexual ideal appears to have freed male love from the archaic necessity of gender, age, or status difference, this appears less true of lesbian relationships. In the 1940s and '50s, lesbian communities were largely dominated by the "butch/femme" culture, which demanded an extreme differentiation in gender roles. Butch lesbians adopted extreme masculine attitudes and appearances, the antipode of that of their "femmes." In the 1970s, the butch/femme model was harshly attacked by the feminist movement, which rejected it as a carbon copy of the old sexist heterosexual standards.[486] Today, to the best of my knowledge, both butch/femme and equal-type relationships coexist among gay women. This difference between male and female modern homosexualities reminds us of a very important point. Male and female homosexualities have undergone distinct evolutionary paths. For men, the main challenge was to reconcile the issue of male ranking with modern morals. For women, the novelty was essentially to enter the public sphere.

Another unexpected innovation of modern homosexuality resides in a widespread aspiration to long-term relationships, including marriage. The heroic struggle of the gay community in its attempt to break through the marital institution demonstrates clearly homosexuals' interest in life-long and sacralized commitments. In the framework of traditional homosexualities, the idea of marriage between two adults of the same sex and status would have been an aberration.

Lastly, modern homosexuality neither rejects nor systemizes gender deviance. Modern homosexuals, both male and female, embrace the entire spectrum of gender roles that is available in and defined by the culture to which they belong. In perfect congruence with the postmodern paradigm, in modern homosexuality the lines between the masculine and feminine and between the insertive and receptive roles, which had defined two distinct classes of individuals in the premodern world, now run through the sexual consciousness of each and every individual.

Finally comes my favorite question: Is there an evolutionary lesson in the emergence of modern homosexuality? Once one gets over the fact that modern homosexuality, egalitarian and versatile, constitutes nothing less than a turning point in the evolution of the human species, one must then admit that modern homosexuality looks a lot like "modern heterosexuality." The specifics of the sexual act aside, modern homosexual relationships value the same principles—mutual and romantic love, long-term partnership, mutual respect, emotional and economical support, integrity, and faithfulness—as modern heterosexual ones. Modern homosexuality, for a large part, has embraced the relational ideal of Judeo-Christianity, an ideal originally brought into existence by the Roman Empire and profoundly reworked by three centuries of modernity and half of century of postmodernity, but a Judeo-Christian ideal nonetheless. The consequence of this is, in my opinion, even more astonishing. Remember that the early Fathers of the Church (in the footsteps of Philo of Alexandria) were the first to coalesce into one unique category all same-sex lovers—pederasts, effeminates, active, passive, male, and female. This directly fostered the emergence of the polymorph archetype of the sodomite, which in retrospect seems to have constituted a transition stage, like a chrysalis. In it, homosexuality accomplished its long metamorphosis from a rank-based to an egalitarian form, and from it emerged the modern homosexual. Hence modern homosexuality was created by the very culture that has relentlessly tried to eradicate same-sex desire from the surface of the earth—Christianity—a fact that neither the Church nor modern homosexuals appear ready to acknowledge.

The transformation of same-sex love took centuries and many innocent lives. But it has bestowed on us the life we have today, the one we are so proud of. One can only salute the extraordinary resilience and inventiveness of homosexual desire, exposed to centuries of homophobic brutality. Reinvented—reborn, indeed—adulterous child of Christianity and (post)modernity, modern homosexuality is fulfilling a spiritual vision, nearly twenty centuries old, which holds love as the most sacred value. History's irony is startling.

Predictably, modern homosexuality is today knocking at the door of churches, temples, and synagogues. In doing so, gay love is logically trying to reconnect with the spiritual womb that had involuntarily nurtured its birth. The question of homosexuality's connection with the sacred is an essential one. As we will see, in all the cultures where homosexual love was integrated in some form or another, homosexual desire was represented through the world of the sacred. And we need now to take a closer look at those representations.

The Missing Myth

If we have now unearthed the contextual logic that underlies the fall from grace of same-sex love in the first centuries and its reemergence two millenniums later, we are still left with a burning question: Why did it work so well? What can explain that homophobia was able to spread like wildfire throughout Christendom and, eventually, throughout the entire planet? As it happens, this simple question, seldom raised, hides many others that are all equally unexplainable.

If, as we have seen two chapters earlier, the desacralization of same-sex love started in Greece around the fifth centuries BCE and gathered even more momentum in the Roman Empire, why was the Greco-Roman civilization still so tolerant of homosexual relationships? In Athens as in Rome homophobia remained for the most part a philosopher's concern. But with the rise of Christianity, the *status quo* does change. Far from being restricted to an "intelligentsia" or institutions (spiritual and political), the hate of the sodomite pervaded popular culture. The entire Christendom hunted sodomites, not just the Holy Inquisition. Why did the anti-homosexual discourse fail to have an effect on people before Christianity? Was Paul so much more convincing than Plato?

As history unfolds, the mystery only deepens. The "barbarian" tribes that invaded Europe and North Africa, causing the collapse of the Roman Empire, appear to have been rather enthusiastic or, at least, unworried about homosexual practices before their conversion to Christianity. Yet they systematically adopted the homophobic mentality of the culture that they had just vanquished and did this in the space of only a few generations.

A millennium later the Protestant reform claimed to recapture Jesus's original teachings. Martin Luther (1483–1546) denounced the crimes and abuse of the papacy, challenging the basic doctrine of the Roman Catholic Church. Priestly celibacy was rejected; the Vulgate—the only official version of the Bible in Latin—was translated in German; and the Virgin Mary was largely demoted from her spiritual position. Those constituted major changes. And yet Luther unambiguously declared that "the heinous conduct of the people of Sodom is extraordinary, in as much as they departed from the natural passion and longing of the male for the female, which was implanted by God, and desired what is altogether contrary to nature. Whence comes this perversity? Undoubtedly from Satan, who after people have once turned away from the fear of God, so powerfully suppresses nature that he beats out the natural desire and stirs up a desire that is contrary to nature."[487] The hate of the Sodomite (or that of the Jew, incidentally) did not die with Luther; in fact, quite the opposite occurred.

Why the philosophers of the Enlightenment and modernity, who rejected religious beliefs as the major source of alienation for people, fell short of their promise to challenge all religion-based prejudice when they examined the case of homosexuality, is even more puzzling. In various ways they all pleaded for more equitable laws against the crime of sodomy. At the same time, most of them made a point to share their disgust and antipathy for homosexual behavior. In his *Spirit of Laws*, nothing really distinguishes Montesquieu's description of the crime against nature: "God forbid that I should have the least inclination to diminish the public horror against a crime which religion, morality, and civil government equally condemn. It ought to be proscribed, were it only for its communicating to one sex the weaknesses of the other, and for leading people by a scandalous prostitution of their youth to an ignominious old age."[488] In his famous *Philosophical Dictionary*, the very anticlerical Voltaire approached the topic of sodomy—in a section titled "Socratic love"—not without ambiguity.[489] On the one hand, he used the matter to discredit the Church ("The monks charged with the education of youth have always exhibited a little of this tendency"). On the other hand, he immediately acknowledged his own skepticism and lack of certitudes regarding this issue ("How could it happen that a vice that, if it were general, would destroy human kind, and that is a despicable offense against nature, should however be so natural?"). Yet Voltaire cannot help finding this subject "odious and disgusting." Even the bravest of all, the English utilitarian philosopher and advocate of law reform Jeremy Bentham (1748–1832), wrote in *Offences Against One's Self: Paederasty* (written in 1785 but only published in 1978), "The act is disgusting and odious . . . not to the man who does it, for he does it only because it gives him pleasure, but to the one who thinks of it."

So, if the philosophers of the Enlightenment advocated for more individual freedom, fairer laws, and the respect of people's privacy, their incomprehension about same-sex love—faked or real—remained reminiscent of the Middle Ages. Despite the absence of prohibition of homosexual acts in post-revolutionary France and a few other countries, one must admit that, overall, modernity embraced the homophobic prejudice with ease, if not conviction (besides, French culture never was particularly homophile either). Modernity "recycled" homophobia, redecorating it with brand new words: "These days, no one doubts that the number of degenerations, of cerebral derailings—expressed by the tendencies toward suicide, by phobias, etc.—results in large part from the fact that in our nation the genital functions are often not accomplished as they should be. Therefore it is necessary, from the point of view of the vitality of the future of the race, to study the morbid causes, to discern the dangerous and evil elements, among which must be ranked for an appreciable part the creature stricken with sexual perversion: the pervert, the feminiform born-invert."[490]

We tend to forget that in the meantime modernity had invented democracy and ended slavery. What was so complicated or so impossible about homosexual love? At odds with the rest of history, the brutal repression of sodomites, which had epitomized centuries of abuse of power by Christian Churches, ended up being relayed, if not amplified, by the modern states very rationally and with the diligent help of their police forces and the medical establishment. From an evolutionary perspective the slaughter of homosexuals in the Nazi camps and the "witch-hunts" in the McCarthy era were the logical conclusion of a process that had started in the Renaissance. Moreover, the irresistible push of homophobia was not confined to the West. And if one may already wonder how Europeans succeeded in exporting homophobia to all the countries they came to dominate, even more incomprehensible is the fact that violence against homosexuals intensified after the withdraw of the colonizing countries, which is currently what we observe in several African and Muslim countries. As for the persecution of homosexuals in communist China during the Cultural Revolution, the logic of this is simply mystifying.

All these examples point to the fact that the dissemination of homophobia is only remotely associated with that of the Christian dogma (e.g., Muslim countries and communist regimes), and that the spread of homophobia in a population does not systematically reflect the homophobic character in dominant intellectual discourse (e.g., the Roman Empire) or the prevalent moral framework of a given culture (e.g., modern democracies). This conclusion leads us to the question: What are the conditions of existence of homosexuality in the sociocultural sphere? In order to resolve this problem that I believe holds the key to our overall endeavor, we will now turn to the works of Carl Jung, Bronislaw Malinowski, Mircea Eliade, and Joseph Campbell, to name only a few, and continue a discussion that we had left on hold in chapter 6. And more specifically, we now need to understand how people know what is true, what is good, and what is beautiful, and what is not.

MYTHS AND MYTHOS

In 1871—well before Jung, Eliade, or Campbell—Sir John Addington Symonds, in one of the first literary works in defense of homosexual love, pointed out the striking difference between the Greek and Christian mythologies. In Greek times, Symonds wrote:

> Eros [. . .] is a youth whose modesty is no less noticeable than his beauty [. . .]
> Eros it may be remembered, was the special patron of paiderastia. Greek art,
> like Greek mythology, embodied a finely graduated half-unconscious analysis

of human nature. The mystery of procreation was indicated by phalli on the Hermae. Unbridled appetite found incarnation in Priapus [. . .] The natural desires were symbolised in Aphrodite, Praxis, Kallipugos, or Pandemos [. . .] The wild and native instincts, wandering, untutored and untamed, which still connect man with the life of woods and beasts and April hours, received half-human shape in Pan and Silenus, the Satyrs and the Fauns.[491]

On the other hand, Symonds observed,

[. . .] the Middle Ages proclaimed through chivalry the truth, then for the first time fully apprehended, that woman is the mediating and ennobling element in human life [. . .] The mythology of Mary gave religious sanction to the chivalrous enthusiasm; and a cult of woman sprang into being to which, although it was romantic and visionary, we owe the spiritual basis of our domestic and civil life.[492]

Can the myths be the missing piece of our puzzle? I believe that they are. Myths hold the keys to homosexual destiny. I intend to show that in any culture the integration of homosexuals, homosexual acts, and homosexual love, whatever sociocultural form they may have taken, is tied to its mythic representation.

We are most familiar with the term "mythology," which designates, according to Joseph Campbell, "an organization of symbolic images and narratives, metaphorical of the possibilities of human experience and fulfillment of a given culture at a given time."[493] Mythologies are composed of distinct subunits, the myths. In chapter 6 we came to understand that the symbolic material of the myths initially aimed to sooth human beings' deepest fear—the unknown—"that for which initially we have no words," specifies Karen Armstrong.[494] Myths, which Bronislaw Malinowski called "a cultural force," are crucial actors in the intersubjective space.[495] Myths explain everything: where human beings are from; where they are going; and how they work; where the world comes from; where it is going; and how it works. They shed light on why and how things are the way they are and why they happen.[496] That is for the etiological function of myths. Mircea Eliade tells us more: "myth narrates a sacred history; it relates an event that took time in primordial Time, the fabled time of the beginnings."[497] Myths are sacred stories that connect human reality to the origins of "Reality."

Of course, not just any story has the chance to become a myth, the same way that not just any piece of metal is a magnet. The sacredness of a story is never guaranteed. Sacredness emerges from the special relationship between a particular story and a people. Myths are absolutely unique in that they are collectively elected by a mechanism that we still do not comprehend, other than the fact that their narrative content "resonates" with the collective psyche.

Because of the unique relationship between myths and the collective mind, another key function of myth is "to reveal exemplary models for all the rites and significant human activities."[498] Malinowski develops the idea further by observing that "an intimate connection exists between the world, the mythos, the sacred tales of the tribe, on the one hand, and their ritual acts, their moral deeds, their social organization, and even their practical activities, on the other."[499]

There appears a third important concept: mythos. In Malinowski's work and nearly everywhere else (including the dictionary), mythos is pretty much the equivalent of mythology. Congruous with pioneer researchers such as Campbell and Eliade, but also popular writers like Karen Armstrong, I will draw a sharp distinction between the two concepts. Mythologies (such as those found in Greek, Viking, Hindu, or Polynesian cultures) are composed of a set of stories—the myths. Altogether, the myths fulfill the various functions that we have just started to lay down: sacred, etiological, and exemplary. We will see however that things become increasingly complicated as societies evolved from traditional, to institutionalized, to modern, and eventually to postmodern stages of cultural development. In fact, we will need an entire new chapter to make sense of the postmodern stage, which is today. So from this point on, I will call mythos that which in the intersubjective space of any culture at any stage of its development plays and perpetuates the role of traditional myths/mythologies, regardless of the fact that what constitutes this mythos may no longer resemble standard mythic narratives. (The relevance of this evolutionary continuity will become increasingly clear in subsequent chapters). So logically, any mythology constitutes a mythos. In contrast, only primitive mythoi can be narrowed down to a particular mythology.

Campbell attributed to myths four distinct functions.[500] Myth's first function is to deal with what mystics have called the *mysterium tremendum et fascinans* ("fearful and fascinating mystery"). As evoked earlier, our distant ancestors opened their eyes to a world that offered no comfort whatsoever. On top of that, human beings have the ability to foresee and also dread miseries to come: war, disease, hunger . . . They know about death. They must have been terrified. We have to understand the extraordinary burden that this must have been. (Even today, we postmoderns are far from coping very effectively with that fundamental aspect of our existence.) From an evolutionary standpoint, awareness is extremely costly. Myths, on the other hand, help "[align] waking consciousness to the *mysterium tremendum* of this universe, as it is." They allow human beings to alleviate the insufferable vulnerability that comes with a higher consciousness. In other words, they reconcile human consciousness with the brutal laws of nature. Myths in all civilizations have provided a familiar representation of all that was inaccessible to human understanding—the enigma of our origin and fate, our birth, death, diseases, time, seasons, strengths and weaknesses, but also passions and desires. They make the infernal swirl of life in which people are desperately trapped comprehensible. They have held a sacred—universal and eternal—representation of everything human beings needed to know about the world, and more importantly, about themselves. They gave meaning to people's lives, and this, despite their unpredictability and unbearable unfairness. Myths did not simply bestow dignity on human beings, they invented it.

The second function of myths is cosmological. Everywhere human beings would otherwise see only disorder and chaos, myths impose structure. They provide an intelligible and reassuring image of the cosmos (comparatively speaking). They describe the shape of the world, how the earth holds still, what keeps the sun, the moon, and the stars up in the sky, what lies beyond the horizon, why the wind blows, and why seasons alternate. But the cosmological order is not merely structural; it is also historical and moral. It explains the origins of the universe, how it was created and by whom, and how the human race came about. Myths tell us what was there at the beginning of time and what happened then that accounts for the situation (usually a mess) in which people find themselves now. They allow human beings to relate with the rest of creation.

Through the cosmological myths, one sees crystallize a "perfect history," perfect first because it is divine, and second because it stems from the origin of the cosmos and the beginning of time. Insofar as they remind people of a perfection they have lost (the "perfection of the origins" that cultures commonly call paradise or golden age), cosmological myths immortalize a symbolic model of how perfection ought to be reestablished in the present. We have actually already encountered this essential dimension of myths when we have studied the key role of the dyad formed by the masculine/dominant principle—Yahveh—and the feminine/submissive principle—the chosen people—in the Jewish cosmology and all the religions of the Abrahamic lineage.

The third function of myths is, in Campbell's words, "to validate and support a specific moral order," and in Malinowski's, "to establish a sociological charter, or a retrospective moral pattern of behaviour."[501] Myths set the moral tone of the culture that keeps them alive.[502] In all human cultures, they have provided a social and moral template, that is, determined the morality of each and every behavior. Faithfully transmitted through the generations, the deeds of gods and heroes delineated the limits between good and bad, appropriate and inappropriate, auspicious and inauspicious. Not only did mythic stories depict the realm of everything that is possible but they simultaneously acted as case laws.

The last and fourth function of myths is "to carry the individual through the various stages and crisis of life—that is, to help persons grasp the unfolding of life with integrity."[503] What Campbell meant by this is that myths play an active role in an individual's psychological development. How is that possible and what does it imply? Jung and Eliade both stressed the "numinous" character of myth. The original meaning of the word "numinous" conveys the idea of some supernatural or divine power. Obviously, this is not exactly what they intended to communicate. In reality, the use of "numinous" hides the embarrassing fact that we simply do not know how myths work. All we know is that living or, more precisely, culturally active myths exert some sort of fascination upon people. The message that they convey is compelling. As a result, myths impose their subtle presence in the individual psyche. One may conclude—we shall say, temporarily—that myths possess a "psychic energy" that is transferred from the collective to the individual psyche, which defines the myth's "numinosity."

In psychological terms, this "psychic energy" is localized inside of what Jung calls archetypes. As a matter of fact, one can view the myths as the stories that give life to archetypes. Archetypes are different from symbols, the other "numinous" constituent of myth (which we will discuss later, in a different context). Symbols are representational elements—object, animal, sign, and so on—that evokes a concept very different from what the element really is. For instance, the moon is often viewed as a symbol of the feminine principle. The moon becomes a symbol by virtue of its association with the feminine principle and generally women, but the moon symbol is not by itself a woman or something feminine. On the other hand, archetypes act in a much more immediate fashion. They are what they represent and do not need to be translated. Take Hercules, for instance, a typical case of hero archetype. The active principle of the Hercules archetype is directly communicated by who Hercules is, what he does, how he behaves, what he seeks, and what he likes or dislikes. In that, mythic archetypes constitute active mirrors of the individual psyche in the intersubjective space.[504] And this role of mirrors goes both ways.

First, myths reflect the human psyche. This movement corresponds to a projection of human psychological realities upon myths (as already touched upon in chapter 6, "the primitive man imagined the outer world in his own image"). Through our myths, human beings gave the unknown a known appearance. More importantly, they conferred on the world that surrounded them and, even more so on the unknown, the same thoughts, emotions, and intentions as those that they experienced inside themselves. The systematic projection of all human mental and physical functions in a plethora of supernatural beings generated such a rich picture of the human psyche that, two millenniums later, psychoanalysts would find in ancient mythologies a precise depiction of nearly all aspects of the psyche and often, a name for it.

Second, the human psyche has mirrored myths. By this I mean that archetypes act as role models. They are not required to be physically real to be active. They just need to be alive in the collective psyche, that is, alive through the myths. Archetypes, like myths, exist in language. In all times archetypes, such as heroes, gods, martyrs, or saints, have delineated the palette of identities available to human beings. And by giving life to a myriad of fundamental archetypes through a fixed narrative, myths constitute a template for being.

Many traditional myths involve various deities and other supernatural beings, all highly personified and all as unpredictable and temperamental as any normally constituted human beings can be—proud, capricious, lustful, violent, loving, jealous, angry, resentful, and so forth—the entire repertoire of our human being-ness. The diversity of human nature reflected upon that of the gods. Each one represented a particular domain of human expertise. In Greek mythology, for example, Zeus embodied power, Athena wisdom and courage, Ares violence and wars, Hades death and the world of the dead, and Apollo the creative skills of arts and medicine. Power, whether social, political, military, or religious, was defined by its connection to a specific mythic representation. In return, myths bestowed sacredness on those honorific functions. Passions and sexual desires, which both spoke through the goddess Aphrodite-Venus and the god Eros, were no exception to the rule.

The mythological depiction of the human psyche—thoughts, emotions and desires—created a nearly perfect parallel between the lives of the gods and those of human beings, thereby establishing myriad connections between human life and the sacred. Thanks to a fluid equilibrium between the human and divine plans, not only did myths recapitulate all that was known about the human soul (as projections) but the soul could only be grasped through a knowledge of the myths (as eternal and universal models). Myths were windows opened on human beings' subjective space, hence, the collective repertoire through which human beings could understand themselves and others. Myths emerged from the discovery of the individual psyche by the group, and ended up being at the same time the mold that the culture imposed on the individual. Understanding this is absolutely crucial.

Ultimately, myths match the particular field of awareness of the culture that holds them as true, what in the worldview was deemed sacred, eternal and universal. They reflect the psychocultural center of gravity of societies, ensuring both coherence and continuity. From one generation to the next, they tell people what is true, good, and beautiful, and what is not. And of course, this vital function of myths far exceeded traditional mythologies; as a matter of fact, throughout history that role has been fulfilled by the mythos.

Mythic Representations of Same-Sex Desire

We have now established that to exist in the collective psyche, that is, to be (1) visible to and (2) understandable by other members of the group, goes hand in hand with being represented in the mythos. It is therefore quite instructive to discover, accordingly, that in cultures where homosexuality was integrated in some form or another, homosexual behavior, desire, and feeling were depicted in the mythic space.

In the Sambia puberty rites one of the (and perhaps the most) developmentally ancient forms of ritualized homosexuality on record, which entails the ritualistic incorporation of acts of fellatio or sodomy involving adult and adolescent males, is dictated by an ancient belief that is quintessentially of magic-mythic nature. Unless boys are fed with the semen of their elders, they may never find the strength to extract themselves from the irresistible attraction exerted by the female world, primarily incarnated by their mothers. The masculinizing power of semen allows boys to grow up as men; otherwise, they may very well fail. Thus the rites perpetuate the fragile balance of power between the male and female sides that governs the Sambia mythic universe. They help maintain the order of the cosmos. For Sambia people, the fact that men enjoy being fellated to the point of reaching orgasm, which is the part that so fascinates us today, is neither good nor bad; it is simply beside the point.

The two-spirit tradition present among Native American populations was similarly undergirded by sophisticated mythologies that incorporated hermaphroditism and sex-transformation. In some tribes, the world could have not been created or agriculture would have not been invented without the gender fluidity of their creators. Two-spirits were often viewed as sacred individuals and believed to possess psychic powers that were manifested primarily through their dreams.[505] Their status was often associated with the transgender characters present in the creation myths and/or with female symbols, such as the moon.[506] Supernatural faculties, such as the ability to converse with the world of spirits, counted among the important attributes of transgender shamans as well.

In all the great civilizations of antiquity it was common to encounter same-sex desire and feelings, gender transgression, or sex transformation in the mythologies: in Greece, the passion of Zeus for Ganymede, Artemis and the nymph Callisto, and Hercules/Heracles' sexual friendship with Iolaus;[507] in Egypt, the competition between Seth and Horus; in Mesopotamia, the adventures of Gilgamesh and Enkidu; and in Japan, Shino No Hafuri and Ama No Hafuri. Deities all over the ancient world symbolized same-sex love—the Greek Eros, the Mayan Chin, and the Aztec Xochipili.[508] For other divine figures, the Indian Shiva or the Chinese Kuan Yin for instance, gender ambiguity was at the core of their spiritual identity.

The case of Asia is particularly edifying. Sexuality always kept an important place in Asian spiritualities. Notwithstanding, none of the major philosophical traditions born from the Axial Age (which in Asia includes Tantrism, Confucianism, and Taoism) considers homosexual behavior as being a noble expression of one's sexual energy. At best, it was seen as manageable. (Homosexual acts were seldom punished, however; they were only sometimes fined at the same level as minor offenses.) In all three schools of thought the complementarity between the masculine and the feminine, manifested through the heterosexual embrace and conception, is held as the basis of the perfect union—the union of the opposites. In that they differ little from Abrahamic religions, Pythagoreanism, and Platonism. Remember that Axial religions are fundamentally dualistic in that they all seek to restore the perfection of the origins through a harmonious synthesis of spiritual opposites—Yin and Yang, male and female, and so on. And yet, because homosexual desires and feelings always kept an honorable place in Asian mythoi, which just like in Classical Greece largely predated the Axial revolution, same-sex eroticism remained viable in one form or another in all Asian cultures of India, China, Tibet, Korea, Japan, and Thailand.

In Japan, for instance, the uninterrupted influence of the Shinto religion, still one of the most sophisticated and resilient forms of pre-Axial spirituality in the world to this day, largely explains the exceptional longevity of homosexual subcultures in the country. Shintoism has been far more concerned with preserving the emergence of the masculine essence from the threatening omnipresence of the feminine essence. In India, *hijras*, who are placed under the protection of the goddess Bahuchara, know that the legendary hero Rama, whose life is depicted in the Hindu epic, the Ramayana, once blessed those people who were neither male nor female. Verses of the famous Kamasutra detail sexual practices to be performed specifically between men and eunuchs. The anthropologist Serena Nanda has captured better than most of her peers why *hijras* have ultimately managed to survive in Indian culture for centuries despite the overt contempt that the rest of Indian society bestows on them:

> Several different aspects of Hindu thought explain both the ability of Indian society to absorb an institutionalized third gender role, as well as to provide several contexts within which to handle the tension between the ideal and real aspects of the role. Indian mythology contains numerous examples of androgynes [. . .], impersonators of the opposite sex, and among both deities and humans individuals with sex changes. Myths are an important part of popular culture. *Sivabhaktis* (worshippers of Siva) give *hijras* special respect because one of the forms of Siva is Ardhanarisvara, ('the lord who is half woman'). *Hijras* also associate themselves with Vishnu, who transforms himself into Mohini, the most beautiful woman in the world, in order to take back the sacred nectar from the demons who have stolen it. Further, in the worship of Krishna, male devotees may imagine themselves to be female, and even dress in female clothing; direct identification with Krishna is forbidden, but the devotee may identify with him indirectly by identifying with Radha, that is, by taking a female form. Thousands of *hijras* identify themselves as Krishna's wives in a ritual performed in South India. These are only a few of the contexts within which the *hijras* link themselves to the Great Tradition of Hinduism and develop a positive definition for their feminine behavior.[509]

Notice also that by putting the emphasis on gender fluidity, Indian culture offers an optimal context for the existence of a third gender, but not of transgenerational homosexual relationships. The opposite is true in ancient Greece, for instance where male relationships were modeled after the love of Zeus and Ganymede.[510] As long as the Greeks believed in their mythology, same-sex relationships between a man and a youth—and only those—remained socioculturally viable. And because neither Pythagoreanism, nor Platonism, nor Neoplatonism really challenged the mythic reality of the Olympian pantheon, those philosophies failed to alter in depth the sexual mores of their contemporaries.

At all times, human life mirrored divine life. The fate of homosexuality has been tied to its mythic representation and connection to the sacred. Whenever homosexual behavior was positively depicted in the mythic narrative, homosexual relationships were maintained inside the field of collective awareness, regardless of the fact that they were not personally experienced by all individuals in the group. Homosexuality remained familiar and safe, hence, socially viable. We are now going to see that, diverging from all other religious traditions, the monotheism of the Abrahamic lineage is singularized by a total absence of homosexuality in the mythos.

A MYTHIC VOID

How did Christianity spread and maintain the automatic association between homosexual acts and the idea of sinfulness so efficiently? The answer is: by modifying its mythos accordingly. And this shift was orchestrated rapidly by Church's leaders who literally purged the Christian mythos of all positive image of homosexuality—acts, desires, and feelings. From this operation resulted what I call a mythic void. Homosexuality's connection to the sacred was severed. And we are going to see how much the departure of homosexuality from the mythic space left little choice to Christians.

Yet, before we get there, you might be surprised to learn that Christian thinkers were actually not the first ones to seek to erase homosexuality from the mythos consciously. Just like his contemporaries Philo and Paul, Musonius, the famous Roman stoic philosopher and ardent proponent of marriage of the first century CE (see chapter 8), rejected any form of same-sex relationship as monstrous and contrary to nature. In order to justify his claim, Musonius did not hesitate to "rearrange" the creation myth originally narrated by Aristophanes in Plato's Symposium. Plato's version goes like this: "The sexes were originally three: men, women, and the union of the two; and they were made round—having four hands, four feet, two faces on a round neck, and the rest to correspond." Unfortunately, Zeus quickly found those creatures much too strong to his taste and decided to "split them as you might split an egg with a hair." From the separation of primordial pairs stemmed the intense longing that occurs between people. "The two halves went about looking for one another, and were ready to die of hunger in one another's arms." This primordial split justifies why some people are attracted preferentially to one sex or the other: "The characters of men differ accordingly as they are derived from the original man or the original woman, or the original man–woman. Those who come from the man-woman are lascivious and adulterous; those who come from the woman form female attachments; those who are a section of the male follow the male and embrace him, and in him all their desires centre. The pair are inseparable and live together in pure and manly affection."[511]

Musonius trimmed Aristophanes' story so as to fit his own agenda: "For what other reason [than marriage] did the demiurge cut apart [. . .] our race and make two sets of genitals, male and female, and instill a strong desire [. . .] and longing [. . .] for association and common relationship with one another?"[512] In Musonius's shortened version, male and female homosexual pairs are simply omitted. Only heterosexual coupling reiterates the gods' original design. Therefore, only heterosexual love complies with the laws of nature. It really was that simple.

Both Aristophanes and Musonius appear to have intuited the crucial relation between moral order and cosmic order. Their creation tales represent typical cases of generative literature, in that their stories have the same narrative texture as a myth. Yet neither Aristophanes's story, nor Musonius's story, achieved a real place in the Greco-Roman mythos. They both failed to impact the collective psyche of their times in a significant manner. They essentially remained literature. And, in retrospect, their failure underlines the formidable success of the early Fathers of the Church even more.

Unlike most of their pagan contemporaries, the early Fathers did not target homosexual love only. They strived to eradicate any form of non-procreative sex. They methodically eliminated all mythic representations of the sexual act in the brand new Christian mythos. In that regard, the works of Clement of Alexandria and Tatian the Assyrian, two theologians with whom we are already acquainted, epitomize the conscious effort of the early Church to fashion the emerging mythic consciousness of Christendom. Yet, when it comes to inventing Christianity, the Jewish Philo of Alexandria contributed among the most brilliant flashes of genius. His reinterpretation of Neoplatonic concepts inside the Judaic worldview greatly facilitated the work of the Christian theologians that succeeded him. His impact on the Christian mythos and the fate of homosexuality is unequalled. Let us now see how they all proceeded.

Philo conflated the biblical "whore" (the "harlot"), the general concept of "Pleasure" (primarily understood as sexual), and the Greek goddess Aphrodite into one unique cosmic principle. For him, Pleasure-Aphrodite incarnates the pervading force that instigates sexual arousal in all living creatures, including human beings. Just like the Greeks, Philo locates this dangerous power in sexual desire, genital contact, and orgasms. By overwhelming the human soul with lust, Pleasure-Aphrodite—"the cosmic madam of religiously alienating sexual desire" as Kathy Gaca elegantly puts it[513]—draws men and women directly into sexual rebellion against God. Pleasure-Aphrodite must therefore be resisted at any cost.

But whereas Philo remained bound to a centuries' old ethnic narrative due to his pledge to the Torah, the early Fathers intuited the formidable powers of their stories, which they quickly sought to compile in what ultimately became the New Testament. In parallel, they undertook to eliminate all concurrent mythoi. When necessary, they did not hesitate to recycle basic elements of preexisting pagan myths into the new emerging mythos of Christianity. Contrary to the Yahveh, the unrepresentable God of the Jews, God-Christ incorporated the various facets of the gods that he was meant to replace, and, first of all, the Greco-Roman pantheon. Christianity re-appropriated numerous elements of the old Greco-Roman imagery, going as far as representing God as a twin brother of Zeus-Jupiter for instance.

Although for many early Christian theologians the pagan gods represented primitive and fragmented versions of the unique and indivisible God of Christianity, they followed in the footsteps of Philo to systematically deny the gods Aphrodite and Eros—the two gods of sexual appetite—a transmutation within the Christian "pantheon."[514] Clement of Alexandria conceptualized the old gods as mere projections of human emotions. He nevertheless stigmatized Aphrodite and Eros as nothing less than demons.[515] Tatian, often at odds with Clement's theological views, saw in the Olympian gods rebellious angels banished by God. Still, he too presented Aphrodite as the most dangerous of those fallen angels because of her power over human beings' libidinous impulses.[516] Clement and Tatian concurred in thinking that Aphrodite is a deceitful temptress *par excellence*—Satan's ally. She represents a threat to reason (logos) and, in consequence, to salvation.

The theological consensus against Aphrodite and Eros increasingly gained momentum during the first centuries. For Christianity the human physical condition—the flesh—is the source of evil. Sex beyond the social and religious duty of reproduction speaks the language of the body, hence the language of Satan. Aphrodite and Eros, who both celebrated carnal pleasures, were at the antipode of the Christian ascetic message. They could not fit into the Christian "pantheon," even discreetly. Now bear in mind that a statue of the god Eros stood in the entrance of the gymnasium, the temple of male love, of which Eros was the protector. It was Eros who inspired the passion of the *erastes* for his *eromenos*.[517] And when many centuries later Eros and Aphrodite were eventually resuscitated in the paintings of the Renaissance, it would be too late; for the Western collective psyche, they had been dead for too long.

The remodeling of the concept of love by early Christian theologians took a linguistic turn as well. Ancient Greek used three different words to express three very distinct flavors of love: "eros" for being in love and all sexual passions; "philia" for friendship and mutual affinity; and "agape" for chaste or divine love. John Boswell reported that the verb corresponding to eros appears only three times in the Septuagint (the Greek translation of the Jewish Bible). Boswell goes on: "[*eran*, the verb form of eros] does not occur at all in the New Testament—a particularly striking absence, since [*eran*] and its derivatives are among the most common subjects of Greek literature of the period. Instead, [*philein*, the verb form of philia] (25 times) and [*agapan*, the verb form of agape] (136 times) are used exclusively as the verbs for a wide variety of emotions, feelings, and desires that would be translated into English as 'like,' or 'love.'"[518] The word "eros"—just like the god that embodied it—was simply deleted by and from a culture that had turned sexual desire into the worst evil. Orwell's "Big Brother" would have not operated more efficiently.

The situation in which Christians found themselves was a historical novelty. Even the Jews, despite the prohibition of male homosexuality, were continually exposed to the mythoi of their neighbors and that of successive invaders of their land—Egyptians, Persians, Greeks, and ultimately Romans. The Bible bears witness to the constant struggle of the Hebrews in order to overcome the seductive power of neighboring cults (i.e., the unforgivable sin of idolatry). Regarding same-sex eroticism, Jews probably never experienced anything like a mythic void, at least not until they found themselves scattered inside Christendom. On the other hand, Christian mythology is fundamentally articulated around concealing sex. Already, the God of Christianity, like that of the Jews, possesses no sexuality whatsoever. Neither God the Father, nor God the Son, nor the Holy Spirit are connected to the sexual energy. Jesus of Nazareth is neither involved romantically nor physically with anyone. The redemption of Mary Magdalene, who originally was a prostitute, glorified the renunciation of any form of sexual activity. The miracle of the birth of Jesus—God's earthly incarnation through a procreative act untainted by genital contact or sexual pleasure—and its reflection in the dogma of Mary's virginity—the Immaculate Conception—epitomized the Christian ideal of purity. Unlike pleasurable sex, reproductive sex found itself miraculously rescued thanks to the ritual of marriage and the celebration of birth. Pleasureless conception, reenactment of the mythic embodiment of Jesus, preserved its connection to the sacred—the eternal and the universal. Everything else was denied the right to be.

SODOM AND GOMORRAH

We now understand how early Christianity orchestrated the emergence of an asexual mythos. The rare references to sex were contextualized in such a way to invite believers to view the renunciation to lust and fornication as the only path to salvation. But when it comes to same-sex love, the early Fathers redoubled their efforts. They did not simply erase homosexual love from the new my mythos; they also inserted one of most popular and enduring myths of Western culture in it: the myth of Sodom and Gomorrah. And, one last time, we must pay tribute to the inventor of this myth in the form in which we know it today, Philo of Alexandria, whose contribution to the Christian mythos is truly unique, at least from a homosexual point of view.

Today scholars largely agree that, before Philo, the crime of Sodom and Gomorrah was not homosexuality per se, but most likely the attempt of male-on-male rape, which represented a highly distasteful violation of the basic rules of hospitality that was highly valued in the cultures of the Middle East.[519] It is therefore the brutal and unwelcoming attitude of the people of Sodom that constituted the unacceptable offense which caused God's brutal ire, not their erotic interest for males specifically. If indeed the original quote from Genesis 19:4-5 is open to multiple interpretations—"all the men from every part of the city of Sodom—both young and old—surrounded the house. They called to Lot, 'Where are the men who came to you tonight? Bring them out to us so that we can have sex ["know" in KJV] them."'—all other biblical references to Sodom leave no ambiguity on how people understood this story prior to Philo.

The prophet Ezekiel, for instance, could not have been clearer: "Now this was the sin of your sister Sodom: She and her daughters were arrogant, overfed and unconcerned; they did not help the poor and needy. They were haughty and did detestable things before me. Therefore I did away with them as you have seen."[520] Ezekiel mentioned neither homosexual behavior nor any text referring to its prohibition. Six centuries later, Matthew and Luke were in alignment with Ezekiel in their understanding the crime of Sodom as being one of inhospitality: "If anyone will not welcome you or listen to your words, shake the dust off your feet when you leave that home or town. I tell you the truth, it will be more bearable for Sodom and Gomorrah on the day of judgment than for that town."[521]

Nowhere in the entire Old Testament or in the Gospels is the crime of Sodom and Gomorrah directly linked to homosexual behavior. In the first century CE, the situation changed. Philo literally rewrote the legend of Sodom and Gomorrah as we commonly understand it today, giving a mythological basis to homophobia in Rabbinic Judaism, Christianity, and Islam.[522] Unlike the original text, Philo's version provides countless details regarding the sex life of the men of Sodom:

> The country of the Sodomites was a district of the land of Canaan, which the Syrians afterwards called Palestine, a country full of innumerable iniquities, and especially of gluttony and debauchery [. . .] As men, being unable to bear discreetly a satiety of these things, get restive like cattle, and become stiff-necked, and discard the laws of nature, pursuing a great and intemperate indulgence of gluttony, and drinking, and unlawful connections; for not only did they go mad after women, and defile the marriage bed of others, but also those who were men lusted after one another, doing unseemly things, and not regarding or respecting their common nature [. . .] the men became accustomed to be treated like women, and in this way engendered among themselves the disease of females, and intolerable evil; for they not only, as to effeminacy and delicacy, became like women in their persons, but they made also their souls most ignoble, corrupting in this way the whole race of man [. . .] But God, [. . .] detesting the unnatural and unlawful commerce of the people of Sodom, [. . .] destroyed those who were inclined to these things, and that not by any ordinary chastisement, but he inflicted on them an astonishing novelty, and unheard of rarity of vengeance.[523]

The contrast with the traditional interpretation of the cause of Sodom's destruction is striking.[524] It is even more shocking to see Philo's reinvented myth of Sodom and Gomorrah disseminate rapidly in Judaism and early Christianity (with the notable exception of Paul; see footnote).[525] In his *Antiquities of the Jews*, completed in 93 CE, Josephus, the prominent Jewish scholar and historian, relays Philo's version without further justification: "Sodomites [. . .] hated strangers, and abused themselves with Sodomitical practices. [. . .] Now when the Sodomites saw the young men to be of beautiful countenances, and this to an extraordinary degree, and that they took up their lodgings with Lot, they resolved themselves to enjoy these beautiful boys by force and violence."[526] And this is only the beginning of possibly the most successful propaganda of all times.

A sermon by the apostle Jude, albeit less specific than Philo and Josephus regarding the exact nature of Sodom's sin, confirms the irresistible impetus of

Philo's version in the new ascetic culture that developed in the first centuries around the Mediterranean: "Sodom and Gomorrah and the surrounding towns gave themselves up to sexual immorality and perversion. They serve as an example of those who suffer the punishment of eternal fire."[527] Peter spoke of "the depraved conduct of the lawless."[528] And in his *Paedagogus*, Clement of Alexandria reiterated the revised version of the story of Sodom and Gomorrah according to Philo as well.[529] Three centuries later, not only had the new interpretation established by Philo remained unchallenged, but it had in fact become the new standard. Philo's reinvented legend of Sodom and Gomorrah became an official myth of Christianity, attesting to the fate of the men and women who defy God's will by abandoning themselves to unnatural pleasures. Let me repeat here Augustine's statement in his *Confessions*: "Therefore are those foul offences which be against nature, to be everywhere and at all times detested and punished; such as were those of the men of Sodom." However, once again, it was John Chrysostom in the fourth century who made it very specific for Christians. For him, the love of boys was clearly the one sin of Sodom and Gomorrah that caused God's wrath. His sermons are worth citing at length for the extraordinary precision and violence that they convey, and because, perhaps, they will sound strangely familiar to some of you:

> If any one disbelieves hell, let him consider Sodom, let him reflect upon Gomorrah, the vengeance that has been inflicted, and which yet remains. This is a proof of the eternity of punishment [. . .] For what have you to say concerning Sodom? Would you wish also to know the cause, for which these things were then done? It was one sin, a grievous and accursed one certainly, yet but one. The men of that time had a passion for boys, and on that account they suffered this punishment. But now ten thousand sins equal and even more grievous than these are committed.[530]

> But if thou scoffest at hearing of hell and believest not that fire, remember Sodom. For we have seen, surely we have seen, even in this present life, a semblance of hell [. . .] Consider how great is that sin, to have forced hell to appear even before its time! For whereas many thought scorn of His words, by His deeds did God show them the image thereof in a certain novel way. For that rain was unwonted, for that the intercourse was contrary to nature, and it deluged the land, since lust had done so with their souls. Wherefore also the rain was the opposite of the customary rain. Now not only did it fail to stir up the womb of the earth to the production of fruits, but made it even useless for the reception of seed. For such was also the intercourse of the men, making a body of this sort more worthless than the very land of Sodom. And what is there more detestable than a man who hath pandered himself, or what more execrable? Oh, what madness! Oh, what distraction! Whence came this lust lewdly revelling and making man's nature all that enemies could? or even worse

than that, by as much as the soul is better than the body. Oh, ye that were more senseless than irrational creatures, and more shameless than dogs! for in no case does such intercourse take place with them, but nature acknowledgeth her own limits.[531]

The example of Sodom of Gomorrah illustrates superbly what Joseph Campbell called "the power of myth." In just three centuries, Christianity eliminated homosexual love from the Western mythos, which generated a mythic void. Concomitantly, it appended a powerful anti-homosexual myth—Philo's revised version of the story of Sodom and Gomorrah—to the traditional Judeo-Christian mythology. Philo's new version of the story of Sodom and Gomorrah resonated with the heart of early Christians, including the early Fathers of the Church. It became real because everybody believed in it. And from that moment on, same-sex love—mythically crippled—was condemned to fight for its own existence.

Before we explore the long-term consequences of the elimination of homosexuality from the Western mythos, let me add a short complement to the above, which further demonstrates the striking correspondence between collective morals and mythic representation. As it happens, Philo's homophobic myth of Sodom and Gomorrah did not constitute an absolute novelty. Another myth had depicted homosexual behavior negatively a few centuries earlier: the cosmological myth of the Zoroastrian religion in ancient Persia. The unambiguous ban on homosexual behavior in the Zoroastrian canon matches exactly its representation in the Zoroastrian cosmology. In the Zoroastrian creation myth, the world is the theater of a war between the forces of good and truth embodied by Ahura Mazda, and the forces of evil led by Ahriman, the symbol of aridity, lies, diseases, and death. According to the myth Ahriman generates a legion of devils, the *daevas*, through self-sodomy. Anal intercourse, with himself in this particular case, becomes then the symbolic act through which Ahriman produces an explosion of evil in the universe.[532] So, on the one hand, Zoroastrian cosmology associates sodomy with evil, and on the other hand, sodomy is punished by death in Zoroastrian law. Here again, the synchrony between mythos and collective morals is edifying.

The Fear of Chaos

Given the correspondence between mythic representation and sociocultural acceptance, what are the consequences of not being depicted in the mythos? In other words, what is the cost of the mythic void in which same-sex love disappeared during the early time of Christianity? We saw that together the myths and their correlates in the interobjective realm, the rituals, constitute the symbolic foundation of cultural kinship. They determine who belongs and who does not (when shared, they include; when betrayed, they divide). As a result, they are fundamental to the social cohesion of a group. They confer a level of predictability in human life and make people feel safe. We also saw that the mythos of a culture gives meaning to everything people experience, and gives a familiar appearance to our greatest foe—the unknown.[533] Human cultures have many names for the unknown—chaos, hell, evil, apocalypse—and for its inhabitants: the "others," the demons, ghosts, and monsters. The mythos thus informs people as to what is true, good, and beautiful and what is not, and it does so in a very detailed and systematic fashion.

As soon as a concept such as the mutual desire between two men or two women disappears from the mythos, it can no longer be comprehended at the collective level. It becomes unfathomable to the great majority of people. In other words, it dissolves into unknown. Now, if same-sex love vanishes in a mythic void, this is less the case of the proto-homosexual figure incarnated by the sodomite. In many ways, the sodomite can be viewed as a mythic "shadow" (in the Jungian sense of it), a negative representation of an incomprehensible element present in the mythos. Why the sodomite archetype is so incomprehensible for early Christians and eventually for practically everybody is twofold. First, as a sexual character, the sodomite conflates under one label the active and the passive role; inevitably, he is suspected to endorse the receptive role, or at least blur the distinction between the two, thereby automatically violating the fundamental rule of male ranking which instinctively associates sexual receptiveness with submissiveness. Thus the sodomite is, by definition, a weak individual and a traitor. Second, by refusing to abide with the cosmic order of Judeo-Christianity (and more generally of the Axial Age) that sees the complementarity between the masculine and feminine principles as being of cardinal importance, the sodomite acts against nature—against what is true, good, and beautiful. He undermines the natural order of things, that to which everything must conform so as to ensure harmony. And in the premodern world, nature is God's creation, and harmony is God's will. Accordingly, the sodomite is a direct offense to God.

Unforgivable in the eyes of male hierarchy, a criminal against nature, and without any mythic alternative other than Philo's legend of Sodom and Gomorrah, the sodomite went down the evolutionary ladder. As we have seen in chapter 7, cultural evolution ensues from a coordinated expansion of the field of collective awareness (the worldview), and the space of cultural kinship (by increasing the level of diversity within a given community). In the case of the sodomite, the dynamic was inverted. Same-sex lovers were simultaneously expelled from the mythos and the space of kinship. Turned into mythic shadows, sodomites became the ultimate "others" just like witches, dragons, sea monsters, and other evil creatures. The membership was broken, and so was the empathic bond. And this had serious implications, as you know: outside the space of kinship, morals no longer apply. And in a culture unable or unwilling to manage those issues, human beings' worst instincts—fear, hate, anger, and violence—were unleashed. And for centuries, the hate of the sodomite united fearful Christians anxious to appease God's wrath.

In this respect, the historian Arthur Gilbert made a pertinent observation by noticing "a link between persecution of homosexuality and perceived or imagined social disaster."[534] We can now understand why that would happen. The sociocultural order, which is the reflection of the sacred order symbolized by the mythos, defined a safe space. That safe space, however, was continuously threatened by the unknown. So the unknown ought to be contained at all costs. Sodomites, rejected from the "empathic space" (or "circle of care," as defined in chapter 7) and completely foreign from a symbolic standpoint, began to trigger irrational fears. They were automatically believed to elicit the divine ire (a belief that is still held true today by the millions of people who still share the same worldview as that of the people of Middle Ages, whether conservative Christians, Muslim fundamentalists, or ultra-orthodox Jews). And that belief was efficiently reinforced by the legend of Sodom and Gomorrah. Let me then remind you that according to our dear fellow Philo, the lover who pursues unnatural pleasures "does his best to render cities desolate and uninhabited by destroying the means of procreation."[535] However, it is the Byzantine Emperor Justinian who gave the most substance to this new rhetorical genre, associating homosexual lust and the terrible catastrophes that people experienced. The following fragment of the Justinian's laws (533 CE) illustrates better than I ever will what happens when same-sex love disappears from the mythos:

> Since certain men, seized by diabolical incitement, practice among themselves the most disgraceful lusts, and act contrary to nature: we enjoin them to take to heart the fear of God and the judgment to come, and to abstain from suchlike diabolical and unlawful lusts, so that they may not be visited by the just wrath of God on account of these impious acts, with the result that cities perish with all their inhabitants. For we are taught by the Holy Scriptures that because of like impious conduct cities have indeed perished, together with the men in them. For because of such crimes there are famines, earthquakes, and pestilences. [We must] inflict on them the extreme punishments, so that the city and the state may not come to harm by reason of such wicked deeds.[536]

THE FAILURE OF MODERNITY

The philosophers of the Enlightenment celebrated the liberating virtue of objective reason. They aimed to break free from the old order. People, they said, must be guided by reason, not by faith, and by science, not by superstitions. For them religion was associated with the dark ages, with centuries of terror and repression and the innumerable atrocities that had been committed in the name of God. Religious beliefs and the myths were held responsible for justifying the blood of innocents, torture, and other crimes. Profoundly indignant, the philosophers fought against the old belief system fiercely. But when the Enlightenment began to challenge the validity of the Christian mythos; it denied the reality of any mythos at all. By refusing to offer new myths that would have embodied and glorified its new value system, the Enlightenment and the age of modernity that followed failed to renew a mythic space that had served as a moral template for so long. They unknowingly left the mythos in the hands of their enemy, religion.

With no mythic representation other than the legend of Sodom and Gomorrah, same-sex love entered modernity with no moral foundation. The open-mindedness of the Enlightenment quickly faded for the simple reason that homosexual love still had no roots in the intersubjective space and no myth to embody it positively. And because modernity did not offer any mythic alternative to represent it, same-sex love remained buried in the unknown—the world of the "others." From sin, homosexuality became a sickness and then a perversion. The epistemological context had changed but not the moral ground because the mythic space, even denied, was left untouched.[537] As a matter of fact, modernity gave homophobia a new youth. The nineteenth century consecrated the planetary success of homophobia as much as that of modernity itself. Ultimately, Communism and Nazism, both ultra-materialist and little interested in Biblical legends, sent more homosexuals to concentration camps than centuries of Christian inquisition had sentenced to the stakes.

In the meantime the Europeanization of the world that ensued from the colonization of the Americas, Africa, Asia, and Oceania, wiped out the old local mythologies to replace them with a triumphant Judeo-Christian mythos. By doing so, Europeans successfully exported a mythic space that was primarily founded on the concepts of the opposition between good and evil and the struggle between the flesh and the divine. It offered no representation of homosexual love except the legend of Sodom and Gomorrah. The European colonization engendered the same shift as the one experienced during the Christianization of the Roman Empire within cultures that previously had little or no concern about same-sex desire. And why did this lately imported homophobia survive the decolonization process so well? The reason is simply that when Europeans departed, they left their mythos behind. Since in many instances the newly liberated nations were not as politically organized and economically developed as their former colonialist countries (see endnote), homophobia often worsened.[538] This explains why, for instance, we have witnessed a strong resurgence of homophobic violence in many African countries.

I cannot end this chapter without addressing another difficult issue, that of the recent upsurge of homophobia in many Muslim countries. Simply consider the fact that countries that apply the death penalty against homosexual behavior today are predominantly Muslim (Saudi Arabia, Iran, Mauritania, Sudan, Somalia, Nigeria, and Yemen, in the year 2011). In these cases it is extremely difficult to incriminate the Christian mythos. Bear also in mind that the Koran (written in the seventh century CE) reproduces Philo's version of the legend of Sodom and Gomorrah almost verbatim already. How can we then make sense of this painful issue?

First of all, the position of Islamic culture toward homosexual behavior has always been imbued with ambiguity. Islam, just like Judaism and Christianity, excludes same-sex love from its mythos. Yet, unlike Christianity and more like Judaism, Islam has shown very little hostility toward sexual pleasure. Moreover, Muslim cultures were marked by a strong segregation of sexes and a quasi absolute dominance of men in the social sphere. From this, one can then understand why they have traditionally demonstrated a well-known tolerance for pederastic relationships, as long as those were kept discreet and as long as the men who indulged in those practices married and reproduced. However, insofar as pederastic relationships were unsupported by the Muslim mythos, we can retrospectively understand why this relative tolerance would remain extremely fragile. The difference between the mythoi of Classical Greece and Islam reveals why pederastic relationships could be praised in one culture but would have to go underground in another.

We can explain why many Muslim countries have "flipped" if we remember that the basic issue behind the acceptance of male homosexual behavior has always been competition among males. In our primate brain, being penetrated is not viewed as "receptiveness," as we tend to regard it today, but as weakness. When transposed at the level of a group—in a tribe, a gang, a religious community, or an entire country—having males allegedly willing to be penetrated sexually within the group is perceived as a sign of collective vulnerability. To the best of my knowledge, homosexual repression in Muslim countries correlates clearly with increasing political tensions with the West. I think that what we see in a large part of the Muslim world as well as in a few Asian and African countries is a transposition of the ranking dynamic at the intercollective level. Inter-male competition is turned into "inter-national" competition, yet the rationale is fundamentally the same. By implementing harsh anti-homosexual laws and eliminating the "weakest" males, those countries reasserted their toughness, that is to say, their maleness. They send a loud and clear signal to all outsiders, just like male gorillas savagely shake the branches of a tree in order to impress undesirable visitors. There are known historical precedents to what we see today: as soon as the competition between antagonistic nations escalates, homophobic anxiety increases.[539] This was the case between France and Germany in the nineteenth century, particularly in the aftermath of the Franco-Prussian war.[540] Exactly the same thing happened in England during World War I and in the United States during the McCarthyism era at the height of the Cold War.

Moreover, it is tempting to interpret the collective trauma caused by colonization directly in sexual terms. The male collective consciousness of the formerly occupied country experiences colonization—retrospectively—as a symbolic rape, an affirmation of dominance by the former colonizing nation, the "victor." Depending on the culture and its level of development, this feeling of humiliation can take a long time to heal, and hopefully it eventually will. Despite its five million year-long expertise in male ranking, the human species greatly lacks experience—to say the least—when it comes to facilitating inter-male reconciliation at a global level.

Here is, I believe, the big lesson of all this: Without a positive representation in the mythos to consolidate its sociocultural existence, homosexuality remains completely vulnerable to a resurgence of homophobia and scapegoating. This naturally brings us to contemplate the absurd paradox in which homosexuals live today. Modern homosexuality, though largely inspired from the Christian concept of marital love, was born in a modern and postmodern culture that has no awareness whatsoever of the importance of the mythos, let alone the dynamics that continuously shape that mythos. Modern homosexuality has no meaning other than its biomedical definition. Thus homosexuality today is still symbolically empty, still absent from the mythos, and still disconnected from the sacred. As a matter of fact, modern homosexuals live today with nearly the same mythic context as the sodomites of the Middle Ages. From a psychocultural viewpoint, this is not just uncomfortable; this is torture.

I hope that you can now realize how much this situation—the mythic void—is collectively and individually unsustainable. Of all the cultural identities that one can name in our current society, homosexuality is the only one deprived of a symbolic base. If you can remember in the preface when I pointed to the persistent malaise of gays and lesbians today, let me offer you now my diagnosis: Without a powerful mythic and symbolic foundation, modern homosexuality will remain socially fragile and homosexuals will continue to feel emotionally incomplete. Why? Because human beings need meaning as much as they need love.

But enough "deconstruction." What is lost is lost forever and there is no way back. It is now time to rebuild. What? The new moral and symbolic foundation of same-sex love.

A Symbolic Existence

Myths do not belong to the past. Our culture, just like any culture, is rooted in a mythic reality. We simply cannot see it (at least not easily) because at any given time the prevalent mythos is not perceived as a collection of myths, but as the truth. As we have seen in earlier chapters, human beings have great difficulty distancing themselves from the cultural context in which they function. This inherent nearsightedness of ours—that is, our inability to perceive our mythos as mythos—is anything but unexpected. The role of the mythos is exactly that: to tell people what is true, good, and beautiful. Only when one has assimilated the fact that Truth, Goodness, and Beauty are culture-bond and evolve through time can one envisage him or herself as being immersed in a mythos. However people hold them, myths exist by virtue of the fact that people believe in them. And one should not deduce from this that people are stupid or weak. From an integral and evolutionary perspective, mythic realities can no longer be labeled as the "the opium of the people" (as professed by modernity) or "instruments of control" (as professed by postmodernity). They are that too, absolutely, but this has never been their primary function. But if we have understood the pivotal role of the mythos in maintaining the psychocultural integrity of human beings, how does this dynamic play out today in today's world? Where are the myths in the current culture and how do they interact with postmodern consciousness? And if we are to give homosexuality a new mythic depth, those are the issues that we must now confront.

MYTHOS VERSUS LOGOS

Intuitively, you might have guessed that the mythos is not equally perceived by everyone. Consider the Christian mythology. The life of Jesus of Nazareth, despite the many claims about its authenticity, is mythic by essence: Jesus rose from the dead; he was born from a virgin; he walked on water, and so forth. Do historians have any evidence to support those claims? They do not. But as stressed earlier, the historical accuracy of myths is irrelevant. What matters is not their objective veracity but how people hold them deep in their souls—their subjective veracity. This is what will decide their existence, strength, and destiny. Henceforth, untroubled by the issue of their historical truthfulness, let us instead now focus on the various ways that people can relate to those myths. And for the sake of clarity, I will continue to use the example of Christianity, but keep in mind that the same reasoning applies to all belief systems.

For so-called fundamentalist Christians, the Scriptures are to be read to the letter: God really created the world in seven days, really conversed with Moses in the form of a burning bush, and really parted the waters of the Red Sea; in the same way, Jesus really walked on water and really turned water into wine. Naturally, fundamentalists tend to believe equally strongly that God really destroyed the ancient cities of Sodom and Gomorrah to punish their inhabitants for their sexual depravity. And this is indeed one possible way of relating to the Christian mythos.

For many other Christians, however, the Bible represents a symbolic rather than a literal truth. God did not reveal himself through historical facts but through allegories. In that case, the spiritual message of the Scriptures must be interpreted so as to decipher God's intention. Yet, there is still only one truth, that of the Holy Scriptures. Today, most major Christian Churches (Roman Catholic, Orthodox, and Episcopalian, for instance) belong to that category. Rarer are the people who maintain that the biblical message is extremely valuable, perhaps even central, but also believe the content of the Scriptures is inevitably contingent upon a particular historical context (which extends from roughly the seventh century BCE to the second century CE in the case of the Holy Scriptures). Hence, the Scriptures ought now to be translated at two levels. The first one requires the symbolic interpretation of the myths; the second evaluates the moral relevancy of the myths in the sociocultural context in which we live today. Often those people also deem as relevant certain spiritual traditions other than Christianity (e.g., Buddhism or Hinduism).

Roughly speaking, those three examples recapitulate a spectrum of opinion that is observed throughout all belief systems, regardless of the specifics of their mythos.[541] So not only do mythoi evolve, but the way human beings relate to their mythos evolves as well. In the first example (the fundamentalists), objective and symbolic realities are conflated into one unique and inalienable truth. In the second one (the Pope), symbolic reality is viewed as being distinct from objective reality. The myth is indeed understood as a symbolic truth, yet that truth is absolute, unique, and hierarchically superior to all other mythic models that diverge from it. In the third case, any symbolic truth is relative and coexists with many other relative truths, which all complement each other. Many of you may have recognized through this progression a familiar trend: As one goes up the ladder of psychocultural evolution, one can hold an increasing number of variables and perspectives. One's relation to the mythos begins with a simple belief (e.g., the belief in one absolute literal truth). As it evolves, that relation becomes increasingly complex (e.g., the belief in multiple and complementary relative symbolic truths, distinct from objective truth). And yet, at whatever stage one is on this spectrum, it is still in the mythos that one looks for what is true, good, and beautiful.

This leads us to discuss an important issue. Observe that despite people's tenacious attachment to their mythoi, there have always been free-spirited individuals (thinkers, philosophers, theologians, and scientists, from ancient Greece to today) to challenge the truthfulness and value of the mythoi of their times. These two radically opposed attitudes do not simply reflect different intellectual priorities. Instead, they remind us of the existence of a dynamic that we have only started to unveil: the interplay between mythos and logos.

I have put in much effort to convince you of the importance of the mythos in order to insure people's spiritual and mental integrity. The mythos acts as a structuring source. By making an entire collection of psychosocial models available, it provides substance and definition to people's psychosocial identity, what Jung called "persona" (related, but not equal, to Freud's notion of "superego").[542] This said, the persona is regarded very differently depending on the culture to which one belongs. In traditional societies, the persona is pretty much all that counts; people are mostly defined by their social role. Myths ensure that social models are faithfully perpetuated from one generation to the next. Sons look like their fathers and daughters like their mothers. Identical personas are replicated over and over. Basically, myths enable a phenomenon that I like to call "psychological cloning." And if we postmodern Westerners may find this prospect horrendous, it is nevertheless how traditional societies (including fundamentalist cultures) have worked for centuries and why they are so tied up with their mythoi. The numinous power of myths is, as you can see, double-edged.

Logos, on the other hand, which we see blossom for the first time in Classical Greek culture (and to some extent all Axial cultures), directly opposes "psychological cloning." Logos promotes self-awareness, self-fulfillment, and the development of one's critical reason. It encourages intellectual independence, personal authenticity, and transgression from the norm. Logos is the key to one's personal freedom. Mythos without logos is a psychological prison, only that without logos no one ever becomes aware of it. The psychological pressure exerted by any traditional mythos would be intolerable in modern society today, including for gays and lesbians, which is why we should not rely too much on traditional myths in order to build our future homosexual mythos. Nobody wants to be reduced to the carbon copy of some old archetype, even if that archetype is Adonis or Aphrodite. Besides, most of the archetypes contained in ancient myths are morally obsolete, if not reprehensible in today's cultural context. For the large part, they are misogynistic, xenophobic, and incredibly violent.[543] We will not solve the current issues by following archaic models but only by going forward on the evolutionary track. This, however, requires us to find out what a healthy interaction between the postmodern psyche and the mythos may look like.

First of all, the persona, our "agent" in the world, so to speak, helps us negotiate a crucial function: telling society what we want it to know about who we are.[544] Indeed, for the self-obsessed individuals that we have become today, who we really are has become far too complicated for anyone (including ourselves) to comprehend. Communicating it would take a lifetime. It would be socially and psychological unmanageable. The persona functions very much like business card. It tells enough about you so that the group can (1) recognize you and (2) guess what can be expected from you in terms of behavior and social interaction. In other words, the persona helps you become familiar and predictable, which coincides exactly with the "grand function" of the mythos. In conclusion, the mythos helps us build a healthy persona able to orchestrate our relation to the outside world.

However, the nurturing role of the mythos is not limited to the formation of the persona. In many ways, the mythos is to the psyche what the DNA is to the body. It provides the basic building blocks necessary for the development of the entire psyche, including the ego. The mythos sums up the vast ontological knowledge—the knowledge about all the different ways human beings can be—that has been accumulated over millenniums of human history. It is the largest ontological database available in any given culture. In the world of being (the ontological realm) just as in the world of knowing (the epistemological realm), we essentially rely on what has been discovered before us. Mostly, we "recycle." If we understand the overall responsibility of mythoi in providing and maintaining the ontological material thanks to which individual psyches can take shape, we will also understand why different cultures, countries, and subcultures, give birth to different kinds of people (for instance, Britons and Italians do not have the same psychocultural center of gravity). The mythos acts as an unconscious ontological framework—a subliminal "ontological mentor"—at all levels of the human psyche.

Diametrically different, logos and mythos could hardly coexist peacefully. For the philosophers of classical Greece, the Enlightenment, modernity, and postmodernity, that is, from Plato to Michel Foucault, logos and mythos have been perceived as two irreconcilable realities.[545] But we can now see that, in fact, mythos and logos constitute two complementary psychic forces. On the one hand, the mythos generates commonality, which results from sharing the same basic psychocultural design. It allows people to belong and relate to others, thereby ensuring both social and mental cohesion. On the other hand, logos allows individuals to reach psychological autonomy—the individuation process, according to Jung's terminology. Both logos and mythos are absolutely and equally necessary. Yet their modes of expression are completely different. Mythos conveys a message that is fundamentally symbolic, emotional, and intuitive, characteristic of an I-WE relation. Logos, on the other hand, relies on evidence, personal experience, and critical thinking, which is more typical of an I-IT relation. In a culture where the cohesive force of mythos predominates, the individual mind (roughly speaking, the ego) suffocates, buried under the weight of the persona, and remains largely unexpressed. Children look, think, and behave just like their parents—like clones. The group, tribe, or nation reproduces faithfully the same sociocultural patterns over time. In contrast, in a culture where the individuating force of logos takes over, people feel emotionally alienated and self-obsessed, two symptoms that have become increasing perceptible in postmodern society.

Now, we also owe logos the fact that the postmodern mythos is far more complex than that of our ancestors. Logos is a powerful creative force. In fact, logos is the transformative force behind the continuous metamorphosis of all the mythoi of humanity. And now that we have clarified the equally important roles of logos and mythos, our logical next task is to lay out the content of the current mythos.

A Global Mythos

To list the various constituents of the postmodern mythos leads us necessarily to touch on many facets of the postmodern worldview. Insofar as we already have substantially inquired into the symbolic frameworks of modernity and postmodernity in the previous chapters, part of the vast and incredibly eclectic material that composes the postmodern mythos will inevitably sound familiar. Perhaps the most striking characteristic of postmodern culture resides in the fact that people are bombarded with information originating from very diverse sources. Never before have people been so exposed, so educated, and so aware. Postmodernity sums up in its mythos the long experience of traditional societies, modernity, adding to it its own discoveries. Note however that a significant number of people have today reached a stage of development beyond mere postmodernity, which I call global postmodernity. Global postmodernity, a tipping point of an increasingly multifaceted civilization, associates the two dimensions of historical experience and unprecedented cultural diversity in a brand new global mythos.

Combining the extraordinary development of the modes of communication with the open-mindedness of postmodern pluralism, a significant portion of the population has now been exposed and has perhaps even integrated multiple traditional mythoi—Christian, Jewish, Buddhist, Hindu, Muslim, and so forth. The number of people whose spiritual beliefs are influenced by more than one mythos is no longer negligible. For instance, Jews compose about 30% of the Buddhist community in the United States.[546] The refreshing popularity of the Dalai Lama around the world, particularly in Western countries, reveals how much the number of individuals capable of integrating more than one mythic framework is clearly on the rise. Today, all the various mythoi of the world are fiercely competing for attention through the media. But all this, as impressive as it may look, only constitutes the tip of the iceberg.

A second massive chunk of the global postmodern mythos is represented by recorded history. From the discovery of the Americas to the landing on the moon, and from Alexander the Great to Winston Churchill, history offers an unprecedented collection of narratives of mythic dimensions. Who are my heroes today?

Neither Hercules nor Gilgamesh, but Mahatma Gandhi, Martin Luther King, Jr., and Nelson Mandela. You can name yours. Being real, or even alive, by no means excludes anything or anyone from reaching the dimension of myth or archetype. This only depends on how something or someone is held in the intersubjective space. Joseph Campbell himself noted the tremendous thrill that he had experienced during the conquest of the moon. And in many ways, space exploration today holds a place similar to that of the Homeric tales in Ancient Greece, in that it unveils the universe of extraordinary possibilities that is opened to us.

The third part, absolutely primordial today, is generated through the arts, first of all literature and cinema, and increasingly, the media. As far back as the Middle Ages, one can trace the emergence of new mythic narratives in literary sources such as the Arthurian romance, the story of the quest of the Holy Grail, the legend of Tristan and Iseult, and that of the Nibelungenlied; and in King Arthur, Lancelot, Percival, Siegfried, or Rabelais's Gargantua the birth of new archetypal heroes. In that regard, medieval Europe did not differ significantly from the Greece of Homer, Hesiod, and Aeschylus. Yet the spectacular popularization of literature that came along with new printing methods and the democratization of education is hardly comparable to anything that preceded it. Suddenly the stories, which for the longest time had been associated with defined rituals, became part of people's daily lives. Not only did the stories begin to proliferate, but they also left the collective space to enter the private sphere.

We may in fact recognize right there a turning point in the evolution of the mythos. We all can see to what extent books, movies, television, the Internet, and other media in general have the power to convey powerful stories, hence potential myths. Joseph Campbell himself recognized George Lucas's blockbuster *Star Wars*, the narrative structure that he had previously discovered in all heroic sagas. *Star Wars* associated all the elements of a hero's journey with a blistering dissemination across the intersubjective space. From Cinderella to Indiana Jones, myths and archetypes of all forms and shapes are swamping us. Their omnipresence is such an ingrained facet of our lives that we tend to forget that such abundance would have probably driven our ancestors insane.

Again, it is impossible to develop here an "integral theory" of myth, and yet, I hope you get the picture. But we are not done yet. You may remember the four functions of myths: (1) to embody the *mysterium tremendum et fascinans*, (2) cosmological, (3) moral, and (4) psychological/ontological. As it happens, these functions are no longer systematically fulfilled through literary-type stories. And that is particularly true of the second (cosmological) and fourth (psychological/ontological) functions of the myths. We must then begin to visualize our current mythos in wider terms.

Accordingly, the fourth piece of our postmodern mythos is to be found in the discourse of social sciences, and very specifically political philosophy and psychology. Political scientist Robert Tucker, the historian and philosopher Mircea Eliade, and others have identified in Marxism-Communism all the constituents of an authentic sociological myth.[547] But because of its evident relevance here, let me focus on the role of psychoanalysis in the current mythos. In my opinion, psychoanalytic theory represents one of the most coherent cases of (post)modern mythology.[548] What gives psychoanalysis its mythic character is not so much the virtual presence of Greek legendary figures, but rather, the fact that people in large numbers started to understand themselves in terms of the conscious and unconscious, the Oedipus and Electra complex, penis envy, unconscious slips, repressed desires, castration fears, and so on. Psychoanalytic concepts may be significantly more abstract than classical myths, yet they still have a mythic form: they unfold with time; they indicate the right path from all the wrong ones; and they reveal the ancestral drama concealed behind people's emotions, anger, and suffering. Life is presented as a series of obstacles to overcome. The twelve labors of Hercules are replaced by new tasks—transcending the Oedipus complex, deciphering the meaning of our dreams, identifying oneself properly with the appropriate gender role, to name only a few—and new rewards—fulfillment, happiness, and why not, orgasms.

One may regret Freud's inability to integrate homosexual desire into his new model other than in a form of a developmental fiasco. Yet Freud's influence was by no means neutral. By theorizing homosexuality as resulting from one's failure to complete one's heroic journey from undifferentiated bisexuality to mature heterosexuality, Freud reiterated Philo's seminal feat: to invent a mythic story that would corroborate the belief in homosexuals' inferiority. Homosexuals had not irritated God this time. They had blown their chances to transcend their Oedipus complex. Quickly, Freud's etiological theory of homosexuality—the overbearing mother, the distant father, and the unresolved Oedipus complex—proved to be at least as powerful and as successful as the legend of Sodom and Gomorrah. And despite Freud's courageous recommendations, the psychoanalytic theory only comforted homophobes in their prejudice.

At the same time, Freud brought to completion a process, well-known to you, which had initiated some twenty five centuries earlier in ancient Greece. This was the time when Greek philosophers desacralized the human mind. Thoughts, emotions, and desires would no longer originate from the gods but from people themselves. In the name of *logos*, the philosophers severed human subjectivity from the realm of the divine, forcing people to become responsible for themselves and their lives. No longer representative of the human soul, Olympian gods progressively lost their attractiveness until, eventually, Christianity banished them from its hegemonic mythos. Freud's feat was to invent a psychological mythology. In the footsteps of the Greeks, two millenniums later, Freud desacralized the mythos itself by creating the first mind-centered mythology. By arguing that gods (including God) were mere psychological projections that resulted from an unresolved collective Oedipus complex, Freud relocated Mount Olympus (as any other pantheon, for that matter) inside the depths of our unconscious. This illustrates another fascinating aspect of Freud's unsurpassed genius. Understanding the fantastic success of psychoanalysis without that insight in mind seems quite difficult otherwise.

The fifth domain of culture (the last one on our list) where myths have emerged and are still emerging, is science. Science, I assert, is the key to the future of our mythos. I know how much my assertion flies in the face of common sense: How can science, modernity's most powerful weapon against myths and other obsolete beliefs, be somehow involved in the current mythos let alone its future? Remember one thing: One of the most crucial functions of the mythos is to provide a symbolic order. It tells why things are the way they are, and not any other way, and gives an answer to the question: where do we come from? The symbolic order—eternal, universal, and sacred, since it was designed by the gods (or God) in the beginning of times—is typically revealed in the form of the cosmological model, after which all things must be modeled. The world, society, and human life in its minute details must abide with the cosmic order so that they remain true, good, and beautiful, which constitutes the very basis of all rituals.

The contradiction in which science finds itself today is not without irony. Science, the "myth killer" of modern philosophers, has largely supplanted religions in their role of guardians of cosmological myths. In fact, many organized religions (including the Roman Catholic Church and many branches of Buddhism), have officially relinquished that authority to scientists.[549] But before going further, let me acknowledge the limits of what I am claiming here. First, many people around the planet still have no or very little access to scientific knowledge. Second, scientific theories—especially when they concern the cosmological order—are fiercely contested by religious fundamentalist groups. They have excellent reasons for doing this, which, I hope, you can now understand (even if fundamentalists cannot). Who holds the myths that best describe the cosmological order holds the "keys to the kingdom," because the cosmological order automatically dictates every other aspect of human life, by telling what is ultimately true, good, and beautiful.

Now consider the case of the big bang theory, probably the most spectacular example of "mythic transmutation" in science history. Never before had science so relied on poetry to grasp its own answer to one of humanity's most ancient riddle: how did the universe come about? The story of the big bang, as it lives in our culture now, is dramatically different from the long, complex, and stern calculus from which the concept originated in the first place. Sometime around the middle of the twentieth century, in one of the most mind-blowing twists of history, the most painful equations of modern physics turned into a fabulous narrative. For postmodern consciousness, the story of the big bang composes none other than the first chapter of a new "Book of Genesis."

The very act of calling the theory "the big bang" was a true flash of genius. Listen to the world that those two words convey. They magically bring to life dozens of images flashing through the mind in a cosmic vision—the birth of our universe: trillions of new particles emerging from nothingness, colliding in a deafening tumult; massive explosions of energy, light, radiation, matter, and stars;

galaxies dancing in slow motion; monstrous black holes devouring all that passes in their vicinity . . . I could certainly go on and on. The big bang today is not just a scientific theory. It is also, and perhaps mainly, a powerful symbolic reality. One can evoke the big bang to describe any type of event—whether an economic crisis, a political upheaval, or a cultural revolution—and everybody will know exactly what is meant by that. Why? Because it is living myth, a key fragment of the postmodern mythos. Notice also that, as far as we can tell, the transmutation of this theory into a mythic narrative does not appear to have been deliberately orchestrated, which only reminds us that what controls the mysterious alchemical reaction that operated that transformation is yet to be fathomed.

This is also true for Darwin's theory of the evolution of species—the second chapter of our new Book of Genesis. Darwin's scientific explanation of the origins of humankind has relegated Adam and Eve to the level of mere tale. Millions (billions perhaps) of people today view the human species as emerging from an evolutionary process rather than a separate creation. We tend to forget how much this cultural innovation broke with thousands of years of human-centered creationism.

Biology-generated myths, as you may have already intuited, will be crucial to a future exploration of homosexuality's symbolic framework. For this reason, I would like to discuss one example of a biology-created symbol: DNA, the molecule also known as deoxyribonucleic acid. Soon after James Watson and Francis Crick discovered its double helix structure in 1953, DNA was proved to be the molecule that supports heredity, that is to say, the material reality of genetic information. Densely packed inside each cell of our bodies, DNA contains all the information necessary for generating an entire living being. Yet, it is less the biological miracle that DNA represents than its extraordinary symbolic significance in today's culture that I would like to highlight now. Here are few scattered, yet representative examples of the symbolic power of words such as DNA, gene, and genome.

"Begin your ancestral journey. Who are you ancestors? Discover your deep ancestral roots using genetic genealogy. Find out where your ancestors come from. Become a part of history."[550] This online advertising contains an interesting offer, new and, at the same time, so ancient: in exchange for just a little bit of DNA, a team of scientists will be able to determine one's complex racial makeup, that is, one's hidden evolutionary past. DNA today is the new Pandora's box in which all our deepest secrets hide, and can be discovered.[551] The traces of our genetic origins, inherited anomalies, potential diseases, and, needless to say, the cause of one's sexual orientation are to be found in our DNA. An advertisement described the U.S. National Guard as the "DNA of America." A Japanese brand of electronics presented an entire line of products named "HDNA" along with the following line: "High definition. It's in our DNA." Certainly, those messages did not target people with a major in biological science only. Whoever conceived these ads knew the impact of the word "DNA" on the general public. In the current mythos, DNA conveys a symbolic dimension that transcends the function of the molecule itself. In postmodern consciousness, DNA holds nearly magical properties that many embrace enthusiastically and that scare others.

Concepts like the big bang, black holes, spacetime dimension, evolution, DNA, genome, and so forth, constitute the new mythic dimension of our age. First generated by teams of scientists, then disseminated in the culture through the media, those concepts were eventually transmuted into myths and symbols. Thanks to that ongoing process—our mythopoeic instinct—science keeps expanding the symbolic diversity of our mythos.

It is equally crucial to notice that scientific myths have no equivalent in the past. They feature no monster to be tamed, no hero to applaud, no miracle to impress believers, or a promise of a bright future. Science-based myths emanate from a type of consciousness that never existed before. The big bang is not a better myth than the Book of Genesis. It is only a myth that fits global postmodern consciousness. Its level of abstraction would have been too far-fetched for our ancestors and even our grandparents. Yet it is the unprecedented subtlety of these concepts that renders science-based myths so true, so good, and so beautiful to many of us. They reflect our inner complexity; they speak to us. Ignoring that important conclusion in our future endeavor to create a new homosexual mythos would condemn us to repeat the errors of the past.

Scientific knowledge affects the way we understand the world, life, and ourselves profoundly, forcing us to rethink boundaries that we thought were inalienable. By doing so, science is changing our vision of the sacred. Today the depth and scope of the global postmodern mythos fills us with awe. Its astonishing complexity reflects that of global postmodern consciousness—"our" consciousness. Today many educated Westerners who belong to, for instance, the Christian tradition are also open to Eastern philosophies and practice yoga, meditate, perhaps believe in karma and reincarnation, and honor the Buddha's teachings. They may even study the Kabbalah or Sufism on the side, and they very naturally believe in the scientific explanations of the origin of the world and life. Often (especially if they live in New York City), they also see a psychoanalyst; like everybody else, they watch television and read books. And I could expand this list far more, only to remind you of the countless facets of postmodern life, and behind it, of the postmodern mythos. For postmodern consciousness, this is a lot to reconcile. This "360° awareness" embraces mythic spaces that were never designed to work together, which may explain why our lives are often so frantic and so fragmented. In comparison, Plato had it easy. Yet, always remember one thing: the mythos should never be reduced to cultural knowledge. That confusion would neutralize the very meaning of the concept of mythos. The mythos is all the knowledge present in a given culture that allows people to connect with the sacred—the True, the Good, and the Beautiful, what is eternal and universal.

In the previous chapter we inquired into the role of postmodernity in fostering the reemergence of homosexuality during the second half of the twentieth century. Now, if the fate of homosexuality is tied to its mythic representation, as I claimed, where is homosexuality present in the current mythos? Since homosexuality is increasingly accepted in Westernized countries, one may anticipate the mythos to be somehow in sync with our evolving morals. And indeed, it is.

HOMOSEXUALITY IN THE GLOBAL MYTHOS

Where is homosexual love to be found in the postmodern mythos? The answer is: increasingly all over the place. As one might guess, homosexuality reappeared first in the arts. Fortunately, visual arts never stopped celebrating the beauty of the body, both female and male, even more so since the revival of the old mythologies in Renaissance arts. The nineteenth century, however, witnessed an unusual display of male nudity, homoerotic scenes, and unambiguous lesbianism in the paintings of well-known European and North American artists. Yet, it is in literature that one can best sense the winds of change. The sexual passion between the poets Verlaine and Rimbaud was anything but a secret for their contemporaries. At the same time, on the other side of the Atlantic, Walt Whitman published his masterpiece, the *Leaves of Grass*. In the twentieth century, major writers such as Oscar Wilde in England, Colette, André Gide, Marguerite Yourcenar, Jean Cocteau, and Jean Genet in France, and Truman Capote, James Baldwin, and Alan Ginsberg in the United States, never hid their taste for partners of their own sex.

Still, Gide was granted the Nobel Prize in literature and Yourcenar was eventually elected to the French Academy. Although they did not all incorporate same-sex desires into their writings, some did. Gide published his *Corydon* in 1924, and Yourcenar published her *Alexis* in 1929 and her extraordinary *Memoirs of Hadrian* (depicting the passionate love of the emperor Hadrian for Antinous) in 1951. In Japan, Yukio Mishima's *Confessions of a Mask* came out in 1948. Edward Morgan Forster's now famous novel *Maurice*, although written around 1913, was not published until 1971 after Forster's death. And since the publication of these groundbreaking masterpieces, homosexuality's presence in modern literature has only taken more ground.

Homosexuality's portrayal in the media and, first of all, on television probably made the biggest difference in homosexuality's social acceptance. You remember that the most basic function of myths is to give a known form to the unknown. Being shown in positive terms on television meant that, for the first time ever, images of homosexuals could potentially reach millions of people at once. For the first time, the homophobic mythos that the traditional culture had imprinted into people's brains for centuries ended up being challenged by something even more powerful than stories: images.

In the space of a few years, television was able to displace the hundreds of received ideas associated with homosexuality. Three television shows are truly emblematic of that process: *Ellen*, in which actress Ellen DeGeneres came out as a lesbian in real life, and then as her character in 1997 (*Ellen* ran for one more year after that time); *Will and Grace*, which was broadcast on the American television network from 1998 to 2006; and the very daring *Queer as Folk*, which was first aired in England in 1999 (1999–2000 in the United Kingdom, then 2000–2005 in the United States). Take the character of Will, from *Will and Grace*, for instance. Will portrayed a typical New Yorker: a successful, charming, and only mildly neurotic young man. His friend Jack, definitely more flamboyant, was not by a long shot any less human and lovable. Ellen, Will, and Jack's wit and sense of humor touched both gay and straight audiences. People could relate to either one of them, or all three, as friends, or even mirrors of themselves. The homosexual lifestyle—whatever that meant for Ellen's, Will's, or Jack's characters, for the producers of these shows, gays and lesbians, or people in general—began to appear not so different from everybody else's lifestyle.

In that process, *Queer as Folk* definitely constituted a step-up. Whoever has seen the first episode of the original British series knows how much its sexual content—quite explicit—constituted a little revolution in itself, introducing straight audiences to practices such as "rimming" probably for the very first time. Prior to that time, only heterosexual sexual practices had been depicted on television in such an explicit fashion. But for the first time in 1999, thousands of heterosexual homes had a chance to stop wondering or imagining what two men can do in bed together and, instead, to see it. Homosexual sex became "visible" again, literally this time, and many people started to wonder what was so revolting about it.

Gay activism had certainly opened the door to a sociocultural change, yet the positive impact of pioneer television shows such as these on the levels of the acceptance of gay people was considerable. Studies confirm that while strongly negative opinions against same-sex relationships started to drop significantly starting in 1992, the most dramatic shift toward warmer feelings for gays and lesbians took place in the years 1996–2000.[552] Political activism often misses the mythic power—the "numinosity"—that television is so better designed to convey. And more than anything else today, the gay cause needs story tellers. Stories, whether they are written or filmed, are simply stories; they only are fragments or approximations of people's lives. It does not matter whether the representation is perfectly accurate or not. What matters is that something positive be associated with the concept of homosexuality in the collective psyche. This is not only what matters but also what we need urgently.

Another significant segment of the current homosexual mythos is directly generated by the news that is distributed by the media uninterruptedly—history unfolding before our eyes. Since the 1970s the wave of "coming-out" of public figures and other celebrities has gained momentum. From singer Elton John to tennis player Martina Navratilova, and from the mayor of Paris Bertrand Delanoë to actress and talk-show presenter Ellen Degeneres, the task of keeping track of gay or lesbian public figures has become nearly impossible. Homosexuality has not only emerged from the unknown; it now has many real faces.

No one today can deny the extraordinarily positive influence of this collective coming-out. The correlation between one's acquaintance with homosexual individuals and one's loss of homophobic feelings is compelling. In fact, one's direct experience of homosexual people—in the right cultural context—appears to constitute the best antidote against homophobia. One must nevertheless admit that the coming-out phenomenon represents a historical oddity. In the wake of gay liberation homosexuals began to disclose their sexuality spontaneously to their family, friends, and coworkers. This wave of confessions has no equivalent in history, even remotely. As homosexuality progressively reintegrates the social sphere, it will be interesting to follow the evolution of this bizarre ritual—a rite of passage, in many respects—in the future (I shall return to this point in a subsequent chapter).

The increasing acceptance of homosexuality in postmodern societies appears to be, for a large part, the product of the higher visibility of homosexuals through the media or in people's social environments. This was made possible by the wave of pluralism that pervaded Western culture since the 1970s. However, we ought to remember that homosexuals enjoyed a relative freedom and some degree of visibility in previous times in history. The burgeoning urban life in Middle Ages Europe fostered a modest, yet promising development of homoerotic literature and the birth of early homosexual subcultures in cities like Florence and Venice. This was eventually crushed by the Holy Inquisition. The Muslim world that once exhibited a remarkable tolerance for homosexual desires, contrasting sharply with the ferocity of Christian Europe in the same period, has made a U-turn regarding its attitude toward homosexuals today. Throughout the centuries, homosexuals have successively been in (rarely) and out (mostly) of the empathic space. The mere visibility of homosexual love in the sociocultural sphere is important, but apparently not enough in the long term. Even visible and tolerated, as long as homosexuals keep being represented as outcasts in the mythos they will remain vulnerable.

THE MISSING MYTH: LOST AND FOUND

Homosexuality's presence in the arts and in the media composes only the most apparent part of a larger edifice. Remember that an essential function of the mythos beyond that of providing a representation of the unknown as well as visibility and predictability, is also to elucidate the mystery of the origins—where do we come from and why are we here? None of what we have reviewed addresses that crucial issue. Homosexuality's representation in the postmodern mythos is therefore incomplete, amputated from all the myths that aim to provide meaning and purpose. The hard-won symbolic visibility of the gay community is still dwarfed by a colossal mythic deficit. I must therefore concede that my "edifice" is mostly empty.

The flames of Sodom and Gomorrah have reduced the homosexual mythos to ashes—ashes that homosexuals are still breathing today. Homosexuality still lacks the vital connection with the eternal and the universal. It still hasn't regained its just place in the realm of the sacred. Today homosexuals—spiritual orphans—are unknowingly mourning this essential link to their origins—the missing myth. We shall revisit that topic more than once and this for a simple reason: It is the key to homosexuality's future. Either homosexuals will undertake the heroic task of reconstructing their broken mythos, or they will be doomed to suffer the fate of eternal outsiders, knowing the risks that such a choice entails. By growing increasingly conscious of the mythic context that supports its existence, a community will proactively foster the birth of its own mythos, perhaps for the first time in history. The truth is, when looking more closely, we can see that a homosexual mythos is slowly materializing. One can distinguish at least three facets of a nascent homosexual mythos. The first one is the mythic dimension of the AIDS epidemic; the second one is the martyrdom of Matthew Shepard; and the third one, which, I believe, has the greatest potential, is conveyed through the extraordinary narrative of homosexuality's natural history. These familiar topics can now be explored from a mythic perspective.

Some readers may have found me a little too silent about the AIDS epidemic. My attitude regarding this issue throughout this book contrasts certainly with the general mood of gay activism and contemporary writings about homosexuality. I must then confess to having been little exposed myself to the devastating effects of AIDS. Yet, I have been exposed to the cultural angst caused by the AIDS epidemic. I certainly shared the dismay, the fear, and the immense sorrow that so many in the gay community have also experienced, and felt empathy for the suffering of my kin.

Yet most studies concur on the strong and ironically favorable impact of AIDS on the public opinion regarding the acceptance of homosexuality. The alarming vulnerability of homosexuals in the face of this nightmare, with their pain, loneliness, despair, and too often their deaths, appeared for the first time on the TV screens of America and Europe. The desperate calls for help of the gay communities were largely broadcast by the media, which brought many homosexuals, the ill and the healthy, as well as many political activists into the limelight. Suddenly, the insufferable social isolation of homosexuals in Western society could no longer be ignored. Many started to feel an unusual compassion. And for the people in the 1980s and 1990s for whom homosexuals were, at best, an inappropriate topic of conversation and, more often, no more than an undesirable species of sex addicts, all this was a total discovery.

I believe that the history of AIDS also has a mythic dimension. The AIDS tragedy is first and foremost a collective martyrdom, and in a Christian culture, martyrdom is a soft spot. The AIDS epidemic—the thousands of homosexuals who either died of it or had to live with its insufferable symptoms—created an image so vivid, so terrible, and so deeply human. It resonated with people because it evoked the mythic source of Christianity, whether in the martyrdom of Jesus depicted in the Gospels or that of thousands of early Christians under Roman rule. A similar phenomenon happened with the Holocaust of the Jews during

World War II. For centuries Jews were persecuted and ostracized by Christians, and this was done without guilt or shame. But after the unthinkable horror of the Nazi concentration camps, people could no longer look at the Jews in the same way because Jewish history had acquired a new mythic dimension—the martyrdom of the Holocaust—which spoke intensely to the Christian collective psyche.

Martyrdom—the ultimate sacrifice of one's life—is a form of heroism particularly revered in Christianity and the martyr is a prime archetype in the Christian mythos. As cynical as this might sound, the unbearable suffering inflicted by the rapid spread of HIV through the gay community reminded people of the "eternal and universal" vulnerability of human beings. Even the death toll acquired a certain divine dimension. And, perhaps against all odds, for an increasing number of people, both homosexual and straight, the AIDS tragedy attained the sacred. It rose to a mythic level.

Because of its mythic resonance, the AIDS tragedy helped crystallize a new vision of homosexuality in people's consciousness. For centuries humanity had abandoned homosexuals, but now with the AIDS epidemic, as it happened earlier when slavery was abolished and in the aftermath of the Holocaust, people realized the devastating effects that denying empathic feelings can cause. Through this terrible experience, homosexuals no longer appeared as perverts hungry for exotic sex. An increasingly large majority discovered homosexuals as human beings who also need love, care, and compassion, and could give all that in return. The media revealed the reality of committed and loving relationships strong enough to resist a total absence of support and recognition, and even the ferocious hostility from the rest of society. And the impact was not any less great on the collective consciousness of homosexuals. The gay community received two formidable lessons thanks to the AIDS tragedy. The first was that it could no longer afford to live exiled at the fringe of society, and the second was that love had to become the centerpiece of what defined homosexuality. And this illustrates better than any theoretical discourse the power of myth.

Then, on October 12, 1998, Matthew Shepherd, a gay student at the University of Wyoming, was kidnapped, beaten, and left to die when tied to a fence for eighteen hours. He was twenty-one years old. I will spare you the horrific details. Once again, we must keep our focus on the specific impact of Shepherd's slaying on the collective psyche. In that respect, the media coverage was without precedent for this "kind" of hate crime. Shepherd's savage murder elicited an intense emotion far beyond the limits of the gay community. The event had a cathartic effect. Shepherd's death inspired books, songs, a play as well as a movie (*The Laramie Project*), and his name was given to an anti-hate crime federal bill, the Matthew Shepard Act. It certainly is difficult to monitor the emergence of a mythic element in such a short time; yet the gay community (at least in the United States) might have found in Matthew Shepherd its first official martyr (the same might be true of Harvey Milk). Shepherd's odious end, his fragile youth, and the natural grace of his face personified the longtime experience of homosexuals torn between two unbearable choices: submitting to secrecy or defying death. I am not the one to proclaim Matthew Shepherd the first gay martyr, even if to the best of my knowledge all the conditions seem met. Only history will tell whether Shepherd will rise to the eternal and the universal, or if he too will eventually be forgotten. But let my heart speak for a moment: Through Matthew Shepherd, I was once young and bold; through him, I was beaten; and through him, I died; I am like him and he is like me. His pain is my pain, still alive deep in my soul. Every time one evokes his name, the memory of Matthew Shepherd reveals my suffering—our suffering—to the entire world. Matthew embodies my revolt, our revolt. And in that too, one may recognize the numinous power of myth.

Myths emerge often in the most surprising places. I would then like to end this chapter with what I believe is the most promising source of myths for (post)modern societies in general, and particularly for the homosexual community: science. I have already explained at length the paradoxical role of the scientific narrative in the new mythos. Most people are seldom aware of this new dimension of science, and scientists themselves, in their great majority, see it as a betrayal of science's original intention. In any case, the increasing presence of scientific concepts in the mythos today is irrefutable. But science does not only talk about the big bang, quasars, black holes, dark matter, and other cosmic creatures. In fact, as you very well know, science has been extremely curious about same-sex behavior. For more than a century and a half now, science—medicine, biology, sociobiology, genetics, and neuroscience—has been utterly engrossed by the homosexual phenomenon and often totally baffled by its allegedly impenetrable logic. Reinterpreted inside the right context (homosexuality as a positive product of evolution that favors both reproduction and the survival of the group), I believe that we have enough data at our disposal to begin to rewrite the natural history of homosexuality. The first part was sorted out in chapter 3 and 4 that covered the biological mechanisms that explain homosexuality's emergence in some individuals. A second part—the evolutionary part, which was explored in chapters 2 and 5, traces the origins and role of homosexual behavior and homosexual identity throughout the biological and cultural evolution of the human species.

All the ingredients of a mythic narrative are there. It only needs to be written, and told. In reexamining the material that is discussed in chapters 3 and 4, for instance, we can easily discern the story behind the scientific logic. We may even recognize the truth, the goodness, and the beauty in this story. Genes have a "numinous" power, as Jung would put it, which is why everybody got so hooked by the search for the gay gene in the first place.[553] Genes have become our link with the beginning of time and the logic of life. They carry within them the memory of our slow emergence in human evolution and in our mothers' wombs. Together, neuroscience, genetics, and evolutionary anthropology offer us the unique chance to retrace the roots of homosexuality back to the two decisive moments, the time of conception and the birth of humanity.

The prospects of the scientific exploration of homosexuality are extraordinary. In the near future, scientific research will most likely bestow on homosexuality a "brand new" natural history of five million years, back to our common ancestor with the chimpanzees and the bonobos. It might also decipher the secret nature of the "loose switch," which sets people's sexual orientation during embryonic life, and tell us how sexual orientation and sexual preference unfold until one reaches adult age. Those are the stories that we will need to assemble and share with the future generations so that, unlike us, they can grow with a profound relationship with their homosexual essence—eternal and universal—and with a deep sense of belonging and sacredness as homosexual beings. Yet gays will have to do the work. Nobody else will do it for them. Recreating the myths is a fantastic opportunity and, at the same time, an incredible responsibility, toward ourselves and even more importantly, our children.

STEREOTYPES

We may now inquire into another ingredient of human culture that until now I have carefully avoided discussing: stereotypes. We all have a sense of what stereotypes look like, and even today it is still difficult to think or talk about homosexuals without stumbling across a whole collection of received ideas. Stereotypes are widespread and come in many different flavors: positive, humorous, neutral, cynical, insulting, or murderous, but also unquestioned, accepted, challenged, or embattled. They are caricatural portrayals of particular categories of people. They are omnipresent. No human mind can escape them—neither you nor I, nor Nelson Mandela, nor even the Dalai Lama. And the same is true of cultures. Virtually anybody who professes the elimination of stereotypes (whether homophobic, racial, or misogynist) inevitably leaves many others totally unquestioned. I have yet to meet a stereotype-free person, and I can explain to you why that does not surprise me.

Just like "nature abhors a vacuum," the human psyche feels compelled to fill in the blank each time it meets the unknown. No culture has ever functioned without some representation of what one may call the "known unknown": what people cannot understand and do not know what it is, let alone what it is up to, and yet know it is there. Neither the mind nor culture is well equipped to confront the unknown as the unknown frontally. How do people satisfy their uncontrollable need for giving a known appearance to the unknown when no objective or symbolic (mythic or archetypal) representation is available in their cultural milieu? The answer is remarkably simple: They guess. They imagine what it is and what it does, based on what they already know; in other words, they extrapolate. When one of those guesses manages to be disseminated in the intersubjective space of "WE," what you get is a stereotype. The stereotype's truthfulness has no importance. All that really matters is the consensus that underlies its existence, that is, that people agree on it and believe in it. Therefore, stereotypes may be defined as oversimplified and imaginary portrayals of categories of people. Mythic archetypes and stereotypes share essential features. They both propagate through populations using the same sociocultural mechanisms. They are communicated from one individual, one group, or one culture to another, and are transmitted through generations. Both find a common origin in the necessity to generate a safe—controllable and predictable—environment. Yet the similarity ends here. Myths and archetypes are poetic metaphors that can hold eternal and universal truths. Stereotypes are only pretenses, urgently designed so as to compensate for our crass ignorance. Unlike mythic archetypes, they have no connection to the sacred. Moreover, and this point is absolutely crucial: they do not have the spiritually, morally, and socially inclusive virtue of myths and archetypes. In the absence of mythic representation, stereotypes are inevitable insofar as only they can relieve human beings' fear of the unknown and their need to predict. They operate like cultural representations by default, for want of anything better.

Stereotypes—those agreed-upon pseudo-truths—are everywhere in the cultural landscape and homosexuals know that from experience. Simply mention words such as homosexual, gay, lesbian, queen, femme, or butch and stereotypes will pop up in the conversation like mosquitoes in the beginning of summer. There is no need to list them here. Nevertheless, I would invite you to judge your experience of stereotypes from a different context. First of all, when it comes to negative stereotypes, gays and lesbians are far from having a monopoly. I do not believe that any category of human being based on race, age, gender, nationality, sexual orientation, physical appearance, social class, education level, geographic origin, and so forth, can be declared exempt from stereotypes. It is not rare to see people endorse stereotypes about categories in which they themselves belong. Stereotypes target everybody because they cost virtually nothing to those who perpetuate them. Do they contain a little bit of truth? Sometimes, yes, they do, even if distorted or partial. And it is that hint of truth that often makes them so plausible, so attractive, and so contagious.

Second, one must humbly acknowledge the fact that it is nearly impossible to function without stereotypes. In other words, let the one who is devoid of any stereotype "be the first to throw a stone." To live without stereotypes would be terribly uncomfortable. We are usually blind to them until someone points them out to us or unless they mock us. Most of the time, stereotypes are just common knowledge. They blend in; they help us fill many blanks; and without them, we would quickly find ourselves in the impossible position of mystics facing the *mysterium tremendum et fascinans*. In the end, stereotypes represent none other than a legitimate effort to transmute what is foreign into something predictable. By the same token, homosexual stereotypes aim at maintaining a cultural reference regarding homosexuals, something people can agree upon and refer to. Not to mention that by virtue of being shared with other members of a group, stereotypes reinforce the sense of membership in the group.

This is why hateful stereotypes are systematically associated with the dynamics of scapegoating. They automatically and efficiently strengthen the cohesion of the other group members who are not being scapegoated.[554]

Stereotypes, however, are neither irreplaceable nor indestructible. Objective information acquired by education or personal experience can efficiently dislodge them. Spend a year in France and your stereotypes about French people are likely to melt away, replaced by a more elaborate knowledge of French culture. Hang out with homosexual friends or discover them on television and in movies, and homophobic stereotypes will dissolve progressively. They might simply disappear (on the other hand, it is equally undeniable that a negative experience can enhance a negative stereotype). But most likely they will simply be exchanged for more positive stereotypes, which is really all that we may wish for. The characters represented by Will and Jack in "Will and Grace" are nothing other than stereotypes. Yet they represent positive and lovable ones.

It is not so much that stereotypes are bad that creates the problem, but rather that they are cut off from the sacred. They are unfinished cultural processes aimed at providing an immediate cultural representation of a particular category of people without regard for the cost to those people. It would be illusory to believe it is possible to suppress all homosexual stereotypes. The problem has never been the stereotypes themselves but the absence of a powerful mythic symbolism to counterbalance their negative message. The power of stereotypes comes from the absence of mythic representation. To vilify the use of stereotypes in people's discourse, although praiseworthy at first glance, hides our inability or our unwillingness to tackle the real roots of the problem. And there is another great lesson to learn from this. Spotting other people's stereotypes is relatively easy. So is taking offense at them. Noticing our own is far more courageous. Let us not mind stereotypes so much. I suggest that we worry more about our myth deprivation.

Rituals

By exploring myths we have uncovered only half of human beings' symbolic existence. The mythos, uncontested king of the intersubjective realm, would terribly lack effectiveness without its correlate in the interobjective realm, the ritualistic space. Rituals are the indispensable complements of the myths. Just like myths, rituals endow human life with the two vital qualities of predictability and meaning. It is the still crucial importance of rituals in today's life that I would like to emphasize now. They are not only, along with myths, the key to homosexuality's integration into society, but they are also behind the fierce political debate on same-sex marriage that agitates many Western countries today.

As originally stated in chapter 6, rituals are culture-specific behaviors with a fixed form, cyclically repeated over time, and meticulously transmitted through the generations. We ought to recognize ritualistic patterns beyond the classic examples: tribal dances, masses, or New Year's Eve parties. Rituals are everywhere cultures actively impose a particular sequence of behaviors upon isolated individuals or groups of people, whether in ancestral rites, traditions, rules by which all abide, superstitious customs, ceremonies, laws, or even institutions. Rituals provide behavioral templates in that they tell people what to do, when, and with whom (just like myths constitute ontological templates). They imply the reiterations of proven, safe, and agreed-upon actions, thereby guaranteeing the success in what is being reenacted. The attractiveness of rituals resides in their ability to generate both a sense of safety and a sense of purpose. They delineate a secure space within the sociocultural sphere. And it is thanks to the scrupulous respect of rituals that the peace and the harmony in the group is preserved over time.

Rituals, masterful conglomerates of symbolic behaviors, embody humankind's dialogue with the unknown. They speak the primordial language of our distant ancestors, thus allowing a direct dialog with the sacred. Myriad rituals reenact the eternal and universal truth contained in the mythos.[555] This symbolic resonance between myths and rituals is crucial. Rituals channel mythic realities into human existence, and, thanks to their inexhaustible repetition through the generations, grant myths longevity. In return, myths give rituals their symbolic depth, that is, their numinosity. As the tangible mirror of the mythic space, rituals concretize the moral and spiritual vision of the society that observes them.[556] Altogether, myths and rituals offer human beings one of the most precious goods: certainty.

Here, the postmodern mind is confronted by an interesting challenge. On the one hand, myths and rituals give human life its symbolic depth. It would be impossible for each generation to reinvent the centuries of sociocultural evolution that they contain. The human journey began thanks to our remarkable ability to inherit increasingly complex cultural information. Without it we would still be reinventing the Stone Age over and over again. Moreover, myths and rituals delimit the safe space on which all of us count if we are to remain sane and functional in our daily life. So, on the one hand, they grant us wisdom and security. But on the other hand, because they are the unavoidable conditions of social membership, they invite us to become predictable, that is to say, docile and shapeable. For the individualistic mind, the dilemma quickly reaches schizophrenic levels. Myths and rituals are double-edged, a conclusion that we have already reached earlier in our conversation about logos. Deprived from them, life is meaningless and the soul is incomplete; but dominated by them, the self suffocates. They grant and limit freedom at the same time. This is the very paradox homosexuals find themselves confronted with today.

As evoked earlier in this chapter, postmodern thinkers were particularly insightful when they understood the overwhelmingly constraining power of cultures. By rejecting any form of labeling—gay, homosexual, lesbian, and so on—queer theorists in particular hoped to escape the cultural stranglehold of a society that they saw as the principal source of homosexual victimization. Queer theorists had however missed an important point: they would never have been able to have that insight if it were not for the cultural baggage that they had inherited from the very society from which they were trying to distance themselves in the first place. The cultural conditioning that they were denouncing is the prerequisite for their discovery of cultural conditioning. They failed to see the full extent of the vicious circle inside of which every human being is trapped.

Now, are human beings really the eternal prisoners of an infernal machinery? One cannot solve a paradox; one can only transcend it. By this formula, I simply mean that we ought to define a larger context inside of which the paradox no longer is one. This is the context that we are only starting to build now. The task will be completed later, in the last part of the book—the Beautiful. In the meantime, what sense shall we make of this complicated situation?

We have seen that mythos and logos could be held not as two irreconcilable forces engaged in a fratricidal combat but as two indispensable and complementary psychocultural dynamics of evolution. In fact, the interplay between mythos and logos is part of a more global dynamic involving the collective and the individual realms. Just like the mythos constitutes an ontological database, the ritualistic space delineates a large repertoire of socially approved behaviors—a behavioral database. These two psychocultural databases, ontological and behavioral are, just like our DNA, the guardians of the extraordinary mass of information selected through several millenniums of cultural evolution. The individual psyche—that is, the self—needs the collective space to fuel its own development. The self picks what best suits it among the large collection of ontological, behavioral, and moral templates available in the mythos and in the ritualistic space. And the richer the collective space is, the more the self finds opportunities to grow. What queer theorists had envisioned as a force of oppression from the collective upon the individual is now replaced by an evolutionary impetus.

This said, the self must in parallel differentiate itself from the collective space thanks to the process that we have called individuation. With the help of logos, the self is able to differentiate the ego and progressively become autonomous. The ego-self is confronted by a fantastic challenge: learning (mainly copying) as much as possible from the available collective psychocultural databases, mythos and ritualistic space, while at the same time systematically reevaluating their form and value, which is for a large part the job of logos. By doing so, the ego-self can integrate the past and grow beyond it. I do not claim that this mechanism works perfectly all the time and for everybody. It certainly can lead to pathologies when the ego-self fails either to individuate properly or, on the contrary, to draw from the collective space the precious information that it needs to develop harmoniously and interact with others.

Given the current mythos and ritualistic space, homosexuals have all the difficulties in the world to find the raw material necessary for building a healthy homosexual self (ego, persona, and so forth), which constitutes a serious psychological handicap. Unlike their heterosexual brothers and sisters, they are condemned to create their identity from scratch, in other words, to reinvent the Stone Age over and over. This is emotionally exhausting and absurd. This situation is fortunately changing, particularly in large urban areas (see chapter 15). But if there is change, it must become a conscious effort on our part and stop relying on population dynamics. It must not only accelerate, but also be made available to all.

To forge a new homosexual mythos and a new homosexual ritualistic space, as I am advocating here, would by no means equate to erecting the bars of a new gilded cage. (In any case, the postmodern self loathes rigidity and uniformity, even in the domain of the sacred). Our brand new homosexual mythic and ritualistic space will have to be vast, diverse, and, most importantly, creative. It will not only contain the raw material thanks to which homosexuals will be given a chance to recognize themselves, but also constitute the means by which the rest of the world will know who homosexuals are and what they are up to—a collective persona, so to speak. It will simultaneously help homosexuals structure their selves and become, to a certain extent, predictable. This said, insofar as "predictability" is largely out of fashion these days, I do not want to end this discussion without specifying what "predictability" would mean in a global postmodern ("integral," possibly) culture, and also without addressing the natural skepticism that this concept might legitimately trigger in many readers.

First, we know that traditional homosexualities were precisely codified. They all imposed a strict behavioral and moral framework, in other words, a "code of conduct" and a "code of honor." Homosexual life—sexual practices, courtship, and relational form(s)—was highly ritualized (especially between men), yet no more than heterosexual life was, and no more than everything else that mattered for the ancients. Conformity to the norm—predictability—was the precondition to social integration and often to one's mere survival. On the flip side of this, transgressions from the established models (e.g., the rules of male ranking) were subject to popular discredit.

How different is modern homosexuality from this? Although no longer based on male ranking, modern homosexuality has a moral framework, even if its boundaries are still blurry. Homosexuals might be resisting some aspect of the prevalent morals. Still, things such as pedophilia, adultery (which entails the absence of mutual consent between partners), sexual abuse, or irresponsibly jeopardizing one's health, are by and large considered unacceptable. I believe homosexuals value love, mutual respect, the emotional and sexual fulfillment of both partners, and moral integrity. Observe that those values were largely foreign to premodern homosexual cultures. As discussed earlier, in ancient Greece and Melanesia, for instance, only the insertive partner was supposed to reach orgasm. In Sambia people, as in imperial Rome, the receptive partners were rarely asked for their permission before being sodomized. If mutual respect occurred in some male relationships, it certainly was not central to the "code of honor" of our homosexual ancestors. Hence, modern homosexuality has its own set of moral values and moral boundaries. It has a "code of conduct" and a "code of honor." We just need to choose collectively and overtly the values that we want to embody and champion in today's society. That is the kind of predictability for which I am campaigning.

Second, thanks to television shows such as *Will and Grace* and *Queer as Folk*, celebrities like Elton John and Ellen DeGeneres, politicians like Harvey Milk and Bertrand Delanoë, and movies like *Brokeback Mountain*, modern homosexuals have already become predictable. Rare are the people today who still wonder what real homosexuals look like and how they behave in public and even in their bedrooms. The bedrock of a homosexual mythos, even if shallow, is already in place. When people think of what two men do in bed, they remember scenes from *Queer as Folk, Brokeback Mountain, Cruising,* or *Happy Together.* They will not ask you or me for details because they already "know." For an increasingly large number of people homosexuals no longer represent an unknown, and that is why less and less people object to gay relationships. Let's face it. Homosexuals no longer are the rebels they used to be, and the alleged "fluidity" of the homosexual desire is just another curiosity from the past that no longer interests anyone.

The reintegration of homosexuality within the sociocultural sphere and the psychological integrity of homosexuals both depend on the same thing: the willingness of the homosexual world to appear safe to the non-homosexual world as much as to itself and, most importantly, on the ability of homosexuality to become sacred again. Modern homosexuality is only at the beginning of a long journey. Today, with gay marriage, gay adoption, and ultimately, I hope, the full recognition of same-sex parent families, homosexuals are gaining access to one of our most emblematic institutions, as I will discuss in the next chapter.

Equal Rights–Different Rites

The integration of same-sex couples into the institution of marriage and the sanctioning of adoption of children by gay couples represents the frontline of a second "gay revolution." Since the 1990s the debate about same-sex marriage has been fierce, and often the incomprehension between the gay community and most religious institutions seems completely hopeless.

I am less interested in giving you another "well-informed" opinion about same-sex marriage than I am in accomplishing an unusual task. First, I would like to reframe the discussion concerning the institution of marriage within the wider dynamic of rituals and myths—since marriage partakes of both—so that one can start to envision same-sex marriage as a multifaceted issue rather than just a moral dispute. Second, I wish to present as clearly as possible what the stakes really are regarding the integration of gay and lesbian couples into the current institution of marriage. I must immediately acknowledge the limited scope of my inquiry. If debates about same-sex marriage are similarly occurring today in non-Christian cultures, in countries like India, China, or Japan, I am, alas, not aware of their existence, let alone of their substance. The analysis of the opposition between gay marriage and religious beliefs that I present here is, therefore, focused for the most part on Judeo-Christianity. I am however inclined to believe that to a large extent the reasoning that I offer here could be applied to other cultures.

Among all rituals, marriage is probably one of the most complex. In it converge many of human beings' most basic needs and deepest anxieties: love, sex, mating, companionship, emotional stability, social recognition, social integration, material security, and so forth. Yet, we tend to forget that marriage has not always been viewed as including all that, and that the priority order in which those various aspects come varies dramatically, depending on the kind of people you discuss it with. One cannot argue about marriage mindless of the fact that the concept has changed significantly throughout history, across cultures, and even subcultures. First, marriage has not always and everywhere been considered as the sacred union between a man and a woman defined only on the basis of biological criteria (see chapter 1). Second, each religion professes its own version of what marriage ought to be. Within Christianity itself, the historical division into many branches—Roman Catholic, Eastern Orthodox, Protestant, and so forth—resulted in a significant diversification of the discourse on marriage, and this, despite common spiritual roots. Third, in most countries, the institution of marriage is not one but two, civil and religious. Hence, today, defining the nature of marriage is a daunting task, for it means something different to different people. More than with any other topics, the issue of marriage in general, and that of same-sex marriage in particular, demands that we hold multiple perspectives at once, and that each one of them be carefully weighted within the particular context from which it emerges.

We already know that marriage consists of two parts, a social-ritualistic one (in interobjective realm) and a mythic-symbolic one (in intersubjective realm). Remember also that moral arguments cannot be resolved at the level at which they were created, for moral views are all equally valid in the context from which they arise. Yet, insofar as the different worldviews that give birth to those different moral views reflect successive stages of psychocultural evolution, let us instead concentrate on the worldviews that underlie the claims of proponents and opponents of same-sex marriage. And, as you are about to discover, the specific reasons that make gay marriage so unacceptable for most religions are by no means unknown to you.

PREDICTABILITY, MEMBERSHIP, AND MEANING

I will spare you a long history of marriage. There is no need to dive into its infinite details to succeed in our enterprise. Let me just lay out some basic facts. First, as far as scholars can tell, marriage predates recorded history. Its origins are lost in the mists of time. Second, just as it was the case for traditional homosexualities, marriage has taken different forms (e.g., monogamy, polygamy, and, in some very rare cases, polyandry) and fulfilled various social functions (e.g., reproductive stability, group alliance, and use of women as bargaining chips).[557] Moreover, if marriage today appears systematically embedded within a particular religious belief system, this was not the case during antiquity or in most polytheistic cultures. For the most part, marriage has involved opposite-sex pairs, but not always. As we know, many North American native tribes and Polynesian cultures celebrated same-sex unions (with the limitations that we know; those unions still involved individuals of opposite genders, at least conceptually). Third, any hasty conclusion drawn from the two previous points so as to justify same-sex marriage in our culture today would be fallacious and meaningless. Each culture has, in the course of history, reinvented its own ritualistic form and generated its own symbolic framework. Hence, the only origin that is relevant for our discussion is not that of marriage, understood as a transcultural and transhistorical reality (which we cannot determine for certain anyway), but only that of the particular ritualistic form of marriage in question inside the current debate. It is therefore on the Western tradition of marriage, which arose in the first centuries from the merging of two major traditions, Roman and Judeo-Christian, that we must focus our attention. All other traditions, although informative and possibly inspirational for gay and lesbian couples today, have no direct place in the current controversy.

In the West, marriage is not one but many. The institutional diversity that we can observe today is the result of the fragmentation of Christianity into multiple denominations and the split between religious and civil marriage. Yet, although the way marriage is defined differs significantly among those institutions, they all have excluded same-sex couples. Most of them still do. It is then in the commonality between all those institutions that we have the best chances to find an explanation to our problem. Our next task is, therefore, to unveil the common purpose of the institution of marriage, often hidden behind the official discourse.

The goal of marriage—whether as a rite, a custom, or an institution—is first to codify the specific sociocultural form that the union of two individuals—almost always between a man and a woman—should adopt in that particular culture. Marriage acknowledges the existence of a novel entity, the couple. This union is not only social. It is also economic. In most cases, partners increase their stability by sharing their material goods. As one may anticipate, marriage fulfills the basic function of rituals, which is to confer predictability and a sense of commonality. In that regard, the institution of marriage can also be seen not as a unique event, but rather as a long chain of rituals: engagement and wedding ceremonies; the right, duties and customs associated with marital life; widowhood; and even divorce. Again the sequence depends on the culture or subculture in question. Rituals offer a clear repertoire of behavioral templates indicating what to do, and when and with whom; in other words, ready-to-go and time-tested solutions for people who choose to marry.

So, marriage aims at making the lives of those who engage in it easier. At the same time, by embracing this ritual, couples signal their willingness to integrate into the community. They agree to become predictable, that is, safe for the rest of the group. Rituals are never about taking risks, at least not on society's side. Opening rituals to "nonbelievers" betrays the very intention of rituals, which is to delineate and guarantee the existence of a safe space. Their role is to keep the unknown at a safe distance, outside the ritualistic space. Those who do not conform to the rituals—as they are designed—do not belong. In traditional (sub)cultures, ancient or current, nothing is more feared than the blurring of the boundaries between the known and the unknown—the safe and the unsafe.

What is then the "safe space" that marriage aims to create and preserve? To answer that question is to shed light on the true essence of traditional marriage, as it ended up being progressively defined in the Roman Empire and, after the collapse of the empire, by the Christian Church. Let me remind you of a few more other things that you probably already know.

THE THREE PILLARS OF TRADITIONAL MARRIAGE

The similitude between the current critics against same-sex marriage and the discourse on the defense of moral virtue in late antiquity is astonishing. The rationales are sometimes indistinguishable, and one could almost forget that two millenniums have passed. Importantly, those coincidences, by betraying the ulterior motive of those who express them, lay bare what truly is at stake with marriage in our culture. As it happens, marriage rests upon three key intentions.

Here is the first one: "marriage is a great social stabiliser of men."[558] This quote is not from Musonius, Seneca, Philo of Alexandria, or Paul the Apostle, as you might expect at first, but from an editorial of *The Economist* of 1996. Consider the following comment made in 1990 by Dennis Prager, a conservative Jewish intellectual and talk-show host:

> Far from being immoral, however, the Torah's prohibition of homosexuality was a major part of its liberation of the human being from the bonds of unrestrained sexuality and of women from being peripheral to men's lives [. . .] Of course Judaism also holds that women need men. But both the Torah statement and Jewish law have been more adamant about men marrying than about women marrying. Judaism is worried about what happens to men and to society when men do not channel their drives into marriage. In this regard, the Torah and Judaism were highly prescient: the overwhelming majority of violent crimes are committed by unmarried men. In order to become fully human, male and female must join.[559]

The historical consistency is truly striking. Man's untamed nature, which already preoccupied numerous great thinkers of antiquity (see chapter 8), remains two thousand years later a central concern. Indeed, the writers of the Torah might have been the first to recognize the virtue of marriage in tempering men. Centuries later, Stoic and Neoplatonic thinkers of the Roman Empire, who also championed marriage, saw in women the qualities that were so dramatically missing in men: overall self-restraint, deference to authority, and parental skills added to an unshakable commitment to their children. Women began to epitomize the way that men ought to relate with the rest of society. By the first century of the Common Era, primarily under the rule of the emperor Augustus, and at a time when Christianity was still an unknown sect, the institution of marriage had already become the cornerstone of a new societal ideal with a declared intention: to channel men's dangerous excesses into their relationship with women.[560]

The second intention of marriage is procreationist. Procreationism, as you know, was first introduced by Pythagorean philosophy and relayed by Plato, and then a few centuries later by Roman Stoics and Neoplatonists. All concurred that human beings are naturally fit to be heterosexually paired in marriage, the only proper institution for sexual activities. By the same token, the only legitimate goal of sexual acts is procreation, not the pleasure that endangers people's reason, and hence jeopardizes the social order.[561] In Roman society it became more than ever a moral obligation for a young man to marry, to be faithful to his wife, and to produce children.[562] The Christian Church, which had just overcome—with difficulty—the perilous internal battle over the issue of sex and reproduction, embraced with evident relief the strict procreationist dogma of Roman Stoics and Neoplatonists. It also recognized in the Roman institution of marriage a chance to fulfill two ambitions at once: to restrict sexual activities among lay people to their strict procreative minimum and, at the same time, perpetuate Christendom. And from an act of civil obedience, marriage among Christians turned into a religious duty.

The third intention of Western marriage is dictated by the principle of religious endogamy, which had originally been enforced by the Hebrews to maintain the integrity of their community that was regularly invaded, deported, and constantly overwhelmed by powerful neighbors (see chapter 8). In light of what we know about rituals, the principle of religious endogamy makes perfect sense. Rituals are designed to reinforce people's cultural identity (internalized as the persona) and counteract the diluting forces to which cultures are inevitably exposed. Paul, whose views on sexuality and marriage proved decisive for Christianity, borrowed the principle of religious endogamy from Judaism with exactly the same intention: to preserve and reinforce the sociocultural coherence of Christendom. Following Paul's lead, the Church instituted marriage as the indissoluble union between a Christian man and a Christian woman. It took centuries for the leaders of the Church to impose their views on Christendom. Nor can one deny the many dissensions regarding those issues among Christian theologians, let alone among Christians themselves. Regardless of this, no one can accuse the Church of not being consistent. Like it or not, the Christian Church has remained, by and large, faithful to the intention of its founders.

The concept of marriage as the union of a man and a woman on the basis of mutual romantic feelings is a recent invention. In her historical study on marriage, Stephanie Coontz concludes unambiguously that "only rarely in history has love been seen as the main reason for getting married."[563] Although the concept of romantic marriage is old enough to look like an ancient tradition to us, the idea was largely foreign to tradition-based cultures that find it far too unpredictable, and thus socially unsustainable. In Ancient Greece, the Roman Empire, medieval Europe, China, and India, the idea of a passionate romance between spouses was never hailed as an ideal, but rather as a threat to the stability typically expected from married couples. The romantic ideal only emerges around the eighteenth and nineteenth centuries. The overly individualistic, almost rebellious spirit of romantic marriage is typical of modern consciousness, but a world apart from traditional (premodern) mentalities. Even if today the concept has been largely incorporated into the Church's marital discourse, the romantic attraction between spouses never was a religious preoccupation to begin with. Romantic marriage is not an invention of Judeo-Christianity. In *Same-Sex Unions in Premodern Europe*, John Boswell continues on the exact same page:

In premodern Europe marriage usually began as a property arrangement, was in its middle mostly about raising children, and ended about love. Few couples in fact married 'for love,' but many grew to love each other in time as they jointly managed their household, reared their offspring, and shared life's experiences. Nearly all surviving epitaphs to spouses evince profound affection. By contrast, in most of the modern West, marriage begins about love, in its middle is still mostly about raising children (if there are children), and ends—often—about property, by which point love is absent or a distant memory.[564]

So, traditional marriage—in its authentic (premodern) Romano-Christian form—has never been about romantic love but only about social responsibility and collective survival, which translated into the three intentions that we discussed above: (1) stabilizing men, (2) procreationism, and (3) religious endogamy. It is undeniable that, for Christian Churches, love has never been a necessary or even a sufficient condition of marriage.

And if you are still unconvinced, I am inviting you to ponder over these two recent quotes from two conservative Catholics: "Certainly mutual love and care are to be encouraged wherever possible. But the justification and rationale for marriage as a social institution cannot rest on the goods of companionship alone [. . .] There are profound social goods at stake in holding together the biological, relational, and procreative dimensions of human love."[565] "Marriage is not, and has never been, primarily about two people—it is and always has been about the possibility of generativity."[566] The times have changed. Yet the worldview remains nearly the same.

One should nonetheless refrain from judging the traditional conception of marriage as being less laudable than our modern vision of it. The socio-economic context of the Middle Ages constrained the Church to make choices very different from those we would make today.

First, by anchoring men to women and embedding people's sexuality within a highly restricted social unit Christian culture succeeded in reducing as much as possible the socially disruptive impact of people's sexual impulses. Bear in mind that before Christianity the rule was not sexual freedom but only the boundless sexual self-gratification of dominant males. The latter were granted the right to "fuck" anyone that was socially and symbolically inferior to them: women, children, class subordinates, defeated warriors, slaves, and so on. Even more significant, perhaps, is the fact that marriage facilitated the emergence of the novel figure—the *paterfamilias*—which was largely absent in the ancient world. Overall, the Romano-Christian institution of marriage accomplished a real tour de force by obliging men to become responsible for the welfare of their families.

Second, why did Christianity, originally so torn about the mere idea of copulation, grow increasingly obsessed with reproductive efficiency? Any limitations on fertility, pregnancy, and childbirth—whether masturbation, non-vaginal sex, or abortion—have been severely condemned by the Church. Again, to understand the logic of early Christianity, we need to compare its procreative credo not to our modern values but to the cultural paradigm it aimed to challenge and replace. We know that Christianity inherited those views from Neoplatonists, fortunately purged of the strong eugenic undertones that are so present in Pythagorean and late Platonic thoughts. We need to remember that in pre-Axial Age cultures, having abundant progeny was interpreted as a sign of male potency. Axial cultures, to which Christianity belongs, turned this paradigm upside down. From then on, childbirth manifested one's deliberate investment in the life and fate of the entire community. At a time when longevity rates plummeted by reason of wars, diseases, and famine, making sure that the next generation would be plentiful represented the best chance to overcome the incessant military and economic competition against neighboring groups. In such a context, procreationism was a clever strategy, and marriage a powerful instrument.

Children became central, not exactly as "children" but as the adults of the future (the concept of "the child as person" that arose with modernity only really took off in the postmodern era). The emphasis on childbirth as the fundamental basis of marriage is not founded on an authentic interest in children but in the collective interest. As a matter of fact, for the Church sterility was a valid reason to break the sacred bond of marriage. Traditional marriage thus has never been rooted in the "love of children," either, and has only been marginally concerned about it. Traditional marriage arose primarily on the basis of a procreative survival strategy perfectly captured by the phrase "number is power." If one understands that, one can also understand why, even today, most Christian Churches oppose altogether any form of contraception, abortion, and same-sex relationships. Notice that procreationism, in the end, appears to have fulfilled its original mission: to make sure that Christendom would thrive.

Today however, the problems that we need to solve urgently are dramatically different. Is procreationism still an appropriate response to issues such as overpopulation, the depletion of our natural resources, deforestation, pollution, or human-induced climate change? Are those views consistent with postmodern consciousness and, of course, with the very new idea that love is the most sacred good of all? I believe not. The world has changed. Needless to say, it would have been impossible for the early leaders of the Church to foresee the problems that we are encountering today. But why are procreationist/anti-same-sex marriage views still so prominent? Why are most religions today still at odds with many realities of our global postmodern world? To answer that question, we need to inquire once more into where people look so that they can know what is true, good, and beautiful: the *mythos*.

THE COSMIC ORDER

It would be impossible to decipher the ritual of marriage and its history without also considering its symbolic meaning. Marriage is not only socio-economic but also, and perhaps foremost, symbolic. Everywhere in the world the marital union of a man with a woman has been modeled upon some eternal and universal, that is, sacred, ideal. According to the *Encyclopedia of Religions*:

> In Samoa the marriage of the creator god Tangaloa with a woman he has created begins the world and, through their union, all of mankind. The Makasar of Indonesia believe that the son of the sky deity was sent to earth on a rainbow to prepare the world for humans. This god married six female deities and their offspring became the peoples of the world. The union of the Japanese gods Izanagi and Izanami consolidates and fertilizes the moving earth. Through their union, they produced the islands of Japan. The marriage of Osiris, one of the greatest of ancient Egyptian deities, with his sister Isis accounts for the continuation of the pharaohs and their practice of marrying their sisters. For Jews, Christians, and Muslims alike, the marriage of Adam and Eve, two beings created by God, generates all of humankind.[567]

By reenacting the primordial sexual union that gave birth to humankind at the beginning of times, marriage restores the perfection of the origins. Uncontestedly, the Adam and Eve pair represents the primordial model for couples in all Abrahamic religions. Yet we have seen that Adam and Eve were only the symbolic manifestation of a more total principle: the cosmic order. In Judaism, Christianity, and Islam, the entire cosmos is organized around the polarity defined by God—the divine principle (Yahveh, Christ, or Allah), which is male, active, and creative—and his creation—earthly/material reality (the "chosen people," the Church, the believers, humanity, the world . . .), which is feminine and receptive.[568] Everything else in the universe, Adam and Eve being no exception, ought to mirror the cosmic order so as to reflect the perfection of God's design. Heterosexual marriage is true, good, and beautiful because it is "in the image of" the sacred cosmic order. It is that simple.

Monotheistic cosmology is also typical of the Axial Age. Many thinkers of that time, from Aristotle to Lao-Tzu, conceptualized the complex energies that animate the world and human life in particular as originating from complementary primordial principles of polar opposites—masculine-feminine, yang-yin, active and passive, and so on. People's suffering—their weaknesses, illnesses, and misfortunes—stem from a disequilibrium between these two fundamental forces. Human beings must then endeavor to reestablish the delicate "energetic" balance. The harmony between these complementary principles reflects the perfection that was present at the beginning of times, hence the perfection that human beings aspire to recreate. Very logically, Axial thinkers favored heterosexual couplings, which ended up being the only one deemed "natural" in the West. Homosexual attractions were viewed as harmless pastimes at best (in the East), more often as repulsive (in the West), and, generally, as being hardly compatible with the community's best interest.

Anybody or any culture whose symbolic mind is still strongly anchored to Hebraic mythology will instinctively strive to model the world after a cosmic order based upon the complementarity between the masculine and the feminine. (Remember that by writing "instinctively" I acknowledge once more that we do not know how the numinous power of myth works.) No one can deny however that many Christian, Jewish, and Muslim thinkers have transcended a strict identification between God and his creation and the masculine-feminine polarity. Regarding Christianity alone, the feminine aspect of Christ's essence and the subtle gender complexity of the Trinity, for example, are equally important aspects of Christian theology. Christianity, Judaism, and Islam are, theologically speaking, very diverse. Throughout history, they have profoundly evolved. Notwithstanding this, the hypnotic power of the Hebraic cosmic order has never faded. None of those religions has made any serious attempt to renew the cosmological model that they have shared for centuries. The founding myth is still identical to what it was three millenniums ago. Efforts to feminize God or, at least, neutralize the gender of the divine principle, which for the most part emanated from feminist thinkers, remains extremely marginal, and at this point their impact on the collective psyche is negligible. The concept of a masculine God keeps dominating the current global postmodern mythos and, along with it, the old cosmic order. If one understands this, one can also understand why decades of feminism and gay liberation have failed to erode a quasi-universal consensus on the spiritual supremacy of the masculine principle and erase the belief that balance and harmony relies on the complementarity between the masculine and the feminine principles.[569] As long as the cosmological myths of the Axial Age will remain in place, proponents of same-sex marriage, gay activists, and feminists will continue to wrestle with an elusive ghost: the cosmic order.

If this situation were not complicated enough already, there is yet another issue, which explains why it is today almost impossible to find a rational solution to the debate on same-sex marriage. The mess was involuntarily caused by modernity. In its legitimate effort to limit the power of the Church, modernity undertook to separate the State from the Church. In the process the institution of marriage ended up being duplicated. Marriage became not one but two rituals, one civil and the other religious. One would have hoped to see marriage be "scientifically" divided along the line that separates the interobjective from the intersubjective realms, that is, split into a strictly social institution, civil marriage, and a strictly symbolic ritual, religious marriage. But this is not what happened.

To explain this imbroglio, let me remind you first that modernity imposed itself despite the many attempts of the Church to contain its irresistible rise. Historically speaking, the divorce between the State and the Church was not pretty. Modernity and the Church seldom saw each other as complementary. Mostly, they were fierce rivals. Second, by denying the validity of any mythos, modernity threw out the baby with the bath water. It created civil marriage to free the institution from the claws of the Church. But, in the process, not only did modernity downplay the spiritual and symbolic significance of marriage; it totally missed the fact that civil marriage would unavoidably end up being tied to a pre-existing mythic framework.

Modernity left the symbolic part of civil marriage in limbo and, as a result, largely in the hands of the Christian Churches. Religious marriage, on the other hand, survived the surgery pretty well, for the Church kept its symbolic raison d'être intact. Then civil marriage started to evolve semi-separately from religious marriage, carrying an increasingly heavy load of "undeclared mythic substance" in its shadow. Gradually and confusingly, civil marriage started to embody the new moral values of modernity, which included the right to divorce (particularly in Roman Catholic countries), the progressive emancipation of women from men's authority and economic domination, and today, the timid recognition of same-sex couples.

Ironically, romantic love—perhaps the most important contribution of (post) modernity to the institution of marriage—ended up being associated with religious marriage more than with civil marriage. Although apparently unfair, this is not surprising. Love is clearly more akin to a sacred vow than it is to a social contract. Unlike city halls, churches and temples invite us to enter into dialogue with the sacred, the eternal, and the universal. They inevitably impose themselves as the natural homes of any celebration of love. In that, modernity was caught by its own contradiction. By privileging logos over mythos in the name of freedom, modernity left people hungry for meaning. Modernity confined the relationship with the sacred to the private domain, ignoring that most people were psychologically unprepared to undertake such a drastic step. In a curious twist of history, religious marriage, which in Abrahamic religions had been built upon the need for social order and rigid procreationist views, became the new champion of romantic love.

Today, the West finds itself with two parallel marital institutions, all at once complementary and competing. Their respective mythic contents, which have been successively denied, usurped, and mixed up throughout history, are now forever confused in the collective psyche. We can no longer tell what belongs to whom. Not only that, but we can also see that all those versions of marriage are rooted, mythically speaking, in the same cosmic order. Most religious institutions are absolutely open about it. They know what their true reference point is. On the other hand, in the secular state, the influence of cosmic order, although omnipresent, remains subliminal. And if one understands that, one also understands why it seems impossible today to find a clean solution to the issue of same-sex marriage.

SAME-SEX MARRIAGE

So, how are we supposed to sort out this mess? As Dan Savage puts it, "straight people have redefined marriage to a point that it no longer makes any logical sense to exclude same-sex couples."[570] Things have already changed dramatically. Same-Sex marriage, either in the form of formal marriage or civil union, is increasingly becoming a reality in parts of Europe, North America (including the complex case of the United States), Latin America, Australia, and New Zealand, not to mention the extraordinary example of South Africa. Yet, regardless of those successes, why does the legalization of gay marriage remain a struggle? According to what we have seen, the issue is twofold.

First, accepting same-sex relationships is perceived as a leap into the unknown. This point was stated by the editors of *The Economist* back in 1996 with a clarity that, I believe, only economists can demonstrate: "Leaving aside (as secular governments should) objections that may be held by particular religions, the case against homosexual marriage is this: people are unaccustomed to it. It is strange and radical."[571] Second, gay relationships are incompatible with the grand cosmic order that is currently held in the mythos. This second issue is the most difficult one. If, as we have seen, people are little by little getting used to the idea that gay relationships are acceptable, the symbolic conflict between same-sex union and the cosmic order is, I am afraid, insurmountable and unlikely to resolve itself without a conscious and courageous effort on everybody's part.

Having all this in the background, what could an integral and evolutionary solution to same-sex marriage look like? In order to answer that important question, I will detail what, in my opinion, could constitute the four basic tenets of a settlement of the issue of same-sex marriage:

- The right of same-sex couples to a social status equal to that of opposite-sex couples is inalienable. As Andrew Sullivan puts it, "same-sex marriage exists in life; it simply doesn't exist in law."[572] Many important benefits to marital status, including social security survivor benefits, tax-free inheritance, spousal immigration rights, and protections against mutual incrimination, are currently denied to same-sex couples, even those living in states or countries that permit same-sex marriage or civil unions. Such discrimination is unacceptable, as would be any discrimination based on race, nationality, social status, wealth, or beliefs. Gay and lesbian people are fully responsible adults and must be treated as such by the rest of society.

- On the other hand, no one should be obliged to acknowledge the symbolic existence or believe in the sacredness of same-sex unions. Insofar as those unions are incompatible with the cosmic order that underlies most of the world's great religious traditions, it would be equally absurd to demand a blind recognition by communities that cannot fundamentally grasp the symbolic reality of same-sex relationships. This by no means diminishes the spiritual values of gay unions. It only means that not everybody would value them as sacred, and that nobody should be forced to hold such a belief. That too is an inalienable right of all human beings.

Interestingly, the current fight over gay marriage has often been compared to the long struggle to legalize interracial marriage in the United States. Yet despite the historical parallel and the legal similarities, I find the comparison misleading.

Nothing in the Judeo-Christian symbolic worldview precludes the existence of interracial unions, as long as the basic rule of religious endogamy is respected. This is not the case with gay relationships. If some Churches are now celebrating same-sex unions, they do so "despite" the cosmic order that they hold as true, not "according to." They courageously choose to value the sacredness of love above that of the cosmic order; yet the basic issue remains unsolved. Even if limited, divorce appears to be a better reference point to address the hostility of Christian churches to same-sex marriage, and help us find a reasonable solution to the problem. We have no problem today accepting the fact that the Roman Catholic Church does not recognize divorce, save for extraordinary circumstances.[573] Divorce is allowed in nearly all predominantly Catholic countries. Yet for the Catholic Church the operation remains invisible. Both worldviews, that of the Catholic Church and that of the secular state, are respected. Gay unions that would be institutionalized by the state but recognized by religious organizations only on a voluntary basis would therefore offer a fair compromise.[574]

• Any claim of authorship of, or ownership over, the institution of marriage is hardly defensible today. If indeed the symbolism of marriage is primarily Christian, we owe most of its moral and social definition to the Roman Empire. Needless to say, the Roman institution of marriage predates the Christian one by several centuries. It is true that after the fall of the Roman Empire, the Church remained the only relatively stable institution amid the political chaos that characterized the early medieval period. As a result, the Church was involved everywhere and tried to control everything. We tend to forget for instance that though the Roman Church created the Holy Inquisition, it also created the first universities. For centuries, the Church strived to impose some social stability on a world that had little, and that effort included enforcing stricter rules for marriage. So, we must give the Church credit for helping the marital institution survive and eventually flourish in the West.

At the same time, the symbolism of marriage is far from being homogenous among the various Christian denominations. Protestant marriage, for instance, which can be officially annulled by divorce, hardly constitutes a valid marriage from a Roman Catholic perspective. In that respect, Catholic and Protestant vows diverge profoundly. The current collusion against gay marriage is far from being based on a common symbolic vision of marriage. Instead, this eclectic coalition is fundamentally opportunistic and primarily built upon a common anxiety in the face of the slow agony of "their" cosmic order.

Many moderate religious leaders have offered to differentiate marriage, which they define as heterosexual, from civil unions, which could include same-sex unions. The request is understandable, somehow reasonable, and yet, in light of what history teaches us, hardly justified. Do religious groups wish to copyright the name "marriage"? On what historical ground could they do that? Nonetheless, rather than settling the thorny question about the authorship of the concept of marriage in a definitive manner, I would invite you to leave it unanswered at this point of our conversation. I believe that this issue hides another far more important one: Whatever its final name will be, what will be the symbolic substance of same-sex marriage?

EQUAL RIGHTS, NOT EQUAL RITES

This last question brings me naturally to disclose the fourth and last tenet:

• It is natural and legitimate for gay and lesbian people, as for any people, to yearn for a sense of sacredness regarding themselves, their relationships, and their families. That too is a fundamental right which cannot be denied. Love without a spiritual dimension is only a crippled version of itself. But here comes the same problem again: not only is same-sex love largely absent from the current mythos, but it also happens to be inconsistent with the predominant mythic cosmic order that we have inherited from the Axial Age.

Same-sex marriage will inevitably imply a profound rethinking of the institution of marriage. In other words, gay unions (either marriage, civil union, or domestic partnership) are symbolically based on a cosmic order that is yet to be discovered. Sooner or later, we will need to explore what lies beyond the reassuring wisdom of Axial thinkers. That is what is really at stake. If homosexuals must have equal rights, they are however not totally identical in essence to heterosexuals. Nor are their relationships. Nor are their families. One can choose to ignore that fact. One can also choose to honor it. Hence, equal rights should never be confused with or reduced to equal rites. That would be missing the point.

I totally understand the desire of gay couples to marry in churches and temples, and I might myself do the same if I were given the opportunity one day. Yet, we also need to stay acutely aware of the fact that the symbolic landscape of those religions is mute, deaf, and blind to the love that we bear in our hearts. Those institutions are anchored in a mythos that makes no reference to homosexual love, and married homosexuals are joining a symbolic space that ignores who they are as homosexual beings. That, I believe, is a serious predicament.[575] Not that this should stop anyone from getting married; on the contrary, that should only remind gay couples, married or not, that a lot more needs to be accomplished. Pioneer theologian James B. Nelson did not hesitate to write that "when existing symbols do not meet legitimate needs, new symbols and rites may be developed."[576] I believe that he is right.

Homosexual love is not in sync with the symbolic meaning of marriage as it is held in our present mythos. This explains why, as discussed in the preface to this book, many gay and lesbian people experience the current sociocultural integration of homosexuals as a dissolution of homosexual identity into the heterosexual norm.

This also explains why many homosexuals today are gripped by a sense of loss. Homosexual couples are missing the myths and the rituals that would allow them to integrate the whole of society without losing their yet-to-be-revealed symbolic contribution. In the meantime, they are "blending in," for want of something better.

It is also tempting, each time a community finds itself at the edge of an evolutionary "precipice," which is the case of gay and lesbian people today, to head backward on the evolutionary track rather than going forward. While evolutionary regression can offer temporary relief, it is never a real solution. Old legends about magic trees, sacred rivers, inseparable pairs of heroic warriors, the moon, Isis, and other goddesses, can no longer affect postmodern consciousness the way that they inspired premodern people in the past. We have no other choice than to leave those ancestral beliefs to those to whom they belong, and instead embrace centuries of psychocultural evolution—from the Neolithic age to postmodernity—and then go beyond. Because we owe it to ourselves and because the stakes are worth the challenge.

If we are now clear about the symbolic meaning of traditional marriage, what will be the symbolic meaning of this "new" marriage? This new marriage ought to be fundamentally different, evolutionarily more aware and more inclusive. Its meaning is deeper, insofar as it includes the original intentions of traditional marriage—ensuring that mothers are protected, empowering males as fathers, and enabling couples to have a political recognition and a solid economical support by the rest of society—but it also transcends those limits. Marriage becomes primarily about the mutual and harmonious development of two human beings united in love, in all three dimensions of body, mind, and spirit. In that space—loving, safe, and nurturing—children find their place naturally, not as a civic or religious duty, but as a creative act. Moreover, in this new context, the creativity of marital love, no longer restricted to the biological realm, can now expand in all domains of human existence. The sacred commitment that marriage represents is itself a creative act.

If the name that this new marriage might take concerns me little, the symbolic substance that it will embody interests me greatly. Of course, the preceding conversation is only a minute fragment of the one we need to have. Millions of gays and lesbians must now speak up.

CHAPTER THIRTEEN

Away from Nature

Between the condemnation of homosexuality as an "act against nature" on the one hand and current claims about the "natural rights" of homosexuals on the other, the concept of "nature" has been used to justify one argument and its exact opposite, and abused to the point where it feels nearly impossible to follow which "nature" is being talked about. When Plato wrote in the *Laws*, through the voice of an Athenian man, "that the pleasure is to be deemed natural which arises out of the intercourse between men and women; but that the intercourse of men with men, or of women with women, is contrary to nature," he unknowingly initiated one of the most lasting controversies in Western history.[577] Plato's philosophy was engrained in the spirit of the Axial revolution, and what he meant by "natural" and "contrary to nature" no longer poses a mystery. More puzzling, however, is the fact that since Plato's statement the concept of nature has had two different meanings in the homosexual debate (and Western culture), in turn conflated and mixed-up, and we have something interesting to learn from sorting this out.

The Real Nature vs. Nurture Debate

Further along in the text, Plato, still through the voice of the Athenian citizen, is more explicit on the anti-natural aspects of same-sex relationships:

> For if any one following nature should [. . .] denounce these lusts as contrary to nature, adducing the animals as a proof that such unions were monstrous, he might prove his point, but he would be wholly at variance with the custom of your states. Further, they are repugnant to a principle which we say that a legislator should always observe; for we are always enquiring which of our enactments tends to virtue and which not. And suppose we grant that these loves are accounted by law to be honorable, or at least not disgraceful, in what degree will they contribute to virtue? Will such passions implant in the soul of him who

is seduced the habit of courage, or in the soul of the seducer the principle of temperance? Who will ever believe this?[578]

First, the Athenian cites animal behavior as evidence that homosexual unions are monstrous. Homosexual behavior is viewed as inconsistent with the way animals operate naturally, that is to say, normally. Nevertheless, Plato does not treat homosexual desire as a mere biological dysfunction. Plato suggests also that same-sex relationships are lustful and disgraceful, and ultimately blames them for ruining one's honor and virtue. Thus, in just a short paragraph, Plato manages to deny Truth, Beauty, and Goodness to same-sex love.

Now we can see that two distinct concepts of nature underlie Plato's discourse. In the first case, "nature" refers to the world of living creatures, all plant and animal species. It is objective nature—the realm of the True. In the second case, Plato refers to one's subjective nature, from which beauty and goodness emerge. This "nature"—our inborn, innate nature, you might call it—constitutes the essence of someone, or something. This is typically what is being expressed in a sentence like "it is not in my nature to do such a thing." So, with Plato and since Plato, homosexuality has been viewed as violating one's biological nature and one's essence, as an intolerable breach of one's physical and spiritual integrity.

We know that Axial thinkers such as Plato conflated the concepts of objective and subjective nature. For them, both manifested the grand design of their gods or God. Christianity embraced the idea of a perfect universal blueprint, which we see culminate with the neo-Aristotelian theology of Thomas Aquinas.[579] Yet despite the fact that Modernity ended the historical confusion between objective and subjective natures some four centuries ago, these two aspects of human nature have been regularly conflated in the discourse on morals, particularly concerning homosexuality, and still to this day both natures are used to justify homophobic views. Notice that nature—either the objective reality of the world of living creatures or the subjective reality of human beings' essence—has systematically been used to justify what seems right. It is therefore the notions of "what is right" and "rights" that I would like to examine with you, in light of what we discovered together in earlier chapters. With this, I will bring the section of this book on the Good to an end. But before getting there, the first thing an integral explorer must attempt to do is to put some order where there is little, that is, to reorganize the various claims and assign them to the respective domain—objective or subjective—to which they belong.

Let us consider nature as objective reality, the world of living creatures. You remember that in the world of things and facts (unlike the world of moral and aesthetic perspectives), the truthfulness of a claim has to be validated experimentally. By arguing that homosexuality is against nature, one suggests that homosexual behavior is not part of our biological design, which is to say, that it does not reflect a "proper" use of the body, a little like saying that a mouse is not made to fly, or a hammer to screw. I suppose that such an allegation rests on two basic ideas. First, all sexual attractions must remain consistent with the possibility of procreation, the meeting of a sperm with an egg; otherwise they are biologically counterproductive (to put it mildly). Second, the vagina is the only orifice able to accommodate a penis; anal and oral penetration are harmful and unhealthy. Obviously, to define the sense of "proper" in a biological context is a delicate task. Human beings have been extremely creative, behaviorally speaking, since they have left the African jungle. Are things as unrelated as drinking alcohol, performing ballet, or remaining chaste proper uses of the human body? The matter is certainly debatable. Yet let us try to answer the question as genuinely as possible. Looking only to Mother Nature for the answer, what is the status of homosexuality in relation to the biological design of the human species?

First, to the best of our knowledge, and despite the obstinate efforts of the nineteenth century medical body to find evidence for it, no homosexual act, whether kissing, mutual masturbation, or oral or anal penetration has ever been reported, in a convincing fashion, as damaging to the body. There are certainly physically hazardous sexual practices, yet they are by no means exclusive to, or even particularly widespread, among homosexuals. Moreover, accusing homosexual acts of unhealthiness seems strangely oblivious to the fact that the most heterosexual act of all, childbearing, is infamous for the chances of physical trauma to which it exposes mothers, not to mention the risk of death during labor.

Second, in numerous animal species, particularly among the most highly evolved, sexual behavior is not limited to reproductive ends. Evolution seems to have used sexual behavior in general and homosexual behavior in particular in order to empower group dynamics. Far from appearing as a gross dysfunction of the animal reproductive instinct, homosexual behavior orchestrates social ranking among males and allows the formation of strong and lasting bonds among females (as discussed in chapter 5).

Third, homosexual behavior plays a non-negligible part in the development of all human beings, including heterosexual development. I am referring here to the "homosexual phase" of adolescence. The odds that the homosexual behavioral repertoire is random and biologically meaningless are extremely low. It is far too sophisticated and organized (as I explained in chapter 5) to support the idea that it constitutes some sort of evolutionary anomaly, let alone a pathology. That Christianity and other fundamentalist movements have developed an uncontrollable aversion to it does not constitute convincing scientific evidence that homosexuality is a biological flaw. Most likely, homosexual behavior is evolutionarily beneficial. Hence, from that point of view, homosexuality is undeniably "natural."

However, the fact that homosexuality is natural, as in "part of nature," even if it sounds like music to the ears of the pro-homosexual camp, only addresses the most flagrant contradictions of the homophobic discourse. Those who wish to use nature as a moral reference point—the myth of lost paradise—would be well-inspired to reevaluate their views. Violence, as you know, is similarly part of the natural design of human beings. Violence is ubiquitous in the animal kingdom, from ants to antelopes. The natural world is brutal and fundamentally amoral. In nature females are raped routinely, males are eaten as snacks by the hungry females right after they have mated, and infants are abandoned and left to die, if not devoured by one of their parents (usually the father). In nature the weakest animals are doomed to beg other members in the group for leftovers or end up being someone's dinner. Even among chimpanzees, our closest relatives, acts of infanticide, war, murder, rape, mutilation, and torture are commonplace. This is nature's solution and nature's true law: everything competes with everything else in order to survive. Harmony in nature results from an implacable balance between life and death, eating and being eaten, mating or failing to mate—a merciless equilibrium of power. Natural history has been shaped by cataclysms, mass destructions, and others bloodsheds. Nature, despite its spectacular beauty, is neither a Garden of Eden nor a reference for moral behavior.

My goal is not to shatter your dreams or even to engage in a deep inquiry into humankind's relation with the natural world. Instead, I intend to persuade you of the fact that the concept of "natural rights," the term "natural" being understood as "in the design of nature," is a largely an illusion. In the natural world there are no rights, only the law that the strongest imposes on others. Ultimately, there is not even a "natural right" to live. Moral principles such as "do not kill," "do not steal," or the basic idea that all humans deserve to be free and happy are completely foreign to the natural world.

We then end up with an interesting paradox. While, on the one hand, homosexual behavior appears perfectly natural, on the other hand, natural rights are absolutely unnatural. What are then the "natural rights" people speak about, those mentioned in the opening statements of two of the most influential texts of modernity, the 1789 French *Déclaration des Droits de l'Homme*—"*les droits naturels, inaliénables et sacrés de l'homme*"—and the 1787 American Constitution—"the Laws of Nature and of Nature's God"? As it happens, those rights—emanating either from nature or from God—were created by the power of a declaration. Words were spoken that gave life to a new idea. When in the 1948 *Universal Declaration of Human Rights* of the United Nations, it is written that "all human beings are born free and equal in dignity and rights," this is not the description of a tangible physical reality. It is a reality as an intention, as a collective belief. Hence, natural rights exist not in nature but only in human consciousness. At any given time of history, those rights reflect people's conception of what is true, good, and beautiful, what is sacred—ideal and inviolable—about human beings everywhere and "everywhen."

Of all those rights, there is one that interests us particularly: the right to be accepted inside the empathic/ritualistic space, in other words, the right to be treated equally. This right, as any other right, is not based on a tangible physical reality but only on a collective agreement. This is really important. Rigorously speaking, acceptance is not some sort of divine birthright, but only a collective agreement on what a given society believes human beings are entitled to. There is no inherent entitlement to being accepted. Acceptance is either granted or it is not, but it is never due to someone unless there is an agreement on the fact that it is. Nobody owes anybody acceptance, or love, or respect, or anything really, unless it is enforced by some cultural consensus—by a law, moral code, peer pressure, etc. For instance, we tend not to respect criminals; to kill an enemy is acceptable; and experimentation on animal is widely performed in pharmaceutical research laboratories. All those non-empathic behaviors are perfectly all right (if not praised) because of the wide agreement on those issues in our society. Opposing them is just a different perspective. Therefore, to accept or reject homosexuals, homosexual behavior, or same-sex marriage is just a perspective also. In the absolute, the right of gay people to marry is no more valid that the right of chickens not to be eaten by humans.

Why do I insist so much on this? Because the feeling of victimization that is still so prevalent in the homosexual community often rests on a sense of entitlement, from feelings that the world has somehow betrayed us. The demand for acceptance is legitimate of course. So is the impatience and so is the occasional anger. I am not talking about being resigned or content, and I believe we should always put up a good fight whenever we have a chance. But the sense of entitlement and the victimization that ensues from it are based on an inaccurate reading of human beings' natural history. Gay activism needs to shift the context of its demand by reevaluating that sense of entitlement. Homosexual rights, which includes equal-opportunity rights, same-sex marriage, gay families, and gay adoption, do not constitute some sort of historical reparations but a cultural creation—a historical novelty. They convey a new vision, around which the homosexual community wants to rally the people of the world. Homosexuals are not victims; they are creative cultural forces.

THE EVOLUTIONARY TELOS

Human rights manifest an ideal, a sacred vision of what it means to be human—our essence as human beings. This essence, far from been some eternal truth (even if almost systematically presented as such), has progressively been revealed and many times altered throughout history. Not only are human rights culture-dependent, but, obeying the laws of immaterial realities, they can be organized hierarchically according to the worldview from which they arise. From an evolutionary standpoint, the emergence of human rights involves two distinct collective dynamics:

The first one is determined by the majority and correlates with the development of the empathic space. When a category of people is assimilated into the space of empathy (as it was the case with the abolition of slavery for instance), what those people represent integrates the sacred ideal of that particular culture.[580] They become a part of our common essence as human beings. From "others," they become "us."

The second one reflects the self-awareness of a marginalized minority—what these people aspire to, yearn for, and what they perceive as essential and sacred (e.g., safety, freedom, happiness, education, and so on). Naturally this awareness also varies as a function of the stage of psychocultural development that people in the minority have reached, and it is limited by the epistemological and symbolic context (i.e., episteme, worldview, and mythos) in which they live.

So, on one side you have the aspiration of a particular category of individuals to be integrated in the community and, on the other, the willingness of that community to do so. Shifts in the moral views occur when those two impetus coincide. The aspirations of a group of people are transmuted into rights by the power of a collective agreement, and this is followed by a solemn declaration and/or some kind of law enforcement.

Now, insofar as empathy represents the antithesis of competition, one can logically conclude that rights (and morals in general) directly oppose the forces of natural selection at work in nature. By constraining people's instinctive propensity to compete, morals alter the order of things. They invite the individual to share and protect within the limits delineated by the empathic space. Because it demands more empathy from people, ethical development can be viewed as unnatural.[581] From the Ten Commandments to the 1948 *Universal Declaration of Human Rights* by the United Nations, the declarations of the basic and inalienable rights of human beings have always imposed more constraints on our natural selfishness. Ethics—rules, laws, rights, interdictions, and obligations—are designed to curb humans' tendency to care only about themselves. When Greek philosophers invited their contemporaries to discipline their unbridled desires, they operated in that exact framework. So did the Buddha who preached the renunciation of all desires. The Golden Rule of the Axial Age—"Do unto others as you would have them do unto you"—overtly challenges humans' animal nature, in other words, humans' biological design.

Ethics have been essential for the harmonious development of human societies, and without them human relationships could not develop beyond self-gratification.[582] But one must therefore concede that, for the most part, ethics puts limits on people's freedom. Yet it does so in exchange for a new space of freedom based upon an entirely new set of sociocultural values: compassion, love, care, honor, dignity, generosity, respect, sharing, relatedness, and so forth. By limiting freedom, ethics create freedom. This paradoxical aspect of human psychocultural growth is fundamental: the leap from one stage of development to the next entails one to relinquish (voluntarily or not) one's current sense of power and freedom to allow the emergence of a new sense of power and freedom, providing more than it deprives. Collective rules overwrite egocentric impulses so that all can benefit from better life conditions, including those who had to renounce some of their power.

So overall, civilization grows in a direction opposite to the one given by our competitive biological nature. Cultural evolution and biological evolution reflect two opposite strategies, two opposite pulls. The first evolutionary pull, psychocultural, is based on empathy and inclusion; the second, biological, is based on competition and selfishness (on "antipathy," one might say). The evolutionary telos of our species (telos means "purposeful end" in Greek) presses human beings to grow simultaneously according to these two apparently contradictory pulls, egocentric/biological and inclusive/cultural, which is not always an easy thing to achieve, as we know.

One could obviously explore that fascinating topic more in depth. Yet I hope you get enough of a sense of what I mean and where I am heading. Given the dual reality of human evolution, one reaches an unusual conclusion: Human cultural development reflected through the evolution of ethics, science, arts, and spirituality, that we unanimously celebrate as humankind's greatest achievement, is actually a movement away from nature, or more precisely away from the limitations of our biological nature. The magic and beauty of human psychocultural development resides in its departure from the world of biological contingencies and the shortsighted strategy of instant gratification. Therefore, being "against nature" understood as "away from nature" is ironically an extraordinary quality.

We must then recognize the pivotal role of homosexual behavior and homosexuality in the cultural pull and as an essentially component in the evolutionary telos. Homosexual love, positively "against nature" for it liberates people from the instinctive obligation to reproduce, partakes directly of this movement. Human beings are no longer mere breeding machines, unlike most and probably all other animal species on the planet. Besides, same-sex behavior has played a key role in maintaining the social cohesion of the group, and the establishment of larger communities were the *sine qua non* condition to the remarkable social and cultural diversification of the human species. In that respect, remember that shamans, the first religious figures of prehistory, were often selected for their ability to express more complex sexual identities. Certainly, homosexuality is not the only factor responsible for the astonishing cultural journey of humankind, yet, homosexuality constituted one important condition to its inception. Ultimately, one must admit that not only is homosexual love strikingly congruent with humankind's psychocultural evolutionary pull, but in fact, it largely epitomizes it.

This can be taken a step further. My conclusion is based on an unnecessary and obsolete dichotomy that we must now transcend. Although the standard opposition between biological and cultural natures has helped me to clarify my point, this division of both human nature and nature itself into two irreconcilable halves is based, as we know, on a fallacy. Culture is part of nature, as much as consciousness is part of life. What is more, empathy, which is widely observed among social mammals as distant as chimpanzees, dogs, and elephants, is as much part of the natural repertoire of animal behavior as competition and selfishness. Empathy is essential to the process of natural selection and the evolutionary success of those species.[583] Nature and culture do not constitute two alien worlds but a subtle continuum. So, I would now like to nuance my conclusion.

In "Nature"—now including its objective and subjective realities—one can recognize two evolutionary forces, which when combined, generate a dual and yet unique evolutionary telos. The first one involves competition and selection, the second, empathy and cohesion. For the longest time (as far as scientists can tell), evolution has relied exclusively on the first force, generating the extraordinary diversity of life forms that we know. That is the survival of the fittest; survival and reproduction are tightly and rigidly coupled at the individual level—to mate or die. But the recent emergence of more complex consciousness in higher mammals and its blossoming in humans opened a second evolutionary front, primarily based on empathy and group dynamics, which promoted the astonishing cultural development that we see today. Inside the community, both empathy and competition applies, one balancing the other; outside of it, only competition does (or, as concluded in a previous chapter, inside the space of empathy, morals apply; outside, they do not). The only reproductive success that counts is that of the whole group, no longer that of each and every individual. Empathy, which I called "unnatural" above, is as much part of our biological design as the competition instinct. One nature, one equilibrium between two evolutionary forces, one telos.

✦   ✦   ✦

We have now finished exploring the realm of the Good, that of shared values, morals, beliefs, myths, and rituals. We have discovered the key factors that have determined the acceptance of homosexuality by human societies and decided its fate. Developmentally "flattened" (i.e., monological and not understood in evolutionary terms), the history of homosexuality is a tragedy. Reconnected to its evolutionary impetus, it becomes again the breathtaking adventure that it always has been, ever since its prehistoric beginning—the heroic journey of the men and women at the forefront of humanity's evolutionary telos. Homosexuals can no longer picture themselves as the innocent prisoners of dynamics that they cannot comprehend. They can, on the other hand, become the conscious actors of evolution.

We are reaching a new frontier. As goodness seamlessly leads to beauty, morals to freedom, and collective values to individual creativity, we are now ready to step into the world of the Beautiful.

PART III

The Beautiful

To Be Free and Free to Be

The Beautiful, at last. The world of "I." I am; I feel; I think; I want; the domain of individual consciousness; the subjective realm. It is here that our thoughts, emotions, desires, and memories occur, without us noticing them most of the time. It is the space from which "I" speaks, consciousness as subject—this indomitable and incessant phenomenon inherent to the state of "awake-ness." But "I" is also the territory that we actively and meticulously examine through introspection, meditation, psychotherapy, remembering our dreams, and artistic creativity. "I"—the Beautiful—is both subject and object.

If we are now about to tackle homosexuality's inner reality, why did we have to wait until this point to explore the variety of the homosexual experience and answer a question as essential as: What are we supposed to do with that? The reason for this is twofold. First, homosexual consciousness is the least explored facet of the homosexual reality. The little we know, principally from the field of psychology, is almost systematically tainted by the pathologization of homosexual desire or, alternatively, the victimization of homosexual people (which is not so different from a pathology, unfortunately). In all cases, it is crippled by a deep ignorance of the sociobiological and symbolic realities of homosexuality.

The Beautiful is best placed at the end of our inquiry for a second reason. Homosexuality's inner substance will have to be "carved out" from its biological ("IT" perspective) and cultural realities ("WE" perspective), and yet, informed by and connected to all that was previously revealed in the True and the Good. By stepping into a conversation about the homosexual self, we are in fact reaching the outskirts of homosexual reality as it stands before us today. Mostly I will attempt to map a still-to-be-discovered territory.

We are also entering now the domain where it all begins and where it all ends. First, where it all begins. Consider the following. For cultures (epistemes, worldview, and mythos altogether) to evolve thanks to an expansion process implies that intersubjectivity is somehow created. If cultural evolution is a creative process, "subjective material" must be generated and then added to the intersubjective space, and this, regularly throughout history. Now, all creative process has a source. Before it disseminates in the intersubjective space, opening new epistemological horizons to all, the creative spark must first emerge from a unique mind, one's individual subjectivity, in other words, the realm of Beautiful (Lacan calls this domain of human reality the "Imaginary" for a good reason). Indeed, history shows us that there have always been people to pave the way for the future. Those extraordinary individuals have embodied (if not channeled) the creative dynamic that has fostered humankind's psychocultural evolution. And if some are remembered, most are not.

The Beautiful is also where it all ends. Remember the great insight of postmodernity: Human consciousness is trapped in its own bubble. If there is indeed a real world "out there"— objective, interobjective, or intersubjective—we can only perceive it through our five senses and experience it using our one and only mind. Human beings are the unaware prisoners of their own subjectivity. We live in our occurrence of the world, which is fundamentally distinct from the world itself (as discussed in the introduction). If we officially owe this essential breakthrough to postmodernity, Axial thinkers appear to have largely intuited the shocking paradox of the human condition. When Siddartha Gautama, the Buddha, taught Indian crowds that what they called reality was nothing less than an illusion, like dreams, this is probably what he had in mind.

The same insight surfaced in Western thought through Plato's allegory of the cave. In a long dialogue between Socrates and Glaucon, Plato, through Socrates's voice, narrates the tale of men, eternal prisoners in a cave. The prisoners, chained to the rock, are immobilized in such a way as to face the back wall of the cave. All they ever see are the shadows of people and animals walking outside, projected onto the wall of the cave thanks to the blazing light of a distant fire. Because they can never see the real people but only their shadows, the prisoners believe that these shadows are real people.[584] They confuse the shadows with the Truth because shadows constitute the only reality that is available to them. And shadows will remain their ultimate reality unless they exit the cave, which is to say, unless they take another perspective.

Plato's allegory symbolizes the predicament of the human condition that postmodernity, somehow, rediscovered. Human reality is like the shadows in Plato's cave and is like our dreams, as the Buddha teaches us. We are only indirectly aware of the realities of the objective world. We, human beings, live in an occurring world. Keep those ideas in mind. They are going to constitute the context of our new exploration. And, grounded again in the reality of the subjective realm, let us start to assemble the last pieces of our puzzle: homosexuality's inner reality.

FREE TO BE, AT LAST

We all knew that sooner or later we would run into a dilemma: how can one reconcile the constraining presence of a collectively defined identity, which is indispensable as I claim here to the psychological development of the homosexual person, with the concept of personal freedom? This important question has tortured an entire generation of gay activists and queer theorists who, like most of postmodernity, went down the "deconstructing" spiral in pursuit of a freedom that they ultimately neither found, nor even less, provided.

If homosexuals are (like everybody else), roughly speaking, biologically determined and culturally shaped as I have argued, is individual freedom still a relevant concept? Is it a mere illusion, as one may logically deduce, or is the apparent contradiction between the reality of biological and cultural determinism on one side and human beings' inherent longing for freedom on the other yet another paradox to overcome? I would like to begin this inquiry exactly where queer theory left off. It seems that, to the best of our knowledge (which is, of course, all relative), the homosexual experience, and human life in general, is subject to three powerful and independent deterministic forces: (1) one's biological nature, (2) cultural imprinting, and (3) one's individual makeup and self-conditioning. I would now like to recapitulate quickly what each of these deterministic forces represents, in the order in which I introduced them.

Let us consider biological imprinting first. The biological origins of homosexual behavior and desire are hard to deny today, and we have extensively explored both the data that support such a claim and the model(s) that could explain how they come into existence. If the genes and specific brain areas involved in this process have yet to be discovered, one can confidently anticipate that, eventually, they will be. (One needs to remember that biological sex, which no one would dare present as being of a minor consequence to the human psyche and as a minor concern in human cultures, is determined by the presence of one gene only, *sry*, carried by the Y chromosome. When *sry* is expressed, you obtain a male; when sry is absent, the default program is activated and produces a female. Those who feel outraged by the notion of biological determinism may meditate on that piece of information.)

However, biological determinism goes far beyond sexuality. Human beings are fundamentally determined by their biological nature. Despite the astonishing heterogeneity observed among individuals as well as populations, everything we like and do oscillates within an invisible yet relatively narrow frame. From language to cooking, the astonishing diversity that human cultures have generated should not hide from view the biological boundaries from which no human being can escape. Biological determination never meant that human beings are directed continually and in the smallest details by their biological makeup. It only means that the biological machinery that ensures the development of the human brain has the power to prime the human soul in an irreversible manner, which culture can constrain but seldom erase. This is not specific to homosexuality or homosexuals; this is, I believe, the human condition.

Regarding the second force, cultural imprinting, I hope that I have provided you with enough evidence so as to persuade you of its equally primordial importance.

Episteme, worldview, and mythos set invisible boundaries that human beings seldom infringe. The invisible umbilical cord that connects us to our intersubjective environment cannot be severed. In fact, our mental well-being depends on this nurturing interaction, and psychiatric institutions are unfortunately packed with individuals who have lost this vital bond. Whoever has read stories of feral children knows how little is left when the cultural environment is not there to give a form to human nature. Human beings' dependency on the intersubjective environment is neither passivity nor addiction; it is built-in.

This said, to grasp the ontological impact of this state of fact in our daily lives takes a little more courage. Look at how much your mind is permeated and shaped by the culture in which it constantly soaks. Try to visualize the countless layers of cultural material that have been imprinted in your psyche. Imagine this process continuing until your last breath. Add together the massive influence of early education by parents, family, and school, the constant exposure to the culture through literature, cinema, television, internet, and other media, and the ongoing influence of communities, their morals, and beliefs. Contemplate all the opinions that you have inherited from your environment and never questioned. Honestly, how much of what we think and say is not a repetition of the past? Sift through your "personal" beliefs about love, men, women, sex, money, career, hierarchy, power, success, etc. How much of that is not something that you have heard or read somewhere before? Mostly, we act like parrots and borrow from our environment. Any attempt to rebel against this situation is a mere illusion of freedom. In the vast majority of cases, one's rebellion against the cultural environment combines cultural conditioning with psychological defensiveness, which is still a form of determinism. Ultimately, the seeker of a homosexual self must first ask himself or herself the following question: What do I know about my sexuality that I did not inherit from my cultural environment? The answer to that question is: almost, if not absolutely, nothing. And that is not the end of the inquiry. It is only the beginning.

The third and last shaping force to which people are inevitably subject is often overlooked, and this is for a simple reason: It is often mistaken for freedom itself. The most pernicious form of determinism is generated from within ourselves, which explains why it mimics free will so well. Yet nothing seems to be able to escape its despotic grip. This "inner determinism," is multiple. First, and this was one of Freud's most brilliant discoveries, people's true intentions often lie deep in their unconscious. Most of the time they are unaware of and have no power over what really motivates their actions. Freud's insight was already a serious blow to the concept of individual freedom; yet it was only the first of a long series. Second, despite the vast gamut of possible ways of being and psychological traits that human beings have at their disposal, it appears that people tend to use a very restricted set of these ways of being preferentially. We call them psychological traits, and their combination varies from one individual to the next. This is how psychologists define psychological types (the ancients called those basic variations "temperaments").

The mechanism behind the genesis of distinct psychological types is still unknown; yet their existence is widely accepted. Human beings are prone to be and behave certain ways and not others. For instance, some people tend to be more extroverted, more cerebral, more social, more intuitive, more controlling, or more passive than others. The life of an extrovert will differ significantly from that of an introvert. Each type finds itself cut off from an entire repertoire of personal experiences that is otherwise available to others. Hence our own psychological makeup dramatically restricts the possibilities that life offers to us.[585]

Human beings go much further in this process of psychological specialization. The combination of our natural psychological tendencies (type or temperament) and life experiences leads quickly to the formation of our so-called personality. Through a set of complex iterations between our psyche and what life exposes us to, we very early on train ourselves to behave and react in certain ways and not others. Often our ways of being become extremely specific. One person always smiles when confronted by an embarrassing situation. Another is always charming in public or always comes up with a solution each time a problem arises. One could certainly "be" differently. But other ways of being appear increasingly remote, and eventually totally foreign: "that's not me." Once again, we split the world of being—the Beautiful—into two irreconcilable halves, self and non-self, into "I" and "not-I." Step by step, the psyche loses its original malleability. We become psychologically unique. We are self-trained and self-limited. We acquire an identity. In the meantime, we forget that we built those boundaries. Rare are the individuals who revisit those boundaries in their lifetimes. For most people, they remain unquestioned, self-evident, like the air that they breathe. They go through life using the same "automatic pilot," whatever the circumstances are. In the end, the individuation process itself, commonly understood as the emergence of ego/identity, is a loss of freedom and a subtle form of determinism. To be unique, to have an identity, or simply to be "oneself" implies to give up most of the freedom that was bestowed on us at birth, or in Freud's terms, to renounce our original "polymorphous" state.

Human existence represents the focal point where three inherent and unavoidable deterministic forces meet—biological makeup, cultural conditioning, and the individuation process—which will alternatively balance each other, synergize, or clash. (Notice that each one of these forces results from the evolutionary dynamic arising from one of the three fundamental realms—biological regarding the True, cultural regarding the Good, and psychological regarding the Beautiful—and inside three different evolutionary time frames a scale of millions of years for the biological, thousands of years for the cultural, and just a lifetime for the individual.) Combined, these forces represent our Karma, if you allow me to redefine Karma as the weight of the past over the present moment. Should the concept of individual freedom be negated or, as I intend to do now, redefined?

First, freedom is not a precise concept but a relative one. Freedom can be defined as a set of conditions that one sees as being necessary in order to feel free. Those conditions vary from one culture and from one individual to the next.

Thus they are always subject to interpretation, which explains why the concept of individual freedom has always been a thorny topic. One's sense of freedom always emerges within a given context. Hence, absolutely speaking, one is never really "free" but only "free from" a particular set of constraints. Yet not any constraint qualifies as a threat to our personal freedom. Rare are the people who see having to eat or sleep every day—which both constitute massive biological constraints on human existence—as limitations on one's freedom. They could however, and logically they should. We choose and pick very carefully the conditions, fulfilled or not, to our freedom.

How we select those conditions to our freedom is what should interest us now. What is the difference between those things that one may see as limiting freedom—cultural conditioning, genes, and unconscious—and those that are almost never perceived as such, and yet, are incredibly constraining—feeding, sleeping, learning, language, and so on? I suggest that the answer to that fundamental question is shockingly simple: We accept and often enjoy the latter but loathe and fear the former. Why does one fear aspects of human existence as fundamental as cultural conditioning, genes, and the unconscious? Because for many people, these things belong to the unknown. It is needless to remind you how human beings feel about the unknown. They would do anything not to have to deal with it.

We have once again to juggle multiple paradoxes. Think about it. Without genes, there would be no brain to think about freedom; without cultural conditioning, our everyday concerns would be that of prehistoric people (to ensure basic survival rather than debating the meaning of freedom); and without the unconscious, humankind would be deprived of its most precious good, creativity. As long as these deterministic forces have not been understood in an evolutionary context, they remain a threat and even sometimes their existence is denied. Deterministic forces are constraining but also nurturing. They limit us only insofar as they propel us at full speed through the evolutionary process that preceded us. They restrict individual freedom because they put us at the very tip of the evolutionary process whether we like it or not. The miracle that human consciousness represents stands on this eternal paradox. Ultimately, one can then see freedom, as relative as that concept might be, not as a static state but instead, as an evolutionary process—another manifestation of telos.

Feeling free has never been about doing "whatever"—anything we want, whenever we want it. Even prehistoric people were already aware of that impossibility. Freedom is not an external thing. Freedom, I suggest, is an inner context, a state of mind from which one chooses to live his or her life. It is the lens through which one sees life. Freedom is a created context. First, freedom arises from deeply valuing the reality of what and who we are. I know that what we understand of ourselves is all relative; yet what and who we are is all that we have and all that we can count on at this point. We can either deny and resist it or, instead, embrace it. Second, freedom results from experiencing oneself as a space of creation. When being involves a conscious creative act, a sense of freedom naturally arises. Ultimately, feeling free comes from the intimate conviction of being the authors of our own existence. This is freedom, inner freedom, the most precious one that there is.

Hopefully the material that I have presented through the discussion of the True and the Good has helped you to discover a new sense of truth, goodness, and beauty about same-sex love. Ideally, this new background should facilitate the emergence of a new sense of freedom. Yet feeling free is primarily your call. You get to choose, regardless of the circumstances. Knowing this, our choice is now twofold: we either participate in the creative process or we remain largely unaware of it, in which case we leave the "automatic pilot" in charge of directing our lives. However, "to participate" implies to befriend the overwhelming reality of the three evolutionary dynamics that continuously fashion our body, mind, and soul. We can no longer ignore them. We must instead become increasingly aware. We then have a new game ahead of us: to search for the areas where we are not free, where we lose the sense of our own inner truth, goodness, and beauty. We must rid the homosexual collective psyche of the disempowering beliefs that soil it—the homosexual shadow. Hence, before exploring the Beautiful, we first have to deal with the ugly.

FAILED HETEROSEXUALS?

It is now time to confront, both individually and collectively, the fact that the homosexual self remains polluted by the lingering belief that homosexuals are failed heterosexuals. "[. . .] when nature had its head together it produces heterosexuals. When it produces homosexuals, something has gone wrong," ironically commented scholars John De Cecco and David Parker.[586] And I am much less concerned when non-homosexuals believe such absurdity than when homosexuals do.

Not such a long time ago, homosexuals' only choices were either to deny their true essence and pass for heterosexuals, or to choose social alienation. Fortunately, things have changed in many countries. However, one cannot ignore that in the same countries today, most homosexuals still have to face the disappointment of their parents, families, co-workers, and friends. Although I am confident that happier situations will eventually become more and more common in the future, rare are the lucky ones whose parents were particularly pleased on the day of their coming-out. For our generation and those who preceded us, the experience was more typically that of shame, betrayal, and grief. In most cases, to be homosexual entails going through a sense of failure for not being the heterosexual that was expected of them. I believe that a vast number of homosexuals still hold such a belief deep in their souls, consciously or not. As a result, homosexual identity is crippled by an endemic low self-esteem—the lingering sorrow that I discussed in the first pages of this book. Homosexuals often have to deal with negative reactions from their environment, whether dismay, incomprehension, rejection, disgust, anger, or hate.

And knowing from experience how unpleasant or even shattering those reactions may be for the individuals who must face them, I would like to reevaluate the way we classically judge these reactions in light of what we have learned previously.

Remember that for humans, as in all other apes, sexual behavior is socially meaningful (see chapter 5). Sexual behavior speaks a language that is diligently scrutinized by all the members of the group. We are biologically and culturally not only equipped but also compelled to "read" the sexual behavior of others. And this is particularly true of homosexual behavior.

First, reproduction is a big deal for human beings. We are biologically and culturally programmed to spread our genes, which means to want progeny, want our progeny to have progeny, want the progeny of our progeny to have progeny, and so on. But because even now the common view remains that homosexuals do not procreate (ignoring the fact that it is instead society that does not let them make the necessary arrangements to achieve reproduction in their own terms), even the best intentioned parents are likely to mourn the loss of their dream of having grandchildren. Even if it appears unpleasant and unfair, one must understand that their disappointment is genuine and legitimate.

Second, and this is particularly true of males, homosexuality has consistently been viewed as a sign of inferiority, which is inherently associated with sexual receptivity. For an adult male, to endorse the passive role constitutes by and large social suicide. It would be inaccurate to assume that human beings are homophobic only because of the cultural conditioning to which they are subjected. The contempt for receptive and effeminate males is deeply ingrained in our ape brains (which by no means implies that all human beings are inclined to homophobic feelings). As for lesbians, their homosexuality has classically been viewed as a rebellion against men's divine authority. Butch lesbians especially have constituted an intolerable challenge (an unmanageable competition, perhaps) to the solely masculine prerogative to penetrate. For the longest time, lesbians were imagined as having enormous clitorises whose size dangerously resembled that of a penis.

When it comes to homosexuality, our parents and relatives have faced the same concerns as all the generations that preceded them. They are, just like us, imprisoned in a "biocultural" paradigm. They are, just like us, human. Homosexuals do not have the exclusivity in that kind of problem, and there are many other ways to disappoint the world. Yet in the process of being hurt, homosexuals often forget that they are not the only ones in that difficult situation, and never have been. Human societies have crushed more than one category of deviants. Both sides tend to take it personally. Parents feel betrayed. Homosexual kid feels betrayed. The truth is, both sides are merely the puppets of the biological and cultural dynamics at work within them.

Homosexual behavior triggers reactions. That is just a fact. I then exhort homosexuals simply to accept the idea that something about themselves needs to be explained, without guilt or resentment. This is being responsible, individually and collectively. This is being adult.

INSULTS

Homophobic insults, like any form of verbal violence, are insufferable. The scars that they leave in people's souls are often indelible. Painful memories haunt the victims for the rest of their lives—a feeling of shame that will not go away. Insults can cause terrible damages. Undeniably and unfortunately, homophobic insults represent a classic ingredient in the lives of homosexuals. Whether hurled at openly gay individuals or at those who inadvertently raise suspicions by ambiguous manners, an awkward twist in the voice, a veiled desire that the eyes betray, a furtive glance, or a disquieting instant of intimacy, insults strike their target swiftly.

My mind is filled with these sort of memories. I remember vividly begging my mother not to send me to play outside with the other kids for fear of becoming once again their target, avoiding crossing the school playground so as to minimize the risk of being noticed by the older boys, always watching who was near me, desperately trying to keep my hips straight when I walked . . . I designed countless strategies to keep myself away from hostile encounters and insults. Not to attract attention, to remain as much as possible invisible, I quickly learned to keep a low profile. I developed a taste for solitary games. When, despite all my efforts, I would become their target, I remember above all the intolerable silence of those who, either entertained or horrified, witnessed those terrible scenes. I remember the burn in my head and in my heart, the humiliation in front of my classmates and, when alone again, the tears, the self-loathing, and those long minutes spent insulting my own reflection in the mirror. I remember the shame and the fear, and, mostly, the loneliness. I know some of you do, too. And yet . . .

We, homosexuals, must grow beyond the experience of social alienation resulting from insults and from the mere anticipation of them. The following statement by French author Didier Eribon, in his book *Insult or the Making of Gay Identity*, illustrates perfectly the ontological fiasco in which so many homosexuals have been trapped: "At the beginning, there is the insult. [. . .] The insult is a verdict. It is a more or less definitive sentence, for life, one that will have to be borne. A gay man learns about his differences through the force of insult and its effects."[587] Eribon's discourse sadly epitomizes what victimhood looks like when it becomes incorporated into the sense of self—the victimized mind. While the anger of the victim of insults is absolutely legitimate, homosexuals must once again shield themselves against the pernicious effects of victimization. To achieve this, my intention is twofold. I would like first to address the recurrent allegation that insult is a constitutive element of the homosexual experience and, second, to revisit the concept of listening from an integral standpoint.

In order to be effective, an insult must first be heard as an insult. As simple as this may sound, it reminds us that the power of insult is fundamentally dependent upon its recognition as insult by the target person. As long as one does not see oneself as a victim, the negative effect of insult is neutralized. While in my early twenties, I once visited a boyfriend who at the time was doing volunteer work in Guinea-Bissau, a tiny country on the Western coast of Africa. While walking on the streets of the capital Bissau, I began to notice the stare of many locals. Most of them looked genuinely surprised by our presence; but in the eyes of a few, I could also detect a frank hostility. The reason for their reaction was not so hard to guess. First, they had seldom had an opportunity to see white people touring the poorest neighborhoods of their city. Second, we displayed all the external signs of privileged people, not to mention the fact that our skin was of the same color as that of the former colonial rulers (Portugal, in this particular case). Nothing particularly surprising about this.

At that point, my boyfriend decided to show me that he and I could hold hands on the street without the smallest consequence. Despite my strong apprehension and immediate reluctance to test the veracity of his claim, he grabbed my hand on the spot and held it. Many "interminable" minutes later, I was still waiting for something terrible to occur. Against all my preconceived ideas and unlike anything I had ever experienced before, nothing happened, neither that day, nor those that followed. As it happens, it is very common for African men to hold hands with their male friends and family members (this is also true in India and in the Middle East). In Europe and the United States, it represented a major risk. Yet in that part of Africa, it was totally innocuous. This was some discovery. The difference of attitude between the West and Africa was mind-blowing for me. My overall experience was that of amazing freedom, one that I had never felt previously in my life, and this, despite the insistent and, occasionally, antagonistic starring.

It is easy to explain why people's staring did not affect my good spirits back then. First, their hostility was largely comprehensible to me insofar as I could empathically relate to their resentment regarding the colonization era. I had therefore a solid context to help me make sense of their reaction to my skin color. I could put myself in their shoes. The second reason is more intriguing. I was being singularized for a feature—the color of my skin—for which I had never developed any low self-esteem. People's responses triggered zero emotional charge for me. I did not mind being seen as different and undesirable as long as it was for something I was comfortable with.

I have since relocated in Harlem, New York, where I still live today, and this paradox keeps amazing me. I have on rare occasions been called racist names, but, once again, despite the probable intention to hurt or intimidate, I never felt victimized. Now, call me a "faggot," and I hit the roof instantly. Something must have happened in the way that I listened to those insults that endowed them with very different qualities and a very different force. As a matter of fact, the context from which I listen—my listening—seems to have much more power than the insults themselves. How I perceive "white butt" is dramatically different from how I perceive "faggot," and the difference is this one: I have constituted myself as a potential victim of homophobic insults but not of racist ones.

Eribon, in his meticulous description of homosexual victimhood, lays bare the pervading impact of insults on their victims: "The effect of insult perpetuates and reproduces itself endlessly, with the wounds that it causes, and the submissions and the revolts that ensue."[588] Eribon is accurate. Little by little, the fear integrates into one's sense of self. The victim identifies itself with the fear. From object, it becomes subject—I. But this, however, cannot be the whole story. Indeed, if this has been my experience of homophobic insults, it has never been the case with racist insults. Someone's hostility toward my being white has never altered my sense of self. My entire perception of the world did not become affected by the fear of reliving the same situation over and over, nor did it occur to me as being an inescapable fate. For me, it remained a circumstance, not a self-defining experience, and the difference is, I believe, crucial.

Unlike real bullets, insults will miss their target if the target dismisses the negative essence of the insult. Any hateful word that one hears or sign that one perceives (such as an insult, a disgusted look, a homophobic joke, or a "God Hates Fags" banner) will inevitably land inside a specific listening, from which one will interpret the experience in the moment. Therefore, it is the "I" that ultimately decides on what it perceives and how it is going to contextualize it. By having the final word, the "I" dictates the meaning of any communication. Accordingly, the power of insults is fundamentally given by the listener's subjectivity. Simply put, it is determined by the listener.[589] Words may come from an intention to hurt or not, but they can touch only those who allow themselves to be touched. It then makes a lot of sense that I would not feel victimized for being insulted for my skin color, nationality, or lack of intelligence, while curiously, I remain so sensitive to homophobic insults.

I do not forget that the meaning of words results primarily from a cultural consensus. Nor do I ignore the fact that, as I evoked earlier, human beings are both compelled and conditioned to perpetuate this consensus. To disengage from it takes both courage and energy. Regardless, to reduce communication to a one-way dynamic and our relationship to language to cultural determinism is to restrict the act of listening to a passive role. It is missing the most important part of the equation, the "I," the domain where it all begins and where it all ends. An insult is an insult because one hears it as such—"consents" to hear it as such.

Acknowledging that one can ultimately control meaning through listening may very well be counter-intuitive; it is however very real. Obviously, the current culture tends to comfort us into a purely docile role, in which listening has little or no creative power. One could, however, choose otherwise. This new mode of listening, which I call conscious listening, obliges us to become responsible for what lands in our own subjective space. Now, given that such a practice remains counter-cultural in today's world, developing conscious listening will require sustained effort from the listener, hence training. The process needs to be nurtured. Inner discipline is indispensable if one wants to experience inner freedom, the freedom to choose what serves us and push away what does not. Listening, just like speaking, is also a creative act.

Now, I am not suggesting here that one can ignore the intended meaning of an injunction and exchange it for another at will. To turn "Faggot!" into "Sorry dude, I feel threatened," while theoretically not impossible I suppose, requires the strength and talent of a saint. One cannot swap the meaning of words as one pleases. The psyche, shaped by years of methodical cultural conditioning, cannot be so easily cheated. Conscious listening is not some kind of positive thinking. It is not about lying to ourselves either. Nor is it about pretending not to be hurt when we are. The only authentic solution to our issue is not to deceive ourselves but, once again, to expand the scope of our awareness. Remember that the basic problem with victimhood is that it is profoundly grounded in a monological view of the world, that is, limited to a self-centered perspective. This is why it is a mental trap.

What saved me from victimization when I was a young man visiting Africa was that, thanks to my upbringing, I had a preexisting understanding of a perspective other than my own. I found legitimate that African people would reject me because of what I might represent for them. This does not validate anything about racism, colonization, or anything else for that matter; it only acknowledges the fact that what they feel is as real as what I feel. I could authentically relate with the experience of another and, therefore, escape the monological nightmare of the victimization process. Conscious listening consists in actively listening to others through a pluralistic lens.

The logic of insult is fundamentally absurd. Although, on the one hand, people in a given category loathe insults targeted at their own group, on the other hand, they seldom shy away from insulting people who belong to other groups. As disturbing as it may sound, I am afraid that if indeed homosexuals refrain from using homophobic insults, they are unfortunately not any different from the rest of the population when it comes to other types of insults—racist, xenophobic, misogynistic, anti-Semitic and so forth. In that regard, homosexuals are by no means special. And the same applies to all sociocultural groups and all people. To be a hate target has never stopped anyone from having his or her own hate targets. We all know that, even if we carefully avoid bringing that to the discussion.

One can consider an even bigger picture. Since the dawn of history words have been used with the intention to cause harm. They have channeled a violence that is far more ancient than language itself. Human beings cannot help hurting each other, for multiple reasons, and in order to do so they carefully select their weapons. Verbal violence, like any other form of violence, is rooted in human nature. It is only the refined expression of a primitive urge, some kind of prehistoric remnant. That verbal violence is natural does not make it acceptable. Yet we ought to grasp its fundamentally mechanical character. Although current culture—postmodern and relativist—appears inexhaustibly fascinated by all its sadistic subtleties, hate speech is hardly different from a dog barking. A dog barks because it intrinsically knows that it will scare you off. Homophobes throw homophobic insults at homosexuals because homophobic insults work on homosexuals, just like racist insults work on people of color, anti-Semitic ones on Jews, and so on (as I said, human beings always select their weapons carefully). An insult does not have to be true; it only needs to be hurtful. From a human perspective, it might sound much more sophisticated than a dog barking, but from a dog's perspective, believe me, it is fundamentally the same.

Should one feel victimized because dogs bark, even though dogs bark all the time and have not demonstrated any intention to quit barking? Why should one feel victimized by something that in the end appears to be so mechanical and fundamentally so meaningless? Put two fingers in an electrical plug and without fail you will get electrocuted. Put a slice of bread in a toaster and it will spit it out one minute later, toasted. Walk by a homophobe and he/she will insult you. No surprise, you just pressed a button. The response is automatic, predictable, and remarkably uninteresting. The homophobe (the racist, the anti-Semite, and so on), the dog, and the toaster all have one thing in common: they act like machines. I concede that dogs and humans are sophisticated machines, but we are giving a lot of importance to something that in the end does not deserve so much of our attention. So, let us enjoy fighting back, but now only because it feels good to do so.

The miscalculation of the homosexual discourse has been to have distinguished homophobic insults as different from insults in general. It surrendered to the temptation of monological thinking. "My wounds are deeper than yours." Homophobic insults became about homosexuals, and not, as you would expect, about homophobes. Let us be very clear: insults, whether homophobic, racist, or sexist, are unacceptable. They are a disgrace for the person who pronounces them and for the culture that tolerates and sometimes encourages them. They have imposed a heavy burden on homosexuals. I feel deeply for the many gay men and lesbians who have been threatened and shamed. Who can deny the pain sometimes unspeakable, caused by a brutal and unsupportive environment?

Yet homophobia reveals only the inner reality of homophobes. For homosexuals, homophobic insults and any other expression of homophobia remain circumstances, even if unpleasant and painful. Homosexuality and homosexuals shall never be defined by circumstances, whether they are historical or personal. Homosexuals cannot let their dignity be set by external factors such as what people think of them, their acceptance into the military, homophobic insults, the AIDS epidemic, or access to the institution of marriage. Not that those issues are not worth fighting for; they just cannot be the prerequisite conditions to one's inner integrity.

What if homophobic insults, like dogs barking, continue forever? (I bet that both will) Would that condemn homosexuals to remain eternal victims? Present-day homosexual discourse has placed homosexuals in an unsustainable situation that must be readjusted urgently. Victimization does not protect homosexuals. It mentally paralyzes them. The cultural victimization of homosexuality mummifies homosexual consciousness at the collective and individual level.[590] It leaves the integrity of the homosexual self up to those who feel threatened by it.

Victimization is a poison that homosexuals are unknowingly administering to themselves.

Ask yourself these questions: Do you see homosexuality as a gift? Are you really conscious of the beauty of the choice that was bestowed upon either you, your child, this friend, or this family member? And if you are gay or lesbian yourself, given a second chance, would you choose to be homosexual again? I invite you, readers, to look deep inside yourselves. Nobody should feel embarrassed to acknowledge doubts, fears, and regrets. Those emotions are normal. But, honestly, I do not anticipate the majority of homosexuals today to answer those questions in the affirmative. Should a woman be delighted to be a woman, a man to be a man, a black person to be black, or a Jew to be a Jew? Without a doubt, they should. How shocking would it be if it were not the case. Why should homosexual identity be different?

My intention, perhaps my only one, is to convince you of the beauty of homosexual love so that homosexuals can begin to experience that aspect of themselves as a source of inner wealth rather than a curse. Homosexuals have no other choice than to undertake the courageous examination of all the darkest recesses of their souls and rid themselves of disempowering beliefs. By jettisoning their identity as victims, homosexuals can finally embrace their inner evolutionary warriors. Yet the metamorphosis is nobody else's responsibility but their own.

Consider Jesuit theology professor James L. Empereur's statement: "Homosexuality is one of God's most significant gifts to humanity. To be gay or lesbian is to have received a special blessing from God. All humans receive their own special graces from their creator, but God has chosen some to be gay or lesbian as a way of revealing something about God-self that heterosexuals do not."[591] Replace the word "God" by "evolutionary telos" if that makes it more acceptable for you. Still, what a superb and unapologetic declaration of independence. We are putting together a new reality, a new vision of homosexuality, true, good, and beautiful, whole and complete, just as it is. Being proud is no longer enough. Being homosexual is an honor and a gift. Homosexuality is sacred, and so is homosexual love.

~

CHAPTER FIFTEEN

The Unfolding of the Homosexual Self

In my never-ending quest to stitch the scattered pieces of my homosexuality back together, I came to wonder if anybody had ever described what the "normal" psychological development of homosexual men and women would look like. Of course, I had read Richard Isay's *Being Homosexual*, which had been recommended to me by an amiable and knowledgeable bookseller at Giovanni's Room Bookstore in Philadelphia. Isay's book had left me profoundly dissatisfied, nearly angry at that time, because of Isay's inability to grasp the fundamentally normal character of homosexuality and depict homosexuals other than as victims constantly dealing with the pathological consequences of growing up in a homophobic culture. Rather, Isay's vision of homosexual experience consisted of a long recovery process. Despite his noble intention, I felt disrespected and, even more painful, misunderstood.

For me, unquestionably, this could not be the end of the story. I was desperately yearning for a mirror, one that would deeply value who I am and stop pitying me—a reflection of my inner beauty. Homosexuals, I intuited, must share similar experiences—the discovery of their "unusual" attractions for same-sex partners, the confrontation with a hetero-centric culture, the marginalization that ensues from that, the coping mechanisms, the coming-out process, and most importantly, the unique specificities of male and female relationships. I had no doubt about this. I decided to email a handful of my most brilliant gay friends, requesting their help in finding a book, an article, or anything really that had outlined the developmental path—de-pathologized and de-victimized—that gay men and lesbians are likely to go through during their lives. Remarkably, all my friends proved clueless about the existence of such a work. None of them had heard about anything like that and most suspected that it probably did not exist. One of them suggested that I find out. So, I did.

Fortunately, although seldom publicized, the development of homosexual identity has been researched and described and models have been developed.

Among those, the works of Vivienne Cass and Richard Troiden clearly stand out, and it is largely a synthesis of their findings that I present here. But as always, to be able to seize the practicality and meaning of any model of homosexual psychological development a solid context is required, and inevitably some clarifications about various controversies that have arisen.

Many people, whether in the Academia or activist circles, have expressed their distrust of any attempt to define a homosexual identity. Regarding queer theorists specifically, their rejection of homosexual (and gay) identity initially constituted a healthy reaction against centuries of theological, medical, and psychoanalytic theorization about same-sex lovers and same-sex desire. For them, to force the idea of homosexual identity upon homosexuals constituted a violation of their individual freedom. Recently, psychologist Ritch C. Savin-Williams went as far as affirming that it is the social pressure resulting from having to espouse gay identity that might in fact explain the alleged high suicide rate among gay teenagers.[592]

Throughout this book, I have instead maintained that social identities such as homosexual identity, even if historically relative and culture-dependent, are indispensable artifacts of human culture and psyche. What we commonly call homosexual identity today is shorthand for modern homosexual identity. Congruent with my choice to reserve the terms homosexual and homosexuality to describe the transhistorical and transcultural reality of same-sex love and desire, homosexual identity unites under one umbrella a vast and diverse range of identities having as a common denominator to have channeled same-sex desire: gay, lesbian, sodomite, bugger, tribade, invert, molly, two-spirit, *erastes* (and possibly *eromenos*), *kinaidos, aikāne, māhū, fa'afafine* . . . the list of homosexual identities is long, yet finite. Notwithstanding, in many cultures, homosexual desire (even essential) did not delineate a particular psychocultural sub-identity. This was typically the case among Melanesians and North American natives where males engaging in insertive homosexual acts were no different from any other males. The same was true in the Greco-Roman world. A man could profess his sexual appetite for boys (and lack thereof for females) without being the least defined by it. In most of the premodern world, male status, hence male identity, was necessary and sufficient to entitle a male to penetrate whoever they wanted, including other males.

How and why a given psychocultural identity emerges in a particular culture is difficult to establish for certain. Often their existence makes sense, but only retrospectively. For instance, one might find eminently logical that human cultures strongly emphasize sexual and gender identities since both are connected in some way or another to the reproductive function. Yet the fact that menopausal women do not constitute a particular category illuminates how much such a hypothesis can hardly explain and even less predict the reality of sexual identities based on reproductive abilities only. As far as I can tell, male ranking and male dominance are the only dynamics that have affected sexual identities in practically all, if not all, known human cultures. Males of adult age who allowed themselves to be sexually penetrated, and thus assumed the receptive role with other males, were universally set apart, and often attributed an inferior status. Elsewhere, how and why particular sexual identities appeared must be approached on a case by case basis, by taking into account the historical and geographical specificities of the culture in question. Future research will hopefully reveal interesting patterns.

Since sexual identities, regardless of their nature and origin, remain stubbornly meaningful for most people today, I find it judicious (if not urgent) that we transform how we hold them in a way that empowers people rather than just labeling them. Consider the following: Chimpanzees do not have sexual identities; they are not less happy than we are for that reason. When it comes to sex, each chimpanzee is fundamentally the instrument of its own particular hormonal makeup. In fact, chimpanzees do not even think of themselves as chimpanzees. As far as scientists can tell (which is always subject to change), chimpanzees have not developed psychocultural identities. Humans certainly have. In fact, they keep inventing new ones. Evolutionarily speaking, psychocultural identities are recent and most likely unique to the human species.

Psychocultural identities, and sexual identities especially, reflect human beings' growing awareness of their own psychological and cultural complexity (provided that there is no reason to believe that they represent random byproducts of human intelligence). In each culture they have constituted what I would call "archetypal landmarks." Like archetypes, they are regularly remodeled, recycled, transformed, or abandoned throughout cultural evolution. They have helped individuals recognize, become aware of, and represent their desire. They have constituted the cognitive prerequisites to people's sexual expression. Indeed, as psychotherapist Willow Pearson suggests: "People deny, fight, and suppress their own desires not only due to a lack of opportunity or a lack of internal acceptance, but because they may not recognize their own desire when it appears."[593] Like archetypes, psychocultural identities act as mirrors of the self. They compose the ontological foundation of the psyche. Keep in mind however that people's relationship to those sexual identities also evolves. Without some degree of self-awareness, these psychocultural identities, just like archetypes, become suffocating (see chapter 11). But without them, individuals are abandoned to the long, solitary, and painful process of seeking images of themselves in order to recognize who and what they are. In the documentary *The Celluloid Closet*, actor-writer Harvey Fierstein expresses his longing for ontological clues better than I ever could:

> There are lots of needs . . . The greatest one is the mirror of our own life and our own existence . . . That hunger that I felt as a kid looking for gay images was 'to not be alone.' I like the sissy. Is it used in a negative way? Yeah but, my view has always been 'visibility at any cost.' I'd rather have negative than nothing. That is just my particular view . . . and also because I am a sissy.

For many (most?) homosexuals, even negative stereotypes have been better than nothing. It's better be an outsider than invisible, or worse, unintelligible to oneself.

Twenty years ago, Gilbert Herdt wisely exhorted us to opt for a more balanced approach to sexual identities: "We must avoid the dangers, both conceptual/intellectual and political, of assuming too much or too little homogeneity."[594] Human beings yearn for a sense of commonality as much as they need to feel unique. One cannot progress in one direction and ignore the other.

Freedom, as I argue, results from experiencing oneself as a space of creation. When being arises as a conscious creative act, when we consent to become the authors of our own existence, our relationship to collective psychocultural identities (and archetypes, for that matter) is forever altered. Suddenly, rigid culturally inherited sexual identities metamorphose into fluid and malleable concepts. They become the canvas, the stone, the clay, the raw material from which one creates his or her own self. One begins to design his/her own evolution. This is the context of my next inquiry.

HOMOSEXUAL IDENTITY, MOVING TARGET

"I" is not a state but a process involving two complementary dynamics: cultural imprinting and individuation. We have largely explored the first one in the Good. We are now going to focus on the second one, the individuation, which I define here in agreement with Jung's theory, as the differentiation process that takes place from childhood all throughout adulthood and that allows individuals to forge a self distinct from collective/parental models.[595] The individual requires the collective to understand oneself. In other words, to become aware, the "I" has no other choice than to rely on the "WE" first. Only later and retrospectively can the "I" undertake the astonishing alchemical process that we call individuation. One must first include, identify with, and then transcend—always in that order, as far as we can tell.

Individuation for homosexuals is twofold.[596] In a first step, homosexuals strive to acknowledge their differences with prevailing heterosexual standards and assert themselves in a hetero-normalized society. This usually results in one's overall identification with homosexual values (identity, cultures, community, and so on). However, this "preliminary" individuation step only brings homosexuals to a position similar to that of their heterosexual peers. Only then can the "true" individuation process begin; that is, a transformative reevaluation of one's homosexual identity that will ultimately disengage the homosexual self from its cultural stranglehold. A few important points can be clarified:

First, although I am discussing primarily homosexual identity, I by no means intend to exclude bisexuals. From the beginning, I have taken for granted that bisexual identity constitutes a true sexual identity, healthy, whole, and complete, just as it is.[597] That some homosexuals appear to hide behind a bisexual persona does not provide a valid argument against the reality of bisexual identity in general. What matters is that for bisexuals, a bisexual identity offers a sense of balance and fulfillment.

Second, for philosophical and other reasons, some people have adopted different sexual identities such as queer, genderqueer, polyamorous, and so on. I am not a specialist in those identities; however, I strongly suspect that the individuation process, as I present it, is not fundamentally different (at least until proven otherwise). I then count on my readers to make the necessary linguistic adjustments and understand that I could not reasonably drag the cohort of all officially declared sexual identities throughout this entire section.

Third, human beings tend, initially, to understand themselves in a modular fashion, homosexual identity being only one piece amid a larger and more complex whole. Ergo, homosexual identity develops as part of a kaleidoscope of identities. The psychologist Vivienne Cass talks about "composite identity": "Self-image is the basic unit upon which identity is built . . . A composite identity may include (and usually does) typological identities. These are organized sets of self-images and attached feelings that an individual holds about self with regards to some social category or type."[598] Cass's point is important. Sexual identity interacts, competes, clashes, or synergizes with other equally powerful psychocultural identities—of race, class, religion, and so on. The development of a gay identity proves quite different depending on whether one is Caucasian or African-American; many African-Americans view gay identity as a betrayal of black identity; and often, African-American homosexuals have to negotiate which identity is going to occupy the forefront. Many find in denial or secrecy the only acceptable solution to an unsolvable dilemma. The complex dynamics that exist among psychocultural identities have been extensively documented in the literature and will not be investigated here. One should never forget, however, that the development of one's homosexual identity always depends on the overall psychocultural context. There are many ways that one can be either proud or closeted, and generic stage descriptions ought to be reinterpreted in accordance with one's personal psychological background, experience, and education.

At this point, gender deserves particular attention. Gender constitutes one of, if not the most, fundamental element of people's psychobiological makeup. Viewed as a typological identity, it will inevitably interact with sexual identity. Inasmuch as sexuality in general already differs between males and females, the homosexual individuation process will unavoidably exhibit gender specificities. For this reason, and for clarity's sake, I chose to treat the characteristic aspects of lesbian identity in a separate chapter.

It is also undeniable that gender deviance is an important—yet not systematic—feature of the homosexual experience. Many studies concur that the majority of gay men and lesbians report having displayed gender atypical interests and behaviors during their childhood. The "sissy boy" and the "tomboy girl" are common realities in the homosexual world. I myself was a "sissy" in my early years. Often those differences lessen later in life, but again, not always. The reason for this is unclear—social pressure, archetypal imprinting, or the natural end of a "gender fluidity phase." Researchers have yet to elucidate those issues.

Regardless, if homosexuality does include a spectrum of gender variance, gender variance is by no means representative of the homosexual experience. If, to the best of my knowledge, gender variance is more prevalent among homosexuals, it is far from being absent among heterosexuals. The two phenomena—homosexuality and gender variance—overlap but do not match, despite claims that they do. Because we live in cultures that have heavily codified the correspondence between gender and sexual roles and because I have yet to come across a theoretical model that explains the role of gender variance in homosexuality convincingly, I have been reluctant, as you might have already noticed, to conflate an exploration of homosexuality with one of gender. Gender deserves an integral exploration of its own, not as an appendage to a study of homosexuality. Ultimately, I believe them to be symbolically independent, which, for me, constitutes the ultimate criterion regarding the content of this book.

Last, it is essential to remember that any model is by definition culture-dependent. Any identity arises inside the cultural space given by a geographical and historical context. Greek *erastoi* did not have to "come out of the closet" for instance. Their homosexual experience was totally different insofar as homosexual behavior was encouraged, represented in their culture and in their mythos, and part of a mainstream sexual identity, namely, male identity. Current models of homosexual identity development are built upon particular historical circumstances. Coming out might become unnecessary in the future; homosexual identity might change or fragment into distinct sub-identities. Human reality is not fixed in stone. Homosexual reality is changing fast. Our models are likely to become obsolete in our lifetime. But despite their inherent historicity, those developmental models, used appropriately and wisely, remain extremely useful.

A MAP OF HOMOSEXUAL DEVELOPMENT

I must reiterate here my original warning: the map is not the territory. One should never confuse the former for the latter. A map is not a faithful portrait but only a tool to help us understand a reality that is often too complex to grasp at the moment when we experience it. Hence, a model of homosexual identity development does not describe the true experience of an individual, nor does it tell us what people should think, feel, and confront at a particular time. Maps and models are symbolic representations of a statistical reality. In other words, a psychological model of homosexual development allows people to position their own unique experience within an ideal common standard. To see those models as restrictive or stereotypical is to miss the point. When one confuses the map for the territory, one will inevitably judge the model as reductive. A model, by definition, must be reductive. However, it must do that intelligently—it must "reduce wisely."

If identities such as homosexual identity constitute archetypal landmarks, one can similarly discern mythic roadmaps in developmental models. Campbell argued that one of the primal functions of myths is "to carry the individual through the various stages and crises of life—that is, to help persons grasp the unfolding of life with integrity."⁵⁹⁹ Psychology has largely taken over that function of myth. At the same time, psychological models, while providing an objective depth that most ancient myths would be unable to offer in a postmodern culture, lack the transcendental dimension and the connection with the sacred that traditional myths use to offer. In many respects, they fail to measure up. Yet, by providing a meticulous description of the heroic journey that awaits us, models of psychological development—those wanna-be myths—remain the best thing our global postmodern culture has to offer in order to help people carry through their lives.

Understood as mythic roadmaps, developmental models can help us contextualize and, consequently, fulfill two fundamental needs: a sense of commonality and directionality. The sense of commonality is directly provided by the collective psychocultural identity, which is, by definition, shared. By identifying as homosexual, homosexuals automatically join a community of people with similar traits and similar life experiences; it creates a sense of belonging and relatedness; and it offers a solid basis for a lasting membership, which is what cultures do best. We often overlook the terrible feelings of loneliness and profound distress of those who were born at a time or place where no homosexual or homosexual-like identity was available. Commonality does not necessarily entail socializing, blending in, or embodying cultural stereotypes. Commonality is about the possibility to connect and bond; it is belonging; it is the ability to love and be loved in return, and this, even if you are an anti-social, introverted rebel.

Directionality is naturally revealed by the progression through the stages of development. Homosexual identity development embodies the same telos as the one that I have analyzed in regard to our cultural and moral development. The developmental telos progresses along two axes: awareness and integrity. Homosexual consciousness grows from undifferentiated, unrecognized, and concealed, to become integrated, complete, self-expressed, and self-generated. Along the way, new pieces of the self will have emerged in the space of awareness, by becoming conscious and visible, and disowned fragments of the self will have integrated one's unified self and self-image. (This process mirrors the evolution of human cultures: worldviews expand and marginalized subgroups progressively integrate the space of kinship.) At every stage, the picture becomes richer, deeper, increasingly coherent, authentic, and interconnected. One might not value them; yet those are the qualities that we see emerging through the evolutionary telos in all aspects of human reality—in the True, the Good, and the Beautiful (which never fails to fill me with awe).

One must not lose sight of an important point. Homosexual identity, thanks to its archetypal properties, is only the mirror through which the individual self can slowly recognize itself.⁶⁰⁰ One may *identify* with homosexual identity; still, who one is is distinct from it. Rigorously speaking, it is not one's homosexual identity that arises through these stages of development but one's increasingly deeper relationship to homosexual identity. If at some point, it really feels like one *is* his gay or her lesbian identity, that is only characteristic of a particular stage (namely, stage 5 or ownership stage) but not of the overall developmental process.

HOMOSEXUAL IDENTITY DEVELOPMENT, HERE AND NOW

Since any model of homosexual identity development is, by definition, context-bound, the historical and cultural circumstances that influence the development of homosexual identity today must be specified first. It is that current "state of affairs" of homosexual development that will be inventoried now.

The first circumstance is what Gilbert Herdt calls the "presumption of heterosexuality."[601] As a rule, parents and society assume and expect youths to fit today's psychocultural norm, that is, to be(come) heterosexual. Exceptions to the rule are rare, to say the least. Most unusual is the case of my friend Dylan, who grew up in a hippie community in the 1970s in New England, and whose mother kept reassuring him throughout his entire youth that it would be totally fine for him to be gay. (Needless to say, this did not make his puberty crisis easier). In this case the presumption of heterosexuality did not apply. But rare are the young homosexuals who have the chance to grow up in such a gay-friendly environment. More often, homosexual youth face a unique conundrum, which is to have to grow up in families and in cultural milieux that are by and large inconsistent with who they are and/or aspire to be. Gay identity is a minority identity, and given homosexuality's demographics, this fact is unlikely to change (see chapter 1). One can hope that in the near future sexuality will be increasingly portrayed as a spectrum of desire through parental education, at school, and in the media. In the meantime, most gay youths have to manage the fact of being "unexpected" and undertake the incredibly peculiar task of, at some point in their lives, "coming out of the closet."

Second, despite some exceptions, homosexual identity development today takes place against a backdrop of a powerful anti-homosexual stigma. Homosexual youths often find themselves in conflict with their immediate environment, family, school, friends, and so on. From isolation, rejection, or expulsion from home, young gays are exposed to unusual complications.[602] A higher suicide rate among gay teenagers has been reported (although the current information is to be taken with a grain of salt because the population samples used in those studies might not have been representative of gay youth in general).

However, and fortunately, this reality is changing—quite rapidly in fact. As Andrew Sullivan pointed out, "A gay child born today will grow up knowing that in many parts of the world and in parts of the United States, gay couples can get married just as their parents did. From the very beginning of their gay lives, in other words, they will have internalized a sense of normality, of human potential, of self-worth—something that my generation never had and that previous generations would have found unimaginable."[603] It is therefore essential to bear in mind the continuously shifting reality of gay youth, especially in Westernized countries.

The third circumstance results from the strong prejudice that our culture perpetuates against interactions between young and adult homosexuals, which I call, the "suspicion of pederasty."[604] The persistent belief that, intrinsically, gay males are potential child molesters has had a massive and disastrous impact on both gay youth and gay adults. On the one hand, gay adults, primarily males, find themselves paralyzed by the idea of being found guilty of having hidden sexual intentions toward a youth. On the other hand, gay youths find themselves cut off from those who have had the life experiences that they so urgently need to hear. While the importance of nurturing relationships between young individuals and adults is acknowledged by virtually all education professionals, gay youth are still condemned to be taken care of by people that are virtually clueless about who they are and how they feel, and most of the time totally unable to provide any real direction with regard to their inner turmoil. Because society succeeds in maintaining an overwhelming pressure against homosexual adult male-youth interactions, scandals like the shameful cases of pederasty among Catholic clergy and male child pornography (regardless of the fact that homosexual pederasty is by no means more prevalent than heterosexual pederasty) remain sadly the most visible examples of what homosexuals have to offer to their youth. This deplorable fiasco is too often overlooked.

The fourth particularity of homosexual psychological development is that it unfolds inside a quasi-mythic void. That crucial point has already been extensively explored in chapters 10 and 11. Unlike their straight friends, gay youths will find very little representation of what they are about to experience in their lives and in their hearts inside the mythos. For them, role models will be scarce, if any. Very early on they will have to hunt consciously for images, stories, books, or movies that depict their feelings and desires. Hopefully the promising changes that we have recently witnessed, especially thanks to the extraordinary creativity in literature and cinema, heralds a more profound mutation of our mythos.

Before delving into the six stages of our model of homosexual identity development, I would like to make an observation regarding the coming out process. Here and there in the specialized literature, the homosexual coming-out process has been compared to a "rite of passage." Yet if one takes into account the true definition of rites and rituals, the claim is largely inaccurate. The statement is, however, fairly intuitive and requires just a little adjustment to hit the mark. Once again, I concur with Gilbert Herdt, who studied homosexual coming-of-age rites among Sambia people for many years and knows probably more than anybody else about the significance of rituals:

> Rites of passage [. . .] structure life crisis [. . .] to adjust people's behaviors to new and appropriate rights and duties, knowledge and identities, as these refashion social relationships with others. [They] also change the person's interior and exterior, thus linking their psychological states and cultural knowledge to their new moral and sociopolitical responsibilities.[605]

Hence rites and rituals are experiential methodologies collectively designed to help individuals undergo all the predictable crises in human life—coming of age, marriage, sex, child bearing, birth, death—the list is long. When one is left completely alone to try to figure out how to manage a time of crisis, which is the case for the homosexual coming out, you do not have a ritual but only a missed opportunity for a ritual. Conceivably, the random confession process that we name "coming out" could be structured into a "rite of coming out." Such a metamorphosis would ease the process a great deal, for both youth and family, and particularly the parents, of course. By offering an exemplary course of action as well as a symbolic framework, a ritualized coming out would help everybody apprehend what they are about to step into with a more positive mind, connected to rather than apart from each other and the rest of the world. Yet, what form(s) a "rite of coming out" might take is still to be determined. It will require respect for all the parties involved, a profound understanding of all the dynamics at play, a fair amount of creativity, and, inevitably, numerous adjustments. In other words, it will necessitate wisdom.

Six Stages of Homosexual Identity Development

The synthetic model that I am about to outline here results essentially from the combination of two models. The first one, and in many respects its backbone, is constituted by the elegant and pioneering six-stage model proposed by Vivienne Cass.[606] The second one is that of Richard Troiden, which contains a wealth of valuable information, yet only four stages.[607] To the best of my knowledge, those two models represent by far the two most relevant descriptions of homosexual psychological development to this day.[608] The combination of these models, presented below, reflects not only my personal experience with remarkable accuracy, but also appears consistent with a lot of what other homosexuals, friends, boyfriends, clients, or acquaintances, have shared with me over the years. Altogether, this model offers a solid and reliable foundation to map out the evolutionary path of homosexual identity.[609]

Remember that these models have focused on gay identity formation; other aspects, such as, for instance, sexual and emotional developments, are not taken into consideration.[610] Each stage describes an ideal psychological state—a statistical average—not an unavoidable destiny or even less a norm. The succession from one stage to the next should be interpreted in a flexible fashion also. The model is expected to unfold in a globally linear fashion; however, one's growth through the stages does not exclude back-and-forth and ups-and-downs. As Richard Troiden puts it: "In many cases stages are encountered in consecutive order, but in some instances they are merged, glossed over, bypassed, or realized simultaneously."[611] Keep in mind also that the progression will be greatly affected by gender, personality type, the presence or absence of a supportive environment, positive or negative early sexual and/or romantic experiences, and so on.

I also try to differentiate the healthy version of each stage from possible problems and pathologies that might appear at that particular step of development. This said, being "healthy" in this specific framework does not always imply feeling comfortable and content, particularly in early stages. Rather, one's degree of happiness and self-fulfillment in relation to homosexual identity climbs through the stages along with increasing levels of awareness and inner integrity. In the same manner, the pathologies that I present do not systematically require psychological assistance; often they resolve themselves in a spontaneous manner as part of one's struggle to grow up and one's quest for happiness. Finally, these six stages are summarized in a table at the end of this section.

Bearing in mind the potential pitfalls inherent to this sort of exploration, one can investigate the following stages of homosexual identity development in the ideal order suggested by Vivienne Cass and Richard Troiden—an order that will reveal, once more, the telos inherent in all aspects of the human adventure.

Stage 1: Sensitization Stage

(identity confusion in Cass's model and sensitization in Troiden's model)
Tentative age: childhood to early adolescence[612]

At this stage, one start to feels different from other kids without knowing precisely why. This feeling remains vague. One is "confused," as Cass puts it.[613] Throughout the first stage, one becomes progressively aware of the source of his or her uneasiness. Their feelings, interests, or even early attraction to same-sex peers—from passionate friendships to sexual play—begin to look suspicious to them. Children with gender atypical behaviors (boys playing with dolls and girls with plastic guns) become self-conscious, usually as a result of being teased or rejected by others. Altogether, the child understands that he/she is not exactly "normal," whether this is revealed through difficulties when interacting with peers or, instead, remains successfully hidden.

On the negative side, this stage often entails feelings of alienation and various degrees of social isolation. Often, but not necessarily, one becomes overly anxious about being perceived negatively by other kids and afraid not to measure up to adult expectations, particularly those of the parents.

Stage 2: Negotiation Stage

(identity comparison in Cass's model; confusion in Troiden's model)
Tentative age: childhood to early adolescence

This stage reflects one's first attempt to rationalize what began to emerge in the first stage. One is going to assess and compare, sometimes obsessively, his/her experience—emotions, feelings, desires, behaviors, and interests—with available cultural models. One no longer just feels; now one also thinks about the problem, and is brought little by little to the idea of perhaps being homosexual.[614] Often, suspicions arise from resemblance to negative stereotypes (faggot, effeminate, queen, dyke, etc.) rather than from the reality of homosexual life that is not always available or visible. At this stage however, "pre-homosexuals" do not identify themselves as homosexual but, instead, keep negotiating their odds of being homosexual. They engage in an endless inner monologue: "Is that such a big deal? It doesn't really count! Am I gay? No, I'm not; what happens doesn't mean anything."

But maybe I am. Maybe I'm just bisexual. What should I do? Who can help me?" It is not uncommon at this stage to prefer labels that do not exclude the possibility of heterosexuality, such as bisexual, open-minded, or rebellious. The cultural stigma and the absence of positive role models encourage the confusion and largely explain it. As a matter of fact, individuals raised in highly insulated subcultures who never hear about the existence of openly gay people face even more difficulties. Stage 2 may also be the time of one's first same-sex sexual experiences.

What are the potential problems at Stage 2? The fear of rejection is generally strong. One struggles to look "normal." Often, but not necessarily, one experiences painful existential doubts, moments of anxiety, feelings of separateness and loneliness, and/or maintains delusive hopes of eventually becoming "normal" again. Self-censoring can cause the self to fragment.

Stage 3: Acknowledgment Stage

(identity tolerance in Cass's model; assumption in Troiden's model)
Tentative age: late adolescence (possibly earlier) to young adulthood

This is the first stage where individuals have the courage to cut from the heterosexual model and acknowledge a homosexual identity. They objectively define themselves as homosexual, lesbian, gay, but mostly in private, or just to themselves. As Cass reminds us, homosexual identity at this point is tolerated rather than embraced. People resign themselves to the idea of being homosexual, which is often perceived as more of a capitulation than a discovery— "So, ok, I'm gay."

Because the acknowledgment stage requires people to have reached reasonable levels of self-recognition, negative/pathological reactions may no longer be as benign as in previous stages. A negative familial and social environment can turn this stage into a life-long nightmare. The person can grow chronically angry or scared. These negative feelings can deteriorate into self-hate. Homosexual attractions may be altogether denied. One then tries to pass for straight, struggling to repress homoerotic impulses. Sometimes one marries in order to reaffirm his/her normality. At this stage, homosexual identity development can simply freeze, hindering the emergence of subsequent stages. As a matter of fact, a significant number of homosexuals do not pass beyond this stage. I also suspect that, under the right cultural conditions—the rise of Nazism, the McCarthy era, and so on—homosexuals at later stages could regress to an unhealthy Stage 3, burying a previously well-developed homosexual identity under layers of denial and self-censorship.

Stage 4: Exploration Stage

(identity acceptance in Cass's model; commitment in Troiden's model)
Tentative age: late adolescence to young adulthood

"If I am gay, what is that about? Who are those gays anyway?" This is the stage where individuals, once they have acknowledged their homosexual identity, look around to meet other gay people—mirrors of themselves. They attempt to exorcize the sense of isolation so characteristic of the previous stages. Now, young homosexuals (young, identity-wise) become more proactive. The potential that had emerged in Stage 3 is slowly blossoming. Thanks to those experiences—cultural, social, romantic, and/or sexual—one's homosexual identity is reinforced. However it is neither rare nor inconsistent with this model to see one's chosen identity (as selected in stage 3) being revisited more than once (e.g., from bisexual to gay/lesbian and vice versa, from gay/lesbian to queer and vice versa, and so on) as additional sexual and romantic experiences, social interactions, and/or greater erudition help the youths become increasingly aware of their patterns of desire. In that case, moving through stage 3 and 4 (and possibly later stages) entails multiple iterations that might confuse their family and peers, as well as psychologists and researchers.[615]

This is often the time when homosexuals come out, at least to a selected circle of close friends and family members. But they also weigh carefully the degree to which this particularly sensitive aspect of their private life is being disclosed to the outer world. Cass writes: "A philosophy of fitting into society, while also retaining a homosexual lifestyle, is adopted and entails the continued maintenance of a passing strategy (pretending heterosexuality) at pertinent times."[616] Notwithstanding this, the silence is broken. Provided that one has reached an appropriate age, Stage 4 may include sex and romance. It is the ideal time to explore being in romantic relationships. In urban areas, Stage 4 often coincides with one's simultaneous discovery of the gay lifestyle and the gay community.

Nevertheless, Stage 4 is not devoid of potential pathologies. Remember that even if coming out is likely to help release a great deal of tension, it does not automatically produce healthy individuals.[617] Although one's homosexual identity has been acknowledged, self-hate can still undermine its fulfillment. In that case, one might engage in self-destructive sexual behaviors. Sex addiction may in fact represent the most typical pathology of Stage 4. People remain emotionally alienated and unable to engage in healthy and fulfilling relationships; in other words, they are incapable of loving.

Stage 5: Ownership Stage

(identity pride in Cass's model; commitment in Troiden's model)
Tentative age: mid twenties, yet this stage tends to occur increasingly earlier in life, as early as adolescence today

Homosexual identity, which before this had mostly been experienced as a burden, becomes much less costly. People at Stage 5 "own" their sexual identity. Whether the culturally defined identity matches one's self-perception precisely or not no longer matters. One endorses the homosexual label despite and beyond individual differences, willingly and, often, proudly. Cass's original description of this stage goes like this: "This stage is characterized by feelings of pride toward one's homosexual identity and fierce loyalty to homosexuals as a group, who are seen as important and creditable while heterosexuals have become discredited and devalued."[618] Congruent with Cass, Troiden notices one's temptation of "aristocratizing homosexual behaviors."[619]

The Stage 5 worldview is characterized by a strong dichotomy between the homosexual and heterosexual worlds. It took much effort for the individual to embrace and assert his/her homosexual identity, but now, the self is strongly identified with the cultural concept called "to be homosexual." It has fully internalized it. In reaction, the heterosexual world ends up representing the alien "other." Although rarely with the same intense animosity, the Stage 5 worldview constitutes, in many respects, a reverse image of the homophobic worldview. At this point, it is not rare for the Stage 5 homosexual to socialize only or at least primarily within the gay and lesbian communities and/or display militant interests in the gay cause.

Stage 5 is of paramount importance for many reasons. This the first stage where homosexuals catch up with heterosexuals in terms of the level of psychocultural development. They are now grounded in and supported by a coherent identity, a community, and a culture—a privilege that heterosexuals never had to fight for. Moreover, homosexual identity is not only integrated into one's sense of self—the ego—but also into one's persona, one's agent in the world (Troiden talks about "presented identity"). In that regard, Stage 5 marks the end of the first individuation cycle of the homosexual differentiation process. Until that point, growing as gay or lesbian had essentially amounted to a long "defragmentation" process. Now, the homosexual self is whole, distinct, and centered, as it is finally discovering what being homosexual and happy means.

Possible negative or pathological aspects of Stage 5 include excessive anger, vengefulness, and a fanatical hatred of the heterosexual world ("heterophobia" so to speak), or, on the other end of the spectrum, disowned anger and shame, and, sometimes a neurotic split between one's militant ego/persona and a deeply victimized soul (as seen in the previous chapter).

Stage 6: Integration Stage

(Identity synthesis in Cass's model)
Tentative age: Adulthood (if it ever happens)

Stage 6, whose very existence was valiantly defended by Vivienne Cass against the opinion of many of her peers, is a complex stage. In my opinion, it comprises an entire new cycle within itself—the second homosexual individuation process. Cass notes how, beyond Stage 5, "positive contacts with non-homosexuals help create an awareness of the rigidity and the inaccuracy of dividing the world into good homosexuals and bad heterosexuals."[620] Hence, if homosexual identity remains a significant aspect of the self, the structural divide between the gay and straight worlds that had characterized the previous stage begins to blur. Homosexuality is no longer opposed to heterosexuality. The former no longer needs to be shielded or protected from the latter. Rather, sexual identity is integrated into the vast gamut of what makes us human beings.[621] At Stage 6, gay men and lesbians make peace with the long and often difficult process that ultimately allows them to affirm their homosexual selves. They can now relate with heterosexual people and the prevailing culture in a different mode. Fundamental differences are not just understood; they are integrated.

Although Stage 6 pathologies are still hard to diagnose at this point, one can nonetheless guess the possible pitfalls. Homosexuals at Stage 6 may end up becoming somehow selfish, a bit in the flavor of "I'm over it," shielding themselves from individuals in earlier stages and their "annoying" issues. They might be exasperated and particularly reactive against the anti-heterosexual vindictiveness often seen in the discourse and behavior of people at Stage 5. Overall, Stage 6 homosexuals might lack compassion completely. They might refuse to take the responsibility to help other homosexuals, especially the youngest generations, for instance, ignoring how valuable it would be if they were to offer themselves as mentors and role models. Eventually, Stage 6 integration may be limited to "blending in"; the individuation process loses its purpose and spirit, for the sake of one's own peace of mind.

Many psychologists have denied the existence of Cass's last stage. Richard Troiden largely missed it, or rather saw it merely as a nuance of Stage 5. In my opinion, the best explanation for this (forgivable) blindness resides in the fact that, in the early 1980s when most of those models were put together, homosexual people at Stage 6 were probably rare. At that time, homosexuality was still struggling to end a long era of social disgrace, and being "out and proud" already constituted an astonishing personal accomplishment. In that respect, one can only bow to Vivienne Cass's visionary prescience.

Yet another reason to explain Stage 6's fragile status might be the following: We need to remember that at any given point of one's development, all "lower" stages are perceived as obsolete, limited, if not barbarian; on the other hand, the stages ahead are perceived as even more dangerous, unsafe, and irrational. So, from a Stage 5 vantage point, Stage 6 is likely to come across as a betrayal of the gay cause, and one damn good reason not to place it at the top of a developmental model of gay identity. Finally, I also suspect that the mere idea that gays and lesbians could naturally outgrow the isolation and the infernal cycle of self-denial for which they were treated may have offended many not-so-enlightened therapists who had made a living from homosexuals' struggle. Hopefully, the time when homosexuals' misery constitutes a lucrative business for some people will soon be behind us.

As hinted at earlier, it is also increasingly apparent that Stage 6 homosexuals reflect altogether a diversity far too vast to be representative of a single stage. All Stage 6 homosexuals have not equally transcended collective archetypes and stereotypes, nor have they all perfectly integrated the homosexual-heterosexual polarity. They have not reached the same depth with respect to their understanding of homosexuality. And rare are those who have totally rid their worldview

STAGES OF HOMOSEXUAL IDENTITY DEVELOPMENT

Stage 1: Sensitization

Cass Stage: Confusion

Troiden Stage: Sensitization

- Begins to notice differences in his/her behavior (something does not feel right)
- Growing sense of alienation
- Often, but not always, exhibits gender atypical behaviors and interests

Negative Aspects:
Anxieties linked to an excessive sense of alienation and fear of rejection

Stage 2: Negotiation

Cass Stage: Comparison

Troiden Stage: Confusion

- Compares his/her behavior with culture-defined identities and stereotypes
- Questions his/her sexual identity, unwilling to see the difference as meaningful ("this shall pass")
- Sometimes, first sexual experiences with same-sex partners
- Often experiences difficult yet natural feelings of fear, low self-esteem, shame, a sense of failure, and difficulties relating with peers

Negative Aspects:
Self-editing, struggles to look normal, excessive fear of rejection

Stage 3: Acknowledgment

Cass Stage: Tolerance

Troiden Stage: Identity Assumption

- Accepts the idea of being gay (coming out to oneself)

Negative Aspects:
Denial, attempts to pass for straight, inner fight to repress homoerotic desires and impulses, homophobia

Stage 4: Exploration

Cass Stage: Acceptance

Troiden Stage: Commitment

- Explores proactively gay/lesbian identity based on collective models, culture, social space, including sexual experiences

- Often, comes out to a restricted circle of trusted people. First friendships based on shared homosexual identity
- Homosexual identity and the feeling of belonging to a community is progressively reinforced

Negative Aspects:
Self-destructive sexual behaviors, feels emotionally alienated from him/herself, self-hate

Stage 5: Ownership
Cass Stage: Pride
Troiden Stage: Commitment

- Gay/lesbian identity becomes a personal (ego) and social (persona) identity
- Often, comes out to the entire world
- Tries to affirm his/her new social identity (militant phase)

Negative Aspects:
Inner Split between a militant ego/persona and a victimized self, unresolved emotional wounds, disowning of anger, unconscious shame, fanatical hatred of the heterosexual world.

Stage 6: Integration
Cass Stage: Synthesis
Troiden Stage: n.a.

- Relativizes the split gay/straight, which no longer defines one's moral boundaries
- Transcends victimization

Negative Aspects:
Rejection or contempt for the previous stages (particularly Stage 5), lack of compassion

After Stage 6: Super-Integrated Stage
Cass Stage: n.a.
Troiden Stage: n.a.

- Manifestation of a universal and eternal homosexual principle through one's unique homosexual self
- Sense of completion regarding the past, homosexual history as much as one's personal history

Negative Aspects:
(too early to be determined)

from the poison of victimization. Stage 6 is the beginning of a new individuation cycle and constitutes a major leap toward higher awareness and deeper integrity. The evolutionary tip of homosexual consciousness (the homosexual telos) continues to move forward, inevitably, differentiating new stages of development along the way. As more depth always lies ahead, I find it useful and desirable to include here a description of what a super-integrated "post-Stage 6" probably looks like, based on what transpersonal and Jungian psychology, and, of course, integral philosophy teach us.

Even at the risk of sounding dangerously mystical (a risk that Jung never hesitated to take however), let me offer the following. What one sees slowly revealing itself throughout the various stages of homosexual development is none other than one's unique homosexual essence, or, rather, the homosexual essence— eternal and universal—being manifested in a totally unique human being. By "essence," I mean something beyond the trait of character, beyond individuality, almost beyond historicity; I mean something of the order of archetypes and myths, symbolic and sacred, something numinous (acknowledging, by inserting this word here, my own ignorance). Fluid, imprecise, nearly invisible, or, on the contrary, intense, consuming, and projected onto the outer world, this unique manifestation of homosexual essence is the Holy Grail of the homosexual individuation process. Those who have embraced their homosexual self, not despite or against, but through and beyond homosexual identity, know exactly what I am talking about, and which is quite challenging to define here. This unusual awareness, seldom described in the field of gay studies, was exquisitely depicted by Jungian psychologist and lesbian Christine Downing when she described her feelings for her partner: "It feels like a *return* [. . .] It feels numinous, sacred, necessary, almost fated. It feels like a gift and blessing and culmination."[622] Echoing Downing, Willow Pearson proclaims that "each individual is a unique manifestation of spirit, while still remaining part of the group to which they truly belong [. . .] The hallmark of such sexual identity is that there is a self to return to, and a self that is ever present."[623]

The final emergence of one's unique and deep homosexual self constitutes the apogee of the long alchemical process in which one ends up recognizing and embracing—within oneself—something much bigger than oneself: the universal and eternal essence of the love that one embodies in his/her flesh—same-sex love. When that happens, one has discovered his/her most sacred core, the homosexual consciousness that emanates through each one of us—whether we are homosexual, bisexual, or heterosexual—if only we let it. In this strange self-embrace, one ultimately discovers a new sense of self-delight, profound and inclusive. This unique homosexual self, individuated, transmuted, numinous and indeed sacred, in turn becomes an inner source, a limitless wellspring of inspiration, a center of gravity. Suddenly something ancient, true, good, and beautiful—eternal and universal, yet unique—shines through you through your homosexual consciousness. Homosexuality is no longer an identity; it is now a cosmic principle.

I ought to confess humbly my struggle to explain what really happens in this process. I must equally acknowledge how much this inner recognition of one's homosexual essence is also, when it happens, irrefutable, grounding, and "home-like"—a return to the origins. If one day you reach that moment of grace, know that you are not the first one to experience it. This inquiry into the spiritual dimension of homosexual consciousness will resume in the next and penultimate chapter of this book. It will not, however, end with this book.

THE LESBIAN SPECIFICITY

To the best of my knowledge, the female homosexual experience, despite its complex and fascinating differences from male homosexuality, remains thoroughly compatible with our six-stage model, if only one refrains from making both reductive and inaccurate assumptions about it. For instance, the model by no means dismisses the possibility that a woman's sexual identity can be of a limited significance amid her overall self-identification; nor does it negate the fact that sexual identity can be more nuanced and revisited more than once throughout one's life; nor does it suspect women of denying their homosexual identity, of lacking authenticity or clarity. Likewise, the ownership stage, Stage 5, which Cass unfortunately yet understandably calls "identity pride," can seldom be reduced to a militant stage (this was, perhaps, more often the case four decades ago). Moreover, for reasons that largely escape me, opponents of the "developmentalization" of homosexual identity have alleged that stage-structured models would unavoidably imply an obligatorily linear progression through the stages, in spite of the recurrent warnings of the authors of those models that this would not necessarily be the case. Based on this series of misconceptions, developmental models were deemed inadequate to account for the many subtleties of female homosexuality.

Having acknowledged this, the lives of many women engaged in romantic and/or sexual relationships with other women have demonstrated the existence of a qualitative difference between male and female homosexuality, which is just another way of saying that overall males and females engage in homosexual relationships with distinct intentions and different desires. For us, this no longer constitutes a surprise. We have seen that male and female homosexualities were already different before the human species even existed. Their evolutionary logics are distinct. Now, how does this translate in terms of identity development?

Compared to that of males, female sexuality in general, and female homosexuality in particular, is singled out for its "fluidity" and its "plasticity," as Lisa Diamond argues in her impressive review on the topic.[624] Virtually all studies concur in that women tend to identify themselves through their relationships with the objects of their affection and desire, while men are much more inclined to define themselves on the basis of the types of sexual acts that satisfy them. "Women have reported that their attractions for women are predominantly emotional or that their sexual desires are usually triggered or enhanced by feelings of emotional connection."[625] Diamond concludes that the female homosexual experience is "particularly sensitive to situational, interpersonal, and contextual factors."[626] This differs strikingly from men, who tend to express an inherent sexual nature through their sexuality.

On the Kinsey scale, men tend to score more toward the extreme (totally heterosexual or totally homosexual); women fall more often in the intermediate categories. As a result, "women are more likely [than men] to report bisexual attractions than to report exclusive same-sex attractions."[627] Yet women's sexuality proves to be more complex than plain bisexuality. Again, Diamond summarizes the female enigma (at least from a male standpoint): "Women's attractions show a greater capacity for change over time and across situations than do men's attractions."[628] Not only that, but women are often "late bloomers." "Women report later ages of first awareness and first questioning of their sexuality than do men [. . .] More striking," Diamonds continues, "are the many cases of women who report no awareness of same-sex attractions altogether until mid- to late adulthood."[629] Eventually, she encapsulates the paradigm of female homosexuality as follows: ". . . nonlinear change over time, spontaneous emergence of novel forms, and periodic reorganizations and phase transitions within the overall system."[630] Certainly, I do not believe that many men will relate to Diamond's statement. Now, what are we supposed to learn from the extraordinary fluidity and plasticity of women's (homo)sexuality?

First, sexual identity must be understood as being a dynamic identity (Diamond elegantly refers to the concept of "dynamic stability").[631] If our model is to represent female specificity fairly, it must be ready to accommodate that new variable—that one's identity can vary throughout one's life—and include the concept of "love object-centered" identity. Second, one can go through the first five (and possibly all six) stages of identity development more than once and each time add a new layer of complexity to her (and possibly his) sexual identity. Still, whatever one's dynamic identity ends up being at a given time in one's life, self-awareness and inner integrity remain the ultimate signs of one's psychological maturity, which will unavoidably manifest into one's ability (not obligation) to share life experiences with others freely and without shame.

The individuation journey gives, to all, the opportunity to become gradually conscious of a dual reality: On the one hand, one is completely unique and distinct from anything else in the universe; on the other hand, one relates with others through shared roots, shared values, and a shared future. Eventually, one becomes ready to endorse the commonality that unites all sentient beings as part of a commonwealth of being. Hence, even fluid and plastic, the evolutionary telos of female homosexuality still points to the same direction. One's sexual identity becomes the unique manifestation of a universal, eternal, and infinitely diverse essence; one's sexual identity becomes the voice of the sacred.

RECLAIMING OUR CHILDREN

Models of psychological development are useless if one's ultimate goal is to sort individuals into rigid categories. To apply those models in order to belittle individuals at early stages would be malicious. Models of psychological development should be used with the sole intention of nurturing one's growth. This is particularly crucial for homosexuals who already have a lot on their plate. Yet the very concept of nurturing one's development is subject to multiple interpretations. For many, to nurture translates into lecturing: in other words, teaching "immature" individuals that they must grow up and telling them how to do so.

If "sermonizing" produces results, those results are always limited. You probably remember that at any given stage of development (psychological or cultural), the subsequent stages are rarely perceived as wisdom. It would be absurd and insensitive to invite young (pre-)homosexuals to prepare themselves to come out, explore the gay world, and eventually transcend the dichotomy between homosexual and heterosexual. They will only listen to you because you are an adult. It will not touch them, at least, not yet. Perhaps, it would be best to let them figure it out by themselves. Despite excellent intentions, we tend to lose sight of simple evidence: Youths do not need anybody's active intervention to become adults. They are designed to become adults. We simply need to let it happen. This may sound like a cliché, and in many ways it absolutely is, but because homosexual identity has been so obsessively "psychologized" in gay-positive culture(s), we have forgotten that homosexual development is just another "normal" aspect of one's psychological development: if nothing comes in the way to hinder one's self-expression, it occurs naturally in the great majority of cases. It requires neither work nor magic. Once this important point is reestablished, a model of homosexual identity development such as the one I have presented finds a new purpose.

First, it endows parents and educators with a reliable "ontological roadmap," a "big picture" of a developmental process that they have most probably never experienced themselves. A developmental model of homosexuality helps us make sense of one's progression through the various steps, see the overall directionality of the whole process, and anticipate the possible multiple iterations that one might undergo before fully discovering oneself. I ardently believe that for many parents the most painful and frightening part is not knowing where their kids are heading, not being able to understand, participate in, or protect who they are and who they become because what they experience is so foreign to them.

Second, it allows us to see the differences along the path of development as necessary steps in the process, and no longer confuse them for deficiencies, signs of one's immaturity, or pathologies. A bud is not a flawed or a failed flower, it is an intermediate structure indispensable to the formation of a flower. Every step plays an important role that must be honored. Yet one must also keep from flattening the evolutionary process. As we know, equally important does not mean equal in value. As one progresses through the stages, one acquires a scope and a depth—a capacity to integrate new perspectives, assimilate new knowledge, and transcend increasingly complex paradoxes—that did not exist earlier. Personal development is a creative act, and that too should be honored. We need to find the right balance between elitism, which only values the end point of the process, and postmodern reductivism, which deconstructs psychocultural mechanisms into scattered parts but loses sight of the directionality, which is to say, the telos inherent in all evolutionary processes.

Third, and this clearly demonstrates a specific moral choice on my part, as well as I would imagine on the part of Vivienne Cass and Richard Troiden, this model of homosexual identity development honors and values fundamental virtues such as self-knowledge, inner authenticity, and personal integrity. It does not shy away from affirming that, for instance, more authenticity is more valuable than less authenticity. It credits the existence of healthy hierarchies of value based on increasing complexity, increasing awareness, and increasing integrity, not to be mistaken for "moralistic" hierarchies. Not everybody shares this philosophy, obviously, and I must respect those differences. I have little to offer to defend mine, other than to me it does sound true, good, and beautiful. It is consistent with my worldview and my stage of development, whatever that is.

In consideration of all this, I still argue that our society and culture can facilitate homosexual identity development, but, perhaps, not the way that you typically hear about it. First, imagine how much easier it is for a child to choose to become a carpenter if he/she has had the chance to witness what happens in a carpenter's workshop—the smell of the wood, linseed oil and varnish, the rich palette of colors, the saws, and the carving tools. To become something, one needs some knowledge about this something. In the world of being, this knowledge has been since the dawn of history provided by two things: role models and archetypes. The biggest difference between heterosexual and homosexual youths is that heterosexual youths are bombarded on a daily basis with information about what it is to be a heterosexual (which undeniably also has its own disadvantages); in comparison homosexual youths live largely in a cultural desert.

Human cultures are highly sexualized; yet since the advent of Abrahamic monotheistic religions and the spread of modernity throughout the entire planet, the male-female sexual polarity has become the unique symbolic standard. From a homosexual perspective, the current mythos is still terribly deficient in myths and archetypes representing same-sex love that would allow homosexuals to connect their identity and their feelings to the sacred. This is problematic for both youths and adults. Who they are has no resonance whatsoever in the symbolic realm, and I believe that we should start to see this as a problem and one that is our responsibility to solve.

We ought to love our youth and honor who they are. Every human being needs love. Gay and lesbian youths need *our* love. While we may not be their biological parents, we still have a great responsibility to help them transform our culture at a global level, so that they can be even freer to be who and what they want to be. The generations that have preceded me made this world a better place for me. Thanks to them, I can express who I am sexually, emotionally, intellectually, and spiritually; I can love; and I can write this book. Today, what gay youths need the most, in addition to stories and heroes with which they can identify, is to hang out with adult homosexuals who are responsible, whole, complete, and fulfilled as homosexual beings.

In that respect, the stigmatic stereotype of the homosexual, especially male, as a potential child molester is no longer bearable. The suspicion of pederasty is nothing short of a disgrace. It forbids the creation of strong and healthy bonds between gay adult males and gay youths. It cuts off gay youths from nurturing relationships with their elders and keeps most gay adult males in a state of total immaturity when it comes to gay youths. When confronted with "their" youths, too many gay men are clueless and paralyzed with guilt. You can probably tell that I have come a long way when it comes to understanding where homophobic fears stem from. I must nevertheless confess that this issue—the suspicion of pederasty—has still the ability to infuriate me. This prejudice simply must end. Society must take its responsibility, just like we must take ours.

.

CHAPTER SIXTEEN

Becoming

*Man positively needs general ideas and convictions that will give a meaning to
his life and enable him to find a place for himself in the universe. He can stand the
most incredible hardships when he is convinced that they make sense; he is crushed
when, on top of all his misfortunes, he has to admit that he is taking part in a
'tale told by an idiot.'*[632]

Carl Jung

One of the reasons gay culture today remains crippled ensues from the fact
that the homosexual discourse, largely dominated by postmodern thought
and queer theory, has invalidated the vital role of homosexual consciousness and
turned homosexual identity into a political product. Prominent queer theorist
David Halperin, who indeed has the courage of his opinions, in his 2007 essay
What Do Gay Men Want? admits the following: "Foreclosing the question of gay
subjectivity was a small price to pay for scuttling a psychological model of homosexual difference premised on sexual abnormality and replacing it with a political
program grounded in a non-psychological notion of gayness as a quasi-ethnic
social identity," a "critical anti-theory [. . .] uncontaminated by normative thinking about gay men's psychology."[633] After religion, psychology became the new
opium of the people.

I certainly do not deny the substantial political gains that resulted from such
rhetoric. I do not agree however that this was a "small price to pay." To enjoin
homosexuals, who had been denied any positive self-representation for centuries,
to embrace the status of eternal outsiders was already brutal; to offer no human-
istic alternative to homosexuals who throughout the world are still fighting for
their basic dignity, if not their own lives, was irresponsible. How long is it going
to take before we realize the disastrous impact of this "small price to pay" on the
gay community?

Today, cyberspace, so efficient and highly profitable, has imposed itself as the
master medium of gay culture.[634] Yet, the gay World Wide Web, largely dominated by the so-called "manhunt culture" and pornography, has constituted
just another trap. Sexual hyper-consumerism gives homosexuals the illusion of
abundance and the illusion of freedom. In the meantime, the ravages of crystal

methamphetamine and the many consequences that follow from its consumption (sexual addition, unsafe sexual practices, and HIV infection) have reached alarming levels in the gay community. Let me remind you that gay men are today ten times more likely to use crystal methamphetamine than the rest of the population (this represents approximately 10 to 20% of gay men).[635] The cost of spiritual depravation in the homosexual community is frightening.

Another reason for this tragedy stems from the fact that modern homosexuality (which really is postmodern rather than modern at this point) arose in the wake of the wave of cultural relativism that liberated social minorities—blacks, women, and gays—all together. But in the process homosexual culture applied moral relativism to itself also. Moral standards were far too reminiscent of the moral oppression that heterosexuals have imposed on homosexuals for centuries. In postmodernity's language, morals are "normative," hence evil. The homosexual discourse presented morals as something that power structures—governments, police forces, schools, the medical institution, and the Church—should reform, but at the same time as something that strangely no longer applied to homosexuals. It was as if the gay community had earned the right to rise above that basic requirement, as if nobody should ever lecture "us" again about how to live our lives, or as if being homosexual made you suddenly immune to the schizophrenic state that inevitably results from lacking a moral framework. Gay culture today offers no moral standards whatsoever to homosexuals, young and old (with the only notable exception of "safe sex" practices).[636] Homosexuals obviously have a strong moral sense, and the extraordinary solidarity displayed during the worst years of the AIDS crisis attest to this fact. Yet the gay community desperately lacks a moral code, a collective moral reference frame for here and now.

So, postmodern homosexuality—deconstructed and soulless—can indeed disappear with the end of gay culture, as Andrew Sullivan predicts; it no longer has any importance. I honor postmodernity's contribution but we can no longer tolerate its current *status quo*, which is as absurd as it is unhealthy. Early in the preface, I asked whether our revolution had not fallen short. The truth is, I believe that our revolution is only starting. Homosexuality today is facing a very simple choice: to give meaning to its existence or, one way or another, to disappear. If as I advocate here, we are to foster a future that reclaims the meaningfulness and integrity of homosexual love, what will be the source of this historic renewal? I would like to review this key issue one last time, in the form of a tribute to Michel Foucault, whose genius regarding imagining homosexuality's future is still largely unequaled to this day.[637]

BECOMING HOMOSEXUAL

Our culture, like the vast majority of human cultures that have existed at one point or another throughout history, command us—relentlessly—to define ourselves and choose among the various psychocultural labels that it offers. In response, or perhaps thanks, to this, individuals undergo the long and demanding process that will catapult their consciousness through thousands of years of cultural evolution and at the same time will allow them to become unique manifestations of human nature—the individuation process. This evolutionary dialectic is especially true with respect to sexual identity, and more generally in how we express and present ourselves in sexual terms. But eventually, as the individuation process seems to get to an end, comes the time when one is offered a singular choice: to remain comfortably nested inside his/her own personal psychocultural consensus or instead to grow beyond it, which is to say, to constitute oneself as a space of onto-logical creation, since we are discussing ways of being. Michel Foucault, clearly ahead of his contemporaries, intuited that deeply spiritual choice:

> Another thing to distrust is the tendency to relate the question of homosexual-ity to the problem of 'Who am I?' and 'What is the secret of desire?' Perhaps it would be better to ask oneself, 'What relations, through homosexuality, can be established, invented, multiplied, and modulated?' [. . .] we have to work at becoming homosexuals and not be obstinate in recognizing that we are.[638]

To be or to become—this may be the ultimate ontological choice that homosexu-als have to confront. Foucault reinvents the concept of homosexuality and iden-tity in general, and not without humor: "If we are asked to relate to the question of identity, it must be an identity to our unique selves. But the relationships we have to have with ourselves are not ones of identity; rather, they must be relationships of differentiation, of creation, of innovation. To be the same is really boring."[639] There is, however, a notable difference between Foucault's invitation and mine. I restrict what Foucault aimed as a "rallying cry" destined to all homosexuals with-out exception, only to those who have reached the end tip of the individuation process (namely, the "super-integrated" stage). It is true, "to be 'gay' [. . .] is not to identify with the psychological traits and the visible masks of the homosexual but to try to define and develop a way of life"[640]—once (I add) one has been able to anchor oneself authentically into a solid psychocultural paradigm and not before. Only then can start what Foucault called, in exquisitely chosen terms, a "homo-sexual ascesis" which "would make us work on ourselves and invent—I [Foucault speaking] do not say discover—a manner of being that is still improbable," which is ultimately, as Foucault reminds us, "up to us."[641] Inner freedom is a choice and a discipline, an ascesis, which continuously obliges us—inner and solitary heroes—to recognize and carve out everything that is not an exercise of our freedom, everything that is not the product of a creative act.

However, one cannot achieve this without first acknowledging the existence of almighty biological and cultural deterministic forces. In fact, one regains the power to create by embracing, not resisting or denying, those forces. Unaware or unable to include them, one can never transcend them, which is precisely what I meant in my discussion about the necessity to transition from being "context determined" to being "context aware" in the introduction to this book. Even more importantly, we would be mistaken to imagine this homosexual ascesis to be some distant fantasy or unlikely exploit. Homosexuality has already demonstrated its ability to turn into a creative process and those are facts that you already know. When modern homosexuality broke free from the ancestral rule of male ranking, which had shaped all traditional forms of homosexuality, this was a generative process. And when homosexual couples today invent new ways of reproducing outside of the heterosexual standard, they are also fostering a creative process. Homosexuals today have been able to overcome two major biological limitations, and from an evolutionary standpoint this already represents an unprecedented leap.

There is a formidable lesson to learn from all this. Individual consciousness—"I," the realm of the Beautiful—apparently so vulnerable, crushed between our impetuous biological nature and remorseless cultural forces, has, in return, the power to alter human biological and cultural realities. Aware of its own structural limitations, the "evolutionary I" imposes itself as the third evolutionary source along with genes and cultures. It becomes a force of nature to be reckoned with. And who better than Pierre Teilhard De Chardin could describe this miracle:

> [...] evolution, by becoming conscious of itself in the depths of ourselves, only needs to look at itself in the mirror to perceive itself in all its depths and to decipher itself. In addition it becomes free to dispose of itself—it can give itself or refuse itself. Not only do we read in our slightest acts the secret of its proceedings; but for an elementary part we hold it in our hands, responsible for its past to its future.[642]

Ultimately, "becoming" is a spiritual choice, which invites us to embrace and embody always more the evolutionary process that carries us away anyway.

Despite the fact that it drives many queer theorists totally crazy, the great majority of homosexuals have no problem with homosexual identity, and the rest of the world seems equally content to use the homosexual or gay labels to recognize same-sex lovers. Hence, it would be most helpful to have the concepts of homosexual identity and "evolutionary I"—to be and to become—reunited under the same umbrella. From an integral vantage point and in agreement with Foucault, homosexuality, which is manifested throughout the whole spectrum of the biological, behavioral, psychological, social, historical, cultural, mythic-symbolic, and spiritual, is first and foremost a space of ontological creation. Therefore, I suggest that we begin relating to homosexual identity no longer as a category but as a created distinction of being, always expanding in depth and scope and as fluid and complex as integral consciousness demands it to be. Homosexual identity, viewed as a created distinction of being and freely chosen by those who recognize themselves through it, emerges from our bodies, minds, and souls, as eternal and yet continuously created—universal and yet always unique. Acting like a gentle gravitational pull, this new, integral, and evolutionary homosexual identity aims to attract gay men and lesbians, or anybody really who wishes to embrace homosexual identity not as a label but as a space of symbolic development. As a natural expression of the body, culturally integrated and meaningful, and socially connected, this new homosexual identity is no longer limited to obsolete stereotypes, but on the contrary is profoundly aware of its archetypal depth and its diversity.

THE MYTHOPOETIC REVOLUTION

To encapsulate the ideas I have explored, the emergence of a homosexual creative space to be complete will require a very particular attention in three specific domains: (1) myths and symbolism, (2) morality, and (3) rituals.

(1) Human beings need meaning just like they need love. Without meaning they find themselves consumed by the fear of the unknown. Human beings are hungry for archetypes with which they can identify and inside of which they can grow. They need myths to give sense to their lives and rituals to function harmoniously within their communities. Neither intellectual limitations nor signs of weakness, those needs are simply inherent to the structure of the human psyche. As we have seen, individuals cannot emancipate themselves from the cultures that have nourished their psyche since birth unless they have acquired enough self-awareness and an epistemological foundation deep enough to support an independent ontological creative process. So, in the meantime, it is essential that the culture provides the psyche its vital nutrients.

Homosexuality must reintegrate the mythos urgently. Joseph Campbell, like Carl Jung before him, understood very well the terrible psychological consequences that result from meaning depravation:

> These symbols stem from the psyche; they speak from and to the spirit. And they are in fact the vehicles of communication between the deeper depths of our spiritual life and this relatively thin layer of consciousness by which we govern our daylight existences. And when those symbols—those vehicles of communication between our greater and lesser selves—are taken away, we are left without an intercom. This split leaves us schizoid; we live in a world up in the head; and the world down below is quite apart. [. . .] they [people] plunge back into the night sea of the realities down there, which they had not been taught about. They're terrified—by demons.[643]

Without myths, one can relate neither with oneself nor with the rest of the world. One is simply left alone to face the unknown. In an interview for the documentary *The Celluloid Closet*, filmmaker Jan Oxenberg wraps the whole issue up in a few words: "We are pathetically starved for images of ourselves." I agree. We need to tackle the mission of generating a new homosexual mythos adapted to integral consciousness. Yet, this will not be sufficient. Most people are far from having reached the postmodern stages, let alone the integral stage. The great majority of people today are split between modern and traditional stages. We cannot then reserve the benefits of a homosexual mythos only to minuscule developmental "elite." We ought to be far more generous and far more creative. We will have to reshape and re-contextualize already existing myths and eliminate others (here of course, I think of Philo's legend of Sodom and Gomorrah). This is exactly what Greek poets did in the sixth and fifth centuries BCE. They did not hesitate to "homosexualize" pre-existing myths, such as the relation between Zeus and Ganymede or the friendship between Heracles and Iolaus.[644] We will also have to invent new ones. Jews and Christians, for instance, have borrowed entire fragments of their mythoi that were often central to their mythologies from their neighbors and predecessors, including the legend of Noah's ark and the Flood, and the legend of a messiah who rises from the dead after three days.[645]

Today heroes no longer levitate, battle dragons, or transmute lead into gold. Instead, they land on the moon, promote world peace, or become the first African-American elected as President of the United States of America. Those are the new heroic acts of today. And no one can predict what those will be in the future. The overall design remains identical (we collectively generate the heroes that we so need) but the substance changes. The same is true of myths.[646] A homosexual mythos will require a new breed of stories and characters that can embody the essence of the homosexual experience, as we live it today.

Herein lies a new difficulty. Myths arise through a mechanism that we have yet to elucidate. We can neither explain nor predict why one element of the culture becomes more successful than another. Schelling, in his *Introduction to Philosophy and Mythology*, had already acknowledged the fundamental mystery that presides over the emergence of mythic realities:

> The mythological ideas are neither invented nor voluntarily taken on. Products of a process independent of thinking and willing, they were of unambiguous and urgent reality for the consciousness subjected to this process. Peoples as well as individuals are only tools of this process, which they do not survey, which they serve without understanding it.[647]

More than two centuries later, despite his unprecedented insights into the human psyche and his discovery of the collective unconscious, Jung reached the same helpless conclusion:

> Symbols are natural and spontaneous products. No genius has ever sat down with a pen or a brush in his hand and said: "Now I am going to invent a symbol." No one can take a more or less rational thought, reached as a logical conclusion or by deliberate intent, and then give it "symbolic" form. No matter what fantastic trappings one may put upon an idea of this kind, it will still remain a sign, linked to the conscious thought behind it, not a symbol that hints at something not yet known.[648]

Scientists in the future will hopefully unravel the subtle alchemy thanks to which some stories take off, disseminate throughout the cultural sphere, and, eventually turn into mythic realities. In the meantime, we can only be certain of one thing: Before they acquire a mythic dimension and become the intersubjective common denominators of entire populations, those stories must first be brought into existence by someone. In spite of our limited understanding of the process underlying the formation of myths, I suggest that we start practicing an art that no culture before us has ever even conceived: that we become conscious actors in the creative process that fosters the emergence of the myths we believe in. This new "mythopoetic consciousness," for which I am advocating, is nothing less than a revolution—the mythopoetic revolution. No culture has ever acknowledged the evolutionary nature of its own mythos before. No culture has ever integrated the idea that what it holds as most sacred—eternal and universal—is inevitably a historical product that evolves. Remember, however, that our ultimate goal is not to desacralize the sacred but instead to embrace an evolutionary vision of the sacred. This is the new challenge that the homosexual cause forces us to take on, or at least, to contemplate.

Science, I believe, will be at the core of this deliberate mythopoeia. In fact, this is already the case. Not only is science the rigorous and demanding methodology that we know, and the best tool that we have at our disposal to help us decrypt the mysteries of the world, but science is also a powerful cultural creative process. As discussed in chapter 11, it is from the scientific narrative that the new myths are arising today—big bang theory, black holes and supernovas, the possibility of other life forms on distant planets, the evolution of species, genes and DNA, the hidden secrets of the human brain . . . the list is only getting longer. Science reveals the beauty of the universe, of life, and of our body, as seen through the delicate spirals of a faraway galaxy or the sublime architecture of the human eye. The depth that science unveils is not just epistemological; it is also profoundly spiritual in essence.

The same thing can and must happen with regard to homosexuality. Investigations led by neuroscientists, geneticists, primatologists, and other scientists have produced a considerable mass of data on homosexual behavior. They need to be reformatted into stories that people can hear—stories that will convey the truth, goodness, and beauty of homosexual love and desire. Science is not only our best ally. It is the instrument thanks to which we will be able to rewrite history and give homosexuality its true place in humankind's adventure since its origins, with all the necessary rigor and integrity.

We must learn from the shortcomings of Classical and modern philosophers. Greek thinkers failed to impact the popular culture of their time mostly because they neglected to offer a mythic alternative that would embody their new worldview. Then, modernity reiterated the same mistake by denying myths altogether. After Jung, Campbell, Lévi-Strauss, Eliade, and many others, it would be unforgivable to lead homosexual culture to another fiasco. Myths are the *sine qua non* condition of homosexuality's long-term integration in society. They are the only true anchors in human's most precious reality: the sacred. And that is true of homosexuality and everything else.

(2) The symbolic reemergence of same-sex love will require more than a mythic etiology of homosexuality. Foucault recognized the double-sided nature of a community's intersubjective space: "It seems to me," Foucault writes, "that a way of life can yield a culture and an ethics."[649] In a separate interview, Foucault details his intuition further:

> It's quite true that there was a real liberation process in the early seventies. This process was very good, both in terms of the situation and in terms of opinions, but the situation has not definitely stabilized. Still, I think we have to go a step further. I think that one of the factors of this stabilization will be the creation of new forms of life, relationships, friendships in society, art, culture, and so on through our sexual, ethical, and political choices. Not only do we have to defend ourselves, not only affirm ourselves, as an identity but as a creative force.[650]

A culture without ethics is inevitably incomplete, uncomfortable, if not unhealthy. Since one of the essential missions of the mythos is to reflect and "stabilize" the moral foundation of the culture that holds it as true, Foucault's reminder could not come at a better time. Foucault never saw rebellion as the final or constitutive state of gay culture. He knew that while periods of sociocultural instability were indispensable so as to allow society's moral development and foster cultural creativity, the vast majority of human beings and regardless of their sexual lifestyle strive for stability. To survive in the long run, all human societies have faced having to fine-tune the balance between form and social cohesion on the one hand, and growth and individual freedom on the other. Excessive control crushes individual liberties and abolishes people's happiness, vitality, and creativity. Too much freedom, however, jeopardizes social harmony and civil peace. In an integral context, both extremes can be viewed as equally immoral. In that regard, homosexuals have jumped from being subject to a code of honor that was smashing their most basic rights to having none, a little like one switches abruptly from suffocation to hyperventilation.

In recent years, voices have risen to regret the lack of an ethical standard in the gay community, and let's face it, especially among gay men: "[. . .] gay men should treat each other as sacred, not merely as disposable sex objects"[651] (Joe Perez in *Soulfully Gay*); "a new ethic of personal relationships that is not exclusively based on sexual gratification or demeaning sexual stereotypes"[652] (Angela Mason, director of the U.K. lobby group Stonewall); "[. . .] the creation of affectionate bonds that imply mutual responsibility and create the obligation of faithfulness—of an uncompromising commitment to the welfare of those involved and to the preservation of the bonds of affection"[653] (Michael Vasey in *Strangers and Friends*). Today homosexuals desperately need a moral code to help them structure, express, and protect themselves and those they love.

We must define those new boundaries, even if we know that those boundaries will have to be revisited by generations to come. It also must be done collectively. It is not my intention here to undertake a conversation about gay morality all by myself. All the men and women who are committed to the healthy development of homosexual people and who no longer fear breaking the absurd taboo that surrounds the very idea of defining sexual moralities in the gay community must speak up and open a new dialogue. Not only that, but this new code of honor, which I am calling forth, will have to be in synchrony with homosexuality's new symbolic foundation, which I am also calling forth.

Homosexuals lack a code of honor in great part because they have no mythos capable of preserving moral standards. And yet, it is also because there is no homosexual mythos that today homosexuals can join their efforts and choose collectively and freely the code of honor by which they want to abide, one that will affirm who they are for now and the time to come—a creative force, a source of truth, goodness, and beauty, for all, including themselves.

(3) The third domain in which homosexuals will inevitably have to reflect and demonstrate their unique ability to adapt and create resides in the future ritualistic expression of homosexuality. Rituals are, as I defined them here, symbolic behavioral scripts. They involve the cyclical reenactment of fixed, safe, and meaningful behaviors, from shaking hands all the way to marriage. Besides granting predictability, rituals possess a second important function: they materialize human beings' connection to the sacred and manifest the symbolic essence of the people involved in those rituals. They are the indispensable and tangible correlate of the mythic space.

The inclusion of gay men and lesbians within the sacrament of marriage—not only institutionally but also symbolically—whatever form or forms this will eventually take, will only constitute the tip of a much larger edifice. In reinventing their mythic reality, homosexual people will naturally seek ways to channel their new symbolic existence into the real world. Rituals will not only materialize homosexuality's new mythic dimension, they will confer upon homosexuality a new sociocultural visibility. Predictably, many of those rituals will be religious, yet one may also anticipate that a significant part of homosexuality's ritualistic reality will unfold in the secular realm, apart from the religious institution.

Ritualistically speaking, we cannot simply "return to the source," revamp ancient rites and assume our job is done. We have been through too many cultural revolutions. It is true, traditional (premodern) rituals do contain something that industrial and post-industrial societies have lost—the familiarity with the sacred—that still resonates with people today. Yet they fail to convey the depth that our culture, despite its current state of confusion, has acquired throughout its history. (In fact, I suspect that the mild "collective schizophrenia" currently experienced by Western culture is the result of having a deficient mythos that is unable to address the depth of postmodern consciousness.) Reintegrating perennial wisdoms is certainly part of the solution but by no means the solution. Homosexuality's new ritualistic reality, I believe, will unfold in a very different context. Despite my reluctance to foretell what this new ritualistic space will or should look like, I wish, however, to discuss the context in which it will arise.

As it happens, when one looks at the various cultural contexts that have shaped the many ritualistic forms that homosexuality has taken throughout history, they all have one particular feature in common. It is surely quite illuminating to discover that in the great majority of cultures (most likely all of them) in which homosexual relationships were integrated in the ritualistic and mythic spaces, not only were those relationships given a particular form, but they were also designed to fulfill a specific and important social function. In other words, homosexual relationships were accepted because they were structured to be beneficial for the group at large, which provided a moral foundation for their existence in return. Yet how and why homosexual relationships profited the rest of the group varied dramatically among cultures.

In the shamanic tradition (including two-spirits), gender transformation was associated with the hazardous duty of conversing with the spirits and the souls of the dead (a position that even the fiercest warriors dreaded). Provided that sexual inversion was always contingent upon social approval, it looks as if the group bartered the right to undergo gender transgression for services of magic nature. In the initiation rites present among numerous Polynesian peoples, feeding the boys with the semen of older males (either orally, anally, or by having their body smeared) allowed the transmission of maleness from one generation the next. In Classical Greece and medieval Japan, the social raison d'être of the pederastic relationship never was sexual pleasure, which would have been deemed distasteful, but first and foremost the education of the youth.[654] Placed under the care and protection of an adult male, the youth learned his future role as a man, while learning how to hunt, grow crops, and fight in battles. The pederastic bond helped the youth gain power and wisdom and in some cultures, achieve spiritual mastery. This explains why transgenerational homosexual relationships were socially paramount in many premodern cultures, fulfilling essential functions that one would expect both school and parents to perform nowadays.

Just like heterosexual relationships or any other type of ritualized/institutionalized bond, traditional homosexual relationships held a defined and exemplary purpose, which in return, ensured their long-lasting integration into the fabric of society. Socially speaking, acceptance, even with open arms, always comes at a price, and in that homosexuality has not been different from the rest of interpersonal dynamics.

Notice now that thus far I have only been talking about premodern ritualistic models. If, as claimed earlier, ancient models seldom constitute a solution, they can still provide us with valuable inspiration. The idea of fulfilling a particular function in exchange for social acceptance, if re-actualized within the context of the current culture, could prove to be decisive for homosexuality's future. The concept of social function, or functionality, is central in traditional societies where collective imperatives largely overshadow individual needs (in agreement with our earlier conversation on the mythos–logos polarity in chapter 11). If the concept remained fairly central in modern culture, the mere idea of having to abide by some predetermined societal model has gotten terrible press in postmodern societies, since more or less the 1960s.

Indeed, we owe it to postmodernity to have repositioned the individual at the center of current morals. Yet the collective requirement of social functionality has not disappeared with the advent of postmodernity. But because the postmodern perspective is different, the creative impetus must also change direction. From an individual vantage point, one no longer conforms to a rigid collective model; instead, one chooses to embody a particular service to others. The new motto of postmodern social consciousness is contribution, which offers many advantages that old traditional values did not have: flexibility, room for personal creativity and self-expression, individual or joint authorship, responsibility, and personal freedom. It would be far more interesting to see homosexuals themselves define the sociocultural impact of homosexuality than have that imposed by some obsolete traditional schemes. If we are interested in reframing the new ritualistic reality of same-sex love in today's multidimensional culture, I do not see a better starting point than the concept of contribution to help us in our task.

My enthusiasm for the extraordinary potential that the concept of contribution offers to homosexual culture would by itself be of little weight if it were not for one television show that illustrates my point brilliantly: *Queer Eye* (originally titled *Queer Eye for the Straight Guy*), which aired in the United States from 2003 to 2007 on the Bravo television channel. In the show, five gay men—known as the "Fab Five," which included a grooming specialist, an interior designer, a fashion adviser, a culture expert, and a food and wine connoisseur—teamed up in each episode to perform a total makeover on a straight man (who could obviously use one). They redecorated his home, changed his clothes and style, and taught him how to be more attractive. The final product of this transformation was, in a nutshell, a man who once again could attract women, which probably was the main reason those straight men accepted being treated as idiots for the entire duration of the episode. Celebrated by some and criticized by others, the success of *Queer Eye* among both gay and straight audiences was impressive and largely unpredicted. *Queer Eye* based most of its humor and, of course, most of its success as well, on the constant use of easy stereotypes, both gay and straight. Yet several scholarly analyses of the show (otherwise totally blind to concepts such as symbols, myths, and rituals) have inadvertently identified many basic properties of rituals. In the quotations that follow, I intentionally put in italic the words that I believe reveal the subtle presence of rituals:

QE [Queer Eye] *puts gay men to the task of* making heterosexual relationships work. [. . .] after all, their primary objective is to cement the bonds between men and women.[655]

[. . .] the show "presents us with a preparation in which gayness has *become domesticated, unthreatening, and constructive to the interests of* heterosexual *fulfillment.*"[656] What matters in this transformation is [. . .] the *modeling of alliances between two groups* (straight and gay men) whose acknowledged mistrust, ignorance, or fear of one another has helped keep homophobia faceless, monolithic, and powerful.[657][. . .] the success of Queer Eye, and for its central achievement: keeping open (within a heteronormative consumer/pop culture) *a space in which authentic connections* between straight and gay men and culture *can be forged and sustained*—and not just between the show's participants but between the homo- and heterosexual men and women who *bond* while watching it together or talking about it at work the next day.[658]

When a behavioral script is repeated publicly and on a weekly basis to promote, (I am quoting others), "sustained" and "authentic connections," "bonds," and "alliances" between members of a group (that is, social cohesion) and displays an "unthreatening and constructive" (hence predictable) image of homosexuality, you have before your eyes something that starts seriously to look like a ritual. When one reads that *Queer Eye* "puts gay men to the task of making heterosexual relationships work" "to the interests of heterosexual fulfillment," how can one not see social contribution as a key element of the show. And when in addition the behavioral script in question is followed by an audience exceeding a million viewers each week and over several years, one may start to wonder what the success of *Queer Eye* was really about.

In spite of this, I do not consider *Queer Eye* to be a canonical model for new rituals. Some authors could not help regretting that "what QE neglects to represent are gay relationships, gay desires, and the homophobia that all too often makes these things unrealizable." But this is slightly beside the point.[659] It would be sad if every media display of gay men or lesbians had to hammer a political agenda. From a symbolic standpoint, *Queer Eye's* major limitation lies elsewhere. It misses an important element: the connection to the sacred. And yet, what sacred representation of homosexuality could the creators of *Queer Eye* have instilled through their show? I wonder.

For all those reasons and despite its numerous limitations, *Queer Eye* is in many ways a ritualistic prototype. First, even if the evocation of homosexuality's sacredness stays rudimentary, to say the least, *Queer Eye* reminds us that celebrating homosexuality does not necessarily require us to return to the woods, bathe in rivers, or chant in a circle. To reconnect with the sacred, homosexuals are by no means limited to using old formulae. The sacred is everywhere one recognizes the presence of the eternal and universal, everywhere one sees truth, goodness, and beauty. It may be found in a television show, on the Internet, in an art performance, in museums, books, or movies . . . imagination is our only limitation. Second, *Queer Eye* demonstrates that to introduce homosexuals, and homosexuality through them, as a "contribution" to the community at large reinforces their integration while insisting on their differences. It includes, without erasing, identity boundaries, which I believe is exactly the virtue that the homosexual rituals of the future should demonstrate.[660]

Ultimately, this is not about becoming safe and predictable. The true goal here is for homosexuals to become responsible for and in control of their visibility in society and their impact in the world. It by no means limits who homosexuals are and what they can do; it only structures the way they are perceived collectively. Will that create expectations on the other side? Certainly, but so what? Rituals based upon the concept of contribution imply that homosexuals have something specific to offer society. And homosexuals do have something specific to offer society.[661] To acknowledge that is not only honoring homosexuals, but also, first and foremost, inventing the reason why they are here in the first place.

PHILIA

The homosexual contribution, I believe, will be primarily symbolic and involve a profound rethinking of the concepts of love, sex, and human relationships. It is therefore with an inquiry on love that I wish to end this chapter on Becoming and this book, as well as complete my modest tribute to Michel Foucault's visionary genius. One might ask why it took me so long to bring the issue of love to the table. My reason for saving love for the end was the following: If I indeed consider homosexuality to be first and foremost a form of love, we first had to attain an authentic sense of completion with respect to homosexual history before a discussion about homosexual love could unfold freely. We had to unveil a clear vision of homosexuality's vast reality, one that exudes truth, goodness, and beauty. We had to feel whole again.

Hitherto unsurpassed in the art of theorizing on love, the Greeks defined four distinct modalities of love—one might say four different love energies. The three major ones are eros, agape, and philia. The last and more minor one is called storge, which in English translates as "affection." Storge is "of all natural loves [. . .] the most catholic, the least finical, the broadest," as Carl S. Lewis defines it.[662] It is the basic love one feels for family members, one's social circle at large, colleagues, acquaintances, and pretty much everybody, to tell the truth. In contrast, eros, agape, and philia have been the topics of ardent philosophical battles throughout history, continually discussed, often redefined, occasionally confiscated, and sometimes ostracized.

Eros symbolizes the love driven by desire, the yearning for a particular target, the love that conveys passion. It is the love when one is "in" love. Like the arrow of the Greek god that shares the name (Eros, or Cupid under his Roman name), eros expresses action and focus. The connection of eros with sexual desire, subliminally and yet so potently conveyed by words such as "erotic" and "erogenous," has in fact been an open dispute since the days of the Greeks. You may remember how Plato urged his contemporaries to free themselves from the tyranny of sexual instinct and instead, redirect the unquenchable energy of eros so as to reach the realm of pure ideas and spiritual beauty. In contrast to Plato, Freud totally identified eros in his concept of sexual drive—libido. And yet Freud also considered eros to be the fundamental life force present in all human beings.

As the antithesis of eros, agape represents the love that cares, embraces, protects, and includes. Agape, which originally constituted a rather secondary matter in Greek philosophy, became central to Judeo-Christianity, which chose it to express God's love for his people and the love of good Christians for their neighbors. While eros was by far the most common form of love depicted in the Classical Greek literature, the word eros and its derivatives were deleted from the vocabulary of both the Septuagint and the New Testament almost completely due to its scandalous association with sexual desire (see chapter 10). Though agape did not preclude sex in Greek culture, and given Christianity's overall horror for all things sexual, agape increasingly came to incarnate "pure" (read asexual) love and virtues such as compassion and selflessness commonly found through God's love, in maternal or more generally parental love, and in caring love. Ultimately, the very Christian C.S. Lewis captured perfectly the difference and complementarity between agape and eros: "Without eros none of us would have been begotten and without [agape] none of us would have been reared."[663]

Over the centuries, the two energies of love that eros and agape embody have come to form a symbolic pair that is still very present in Christian theology, and, more generally, Western spirituality. Eros sparks from one's desire for a specific target and seeks union with the object of its affection in order to become whole again: the love of the lover for his/her beloved (either sexual or platonic), of the believer toward God, or of God for one of his particular sons or daughters. It is the transcending power of the divine as Plato understood it and that modern Christianity calls the "ascending path to God." On the other hand, agape flows freely regardless of the quality and identity of those who receive it—the unconditional love of parents for their children, of a preacher for his flock, of God for all his children, what modern Christianity recognizes as the "descending path."[664] Yet, in my opinion quantum physics, thanks to its dual theory of matter, offers the best analogy to help us grasp the fundamental difference between eros and agape: Eros is like a particle; it has a location and a trajectory; and when accelerated by invisible forces (whether attractive or repulsive) it hits its target in a blazing collusion. Agape, on the other hand, is of the same nature as a wave; it radiates in all directions blindly, fluid, impalpable. It merges, bounces, and reshapes itself endlessly.

When discussing love and sex, the powerful dynamic generated by eros and agape inevitably unfolds in the backdrop of another fundamental symbolic duality of Western culture: the gender polarity, that is, the masculine and the feminine. In many ways, the masculine and the feminine are none other than the Western version of the Yin and Yang central to Eastern philosophy. Remember that Axial thinkers unanimously envisioned the universe in terms of symmetries, complementary opposites, and hierarchies. For them, the world was split between the masculine/yang—active, bright, hot, and dry—and the feminine/yin—passive, dark, cold, and moist. Rare were the substances, objects, or individuals that partook of both equally—the androgyne archetype (the god Hermes is a typical example). Almost everything and everyone had to fall into one camp or another. If the nature of the masculine and feminine principles and their relevance regarding male and female natures have again become debatable matters today, thankfully, Western thinkers traditionally saw, in those two principles, the fundamental source of the differences between the male and female genders, that is, men and women (bear in mind however that ancients were also able to conceptualize gender inversion, as we have seen in previous chapters). This fundamental polarity explained not only why men and women are the way they are, but it also indicated the "natural order" by which both sexes must abide.

Sexual behavior (if not all human behaviors) was always interpreted through the lens of gender polarity and gender conformity, that is, male (or male-like) with female (or female-like), symbolically heterosexual no matter what, regardless of the biological and psychological sex of the people involved in the relationship. And if one understands this, one also understands why for centuries homosexual desire was understood in terms of gender inversion, that of the subject—the lover—or that of the object—the beloved. This is why, for instance, tribades were masculine women with penis-size clitorises, or why, according to Philo, the partner of the pederast was by necessity an effeminate man or boy. In reality, none of that was true, but those were the best concepts people of the time were able to devise so as to understand the world. From Aristotle's physics to Carl Jung's notion of animus-anima, this gender dichotomy has dominated Western symbolic culture ever since. Today, it is still strongly implanted in modern psychology and remains a given in the Judeo-Christian cosmology (see chapters 8 and 9).

I find it informative to report here the claims of two prominent twentieth century thinkers who both sought to match the eros-agape dynamic with the gender polarity. The first one is Carl Jung, who saw in eros a quintessentially feminine quality—the drive to create relationships—that he opposed not to agape, however, but to logos, which for him represented best the masculine principle of transcendence (that in many ways is also what platonic eros is about).[665] The second is Ken Wilber, who correlates the unquenchable thrust of eros and the all-encompassing embrace of agape with the masculine and feminine principles, respectively (opposing not only Jung, but also centuries of Christian theology, which never saw a contradiction between the fundamentally masculine nature of God-Christ and agapic love).[666] One cannot help concluding from this puzzling heterogeneity of opinion that the relation between love, sex, and the divine is far from having been sorted out.

However the Greeks had more to say about love than just debating about eros and agape. Philia, the third major form of love (commonly translated as friendship), was first theorized by Aristotle in his *Nicomachean Ethics*, but not well differentiated yet from the mere affection otherwise symbolized by storge. Philia's true depth would be revealed and celebrated only later in history.[667] For that matter, we owe Michel de Montaigne, French humanist of the sixteenth century, one of the most splendid, touching, and authentic accounts on friendship between two men. In one chapter of his *Essays* titled "De l'Amitié" ("Of Friendship"), Montaigne unveils the intimate bond that he had once shared with his friend Etienne de la Boétie, who unfortunately died a few years prior to the publication of Montaigne's masterpiece:

> In the friendship I speak of, our souls mingle and blend with each other so completely that they efface the seam that joined them, and cannot find it again. If you press me to tell why I loved him, I feel that this cannot be expressed, except by answering: Because it was he, because it was I.[668]

> He and I made our alliance a brotherhood.[669]

> He is myself.[670]

> One soul in two bodies.[671]

Philia's love—friendship—represents a radical departure from the love conveyed through eros or agape. One cannot miss the fundamental asymmetry that exists between subject and object inherent to both eros and agape. They both entail an imbalance between subject and object. None of that is present in philia. Philia is intrinsically characterized by a deep sense of mutuality, that is, a similar status and nature between the two members of the pair. Eros and agape require differences between subject and object; philia, on the other hand, dwells on sameness. When romantic passion relies on inequality ("in love there is nothing but a frantic desire for what flees from us"[672]), Montaigne remarked, "friendship feeds on communication."[673]

Certainly, the similitude between philia—so clearly encapsulated in the words sameness and mutuality—and modern homosexual love is unmistakable, stunning, and unavoidably, challenges us to clarify our thought. In fact, "homophilia," first coined in 1924 by the German astrologer and psychoanalyst Karl-Günther Heimsoth, was the term of choice among political organizations to designate homosexuality in the 1950s and 1960s in what would later be remembered as the Homophile Movement.[674] (Shortly after, the word "gay" imposed itself as the main alternative to "homosexual." The word "homophilia" sounded disturbingly like other less honorific sexual philias, such as zoophilia or necrophilia.)

However, when one speaks of symbolic resonance between homosexuality and friendship, it is Michel Foucault once again who offered the first and by far most visionary insights on the topic. In an interview to the French homosexual magazine *Gai Pied* in April 1981, he declared boldly that "the development towards which the problem of homosexuality tends is the one of friendship" (remember that in Foucault's discourse the term homosexuality relates essentially to modern homosexuality).[675] With little justification to his bold assertion, Foucault introduced a new query in the homosexual discourse—what is homosexuality's essence?—and a new context to address that question—homosexuality's essence is not to be discovered but to be created.

To unveil the profound and ancient connection between philia and homosexual love, one needs to trace the emergence of philia during evolution. Eros manifested first in the biological world very early (before the split between plant and animal species perhaps) through the sexual impulse; storge might represent the basic cohesion force present in all gregarious animal species, whether termites, geese, wolves, or human beings;[676] agape started to emerge later through the care of mothers for their progeny or the selfless sacrifice of males to defend their territory and other members of their group. Philia appeared last in animal evolution, no earlier than the last million years. In chapter 5, I described philia's emergence in great apes, especially chimpanzees and bonobos, through the establishment of lasting alliances between males and between females (I do not however preclude the existence of similar bonds in other highly evolved species other than apes).

In accordance with anthropological and early historical data of his time, C.S. Lewis discerned the origins of friendship in the "cooperation of the males as hunters or fighters."[677] But insofar as he could not have possibly known about the incredible social power and exuberant sexuality of female bonobos, Lewis must be forgiven for missing the evolutionary inception of friendship among females ("What were the women doing meanwhile? [. . .] I am only guessing. I can trace the prehistory of friendship only in the male line," Lewis confessed).[678] Interestingly, he inferred immediately that what makes the philia-friendship bond so evolutionarily unique is its very independence from the reproductive process, in which both eros and agape are so desperately trapped. Lewis is, once again, worth quoting: "Friendship," he says, "is [. . .] the least natural of loves; the least instinctive, organic, biological, gregarious and necessary. [. . .] The species, biologically considered, has no need of it."[679] The concordance between Lewis's conclusion and my own regarding the place of homosexuality in evolution is striking. (Homosexuality, I wrote earlier in the chapter titled *Away from Nature*, constitutes a "departure from the world of biological contingencies and the shortsighted strategy of instant gratification.") Philia, Lewis concludes, "of all the loves, seemed to raise you to the level of gods or angels."[680] I could not formulate it better.

One then cannot help noticing how much, all throughout history, the concept of friendship kept flirting with that of homosexual relationships. In Classical Greece the romantic relationship between the *erastes* and his *eromenos*, once the *eromenos* reached the age limit, was destined, ideally, to turn into a deep and lasting friendship. Moreover, the *eromenos* was supposed to respond his *erastes's* eros not with eros, but with philia (understood as moral, emotional, and intellectual but sexually uninterested; more generally however, philia and sexual desire were not mutually exclusive in Greek culture).[681] A similar transformation was observed in many tribal forms of homosexuality around the world: homosexual relationships often yielded to solid friendships in adulthood, which would forever stand out above any other clan bonds.

Philia-friendship permeates the love of heroes that populate ancient mythologies in the occasionally sexual friendship between Gilgamesh and Enkidu, the sexually ambiguous love between Achilles and Patroclus, and the passionate and yet chaste (my guess) friendship between David and Jonathan.[682] The love between heroes, as Montaigne contends in *De l'Amitié*, "constituted the strength of the countries which accepted the practice, and the principal defense of equity and liberty: witness the salutary loves of Harmodius and Aristogeiton [the two lovers who freed Athens from tyranny mentioned in Chapter 9]. Therefore they [people] call it sacred and divine."[683]

For better or worse, friendships stand out from the realm of common human relationships (storge). Some friendships are deemed divine and sacred, others sulfurous, uncontrollable, or even potentially destructive. "Every real friendship is a sort of secession, even a rebellion," asserts C.S. Lewis, who perfectly seized the ambiguous virtue of friendship.[684] And Montaigne, who talked about "friends more than citizens, friends more than friends or enemies of their country or friends of ambition and disturbance, [having] committed themselves absolutely to each other, they held absolutely the reins of each other's inclination," already knew that.[685] So two human beings linked by the sacred bond of philia-friendship may very well rebel against the social order and injustice. Regardless of what those legendary men or heroes did together in bed or not, their love—true, good, and beautiful, deep, intense, uncompromising, and committed—still inspires us. And nothing prevents us from appropriating the archetypal essence of heroic love so as to help us give homosexuality its new symbolic shape.

Remember however that the Greeks, just like the rest of the ancient world, never welcomed the possibility of sexual friendships involving two men or two women on an equal footing. Halperin visualized very clearly the direct symbolic contradiction that exists between traditional forms of homosexuality (and heterosexuality, for that matter) and the concept of friendship: "sexual love [in antiquity] is all about penetration and therefore all about position, superiority and inferiority, rank and status, gender and difference [. . .] It is this very emphasis on identity, similarity, and mutuality that distances the friendship tradition, in its original social and discursive context, from the world of sexual love."[686] In the sixteenth century Montaigne, in his curiously mellow critique of Greek love, made a very interesting point: "Since [Greek love] involved, moreover, according to their practice, such a necessary disparity in age and such a difference in the lovers' functions, it did not correspond closely enough with the perfect union and harmony [friendship] that we require here."[687] He then goes on by citing one of Cicero's great lines: "Why does no one love either an ugly youth, or a handsome old man?"[688]

For their minds and hearts entirely submitted to the rule of male ranking, not a single traditional culture, as far as I can tell, has ever succeeded in reconciling sexual desire with the concept of friendship among male adults, let alone females. The very devout C.S. Lewis could not bear the idea of homosexual friendships either, which he conceptualized as philia combined with "abnormal" eros.[689] But today, no longer preoccupied with the issue of male ranking, or obsessed with confining women in their homes and in pleasureless sex lives, and now free to love and desire any responsible and consenting adult, after having transcended fifty million years of sociobiological and cultural baggage (quite a feat), we are ready to explore the symbolic dimension of homosexual love within the concept of philia-friendship.

Can one reconcile eros, agape, and philia, heterosexuality and homosexuality, sex, love, and the divine-Spirit-God into a comprehensive model?[690] What I would like to do now, is to draw the grand lines of a model that could integrate all those elements, one that could function as our "working hypothesis" and, perhaps, a foundation for subsequent works.

Our model must first embrace the idea that sex is not eros's exclusive register. The Greeks never viewed it that way. Christianity, at its inception, used eros to evacuate sex from the sacred, but, if we now understand the Church's particular intention behind demonizing sex through eros, we equally understand that we no longer need to repress sexual desire or forbid the pleasures of the flesh in order to protect logos. Even the Catholic Church today has rehabilitated eros as being the yearning for God, the "ascending path." Eros includes the sexual impulse but should not be reduced to it. This is, I believe, a step in the right direction, but the first one only.

From this point on, I will posit that eros, agape, and philia all have the ability to express love through three distinct media: the love through the body that is sexual expression; the love through the mind, or the feeling of love (what we commonly call love); and the love through spirit, which I call here mystic love. In this model, loves end up being channeled through nine distinct forms or modalities— three distinct love energies through three different media—while the current culture gives us only three (sexual love exclusively through eros; agape as divine and parental love, sexually uninvolved and morally superior to all other forms of love; and philia as strictly asexual friendship). And in order to convince you further that this "love matrix" is by no means a mere abstraction, let me give you a glimpse of what those nine modalities may look like in human reality.

Eros expressed through the body is classically thought of as sexual desire, what Freud defined as the libido (the Latin word for desire). Through the mind eros generates longings and passions—the quasi-painful feeling of being in love as much as the intense desire for that beautiful Mercedes you can no longer live without. Eros "wants"—a beloved, a coveted object, money, or success—and it will make you run after what it wants. It might inspire, torture, or even destroy you, but it will not cease until you reach its goal. Through S/spirit, eros fuels one's ardent yearning for the mystic union with the divine (the ascending path). Eros is also found through God's penetrating and almighty power, which pierces the human soul like a sword when God, by revealing himself, burns you from the inside. When Yahveh appeared to Moses in the form of a burning bush, when the angel Gabriel announced to Mary that she was to bear God's son, and when Christ's sudden apparition blinded Paul on the road to Damascus—that is divine eros or, to put it bluntly, God's erotic power.

Let us now explore agape. Everywhere eros generates intensity, agape provides depth. Revealed through the body, agape is the sexual abandonment that no longer craves the inaccessible other, the sexual embrace with nothing more at stake other than embracing, caring, and giving. Agapic sex is the sex between lovers who know each other well. It is sacred sexuality, when sex is performed and offered as a mystic experience. Perhaps also, it is the sexual enjoyment one receives from a prostitute who authentically embodies his/her profession as a pleasure giver . . . who is to judge? Agapic sex is sex offered as a gift. But beware: agapic sex is not to be confused with passive sexuality, let alone female sexuality. Those two concepts may occasionally overlap with what I described above, yet they are very different. Agapic sex is fundamentally an active behavior—a liberated energy.

In human relationships, that is, through the mind, agapic love cares and protects, listens and understands, and does so without demanding anything particular in return: a mother's unconditional love for her children, the patriotic love of a warrior who is willing to die on the battlefield, the love of our great peace leaders for their people—Gandhi, Martin Luther King, and Mother Teresa. In its mystic form, so elegantly theorized by Christian theologians, agapic love is God's love for his people (the descending path) and its counterpart, one's surrendering to God's infinite and immanent love. Mystic agape is the total abandonment to the divine presence.

Now, what about philia? Remember that philia's key words are mutuality and sameness. The difference between subject and object, which is inherent to both eros and agape, is in philia reduced to the point of disappearing. Philia requires symmetry, that is, equal contributions from the two parties involved. Embodied in the flesh and expressed sexually, philia becomes a game, an exploration, or an adventure shared by two friends seeking intimacy and pleasure. Both parties play equivalent parts, unattached to a particular sexual role, intrinsically interchangeable. One does not win over the other, as with eros, and nobody loses oneself (other than in the intensity of the sexual act itself, of course), as with agape. Among men, when philia-friendship, the love of heroes, embraces sexual desire, it transmutes itself into the "love of comrades" so dear to Walt Whitman. It becomes modern homosexuality.

But notice how much lesbian love, more than any other form of love, has embodied philia. As a matter of fact, the symbolic resonance between the two is astonishing. I cannot help thinking about female bonobos and the playful and mutually empowering nature of their sexual relationships. Compare it to what Simone de Beauvoir wrote on the love between women in *The Second Sex*, her historic masterpiece: "Between women, love is contemplative; caresses are intended less to gain possession of the other than gradually to re-create the self through her; separateness is abolished, there is no struggle, no victory, no defeat; in exact reciprocity each is at once subject and object, sovereign and slave; duality becomes mutuality."[691] Echoing this, Jungian psychologist Christine Downing observed "how important to Sappho's understanding of love among women is the theme of reciprocity."[692] In other words, one cannot but recognize the historic and inspirational role of lesbianism in inventing homosexuality as we know it today.

Now, philiac sexuality is by no means restricted to homosexuality, nor, obviously, are all homosexual relationships philiac in nature. Philiac sexuality is also the sex that good friends, regardless of their sex, whether in a relationship or not, can venture into if they are not too afraid that eros might mess everything up (a situation that is not to be mistaken with two eros impulses happily responding to each other), or the sex that two longtime partners share when passion has turned into mutual trust and friendship, and when dominance is no longer at stake.

Love through the lens of philia and that of the mind is, we have seen, friendship—the deep and lasting bond between two friends, two partners, or two siblings: Montaigne and Etienne de le Boétie, Achilles and Patroclus, David and Jonathan, but also Simone de Beauvoir and Jean Paul Sartre. Now what is philia through spirit, philia in the mystic realm? That last question is not a common topic in theological discussion, and we can historically guess why. Literally, mystic philia symbolizes mutuality with the divine. It is relating to God on an equal footage, from spirit to "Spirit." Mystic philia no longer feels the burning desire to unite with God, nor is it liquified through its surrendering to God, but instead, it recognizes the possibility or, perhaps, the reality of an intimate friendship with God.

This said, do not forget that mutuality is distinct from total equality, let alone total identity. One has to be very careful about what equal footage means when relating with the divine. Mutuality is equality and sameness in the relating. In mystic philia, the human soul mirrors God, just like the human body mirrors the cosmos. Men and women constitute the microcosmic extremity of a divine macrocosm. Mystic philia abolishes the duality between humankind and God.

So, we now have a three by three matrix of what love can look like in the human universe:

[eros, agape, philia] x [body (sex), mind (feeling of love), spirit (mystic love)]

Both homosexual love and heterosexual love have the ability to tune into eros, agape, philia, or a combination of those three. This will depend on the people involved and the state of the relationship, but also on the prevailing cultural standards. Traditional forms, whether homosexual or heterosexual, have largely favored eros (although sexually repressed in the West) and, to some extent, agape. The historic emphasis on eros and agape both relied on and exacerbated the asymmetry between the male and female or male-like and female-like roles. On the other hand, the current model of romantic relationship, which we commonly call "modern" but truly is postmodern at this point, grants philia a more visible place in the couple's dynamic, due in great part to women's liberation and the rise of modern homosexuality. But when one observes things more closely, this apparent uniformity hides some striking disparities.

In heterosexual relationships, the inevitable difference between the male and female bodies precludes the full experience of philia at the sexual level. The female genital organs are not naturally equipped to penetrate the male body; hence heterosexual partners cannot reciprocate (assuming that the male partner might be interested, which is by no means a given). In other words, heterosexual couples may be able to experience philia at the level of the mind but hardly at the level of the body. However, the inherently asymmetrical heterosexual coupling possesses a unique and unequaled power: the ability to reproduce and generate new life, which homosexual coupling cannot do at the level of the body. Therefore, heterosexual love personifies eros.

On the other hand, homosexual partners can do exactly the same things to each other sexually. Thanks to the symmetry between their bodies and desires, modern homosexual lovers epitomize very naturally the love symbolized by philia. However, just like heterosexual couples need some sort of technical help in order to overcome their inherent insertive-receptive sexual polarity (sex toys) or impede the reproductive process (contraception), homosexual couples require assistance to break through the limits of conventional reproduction. In other word, they cannot count on the body alone. To bypass the issue of reproduction, they need to switch gears and use the mind—logos.

Evolutionarily speaking, eros and agape represent two distinct facets of the reproductive instinct. Eros finds the mate, and agape takes care of the young, as C.S. Lewis rightly puts it. Philia, as we have seen, is the first love to escape the weight of procreation, choosing instead to relate for the sake of relating only, at the levels of the body, mind, or spirit. For that reason it is a, if not the, central driving force in human culture. Yet philia would never have existed in the first place without eros and agape. Hence the three forms of love—eros, agape, and philia—are distinct and at the same time interdependent—another beautiful paradox in the integral landscape.

Modern homosexual love—philia's full embodiment—shifts the central concern of human relationships away from the strictly biological realm. If, from a symbolic standpoint, the creative power of heterosexual love is expressed in the miracle of procreation, the magic of homosexual love originates in that it liberates human beings from the reproductive process. When sexual culture denies homosexuality, that is, the sexual expression of philia, it unavoidably reduces heterosexual love to the love of "breeders." But when sexual culture embraces homosexual love in its bosom, it takes on an entirely new dimension. Homosexuality is by no means superior to heterosexuality. However, a vision of love that includes the entire spectrum of heterosexual and homosexual love—eros, agape, and philia— is evolutionarily infinitely superior.

Procreation viewed through the lens of philia arises as a creative act, not as the fulfillment of an instinct or a social duty. In a symbolic context that includes eros, agape, and philia, the procreative drive, although initially biological, becomes first and foremost a quest for beauty— that is, a creation in the three domains of body, mind, and spirit. Children are no longer the only valid justification for romantic pairing but instead a natural and authentic expression of the union between two human beings founded on love.

At the same time, it would be both reductive and inaccurate to believe that homosexual love is spiritual in essence or simply more spiritual than heterosexual love. The "love matrix" that I have presented earlier reminds us that eros, agape, and philia can all relate to the divine, even if they do so very differently. However, philia, the essence of modern homosexual love, allows human beings to transcend a relationship with the divine exclusively based on a symbolic scheme modeled after the procreative act—penetration or abandon, active or passive, male or female, and so forth. Philia's symbolic creative power extracts love, whether expressed through the body, the mind, or spirit, from the limitation of our biological nature—the evolutionary telos revealed in all its splendor.

✦ ✦ ✦

As Carl Jung justly observed, "Man cannot stand a meaningless life."[693] The absence of meaning, just like the absence of love, is inhuman. For that reason it was urgent to undertake a rigorous analysis of the homosexual phenomenon based on one central intention: to make sense of homosexuality, to reveal its truth, its goodness, and its beauty, without which not a single human being can function properly. Meaningfulness is a *sine qua none* condition to our happiness. I hope to have provided the beginning of an epistemological foundation upon which others will continue to build.

Homosexuality's history is nothing short of outstanding. From Socrates to Michel Foucault, from Leonardo da Vinci to Francis Beacon, and from Allen Ginsberg to Marguerite Yourcenar, homosexuals can be proud of their collective past. Their legacy in the realms of philosophy, art, science, and spirituality is extraordinary. Those men and women are our roots; we are their heirs. This is both a source of pride and a profound responsibility. Today, the many and invaluable contributions of scientists, theologians, psychologists, anthropologists, philosophers, and political activists all play their part in homosexuality's current evolution, one way or another.

Homosexuality will prevail as a creative force because it has always been one, even if that reality has seldom been acknowledged in our culture. It will survive its current identity crisis. Homosexual love is a process of inventing—of giving birth to—a love that encompasses the entire spectrum of body, mind, and spirit, free from all limitations. More than anybody else, Michel Foucault grasped homosexuality's critical role within the larger context of human relationships: "[. . .] gay culture," he intuited, "will not only be a choice of homosexuals for homosexuals—it would create relations that are, at certain points, transferable to heterosexuals. We have to reverse things a bit. [...] By proposing a new relational right, we will see that non-homosexual people can enrich their lives by changing their own schema of relations."[694] Then, at some point in the interview, Foucault muttered what is, I believe, one of the most profound statements ever made about homosexuality: "I'm not sure that we have to create our *own* culture. We have to *create* culture."[695]

Homosexual love is one of the many faces of the divine. It is sacred, universally present, eternally created, and the spiritual privilege of those who have no choice other than honoring its presence in their own flesh, mind, and soul. Homosexual love is not a gift to homosexuals only. It is the power of any who choose to love from an ontological and spiritual—human and divine—context that embraces homosexual love. Free from any constraint and reinvented as a space of conscious contribution to human evolution, homosexuality comes forth as a fertile soil where new meanings for what it is to be human will emerge. The task that lies before us is extraordinary. We have an entire culture to reinvent. And here, following Michel Foucault's advice to himself, I will end with his words:

> [...] the idea of a program of proposals is dangerous. As soon as a program is presented, it becomes a law, and there's a prohibition against inventing.[696]

> [...] I am wary of imposing my own views or of setting down a plan, or a program. I don't want to discourage invention, don't want gay people to stop feeling that it is up to them to adjust their own relationship by discovering what is appropriate in their situations. [...] Gays have to work out some of these matters themselves.[697]

REFERENCES

Adam, Barry D. 1986. "Age, Structure, and Sexuality: Reflections on the Anthropological Evidence on Homosexual Relations." In *Anthropology and Homosexual Behavior*, edited by Evelyn Blackwood, 19–33. New York: Haworth Press.

Adriaens, Pieter R. and Andreas De Block. 2006. "The Evolution of a Social Construction: The Case of Male Homosexuality." *Perspectives in Biology and Medicine* 49: 570–85.

Allen, Laura S. and Gorski, Roger A. 1992. "Sexual Orientation and the Size of the Anterior Commissure in the Human Brain." *Proceedings of the National Academy of Science* 89:7199–202.

Allen, Laura S., M. Hines, J.E. Shryne, and R.A. Gorski. 1989. "Two Sexually Dimorphic Cell Groups in the Human Brain." *Journal of Neuroscience* 9:497–506.

Allen, Robert H. 2006. *The Classical Origins of Modern Homophobia*. Jefferson: McFarland &. Company.

Amstrong, Karen. 2005. *A Short History of Myth*. Edinburgh: Canongate.

Atsalis, S. and S.W. Margulis. 2008. "Perimenopause and Menopause: Documenting Life Changes in Aging Female Gorillas." *Interdisciplinary Topics in Gerontology* 36:119–46.

Axel, Richard. 1995. "The Molecular Logic of Smell." *Scientific American* 273:130–37.

Bagemihl, Bruce. 1999. *Biological Exuberance: Animal Homosexuality and Natural Diversity*. New York: St. Martin Press.

Bailey J. Michael, R.C. Pillard, K. Dawood, M.B. Miller, L.A. Farrer, S. Trivedi, and R.L. Murphy. 1999. "A Family History Study of Male Sexual Orientation Using Three Independent Samples." *Behavioral Genetics* 29:79–86.

Bailey, J. Michael and Richard C. Pillard. 1991. "A Genetic Study of Male Sexual Orientation." *Archives of General Psychiatry* 48:1089–96.

Bailey, J. Michael, Michael P. Dunne, and Nicholas G. Martin. 2000. "Genetic and Environmental Influences on Sexual Orientation and its Correlates in an Australian Twin Sample." *Journal of Personality and Social Psychology* 78:524–36.

Bailey, J. Michael, Richard C. Pillard, Michael C. Neale, Yvonne Agyei. 1993. "Heritable Factors Influence Sexual Orientation in Women." *Archives of General Psychiatry* 50:217–23.

Bajko, Matthew S. 2007. "Castro Boosters Look over the Rainbow." *Bay Area Reporter* online, May 17. Accessed Jun 4, 2012. http://www.ebar.com/news/article.php?sec=news&article=1657.

Bamford, Helen. 2007. "Cape Straight Invade Gay Patch." *Sunday Tribune*, February 11, p.7

Banbury, Samantha. 2004. "Coercive Sexual Behaviour in British Prisons as Reported by Adult Ex-Prisoners." *The Howard Journal* 43:113–30.

Bateman, Robert Benjamin. 2006. "What Do Gay Men Desire? Peering Behind the Queer Eye." In *The New Queer Aesthetic on Television*, edited by James R. Keller and Leslie Stratyner, 9–19. Jefferson: McFarland.

Baum, Michael J. 2006. "Mammalian animal models of psychosexual differentiation: When is 'translation' to the human situation possible?" *Hormones and Behavior* 50:579–588.

Baum, Robert M. 1993. "Homosexuality and the Traditional Religions of the Americas and Africas." In *Homosexuality and World Religions*, edited by Arlene Swider, 1–46. Harrisburg: Trinity Press International.

Beauchamp, Gary K. and Julie A. Mennella. 2009. "Early Flavor Learning and its Impact on Later Feeding Behavior." *Journal of Pediatric Gastroenterology and Nutrition* 48:25–30.

Beck, Don and Christopher Cowan. 1996. *Spiral Dynamics: Mastering Values, Leadership, and Change*. Malden: Blackwell.

Berglund, Hans, Per Lindström, and Ivanka Savic. 2006. "Brain Response to Putative Pheromones in Lesbian Women." *Proceedings of the National Academy of Science* 103:8269–74.

Berman Louis A. 2003. *The Puzzle, Exploring the Evolutionary Puzzle of Male Homosexuality*. Wilmette: Godot Press.

Bérubé, Allan. 1989. "Marching to a Different Drummer: Lesbian and Gay GIs in World War II." In *Hidden from History: Reclaiming the Gay and Lesbian Past*, edited by M.B. Duberman, M. Vicinus, and G. Chauncey, 383–94. New York: New American Library.

Blackwood, Evelyn. 1986. "Breaking the Mirror: The Construction of Lesbianism and the Anthropological Discourse on Homosexuality." In *Anthropology and Homosexual Behavior*, edited by Evelyn Blackwood, 1–17. New York: The Haworth Press.

Blanchard, Ray. 2004. "Quantitative and Theoretical Analyses of the Relation between Older Brothers and Homosexuality in Men." *Journal of Theoretical Biology* 230:173–87.

Blankenhorn, David and Jonathan Rauch. 2009. "A Reconciliation on Gay Marriage." *New York Times*, February 22. Accessed January 23, 2012. http://www.nytimes.com/2009/02/22/opinion/22rauch.html.

Bocklandt, Sven and Eric Vilain. 2007. "Sex Differences in Brain and Behavior: Hormones Versus Genes." *Advances in Genetics* 59:245–66.

Bocklandt, Sven, Steve Horvath, Eric Vilain, and Dean H. Hamer. 2006. "Extreme Skewing of X Chromosome Inactivation in Mothers of Homosexual Men." *Human Genetics* 118:691–94.

Bogaert, Anthony F., Chris Friesen, and Panagiota Klentrou. 2002. "Age of Puberty and Sexual Orientation in a National Probability Sample." *Archives of Sexual Behavior* 31:73–81.

Borris, Kenneth. 2008. "The Prehistory of Homosexuality in the Early Modern Sciences." In *The Sciences of Homosexuality in Early Modern Europe*, edited by Kenneth Borris and George Rousseau, 1–40. New York: Routledge.

Bosnak Robert. 1993. "Individuation, Taboo, and Same-Sex Love." In *Same-Sex Love and the Path to Wholeness*, edited by Robert H. Hopcke, Karin Lofthus Carrington, and Scotte Wirth, 264–272. Boston: Shambhala.

Boswell, John. 1980. *Christianity, Social Tolerance, and Homosexuality*. Chicago: University of Chicago Press.

Boswell, John. 1994. *Same-Sex Unions in Premodern Europe*. New York: Vintage Books.

Boyarin, Daniel. 2007. "Against Rabbinic Sexuality." In *Queer Theology, Rethinking the Western Body*, edited by Gerard Loughlin, 131–46. Malden: Blackwell.

Brewer, Paul R. 2003. "The Shifting Foundations of Public Opinion about Gay Rights." *Journal of Politics* 65:1208–20.

Bronner, Ethan. 2008. "Ancient Tablet Ignites Debate on Messiah and Resurrection." *New York Times*, July 6. Accessed January 24, 2012. http://www.nytimes.com/2008/07/06/world/middleeast/06stone.html.

Brooten, Bernadette. 1996. *Love Between Women*. Chicago: The University of Chicago Press.

Brown, Judith. C. 1989. "Lesbian Sexuality in Medieval and Early Modern Europe." In *Hidden from History: Reclaiming the Gay and Lesbian Past*, edited by M.B. Duberman, M. Vicinus, and G. Chauncey, 67–75. New York: New American Library.

Brown, Robert and Ruth Washton. 2010. "The Gay and Lesbian Market in the U.S.: Trends and Opportunities in the LGBT Community, 6th Edition." Packaged Facts published by MarketResearch.com. Accessed January 18, 2012. http://www.marketresearch.com/Packaged-Facts-v768/Gay-Lesbian-Trends-Opportunities-LGBT-2690458.

Brown, Tom. 2002. "A Proposed Model of Bisexual Identity Development that Elaborates on Experiential Differences of Women and Men." *Journal of Bisexuality* 2:67–91.

Bullough, L.V. 1976. *Sexual Variance*. Chicago: University of Chicago Press.

Bullough, Vern L. and Bonnie Bullough. 1995. *Sexual Attitudes: Myths and Realities*. Amherst: Prometheus Books.

Burg, Barry Richard. 1984. *Sodomy and the Pirate Tradition: English Sea Rovers in the Seventeenth-Century Caribbean*. New York: New York University Press.

Byne, William, Stuart Tobet, Linda A. Mattiace, Mitchell S. Lasco, Eileen Kemether, Mark A. Edgar, Susan Morgello, Monte S. Buchsbaum, and Liesl B. Jones. 2001. "The Interstitial Nuclei of the Human Anterior Hypothalamus: An Investigation of Variation with Sex, Sexual Orientation and HIV Status." *Hormones and Behavior* 40:86–92.

Byne, William. 1994. "The Biological Evidence Challenged." *Scientific American* 270:50–55.

Byrne, Richard W. 2007. "Ape Society: Trading Favours." *Current Biology* 17:R775–R776.

Campbell, Denis. 2005. "3,6m People in Britain Are Gay - Official." *Guardian*, December 10. Accessed January 13, 2012. http://www.guardian.co.uk/uk/2005/dec/11/gayrights.immigrationpolicy?INTCMP=SRCH

Campbell, Joseph. 2001. *Thou Art That*. Novato: New World Library.

Campbell, Joseph. 2004. *Pathway to Bliss*. Novato: New World Library.

Camperio-Ciani, Andrea, Francesca Corna, and Claudio Capiluppi. 2004. "Evidence for Maternally Inherited Factors Favouring Male Homosexuality and Promoting Female Fecundity." *Proceedings of the Royal Society of London B* 271:2217–21.

Canadé Sautman, Francesca. 1996. "Invisible Women." In *Homosexuality in Modern France*, edited by Jeffrey Merrick and Bryant T. Ragan, Jr., 177–201. New York: Oxford University Press.

Cass, Vivienne C. 1979. "Homosexuality Identity Formation." *Journal of Homosexuality* 4:219–35.

Cass, Vivienne C. 1984a. "Homosexual Identity: A concept in Need of Definition." *Journal of Homosexuality* 9:105–26.

Cass, Vivienne C. 1984b. "Homosexual Identity Formation: Testing a Theoretical Model." *Journal of Sex Research* 20:143–67.

Cloud, John. 2005. "The Battle over Gay Teens." *Time Magazine*, October 2. Accessed November 9, 2007. http://www.time.com/time/printout/0,8816,1112856,00.html.

Conner, Randy P. 1993. *Blossom of Bone, Reclaiming the Connections Between Homoeroticism and the Sacred*. San Francisco: HarperCollins.

Conner, Randy P., David Hatfield Sparks and Mariya Sparks. 1997. *Cassell's Encyclopedia of Queer Myth, Symbol, and Spirit*. London: Cassell.

Coontz, Stephanie. 2006. *Marriage, a History: How Love Conquered Marriage*. New York: Penguin.

Crompton, Louis. 2003. *Homosexuality and Civilization*. Cambridge: The Belknap Press.

Csikszentmihalyi, Mihaly. 1996. *Creativity*. New York: Harper Perennial.

Culbertson, Philip L. 1996. "Men and Christian Friendship." In *Men's Bodies, Men's Gods: Male Identities in a (Post) Christian Culture*, edited by Björn Krondorfer, 149–80. New York: New York University Press.

Dalai Lama. 2005. *The Universe in a Single Atom*. London: Abacus.

Davidson, James. 2007. *The Greeks and Greek Love*. London: Phoenix.

de Beauvoir, Simone. 1953 (reprinted 1989). *The Second Sex*. New York: Vintage.

De Cecco, John P. and David Allen Parker. 1995. "The Biology of Homosexuality: Sexual Orientation or Sexual Preference?" In *Sex, Cells, and Same-Sex Desire: The Biology of Sexual Preference*, edited by John P. De Cecco and David Allen Parker, 1–27. Binghamton: Haworth Press.

de Waal, Frans. 1986. "The Integration of Dominance and Social Bonding in Primates." *Quaterly Review of Biology* 61:459–79.

de Waal, Frans. 1995. "Sex as an Alternative to Aggression in Bonobo." In *Sexual Nature Sexual Culture*, edited by Paul R. Abramson and Steven D. Pinkerton, 37–56. Chicago: University of Chicago Press.

de Waal, Frans. 2000. "Primates—A Natural Heritage of Conflict Resolution." *Science* 289: 586–90.

de Waal, Frans. 2005. "A Century of Getting to Know the Chimpanzee." *Nature* 237:56–59.

de Waal, Frans. 2009. *The Age of Empathy: Nature's Lessons for a Kinder Society*. New York: Three Rivers Press.

de Waal, Frans. 2010. "Morals Without God." *New York Times* online, the Opinion Pages, October 17. Accessed January 23, 2010. http://opinionator.blogs.nytimes.com/2010/10/17/morals-without-god.

Diamond, Lisa M. 2007. "A Dynamical Systems Approach to the Development and Expression of Female Same-Sex Sexuality." *Perspectives on Psychological Science* 2:142–61.

Diamond, Milton. 1993. "Homosexuality and Bisexuality in Different Populations." *Archives of Sexual Behavior* 22(4), 291–310.

Dixson, Alan. 1998. *Primate Sexuality: Comparative Studies of the Prosimians, Monkeys, Apes, and Human Beings*. New York: Oxford University Press.

Donaldson, Stephen. 1990. "Rape of Males." In *Encyclopedia of Homosexuality*, edited by Wayne R. Dynes. New York: Garland, 1990. Accessed January 18, 2012. http://www.williamapercy.com/wiki/index.php/Portal:EOH.

Doty, G. William. 2000. *Mythography*. Tuscaloosa: University of Alabama Press.

Douglas, Mary. 1966. *Purity and Danger*. London: Routledge.

Dover, Kenneth J. 1978. *Greek Homosexuality*. Cambridge: Harvard University Press.

Dover, Kenneth J. 1997. "Greek Homosexuality and Initiation." In *Que(e)rying Religion: a Critical Anthology*, edited by Gary David Comstock and Susan E. Henking, 19–38. New York: Continuum.

Downing, Christine 1989. *Myths and Mysteries of Same-Sex love.* New York: Continuum.

Downing, Christine. 1993. "Coming Home. The Late-Life Lesbian." In *Same-Sex Love and the Path to Wholeness*, edited by Robert H. Hopcke, Karin Lofthus Carrington, and Scotte Wirth, 28–37. Boston: Shambhala.

Downing, Christine. 1997. "Lesbian Mythology." In *Queering Religion*, edited by Gary David Comstock and Susan E. Henking, 415–40. New York: Continuum.

Duffy, Kimberly G., Richard W. Wrangham and Joan B. Silk. 2007. "Male chimpanzees exchange political support for mating opportunities." *Current Biology* 17:R586–R587.

Dulac, Catherine and Thomas Torello. 2003. "Molecular Detection of Pheromone Signal in Mammals: From Genes to Behaviors." *Nature Neuroscience* 4:551–62.

Duran, Khalid. 1993. "Homosexuality and Islam." In *Homosexuality and World Religions*, edited by Arlene Swider, 181–97. Harrisburg: Trinity Press International.

Eglinton, J.Z. 1964. *Greek Love.* New York: Oliver Layton Press.

Elegant, Simon. 2008. "Post Card: Beijing." *New York Times*, January 24. Accessed February 8, 2008. http://www.time.com/time/printout/0,8816,1706776,00.html.

Eliade, Mircea. 1957. *Mythes, Rêves, et Mystères.* Paris: Gallimard.

Eliade, Mircea. 1963 (reprinted 1998). *Myth and Reality.* Long Grove: Waveland Press.

Eliade, Mircea. 1968. *The Sacred and the Profane.* New York: Houghton Mifflin Harcourt.

Empereur, James L. 1998. *Spiritual Direction and the Gay Person.* New York: Continuum.

Eribon, Didier. 1999. *Reflection sur la Question Gay.* Paris: Fayard.

Feldmesser, Ester, Dani Bercovich, Nili Avidan, Shmuel Halbertal, Liora Haim, Ruth Gross-Isseroff, Sivan Goshen and Doron Lancet. 2007. "Mutations in Olfactory Signal Transduction Genes Are Not a Major Cause of Human Congenital General Anosmia." *Chemical Senses* 32:21–30.

Fone, Byrne. 2000. *Homophobia.* New York: Picador.

Foster, Thomas A. 2011. "The Sexual Abuse of Black Men under American Slavery." *Journal of the History of Sexuality* 20:445–64.

Foucault, Michel. 1970 (reprinted 1994). *The Order of Things.* New York: Vintage Books.

Foucault, Michel. 1978. *History of Sexuality, Volume 1: An Introducion.* New York: Random House Pantheon Books.

Foucault, Michel. 1985. *History of Sexuality, Volume 2: The Use of Pleasure.* New York: Random House Vintage Books.

Foucault, Michel. 1986. *History of Sexuality, Volume 3: The Care of Self.* New York: Pantheon Books.

Foucault, Michel. 1997. *Ethics: Subjectivity and Truth*, edited by Paul Rabinow. New York: New Press.

Fox, Elizabeth A. 2001. "Homosexual Behavior in Wild Sumatran Orangutans (Pongo pygmaeus abelii)." *American Journal of Primatology* 55:177–81.

Fraga, Mario F., Esteban Ballestar, Maria F. Paz, Santiago Ropero, Fernando Setien, Maria L. Ballestar, Damia Heine-Suñer, Juan C. Cigudosa, Miguel Urioste, Javier Benitez, Manuel Boix-Chornet, Abel Sanchez-Aguilera, Charlotte Ling, Emma Carlsson, Pernille Poulsen, Allan Vaag, Zarko Stephan, Tim D. Spector, Yue-Zhong Wu, Christoph Plass, and Manel Esteller. 2005. "Epigenetic Differences Arise during the Lifetime of Monozygotic Twins." *Proceedings of the National Academy of Science* 102:10604-49.

Francks, C., S. Maegawa, J. Lauren, B.S. Abrahams, A. Velayos-Baeza, S.E. Medland, S. Colella, M. Groszer, E.Z. McAuley, T.M. Caffrey, T. Timmusk, P. Pruunsild, I. Koppel, P.A. Lind, N. Matsumoto-Itaba, J. Nicod, L. Xiong, R. Joober, W. Enard, B. Krinsky, E. Nanba, A.J. Richardson, B.P. Riley, N.G. Martin, S.M. Strittmatter, H.J. Moller, D. Rujescu, D. St Clair, P. Muglia, J.L. Roos, S.E. Fisher, R. Wade-Martins, G.A. Rouleau, J.F. Stein, M. Karayiorgou, D.H. Geschwind, J. Ragoussis, K.S. Kendler, M.S. Airaksinen, M. Oshimura, L.E. DeLisi and A.P. Monaco. 2007. "LRRTM1 on Chromosome 2p12 is a Maternally Suppressed Gene that is Associated Paternally with Handedness and Schizophrenia." *Molecular Psychiatry* 12:1129–39.

Freud, Sigmund. 1910. *Three Contributions to the Sexual Theory.* New York: The Journal of Nervous and Mental Disease Publishing Company.

Freud, Sigmund. 1916 (reprinted 2001). *Leonardo da Vinci.* New York: Routledge.

Friederici, Angela D., Christian J. Fiebach, Matthias Schlesewsky, Ina D. Bornkessel and D. Yves von Cramon. 2006. "Processing Linguistic Complexity and Grammaticality in the Left Frontal Cortex." *Cerebral Cortex* 16:1709–17.

Fry, Peter. 1986. "Male Homosexuality and Spirit Possession in Brazil." In *Anthropology and Homosexual Behavior,* edited by Evelyn Blackwood, 137–53. New York: Haworth Press.

Gaca, Kathy L. 2003. *The Making of Fornication: Eros, Ethics, and Political Reform in Greek Philosophy and Early Christianity.* Berkeley: University of California Press.

Gates, Gary J. 2006. "Same-sex Couples and the Gay, Lesbian, Bisexual Population: New Estimate for the American Community Survey." The Williams Institute. Accessed on January 14, 2012. http://escholarship.org/uc/item/8h08t0zf#page-1.

Gates, Gary J. 2010. "Sexual Minorities in the 2008 General Social Survey: Coming Out and Demographic Characteristics." The Williams Institute. Accessed on January 14, 2012. http://williamsinstitute.law.ucla.edu/wp-content/uploads/Gates-Sexual-Minorities-2008-GSS-Oct-2010.pdf.

Gates, Gary J., Ost, Jason. 2004. *Gay and Lesbian Atlas.* The Urban Insitute.

Gatewood, Jessica D., Aileen Wills, Savera Shetty, Jun Xu, Arthur P. Arnold, Paul S. Burgoyne, and Emilie F. Rissman. 2006. "Sex Chromosome Complement and Gonadal Sex Influence Aggressive and Parental Behaviors in Mice." *Journal of Neuroscience* 26:2335–42.

Gay, Judith. 1986. " 'Mummies and Babies' and Friends and Lovers in Lesotho." In *Anthropology and Homosexual Behavior,* edited by Evelyn Blackwood, 97–116. New York: The Haworth Press.

Gellman, Jerome. 2006. "Gender and Sexuality in the Garden of Eden." *Theology and Sexuality* 12:319–36.

Gettleman, Jeffrey. 2009. "Symbol of Unhealed Congo: Male Rape Victims." *New York Times,* August 4. Accessed on January 18, 2012. http://www.nytimes.com/2009/08/05/world/africa/05congo.html.

Ghadami, Mohsen, Keyvan Majidzadeh-A, Saeid Morovvati, Elia Damavandi, Gen Nishimura, Kazuki Komatsu, Akira Kinoshita, Mohammad-Taghi Najafi, Norio Niikawa, and Koh-ichiro Yoshiura. 2004. "Isolated Congenital Anosmia With Morphologically Normal Olfactory Bulb in Two Iranian Families: A New Clinical Entity?" *American Journal of Medical Genetics* 127:307–09.

Gilbert, Arthur N. 1977. "Sexual Deviance and Disaster During the Napoleonic Wars." *Albion* 9:98–113.

Gilbert, Arthur N. 1981. "Conception of Homosexuality and Sodomy in the Western World." In *Historical Perspectives on Homosexuality*, edited by Salvatore J. Licata and Robert P. Petersen, 57–68. New York: Harthworth Press & Stein and Day.

Gilbert, Arthur N. and Michael Barkun. 1981. "Disaster and Sexuality." *Journal of Sex Research* 17:288–99.

Gomes, Cristina M. and Christophe Boesch. 2009. "Wild Chimpanzees Exchange Meat for Sex on a Long-Term Basis." *PLoS ONE* 4:e5116.

Gooren, Louis. 2006. "The Biology of Human Psychosexual Differentiation." *Hormones and Behavior* 50:589–601.

Gorski, Roger A., J.H. Gordon , J.E. Shryne , and A.M. Southam. 1978. "Evidence for a Morphological Sex Difference within the Medial Preoptic Area of the Rat Brain." *Brain Research* 148:333–46.

Greenberg, David F. 1986. "Why Was the Berdache Ridiculed?" In *Anthropology and Homosexual Behavior*, edited by Evelyn Blackwood, 178–89. New York: The Haworth Press.

Greenberg, David F. 1988. *The Construction of Homosexuality*. Chicago: University of Chicago Press.

Greenberg, David F. and Marcia H. Bystryn. 1982. "Christian Intolerance of Homosexuality." *American Journal of Sociology* 88:515–48.

Greenberg, Steven. 2004. *Wrestling with God and Men, Homosexuality in the Jewish Tradition*. Madison: University of Wisconsin Press.

Gross, Michael Joseph. 2008. "Has Manhunt destroyed Gay Culture?" *Out*, August 4. Accessed August, 29, 2008. http://www.out.com/entertainment/2008/08/04/has-manhunt-destroyed-gay-culture.

Haggerty, George E., editor. 2000. *Gay Histories and Cultures: An Encyclopedia*. New York: Taylor & Francis.

Hahn, Matthew W., Jeffery P. Demuth, and Sang-Gook Han. 2007. "Accelerated Rate of Gene Gain and Loss in Primates." *Genetics* 177:1941–49.

Halperin, David M. 1990. *One Hundred Years of Homosexuality*. New York: Routledge.

Halperin, David M. 2002. *How to do the History of Homosexuality*. Chicago: The University of Chicago Press.

Halperin, David M. 2007. *What Do Gay Men Want? An Essay on Sex, Risk, and Subjectivity*. Ann Arbor: University of Michigan Press.

Halperin, David M. 2012. "Normal as Folk." *New York Times*, June 21.

Hamer, Dean H., Stella Hu, Victoria L. Magnuson, Nan Hu, Angela M.L. Pattatucci. 1993. "A Linkage between DNA Markers on the X Chromosome and Male Sexual Orientation." *Science* 261:321–27.

Hammer, Michael F., Fernando L. Mendez, Murray P. Cox, August E. Woerner, Jeffrey D. Wall. 2008. "Sex-Biased Evolutionary Forces Shape Genomic Patterns of Human Diversity." *PLoS Genetics* 4:1–8.

Harris, W. C. 2006. "Queer Eye on the Prize: The Stereotypical Sodomites of Summer." In *The New Queer Aesthetic on Television*, edited by James R. Keller and Leslie Stratyner, 20–42. Jefferson: McFarland.

Herdt, Gilbert and Robert J. Stoller (1990). *Intimate Communications: Erotics and the Study of Culture*. New York: Columbia University Press.

Herdt, Gilbert. 1984. "Ritualized Homosexual Behavior in the Male Cults of Melanesia, 1862–1983: An Introduction." In *Ritualized Homosexuality in Melanesia*, edited by Gilbert Herdt, 1–82. Berkeley: University of California Press.

Herdt, Gilbert. 1989. "Introduction: Gay and Lesbian Youth, Emergent Identities, and Cultural Scenes at Home and Abroad." In *Gay and Lesbian Youth*, edited by Gilbert Herdt, 1–42. Binghamton: Harrington Park Press.

Herdt, Gilbert. 1991a. "Representation of Homosexuality: An Essay on Cultural Ontology and Historical Comparison, Part I." *Journal of the History of Homosexuality* 1:481–504.

Herdt, Gilbert. 1991b. "Representation of Homosexuality: An Essay on Cultural Ontology and Historical Comparison, Part II." *Journal of the History of Homosexuality* 1:603–32.

Herrada, Gilles and Catherine Dulac. 1997. "A Novel Family of Putative Pheromone Receptors in Mammals with a Topographically Organized and Sexually Dimorphic Distribution." *Cell* 90:763–73.

Herrada, Gilles. Forthcoming. "Up and Beyond Gay Pride." In *Integral Perspectives on Diversity*, edited by Toni Gregory and Michael Raffanti. Albany: SUNY Press.

Herzer, Manfred. 1986. "Kertbeny and the Nameless Love." *Journal of Homosexuality* 12:1–26.

Hocquenghem, Guy. 1978 (reprinted 1993). *Homosexual desire*. Durham: Duke University Press.

Hoffman, Richard J. 1984. "Vices, Gods, and Virtues." *Journal of Homosexuality* 9:27:44.

Hopcke, Robert H. 1995. *Persona: Where Sacred Meets Profane*. Boston: Shambhala.

Hu, Stella, Angela M. Pattatucci, Chavis Patterson, Lin Li, David W. Fulker, Stacey S. Cherny, Leonid Kruglyak, Dean H. Hamer. 1995. "Linkage between Sexual Orientation and Chromosome Xq28 in Males but not in Females." *Nature Genetics* 11:248–56.

Hubbard, Thomas. 2003. *Homosexuality in Greece and Rome: A Sourcebook of Basic Documents*. Berkeley: University of California Press.

Imani, Ko. 2003. *Shirt of Flame: The Secret Gay Art of War*. Ypsilanti: Goko Media.

Isay, Richard A. 1989. *Being Homosexual*. New York: Avon Books.

Isay, Richard A. 2006. *Commitment and Healing: Gay Men and the Need for Romantic Love*. Hoboken New Jersey: Wiley & Sons.

Jablonka, Eva and Marion J. Lamb. 2006. *Evolution in Four Dimensions: Genetic, Epigenetic, Behavioral, and Symbolic Variation in the History of Life*. Cambridge: MIT Press.

James, Scott. 2011. "Change With a Straight Face Barrels Into the Castro." *New York Times*, May 8, 2011.

Jepsen, Gary R. 2006. "Dale Martin's 'arsenokoitai and malakos': Tried and Found Wanting." *Currents in Theology and Mission* 33:397–405.

Joost-Gaugier, Christiane L. 2006. *Measuring Heaven: Pythagoras and His Influence on Thought and Art in Antiquity and the Middle Ages*. Ithaca: Cornell University Press.

Jung, Carl G. 1964 (Reedition 1968). "Approaching the Unconscious." In *Man and His Symbols*, edited by Carl G. Jung. New York: Dell Publishing.

Jung, Carl. 1953 (reprinted 1990). *Two Essays on Analytical Psychology*. London: Routledge.

Jung, Carl. 1989. *Aspects of the Masculine*. Princeton: Princeton University Press.

Kallmann, F. J. 1952. "Comparative Twin Studies on the Genetic Aspects of Male Homosexuality." *Journal of Nervous and Mental Disease* 115:283–98.

Kandel, Eric R. and Thomas M. Jessel. 1995. "Sensory Experience and the Formation of Visual Circuits." In *Essentials of Neural Science and Behavior*, edited by Eric R. Kandel, James H. Schwartz, and Thomas M. Jessel, 469–84. Norwalk: Appleton and Lange.

Karama, Sherif, Andre Roch Lecours, Jean-Maxime Leroux, Pierre Bourgouin, Gilles Beau-doin, Sven Joubert, and Mario Beauregard. 2002. "Areas of Brain Activation in Males and Females During Viewing of Erotic Film Excerpts." *Human Brain Mapping* 16:1–13.

Kegan, Robert and Lisa Laskow Lahey. 2001. *How the Way We Talk Can Change the Way We Work*. San Francisco: Jossey-Bass.

Kendler, Kenneth S., Laura M. Thornton, Stephen E. Gilman, Ronald C. Kessler. 2000. "Sexual Orientation in a U.S. National Sample of Twin and Nontwin Sibling Pairs." *American Journal of Psychiatry* 157:1843–46.

Kennedy, Hubert. 1997. "Karl Heindrich Ulrichs, First Theorist of Homosexuality." In *Science and Homosexualities*, edited by Vernon A. Rosario, 26–45. New York: Routledge.

King, Michael, and Elizabeth McDonald. 1992. "Homosexuals Who are Twins. A Study of 46 Probands." *British Journal of Psychiatry* 160:407–09.

Kinnunen, Leann H., Howard Moltz, John Metz, and Malcolm Cooper. 2006. "Differential Brain Activation in Exclusively Homosexual and Heterosexual Men Produced by the Selective Serotonin Reuptake Inhibitor, Fluoxetine." *Brain Research* 1024:251–54.

Kirkpatrick, R.C. 2000. "The Evolution of Human Homosexual Behaviors." *Current Anthropology* 41:385–413.

Knauft, Bruce M. 2003. "What Ever Happened to Ritualized Homosexuality? Modern Sexual Subjects in Melanesia and Elsewhere." *Annual Review of Sex Research* 14:137–59.

Kohl, James Vaughn and Robert T. Francoeur. 1995. *The Scent of Eros*. New York: Continuum.

Kuhl, Patricia and Maritza Rivera-Gaxiola. 2006. "Neural Substrates of Language Acquisition." *Annual Review of Neuroscience* 31:511–34.

Laumann, Edward O., Gagnon, John H., Michael, Robert T., and Michaels, Stuart. 1994. *The Social Organization of Sexuality Sexual Practice in the United States*. Chicago: The University of Chicago Press.

Layard, John. 1959. "Homo-Eroticism in Primitive Society as a Function of the Self." *Journal of Analytical Psychology* 4:101–15.

Lee, Ryan. 2007. "Demolished Gay Bars Make Way for Midtown's Future." *Southern Voice*, March 9, p. 5–8.

Lestrade, Didier. 2007. "1001 Secrets de la Culture Gay." *Têtu*, November 1.

LeVay, Simon. 1991. "A Difference in Hypothalamic Structure between Heterosexual and Homosexual Men." *Science* 253:1034 –37.

LeVay, Simon. 1993. *The Sexual Brain*. Cambridge: MIT Press.

LeVay, Simon. 2010. *Gay, Straight, and the Reason Why: The Science of Sexual Orientation*. New York: Oxford University Press.

Lewis, Carl S. 1960 (reprinted 1971). *The Four Loves*. San Diego: Harcourt.

Leypold, Bradley G., C. Ron Yu, Trese Leinders-Zufall, Michelle M. Kim, Frank Zufall, and Richard Axel. 2002. "Altered Sexual and Social Behaviors in trp2 Mutant Mice." *Proceedings of the National Academy of Science* 99:6376–81.

Licata, Salvatore J. 1981. "The Homosexual Right Movement in the United States. A Traditionally Overlooked Area of American History." In *Historical Perspectives on Homosexuality*, edited by Salvatore J. Licata and Robert P. Petersen, 161–90. New York: Harthworth Press & Stein and Day.

Licata, Salvatore J. and Robert P. Petersen. 1981. "Introduction." In *Historical Perspectives on Homosexuality*, edited by Salvatore J. Licata and Robert P. Petersen, 3–10. New York: Harthworth Press & Stein and Day.

Liu, Yan, Yun'ai Jiang, Yunxia Si, Ji-Young Kim, Zhou-Feng Chen, and Yi Rao. 2011. "Molecular Regulation of Sexual Preference Revealed by Genetic Studies of 5-HT in the Brains of Male Mice." *Nature* 472:95–99.

Lockard, Denyse. 1986. "The Lesbian Community: An Anthropological Approach." In *Anthropology and Homosexual Behavior*, edited by Evelyn Blackwood, 83–95. New York: The Haworth Press.

Long, Ronald E. 2004. *Men, Homosexuality, and the Gods: An Exploration into the Religious Significance of Male Homosexuality in World Perspective*. Binghamton: Harrington Park Press.

Loughlin, Gerard. 2007. "Introduction: The End of Sex." In *Queer Theology*, Rethinking the Western Body, edited by Gerard Loughlin, 1–34. Malden: Blackwell.

Loughlin, Gerard. 2007. "Omphalos." In *Queer Theology*, Rethinking the Western Body, edited by Gerard Loughlin, 115–27. Malden: Blackwell.

Lovejoy, C. Owen. 1981. "The Origin of Man." *Science* 211:331–50.

Malinowski, Bronislaw. 1954. *Magic, Science and Religion and Other Essays*. New York, Doubleday Anchor Book.

Manning, John T., Andrew J. G. Churchill and Michael Peters. 2007. "The Effects of Sex, Ethnicity, and Sexual Orientation on Self-Measured Digit Ratio (2D:4D)." *Archives of Sexual Behaviors* 36:223–33.

Martin, Dale B. 1996. "Arsenokoitai and Malakos: Meanings and Consequences." In *Biblical Ethics and Homosexuality: Listening to Scripture*, edited by Robert L. Brawley, 117–36. Louisville: Westminster John Knox.

Martin, James T. and Duc Huu Nguyen. 2004. "Anthropometric Analysis of Homosexuals and Heterosexuals: Implications for Early Hormone Exposure." *Hormones and Behavior* 45:31–39.

McDonald Pavelka, Mary S. 1995. "Sexual Nature: What Can We Learn from a Cross-Species Perspective?" In *Sexual Nature Sexual Culture*, edited by Paul R. Abramson and Steven D. Pinkerton, 17–36. Chicago: University of Chicago Press.

Mennella, Julie A., Coren P. Jagnow, and Gary K. Beauchamp. 2001. "Prenatal and Postnatal Flavor Learning by Human Infants." *Pediatrics* 107:e88.

Michaelson, Jay. 2008. "Chaos, Law, and God: The Religious Meanings of Homosexuality." *Michigan Journal of Gender & Law* 15:41–19.

Miller, Neil. 1995 (reprinted 2006). *Out of the Past, Gay and Lesbian History from 1969 to Present*. New York: Alyson Books.

Mitani, John C. and David P. Watts. 2001. "Why Do Chimpanzees Hunt and Share Meat?" *Animal Behaviour* 61:915–24.

Morris, John A., Cynthia L. Jordan and S. Marc Breedlove. 2004. "Sexual Differentiation of the Vertebrate Nervous System." *Nature Neuroscience* 7:1043–39.

Murray, Stephen O. 2000. *Homosexualities*. Chicago: University of Chicago Press.

Murray, Stephen O. 2002. *Pacific Homosexualities*. Lincoln: iUniverse.

Murray, Stephen O. and Will Roscoe. 1998. *Boys-Wives and Female Husbands.* New York: Palgrave.

Muscarella, Frank. 1999. "The Homoerotic Behavior That Never Evolved." *Journal of Homosexuality* 37:1–18.

Muscarella, Frank. 2000. "The Evolution of Homoerotic Behavior in Humans." *Journal of Homosexuality* 40:51–77.

Mustanski, Brian S., Meredith L. Chivers, J. Michael Bailey. 2002. "A Critical Review of Recent Biological Research on Human Sexual Orientation." *Annual Review of Sex Research* 13: 114–15.

Mustanski, Brian S., Michael G. DuPree, Caroline M. Nievergelt, Sven Bocklandt, Nicholas J. Schork and Dean H. Hamer. 2005. "A Genomewide Scan of Male Sexual Orientation." *Human Genetics* 116:272–78.

Nanda, Serena. 1986. "The Hijras of India: Cultural and Individual Dimensions of an Institutionalized Third Gender Role." In *Anthropology and Homosexual Behavior*, edited by Evelyn Blackwood, 35–54. New York: The Haworth Press.

Neiman, Susan. 2008. "Idealism for Grown-ups." Interview with Susan Neiman by Elizabeth Debold. *EnlightenNext*, December. Accessed January 20, 2012. http://www.enlightennext. org/magazine/j42/neiman.asp.

Nelson, James B. 1978. *Embodiement.* Minneapolis: Augsburg Publishing House.

Neumann, Erich. 1954. *The Origins and History of Consciousness.* Princeton: Princeton University Press.

Nielsen, Rasmus, Carlos Bustamante, Andrew G. Clark, Stephen Glanowski, Timothy B. Sackton, Melissa J. Hubisz, Adi Fledel-Alon, David M. Tanenbaum, Daniel Civello, Thomas J. White, John J. Sninsky, Mark D. Adams, Michele Cargill. 2005. "A Scan for Positively Selected Genes in the Genomes of Humans and Chimpanzees." *PLoS Biology* 3:976–85.

Nishida, T. and K. Hosaka. 1996. "Coalition Strategies among Adult Male Chimpanzees of the Mahale Mountains." In *Great ape societies*, edited by Linda Frances Marchant and Toshisada Nishida, 114–32. Cambridge: Cambridge University Press.

O'Hara, S.J. and P.C. Lee. 2006. "High Frequency of Postcoital Penis Cleaning in Budongo Chimpanzees." *Folia Primatologica* 77:353–58.

O'Neill, John 1996. "Marxism and Mythology." *Ethics* 77:38–49.

Olyan, Saul M. 1994. "'And with a Male You Shall Not Lie the Lying down of a Woman': On the Meaning and Significance of Leviticus 18:22 and 20:13." *Journal of the History of Sexuality* 5:179–206.

Pakaluk, Michael, editor. 1991. "Montaigne, 'Of Friendship.'" In *Other Selves: Philosophers on Friendship*, 185–99. Indianapolis: Hackett.

Paul, Thomas, Boris Schiffer, Thomas Zwarg, Tillmann H.C. Krüger, Sherif Karama, Manfred Schedlowski, Michael Forsting, and Elke R. Gizewski. 2008. "Brain Response to Visual Sexual Stimuli in Heterosexual and Homosexual Males." *Human Brain Mapping* 29:726–35.

Pearson, Willow. 2006. "The Development of Desire." *AQAL* 1:276–96.

Perez, Joe. 2007. *Soulfully Gay.* Boston: Integral Books.

Perkins, Anne and Charles E. Roselli. 2007. "The Ram as a Model for Behavioral Neuroendocrinology." *Hormones and Behavior* 52:70–77.

Peters, N.J. 2006. *Conundrum: The Evolution of Homosexuality.* Bloomington: AuthorHouse.

Pigliucci, Massimo. 2008. "Is Evolvability Evolvable?" *Nature Reviews Genetics* 9:75:82.

Pillard, Richard C, James D. Weinrich. 1986. "Evidence of Familial Nature of Male Homosexuality." *Archives of General Psychiatry* 43:808–12.

Pinker, Steven. 1994. *The language Instinct*. New York: Harper Perennial Classics.

Pinker, Steven. 2007. "A History of Violence." *New Republic*, March 19. Accessed January 25, 2012. http://pinker.wjh.harvard.edu/articles/media/2007_03_19_New%20Republic.pdf.

Pinker, Steven. 2009. "My Genome, My Self." *New York Times*, January 11.

Ragan, Bryant T. Jr. 1996. "The Enlightenment Confronts Homosexuality." In *Homosexuality in Modern France*, edited by Jeffrey Merrick and Bryant T. Ragan, Jr., 8–29. New York: Oxford University Press.

Rahman, Qazi. 2005. "The Neurodevelopment of Human Sexual Orientation." *Neuroscience and Biobehavioral Reviews* 29:1057–66.

Ray, Nicholas. 2006. "Lesbian, Gay, Bisexual and Transgender Youth: An Epidemic of Homelessness." Report by The National Gay and Lesbian Task Force Policy Institute and the National Coalition for the Homeless. Accessed December 15, 2011. http://www.thetask-force.org/downloads/HomelessYouth.pdf.

Rice, George, Carol Anderson, Neil Risch, and George Ebers. 1999. "Male Homosexuality: Absence of Linkage to Microsatellite Markers at Xq28." *Science* 283:665–67.

Rickman, John, editor. 1957. *A General Selection from the Works of Sigmund Freud*. New York: Doubleday Anchor Books.

Ringrose, Kathryn. 1993. "Living in the Shadows: Eunuchs and Gender in Byzantium." In *Third Sex Third Gender*, edited by Gilbert Herdt, 85–109. New York: Zone Books.

Rist, John M. 1982. *Human Value: A Study in Ancient Philosophical Ethics*. Laiden: E.J. Brill.

Robbins, Andrew M., Martha M. Robbins, Netzin Gerald-Steklis, and H. Dieter Steklis. 2006. "Age-Related Patterns of Reproductive Success Among Female Mountain Gorillas." *American Journal of Physical Anthropology* 131:511–21.

Rogers, Carl. 1959. "A Theory of Therapy, Personality and Interpersonal Relationships, as Developed in the Client-Centered Framework." In *Psychology: A Study of Science(3)*, edited by Sigmund Koch. New York: McGraw Hill.

Rogers, Eugene F. Jr. 2007. "Bodies Demand Language, Thomas Aquinas." In *Queer Theology, Rethinking the Western Body*, edited by Gerard Loughlin, 176–87. Malden: Blackwell.

Rosario, Margaret, Eric W. Schrimshaw, Joyce Hunter, and Lisa Braun. 2006. "Sexual Identity Development among Gay, Lesbian, and Bisexual Youths: Consistency and Change Over Time." *Journal of Sex Research* 43:46–58.

Rosario, Vernon A. 1996. "Pointy penises, Fashion Crimes, and Hysterical Mollies." In *Homosexuality in Modern France*, edited by Jeffrey Merrick and Bryant T. Ragan, Jr., 146–76. New York: Oxford University Press.

Rosario, Vernon A. 2009. "Quantum sex: Intersex and the Molecular Deconstruction of Sex." *GLQ: A Journal of Lesbian and Gay Studies* 15:267–84.

Roscoe, Will. 1998. *Changing Ones: Third and Forth Gender in Native North America*. New York: St. Martin Press.

Roselli, Charles E., Henry Stadelman, Reed Reeve, Cecily V. Bishop and Fred Stormshak. 2007. "The Ovine Sexually Dimorphic Nucleus of the Medial Preoptic Area Is Organized Prenatally by Testosterone." *Endocrinology* 148:4450–57.

Rouquier, Sylvie, Antoine Blancher, and Dominique Giorgi. 2000. "The Olfactory Receptor Gene Repertoire in Primates and Mouse: Evidence for Reduction of the Functional Fraction in Primates." *Proceedings of the National Academy of Science* 97:2870–74.

Rupp, Leila J. 2009. *Sapphistries*. New York: New York University Press.

Russell, Stephen T., Thomas J. Clarke, and Justin Clary. 2009. "Are Teens ''Post-Gay''? Contemporary Adolescents' Sexual Identity Labels." *Journal of Youth and Adolescence* 38:884–890.

Saewyc, Elizabeth M. 2011. "Research on Adolescent Sexual Orientation: Development, Health Disparities, Stigma, and Resilience." *Journal of Research on Adolescence* 21:256–272.

Sanello, Frank. 2005. *Tweakers*. Los Angeles: Allyson Books.

Sankar, Andrea. 1986. "Sisters and Brothers, Lovers and Enemies: Marriage Resistance in Southern Kwangtung." In *Anthropology and Homosexual Behavior*, edited by Evelyn Blackwood, 68–81. New York: The Haworth Press.

Savage, Dan. 2005. *The Commitment*. New York: Penguin.

Savic, Ivanka and Per Lindström. 2008. "PET and MRI Show Differences in Cerebral Asymmetry and Functional Connectivity between Homo- and Heterosexual Subjects." *Proceedings of the National Academy of Science* 105:9403–08.

Savic, Ivanka, Hans Berglund, and Per Lindström. 2005. "Brain Response to Putative Pheromones in Homosexual Men." *Proceedings of the National Academy of Science* 102:7356 –61.

Savic, Ivanka, Hans Berglund, Balazs Gulyas, and Per Roland. 2001. "Smelling of Odorous Sex Hormone-like Compounds Causes Sex-Differentiated Hypothalamic Activations in Humans." *Neuron* 31:661–68.

Savin-Williams, Ritch C. 2005. *The New Gay Teenager*. Cambridge: Harvard University Press.

Savolainen, Vincent and Laurent Lehmann. 2007. "Genetics and Bisexuality." *Nature* 445: 158–59.

Schüklenk, Udo and Michelle Murrain. 2000. "Scientific Approaches to Homosexuality." In *Gay Histories and Cultures: An Encyclopedia*, edited by George E. Haggerty, 781–85. New York: Garland Publishing.

Sergent, Bernard. 1996. *Homosexualité et Initiation chez les Peuples Indo-Européens*. Paris: Payot.

Serpenti, Laurent. 1984. "The Ritual Meaning of Homosexuality and Pedophilia among the Kiman-Papuans of South Irian Jaya." In *Ritualized Homosexuality in Melanesia*, edited by Gilbert Herdt, 292–317. Berkeley: University of California Press.

Shah, Nirao M., David J. Pisapia, Silas Maniatis, Monica M. Mendelsohn, Adriana Nemes, and Richard Axel. 2004. "Visualizing Sexual Dimorphism in the Brain." *Neuron* 43:313–19.

Shumaker, R.W., S.A. Wich, L. Perkins. 2008. "Reproductive Life History Traits of Female Orangutans (Pongo spp.)." *Interdisciplinary Topics in Gerontology* 36, 147–61.

Schelling, Friedrich Wilhelm Joseph Von. 2007 (Reedition). *Historical-Critical Introduction to the Philosophy of Mythology*. Albany: State University of New York Press.

Sibalis, Michael David. 1996. "The Regulation of Male Homosexuality in Revolutionary and Napoleonic France, 1789–1815." In *Homosexuality in Modern France*, edited by Jeffrey Merrick and Bryant T. Ragan, Jr., 80–101. New York: Oxford University Press.

Singer, Peter. 1981 (reprinted 2011). *The Expanding Circle: Ethics, Evolution, and Moral Progress*. Princeton: Princeton University Press.

Sivakumaran, Sandesh. 2007. "Sexual Violence Against Men in Armed Conflict." *European Journal of International Law* 18: 253–76.

Sommer, Volker and Paul L.Vasey. 2006. "Part 1, Introduction." In *Homosexual Behaviour in Animals - An Evolutionary Perspective*, edited by Volker Sommer and Paul L.Vasey. Cambridge: Cambridge University Press.

Stanford, Craig B. 1999. *The Hunting Apes*. Princeton: Princeton University Press.

Stener Carlson, Eric. 1997. "Sexual Assault on Men in War." *Lancet* 349:29.

Stern, Kathleen and Martha K. McClintock. 1998. "Regulation of Ovulation by Human Pheromones." *Nature* 392:177–79.

Storr, Merl. 1999. *Bisexuality: A Critical Reader*. New York: Routledge.

Stowers, Lisa and Darren W. Logan. 2010. "Olfactory Mechanisms of Stereotyped Behavior: On the Scent of Specialized Circuits." *Current Opinion in Neurobiology* 20:274–80.

Stowers, Lisa, Timothy E. Holy, Markus Meister, Catherine Dulac, and Georgy Koentges. 2002. "Loss of Sex Discrimination and Male-Male Aggression in Mice Deficient for TRP2." *Science* 295:1493–500.

Sullivan, Andrew. 1996. *Virtually Normal*. New York: Vintage.

Sullivan, Andrew. 1997. *Same-sex Marriage: Pro and Con, a Reader*. New York: Vintage Book.

Sullivan, Andrew. 2005. "The End of Gay Culture and the Future of Gay Life." *New Republic*, November 1. Accessed January 13, 2012. http://sullivanarchives.theatlantic.com/main_article.php.artnum-20051101.html.

Swaab, Dick F. 2008. "Sexual Orientation and its Basis in Brain Structure and Function." *Proceedings of the National Association for Science* 105:10273–74.

Swaab, Dick F. and Eric Fliers. 1985. "A Sexually Dimorphic Nucleus in the Human Brain." *Science* 228:1112–15.

Symonds, John Addington. 1928 (reprinted 2003). *Studies in Sexual Inversion Embodying: A Study in Greek Ethics and A Study in Modern Ethics*. Whitefish: Kessinger Publishing.

Tacey, David J. 1993. "Homoeroticism and Homophobia in Heterosexual Male Initiation." In *Same-Sex Love and the Path to Wholeness*, edited by Robert H. Hopcke, Karin Lofthus Carrington, and Scotte Wirth, 246–63. Boston: Shambhala.

Tarnas, Richard. 2006. *Cosmos and Psyche*. New York: Viking.

Taylor, Timothy. 1996. *The Prehistory of Sex*. New York: Bantam Books.

Teilhard De Chardin, Pierre. 1959. *The Phenomenon of Man*. New York: HarperCollins.

Thompson, Melissa Emery, James H. Jones, Anne E. Pusey, Stella Brewer-Marsden, Jane Goodall, David Marsden, Tetsuro Matsuzawa, Toshisada Nishida, Vernon Reynolds, Yukimaru Sugiyama, and Richard W. Wrangham. 2007. "Aging and Fertility Patterns in Wild Chimpanzees Provide Insights into the Evolution of Menopause." *Current Biology* 17: 2150–56.

Tirindelli, Roberto, Michele Dibattista, Simone Pifferi, and Anna Menini. 2009. "From Pheromones to Behavior." *Physiology Review* 89:921–56.

Tobin, Robert D. 2005. "Kertbeny's 'Homosexuality' and the Language of Nationalism." In *Genealogies of Identity: Interdisciplinary Readings on Sex and Sexuality*, edited by Margaret Sönser Breen and Fiona Peters, 3–18. Amsterdam: Rodopi BV.

Tovée, Martin J. 1996. *An Introduction to the Visual System*. Cambridge: Cambridge University Press.

Troiden, Richard. 1989. "The Formation of Homosexual Identities." In *Gay and Lesbian Youth*, edited by Gilbert Herdt, 43–74. Binghamton: Harrington Park Press.

Troiden, Richard. 1998. "A Model of Homosexual Identity Formation." In *Social Perspectives in Lesbian and Gay Studies: A Reader*, edited by Peter M. Nardi and Beth E. Schneider, 261–78. New York: Routledge. (Originally published in 1988 as Gay and Lesbian Identity: A Sociological Analysis. Dix Hills: General Hall).

Trumbach, Randolph 1993. "London's Sapphists: From Three Sexes to Four Genders in the Making of Modern Culture." In *Third Sex Third Gender*, edited by Gilbert Herdt, 111–36. New York: Zone Books.

Trumbach, Randolph. 1989. "The Birth of the Queen: Sodomy and the Emergence of the Gender Equality in Early Modern Culture." In *Hidden from History: Reclaiming the Gay and Lesbian Past*, edited by M.B Duberman, M Vicinus, and G. Chauncey, 129–40. New York: New American Library.

Tucker, Robert. 1961. *Philosophy and Myth in Karl Marx*. Cambridge: Cambridge University Press.

Turner, Edith and Pamela R. Frese. 2005. "Marriage." In *Encyclopedia of Religions*, second edition, edited by Lindsay Jones, volume 8, 5724–27. Farmington Hills: Thomson Gale.

van Agtmael, Tom, Susan M. Forrest, Jurgen Del-Favero, Christine Van Broeckhoven, and Robert Williamson. 2003. "Parametric and Nonparametric Genome Scan Analyses for Human Handedness." *European Journal of Human Genetics* 11:779–83.

Vasey, Paul and Volker Sommer. 2006. "Homosexual Behaviour in Animals: Topics, Hypotheses and Research Trajectories." In *Homosexual Behaviour in Animals an Evolutionary Perspective*, edited by Paul Vasey and Volker Sommer, 3–42. Cambridge: Cambridge University Press.

Vasey, Paul L. 1995. "Homosexual Behaviors in Primates: A Review of Evidence and Theory." *International Journal of Primatology* 16:173:204.

Vasey, Paul L. and James G. Pfaus. 2005. "A Sexually Dimorphic Hypothalamic Nucleus in a Macaque Species with Frequent Female–Female Mounting and Same-Sex Sexual Partner Preference." *Behavioural Brain Research* 157:265–72.

Vasey, Paul L., David S. Pocock, Doug P. VanderLaan. 2007. "Kin Selection and Male Androphilia in Samoan Fa'afafine." *Evolution and Human Behavior* 28:159–67.

Vernon, Mark. 2000. "What Are Gay Men for?" *Theology and Sexuality* 7:63–76.

Videan, E.N., J. Fritz, C.B. Heward, J. Murphy. 2008. "Reproductive Aging in Female Chimpanzees (Pan troglodytes)." *Interdisciplinary Topics in Gerontology* 36:103–18.

Voracek, Martin, John T. Manning, and Ivo Ponocny. 2005. "Digit Ratio (2D:4D) in Homosexual and Heterosexual Men from Austria." *Archives of Sexual Behavior* 34:335–40.

Wainberg, Milton L., Frederick Muench, Jon Morgenstern, Eric Hollander, Thomas W. Irwin, Jeffrey T. Parsons, Andrea Allen, and Ann O'Leary. 2006. "A Double-Blind Study of Citalopram Versus Placebo in the Treatment of Compulsive Sexual Behaviors in Gay and Bisexual Men." *Journal of Clinical Psychiatry* 67:1968–73.

Walsh, Jerome T. 2001. "Leviticus 18:22 and 20:13: Who Is Doing What to Whom?" *Journal of Biblical Literature* 120:201–09.

Wang, Sijia, Nicolas Ray, Winston Rojas, Maria V. Parra, Gabriel Bedoya, Carla Gallo, Giovanni Poletti, Guido Mazzotti, Kim Hill, Ana M. Hurtado, Beatriz Camrena, Humberto Nicolini, William Klitz, Ramiro Barrantes, Julio A. Molina, Nelson B. Freimer, Maria Cátira Bortolini, Francisco M. Salzano, Maria L. Petzl-Erler, Luiza T. Tsuneto, José E. Dipierri, Emma L. Alfaro, Graciela Bailliet, Nestor O. Bianchi, Elena Llop, Francisco Rothhammer, Laurent

Excoffier, Andrés Ruiz-Linares. 2008. "Geographic Patterns of Genome Admixture in Latin American Mestizos." *PLoS Genetics* 4:1–9.

Watanabe, John, and Barbara Smuts. 1999. "Explaining Religion without Explaining It Away: Trust, Truth, and the Evolution of Cooperation in Roy A. Rappaport's 'The Obvious Aspect of Ritual.'" *American Anthropologist* 101:98–112.

Watts, David P., Martin Muller , Sylvia J. Amsler, Godfrey Mbabazi, and John C. Mitani. 2006. "Lethal Intergroup Aggression by Chimpanzees in Kibale National Park, Uganda." *American Journal of Primatology* 68:161–80.

Whitam, Frederic L., Milton Diamond, and James Martin. 1993. "Homosexual Orientation in Twins: A Report on 61 Pairs and Three Triplets Sets." *Archives of Sexual Behavior* 22: 187–206.

Whiten, A., J. Goodall, W. C. McGrew, T. Nishida, V. Reynolds, Y. Sugiyama, C.E.G. Tutin, R.W. Wrangham and C. Boesch. 1999. "Cultures in Chimpanzees." *Nature* 399:682–85.

Wilber, Ken. 2000 (second edition, revised). *Sex, Ecology, and Spirituality*. Boston: Shambhala.

Williams, Craig A. 1995. "Greek Love at Rome." *Classical Quaterly* 45:517–39.

Wilson, David Sloan and Edward O. Wilson. 2007. "Rethinking the Theoretical Foundation of Sociobiology." *The Quarterly Review of Biology* 82:327–48.

Wilson, Edward O. 1963. "Pheromones." *Scientific American* 5:2–11.

Wilson, Edward O. 1975. *Sociobiology: The New Synthesis*. Cambridge: Belknap.

Wilson, Edward O. 1978. *On Human Nature*. Cambridge: Harvard University Press.

Wilson, Glenn and Qazi Rahman. 2008. *Born Gay*. London: Peter Owen.

Witham, Larry. 2005. *The Measure of God: History's Greatest Minds Wrestle with Reconciling Science and Religion*. New York: HarperCollins.

Wrangham, Richard and Dale Peterson. 1996. *Demonic Males*. New York: Houghton Mifflin Company.

Yamagiwa, Juichi. 2006. "Playful Encounters: The Development of Homosexual Behaviors in Male Mountain Gorillas." In *Homosexual Behaviour in Animals: An Evolutionary Perspective*, edited by Paul Vasey and Volker Sommer, 273–93. Cambridge: Cambridge University Press.

Zawati, Hilmi M. 2007. "Impunity or Immunity: Wartime Male Rape and Sexual Torture as a Crime against Humanity." *Torture* 17: 27–47.

NOTES

1 "If a man also lie with mankind, as he lieth with a woman, both of them have committed an abomination: they shall surely be put to death; their blood shall be upon them." Leviticus 20:13 (King James Version).
2 "And the Lord spoke to Moses, saying, 'Take outside the camp him who has cursed; then let all who heard him lay their hands on his head, and let all the congregation stone him. 'Then you shall speak to the children of Israel, saying: 'Whoever curses his God shall bear his sin. And whoever blasphemes the name of the Lord shall surely be put to death. All the congregation shall certainly stone him, the stranger as well as him who is born in the land. When he blasphemes the name of the Lord, he shall be put to death." Leviticus 24:13–16. Unless specified, biblical quotes are from the New International Version.
3 "Anyone who curses his father or mother must be put to death." Exodus 21:17.
4 "A man or woman who is a medium or spiritist among you must be put to death. You are to stone them; their blood will be on their own heads." Leviticus 20:27.
5 "Then the Lord said to Moses, 'Say to the Israelites, 'You must observe my Sabbaths. This will be a sign between me and you for the generations to come, so you may know that I am the Lord, who makes you holy. 'Observe the Sabbath, because it is holy to you. Anyone who desecrates it must be put to death; whoever does any work on that day must be cut off from his people." Exodus 31:12–14.
6 "But if out in the country a man happens to meet a girl pledged to be married and rapes her, only the man who has done this shall die." Deuteronomy 22:25. However, the severity of the punishment varies dramatically whether the women is "pledged to be married" or not: "If a man happens to meet a virgin who is not pledged to be married and rapes her and they are discovered, he shall pay the girl's father fifty shekels of silver. He must marry the girl, for he has violated her. He can never divorce her as long as he lives." Deuteronomy 22:28–29.
7 Isay 1989, 133.
8 Isay 2006, 132.
9 Lestrade 2007, 84 (translated by the author).
10 Cloud 2005.
11 Lestrade 2007, 84 (translated by the author).
12 Savin-Williams 2005
13 Savin-Williams 2005
14 A 2009 study shows that about a third of non-heterosexual youth (10th–12th grades) does not identify with historically typical sexual identities (i.e., gay, lesbian, and bisexual) and prefer other less typical or undefined qualifiers (e.g., queer [5%], "questioning" [13%], pansexual, "everything," "anything," "open," 'hetero-flexible," "bisexually gay," "bi-curious," and so forth). Yet the same study does not investigate whether the youths among the two-third that identifies as either gay/homosexual, lesbian, or bisexual are actually satisfied with their adopted identity. Russel *et al.* 2009.
15 Cloud 2005.
16 "It is indeed hard not to feel some sadness at the end of a rich, distinct culture built by pioneers who braved greater ostracism than today's generation will ever fully understand." Sullivan 2005.
17 Regarding this matter, one can read David Halperin's recent article in the *New York Times* that also discusses the issue of integrity versus integration. Halperin 2012.

18 Sullivan 2005. Author's personal observations.

19 Author's personal observations.

20 Author's personal observations.

21 Lee 2007.

22 Sullivan 2005.

23 Bamford 2007.

24 Bajko 2007. James 2011.

25 Sullivan (who is only two years apart from me in age, I believe) reports similar impressions. Sullivan 2005.

26 Sullivan 2005.

27 Sullivan 2005.

28 Sullivan 2005.

29 Elegant 2008.

30 Sullivan 2005.

31 One can read the 2011 Report of the United Nations High Commissioner for Human Rights, *Discriminatory laws and practices and acts of violence against individuals based on their sexual orientation and gender identity*. Accessed November, 17, 2011. http://www2.ohchr.org/english/bodies/hrcouncil/docs/19session/a.hrc.19.41_english.pdf.

32 Gerard Loughlin, drawing on David Halperin writings, summarized the aversion of queer theory (and his own, I believe) for the concept of homosexual essence. Loughlin 2007, 9.

33 Kegan and Lahey 2001.

34 Randy Conner gives an exhaustive list of books and groups recapitulating very conveniently this particular approach to gay spirituality: "Since the 1970s, literary texts focusing on our domain have proliferated. Indeed, a canon of such works is emerging. It includes Arthur Evans's Witchcraft and the Gay Counterculture, Mitch Walker's Visionary Love, Larry Mitchell's The Faggots and Their Friends Between Revolutions, Judy Grahn's Another Mother Tongue, Mark Thompson's Gay Spirit, Walter Williams's The Spirit and the Flesh, Will Roscoe's Living the Spirit (with Gay American Indians) and The Zuni Man-Woman, Bradley Rose's Of Intermediate Concern, the essays of Harry Hay and John Burnside, and the journals RFD, Ganymede, The Crucible, White Crane, Marilyn Medusa, New Uranian, Coming Out Pagan, and Lavender Pagan. Also since the 1970s, fueled in part by the emergence of the neopagan, gay, and feminist-spiritual movements, groups and gatherings embracing the interrelationship of homoeroticism, gender variance, and sacred experience have proliferated. These have included Gay Voices and Visions, the Yellow Rose Tribe, the Radical Faeries, the Congregation of Hermes, Tayu Center for Gay Spirituality, Body Electric School of Massage, the Gay Metaphysical Spiritual Association, COGS (Conference of Gay Spirituality), EroSpirit, Treeroots, Shaman's Circle, Gay Spirit Journeys, Heart and Fire Gay Men's Gatherings, Light Touch Retreats, Wicca for Gay Men, the Queer (or lavender) Pagans, and Faggot Witch Camp. Gatherings of these groups, often held outdoors, frequently include self- and group-empowering rituals blending ancient wisdom with contemporary psychological and political perspectives." Conner 1993, 11–12.

35 Modern justice dedicates a lot of energy trying to determine the real intention of a criminal. This issue is also central to modern psychology and, in general, therapeutic techniques, which all aim at unveiling one's true intentions, true thoughts, and true feelings.

36 Humanist psychologist Carl Roger defines empathy as followed: "The state of empathy, or being empathic, is to perceive the internal frame of reference of another with accuracy and with the emotional components and meanings which pertain thereto as if one were the person, but without ever losing the 'as if' condition. Thus, it means to sense the hurt or the pleasure of another as he senses it and to perceive the causes thereof as he perceives them, but without ever losing the recognition that it is as if I were hurt or pleased, etc. If this 'as if' quality is lost, then the state is one of identification." Rogers 1959, 210–211.

37 Foucault 1970, 157.

38 Hocquenghem 1978, 55.

39 Halperin 2002, 10.

40 Introducing the first volume of his *History of Sexuality*, Foucault proclaimed that his "main concern will be to locate the forms of power, the channels it takes, and the discourses it

permeates in order to reach the most tenuous and individual modes of behavior, the paths that give it access to the rare or scarcely perceivable forms of desire, how it penetrates and controls everyday pleasure-all this entailing effects that may be those of refusal, blockage, and invalidation, but also incitement and intensification: in short, the 'polymorphous techniques of power.' And finally, the essential aim will not be to determine whether these discursive productions and these effects of power lead one to formulate the truth about sex, or on the contrary falsehoods designed to conceal that truth, but rather to bring out the 'will to knowledge' that serves as both their support and their instrument." Foucault 1978, 15–16.

41 Wilber 2000, 149. To Wilber's list, I would add the three domains of human experience defined by Jacques Lacan: the Imaginary, the Symbolic and the Real, which roughly correspond to the I, the we, and the it.

42 Men and women included. Campbell 2005.

43 BBC online. Accessed Jan 14, 2012. http://www.bbc.co.uk/news/uk-11398629

44 A study conducted in 1994 estimated the U.S. gay and lesbian population to 2.8% and 1.4% retrospectively (Laumann et al. 1994, 295). Another survey by the National Survey of Family Growth realized in 2006 reported 4.1% of men and women between 18 and 45 years old are self-declared homosexuals and bisexuals (Gates 2006).

45 Gates and Ost 2004, 18–21. Gates 2010. See also 2011 update from The Williams Institute online, accessed on January 14, 2012 http://williamsinstitute.law.ucla.edu/press/in-the-news/ transgender-by-the-numbers. Bisexuals represent 1.1 to 1.8% of the adult population.

46 Indeed, a significant number of people primarily or even exclusively engaged in same-sex relationships don't identify as gay, lesbian, or bisexual (~1% according to Gates 2010). 0.5% selected "other" and 3% either did not know or did not answer in the UK survey by the Office for National Statistics. See also Gates and Ost 2004, 18–21. Data consistently show higher scores for male compared to female homosexuality (Milton 1993) however this is not the case in Gates 2010 (1.8% among women vs. 1.5% among men).

47 Kinsey Institute website. Accessed on December 29, 2008. http://www.kinseyinstitute.org/ research/ak-data.html.

48 8.2% in the US according to the 2011 update from The Williams Institute online, accessed on January 14, 2012 http://williamsinstitute.law.ucla.edu/press/in-the-news/transgender-by-the-numbers. 15% in the UK, according to a IPSOS MORI poll realized for *The Observer, accessed* on January 15, 2007. http://www.ipsos-mori.com/polls/2006/sa.shtml. Gates 2010 claims that 5.8% of the US adult population self-identify as heterosexual but report some same-sex sexual experiences.

49 Kirkpatrick 2000, 385.

50 Bagemihl 1999.

51 Taylor 1996, 173.

52 Hammer *et al.* 1993.

53 In the future, we might be able to identify what neurological structure correlates with homosexual identity. One could then attempt to trace the genetic footprint of such a structure in the genome of our distant ancestors. For instance, we know that experiencing fear is correlated with the activation of a particular brain area called amygdala. As a result, scientists can sensibly extrapolate the fact that any animal species that possesses a neural structure similar to the amygdala is likely to experience a subjective sensation close to what human beings name fear. So if one day (1) a particular structure in the brain is proved to host the neuronal activity correlated with homosexual identity, and if (2) the genetic information responsible for the formation and the functioning of such a structure is identified clearly, only then would one have a chance.

54 Greenberg 1988 and Stephen O. Murray 2000.

55 Greenberg 1988, 63.

56 Kirkpatrick 2000, 397.

57 Murray 2000.

58 Halperin 1990, 15–40.

59 Trumbach 1989, 137.

60 Adam 1986. Herdt 1991a, 483.

61 Greenberg 1988. Murray 2000.

62 Even in the most permissive case of homosexual relationships, such as those encountered among Amazonian tribes where (mostly but not only unmarried) young men freely and publicly engaged in playful sexual interactions, it appears that those relationships occur principally between current or future brothers-in-law, thereby playing a significant role in the social structure of the tribe. Murray 2000, 373.

63 I strongly agree with Murray when he writes that "while normative models may channel perception of others and conception of self, they do not determine these." Murray 2000, 7.

64 Regarding the Indo-European lineage specifically (pre-Dorian Greece, Goths, Celts, Germans, and Scandinavians), see Sergent 1996.

65 Herdt 1991b, 604.

66 In general, inserted did not systematically imply anal penetration. In Athens for instance, intracrural (i.e., between the thighs) sex was preferred to anal penetration.

67 Herdt 1984.

68 Herdt 1991b, 611.

69 "[. . .] with fatherhood, sexual relations with boys are to cease by ritual edict." Herdt 1991b, 611.

70 Herdt 1991b, 611.

71 The word "berdache" is still the most commonly used name for cross-gendered homosexuals in pre-European North America. However, the word was derived from the Arabic *bardag*, which means slave (Murray 2000, 348 footnote 73), or male prostitutes. It started to be used by Europeans to describe North American effeminate natives without consideration for the various original names that North American tribes used. The unique term "two-spirit" is slowly imposing itself as a reaction to the negative meaning that the word berdache originally conveyed. I personally prefer the word "two-spirit" essentially because it appears to recapture the original identity of native cross-gendered homosexuals better than the term berdache. See also Greenberg 1988, 41.

72 Ringrose 1993, 85–109.

73 Roscoe 1998.

74 I am aware of the existence of pre-modern egalitarian homosexuality cases. Going through the list in Murray 2000, it appears that most of those cases described situations that are either unusual or anecdotical. In their great majority, the list of pre-modern egalitarian same-sex relationships involved teenagers and young adults. In my opinion, none of those represent a convincing cultural form of adult homosexuality. However, the Hawaiian *aikānes* constitute an interesting exception and deserve our attention. *Aikānes* were noble men carefully selected to join the harem of the local chief (*ali'i*). *Aikāne's* masculine status was kept absolutely intact and the sexual relationship did not seem to involve a particular polarity. However, Murray justly insisted on the recurrent difference in status and very often in age between the *aikāne* and the *ali'i*, which makes the *aikāne* an intermediate class, intriguing but also isolated.

75 Murray 2000, 357.

76 Murray 2000, 377.

77 Murray 2000, 357 and 378–381.

78 Murray 2000, 204–211 and 220–254.

79 "Lesotho is a country completely surrounded by the Republic of South Africa. The dominant feature of its socioeconomic life is male migrant labor. About half of Lesotho's adult male labor force migrates to South Africa, leaving women in Lesotho for most of their lives as daughters without fathers, sisters without brothers, wives without husbands, and mothers without sons." As a result, "young girls in the modern schools develop close relationships, called 'mummy-baby,' with slightly older girls." Those relationships, which occasionally entail sexual intimacy, eventually evolve into life-long friendships, providing emotional support prior to and after marriage between adult women. Gay 1986, 97–98. Murray 2000, 210–211.

80 Murray 2000, 243.

81 "From approximately 1865 through 1935 in three districts of the Pearl River Delta, there arose a singular social phenomenon [. . .] called the 'marriage resistance movement.' Women who chose not to marry were called *sou hei*, 'self-combers,' referring to the fact that they combed their own hair in the fashion of married women rather than having it done for them in a marriage ceremony. Most *sou hei* formed sisterhoods which, if successful, served as a substitute for the family throughout their lives. The movement was spontaneous and unorganized, spurred by

the economic leverage which some women gained through the wages earned in the production of silk, and popularized through song and story. At its height, in the early twentieth century, the movement may have included up to 100,000 women." Eventually, the marriage resistance movement ended with the collapse of the silk market in the international depression of the nineteen thirties and the Japanese invasion. Sankar 1986, 69. Murray 2000, 243

82 Blackwood 1986, 13. Murray 2000, 236. Roscoe 1998.

83 Blackwood 1986, 7.

84 Brooten 1996, 23–24. Halperin 2002, 78.

85 See also Rupp 2009, 143.

86 Blackwood 1986, 10.

87 Blackwood 1986, 10.

88 In agreement with Rupp 2009, 228.

89 Peters 2006.

90 Berman 2003.

91 In 2007, one can still read in the highly respectable scientific journal Nature: "how can genes influencing homosexual—and so non-reproductive—behaviour be favoured by natural selection." Savolainen and Lehmann 2007, 158. See also Adriaens and De Block 2006, 572, and references within.

92 Murray 2000, 70.

93 Walter L. Williams in *The Spirit and the Flesh*, cited in Sullivan 1997, 40–41. Greenberg 1986, 179–189. A similar pattern was also found in Sudan. Murray and Roscoe 1998, 24.

94 Herdt and Stoller 1990, 80.

95 Gates 2006.

96 Knauft 2003.

97 Murray 2000, 393–418. Murray 2002, 287–325.

98 International Lesbian, Gay, Bisexual, Trans and Intersex Association (ILGA). Accessed January 17, 2012. http://old.ilga.org/Statehomophobia/ILGA_map_2011_A4.pdf.

99 Ibid.

100 Campbell 2005.

101 Brown 2010.

102 Sullivan 2005.

103 In that sense, I differ from Frank Muscarella who offered to use "the term homosexual behavior [. . .] to refer to any same-gender sexual behavior, irrespective of its motivation." Yet, his distinction between homosexual behavior on the one hand and homosexuality as being "the state of a predominantly same-gender sexual attraction and to the pattern of same-gender sexual behavior associated with it" on the other, is fairly on the same lines. Muscarella 1999, 2. See also Cass 1984a.

104 In that regard, my definition of homosexual identity matches that of "sexual orientation identity" presented by Vasey and Sommer: "Sexual orientation identity refers to the sexual orientation that an individual considers themselves to have." Sommer and Vasey 2006.

105 Herdt 1991b, 611. Original data can be found in Herdt and Stoller 1990, 279.

106 Rahman 2005, 1063.

107 Kirkpatrick 2000, 390 and 397.

108 Murray and Roscoe 1998, 178–182.

109 Human Right Watch. Accessed January 18, 2012. http://www.hrw.org/reports/2001/prisons; http://www.hrw.org/reports/1997/venez; and http://www.hrw.org/reports98/brazil/Brazil-10. htm. *In the Shadow, Sexual Violence in U.S. Detention Facilities*, 2006 report by Just Detention international. Accessed January 18, 2012. http://www.justdetention.org/pdf/in_the_shadows. pdf. Banbury 2004. Murray and Roscoe 1998, 24.

110 Donaldson 1990.

111 Stener Carlson 1997. Sivakumaran 2007, 257–58. Zawati 2007. Gettleman 2009.

112 Foster 2011.

113 Lockard 1986, 84.

114 Despite the similarity in the terminology, the concept of "optional" homosexual behavior (and desire), as I define it here, is not be confused with that of "facultative" homosexuality.

In most cases, "facultative" homosexuality (which is also called "functional," "deprivational", or "accidental" homosexuality in the specialized literature) is equivalent to what I refer as "situational" homosexuality and qualifies homosexual behavior that results from the lack of opposite-sex partners, but not from a free choice between same and opposite-sex partners. In situational homosexuality, homosexual behavior is optional if it is motivated by an authentic desire. In most cases however, the partner appears to be a mere functional substitute, in other words, a temporary sexual outlet *faute de mieux*. This said, remember that in everything that concerns human subjectivity and sexual desire, boundaries are rarely clear and defining one's authenticity with certainty is a quasi impossible task.

Likewise, my definition of "essential" homosexual behavior (and desire) is not directly related to the notion of "obligative homosexuality," which is occasionally found in the psychological literature and describes people that are exclusively interested in same-sex partners.

115 Herdt 1991b, 612.

116 Here is a typical example: ". . . it is clear that the assumption that 'gay men are like women' (and the concomitant assumption 'lesbian are like men,' although there has been very little research on lesbians) underlies much of this research. Yet that assumption is really based on societal biases . . . this assumption produces biases in the way the questions are asked, the way the research is carried out, and the manner in which the data are analyzed." But it actually gets even better: "Biological sexual orientation research serves no immediate medical purpose . . . There is no immediate medical need to conduct biological sexual orientation research simply because no human pain is supposed to be alleviated. Previous research into the causes of homosexuality emerged from a desire to eradicate homosexuality." "Arguments in favor of research into the causes of homosexuality have been proposed most notably by U.S.-based researchers trying to further a domestic political agenda." "Hamer's argument [Dean Hamer is one of the researchers that proposed the first chromosomal location for a possible gay gene. He believed that his research would help proving that homosexuality is normal] is philosophically unsound constituting a good example of a naturalistic fallacy." Schüklenk and Murrain 2000, 781–783.

117 Schüklenk and Murrain 2000, 785.

118 Borris 2008, 22–24. Brooten 1996, 115–142.

119 LeVay 1993, 110.

120 Gooren 2006, 592–93.

121 Martin 2004.

122 Rahman 2005, 1058

123 Endocrine disorders linked to an impairment of the androgen signaling pathway such as congenital adrenal hyperplasia confirm that the 2D:4D ratio decreases with prenatal exposure to an excess of androgen.

124 Rahman 2005, 1059

125 "Mean 2D:4D varied across ethnic groups with higher ratios for Whites, Non-Chinese Asians, and Mid- Easterners and lower ratios in Chinese and Black samples." Manning 2007.

126 Manning et al. 2007, 232. Voracek et al. 2005.

127 Keep in mind that how individuals end up being defined as homosexuals is rarely consistent among studies. One has to check the methodological procedure of each study attentively to find out which of either homosexual behavior or self-identification as gay and lesbian was used. Often, it is hard to tell what aspect of homosexuality is being traced. As default, I will use the concept of sexual orientation.

128 Unsurprisingly, studies regarding the higher incidence of adult homosexual orientation of women with congenital hyperplasia syndrome are contradictory. The variation was observed in one study but not in another. Bocklandt and Vilain 2007, 255.

129 Morris et al. 2004, 1038. Baum 2006, 581.

130 Rahman 2005, 1059. Levay 2010.

131 Gorski et al. 1978.

132 Swaab and Fliers 1985. Allen et al. 1989.

133 LeVay 1991. LeVay 1993, 120.

134 Byne et al. 2001.

135 Karama et al. 2002.

136 Paul et al. 2008.
137 Savic et al. 2005. Berglund et al. 2006.
138 Perkins and Roselli 2007.
139 In the literature, those males are described as "male-oriented." I prefer to use here the term "homosexual" for the stake of consistency. Those so-called "male-orientated" sheep do exhibit exclusive homosexual behavior. Almost certainly, this behavior has its counterpart in the sheep's subjectivity, made of desire and pleasure. We can safely call this a sexual preference. Yet, as far as we can tell, those rams do not possess a homosexual identity—they do not know themselves as rams which like rams. It is therefore risky to talk about homosexual orientation as I have defined it in a previous chapter. To talk about sexual orientation in this case, one would have to make sure that rams homosexual behavior is essential in nature, which remains hard to guess from reading the various scientific publications on the topic.
140 Roselli et al. 2007.
141 Interestingly, but in mice this time, a molecular approach of sexual dimorphism in rodents' hypothalamus has revealed that the androgen receptor, which is suspected to be behind the 2D:4D ratio variation, is differentially expressed in rodents' hypothalamus at much higher levels in males than in females. Shah et al. 2004.
142 Allen and Gorski 1992.
143 Savic and Lindström 2008.
144 Rahman 2005, 1062.
145 The dictionary defines tropism as "the turning or bending movement of an organism or a part toward or away from an external stimulus, such as light, heat, or gravity." Accessed January 18, 2012. http://www.thefreedictionary.com.
146 Crompton 2003, 65.
147 "In all our male homosexual cases the subjects had had a very intense erotic attachment to a female person, as a rule their mother, during the first period of childhood, which is afterward forgotten; this attachment was evoked or encouraged by too much tenderness of the mother herself, and further reinforced by the small part played by the father during their childhood [. . .] The boy represses his love for his mother: he puts himself in her place, identifies himself with her, and takes his own person as a model in whose likeness he chooses the new objects of his love. In this way he has become homosexual. What he has in fact done is to slip back to auto-erotism: for the boys whom he now loves as he grows up are after all only substitute figures and revivals of himself in childhood—boys whom he loves in the way in which his mother loved him when he was a child." Freud 1916, 50–51.
148 Pillard 1986. This study was preceded by Kallmann 1952.
149 Rahman 2005, 1062.
150 A: Pillard and Weinrich 1986. B: Hamer et al. 1993. C: Bailey et al. 1999. D: Bailey and Pillard 1991. E: Whitam et al. 1993. F: Bailey et al. 2000. G: Kendler et al. 2000. H: King and McDonald 1992. E: Bailey et al. 1993.
151 Bailey et al. 2000.
152 Mustanski et al. 2002.
153 Hamer et al. 1993.
154 Hu et al. 1995.
155 Rice et al. 1999.
156 Mustanski et al. 2005.
157 See the data comparison in Bocklandt and Vilain 2007, 258.
158 Molecular Genetic Study of Sexual Orientation. Accessed on Jan 18, 2012. http://www.gaybros.com.
159 Bocklandt et al. 2006.
160 Camperio-Ciani et al. 2004.
161 Reviewed in Bocklandt and Vilain 2007.
162 Blanchard 2004.
163 See also Gooren 2006, 598.
164 Mustanski 2002.
165 Reviewed in Wilson and Rahman 2008, 20–42.

166 In an interesting critical article about Simon LeVay and Dean Hamer's research, published in Scientific American, William Byne offered a typical example of the discourse of opponents to a biological determinism of homosexuality. There, he argued that "myriad experiences (and subjective interpretations of those experiences) could interact to lead different people to the same relative degree of sexual attraction to men or to women." Still he did not offer a possible list of candidates that might be tested experimentally. He later continued: "Instead particular genes might influence personality traits that could in turn influence the relationships and subjective experiences that contribute to the social learning of sexual orientation. One can imagine many ways in which a temperamental difference could give rise to different orientations in different environments." He then offered a surprising example: "One could combine these observations to speculate that a genetically based aversion to rough-and-tumble play in boys could impair rapport with fathers who demand that they adhere to rigid sex-role stereotypes. Fathers who made no such demands would maintain a rapport with their sons. As a result, the hypothetical gene in question could affect sexual orientation in some cases but not in others." First, putting a genetic inheritance of rough-and tumble play, for which we have not even the slightest indication, at the same level of likeliness with that of sexual orientation is by itself lacking judgment. But the most puzzling aspect of his argumentation appears in the absence of credible counter theory. Byne 1994, 50 and 55.

167 Fraga et al. 2005.

168 Francks et al. 2007.

169 Van Agtmael 2003.

170 Recent observations made in Japanese macaques demonstrate how far we still are from having pinned down the switch that gives sexual orientation/preference its unique distribution: like humans, Japanese macaques exhibit sexual dimorphism in the anterior hypothalamus, larger and more populated in males than in females. Nevertheless, while as many as 50% of female Japanese macaques appear to be more interested in mounting other females than playing with males, their anterior hypothalami exhibit no particular shift on the average toward "masculinization." Thus, size alone cannot help us predict sexual behavior with certainty. Vasey and Pfaus 2005.

171 The neurotransmitter serotonin (5-HT) is a likely candidate. Liu et al. 2011. Kinnunen et al. 2006. Wainberg et al. 2006.

172 Gatewood et al. 2006.

173 Swaab 2008.

174 Kandel and Jessel 1995, 470.

175 Tovée 1996, 98–99.

176 Pinker 1994. See also the references to the work of Noam Chomsky and other psycholinguists in Wilson 1978, 63.

177 Kuhl and Rivera-Gaxiola 2006, 523. Friederici et al. 2006.

178 Isay 1989, 20.

179 Byne 1994, 50.

180 Beauchamp and Mennella 2009.

181 Rosario 2009.

182 Rouquier et al. 2000.

183 Ghadami et al. 2004.

184 Feldmesser et al. 2007.

185 Axel 1995.

186 Wilson 1963. Herrada and Dulac 1997.

187 Dulac and Torello 2003. Tirindelli et al. 2009.

188 Reviewed in Dulac and Torello 2003.

189 Stowers et al. 2002. Leypold et al. 2002.

190 I am well aware of the classic distinction between an olfactory system specialized in detecting common odors and a vomeronasal system dedicated to the recognition of pheromones (as evidenced in Herrada and Dulac 1997). However, recent studies have clearly demonstrated that such a dichotomy no longer applies. Ergo, the absence of a functional vomeronasal organ in

humans does not preclude that humans can discern pheromonal cues. For review, see Tirindelli et al. 2009, Stowers and Logan 2010.

191 Stern and McClintock 1998.

192 Kohl and Francoeur 1995, 70.

193 Kohl and Francoeur 1995.

194 Savic et al. 2001 showed that female and male pheromones did not activate exactly the same regions in the hypothalamus. For the "connoisseur," the subregions of the hypothalamus that reacted were either in the preoptic and ventromedial nuclei in female subjects or the paraventricular and dorsomedial nuclei in male subjects.

195 Kohl and Francoeur 1995, 79.

196 Mennella et al. 2001. Beauchamp and Mennella 2009.

197 The primate family also includes Aye-aye, lorids, galagos, and tarsiers.

198 Gibbons are categorized as lesser apes and stands somewhere in the middle, between great apes and monkeys

199 Vasey 1995, 195–96.

200 Translation by Theodore Besterman (Besterman, T. 1972. *Voltaire. Philosophical Dictionary*. Harmondsworth: Penguin). Original French text from Gallica, Bibliothèque National de France. Accessed January 18, 2012. http://gallica.bnf.fr/ark:/12148/bpt6k37533m/f286.table. Curiously, Besterman's English version omits to translate the short segment about onanism that is present in Voltaire's original text and that I added in brackets. This omission is also found in another anonymous translation ("it is blind youth, which at the end of childhood, by an unaccountable instinct, plunges itself into this enormity") and even in John Fletcher's translation published in 2011 ("it affects blind youth which, not having worked out where its instinct lie, rushes into this perversion when barely out of short trousers"). However, these anomalies are nothing compared to the way William F. Fleming (19th century) appears to reinvent (rather than translate) this section on Socratic Love entirely: "It is a certain as the knowledge of antiquity can well be, that Socratic love was not an infamous passion. It is the word "love" which has deceived the world. Those called the lovers of a young man were precisely such as among us are called the minions of our princes—honorable youths attached to the education of a child of distinction, partaking of the same studies and the same military exercises—a warlike and correct custom, which has been perverted into nocturnal feasts and midnight orgies."

201 Hahn et al. 2007.

202 Nielsen et al. 2005.

203 Whiten et al. 1999.

204 O'Hara and Lee 2006.

205 de Waal 2000.

206 Wrangham and Peterson 1996, 132–143.

207 Fox 2001.

208 Bagemihl 1999, 285.

209 Wrangham and Peterson 1996, 134.

210 MacKinnon cited in Wrangham and Peterson 1996, 135–136.

211 Bagemihl 1999, 281.

212 Bagemihl 1999, 281.

213 de Wall 1995, 38.

214 Bagemihl 1999, 283.

215 Wrangham and Peterson 1996, 148.

216 Wrangham and Peterson 1996, 17.

217 Watts et al. 2006, 167.

218 Wrangham and Peterson 1996, 24.

219 Wrangham and Peterson 1996, 7. It is interesting to put this particular female chimpanzees' behavior together with studies that were realized in Israeli kibbutzim which showed that a sexual aversion automatically develops between people who have lived together when one or all grew to the age of six. No marriage was recorded between members of the same kibbutz who had been together since birth. Wilson 1978, 36.

220 Wrangham and Peterson 1996, 24.

221 In about 75% of societies studied by anthropologists, the bride is expected to move from the location of her own family to that of her husband, while only 10% require the reverse exchange. Wilson 1978, 128.

222 de Waal 2005, 58.

223 Wang et al. 2008.

224 Watts et al. 2006, 162.

225 Wrangham and Peterson 1996, 16.

226 As bravely stated by Wrangham and Peterson (1996, 125), "Patriarchy has its ultimate origins in male violence, but it doesn't come from man alone, and it has its sources in the evolutionary interests of both sexes." Likewise, Ken Wilber observed that "Viewing [this issue] in this evolutionary light allows us to bypass much of the standard and useless rhetoric that men have been oppressive pigs from day one, with the unavoidable implication that women have been herded sheep." Wilber 2000, 167.

227 Bagemihl 1999, 276–77.

228 Gomes and Boesch 2009.

229 de Waal 2005, 58. Gomes and Boesch 2009.

230 Depending on the species, postconflict reunions may include mouth-to-mouth kissing, embracing, sexual intercourse, clasping the other's hips, grooming, grunting, and holding hands. de Waal 2000, 587. de Waal 1986.

231 de Wall 1995.

232 de Wall 1995, 51.

233 de Wall 2000, 589.

234 Wrangham and Peterson 1996, 205.

235 Wrangham and Peterson 1996, 209–10.

236 McDonald Pavelka 1995, 51.

237 Reviewed in Muscarella 1999.

238 Louis Berman's nearly 600 pages book, *The Puzzle*, offers a typical example of this sort of approach. Berman 2003.

239 Wilson and Wilson 2007. Pigliucci 2008, 80.

240 Wilson and Wilson 2007, 338.

241 I however wish to honor Edward O. Wilson's tentative theory on homosexuality (Wilson 1975). In his courageous and pioneer attempt to explain the evolutionary logic of homosexual behavior, Wilson argued that homosexuals, by withdrawing themselves from the reproductive pool, would become available as caretakers—uncles and aunts—providing assistance to other family members and especially mothers, and thus, increase the chances of the survival of his or her own kin. Yet, this theory exemplifies a somewhat naive concept of altruistic behavior. Field data have seriously challenged its validity (Vasey et al. 2007). Moreover, Wilson's theory was based on an inaccurate understanding of homosexual sociocultural and historical reality, as we have seen.

242 de Waal 2000.

243 Lovejoy 1981, 347.

244 de Waal 2005, 57.

245 Wrangham and Peterson 1996, 222.

246 Stanford 1999, 199–217.

247 Gomes and Boesch 2009. Mitani and Watts 2001 and references within.

248 Kirkpatrick 2000, 396. Muscarella 2000, 60.

249 Kirkpatrick 2000, 393.

250 Herdt 1984, 69–71.

251 Burg 1984.

252 Frank Muscella's commentary on Kirkpatrick 2000, 401.

253 "When homosexual desire is routinized, it attains a place and meaning consistent with overall kinship logic." Adam 1986, 20.

254 Wrangham and Peterson 1996, 211.

255 Let me address here Vasey's (Vasey 1995, 190–91) relative cautiousness and Bagemihl's (Bagemihl 1999, 285) open hostility regarding the role of male dominance in homosexual behavior. I agree with both authors that asserting dominance is neither the cause nor the goal of homosexual behavior among primates, and even less in the animal kingdom in general. Homosexual interactions cannot be reduced to ranking displays. However, to reject naive generalization and inaccurate association between dominance and same-sex behavior should not hinder researchers to undertake a species-by-species examination of the organization of homosexual interactions. More measured, Vasey does not deny that dominance plays a role in some species of primates, and appears to agree on its central role in humans (Vasey and Sommer 2006, 22). Bruce Bagemihl, on the other hand, is strangely discreet about the unequivocal impact of the ranking order on the organization of male same-sex interactions among gorillas, macaques, and baboons, for instance (Watanabe and Smuts 1999, 103). Notwithstanding his reasons, Bagemihl's overall denial concerning the role of dominance in homosexual behavior whatever the species is just another excessive generalization. One will find a more balanced review on this matter in Dixon 1998, 146–153.

256 de Wall 1995, 51. Nishida and Hosaka 1996 shows that lower-rank male chimpanzees are mounted by higher-rank peers more often than they mount them (Table 9.7), a bias that is not found with regard to grooming behavior (Table 9.14b). However, they also show that there is no strict correlation between rank and mounting polarity. In particular, if the alpha and beta males, fierce rivals, never mounted each other, the gamma male mounted and was mounted by both the alpha and the beta male, which presented nearly 93% of the total number of male-male mountings in the group.

257 Muscarella 2000, 58, and references within.

258 Yamagiwa 2006, 289.

259 Fox 2001, 180.

260 Wrangham and Peterson 1996, 211.

261 Trumbach 1989, 129. Muscarella 2000, 60.

262 Murray 2000, 70–80.

263 Murray 2000, 197. Murray and Roscoe 1998, 142.

264 Fry 1986, 142. Murray and Roscoe 1998, 24.

265 Regarding the African continent, Murray and Roscoe observe that almost all reports of mutual homosexual relations between men during colonial times involve lower status males (e.g., slaves), youth, and bachelors (Murray and Roscoe 1998, 269).

266 Human Right Watch. Accessed January 18, 2012. http://www.hrw.org/reports/2001/prisons; http://www.hrw.org/reports/1997/venez; and http://www.hrw.org/reports98/brazil/Brazil-10. htm. *In the Shadow, Sexual Violence in U.S. Detention Facilities*, 2006 report by Just Detention international. Accessed January 18, 2012. http://www.justdetention.org/pdf/in_the_shadows. pdf.

267 "[. . .] interestingly enough, the inmates of men's prisons are organized more loosely into institution-wide hierarchies and castes, in which dominance and rank are paramount. Sexual relationship are quite common among these men, but the more passive partners, who play the female role, are ordinarily treated with contempt." Wilson 1978, 137.

268 Muscarella 2000, 64.

269 Interestingly, a very similar dynamic has been described among male Rhesus monkeys. Muscarella 2000, 57, and references within.

270 Muscarella 2000, 57.

271 Blackwood 1986, 10.

272 Sankar 1986.

273 Muscarella 2000, 65–66, and references within. Gay 1986.

274 In that sense I very much agree with Muscarella 2000, 64–65.

275 de Waal 2000.

276 Byrne 2007.

277 Duffy et al. 2007.

278 Also suggested in Muscarella 2000, 55 and 61.

279 Hammer 2008.

280 Frank Muscarella 2000, 61–62. Adam 1986, 20. Murray and Roscoe 1998, 92.

281 This theory is reminiscent of Vasey 1995, 197: "Perhaps such homosexual interactions influence patterns of heterosexual copulation, which, in turn, could effect the combination of genes that are contributed to the next generation."

282 Kirkpatrick 2000, 407.

283 Murray 2000, 181.

284 Paul Vasey suggests that "at some point during or after the late Miocene-early Pliocene certain hominid or proto-hominids individuals evolved the behavioral potential to engage in exclusive homosexual behaviors and consort bonding." Vasey 1995, 195–196.

285 Thompson et al. 2007.

286 Robbins et al. 2006.

287 Shumaker et al. 2008.

288 Atsalis and Margulis 2008.

289 Videan et al. 2008.

290 Thompson et al. 2007.

291 Walter L. Williams's commentary in Kirkpatrick 2000, 403.

292 Fone 2000, 7.

293 Yet, if this polarity is crucial between sexually mature adults, it affect younger males very little. As we have seen, sexually involved youth, teenagers, and sub-adult, in gorillas, orangutans, and chimpanzees, are quite oblivious when it comes to the polarity of anal penetration. In fact, anything goes. Adulthood quickly puts an end to that state of innocence.

294 Wilson and Wilson 2007, 343.

295 Greenberg 1988, 127 and 130.

296 Murray 2000, 256

297 Conner 1993, 100.

298 Crompton 2003, 53.

299 "Consciousness naturally resists anything unconscious and unknown. I have already pointed out the existence among primitive peoples of what anthropologists call 'misoneism,' a deep and superstitious fear of novelty. The primitives manifest all the reactions of the wild animal against untoward events. But 'civilized' man reacts to new ideas in much the same way, erecting psychological barriers to protect himself from the shock of facing something new." Jung 1964, 17.

300 Wilson 1978, 119.

301 Wrangham and Peterson 1996, 194–95.

302 Wilson 1978, 119.

303 Wilson 1978, 18–22.

304 Wilson 1978, 18 and 78.

305 Wilson 1978, 70.

306 Dulac and Torello 2003, 553.

307 Wilson 1978, 106.

308 Eliade 1957, 246

309 de Waal 2000, 588.

310 Jung 1964, 83. Neumann 1954.

311 "[. . .] early man seeks above all to control the course of nature for practical ends [. . .] compelling wind and weather, animals and crops to obey his will." Malinowski 1954, 19.

312 Malinowski 1954, 18.

313 I am well aware that the evolutionary continuity that I establish here between innate symbolic behaviors and cultural rituals, which I find extremely important to help us understand the primordial reason human beings are instinctively driven to converse with the world on a symbolic mode, is broad at best and would deserve a more extensive argumentation. That would unfortunately be beyond the scope of this book. I found therefore useful at this point to quote E.O. Wilson: "Consider rituals. Stirred by an early enthusiasm for Lorenz-Tinbergen ethology, some social scientist drew an analogy between human ceremonies and the displays of animal communication. The comparison is at best imprecise. Most animal displays are discrete signals

that convey limited meaning. They are commensurate with the postures, facial expressions, and elementary sounds of human non-linguistic communication. A few animal displays, such as the most complex forms of sexual advertisement and bond formation in birds, are so impressively elaborate that they have occasionally been termed ceremonies by zoologists. But even here the comparison is misleading. Most human rituals have more than just an immediate signal value. As Durkheim stressed, they not only label but reaffirm and rejuvenate the moral values of the community." Yet, a few lines downs, he also wrote that "the anticipatory action [of the rituals] is comparable to the intention movements of animals, which in the course of evolution have often been ritualized into communicative signals." Wilson 1978, 179.

314 I highly recommend Douglas 1966 to readers interested in the general theory of rituals and symbolic systems. See also Malinowski 1954, 37; de Waal 2000, 590; Wilson 1978, 70.

315 Eliade 1957, 22.

316 Malinowski 1954, 53.

317 Amstrong 2005, 3.

318 Jung 1964, 68.

319 Malinowski 1954, 41.

320 Malinowski 1954, 40–41.

321 Murray 2000, 303.

322 Murray 2000, 295–96 and 298–99.

323 Murray 2000, 286.

324 Murray 2000, 314 and 348.

325 Walter L. Williams, *The Spirit and the Flesh* (1986) cited in Sullivan 1997, 40–41.

326 Rist 1982, 26, 143 and144.

327 Beck and Cowan 1996. Wilber 1995.

328 Beck and Cowan 1996, 17.

329 Layard 1959, 101. Herdt and Stoller 1990, 94.

330 "In general, primitive men divide the world into two tangible parts, the near environment of home, local villages, kin, friends, tame animals, and witches, and the more distant universe of neighboring villages, intertribal allies, enemies, wild animals, and ghosts. This elemental topography makes easier the distinction between enemies who can be attacked and killed and friends who cannot. The contrast is heightened by reducing enemies to frightful and even subhuman status." Wilson 1978, 111.

331 Matthew 7:12. Most religious traditions offer similar moral precepts as center piece of their moral system.

332 Matthew 22:39.

333 Wilson 1978, 163. Wilson concludes elsewhere that: "Primitive men cleaved their universe into friends and enemies and responded with quick, deep emotion to even the mildest threats emanating from outside the arbitrary boundary." Wilson 1978, 116.

334 Singer 1981.

335 Pinker 2007.

336 Fone 2000, 3.

337 Neiman 2008.

338 Sullivan 1997, 278–282.

339 Serpenti 1984, 306.

340 Greenberg and Bystryn 1982.

341 Greenberg 2004, 231–232.

342 Greenberg and Bystryn 1982.

343 The lack of visibility of lesbian relationships extends to the Middle Ages. Brown 1989.

344 Fone 2000, 7.

345 I purposefully quote the King James Version of the Bible here for it uses of the word "abomination." I do so insofar as this word constitutes today an inevitable landmark in the homosexual discourse, be it pro or con. However, the English word "abomination" poorly translates the original Hebrew "to'ebah" (also "*toevah*"), which is more closely related to the concept of taboo. For an extensive exploration of the meaning of "to'ebah," see Michaelson 2008.

346 Boyarin 2007, 131–146 and 132. Olyan 1994. Walsh 2001.

347 Detailed accounts of sexual standards in ancient Middle-Eastern cultures can be find in Bullough 1976 and Greenberg 1984.

348 The Mesopotamian period includes the Sumerian and Babylonian periods, fifth to third and second millennium BCE respectively.

349 Greenberg and Bystryn 1982.

350 Chester Beatty papyrus I. Accessed January 20, 2012. http://www.reshafim.org.il/ad/egypt/texts/horus_and_seth.htm.

351 Avesta:Vendidad:Fargard 8. Funerals and Purification, Unlawful Sex. Accessed January 20, 2012. http://www.avesta.org/vendidad/vd8sbe.htm.

352 Hoffman 1984, 36. Loughlin 2007.

353 Gaca 2003, 3. Hoffman 1984, 29 and 35.

354 Hoffman 1984, 36.

355 Armstrong 2005, 20–21. Eliade 1957, 163.

356 One can find an excellent discussion about this topic in Gellman 2006.

357 Hoffman 1984, 31.

358 Gaca 2003, 122.

359 "When the Lord your God brings you into the land you are entering to possess and drives out before you many nations—the Hittites, Girgashites, Amorites, Canaanites, Perizzites, Hivites and Jebusites, seven nations larger and stronger than you and when the Lord your God has delivered them over to you and you have defeated them, then you must destroy them totally. Make no treaty with them, and show them no mercy. Do not intermarry with them. Do not give your daughters to their sons or take their daughters for your sons, for they will turn your sons away from following me to serve other gods." *Deuteronomy* 7:1–4.

360 Gaca 2003, 132. Douglas 1966, 84–89.

361 King James Version, for the same reasons as before.

362 Hoffman 1984, 37–38.

363 Crompton 2003, 39–42. Conner 1993, 78.

364 Leviticus 15:19–35.

365 In this section, I focus my attention on the Athenian male relational model, emblematic and, with respect to the traits that interest me here specifically, representative of Greek homosexuality at large. However, Greek homosexuality is better accounted for as a constellation of local cultural variants (Davidson 2007). Each city, be it Athens, Sparta, Elis, or Thebes, was not only proud of its own homosexual subculture but also often dismissive of others.

366 Dover 1978, 16.

367 Crompton 2003, 4.

368 Long 2004, 30.

369 Foucault 1978, 61.

370 Dover 1978.

371 Allen 2006, 9.

372 Crompton 2003, 18.

373 Murray 2000, 256

374 Conner 1993, 100.

375 Crompton 2003, 53.

376 Miller 2006, 91.

377 Miller 2006, 95.

378 Gaca 2003, 132.

379 Gaca 2003, 65.

380 Body-soul dualism and asceticism, which epitomize Pythagorean philosophy, echo similar beliefs found in Orphic Religion, which developed in Greece at about the same time. See Bullough 1976, 161; Bullough and Bullough 1995, 12–13.

381 Gaca 2003, 96.

382 Gaca 2003, 94.

383 Gaca 2003, 96

384 Gaca 2003, 108.

385 Joost-Gaugier 2006, 169.

386 Plato. Symposium. Translation by Benjamin Jowett.

387 Plato. Laws.

388 Gaca 2003, 28.

389 Gaca 2003, 30.

390 "The friendship which arises from contraries is horrible and coarse, and has often no tie of communion; but that which arises from likeness is gentle, and has a tie of communion which lasts through life. As to the mixed sort which is made up of them both, there is, first of all, a difficulty in determining what he who is possessed by this third love desires; moreover, he is drawn different ways, and is in doubt between the two principles; the one exhorting him to enjoy the beauty of youth, and the other forbidding him. For the one is a lover of the body, and hungers after beauty, like ripe fruit, and would fain satisfy himself without any regard to the character of the beloved; the other holds the desire of the body to be a secondary matter, and the desire of the body to be a secondary matter, and looking rather than loving and with his soul desiring the soul of the other in a becoming manner, regards the satisfaction of the bodily love as wantonness; he reverences and respects temperance and courage and magnanimity and wisdom, and wishes to live chastely with the chaste object of his affection." Plato. *Laws.*

See also Gaca 2003, 24 and 29. "This orientation of Platonic eros away from sexual physicality is motivated by Plato's stance that the immortal soul must struggle to loosen the shackles of the sexual body in order to glimpse pure Being." Gaca 2003, 64.

391 Gaca 2003, 49.

392 Gaca 2003, 69. Bullough 1976, 166.

393 Gaca 2003, 63 and 76.

394 Gaca 2003, 76.

395 Gaca 2003, 77.

396 Epicurus. Letter to Menoeceus. Reproduced in Diogenes Laertius, Lives of Eminent Philosophers, Book X. Accessed January 20, 2012. http://www.epicurus.info/etexts/Lives.html#I40.

397 Foucault 1985, 253.

398 Foucault 1985, 200.

399 Marcus Aurelius. Meditations 1.16.1. cited in Hubbard 2003, 467.

400 Foucault 1985, 17.

401 Gaca 2003, 85.

402 Gaca 2003, 85.

403 Boswell 1994, 40.

404 Boswell 1994, 40–41.

405 Foucault 1986, 73, 77, and 148.

406 Foucault 1986, 77.

407 Williams 1995, 533.

408 Cited in Crompton 2003, 124.

409 Cited in Williams 1995, 520.

410 Bullough 1976, 149. Sergent 1996, 540–41.

411 Williams 1995, 525.

412 Cited in Allen 2006, 109.

413 Boswell 1994, 97.

414 Crompton 2003, 131.

415 Crompton 2003, 81.

416 For instance, David Greenberg largely missed that important fact when he writes: "Some scholars have maintained that homosexuality never found the same acceptance among the Romans as among the Greeks [. . .]; however, Boswell [. . .] has amassed considerable evidence challenging this conclusion. Although expressions of distaste for homosexuality can be found in Roman literature, negative attitudes seem to have centered on effeminacy, coercion, the seduction of minors, and the participation of citizens, but not foreigners or slaves, in prostitution. There was probably no law against homosexuality per se until fairly late in the Empire." Greenberg and Bystryn 1982, 518.

417 In a discussion about the issue of marriage and divorce (Matthew 19), Jesus uses the term "eunuch" several times:

Some Pharisees came to him [Jesus] to test him. They asked, "Is it lawful for a man to divorce his wife for any and every reason?" "Haven't you read," he replied, "that at the beginning the Creator 'made them male and female,' and said, 'For this reason a man will leave his father and mother and be united to his wife, and the two will become one flesh'? So they are no longer two, but one flesh. Therefore what God has joined together, let no one separate." "Why then," they asked, "did Moses command that a man give his wife a certificate of divorce and send her away?" Jesus replied, "Moses permitted you to divorce your wives because your hearts were hard. But it was not this way from the beginning. I tell you that anyone who divorces his wife, except for sexual immorality, and marries another woman commits adultery." The disciples said to him, "If this is the situation between a husband and wife, it is better not to marry." Jesus replied, *"Not everyone can accept this word, but only those to whom it has been given. For there are eunuchs who were born that way, and there are eunuchs who have been made eunuchs by others—and there are those who choose to live like eunuchs for the sake of the kingdom of heaven. The one who can accept this should accept it."* (italic is mine).

Given the context (i.e., marriage and the legitimacy of divorce), "eunuch" seems to be used to describe (1) men who are either impotent or uninterested in sex and/or women, (2) castrated men (and possibly men whose sexuality or reproductive power is limited, such as slaves), and (3) men choosing to become celibate for religious reasons. I find it hard to read in Matthew 19 a backing of homosexuality. However, given the historical context, I find it equally hard to believe that Jesus or the writer(s) of the Gospel of Matthew did not know that castrated males (eunuchs) often played the receptive role with other males. It is then the absence of commentary regarding the sexual receptivity of males that I find most revealing. Neither backing nor condemnation, Matthew 19 seems simply unconcerned about the issue of homosexual relationships, or at least appears to regard it as subordinate to the many other ethical issues that are presented in this Gospel.

Scholars have also discussed the word *raca* that appears in Matthew 5:22: "But I tell you that anyone who is angry with his brother will be subject to judgment. Again, anyone who says to his brother, 'Raca,' is answerable to the Sanhedrin [the highest court of justice and the supreme council in ancient Jerusalem]. But anyone who says, 'You fool!' will be in danger of the fire of hell." *Raca* appears to be derived from the raqa, which means "brainless." Its resemblance with the Hebrew word *rakh* or *rakha*, which means "soft," and the Greek *racha*, "wicked man," authorized some scholars to assimilate *raca* to *malakos*, which it to say, effeminate men. The evidence is faint and the logic questionable, to say the least. At any rate, in the context of Matthew 5:22, raca appears as an insult less harmful than "you fool." Allen 2006, 156. Fone 2000, 94–95.

418 Gaca 2003, 194.

419 Philo of Alexandria. On the Creation 151–52. Accessed November 4, 2010. http://www.earlyjewishwritings.com/text/philo/book1.html.

420 Allen 2006, 145.

421 Gaca 2003, 148.

422 Gaca 2003, 139.

423 Foucault 1985, 50.

424 As far as I can tell, Jainism represents a remarkable exception to my claim.

425 Gaca 2003, 15 and160.

426 Greenberg and Bystryn 1982, 525. Bullough 1976, 182–195.

427 And yet, the coercion over women's sexuality barely has any equivalent in the men's world. Christianity maintained the superior status of wives, which it had inherited from Roman aristocratic class. However, it stopped there. Christianity inherited the same anxiety regarding female adultery and random childbearing as all other civilization before and after it. Females' chastity and bride's virginity—but rarely males'—became a recurrent concern in Christian culture. In a world where tight control was demanded over reproduction, females sexual freedom constituted an obvious danger. We need to keep in mind that, when it comes to sexuality, women paid by far the highest price for their transgressions.

428 Gaca 2003, 9.

429 Musonius, from a short essay titled "On Sexual Matters." Cited in Hubbard 2003, 395.

430 Brooten 1996, 29.

431 Philo of Alexandria, The Special Laws, cited in Allen 2006, 144.

432 See also Philo of Alexandria, The Special Laws III-VII: "Moreover, another evil, much greater than that which we have already mentioned, has made its way among and been let loose upon cities, namely, the love of boys, which formerly was accounted a great infamy even to be spoken of, but which sin is a subject of boasting not only to those who practise it, but even to those who suffer it, and who, being accustomed to bearing the affliction of being treated like women, waste away as to both their souls and bodies, not bearing about them a single spark of a manly character to be kindled into a flame, but having even the hair of their heads conspicuously curled and adorned, and having their faces smeared with vermilion, and paint, and things of that kind, and having their eyes pencilled beneath, and having their skins anointed with fragrant perfumes (for in such persons as these a sweet smell is a most seductive quality), and being well appointed in everything that tends to beauty or elegance, are not ashamed to devote their constant study and endeavours to the task of changing their manly character into an effeminate one. And it is natural for those who obey the law to consider such persons worthy of death, since the law commands that the man-woman who adulterates the precious coinage of his nature shall die without redemption, not allowing him to live a single day, or even a single hour, as he is a disgrace to himself, and to his family, and to his country, and to the whole race of mankind. And let the man who is devoted to the love of boys submit to the same punishment, since he pursues that pleasure which is contrary to nature, and since, as far as depends upon him, he would make the cities desolate, and void, and empty of all inhabitants, wasting his power of propagating his species, and moreover, being a guide and teacher of those greatest of all evils, unmanliness and effeminate lust, stripping young men of the flower of their beauty, and wasting their prime of life in effeminacy, which he ought rather on the other hand to train to vigour and acts of courage; and last of all, because, like a worthless husbandman, he allows fertile and productive lands to lie fallow, contriving that they shall continue barren, and labours night and day at cultivating that soil from which he never expects any produce at all. And I imagine that the cause of this is that among many nations there are actually rewards given for intemperance and effeminacy. At all events one may see men-women continually strutting through the market place at midday, and leading the processions in festivals; and, impious men as they are, having received by lot the charge of the temple, and beginning the sacred and initiating rites, and concerned even in the holy mysteries of Ceres. And some of these persons have even carried their admiration of these delicate pleasures of youth so far that they have desired wholly to change their condition for that of women, and have castrated themselves and have clothed themselves in purple robes, like those who, having been the cause of great blessings to their native land, walk about attended by bodyguards, pushing down every one whom they meet. But if there was a general indignation against those who venture to do such things, such as was felt by our lawgiver, and if such men were destroyed without any chance of escape as the common curse and pollution of their country, then many other persons would be warned and corrected by their example. For the punishments of those persons who have been already condemned cannot be averted by entreaty, and therefore cause no slight check to those persons who are ambitious of distinguishing themselves by the same pursuits." Translation by C. D. Yonge. Accessed January 20, 2012. http://www.earlyjewishwritings.com/text/philo/book29.html.

433 The word *arsenokoitai* is also used in 1 Timothy 1:10.

434 The Greek word *malakos* means literally "soft." When applied to men (*malakoi*), it is the equivalent of *kinaidos*, which is to say, an effeminate man—a man who typically accepts and/or enjoys being penetrated by other men, which the Greeks had in horror.

435 Allen 2006, 177. For more details, I suggest reading these two contradicting articles: Martin 1996. Jepsen 2006.

436 It is worth mentioning here that the words "*arsenos*" and "*koiten*," which compose the roots of Paul's new term "*arsenokoitai*," are also found in the verses Leviticus 18:22 and 20:13 of the Septuagint, the Greek translation of the Jewish Bible. This said, nobody ever doubted the fact that Paul knew the Septuagint. In fact, his use of the same Greek words as in Leviticus 18:22 and 20:13 to define the target of his criticism of same-sex relationships only highlights the fact that on the other hand he did not bother quoting Leviticus. Nor did Paul use the word "*bdelygma*,"

"a detestable thing" ("*abominatio*" in the Latin Vulgate, "abomination" in the King James version of the Bible). Instead he uses the Platonic term *para physin*, against nature.

437 Brooten 1996, 237.
438 Brooten 1996, 66–70.
439 Fone 2000, 102.
440 Brooten 1996, 331.
441 The term arrenomixia is also used by the Skeptic philosopher Sextus Empiricus who lived around the same time as Clement (circa 160-210 CE), showing that the conceptual shift was not limited to Christianity. Boswell 1980, 66 and 346.
442 John Chrysostom. Homilies on Titus, Homily V, 538. In NPNF1-13 Saint Chrysostom: Homilies on Galatians, Ephesians, Philippians, Colossians, Thessalonians, Timothy, Titus, and Philemon. Edited by Philip Schaff. Christian Classics Ethereal Library. Accessed January 20, 2012. http://www.ccel.org.
443 Fone 2000, 103.
444 John Chrysostom. Epistle to the Romans, Homily IV, 355–356, on Roman 1:26–27. In NPNF1-11. In Saint Chrysostom: Homilies on the Acts of the Apostles and the Epistle to the Romans. Edited by Philip Schaff. Christian Classics Ethereal Library. Accessed January 20, 2012. http://www.ccel.org.
445 Augustine. The Confessions of Saint Augustine, translated by Edward B. Pusey. Christian Classics Ethereal Library. Accessed January 20, 2012. http://www.ccel.org.
446 Thomas Aquinas. *Summa Theologica*, Question 154: Of the Parts of Lust. Accessed January 20, 2012. http://www.ccel.org. http://www.sacred-texts.com/chr/aquinas/summa/sum411.htm.
447 I share that conclusion with Bernadette Brooten (1996, 331).
448 For more information, consult Bullough 1976, 245–310.
449 Boswell 1980, 207–241.
450 See also Douglas 1996, 159.
451 Symonds 1928, 86–87.
452 Licata and Petersen 1981, 7.
453 Malinoski 1954.
454 Cited in Symonds 1928, 122.
455 Symonds 1928, 143.
456 Rosario 1996, 149–150.
457 Herzer 1986, 6.
458 Canadé Sautman 1996, 179.
459 Kennedy 1997, 30. Symonds 1928, 164.
460 The terms urning and dioning are derived from Ouranos and Dione respectively. In Plato's *Symposium*, Pausanias opposes Heavenly Aphrodite, daughter of the god Ouranos, and common Aphrodite, daughter of Zeus with the mortal Dione. Heavenly Aphrodite presides over male love, while common Aphrodite symbolizes the "common" love of men for women.
461 Freud 1910, 10.
462 Cited in Tobin 2005, 12.
463 Rosario 1996, 161–163.
464 Bryson 2003, 85.
465 Sigmund Freud, "Note on the Unconscious in Psychoanalysis," cited in Rickman 1957, 46–53.
466 See similar observations in Csikszentmihalyi 1996, 94; Witham 2005.
467 "This contains a new contradiction to the popular belief which assumes that a human being is either a man or a woman [...] The importance of these abnormalities [hermaphroditism] lies in the fact that they unexpectedly facilitate the understanding of the normal formation. A certain degree of anatomical hermaphroditism really belongs to the normal [...] It was natural to transfer this conception to the psychic sphere and to conceive the inversion in its aberrations as an expression of psychic hermaphroditism." Further, Freud confirms his interest in the concept of original bisexuality: "Since becoming acquainted with the aspect of bisexuality I hold this factor as here decisive [Freud is talking here about autoerotism], and I believe that without taking into account the factor of bisexuality it will hardly be possible to understand the actually observed sexual manifestations in man and woman." Freud 1910, 7, 8, and 68.

468 Storr 1999, 21.
469 Crompton 2003, 504–512.
470 Ragan 1996, 17.
471 Sibalis 1996, 80.
472 Crompton 2003, 528.
473 Crompton 2003, 533.
474 Haggerty 2000, 705.
475 Wikipedia. Accessed January 21, 2012. http://en.wikipedia.org/wiki/Magnus_Hirschfeld.
476 Bérubé 1989. Miller 1995, 210–218.
477 Neil Miller 1995, 234–250.
478 Neil Miller 1995, 314.
479 Licata 1981.
480 Boswell 1994, 61. Crompton 2003, 25–28.
481 Boswell 1994, 60.
482 Trumbach 1989, 1993.
483 Sibalis 1996, 93.
484 Karl Maria Kertbeny cited in Tobin 2005, 12.
485 Miller 1995, 11.
486 Miller 1995, 290–296.
487 Fone 2000, 188.
488 Montesquieu. The Crime Against Nature. Spirit of Laws, Book 12, Chapter 6, Section 6. Later Montesquieu adds that the crime of sodomy should be proscribed according to a fair policy, like any violation of sexual mores ("qu'on le proscrive par une police exacte, comme toutes les violations des mœurs").
489 Voltaire. Socratic Love, in *Philosophical Dictionary*.
490 Rosario 1996, 160–161.
491 Symonds 1928, 86–87.
492 Symonds 1928, 99.
493 Campbell 2001, 1–2.
494 Armstrong 2005, 4.
495 Malinowski 1954, 143.
496 Malinowski 1954, 109.
497 Eliade 1963, 5.
498 Eliade 1963, 9.
499 Malinowski 1954, 96.
500 Campbell 2001, 1–9.
501 Campbell 2001, 5. Malinowski 1954, 144.
502 "[. . .] myth is, therefore, an indispensable ingredient of all culture. It is [. . .] constantly regenerated; every historical change creates its mythology, which is, however, but indirectly related to historical facts. Myth is a constant byproduct of living faith, which is in need of miracles; of social status, which demands precedent; of moral rule, which requires sanction." Malinowski 1954, 146.
503 Campbell 2001, 5.
504 Richard Tarnas provides an excellent "transhistorical" definition of archetypes: "Archetypes thus can be understood and described in many ways, and much of the history of Western thought has evolved and revolved around this very issue. For our present purposes, we can define an archetype as a universal principle or force that affects—impels, structures, permeates—the human psyche and the world of human experience on many levels. One can think of them in mythic terms as gods and goddesses (or what Blake called 'the Immortals'), in Platonic terms as transcendent first principles and numinous Ideas, or in Aristotelian terms as immanent universals and dynamic indwelling forms. One can approach them in a Kantian mode as a priori categories of perception and cognition, in Schopenhauerian terms as the universal essences of life embodied in great works of art, or in the Nietzschean manner as primordial principles symbolizing basic cultural tendencies and modes of being. In the twentieth-century context, one can conceive of them in Husserlian terms as essential structures of human experience, in

Wittgensteinian terms as linguistic family resemblances linking disparate but overlapping particulars, in Whiteheadian terms as eternal objects and pure potentialities whose ingression informs the unfolding process of reality, or in Kuhnian terms as underlying paradigmatic structures that shape scientific understanding and research. Finally, with depth psychology, one can approach them in the Freudian mode as primordial instincts impelling and structuring biological and psychological processes, or in the Jungian manner as fundamental formal principles of the human psyche, universal expressions of a collective unconscious and, ultimately, of the *unus mundus*." Tarnas 2006, 84.

505 Baum 1993, 8–9.

506 Roscoe 1998, 132.

507 Regarding Classical Greece specifically, see Sergent 1996.

508 Downing, 1989. Conner et al. 1997. Hoffman 1984, 30.

509 Nanda 1986, 50.

510 Downing 1989, 146–47.

511 Plato. *Symposium*. Translated by Benjamin Jowett.

512 Cited in Gaca 2003, 83–84.

513 Gaca 2003, 203–204.

514 By Christian "pantheon," I mean to convey the idea of God the father, Jesus-Christ, the Virgin Mary, archangels, angels, and saints, in other words, all the mystic creatures represented and worshipped in the Christian Church.

515 Gaca 2003, 261.

516 Gaca 2003, 235.

517 Dover 1997, 28.

518 Boswell 1994, 8.

519 Boyarin 2007, 138–141. Fone 2000, 75–89. Allen 2006, 135. Crompton 2003, 36–38. Long 2004, 65. And references within.

520 Ezekiel 16:49–50.

521 Matthew 10:14–15. Similar version can be found in Luke 10.

522 Duran 1993, 181–182.

523 Philo. On Abraham. XXVI-XXVII. Accessed January 21, 2012. http://www.earlyjewishwritings.com/text/philo/book22.html.

524 Note the Neoplatonic influence through (1) the association between gluttony, drinking, and unlawful connections and (2) the many references to nature, the laws of nature, common nature, and unnatural.

525 Paul is absolutely silent on both the Leviticus prohibition and Sodom and Gomorrah. Unlike his contemporary Philo and despite their common Neoplatonic views and striking convergence regarding sexual matters, always bear in mind Paul discharged Christians from the old Jewish covenant contained in the Torah, the Ten Commandments being the only exception. Philo aimed at reinforcing Mosaic Judaism by highlighting its concordance with Neoplatonic concepts. Paul worked the other way around by merging his primarily Neoplatonic spiritual worldview with the Jewish monotheistic cosmology. He had no need to validate his claim by using the Jewish Bible.

526 Josephus. Antiquities of the Jews, Book I, Chapter 11:1–3. Accessed January 21, 2012. http://www.ccel.org/j/josephus/works/ant-1.htm.

527 Jude 1:7.

528 2 Peter 2:6–7.

529 "The Sodomites having, through much luxury, fallen into uncleanness, practising adultery shamelessly, and burning with insane love for boys" Clement of Alexandria. Paedagogus. Book III:8. Accessed January 21, 2012. http://www.newadvent.org/fathers/02093.htm.

530 John Chrysostom. Homilies on Thessalonians, Homily VIII, 358. In NPNF1-13 Saint Chrysostom: Homilies on Galatians, Ephesians, Philippians, Colossians, Thessalonians, Timothy, Titus, and Philemon. Edited by Philip Schaff. Christian Classics Ethereal Library. Accessed January 21, 2012. http://www.ccel.org.

531 John Chrysostom. Epistle to the Romans, Homily IV, 358, on 1 Roman 26–27. In NPNF1-11. Saint Chrysostom: Homilies on the Acts of the Apostles and the Epistle to the Romans. Edited

by Philip Schaff. Christian Classics Ethereal Library. Accessed January 21, 2012. http://www.
ccel.org.

532 Long 2004, 68. Sergent 1996, 550–563.

533 Neumann 1954.

534 Gilbert 1981, 61. Gilbert and Michael 1981. Gilbert 1977.

535 Philo of Alexandria, The Special Laws, cited in Allen 2006, 144.

536 Cited in Fone 2000, 115–116. Justinian reiterated the same menace in his Novella 77: "Therefore We order all men to avoid such offences, to have the fear of God in their hearts, and to
imitate the example of those who live in piety; for as crimes of this description cause famine,
earthquake, and pestilence, it is on this account, and in order that men may not lose their souls,
that We admonish them to abstain from the perpetration of the illegal acts above mentioned."
Justinian, *Novella* 77. Cited in Crompton 2003,146.

537 In his remarkable historical survey of sexual behavior, *Sexual Variance*, Vern Bullough noted
the striking consistency of western sexual morals throughout history: "Early peoples and cultures usually made assumptions about the nature of creation, the need for reproduction, and the
importance of sex act that exercised great influence long after their original basis had been discarded. [. . .] Western assumptions about sexuality, first formulated by the Greeks, if not before,
were given new impetus by the early Christian Fathers, reaffirmed by the Protestant reformers,
and accepted by the scientific community of the eighteenth, nineteenth, and even twentieth
centuries with little basic changes. Bullough 1976, ix.

538 After the wave of decolonization that followed World War II, most African countries adopted
authoritarian regimes, often incredibly brutal, and many of those countries experienced wars
and dramatic famines. Ethnic conflicts were common. Similarly, India and several South East
Asian countries were ravaged by wars, civil wars, dictatorship, and/or malnutrition issues.
Because life conditions went down, so did the average level of cultural development. In the
meantime, European countries initiated an unprecedented economical and political integration process; they gave rights to their minorities; democratic institution were held as the only
acceptable standard; and so forth.

539 Rosario 1996, 167.

540 In the respect, Walter L. Williams makes a pertinent comment in Kirkpatrick 2000 (p 404): "Let
me suggest another hypothesis to account for the rise of compulsory heterosexuality: it helped
to maximize population increase for competing European nation-states that wanted to expand
their political and economic dominance in Europe and into colonial empires around the
world. In this expansionist value system any form of non-procreative sex (for example, masturbation, birth control, abortion, oral sex) becomes stigmatized in favor of penile-vaginal sex
as the only acceptable form of sex for everyone. This hypothesis could explain why the most
expansionist modern nation-states (for example, the United States, Nazi Germany, and the
Soviet Union) and the most expansionist missionary-oriented Christian churches (for example,
Catholics, Mormons, and fundamentalist Protestants) are associated with severe discrimination against homosexuality. That is, homophobia is, to a great extent, a product of expansionist
missionary imperialism. This hypothesis could also explain why Japan, once one of the world's
most accepting cultures of same-sex love [. . .], has become so homophobic in the period since
it began its expansionist empire. Social pressure to reproduce also explains why such high per-
centages of Japanese bisexuals and homosexuals marry heterosexually and have children. In
the post-1945 world, as colonial empires have started falling apart and population growth is
no longer the prime need, sanctions against non-procreative sexuality have declined. Non-
imperialistic European nations like those of Scandinavia and (after 1950) Holland have not
surprisingly led the way in repealing laws against homosexuality."

541 Another way to deal with myths is to disregard them as being totally irrelevant to human life. In
that respect, people who deny the reality or the importance of subjective truths operate a lot like
fundamentalists. Claiming that myths are mere lies is not very different from pretending that
Jesus really walked on water because it is written. Both camps (extremist materialists and fundamentalists) cannot grasp the coexistence of two levels of reality, subjective and objective. For
them, reality ought to be monolithic, simply revealed, either through religion or science but not
both. Including the other side is perceived as a dangerous fragmentation, that is to say, chaos.

542 Jung 1953.

543 While we differ on the definition and role of archetypes, I largely concur with the analysis of constructivist thinker Björn Krondorfer in his well-thought critic of the use of past masculine archetypes by what he calls alternatively neo-Jungians, essentialists, and men mythopoetic movements. To re-actualize old archetypes can only resuscitate old psychocultural patterns, which are, for the most part, morally and epistemologically unsuited for our postmodern culture. Unfortunately, Krondorfer appears unaware that, by definition, the concept of mythopoeia implies the "creation" of new myths, not so much the reprocessing of old ones, and the same logic applies to archetypes.
Krondorfer, Björn. 1996. Introduction. In Men's Bodies, Men's God. New York University Press (1996) p. 15.

544 For a deeper analysis of the Jungian concept of persona, see Hopcke 1990.

545 When queer theorists argue that sociocultural labels, such as gay, lesbian, or homosexual, represent limitations imposed upon individuals so as to control them, they are directly challenging the dominance of our current archetypes and mythos. I agree with them: sociocultural identities have the power to imprint a fragment of the mythos—a piece of the collective imagery—on people's souls. Notwithstanding this, queer theorists have failed to realize that an anti-identity still constitutes an identity; that an anti-culture still is a culture; that queer politics is also oppressive, even if its intention is to free gays and lesbians from society's normative compulsive needs; and that ultimately, "queer" is just another normative label, and so is "no label;" any discourse is normative; we are all compelled to control our environment—if only we are given a chance—be we societies, individuals, or queer theorists.

546 According to the 1999 documentary Jews and Buddhism: Belief Amended, Faith Revealed. Wikipedia. Accessed January 23, 2012. http://en.wikipedia.org/wiki/Jews_and_Buddhism_ (documentary).

547 Mircea Eliade's comment on Communism is revealing: "For but one example we need only refer to the mythological structure of communism and its eschatological content. Marx takes over and continues one of the great eschatological myths of the Asiatico-Mediterranean world—the redeeming role of the Just (the 'chosen,' the 'anointed,' the 'innocent,' the 'messenger'; in our day, the proletariat), whose sufferings are destined to change the ontological status of the world. In fact, Marx's classless society and the consequent disappearance of historical tensions find their closest precedent in the myth of the Golden Age that many traditions put at the beginning and the end of history. Marx enriched this venerable myth by a whole Judaeo-Christian messianic ideology: on the one hand the prophetic role and soteriological function that he attributes to the proletariat; on the other, the final battle between Good and Evil, which is easily comparable to the apocalyptic battle between Christ and Antichrist, followed by the total victory of the former." Eliade 1968, 206–207. See also Tucker 1961; O'Neill 1996; and Wilson 1978, 190–91.

548 William Doty expresses a similar point of view in his massive Mythography. See Doty 2000, 169, and references within.

549 This list is by no means exhaustive. The article on the "Catholic Church and evolution" from Wikipedia (accessed January 21, 2011; http://en.wikipedia.org/wiki/Catholic_Church_and_ evolution) includes many quotes from the two most recents Popes, John Paul II and Benedict XVI. Others sources can be found in the article "Relationship between religion and science" (accessed January 21, 2011; http://en.wikipedia.org/wiki/Relationship_between_religion_and_ science). See also Dalai Lama (2005).

550 Genetic Genealogy. Accessed January 23, 2012. http://www.dnaancestryproject.com.

551 I highly encourage reading Steven Pinker's witty account regarding his own quest for his genetic origins. Pinker 2009.

552 Brewer 2003.

553 In a book that otherwise makes no mention of myth, mythos, or anything distantly related to those concepts, authors Eva Jablonka and Marion Lamb (2006, 381) observe (almost with regret, in fact) that "genes are seen as links to our ancient past, to our ancestors, which govern us in an irrational and mysterious manner. There is something very romantic in that notion—in the eternal dark and deep guiding force of the genes."

554 Eglinton 1964, 48.

555 This correspondence between mythos and rituals should not be viewed as being systematic. Many rituals appear to lack a mythic counterpart, either because it was lost during history or because there never was one to start with (see chapter 6). By the same token, myths are not all embodied in a given ritual.

556 Amstrong 2005, 89.

557 Turner and Frese 2005, 5724–25.

558 The editors of the *Economist*, cited in Sullivan 1997, 183–5.

559 Dennis Prager, cited in Sullivan 1997, 62, 64, and 65.

560 Brooten 1996, 42.

561 Gaca 2003, 108–116.

562 Gaca 2003, 83 and 87.

563 Coontz 2006, 15–17.

564 Boswell 1994, xxii.

565 From the editors of Commonweal, cited in Sullivan 1997, 55.

566 Jean Bethke Elshtain, cited in Sullivan 1997, 59.

567 Turner and Frese 2005, 5727.

568 Nelson 1978, 50.

569 See also Bullough 1976, 4.

570 Savage 2005, 126.

571 The editors of the *Economist*, cited in Sullivan 1997, 185

572 Sullivan 1997, 295.

573 "Therefore what God has joined together, let man not separate." Mark 10:9.

574 A very similar conclusion, based on a significantly different rationale however, was expressed in an article by David Blankenhorn, president of the Institute for American Values and the author of *The Future of Marriage*, and Jonathan Rauch, the author of *Gay Marriage: Why It Is Good for Gays, Good for Straights and Good for America*. Blankenhorn and Rauch 2009.

575 Journalist and writer Mark Vernon understood the true scale of the gay marriage predicament: "The problem is that if same-sex acts are just legally permitted then the symbolic truths that are attached to gayness are likely to be left untouched. In fact, inserting rights where before there was a crime might actually perpetuate the social order since gayness continues to be treated as an exceptional case, against which what is normal continues to be defined." Mark Vernon is right, and the legalization of gay marriage, albeit legitimate, is only rendering the task ahead of us more complicated. Vernon 2000, 68.

576 Nelson 1978, 208.

577 Plato. *Laws* 636.

578 Plato. *Laws* 836.

579 Eugene F. Rogers Jr. noticed in Thomas Aquinas the typical medieval conflation between one's physical body and one's essence: "Homosexuality, one infers, is for Thomas [Aquinas] in some respects a lie of the body." Rogers 2007, 184.

580 Note that I am forced to simplify a process that is far more complex, fragmented, and layered than what I describe here. For instance, the integration of African slaves in the empathic space took more than one step: abolition of slavery, civil rights, and one might assert that this process is far from complete today. The same is true of women. Women were by no means absent from the space of empathy when they were given the same civic right as men. Cultural phenomenon are never simple. The empathic space encompasses multiple and intricate hierarchies among various groups, sub-group, sub-sub-group . . . Yet, I believe that the same dynamic repeats itself indefinitely each time one encounters an empathic boundary, between those inside and those outside a given circle.

581 E.O. Wilson, commenting on the sixth and highest stage of ethic development defined by the educational psychologist Lawrence Kohlberg, acknowledges that it is "the most nearly nonbiological." Wilson 1978, 166–67.

582 Equally true is the fact that cultures and ethics are far from channelling empathic intentions only. Egocentric/selfish needs are as much codified in human laws as empathic concerns, even if, throughout cultural evolution, the former tends overall to recede in favor of the latter.

583 de Waal 2009, 2010.

584 Plato. *The Republic*, Book VII, On Shadows and Realities in Education.

585 See similar views in Csikszentmihalyi 1996, 358–59.

586 De Cecco and Parker 1995, 14.

587 Translated by the author. Eribon 1999, 29–30.

588 Translated by the Author. Eribon 1999, 109.

589 Sullivan makes a nearly identical observation: "For [hatred] to be effective psychologically, it requires, to some extent, the acquiescence of the victim." Sullivan 1996, 165.

590 "Part of the problem with casting homosexuals constantly as victims [. . .] is that it helps remove the responsibility for change from homosexual shoulders and put it onto others, and therefore makes this catharsis less, rather than more, likely." Sullivan 1996, 166.

591 Empereur 1998, 1.

592 Savin-Williams 2005, 180–181.

593 Pearson 2006, 282.

594 Herdt 1989, 20.

595 Jung 1953.

596 To the best of my knowledge, David J. Tacey (1993) and Robert Bosnak (1993) were the first to suggest the existence of a "homosexual individuation" process.

597 For a detailed review on bisexual identity and its development, see Brown 2002.

598 Cass 1984b.

599 Campbell 2001, 5.

600 Cass 1984a.

601 Herdt 1989, 5.

602 "Of the estimated 1.6 million homeless American youth, between 20 and 40 percent identify as lesbian, gay, bisexual or transgender (LGBT). Why do LGBT youth become homeless? In one study, 26 percent of gay teens who came out to their parents/guardians were told they must leave home; LGBT youth also leave home due to physical, sexual and emotional abuse. Homeless LGBT youth are more likely to: use drugs, participate in sex work, and attempt suicide. Also, LGBT youth report they are threatened, belittled and abused at shelters by staff as well as other residents." Ray 2006.

603 Sullivan 2005.

604 Herdt 1989, 30.

605 Herdt 1989, 21.

606 Cass 1979, 1984b.

607 Troiden 1998, 261.

608 A review of the various models of homosexual identity development is available in Brown 2002.

609 A detailed analysis of homosexual identity development in comparison with other models of development (e.g., cognitive and moral developmental lines) can be found in Herrada, forthcoming.

610 Few studies have claimed the existence of differences in the timing of sexual development (which includes sexual attraction and activity) between homosexuals and heterosexuals. However, those differences accounted statistically for no more than half a year among males, and they were clearly below significance among females. In my opinion, nothing interesting has yet emerged from this research. Bogaert et al. 2002.

611 Troiden 1989, 48.

612 I chose to mention the period of human life when each stage is most likely to be encountered. This age frame is tentative only, mostly applicable in Europe, North America, and other nations where homosexuality is culturally present and moderately accepted. Everywhere else (including in highly conservative subcultures), it ought to be taken cautiously. Cultural contexts, psychological types, individual personalities, and early experiences all have the power to alter the speed at which one progresses through the stages in a very significant manner.

613 Cass 1984b, 147.

614 "[. . .] the difference between self and non-homosexual others becomes clearer." Cass 1984b, 151.

615 Rosario *et al.* 2006. Also reviewed in Saewyc 2011.

616 Cass 1984b, 151. In Gates 2010, we learn that nearly 13% of lesbians, gays, and bisexuals in the US have never told anyone about their sexual behavior; ~35% had told someone before turning 18 and ~53% not before adult age.

617 Empereur 1998, 120.

618 Cass 1984b, 152.

619 Troiden 1998, 273.

620 Cass 1984b, 152.

621 Jungian psychologist Robert Hopcke reached a similar conclusion on the need to transcend community conventions and stereotypes: "These personas, by their very collectivity, can represent, on the one hand that healthy, socially transformative, in-your-face kind of self-presentation which is the best part of persona development. Nevertheless, such wholesale adoption of a community, which is to say, collective way of being in the world, particularly as a compensatory overstatement, can simply be yet another falsification of the gay and lesbian individual's true self. To substitute conformity to heterosexual conventions with conformity to gay or lesbian community conventions is no great psychic gain and can lead to as much unhappiness and emotional vacuity. Unfortunately, often these new and so often overblown personas of 'professional homosexuals,' whatever the variety, can be clung to with great tenacity as a security blanket not simply against homophobia but against the demands of individuation itself, which requires a toleration of complexity and conflict that many gay men and lesbians simply do not have after years of being worn down by homophobia, discrimination, fear, and self-loathing. In the best-case scenario, which in my experience is by far the most common, the development of such community-based personas is but a middle phase in the coming out process, modified and abandoned altogether as the individual grows more comfortable and mature as an out gay man or lesbian. In a manner of speaking, I find that the coming out process in some ways recapitulates the adolescent and young-adult developmental process, no matter what age the individual, so that such persona-based peer solidarity, normal among teenagers and college-age individuals, is likewise normal for gay men and lesbians who after coming out live out a kind of second, more authentic adolescence on the road to maturity." Hopcke 1995, 143–44.

622 Downing 1993, 31.

623 Pearson 2006, 288.

624 Diamond 2007, 143.

625 Diamond 2007, 149.

626 Diamond 2007, 144.

627 Diamond 2007, 144.

628 Diamond 2007, 144.

629 Diamond 2007, 146.

630 Diamond 2007, 142.

631 Diamond 2007, 151.

632 Jung 1964, 76.

633 Halperin 2007, 5 and 104.

634 "In 1993, 2.3% of gay men found their first male sexual partner online. In 2003 the number was 61.2%. These figures come from the United Kingdom, and there's been no parallel study in the United States, but sociologists believe the findings here would be similar." Gross 2008.

635 Breaking the Grip: Treating Crystal Methamphetamine Addiction Among Gay and Bisexual Men. Report by the Gay and Lesbian Medical Association, November 2006. Accessed on January, 23, 2012. http://glma.org/_data/n_0001/resources/live/BreakingtheGrip.pdf.
"'Sex and Love,' a survey conducted by the Center for HIV Education Studies and Training (CHEST) at Hunter College of the City University of New York, found that out of the 2,335 gay and bisexual men interviewed in the fall of 2003 and spring of 2004, 22% had used meth and 10.4% had used it in the past three months. The study also found that the younger the man, the more likely it was that he had used recently (the study polled men ages 18 to 84). [. . .] crystal is 'probably the [number 1] cause of HIV transmission. We're not finding high rates of new infection among gay men who aren't crystal users.' The 'Sex and Love' study concurs, showing that 'the HIV-positive men reported much higher rates of having used crystal (39.2% vs. 18.9%) and more recent use of crystal (20.8% vs. 9%) compared to HIV-negative men.' Also, the study

finds that only 22.1% of HIV-negative men said they had unprotected and receptive sex with a partner who was HIV-positive while on crystal, but 57.4% of HIV-positive men said they'd had unprotected and receptive sex with an HIV-negative partner while on crystal." Sanello 2005, 4–5.

636 In *Soulfully Gay*, Joe Perez voices a similar verdict: "Many gays," he writes, "are unsatisfied with the shallowness and negativity that we have experienced." Later Perez adds: "We must bring healing from the antigay fear, shame, and hatred buried within the heart of every person, transmitted in the very fabric of our families and culture, and institutionalized in our laws and other social structures. Our liberation must make us vessels of healing and transformation in the world, and our soul searching must take us to the Source of All." Perez 2007, 90 and 284.

637 Foucault died of AIDS, in 1984, only three years after giving this visionary interview "Friendship as a way of life" for the now defunct gay magazine *Gai Pied*. Foucault 1997, 135–40.

638 Foucault 1997, 135–136.

639 Foucault 1997, 166.

640 Foucault 1997, 138.

641 Foucault 1997, 137.

642 Teilhard De Chardin 1959, 226.

643 Campbell 2004, 24–25.

644 Dover 1978, 196–200.

645 Bronner 2008.

646 I do not share all Campbell's ideas on the nature and role of myths and symbols in modern societies. Campbell, unlike myself, still believed in the power of ancient myths on (post)modern consciousness: "When these symbols disappear, we have lost the vehicle for communication between our waking consciousness and our deepest spiritual life. We have to reactivate the symbol, to bring it back to life, and to find what it means, to relate it to ourselves in some way or another." Campbell 2001, 94.

647 Schelling 2007, 135.

648 Jung 1964, 41.

649 Foucault 1997, 138.

650 Foucault, 1997, 164.

651 Perez 2007, 284.

652 Cited in Vernon 2000, 74.

653 Cited in Vernon 2000, 75.

654 Regarding Classical Greece specifically, see Sergent 1996.

655 Bateman 2006, 11.

656 Sociologist Melinda Kanner cited in Harris 2006, 20.

657 Harris 2006, 24.

658 Harris 2006, 26.

659 Bateman 2006, 11.

660 Ko Imani's call for a "voluntary redemptive service" (which Imani conceives essentially in terms of social service—helping the poor, the hungry, the sick—and also in political terms—helping revitalize cities, protecting endangered lands, mentoring, and so forth) comes really close to the type of ritual we need, yet, it is far too limited and ignores the fact that postmodern consciousness will only reluctantly adopt this sort of role unless it becomes a medium of self-expression. Yet Imani is the only one I know who intuited the power of social contribution to help us transcend the gay-straight face-off. Imani 2003, 96.

661 I believe Andrew Sullivan and I are on the same page on that issue. "We need nothing from you, but we have much to give back to you." Sullivan 1996, 177.

662 Lewis 1960, 37.

663 Lewis 1960, 58.

664 Pope Benedict XXVI. Encyclical Letter: Deus Caritas Est. Accessed January 24, 2012. http://www.vatican.va/holy_father/benedict_xvi/encyclicals/documents/hf_ben-xvi_enc_20051225_deus-caritas-est_en.html.

665 Jung 1989.

666 Wilber 2000.

667 A short, yet detailed, review on how friendship (essentially among males) was held by various authors from antiquity to the twentieth century can be found in Culbertson 1996, 152–53

668 Pakaluk 1991, 192.

669 Pakaluk 1991, 189.

670 Pakaluk 1991, 195.

671 Pakaluk 1991, 194.

672 Pakaluk 1991, 190.

673 Pakaluk 1991, 188.

674 Philia, used a prefix or suffix, always express attraction and affinity: pedophilia, hemophilia, the adjective Francophile, cinephile, and thermophilic, but also words such as philosophy, philately, or philanthropy.

675 Foucault 1997, 136.

676 Alternatively, *storge* may be the force that hold multicellular organisms together. In that case, it would represent the most ancient form of binding energy or love, older that sex, hence older than eros.

677 Lewis 1960, 63.

678 Lewis 1960, 64.

679 Lewis 1960, 58.

680 Lewis 1960, 59.

681 Dover 1978, 52.

682 The interminable debate on whether those friendships were sexual or not is beside the point. There will never be definitive historical proofs, neither of what really happened nor of what people really believed happened. On that issue, I concur with David Halperin wise comment: "It is difficult for us moderns—with our heavily psychologistic model of the human personality, our notion of unconscious drives, our tendency to associate desire with sexuality, and our heightened sensitivity to anything that might seem to contravene the strict protocols of heterosexual masculinity—it is difficult for us to avoid reading into such passionate expressions of male love a suggestion of 'homoeroticism' at the very least, if not of 'latent homosexuality,' those being the formulations that often act as a cover for our own perplexity about how to interpret same-sex emotions that do not quite square with canonical conceptions of sexual subjectivity." Halperin 2002, 120.

683 Pakaluk 1991, 192.

684 Lewis 1960, 80.

685 Pakaluk 1991, 195.

686 Halperin 2002, 121.

687 "And that other, licentious Greek love is justly abhorred by our morality" is about as far as Montaigne goes in his condemnation of Greek pederasty. Remember however that Montaigne was a humanist and a stoic. Pakaluk 1991, 191.

688 Pakaluk 1991, 191.

689 This said, C.S. Lewis does not attempt to make a strong case against homosexuality, rather, he struggles to subtract friendship between men from suspicion of homosexuality, which I find both reasonable and legitimate.

690 Perez identifies heterosexuality with eros and homosexuality with agape, which I personally find unsatisfying, to say the least. Perez 2007, 52.

691 de Beauvoir 1953, 416.

692 Downing 1997, 438.

693 Carl Jung in "Face to Face," an interview to the BBC, October 1959.

694 Foucault 1997, 160.

695 In italics in the original text. Foucault 1997, 164.

696 Foucault 1997, 139.

697 Foucault 1997, 154.

INDEX

ABOUT THE AUTHOR

Gilles Herrada, PhD, began his career as a research biologist after receiving his academic degrees from the University of Nice and the Pasteur Institute in Paris. His research as a scientist at Columbia and Harvard universities in the fields of reproductive molecular biology and molecular neuroscience has been published in top scientific journals, such as *Cell*, one of the leading journals in molecular biology, and *Proceedings of the National Academy of Sciences of the United States of America*, the official journal of the National Academy of Sciences. His important accomplishments in scientific research include his discovery in 1997 of a family of more than one hundred genes encoding for receptors to pheromones, which are biochemical cues contained in bodily secretions and involved in triggering sexual and dominance behaviors in animals.

Today, Gilles Herrada dedicates his time to his transdisciplinary research project, applying integral philosophy to understanding human sexuality and the evolution of symbolic realities in human cultures, as well as his business as a life coach. (See www.lifeasacreation.com). Gilles Herrada lives in New York City.

For more information about his book, visit: www.themissingmyth.com.